Listening and Interpreting

The Challenge of the Work of Robert Langs

Listening and Interpreting

The Challenge of
the Work of
Robert Langs

Edited by
James Raney, M.D.

Jason Aronson, Inc.
New York and London

The Reflective Potential of the Patient as Mirror to the Therapist
© 1984 by Patrick Casement

Copyright © 1984 by Jason Aronson, Inc.

10 9 8 7 6 5 4 3 2 1

Library of Congress Cataloging in Publication Data
Main entry under title:

Listening and interpreting.

    "Chronological bibliography of the writings of
Robert Langs": p. 491
        Includes index.
        1. Psychotherapy.   2. Psychoanalytic interpretation.
3. Listening.   4. Langs, Robert J.   I. Raney, James
[DNLM: 1. Psychoanalytic therapy—Methods.   2. Communi-
cation. WM 460.6 L773]
RC480.5.L574   1983   616.89'14   83-8816
ISBN 0-87668-624-2

Manufactured in the United States of America.

To Carolynn

CONTENTS

PREFACE

> . . . to develop, it is necessary to liberate ourselves from our parents, our analysts, and our teachers.
>
> John Klauber (1981, p. xxi)

In a little more than a decade, Robert Langs has made a remarkable contribution to the field of psychoanalytic psychotherapy. As a result of his determined search for the unconscious meanings of emotional disturbance, he has reworked older psychoanalytic ideas and introduced major innovations in psychotherapeutic understanding and technique. His visionary theory and systematic clinical approach are both appealing and challenging.

The most important of his many innovations is the view that dreams and communication in psychotherapy have properties in common (Langs 1971, 1982). Langs approaches the therapy session as Freud (1900) did the dream. He has shown that the manifest content of a patient's associations in a therapy hour is like the manifest content of a dream. Both are created from underlying unconscious meanings through the mechanisms of condensation, displacement, considerations of representability, symbolization, and secondary revision.

Langs thus has amplified Freud's idea (Freud 1900, p. 507) that waking thought (manifest content) is different from dream work (those mechanisms that transform the unconscious latent or raw images into manifest material). To understand unconscious meaning, the logic of the manifest (waking) thought must be treated much as the logic of the manifest dream. Therapists should consider that the same processes that compose the dream are at work in the form, composition, and subject matter of the expressed thought and feelings—the crucial communications—of the therapy hour. Accordingly, to treat only rational waking thought for purposes of therapeutic understanding and intervention, as a majority of therapists, even psychoanalysts, appear to do, is quite incorrect. Latent implications must be detected, and Langs has detailed systematically the means to do so. Langs's entire psychoanalytic therapeutic approach is based on these premises.

Langs acknowledges a great debt to his psychoanalytic predecessors. Nevertheless, he departs from them all by considering *interventions of the therapist* not only as stimuli for subsequent material, but also as unconscious components of virtually every image and association from the patient. According to Langs, interventions are more than innocuous "day residues" that stimulate associations. They are for the patient *adaptation-evoking contexts*—powerful, organizing, often conflicted (especially if erroneous to any degree), unconsciously linked "dream thoughts" (dangerous raw images and perceptions) that must be acknowledged as a part of each therapeutic interpretation.

Sources and foundations of other concepts developed by Langs can be found throughout earlier psychoanalytic writings. The communicative field ideas, for example, can be traced to the British school, especially the writings of Bion (1970). These and many other influences have led, by way of Langs's ingenuity, to a comprehensive, documented, and systematic approach to the therapy hour that equals and probably surpasses the method and theory developed by Freud to understand and interpret dreams.

Langs has documented his ideas extensively and grounded them firmly in classical psychoanalytic clinical theory. His approach is now being investigated through study, writing, and amplification by others. Expansion of the base of independent assessments of Langs's ideas and application of his ideas to other areas of clinical work and related fields, clearly has begun.

After discussions with Jason Aronson, I invited talented and creative people known to be thinking about, studying, and working with Langs's ideas to write for a single collection. We anticipated that, by coalescing and communicating their experiences and ideas, an example and broadened base would be established for others working with Langs's concepts to evaluate, validate, extend, or revise Langs's propositions. The broad range of applications to be found in this volume is testimony to the fertile interest in and wide utilization of Langs's ideas.

The contributors include psychotherapists of several disciplines: social work, psychology, psychiatry, and psychoanalysis. Professors and students of English, linguistics, and philosophy are also represented. The authors extend, criticize, and apply Langs's ideas in novel areas from their unique clinical perspectives. They write about experiences with the frame, adaptive context, and other concepts in various clinical settings and with several diagnostic categories of patients. Several find Langs's concepts applicable to observations and reflections about such diverse fields as child development, psycholinguistics, and dramatic criticism.

The novice and experienced therapist, the student of Langs, and the interested scholar will be certain to discover provocative ideas in all that follows.

REFERENCES

BION, W. (1970). *Seven Servants*. New York: Jason Aronson.

FREUD, S. (1900). The interpretation of dreams. *Standard Edition* 4/5.

KLAUBER, J. (1981). *Difficulties in the Analytic Encounter*. New York: Jason Aronson.

LANGS, R. (1971). Day residues, recall residues, and dreams: reality and the psyche. *Journal of the American Psychoanalytic Association* 19:499–523.

—— (1982). *Psychotherapy: A Basic Text*. New York: Jason Aronson.

ACKNOWLEDGMENTS

The creation of this book would not have been possible without the help of many people. Those who provided essential indirect support and encouragement were Edith Fredrickson, Hazel Kellson, Dick Hannula, Roger Eddy, and two patient analysts. Others too numerous to name also provided sources and stimuli for this project.

Several people encouraged the project specifically by aiding in the task of assembling such a wide-ranging and diverse group, by giving valuable advice at crucial points, and by reading all or parts of the manuscript once or, in some instances, several times. These include Bob Langs, Jason Aronson, Joan Langs, Bob Watt, Ted Dorpat, Heinz Kohut, Susan Raney for her assistance with the index, and, most important of all, the authors of the chapters. The patience and diligence of the contributors cannot be credited enough. To them are dedicated the hopes and prospects of this book.

Finally, a great debt is due my family and the families and associates of all of the contributors, who suffered our physical and affective absences during the writing, editing, and assembly of the manuscript.

CONTRIBUTORS

LEON S. ANISFELD, D.S.W., is a psychoanalyst practicing in New York City. He is a senior faculty member of the Lenox Hill Hospital Psychotherapy Program, where he teaches courses on psychosis, depression, and mania. He also conducts a workshop on the psychoses for the Society for Psychoanalytic Psychotherapy, in New York City. *New York, N.Y.*

JAMES BEATRICE, PH.D., provides psychoanalytic psychotherapy to adults and children in San Diego, California. *San Diego, Calif.*

LARS BEJERHOLM, PH.D., is Assistant Professor of Philosophy at the University of Lund, Sweden, and Managing Director of the Bureau of Psychology in Malmö, Sweden. *Malmö, Sweden*

RICHARD M. BILLOW, PH.D., is Associate Professor of Psychology at the Institute of Advanced Psychological Studies, Adelphi University, and is on the postdoctoral faculty in the child-adolescent and adult programs. He is a lecturer in the Department of Psychiatry at the College of Medicine, Downstate Medical Center, State University of New York. He is currently in private practice in Great Neck, New York. *Great Neck, N.Y.*

RONALD D. BROWN, M.D., F.R.C.P.(C), is Assistant Professor in the Department of Psychiatry, McGill University, and is the Coordinator of Psychotherapy Training Programs at the Sir Mortimer B. Davis Jewish General Hospital in Montreal, Quebec. *Montreal, Que., Canada*

PATRICK CASEMENT, M.A., is a member of the British Association of psychotherapists as well as of the British Psychoanalytical Society. He is a practicing psychotherapist and psychoanalyst. *London, England*

LORNA GALE CHEIFETZ, PSY.D., is an adjunct faculty member at the Illinois School of Professional Psychology. She is a member of the American Psychological Association, the Chicago Association for Psychoanalytic Psychology, and the Society for Psychoanalytic Psychotherapy. Dr. Cheifetz is also a practicing clinical psychologist employed by the City of Chicago. *Chicago, Il.*

DOUGLAS DETRICK, PH.D., is a clinical instructor in the Department of Psychiatry, Stanford University School of Medicine, and is in private practice in San Francisco and Palo Alto, California. *Portola Valley, Calif.*

THEODORE L. DORPAT, M.D., is Clinical Professor of Psychiatry at the University of Washington School of Medicine and a training analyst at the Seattle Psychoanalytic Institute. *Seattle, Wash.*

JOAN BALOGH ERDHEIM, PH.D., is an instructor and supervisor at the Training Institute for Mental Health Practitioners in New York City. *New York, N.Y.*

MERTON M. GILL, M.D., is Professor of Psychiatry at the University of Illinois College of Medicine. He is also a supervising analyst and on the faculty of the Institute for Psychoanalysis in Chicago. *Chicago, Ill.*

MARTIN GREENE, D.S.W., is a faculty member of the Lenox Hill Hospital Psychotherapy Program and of the Society for Psychoanalytic Study and Research, and he is a professor at the Adelphi University School of Social Work. He is currently in the private practice of psychoanalytic psychotherapy. *Great Neck, N.Y.*

JAMES S. GROTSTEIN, M.D., is Associate Clinical Professor of Psychiatry at the University of California School of Medicine at Los Angeles and a training and supervising analyst at the Los Angeles Psychoanalytic Society/Institute. He is an attending psychiatrist at the Cedars-Sinai Medical Center and Director of the Interdisciplinary Group for Advanced Studies in Psychotic, Borderline, and Narcissistic Disorders. *Beverly Hills, Calif.*

A. GERRY HODGES, M.D., is a psychiatrist in private practice with an emphasis on psychoanalytic psychotherapy. *Altamonte Springs, Fla.*

VERA JIJI, PH.D., is Director of the Program for Multimedia Studies in American Drama at Brooklyn College, where she also teaches courses in drama and a course entitled Literature and Psychology. *New York, N.Y.*

CYNTHIA KEENE, PSY.D., is Chief of the Evening Hospital at the Treatment Center of the Martha Washington Hospital in Chicago and is a member of the adjunct faculty of the Illinois School of Professional Psychology. She is also in private practice in psychoanalytic psychotherapy. *Chicago, Ill.*

M. MASUD R. KHAN, M.A., is a member of the British Psychoanalytic Society and Director of the Sigmund Freud Copyrights. He is also Foreign Editor of the *Nouvelle Revue de Psychoanalyse* and a consulting associate editor for the *International Journal of Psycho-Analysis* and the *International Review of Psycho-Analysis. London, England*

ROSEMARIE KRAUSZ, M.P.s., is a doctoral candidate at the University of Montreal. She is a clinical psychologist in private practice in Montreal, Quebec, where she practices psychoanalytic psychotherapy. *Montreal, Que., Canada*

JILL GRANT LOVETT, M.A., is a doctoral candidate in clinical psychology at the Institute of Advanced Psychological Studies, Adelphi University. *Great Neck, N.Y.*

MARC LUBIN, Ph.D., is currently Dean of Faculty of the Illinois School of Professional Psychology. He is also in part-time private practice. *Chicago, Ill.*

MAURY NEUHAUS, Ph.D., is an adjunct professor at the School of Professional Psychology of the Florida Institute of Technology. He is Associate Director of the Lenox Hill Hospital Psychotherapy Program and Director of the West Side Psychological and Educational Center in New York City. *New York, N.Y.*

JAMES RANEY, M.D., is on the faculty of both the Seattle Psychoanalytic Association and the Lenox Hill Hospital Psychotherapy Program. He is Clinical Assistant Professor at the University of Washington, Department of Psychiatry and Behavioral Sciences, and is in the private practice of psychiatry and psychoanalysis in Seattle. *Seattle, Wash.*

EUGENE A. SILVERSTEIN, M.D., is in the private practice of psychoanalytic psychotherapy in Orlando, Florida, and he is a consultant and teacher for the Seminole County Mental Health System. *Winter Springs, Fla.*

MARK VLOSKY, Ph.D., is currently on the psychology staff of Kaiser-Permanente, Denver. He also is in private practice. *Denver, Colo.*

GUNNAR WINDAHL, Ph.D., is a research psychologist at the University of Lund in Sweden, and he teaches and supervises psychotherapy at the Psychiatric Clinic of Boden. *Boden, Sweden*

Part I

Using the Adaptive Context

CHAPTER 1

The Higher Implications of Langs's Contributions

James S. Grotstein, M.D.

Robert Langs has presented a steady series of writings that have examined the very foundations of psychotherapy. His first contributions were attempts to rescue psychoanalytic psychotherapy from its status as an inferior offspring of psychoanalysis, but later he more ambitiously examined psychoanalytic technique itself. His contributions have been so prolific and rapid that definitive critiques and decisive responses have not yet been possible.

His recent contribution entitled "Modes of 'Cure' in Psychoanalysis and Psychoanalytic Psychotherapy" (Langs 1981) not only epitomizes his current beliefs but is a challenge to all psychoanalysis and all psychotherapy. Langs's rhetoric urgently challenges all practitioners to reexamine the meaning of the therapy they do, the transferences they interpret, the theories behind their interpretations, their interventions and silences—in short, every aspect of their procedures.

Fundamentally, Langs is concerned with what Bion (1970) has termed therapy based upon the truth as opposed to therapy based upon the lie. He holds that most therapists practice forms of therapy and analysis that either adhere mainly to manifest content themes, at the expense of latent content, or deal with unconscious derivatives of manifest content in a way that maintains the theater of the analysis solely within the patient, who alone is considered the agent of distortion. At issue is Langs's belief that psychoanalysis occurs in a bipersonal field, a term he borrowed from the Barangers (1966) that designates the phenomenon of two people acting upon each other in the analytic framework. Yet it is not an "I–Thou" communication, in which there is mutual free-associative conversation. The field Langs believes occurs in psychoanalysis and psychoanalytic psychotherapy is somewhere between (1) the classical notion of the patient as the sick one and the psychoanalyst as the umpire who keeps score in an adversary conversation (conflict) between two different aspects of the patient and (2) the "I–Thou" shared intimacy between therapist and patient.

These unconscious elements, or derivatives, reflect a blend of past (genetic) events and currently active instinctual elements that are a part not only of these events but also of here-and-now experiences. The unconscious content or communication, however, speaking through the derivatives (manifest content), includes perceptions of the intimacy-evoking frame itself, the evocations by the analyst. Thus Langs negates analyst or therapist as "umpire" and acknowledges transference as a displacement of past object choices. He also, however, acknowledges the importance of the here-and-now, instinctual choices of the patient's unconscious as well as those of the therapist. He strongly contends that even normally the analyst's *being and activity* are reflected in the manifest content of the patient. He believes this is especially true when the analyst or therapist performs errors of commission or omission, among which are attacks on the integrity of the framework binding the patient and the therapist.

Of central importance is Langs's thesis that the patient's manifest content virtually always reflects the patient's experience of the analyst's presence, especially the patient's unconscious response to the analyst's interpretations and interventions. In other words, whatever the analyst does or does not do is reflected to some degree in the manifest content of the patient's associations as unconscious derivatives. The analyst may choose to talk about the patient's associations on the manifest level, which ignores the unconscious, or may choose to interpret what Langs calls a Type One derivative, which is transferential but which concentrates solely on the patient. A Type Two derivative, in contrast, is the analyst's interpretation of the analyst–patient relationship and of the patient's response to the analyst's intervention, interpretation, silence, or error. It is followed, Langs states, by a clarification and resumption of the bipersonal field.

Another important assumption in Langs's theory is central to psychoanalysis itself: that the patient is a generator of meaning, that his or her free associative manifest content is always attempting to surface and to communicate with the therapist to permit therapist intervention or interpretation that will restore lost aspects of the patient. Exceptions to this pattern, according to Langs, are patients with narcissistic personality disorders. Such patients are characterized by Type B fields, in which projective identification is used to evacuate mental content, and Type C fields, in which meaning itself must be abolished in order to preserve the lie as a barrier against catastrophic truth. Such a field is often a prelude to a psychotic sequela and is a notion for which Langs acknowledges his debt to Bion (1970). Complicating Type B and C resistance fields are therapists who themselves are predisposed, by their own pathology or their countertransferential responses, to collude with such patients in their resistance endeavors so as to achieve a pathological, parasitic relationship. Langs believes that a steadfast adherence to a Type A field, that is, listening to the material for Type Two derivatives, offers the only hope for a proper resolution of Type B and C fields. Specifically, he recommends that the therapist maintain the Type Two derivative interpretive mode for the Type B field but construct a holding environment for the Type C field.[1]

Langs's extensive critiques of supervisees and of discussions of technique reflect a deep questioning of what is meant by a transference interpretation. For instance, interpretations of feelings and impulses toward the analyst as the displacement of past (genetic) object cathexes may seem correct, but how does this kind of interpretation cause basic changes in the therapeutic process? Langs believes that the analyst's presence and stimulation of these feelings, and his or her participation and interpretation of this participation, is the evoking instrument. Relegating this role to past object cathexes dilutes the here-and-now transference and the role of the analyst in producing such transference. Thus, the underlying basis of Langs's interventions seems to be a bipersonal field that reflects a constant, dynamic interaction between patient and therapist. Ultimately, all the patient's material will reflect to some degree this active dyad, an invariant which Langs calls the adaptive context.

Langs has examined meticulously the works on technique of such authors as Freud (1909 [1910], 1910), Greenson (1965), Searles (1956, Searles and Langs 1980) Little (1981), Brenner (1976), Blanck and Blanck (1974), and Goldberg (1978). He has listed example after example from students, super-visees, colleagues, and well-established current analysts and has found all of them wanting in terms of technique. At worst, he finds some of them collusively adherent to manifest content themes. At best, he finds most of them dealing with Type One derivatives, acknowledging transference mainly from the past and at the expense of the here-and-now contributions, especially the distortions, that the analyst adds to the transferential theme. Dr. Langs stated to me just prior to his Franz Alexander lectureship in Los Angeles, "Present me with any material, your own or anyone else's. I promise to surprise you!" What I thought at the time to be a brash, theatrical statement actually contains a sad truth. One inference from Dr. Langs's statement is that many therapists and analysts are not emotionally qualified, by reason of personality, insufficient analysis, or both, to conduct analyses. These are the therapists most likely to use Type B and C field defenses, even though they occasionally may analyze in the symbolic mode in the

---

[1]It is important to differentiate a *holding environment* as Winnicott (1960) meant it and the *containment* of the infant's anxiety by the mother as Bion (1970) meant it. The former is a silent and silencing holding of the infant's being; the latter is an absorption *and* transformative translation of the infant's cries into meaning and meaningful responses.

Type A field and use Type One and, on fewer occasions, Type Two derivatives. I believe that Langs is addressing one of the most crucial elements in psychoanalytic therapeutics: How do we cure a patient? How do we derive optimal benefit from the transference? Put another way, how do we metapsychologize the interaction between patient and therapist and use what Greenson (1965) was one of the first to consider: the real relationship to the patient? Langs is addressing a central problem in psychoanalytic training and conceptualization, the issue of the single direction of analytic inquiry from the analyst's standpoint. Langs seems to be decrying the superficiality and one-sidedness of traditional transference, and especially nontransference, interpretations. Most traditional analysts seem to believe that a mere reference to transference feelings is enough to allow a therapeutic discharge. Thus, Langs's first challenge is directed toward the lack of mutuality in psychoanalytic conceptualization.

His second major challenge concerns the inability to be analyzed of those patients who cannot yet participate in a Type A communicative field. Yet he offers psychoanalytic formulations that allow them a place. Does a reverence for psychoanalysis learned in our institute training make criteria of analyzability loom so large that we suspend analysis of so-called nonanalyzable patients, and even of nonanalyzable sectors or moments during the analyses of analyzable patients? In short, do we still have, by virtue of our training, too much respect for unanalyzability and too little respect for analyzability?

Another question concerns how well schooled we are in the ultimate purposes of analytic treatment. Do we really understand the deeper meaning of symbolism, of analogical thinking, of metaphors as transactional phenomena in the analytic situation? There are many possible reasons for psychoanalysts and psychotherapists to be guilty of Langs's indictments, and my own suggestions barely scratch the surface. Furthermore, I adhere to Christ's admonition, "He that is without sin among you, let him first cast a stone"(*John* 8:7). Nevertheless, something seems to be very seriously wrong with the teaching and practice of psychoanalysis and psychotherapy today. I paraphrase Langs when I say that we have withdrawn our belief in the unconscious and merely pay lip service to it.

Yet further explanations might cast light on this dilemma. Perhaps the problem goes back to Freud, the originator of psychoanalysis, who as such has come down to us as an oracle and whose oracular ambiguity is representative of 19th-century epistemology. Our apprehension of truth itself is ambiguous rather than certain. Freud probably did not know that he was the discoverer of a superordinating science that would give credence to ambiguity. His discovery of psychoanalytic observation constituted the greatest single shift in scientific epistemology since Descartes: it enfranchised two separate bodies of experience, that of the rational world and that of the irrational world. In his discovery he anticipated the psychology of the nondominant hemisphere by focusing, along with Breuer (Breuer and Freud 1893–1895), on the phenomenon of double consciousness ("double conscience"). This amounted to a discovery that the data of experience could be observed via both detached and subjective observation.

As psychoanalytic technique evolved, however, Freud and his followers relied increasingly on detached observation. Although seemingly respecting subjective observation by the patient of his or her own experience as analysand, the analyst fell back more and more onto the older scientific method of detached observation. And, unfortunately, Freud depersonified, mystified, alienated, and disenfranchised his discovery, calling it the "id" ("it"). He then biologized it as an experience-distant phenomenon, and this phenomenon was to remain experience distant until properly tamed and "worthy to eat at the table in the house of the ego." What was probably behind Freud's unfortunate mistreatment of the second portion of the personality, I believe, was his rigid adherence to the scientific precepts of his time, those of Bruecke, of von Helmholtz, and particularly of Newton, all descended from the materialistic world of Descartes, who had compared the universe to a "great machine." It was Newton who was to describe the physical laws of this great machine.

One of the features of Cartesian–Newtonian materialistic physical science is a universe in which there are objects—discrete entities—subject to such immutable laws as gravity, inertia of motion, inertia of rest, and attraction-repulsion. One further feature is that these objects can be observed and that each observer can observe the same phenomena, having not altered the immutable laws, cycles, and trajectories of these objects. The observer is independent of the cosmos of the objects. This principle—Newtonian mechanics—has dominated Western science since Descartes.

While Freud was pondering the unconscious, however, physicists in Europe were already beginning to be puzzled by phenomena that were to conflict with Newtonian mechanics, and in the early part of this century, the study of atomic structure was beginning to shed an entirely new light on physics. Finally, quantum mechanics was born as a separate set of cosmic laws of subatomic particles, which were found to obey laws other than those of Newtonian mechanics. In trying to observe the hydrogen atom, Bohr found that he altered the atom by the very radiation he had to use to illuminate his object. This finding had far-reaching significance: in the realm of subatomic particles, the observer alters the observed object through the very act of observation. One of the most important derivatives of this point is that, if the observer alters the object by observing it, the very act of observation unifies and closely connects the observer and what is observed.

The philosophy of Descartes, the laws of Newton, and the principles of von Helmholtz and Bruecke allowed Freud to be the observer who was independent of the observed. Having discovered subjective observation, he seems to have separated it and assigned it to the patient, reserving detached observation for the analyst. This position was to be challenged by Sullivan's "participant observation" (1956) and Kohut's "empathic observation" or "vicarious introspection." Freud's detached observation was based on the phenomenon of biological instincts, which, obeying the second law of thermodynamics (the drift toward entropy), discharged from a higher level of energy to a lower one via the facilitation of an object. I believe this last point is of considerable importance in the development of the one-sidedness of psychoanalysis to which Langs refers. At one time the orthodox, and now classical, analyst was content to allow the unconscious to unfold (discharge). As Freud (1923) expressed it, "It is the destiny of the instinct to be expended in the cathexis of its descendents." Therefore, orthodox or classical analysts saw their sole role to be to remove impediments to the dischargelike unfolding of the unconscious, rather than to contribute to this process. They believed that in this way they maintained the desired surgical sterility of the field. Analysts' errors in technique, therefore, impeded the discharge of the unconscious by virtue of giving interpretations that, because of inappropriate timing and presentation, were unable to resonate with the unconscious element. As a result, they would collude with the defensive resistances rather than facilitate their removal (Glover 1955). An impulse–discharge phenomenon goes only one way, and orthodox or classical analysts could not conceive of the therapist, as well as the patient, as a discharging entity in the analytic situation. Countertransference has been discussed more and more over the years, but as a contaminant. The idea of a two-track bipersonal field had to await the Barangers' important work and Langs's discovery, in turn, of their realization.

Another aspect of Newtonian physics that seems to have dominated psychoanalysts and psychotherapists has been the theory of resonance. In our psychoanalytic training, we were taught to believe that, if we found the right interpretation in the right verbal form, it would "resonate" with its unconscious counterpart and force the latter to the surface in the form of discharge. Resonance was thus connected with discharge, a central issue in Freud's theory of psychoanalysis. For many years, he called psychoanalysis the cathartic method. Even his instinctual theory was based on discharge cathexis, and the object was needed in order to facilitate this discharge. Freud had not sufficiently conceived of the unconscious as populated with "subatomic particles" of potential meanings or preconceptions, as Bion (1970) was later to do, or as Peterfreund (1975) was to suggest from another point of view. In other words, Freud did not see the brain (or the mind) as a communicating network where ideas either were dormant or were pulsating and waiting to be realized by their counterparts in experience—or, once experienced and the experience found to be overwhelming, pretentiously turned into nonexperienced noncommunications. These Bion was to call beta elements, or lies that circumscribe a disaster area.

It is the truth and the lie that I would like now to address, because these concepts are so central in Langs's thinking as well as in Bion's. To condense Langs's thinking: There are patients who tell the truth through manifest content that betrays truthful unconscious derivatives. A truth-abiding therapist who chooses to adhere to Type Two derivatives can interpret these derivatives. There is also an analyst who clings to manifest content or Type One derivatives, uses Type B-field projective identifications (his or her own onto the patient), or colludes with the patient's projections into the analyst. Such an analyst conceives of therapy as the cathartic method in its most concrete simplicity. The third kind of patient and analyst are liars who revere the truth of the lie and the lie of the truth. Although Langs at times may seem moralistic on this issue (and moralistic he has a right to be when it comes to the application of analytic technique to a patient), he nevertheless acknowledges Bion's important contributions to the conceptions of the lie and the truth as ways of talking about a catastrophe that cannot be faced.

Another important principle began to emerge from the subatomic cosmos of quantum mechanics when Heisenberg discovered the uncertainty principle: subatomic particles cannot be particulated individually. One can measure either their momentum or their position, not both; therefore, no single subatomic particle can be located in terms of both position and momentum. Stochastic laws of probability had to be discovered that would account for the probability of their position *and* momentum. One of the main ramifications of the Heisenberg uncertainty principle is, therefore, that subatomic particles can be considered only in groups, not individually.

We have long considered "individual psychotherapy" an entity quite distinct from "group psychotherapy." I suggest that quantum mechanics can be used as a model to help us resolve the dilemma that Langs defines for us. Or perhaps Langs has found his way into quantum mechanical thinking without actually having realized it. I think he has, and I think Bion and Kohut have as well. Let me be specific: First, individual psychotherapy or individual psychoanalysis is a group phenomenon (a bipersonal field). Second, psychoanalysis, as an act of observation by both the analyst and the patient of themselves and of each other, is a complex observational experience that, like the impact of radiation on the orbits of an atom, alters the very object it observes.

Thus, psychoanalysis is a special form of observation in which the subject of observation and the object of observation are both altered by the act of observation. In this instance I am going somewhat beyond Langs's formulations. The analyst's observation of the patient changes the patient. The patient's self-observation changes the patient. The patient's observation of the analyst, however, is another important factor in the patient's progress and can be a beneficent change or a malevolent stagnation. Thus, psychoanalysis is more like a subatomic field of probability–particle groupings constantly acting on one another, and Langs exhorts us to examine the patient's productions while viewing the patient not merely as a transmitter but as a participant in a continuing dialogue on varying levels of consciousness. In other words, there are two transmitters, not just one, and they (as well as the two receivers) are not so far apart as psychoanalytic theory has suggested.

Perhaps the first consideration of the bonding between the therapist and the patient was Harry Stack Sullivan's discussion of participant observation and consensual validation (1956). Zetzel (1963) and Greenson (1965) talked about such bonding peripherally in terms of the therapeutic alliance or the real relationship. Winnicott (1960) and Bowlby (1969, 1973, 1980) have hinted at it strongly in terms of the theory of bonding. Bion (1962) was addressing it when he discussed the concept of the container and the contained. Kohut (1971, 1977) has expanded the idea considerably in his theory of empathic communication. Thus, vicarious introspection and the impact its intimacy has on the observed object (as well as the observing subject) have become the substance of three psychoanalytic psychologies: (a) the interpersonal psychology of Harry Stack Sullivan, (b) the empathic communication of the self psychology of Kohut, and (c) the bipersonal field of Langs.

With what does this mode of communication contrast in classical psychoanalysis? With detached observation, the kind of observation that is the purest product of the Cartesian-Newtonian cosmos. Is one to replace the other? Undoubtedly not. Langs, even more than Kohut, stresses the maintenance of detached (Newtonian) observation to permit the detection of the errors and pitfalls inherent in the empathic and intimate bonding of therapist and patient. Kohut, however, although also emphasizing the empathic errors implicit in such an intimate bonding, sees this very empathic bonding to be of crucial importance. Later, I will compare the psychologies of Kohut and Langs. What I wish to emphasize at this point is that psychoanalytic observation itself is more complicated than we had thought: it comprises detached observation as well as empathic or vicarious introspection. Detached observation, the product of our Cartesian-Newtonian heritage, bids us abandon memory and desire, as Freud hinted and Bion specified, in order to allow mysterious, obscure, or hidden particles of truth to emerge and be perceived by the analytic observer.

Our capacity to abandon memory and desire so as to achieve detached observation is one of the gifts we offer our patients, and it is at the same time their entitlement. It serves to permit the establishment of an analytic space, a transitional space between the therapist and the patient where the analytic scenario can take place, a scenario that, whatever else, is always revelatory. This space bespeaks a hallowed and revered area between the patient and the therapist much like the space between the infant and its mother where nursing takes place. The empathic, vicarious, participant observation metaphor, however, conveys a bonding, a postnatal continuation of umbilical at-one-ment, if you will.

That there are two ways of listening to a patient—and of listening to oneself while listening to a patient—suggests a specific application of a dual-track theory of human existence, a concept that is as old as psychoanalysis but that Freud unfortunately ignored when he depersonalized and disenfranchised the unconscious as an inferior function, making it an "object" of inquiry rather than allowing it to be the ego's partner and "co-subject."

Bion (1970) draws an analogy between maternal reverie and the group establishment; it is a container that is to withstand the impact of the infant's fear of dying and diminish it by acknowledging its meaning through translation and through remedial understanding. Yet a container, especially in its establishment function in groups (and psychoanalysis is precisely the group I am talking about), may so revere truth that it seeks to protect it against all challenges, one of which is the messiah challenge. Yet Bion suggests that the establishment container also must prepare for the messiah—or the messiah thought—in order to protect the people under its charge. In other words, the establishment container must prepare the people for a new truth with which the present truth is no longer congruent. Thus far, this discourse is simply a way of talking about the fact that truth changes, but that the need to revere and protect truth misfires and, more often than not, converts the truth into a lie by ritualizing it, devitalizing it, and suffocating it.

We can posit that Langs's beliefs constitute a messiah thought that the psychoanalytic establishment has interdicted, having become a ruling body of pious old men protecting truth from blasphemy—and from change. In the grammar of existence, this is the negative transformation from the verb of change to the noun of stasis. If the messiah is truly a messiah or truly carries the messiah message, then he or she represents truth. The problem is, however, that there is not only the new truth contending for acceptance, but a deeper truth as well: the establishment must protect its populace from truths of the future, which it knows it cannot tolerate, as well as from truths of the past, which it knows it cannot hear. Here again I would like to detour into physics to invoke Hooke's law: stress equals strain times the coefficient of elasticity. The estimate of the elasticity of the establishment container—or individual psyche—is the ultimate truth of the present. The beleaguered self is unable to remember experience arising from confrontation with the messiah truth, although when the experience comes back in the "return of the repressed," the effect will be devastating and catastrophic. It may be true that the establishment container knows the truth of its coefficient of elasticity, especially its limitations and thresholds of tolerance, and may actually be appraising the situation accurately without our realizing it. Thus, if we invoke Hooke's law, the establishment container, the precursor of the beleaguered patient's resistance to insight, is correct in resisting insight because of the anticipation of certain disaster.

We must now cross over into quantum mechanics psychology—to the laws of bonding, of probability, of groups—and invoke the second model of being, that of umbilical at-one-ment, of empathic vicariousness, of self-object-hood, that allows two people acting as one to bear the pain of one. Using this principle, we can see how the establishment container, either that of the interpersonal group or the psyche of the patient, can experience a higher threshold for disaster because it is able to tap into an at-one-ment with another caring, concerned person. This person's bonding ensures that the patient (a) does not have to face the problem alone and (b) can receive a "second opinion" about the problem that offers other options and possibilities, and is not left with "no exit." Problems of absolute disaster with no exit frequently change into problems that can be faced if there is a caring therapist with whom the patient can bond temporarily or quasi-permanently, an experience of which psychoanalysis and psychoanalytic psychotherapy avail themselves.

Psychoanalysis is not an isolated interpretative exercise; it is more like an ongoing symbiotic crucifixion. Elsewhere I have examined the profounder meaning of the word *transference* and tried to convey that it is to be taken more literally than it has been—that *transference* means a transfer of mental pain, a translocation of the experiencing of an event that takes place only in that indescribable, holy atmosphere inadequately described as bonding (Grotstein 1981). Transference can occur only when there is an at-one-ment simultaneously with a separateness, a dual-track conception.

What, then, is the purpose of the repetition compulsion in the transference? Freud stated that the repetition compulsion provided an opportunity to relive an experience that had been met passively and to try to master it. Particularly in the catastrophic state, he suggests, the victim does not experience sufficient signal anxiety to permit preparation for the experience;

therefore, repetition compulsions, particularly nightmares, for instance, are an attempt to develop the anxiety that was insufficient and thus nonprotective at the time of the event. Again, this externalization borrows from Newtonian psychology.

Quantum psychology suggests that the repetition is an externalization of an internalized foreign body: overwhelming and therefore incompletely experienced events, bad internal objects, bad introjects, etcetera. In the externalization, the foreign body first is brought to the surface and then translocated into some other body: the outside world in the sense of either the atmosphere or, more personally, the mother's body. We are best able to complete an experience—and to mourn it, say good-bye to it, and forget it—when we know that there is an object present who is attuned to us in an empathic bond and yet separate from us, and who is sufficiently unvictimized to convince us that he or she has survived personal experiences and can pull us into our future safely.

The repetition compulsion, therefore, is the externalizing agent of not only past unexperienced events, but also incompletely experienced events of the present. In the analytic situation, these unexperienced events will be elements of the "me–not me" phenomenon. Intrusive or unempathic participation by the analyst in the adaptive context frame will be internalized— made into "me"—as a "not me" element that becomes either a pathological introjection, a pathological identification, or both. The repetition compulsion is part of the patient's desire for health and cure; it seeks to reexternalize this pathological internalization through repetitive acting-out or repetitive symptomatology, to which a "restored" analyst may be attuned. Until then, the patient's material will reflect varying misconceived "me–not me" elements. Any interpretation, transferential or otherwise, will constitute what Langs calls *transversal interpretations*, interpretations that ignore the truth and confirm the lie. This process will continue until the adaptive context is beneficently and honestly restored in the transitional space.

To this point, we have discussed the patient as one who sends meanings in the cryptic language of manifest content and in a manner that reveals two truths to the therapist, who listens in at least two separate ways, empathic and detached. We now, thanks to Langs, accede to the notion that the therapist not only listens in two ways but also "sends" in two ways: helpful truths and deceitful lies. Implicit in all the previous discussion, however, is Langs's emphasis on symbolic logic, that is, his belief that manifest content is part of a cryptology whose purpose is to reveal the truer unconscious meaning, both in its own right and in the context of the bipersonal field with the analyst.

I would now like to add another dimension. One can infer from the vast new literature on self psychology that one of the principles of empathic listening or vicarious introspection is to accept the patient's account as being the way an event was experienced. Such an act on the part of the therapist does not necessarily mean agreement with the patient as to the report of the event; it merely means the experience of the event is to be acknowledged and vouchsafed. This empathic vouchsafing amounts to a notarization of the experience, not as the truth but as the patient's actual experience of the event. An interpretation of the patient's unconscious inescapably suggests that, for example, "Yes, I know that's the way you experienced the way your wife talked to you today; however, it might also mean that she represents (a) an angry aspect of yourself, (b) a latter-day version of your unempathic mother, and/or (c) an aspect of me that may be critical of you."

An interpretation that, no matter how well meaning, goes further than the patient's experience—that is, further than the manifest content of the experience—may undermine the vouchsafement or notarization of the experience and suggest that the analyst knows more about what goes on inside the patient than the patient does, thereby leading to a situation rife with intimidation and consequent envy. If my summary of the self-psychology perspective is correct, a serious obstacle is placed in Langs's path. In addition, we have even further to go to redefine what is meant by an interpretation. The point here, however, is simply that there may be more to be said for manifest content than is immediately apparent. Often we must be content with that which is manifest, because what is manifest to us may be profound for the patient and not yet manifest until we make it so, not through collusion or approval, but through empathic vouchsafement. Furthermore, a reading of Kant reassures us that manifest content, the diary of experiences with seemingly external objects, contains a mystery of its own. Objects of reality are not knowable via the senses or even by intuition. We can only gain knowledge about them (Bion 1962). Interpretations that ignore the overt meaning of manifest content are in danger of ignoring the patient's concerns of the moment. Even though one may wait for bridges to the adaptive context, therapists demonstrate their value systems in what they interpret and what they do not. Once patients begin to divine therapists' values, they will not take long to respond to them. They will learn what is personally important to the analyst, and what is unimportant. Once again, I believe that a dual-track conception is very important here. But the emerging technique that can employ a dual track has yet to be delineated.

Perhaps the mistake we all make, if it is a mistake rather than a human propensity, is to see things from one point of view. We now know we have two cerebral hemispheres and, therefore, two "minds" and even two separate consciousnesses associated with them. We can judge the data of internal and external experience from two different points of view. By achieving such a differentiation between personal meaning and abstract meaning, we are led toward ultimate meaning. We all know we have two eyes and two ears, but we see a single object or hear a single sound—for perceptual simplicity. The price we pay for this perceptual simplicity is the eclipsing of the full significance of having perceived from at least two, if not more, points of view. If there is a thesis and an antithesis, then we must optimistically assume they once were harmonious and also that they are pointing toward a future reconciling synthesis. Behind Langs's diligence in promoting the bipersonal field is his sense of fairness toward the patient. His ethical philosophy reminds one of Kohut and his followers in self psychology. Their conceptions of empathic understanding, which I have alluded to earlier in this chapter, also predicate a dual-track theory in which the therapist is as important as the patient in the therapy. Further, Kohut and his followers have described in great detail the consequences of empathic failures by therapists as well as by parents on the patient's progress and the child's development.

Certainly Langs and Kohut seem to be in full agreement as to the therapists' potential in the therapeutic transaction. Where do they differ, however? Kohut seems to have developed a second path of empathic observation (vicarious introspection) separate from the detached observation of classical analysis. Langs, in contrast, maintains the detached observation of classical analysis and carries it several steps further, by (1) unifying it with the primitive mental mechanisms of splitting and projective identification that have been discovered and explored by Klein and her followers; (2) considering the concepts of the container and the contained and of lie therapy contributed by Bion; and (3) incorporating the empathic me–not me interface to protect the patient from misidentification with the analyst's countertransference. By holding to a veridical extension of classical analysis rather than a modified form of it, Langs has offered a dual track for psychoanalysis, a bipersonal field in which there are two people interacting in an ongoing dialogue, participating all the while in what Vico (1968) called spiraling synthesis.

Kohut implicitly acknowledges the presence and importance of a bipersonal field, as Langs does, and consequently is aware of the importance of the nontransferential interaction of the therapist with the patient. In addition, however, he has located two primitive selfobject transferences that are important in helping to understand Langs's Type B and Type C fields. These fields identify victims of deficient or intrusive selfobjects who can be repaired and restored, one hopes, via the bipolar selfobject transferences. Thus, the ultimate difference between Kohut and Langs is that empathy for the patient by the analyst is implicit with Langs and explicit with Kohut—

and by empathy I do not mean compassion, but rather that attunement to and validation of the patient's experiencing of his or her experience. Winnicott (1960) commented more succinctly that the best "support" is the patient's knowledge that he or she is being well analyzed. The two paths of empathic observation can function together as a dual track. I believe they need each other and are complementary.

There is yet another serious stumbling block in Langs's path to explication, that of the influencing pressures on the patient in psychoanalysis—in other words, "brainwashing." I do not think that it is pleasant for any of us to consider what is behind that entity known as the setting, or the frame, of the analysis that Langs holds as holy. This frame is the definition that the analytic therapist gives to the way the patient and therapist are to meet, that is, regular sessions of 50 minutes two to five times per week, at a certain fee. Those are the explicits (with the addition of arrangements for holidays and regular, anticipated breaks). What is implicit in the arrangement is that the patient is to come into the analysis, present free associations about his or her state of mind, but be directed by the nature of the analytic treatment into presenting his or her complaints. Analysis thus by its very structure emphasizes the selective mobilization of complaints, pains, and agonies at the expense of positive aspects of the self, which are purposely pushed aside. Further, the patient responds to the analyst's cues, as Langs so carefully tells us. What are these cues? The analyst's silence tells us what is not of interest. The analyst's interpretations are a clear revelation of his or her values. Before long a dialogue is established in which the patient has already become conditioned to the values implicit and explicit in the analytic setting and is increasingly prone to self-incrimination.

At issue, I suggest, is that psychoanalysis and psychoanalytic psychotherapy are at best brainwashing exercises, albeit for the eventual benefit of the patient, that necessarily convince the patient to cooperate with the therapist in a way that will produce a regressive transference via the therapist's induction. Adherence to the Type Two derivatives that Langs recommends, although a highly commendable technique on one hand, is on the other a powerful instrument of regressive induction into a psychoanalytic brainwashing trance not unlike a hypnotic state. Those patients who are capable of tolerating these trancelike states, the patients whom Langs assigns to a Type A field, may be those who can benefit from such states because of their inherent capacity to resist deeper states of influence within the trance ("me–not me").

Those patients whom Langs typifies as Type B and Type C, however, may have personalities so fragile that they are more vulnerable to hypnotic induction and brainwashing and therefore all the more realistically endangered by psychoanalytic brainwashing induction. I use the loaded, provocative term *brainwashing* to emphasize the central issue of adherence to a framework of therapeutic reference that constitutes a dangerous instrument. Yet the paradox with which Langs presents us is his own recognition that patients can be badly influenced or malinduced by incomplete or bad analytic technique. So his recommendations, though rigorous and therefore inductive, are also protective.

There is a very important general issue regarding the context of Langs's contributions to psychoanalysis. Where do they fit in, in the history of psychoanalytic theory and practice? In considering this question, I was reminded of an epistemological battle that takes place in Thomas Mann's *Magic Mountain*, in which the highly traditional representative of European scholasticism, Naphta, becomes so angered with Settembrini, the humanist, that he challenges him to a duel. The duel represents the battle between these epistemological forces that has beset Western learning since antiquity. The battle seems to have repeated itself in the history of the psychoanalytic movement. Vienna, the originating site of psychoanalysis, began and continued in a scholastic vein, whereas Budapest, especially under Ferenczi's influence, became more and more humanistic. Some of his followers, such as Franz Alexander, were then to go to Berlin and ultimately to Chicago to conduct a humanistic modification of psychoanalytic scholasticism. Franz Alexander's "corrective emotional experience" had, I believe, much to do with the spawning of the humanism of the self-psychology movement today. Another follower of Ferenczi's, Imri Hermann, began the object relations movement, influenced Balint and Bowlby, and thus inspired the British object relations school.

Psychoanalysts today seem to be divided between a scholastic approach to their patients and a holistic–humanistic one. Langs's criticism extends especially to the humanistic, but also even to the classical scholastic, for not being scholastic enough. Humanism, however, may ultimately present a spectrum of possibilities for the relation of therapist to patient, extending from a playful interaction within the adaptive context to an "I–thou" actual participation. In this regard, Langs's critique is of great importance. Yet so is the concept of play. The analyst and the patient are locked into an important, profoundly intimate situation. How is the analyst to experience this profound situation? I suggest that all analysts try to be as serious as possible but, at the same time, have impulses to be playful. By *playful*, I do not mean "kidding" with the patient as a collusive departure from the serious work of analysis. I am referring to Winnicott's (1967) conception of the analytic play space as a derivative of the transitional space between the infant and its mother (1957)—his conception that creative work is playful, that it may be playfully serious and seriously playful. In other words, analytic work has to be in part enjoyable, both to patient and to analyst. This is probably another requirement of the adaptive context. It is not clear how this concept fits into Langs's views of the relationship between the patient and the analyst, however.

SUMMARY

I have tried to address the higher issues that Langs's contributions to psychoanalysis and psychoanalytic psychotherapy have evoked. One of the most important of these issues is the establishment of a newer therapeutic paradigm known as the bipersonal field, which he offers in place of the older paradigm in which the analyst is the objective umpire and the patient is the only object of observation. He is stating, to paraphrase Winnicott, that there is no such thing as a patient alone; there is only a patient and a therapist. A consequence of the bipersonal field is the alteration of transference interpretations to emphasize the adaptive context, which is the ongoing study of the therapist's impact on the patient. This context includes distortions coming from the analyst, either endogenous to the analyst or secondary to the effect of the patient on the analyst, that result in the analyst's "acting out" his or her countertransference by breaking the rules of the frame, either in deed or by unwarranted interventions. Thus transference must now be seen in the transference–countertransference–therapeutic alliance continuum. Langs's concept of the adaptive context seems to restrict the study of the unconscious to this bipersonal field. At the same time, it emphasizes an awareness of the reality of the interaction between therapist and patient and thereby provides a specific reality–unconscious unit suitable for analytic study. Langs's suggestions are rigorous, demanding the analyst's honesty and diligence in searching his or her own contributions to the patient's free associative responses. One of the casualties of this new requirement may seem at first to be the analyst's freedom for playful imagination and innovation. Once this new "self-consciousness" is integrated into the analyst's technique, however, this fear may be obviated.

I have also tried to illuminate the relationship between detached observation and empathic observation, the discharge model of psychoanalysis as opposed to the communicative interpersonal model, and the issue of brainwashing, which Langs's technique invokes and also responds to.

REFERENCES

BARANGER, W., AND BARANGER, M. (1966). Insight in the analytic situation. In *Psychoanalysis in the Americas*, ed. R. Litman, pp. 56–72. New York: International Universities Press.

BION, W. R. (1962). *Learning from Experience*. London: Heinemann.
———— (1970). *Attention and Interpretation*. London: Tavistock.
BLANCK, G. AND BLANCK, R. (1974). *Ego Psychology: Theory and Practice*. New York: Columbia University Press.
BOWLBY, J. (1969). *Attachment and Loss*, Vol. 1: *Attachment*. New York: Basic Books.
———— (1973). *Attachment and Loss*, Vol. 2: *Separation: Anxiety and Anger*. New York: Basic Books.
———— (1980). *Attachment and Loss*, Vol. 3: *Loss: Sadness and Depression*. New York: Basic Books.
BRENNER, C. (1976). *Psychoanalytic Technique and Psychic Conflict*. New York: International Universities Press.
BREUER, J., AND FREUD, S. (1893-1895). Studies on hysteria. *Standard Edition* 2.
FREUD, S. (1909 [1910]). Five lectures on psycho-analysis. *Standard Edition* 11.
———— (1910). The future prospects of psycho-analytic therapy. *Standard Edition* 11.
———— (1923). The ego and the id. *Standard Edition* 19.
GLOVER, E. (1955). *The Technique of Psychoanalysis*. New York: International Universities Press.
GOLDBERG, A. (1978). *The Psychology of the Self: A Clinical Casebook*. New York: International Universities Press.
GREENSON, R. (1965). The working alliance and the transference neurosis. *Psychoanalytic Quarterly* 35:155-181.
GROTSTEIN, J. S. (1981). *Splitting and Projective Identification*. New York: Jason Aronson.
KOHUT, H. (1971). *The Analysis of the Self*. New York: International Universities Press.
———— (1977). *The Restoration of the Self*. New York: International Universities Press.
LANGS, R. (1972). A psychoanalytic study of material from patients in psychotherapy. *International Journal of Psychoanalytic Psychotherapy* 1(1):4-45.
———— (1973a). The patient's view of the therapist: reality or fantasy? *International Journal of Psychoanalytic Psychotherapy* 2:411-431.
———— (1973b). *The Technique of Psychoanalytic Psychotherapy*. Vol. 1. New York: Jason Aronson.
———— (1974). *The Technique of Psychoanalytic Psychotherapy*. Vol. 2. New York: Jason Aronson.
———— (1975a). The patient's unconscious perception of the therapist's errors. In *Tactics and Techniques in Psychoanalytic Therapy*, Vol. 2: *Countertransference*, ed. P. L. Giovacchini pp. 239-250. New York: Jason Aronson.
———— (1975b). Therapeutic misalliances. *International Journal of Psychoanalytic Psychotherapy* 4:77-105.
———— (1975c). The therapeutic relationship and deviations in technique. *International Journal of Psychoanalytic Psychotherapy* 4:106-141.
———— (1976). *The Bipersonal Field*. New York: Jason Aronson.
———— (1978a). *The Listening Process*. New York: Jason Aronson.
———— (1978b). *Technique in Transition*. New York: Jason Aronson.

—— (1978c). Some communicative properties of the bipersonal field. *International Journal of Psychoanalytic Psychotherapy* 7:87–135.

—— (1979a). *The Supervisory Experience*. New York: Jason Aronson.

—— (1979b). *The Therapeutic Environment*. New York: Jason Aronson.

—— (1980a). *Interactions: The Realm of Transference and Countertransference*. New York: Jason Aronson.

—— (1980b). Truth therapy/lie therapy. *International Journal of Psychoanalytic Psychotherapy* 8:3–34.

—— (1981). Modes of "cure" in psychoanalysis and psychoanalytic psychotherapy. *International Journal of Psycho-Analysis* 62:199–214.

LITTLE, M. (1981). *Transference Neurosis and Transference Psychosis*. New York: Jason Aronson.

PETERFREUND, E. (1975). How does the analyst listen? On models and strategies in the psychoanalytic process. *Psychoanalysis and Contemporary Science* 4:59–101.

SEARLES, H. (1956). The psychodynamics of vengefulness. In H. Searles, *Collected Papers on Schizophrenia and Related Subjects*, pp. 177–191. New York: International Universities Press, 1965.

SEARLES, H., AND LANGS, R. (1980). *Intrapsychic and Interpersonal Dimensions: A Clinical Dialogue*. New York: Jason Aronson.

SULLIVAN, H. S. (1956). *Clinical Studies in Psychiatry*. New York: Norton.

VICO, G. (1968). *The New Science of Giambattistia Vico*. 3rd rev. ed. Trans. T. Bergin and M. H. Fisch. Ithaca, N.Y.: Cornell University Press.

WINNICOTT, D. W. (1960). The theory of the parent-infant relationship. In D. W. Winnicott, *The Maturational Processes and the Facilitating Environment*, pp. 37–55. New York: International Universities Press, 1965.

—— (1967). The location of cultural experience. In D. W. Winnicott, *Playing and Reality*, pp. 112–121. London: Tavistock, 1980.

ZETZEL, E. (1963). The significance of the adaptive hypothesis for psychoanalytic theory and practice. *Journal of the American Psychoanalytic Association* 11:652–660.

CHAPTER 2

The Patient's Unconscious Perceptions of the Therapist's Disruptions

Ronald D. Brown, M.D., F.R.C.P.(c), and Rosemarie Krausz, M.Ps.

This chapter is an attempt to explore patients' unconscious and conscious perceptions of therapists. Specifically, we present clinical data relating to patients' responses to a therapist's depression following the onset of Bell's palsy.[1] We explore the way this situation was handled in the clinical and supervisory settings.

The relatively limited literature on patients' veridical perceptions of their therapists or analysts has been reviewed previously by Langs (1973, 1975). Freud (1922) recognized that even in delusional paranoid states, there is a kernel of truth to the delusional projections: "they project outwards on to others what they do not wish to recognize in themselves . . . but they do not project it into the blue, so to speak, where there is nothing of the sort already" (p. 226). Searles has contributed a number of articles to this literature. For example, in a paper entitled "The Function of the Patient's Realistic Perceptions of the Analyst in Delusional Transference," Searles (1979) explains his main point as "the awesome extent to which the reality of the analyst's personality gives rise to the whole, seemingly so-delusional, world of the patient" (p. 211).

In an earlier paper, Searles (1965) explores a similar topic and asserts that his experience with nonschizophrenic patients has led him "to surmise that the relatively dramatic phenomena to be presented here have analogues, less dramatic and less easily detectable, but of much importance none the less, in other varieties of psychiatric illness" (p. 193). Limentani (1956) touches on this area: "Richard was so keenly aware of his therapist's mood and re-

[1]R. K. was doing the therapy as part of a postdoctoral training program on the Youth Service of the Department of Psychiatry, Sir Mortimer B. Davis Jewish General Hospital, Montreal, Quebec. R.D.B. supervised.

The authors thank Dr. R. Langs for his comments on an early version of this paper.

produced it so closely that the therapist at times gained from the interviews with the patient awareness of how he himself felt" (p. 233). Margaret Little (1951) makes a similar point: "We often hear of the mirror which the analyst holds up to the patient, but the patient holds one up to the analyst too . . ." (p. 37). Later in the paper, she assigns to the analyst the task of bringing to consciousness the "great deal of truth about [the analyst] both actual and psychic" (p. 38) that analysands unconsciously possess. She notes that the analyst may have great resistances to doing so.

Anna Freud (1954), in commenting on the importance of the "real personal relationship" between analyst and patient, adds the statement: "But these are technically subversive thoughts and ought to be handled with care" (p. 373). Greenson and Wexler (1969), in raising issues surrounding the nontransference relationship, express a similar sentiment regarding "the sensitive nature of the problem." They elaborate on the therapeutic alliance inherent in the nontransference relationship and pursue the idea of the patient's realistic, valid perceptiveness regarding the analyst. In a statement reminiscent of Margaret Little's advice, they posit that the "analyst must help the patient's beleaguered ego distinguish between what is appropriate and distorted, correct and false, realistic and fantastic in regard to his reactions to people, above all toward his psychoanalyst" (p. 193).

Greenson's clinical examples in this paper and a later one (1972) are all instances in which the patient makes a conscious assessment of the analyst. Langs (1973, 1975) has extended this area of exploration considerably. He emphasizes the patient's unconscious veridical perceptions of both the therapist's valid functioning and the therapist's erroneous interventions. These perceptions generally remain unconscious and are expressed through disguised derivatives via displacements, although other reactions to erroneous interventions, such as "ruptures in the therapeutic alliance; various forms of acting-in against the therapist; premature termination of treatment; erotic responses to the therapist; acute symptoms and symptomatic regression of all kinds; and major and minor episodes of acting-out" (1975, p. 240), may occur. Langs emphasizes, and offers much clinical data confirming, the necessity of monitoring the patient's associations for manifest and, especially, latent themes relating to the therapist, the therapeutic alliance, and the therapeutic atmosphere.

CLINICAL MATERIAL

We present extensive clinical material from two cases that were in supervision with R. D. B. and one that was brought to another supervisor. The major manifestation of the Bell's palsy suffered by R. K. was an inability to close her right eyelid, necessitating use of eyedrops every half hour, and thus at least once during each therapy session, for 14 days. Each patient was told that there was something temporarily wrong with the therapist's eye that required the use of drops. The therapist became aware of her depression some time after the onset of the acute facial nerve palsy, although each of the patients seemed to be aware of it from its onset.

Case 1: Miss E.

A 20-year-old woman had first presented herself to the clinic at age 17 with complaints of excessive anxiety and depression upon entering junior college. She was seen for several months, until the clinic worker left the clinic. She presented herself again two years later, with complaints of crying easily and of an inability to concentrate on her schoolwork. She was seen in supportive psychotherapy for six months, at which time she was referred to our day hospital because of her regression, manifested in constant crying and brooding over her failed year at the university and by withdrawal into a suicidal isolation. She had taken an overdose of 12 antidepressants early in the supportive therapy. She left the day hospital prematurely after finding a summer job.

She began the therapy reported here after presenting herself to the clinic six months later with easy crying, fear of failure at the university, inability to concentrate, withdrawal from personal relations, and mild suicidal urges. The central dynamics revolved around her attempts to break out of an enmeshment with her Italian immigrant parents, who were depicted by the patient as intolerant of any expression of emotion or attempt to make anything of her life outside the family. The mother had told Miss E. directly that if she left, she (the mother) would die.

After the first year of this therapy, the patient worked as a mother's helper for a family in California. This experience both bolstered her self-esteem and made her aware of how depriving and depressed her own family had been. After her return, this awareness developed into a depression, one aspect of which was an intense fear that the therapist, like her parents, would not be able to tolerate her sadness and rage and would attack her for these feelings and her dependency needs. This fear was expressed in the therapy by her coming for two weeks and then calling and having a session on the telephone the third week.

The first session after the Bell's palsy was diagnosed took place on the telephone. In the middle of it, a series of associations occurred that could be organized meaningfully around Miss E.'s early perception of the therapist's depression as well as around the therapist's having accepted the idea of telephone sessions. In this session the patient talked about her mother, who was doing nothing, just lying around the house; she talked about feeling very alone and disillusioned with how her parents' lives were "stuck": "I feel like I'm passing my parents and I don't have time to stop and teach them what I've learned." She went on, "I know she can't help me anymore, she can't even help herself." She talked about feeling that she either had to give in to her mother or withdraw.

In supervision we hypothesized that, although manifestly the patient was talking about her parents and probably with much valid perceptiveness, in doing so she was articulating, in derivative fashion, an evaluation of the therapist's inner state based on the therapist's handling of the missed sessions, the telephone contact, and an unconscious perception of the therapist's withdrawal in the session being reported. These reactions and perceptions she was beginning to elaborate as follows: "I sense you are withdrawn and preoccupied and I worry that you will do nothing for me; you will become as stuck as my mother who just lies around the house and will not be available to help me anymore; once again I will be left alone to try to get on with my life."

The next sessions, which were in the therapist's office, contained an underlying theme of lifelong deprivation linked to an inability to learn, to feeling stupid, and to depression and rage, which she had been deprived of expressing. She said, "When I was a little girl, they never let me have bad feelings. When I would hurt my knee, it would feel good to cry, but they wanted me to stop, they didn't want me to cry." She spoke of her time in California, which represented a place to make up for life's deprivations, and how she had deliberately become sunburned in order to feel the pain.

In her associations to these themes, there were references to her parents having catastrophized her feelings: a bit of depression, anger, or pain would be blown out of proportion. These themes built to a climax over several weeks, leading to the patient's missing a session. The therapist called the patient and interpreted that the patient was staying away to protect the therapist, who, she felt, like her parents, could not tolerate the patient's depression. The patient returned for her next session and talked about how alone she had felt over the previous several weeks: "I've discovered how alone I am in the world, how alone I've been all my life." She talked about being used by and withdrawing from her friends, who seemed empty and unable to understand her. The therapist then made the following intervention: "Perhaps you are feeling lately that I don't understand you either." The patient replied, "Yes, but the reason is hard to talk about." The supervisor felt that the patient was communicating her unconscious evaluation that the therapist was still not making a full enough interpretation, that is, that it was the therapist who was finding it hard to talk about the precipitants within the therapy for the patient's feelings of being with someone who had withdrawn, seemed empty, and was unable to understand. The therapist's skills of detachment, which promote observation, hypothesis construction and synthesis (Lewis 1978), had regressed under the burden of her depression. Also, she was not making complete interpretations: she was neither alluding to her withdrawal as reflected in the patient's material nor indicating the patient's perceptions, both valid and distorted. It therefore was decided in supervision that an explicit reference to her depression would be made by the therapist. The avoidance of any reference to her state might have constituted a repetition of the pathogenic effect on the growing patient of the parent's disrupted moods and their denial of these.

In a later session the patient began by talking about a letter from a man she had been involved with in California. She wondered what he could want from her—perhaps her return the following summer. That would be a step backward, and she did not want to go backward after having made some gains. The therapist commented on her fears that her gains in therapy would be taken away from her and that they could not possibly last. The patient responded by saying, "But do you think I will be depressed forever, or will it go away? When did it start anyway? I think it started back in November, no?" The therapist then told the patient that she, the therapist, had been depressed at that time, that the patient seemed not to be sure the therapist was over it. She added that, as with the gentleman from California, the patient was concerned about being used by the therapist to undepress herself, as the patient had been used by her mother as an antidepressant and scapegoat. This scapegoating had led the patient to feel a guilty responsibility for her mother's depressions, and this was how she had been feeling toward the therapist.

Monitoring the patient's response to this self-revelation for Type Two derivative validation (Langs 1981) revealed a mixed picture. Among the patient's initial associations was a reference to her parents' saying to her, "Look at E.—the facade is down and it's all coming out—she probably had it hidden away for years." This was a clear reference to the self-revealing nature of the intervention. She added new material about physical abuse by her father—a commentary on the abusive nature of the self-revelation. Also, however, she responded in this session by referring to her hypothyroidism and her neglect of having it monitored. Although this comment contained an implicit message to the therapist that she had not been taking good care of herself or the patient, there was also an increased interest in her own health. Between sessions she did see her endocrinologist, who increased her thyroid medication. As well, she began to look actively for a job and to make plans to move out on her own, something she had been avoiding for months. She wrote to the man in California and told him it was unlikely she would return, and she was curious as to his response once she had removed the possibility of his directly using her. These actions contained elements of validation.

The therapist's subjective response to this self-revelation was one of anxiety and relief. The disclosure seemed to have had an unburdening effect and to have helped her resume her usual mode of functioning. Miss E.'s renewed efforts to care for herself, to disentangle herself from her parents, and to set straight the relationship with the man in California certainly may have reflected the therapist's own unburdened state; after an initial working over of the acknowledgment as an abusive projection, the patient may have been no longer burdened by the introjection of the therapist's depression.

The therapist's depression was a trauma to this patient, one that the patient elaborated as a withdrawal of love based on something bad within herself, a negative introject. The explicit acknowledgment of it, although experienced in part as an impingement, did seem to have positive unconscious connotations for the patient and allowed the therapist to settle back into her usual style.

Case 2: Mr. L.

A 20-year-old man had been in once-a-week therapy for about a year prior to the period being reported. He had been referred from the ward, where he had been admitted after taking an overdose of 1,000 mg of a tricyclic antidepressant. At that time he was depressed, very withdrawn, and doing poorly in school, and had no friends. He experienced his mother as overly intrusive and bossy, his father as absent, and his 16-year-old brother as admirably extroverted and successful.

He had been in therapy at age 17 for one-and-a-half years with a Dr. W., who seemed to have attempted to strike up a friendly relationship with the patient by playing checkers and basketball and betting with him on sports events.

In the present therapy he was a silent patient, as he had been on the ward. This behavior required the therapist to make full use of her feelings that seemed to be a response to his general silence and nonverbal language. Interpretations formulated from these presumably induced feelings were usually met with silence or a tentative, drawn-out "maybe" up to ten minutes later. With the therapist's continued use of this technique, the patient began to emerge from his shell, talking more and more, even tentatively expressing some of his feelings. This development was continuing in the period prior to the therapist's developing Bell's palsy.

The time of the first session after the onset of the Bell's palsy had been changed. The patient started by asking if he would have his regular time the following week. He asked what he should talk about. Then he said, "Well, I'm depressed this week." *Both patients, and a third, unreported one, made fairly clear references to depression in the first or second session after the onset of the palsy. Such references were highly unusual, especially for Mr. L.*

Mr. L. went on in this session to talk about the antidepressants he had been given in the hospital. The therapist directly encouraged him to talk about his depression and confronted him with ways he had of avoiding doing so. At the beginning of the next session, he asked, "Are we going to take up where we left off? Where were we?" When the therapist, in an uncharacteristic response, indicated that she did not remember, he seemed to be disrupted, sighed, and looked angry. He talked positively about his former psychologist, wanted to play checkers, and later began giggling and muttering private jokes. Toward the end of the session, he wondered aloud if the therapist enjoyed being a psychologist.

Supervision included a discussion of the very quick perception of the therapist's depression, reflected in the derivative communication of the patient's feeling depressed and having needed antidepressants. The latter derivative referred as well to his noticing the therapist's use of eye drops. There was discussion as well of the patient's disrupted state, manifested in his angry sigh and withdrawal to private jokes as a response to the therapist's depression and the ensuing deviations, including her questioning confrontational technique and her failure to handle his question about the previous session interpretively. His disrupted state was further expressed in the next session by his coming late for the first time.

In the subsequent session the therapist responded to his continued state of disruption with the following self-revelation/interpretation: "I have the feeling that you have noticed a problem with my eye and how my mood has been somewhat down. Perhaps you are afraid I won't be able to support you when you are feeling depressed if I'm down myself." He responded by asking if the condition was an infection and if the therapist was seeing a psychologist. He suggested she could go to his ward psychiatrist, who had been of no help to him. In this way he expressed his hostility toward the therapist and his perception that she was not being of any help to him.

This formulation was affirmed in the following interchange at the beginning of the next session:

P: There is a strike in the hospital. I heard someone committed suicide. Is that true?
T: Yes. Do you have any thoughts about it?
P: Was it because of the strike?
T: I don't know; what do you think?
P: I guess no one was taking care of him.

Here, in an only mildly disguised derivative form, the patient reveals his perception and concern that the therapist has gone on strike, that she is depressed (suicidal) and unavailable to him. Although the explicit self-revelation had been part of an increasing series of deviations resulting from her depression, only after it did the therapist become able to deal with issues surrounding her recent unavailability to the patient, so poignantly expressed in the derivative of a strike resulting in a suicide. As well, it seemed to allow her to regain a more interpretive stance.

Over the next weeks the patient raised these abandonment concerns by referring to a sense of failure to progress in therapy and by talking about his uncaring ward psychiatrist. He was increasingly able to express and work through his anger about all these failures in caring. In the middle of February, long after the therapist had recovered from her palsy and the associated depression, the patient noticed the therapist rubbing her eye, asked if she was wearing contact lenses, and then said, "I wouldn't want you to get sick again. You weren't as energetic as you usually are." Because the therapist had gone back to her usual way of therapeutic functioning some time previously, this and other continuing references to the period of her depression afforded an opportunity to tease out reality perception and transference distortion. The patient's ongoing wariness of the therapist's mood represents a transference from an earlier phase of therapy to a later one, as well as from the patient's more remote past. Recognizing this transference and the validity of his earlier perceptions as the origins of his present wariness, the therapist is able to handle his deep abandonment fears more sensitively.

Case 3—A Clinical Control: Miss H.

The following history is taken from detailed notes of a case that the same therapist brought to a different supervisor. In this therapy the derivative references to the therapist's withdrawal and its manifestation in her management of the ground rules and interpretable content of the therapy are not examined. In this way the case provides a clinical control.

Miss H., a 16-year-old girl, was living with her parents. She was referred for therapy when her parents became alarmed about her membership in a gang that used drugs and was sexually promiscuous and involved in acts of violence. Her chaotic family used excessive controls reflecting sadomasochistic trapping enmeshments; for example, Helen's mother had once locked her in the house, removed the speakers from the telephone, and activated the burgler alarm so that she could not leave.

This therapy started in the fall, and the first four sessions were dominated by associations to her mother's intrusiveness. The fifth session was the first after the onset of the Bell's palsy and, as did the other patients described, the patient for the first time in the therapy talked about being depressed; she was daydreaming a great deal, and her group of school friends was drifting apart.

She started the next session by saying she was still gloomy and that she could not concentrate. She said, "I feel I daydream a lot, like now, I feel I'm here, but my mind is outside of the room." She went on about feeling "spacy" lately, wanting to cry all the time and to get away or to sleep. She felt confused about what it could mean. After reading the transcript, R. D. B. felt that although the patient manifestly was talking about herself, these derivatives suggested a latent unconscious perception and elaboration of the therapist's mood, withdrawal, and consequent missed interventions. In this therapy the therapist made no references to the derivatives or adaptive contexts.

In the eighth session, the patient started by talking about renewed temptation to take drugs, to get back "that feeling," that seemed to represent a wish to regain a feeling of connection to the therapist. She then said that she was upset with her brother because he was seeing less and less of her and was preoccupied with his girlfriend. She continued by talking about getting out of the gang she had belonged to and about having gone to live with her brother's girlfriend's family at that time so that the gang could not locate her, and of how "crazy" that family had been.

In this session the patient represents her wish to make a contact with the therapist that will impart "that feeling" to her. She goes on to say, in disguised derivatives, that the therapist (brother) seems preoccupied and that she is beginning to feel that the place (therapist, brother's girlfriend's family) she has gone to as a refuge and way station in her attempts to extricate herself from crazy enmeshments has turned out to be just as crazy.

This network of derivative communications about the therapy continued in the next session. She started by talking about a fight with her parents over the weekend, in which she had confronted them with their own fears and feelings.

In all of these sessions, the themes being elaborated around the therapist's depression are not being "heard." Without such a recognition, the patient was bound to become more depressed and confused.

In the tenth session the patient again talked about being depressed and moody and about how easily she cried. She did not understand what was going on. She had felt ignored and excluded at a family dinner, even having a conversation with herself to prove that no one was listening. Then, following an urge to sit next to her mother, she had asked her father to change seats. When her mother appeared disgusted by this, she had fled to the bathroom and burst into tears. A woman had come to her in the bathroom and implored her to not cry. The patient's problems, the woman said, could not be as bad as her own, and she had proceeded to relate all of them to the patient. Perplexed, the patient asked the therapist, "Why did this happen?"

In her increasingly clear derivates, the patient seems to be saying that the therapist does not know what is going on, that she (the patient) is not being listened to and so is talking to herself, and that, like the woman in the bathroom, the therapist has problems worse than her own that are being dumped by the therapist into the therapy. In the same session the patient said, "I get so mad at mother lately; I swear at her; I'm hostile—I was *never* like that—and I'm depressed—up and down—what's going on?" In this material the patient offers a rich derivative complex relating to her unconscious perception of and affective reactions to the therapist. She then seems to ask the therapist to interpret the derivative complex: "What's going on?"

She went on to say that she just wanted to get rid of her family and hoped to go abroad for Christmas to see her boyfriend, who had not written for 27 days. Here the derivative communication suggests that she is considering leaving therapy to get rid of the therapist, whom she feels has not really communicated with her for the last four weeks.

The patient then talked about her mother's inability to mother and how a nanny had been delegated this job. She cherished the nanny, who had left when the patient was 10. The therapist related this to a composition the patient had written in school in which she had depicted herself as a child whose real mother had died. She further related it to the patient's style of feeling herself to actually be that girl who had lost an ideal, caring mother.

This dynamic content around the loss of the beloved replacement mother–nanny was of central importance to this patient, but the interpretation did not have the desired effect. To the contrary, after this session a series of latenesses and cancellations culminated in a premature termination. This result may have occurred because the context of the therapist's disrupting input was left out. The patient had been saying through derivatives that for the last four weeks the therapist had become the preoccupied mother, unable to hold the therapeutic situation, from whom she wanted to flee both forward in time to Europe for Christmas and backward in time to the beloved nanny. In retrospect, it seems that well before this session the time would have been right to allude to the patient's perception, and reaction to the perception, of the therapist's state. At this point in the therapy, some reference to her dissatisfaction with the therapy and her growing, although unconscious, impulse to flee from it might have been helpful.

That the patient was considering leaving therapy seemed confirmed in the very next session. She was late for the first time and started with the following question: "Do you think it's more important to keep friends you don't like or to drop them and be lonely?" The patient's cancelling the next session was followed by a two-week Christmas break, after which the patient cancelled another session.

In the first session after the break, she talked mainly about the family vacation south and their involvements with one another. She said she had often felt like crying there. She was better, although she had felt very tired the day of the session. The therapist commented on the depression underlying all she had been talking about and on her attempts to avoid it, and suggested she had missed the previous session as part of this avoidance. The patient disagreed and said, "I don't know why I'm depressed. I think it's my family, not me. . . . I can hardly wait to leave, to go to Europe." The therapist may certainly be right about the patient's underlying depression and in viewing the patient's saying "I think it's my family" as a manifestation of an externalizing defense. Nevertheless, the patient's comment also communicates a valid perception about the therapist—"I think it's my therapist" —and contains a warning that she will soon break off therapy: "I can hardly wait to leave. . . ." This valid perception should have been addressed first. The next week the patient called five minutes before the time of the session to cancel.

In the session after the cancellation, she related three complex dreams in which she was asked to cope alone with situations for which she had not been prepared. The next few sessions were taken up by descriptions of a battle between her mother and her brother's fiancée, a battle that had resulted in the breaking of the engagement. Through this period the mother and brother were functioning poorly, and the patient had become the coping member of the family. She then missed three sessions in a row. When she returned she again talked about her "crazy" family. She talked about her brother, who was still depressed after breaking up with his fiancée and who was lessening the depression by chasing women. She complained about his telling her about his escapades, saying, "I'm his sister, not his buddy." Here she is talking about a situation in which one person uses another to make himself feel better. She is not able to maintain the appropriate relationship to herself and is thus in derivative fashion telling the therapist of her feelings of being used in the therapy and of a reversal of the therapist-patient axis. She went on about her family, saying, "Everyone is crazy, I can hardly wait to get away; I'll never come back." She never did.

In this case, in contrast with the others, the therapy was in its opening phase when the Bell's palsy struck, and this may have been an important factor in determining the outcome. The therapist had other patients in treatments in which she made no intervention around the patient's unconscious perception of her depression that did not end prematurely. It seems, however, that had the latent references to the therapist's effect on the therapeutic field in this therapy been handled in an interpretive fashion, including a use of the therapist's disrupting influence as the central meaningful organizer of the patient's displaced perceptions and reactions to those perceptions, the premature termination might have been avoided and the central issue—the loss of and longing for the good mothering figure—worked through more effectively.

DISCUSSION

In our examples the therapist has an ongoing disruptive effect on the communicative interaction that unconsciously is perceived, reacted to, and expressed in derivatives and action discharge patterns by each of the patients.

Recognition of the therapist's effect on the bipersonal interaction requires the therapist's hearing all the patient's self and object references as applying to the therapist. The level of development of the object relatedness manifest or implied in the patient's material must also be monitored as a depiction of the "here-and-now" state of the therapeutic relationship. In particular, regressive changes in the level of these representations should alert the therapist to potentially disruptive elements of his or her technique. The therapist must then make a judgment as to the relative validity of the patient's unconscious perceptions. This judgment rests on self-knowledge, including the therapist's initial subjective responses to interventions, and on cognitive and affective responses to the ongoing material. He or she must be open to an awareness of deviations from a therapeutic mode of functioning that may have precipitated the ongoing material and be open to the possibility that the therapist's usual mode of working may contain elements that are pathologically gratifying or disruptive and that unconsciously will be perceived as such by the patient (Langs 1981). The therapist must also analyze the origins within the therapist and the patient not only of the patient's perceptions but also of the shift in his or her usual style.

The following catalog of the kinds of derivative responses to therapist's disruptions may help us to recognize their presence:

Allusions to failures of "holding." In case 3, the patient refers to the place she went to for refuge as being as crazy as the situation she was fleeing; in case 2, the patient refers to the hospital strike and its disastrous consequences.

Allusions to inappropriate use of one person by another. In case 3, the patient refers to her brother's use of women to bolster his self-esteem; in case 1, the patient refers to her father's physical abuse and her mother's psychologically abusive entrapments.

Allusions to reversals of the parent-child axis. In case 1, the patient says, "I feel like I'm passing my parents and I don't have time to stop and teach them what I've learned"; in case 3, the patient refers to her parents and brother as functioning poorly and herself as having to compensate for their failures.

Allusions to the self state of the subject or others that may reflect a view of the therapist. In case 1, the patient refers to her mother as doing nothing, just lying around the house; in case 2, the patient for the first time in the therapy refers to being depressed; in case 3, the patient, also for the first time in therapy, refers to being depressed.

First appearance of action-discharge patterns, or an increase in their incidence. In case 2, the patient arrives late to a session for the first time; in case 3, the patient also is late for the first time and cancels subsequent sessions.

Derivative fantasy elaborations of the patient's view of the motive of the therapist. In case 1, the patient says, "When I was a little girl, [my parents] never let me have bad feelings," possibly reflecting the patient's understanding that the therapist has withdrawn in order to avoid the patient's bad feelings; in case 3, the patient details how the woman in the bathroom dumped her own problems onto the patient, reflecting the patient's sense of the therapist's projective identification defenses (Levy and Brown 1980).

Regressions in the object relational level of the communicative properties of the patient's material. In case 2, the patient becomes relatively autistic, giggling and muttering private jokes.

The therapist should become aware quickly of the patient's unconscious perceptions of his or her disruptions and handle the situation interpretively, acknowledging both the therapist's role and the transferences in the patient's responses. The therapist in the clinical examples was just learning about technique and was then further burdened by depression. Her affective state made hearing her patient's responses more difficult. Her depression may have led her to make a number of uncharacteristic noninterpretive interventions that seemingly were attempts to repair the therapeutic disruption. Instead, these interventions fed the cycle of withdrawal, derivative response by the patient, and attempts at repair via gratifications that unconsciously were perceived by the patient as a further withdrawal or as impingements.

The situation provided a unique opportunity in the supervision. Although R.D.B. considers supervision closer to teaching than to therapy, flexibility in this perspective was required and even demanded by the Type Two derivative listening mode. It was important to provide a secure holding situation, both in the supervision and on the clinical service. What proved very helpful to the therapist was the monitoring, in supervision, of the patient's derivative recognitions of the therapist's affect. It allowed the therapist to relax her attempts at hiding her state and become intellectually interested in her patients' unconscious perceptions. This intellectual interest was encouraged further by the suggestion of using the material for this clinical paper and a companion one on countertransference (Krausz and Brown 1983). Because the therapist's intellectual grasp of the material did not lead to interpretive intervention, the supervisor recommended the relatively explicit acknowledgment of her depressed state. Although this self-revelation is itself a deviation in technique and was met, for example, with associations to an abusive parent by the first patient, it did seem to "clear the air" and allow a shift of the field toward the pathology of the patient. In the "control" case, where no such reference was made, there was a premature flight from therapy.

We have presented detailed clinical material illustrating the effects of an acute disruption of the therapist's mood. We have noted its effect on her functioning, including her attempts at noninterpretive repair. We have traced the unconscious responses of her patients and have presented the manner in which the situation was handled in the clinical and supervisory settings.

REFERENCES

FREUD, A. (1954). The widening scope of indications for psychoanalysis: discussion. *Journal of the American Psychoanalytic Association* 2:607–620.

FREUD, S. (1922). Some neurotic mechanisms in jealousy, paranoia and homosexuality. *Standard Edition* 18.

GREENSON, R. (1972). Beyond transference and interpretation. *International Journal of Psycho-Analysis* 53:213–216.

GREENSON, R., AND WEXLER, M. (1969). The nontransference relationship in the psychoanalytic situation. *International Journal of Psycho-Analysis* 50:27–40.

KRAUSZ, R., AND BROWN, R. D. (1983). Countertransference: exploring an avoided aspect. Submitted for publication.

LANGS, R. (1973). The patient's view of the therapist: reality or fantasy? *International Journal of Psychoanalytic Psychotherapy* 2:411–431.

——— (1975). The patient's unconscious perception of the therapist's errors. In *Tactics and Techniques in Psychoanalytic Therapy*, Vol. 2: *Countertransference*, ed. P. L. Giovacchini, pp. 239–250. New York: Jason Aronson.

——— (1981). *Resistances and Interventions: The Nature of Therapeutic Work*. New York: Jason Aronson.

LEVY, J., AND BROWN, R. D. (1980). The uncovering of projective identification in the treatment of the borderline adolescent. *International Journal of Psychoanalytic Psychotherapy* 8:137–149.

LEWIS, J. (1978). *To be a Therapist: The Teaching and Learning.* New York: Brunner/Mazel.

LIMENTANI, D. (1956). Symbiotic identification in schizophrenia. *Psychiatry* 19:231–236.

LITTLE, M. (1951). Countertransference and the patient's response to it. *International Journal of Psycho-Analysis* 32:32–40.

SEARLES, H. (1965). The schizophrenic's vulnerability to the therapist's unconscious processes. In H. Searles, *Collected Papers on Schizophrenia and Related Subjects,* pp. 192–215. New York: International Universities Press.

—— (1979). The function of the patient's realistic perceptions of the analyst in delusional transference. In H. Searles, *Countertransference and Related Subjects: Selected Papers.* pp. 196–227. New York: International Universities Press.

CHAPTER 3

The Therapist's Disability as an Adaptive Context

Leon S. Anisfeld, D.S.W.

What are the stimuli that evoke the patient's unconscious communications in the psychotherapeutic situation? What meaning do these stimuli have for the patient's adaptational and intrapsychic functioning? This chapter will explore the impact of the therapist's disability on the treatment by assessing patients' attempts to communicate their experiences of it and will illustrate how exploration of this issue furthers the positive course of treatment.

From the time of Freud's discovery of transference, based on the "false connection" and "mésalliance" of the hysterical patients he discussed in "Studies on Hysteria" (Freud and Breuer 1895, pp. 67–70, 301n), analysts have attempted to find the stimuli for the patient's unconscious verbal and symptomatic communications in the pathological unconscious distorting effects of the patient's fantasies, memories, and introjects. This approach was expanded to include consideration of the analyst's pathological unconscious fantasies, memories, and introjects (countertransference). This model of transference/countertransference phenomena made it possible to conceive of the therapeutic setting as one in which the patient projected onto the analyst the content of the patient's fantasies, memories, and introjects, thereby distorting the analyst's image and developing pathologically distorted perceptions of the analyst–analysand relationship. On the basis of this transference, the analyst could reconstruct the patient's history and explain its pathological repetition in the present. The model failed to elucidate comprehensively the therapeutic relationship, however, in two very significant ways: (a) by failing to explain the nature of the conscious/unconscious communicative interaction and (b) by neglecting to consider reality factors impinging on the therapy setting to which patient and analyst respond

---

I am indebted to Dr. Robert Langs and Ms. Janet Fisher for their useful suggestions in revising this paper.

interactionally and that cannot be understood by referring solely to the genetic past or neurotic distortions of the patient.

The work of Langs (1976a, 1978, 1980, 1982) has altered radically the conventional view of the analytic situation and, consequently, of the stimuli that evoke the patient's unconscious communications. By viewing the analytic situation as a bipersonal field in which therapist and patient interact and in which both attempt to adapt to the qualities of the field, Langs (1978, 1982) has made clear that specific reality stimuli contributed by the analyst (the adaptive context) evoke in the patient an intrapsychic response that must be analyzed and, when the therapeutic frame is broken, rectified before further analytic investigation is possible (Langs 1978, 1979, 1982). This adaptive context may include anything the therapist says or does and also, as I will demonstrate in this chapter, who the analyst is, his or her personal attributes.

In his biography of Freud, Jones (1957) states:

> Eva Rosenfeld has told me [Jones] of an incident during this time [circa September 1930], and I shall relate it in her own words: "At the end of the summer Professor Freud was far from well, and Ruth Brunswick, evidently forgetting that I was at that time in analysis with him, confided to me her anxiety lest his symptoms were of a serious nature. I was much perturbed and tried not to disclose this during my next interview. Freud of course sensed my hesitation and after he had wrested my unhappy secret from me he said something which has ever since remained my most significant 'lesson' in analytic technique. It was this: 'We have only one aim and only one loyalty, to psychoanalysis. If you break this rule you injure something much more important than any consideration you owe to me.'" (p. 153)

In this paragraph we may note several important facts in addition to Freud's courage and search for truth. There are at least three adaptive contexts: first, the extratherapeutic relationship between the analyst and his patient/disciple; second, the alteration of the anonymity of the analyst; and third, the patient's fear for the analyst's life, which, it seems, necessitates that the analyst "wrest" a secret from her, perhaps because of the patient's fear of upsetting and even harming him. We may understand each of these adaptive contexts as a possible stimulus for the patient's distorted unconscious fantasies about Freud. More immediately, the analyst's physical illness, known to the patient, served as the adaptive context for her attempts to withhold from him a chain of free associations that very likely would have enabled both patient and analyst to uncover the meaningful adaptive and intrapsychic factors underlying her evident idealization of Freud. We see in this incomplete analysis the possible role of a therapist's illness as an adaptive context that creates in the analysis a sector of misalliance between analyst and patient, a barrier to the further exploration of the analyst's vulnerability and the patient's communications about it. The failure to acknowledge and interpret Ms. Rosenfeld's unconscious perception of Freud's physical illness created a barrier to the patient's free association.

REVIEW OF THE LITERATURE

The therapist's state of health or disability has been relatively neglected as a subject of theoretical investigation. It is likely that the same concerns that have inhibited exploration of this issue in professional writings have interfered with clinical investigations of the effect of the therapist's disability on patients: fear of illness and death, the need to preserve the illusion of the therapist's omnipotence, the belief that such exploration would destroy the therapist's anonymity, and so forth. Several authors, however, have attempted to address this issue.

Little (1967) describes his treatment of a female patient that was interrupted for six months because of his myocardial infarction. He responded to the patient's expressions of anger with transference interpretations connecting her anger to earlier losses of father and uncle, ignoring the current stimulus for the affective response and the appropriate (i.e., nonneurotic) aspect of such a reaction to real abandonment. Later, Little recognized his countertransference fear that the patient's intense affect would induce in him a second attack. Nonetheless, he states that the patient's transference anger and his genetic interpretation of it adaptively enabled the analysis to survive the six-month hiatus. One can offer an alternate hypothesis: that the genetic interpretation was offered in an attempt to banish further expressions of hostility, and that the patient accepted this interpretation and remained in treatment because she understood that her analyst felt her anger might threaten his health and she did not wish to kill him. By extending Glover's concept (1955) of inexact interpretations that protect the patient from knowledge of his or her core conflicts, we can postulate that patient and therapist here colluded in believing that anger would hurt the therapist. This protected both parties from their fear of the patient's anger, a collusive arrangement that would certainly have been brought into the treatment had the patient's reality-oriented perception of the analyst's illness and absence been interpreted as a stimulus (adaptive context) for her anger.

Hannett's discussion (1967) of Little's paper points to the "mutual compliance" between patient and analyst designed to avoid the source of the patient's anger. Tower (1967) draws an analogy between the analyst's efforts to protect the patient and parents' attempts to shield their children from significant life stresses. The analyst's overprotectiveness, resented by the patient and inducing in her a sense of frustration, anger, and unpreparedness to deal with life's realities, is not brought into the therapeutic setting. As Wahl (1967) points out in another discussion of the Little paper, countertransference feelings may prevent the patient from dealing with the analyst's fallibility and vulnerability, a situation that hinders growth in the patient and shields the analyst from his or her vulnerabilities in this area.

Grotjahn's 1964 paper, "On Being a Sick Physician," relates his experience when afflicted with a kidney stone. He speaks of his efforts to keep his illness out of sessions, feeling "that a sick physician is a contradiction in the eyes of a patient," that the ill physician feels guilty and defeated, and that his or her sense of omnipotence has been reduced by the disability. This sense of injured narcissistic omnipotence points to the therapist's frequent dichotomization of the therapeutic interaction into a situation that involves a superior/healthy therapist and a dependent/inferior/sick patient. One of the results of this view of the therapeutic dyad is the suppression of the patient's gratification in not being the sick member of the dyad. Consequently, exploration of this issue is discouraged. Although Little and the discussants of his paper, and Grotjahn in his paper, acknowledge the pathological unconscious distortions of both patient and therapist that may emanate from past memories, fantasies, and introjects, the here-and-now stimulus of the analyst's illness for the production of specific patient responses generally is ignored.

Singer (1970) discusses how the revelation of a crisis in the life of the analyst (the illness of his wife, which occasioned his cancellation of sessions for a period of time) mobilized patients' important areas of positive functioning, to both their own and the analyst's benefit. Patients responded in accord with their own character structures and pathology, and the experience was viewed as a stimulus not only for eliciting otherwise latent areas of ego-adaptive behavior, but also for uncovering, exploring, and working through various unconscious themes in the patients' pathology. Although the interactive and adaptive nature of the analytic situation is certainly well described in this paper and the gratification to the analyst and patient of a particular breach in the analyst's anonymity is explored, we are not informed of the effect of the adaptive context on the patients' anger toward the analyst or on the patients' possible views of the analyst as an insufficient or damaged container for the metabolization of the patients' projective identifications. Undoubtedly, the patient is mobilized to serve as the container for the analyst's real life crisis and to find his or her own resources and a sense of usefulness to aid the analyst. But what happens to the dependency and separation needs of the patient after the analyst has provided an adaptive context that has elicited a role reversal of the type described by Singer? Should the analysis be terminated at a point soon after an interaction of this type has occurred? What enduring effects will the experience have on the patient's future communications, interactions, and adaptive responses? These questions are not addressed in Singer's paper, because the discussion of patients' responses to his absence occurs on a manifest content level, utilizing surface reactions to his "disability" and not true unconscious indirect and derivative reactions.

In a paper by Farber (1953) describing certain modifications made in the treatment situation because of the deafness of the analyst, the author concludes that the patient's free association via written communication with him made little difference in the treatment experience. Written communication from patients made it easier to demonstrate the use of denial or repression, to examine material more carefully, to retain, through visual memory, the associations of patients, to find additional clues, and to uncover a number of resistances and unconscious meanings in slips of the pen.

The modus operandi of the analyses conducted by Farber is indeed fascinating, courageous, and certainly revealing along a number of lines. Although the author recognizes that his patients' resistances to this type of treatment did have various unconscious meanings related to the patients' own intrapsychic conflicts, there is no consideration of the effects of non-transference perceptions (valid unconscious perceptions) of the analyst's disability on the nature of these patients' experiences and communications. How often, we may wonder, did his patients communicate a feeling of being ignored, of speaking in a language different from important persons in their environments, and of not being able to make sense to others? And more important, how often were these communications interpreted solely along genetic lines—for example, that mother and father did not understand the patient, were different from the patient, ignored the patient, or forced him or her to accommodate to their ways, to their desires? I ask these questions not so much to illuminate the nature of Farber's specific interpretations to his patients as to question the manner in which we, as analysts, often convert our patients' unconscious perceptions of the stimuli we introduce into the analytic situation into genetic interpretations that presumably unlock the mysteries of our patients' pathology. Although these genetic interpretations may in fact be etiologically correct, their usefulness in producing insight and adaptive structural change may be limited if we ignore our contribution in stimulating the patients' free associations in the present analytic setting.

By overlooking these precipitants in the here-and-now, we may be re-creating the stance of parents who in the past blamed the patient for actions for which the parents themselves were responsible. By underestimating his or her own contribution (stimulus) to the patient's associations and by focusing on the transference to the exclusion of the nontransference responses of the patient, the therapist engages in a denial of the patient's encoded reality-oriented perceptions and the responses emanating from them. Often the therapist will go so far as to refer to the patient's perceptions and responses as resistances to the therapist's interpretations (Langs 1976b, pp. 164–165), ignoring the stimuli that have called them forth and the manner in which the patient has selectively elaborated on these stimuli. This failure on the part of the therapist tends to suppress an accurate genetic reconstruction and dynamic assessment of the meaning of the associations to the patient, which can be formulated properly only in view of the immediate precipitants of the associations.

THE ANALYST'S DISABILITY

In order to demonstrate how the traditional approach can be modified, I will concentrate on how a physical disability that was obvious in me evoked specific communications and internalizations in several of my patients. I will illustrate how my physical condition and my countertransferential responses to that condition served as an adaptive context for the material produced by the patient and for various behaviors, internalizations, and fantasies, both positive and negative, communicated within the analytic situation.

Several years ago I experienced a physical condition that required my using a cane to walk. I was aware at the time that my patients would notice the cane, and when they referred to it by questioning me about what was wrong, I maintained a basically neutral and anonymous position, interpreting their concerns about me and about my future (and therefore my ability to continue to care for them) as manifestations of the transference, i.e., as concerns displaced onto me from parental figures from the past. With those patients who were too guilty, frightened, or ashamed to speak openly of my disability, I maintained a silence that, I was to learn later, represented a collusion of mutual convenience: for me, the disability would be ignored and I could feel normal, totally capable of being the proper container for my patients' projective identifications, and in control; for the patient, feelings of insecurity, of not having a therapist who could contain their feelings of rage and helplessness, could be ignored, and the pain attending these feelings suppressed.

Several papers that I read at this time led me to modify this collusive arrangement. Searles (1975) has examined the patient's innate need to care for and cure the analyst (mother). This discussion helped alert me to a number of direct and indirect indications from my patients that they wished to care for me and that my avoidance of their efforts had more to do with self-protection than with concern for them or the maintenance of an uncontaminated analytic setting.

At about the same time I read several of Langs's writings (1975a, 1975b, 1976a, 1978, 1979) that spoke of the collusion of patient and therapist in creating barriers to communication. Even more important, Langs's concept of the adaptive context pointed to the very significant stimuli that the therapist provides for the patient's unconscious and conscious communications in the therapeutic setting. Working with Langs, I became aware after a short time that my disability did not simply trigger distorted unconscious pathological (transference) responses in the patient, but that it was also (mainly) a stimulus for patients' communications that included valid unconscious perceptions of me. These unconscious perceptions were then elaborated along lines that expressed each patient's particular genetic and characterological background and various unconscious fantasies about me and about the patient (Langs's concept of the "me–not me" interface is relevant here). Clinically, it became evident that the patient's response to my disability and the use of my disability as a stimulus for his or her associations had to be viewed first in terms of unconscious veridical perceptions and only later as these reactions were elaborated in terms of the transference. Thus the unconscious, veridical nature of the perception had to be interpreted first; if not, the transference interpretation would be denied or accepted only intellectually, with little insight or structural change.

Patient 1

The first vignette illustrates how the adaptive context of my disability is represented by the patient, and how it is related to his unconscious perception of me and of himself, to his unconscious fantasies, memories, and introjects, and to the ways in which these unconscious elements connect to those perceptions.

The patient, an obsessional professional man in his mid-thirties, had been in analysis with me for four years. He had been in therapy before my disability became obvious and in fact had seen me bicycling to my office. In the sessions preceding the one I will report, he had spoken of his preoccupation with time and how it was necessary for him to be in control of every moment of his waking life.

The patient began this session with a denial of his difficulties in managing his schedule and then admitted that in fact he has felt quite "lame" at work. His denial, he said, was meant to impress me with his perfection, because he felt for some reason a need to show no weakness to me. This was the case, he said, in other situations as well, especially in his sexual relations, in which he viewed each encounter as his first. He then spoke of an incident that had occurred when he was 5 years old and that he had discussed on a number of previous occasions. His mother had feigned a heart attack when the patient, as a young boy, had disobeyed her. His next association was to jogging in the park, which he did daily. The previous day a man had come over to him and asked if he could run alongside the patient, because the man had recently been mugged. The patient had agreed, "and then," he said, "I mugged him. It's just a joke, but a lot of women are raped by guys who run next to them in the park. And this guy later told me that he had also been attacked while cycling through the park."

At this point I said to the patient that he had begun by telling me that he didn't want to appear lame or show any weakness to me, and that my "lameness" might have some connection with this. I then pointed out how he had spoken of feeling as though each sexual encounter was his first and then about his mother's supposed heart attack. His next association had concerned a man asking to run alongside him and how women are often tricked and then raped by similar means. Was there some connection between my lameness, his need to hide his imperfections from me, and his being hurt?

The patient spoke of how he sometimes wondered whether he could trust me, as though, like his mother, my disability was an attempt to trick him into doing or saying something. In fact, he distrusted many people. He then spoke of his sadness about the death of a friend who, ill for many years, had died recently. He had had a dream from which he had awakened crying the previous night about this friend's death. "And if you [the analyst] died I would feel such loss, as though you abandoned me." He spoke next of how he felt abandoned by a former girlfriend who had recently married. It was "shocking to see her again." He then spoke of how inadequate he felt when his present girlfriend demanded that he satisfy her sexually. The demands that people made of him always seemed to come as surprises, like his mother's feigned heart attack. He felt that to safeguard himself from these sudden demands, he had to be always in control, always perfect. At the same time he had to put everyone on a pedestal, so that they would never fool him as his mother had.

The use of my disability as an adaptive context led in this session to a new understanding by the patient of the effects of his mother's "heart attack." The linking of his need for perfection in both self and object representations to the warding off of the early trauma of a threatened loss of the loved mother may be viewed as a "selected fact" (Bion 1962). As subsequent sessions were to make clear, the patient's obsessional concern with time and control was a defensive maneuver designed to ward off the traumatic effect of the feigned heart attack and the mother's devious means of controlling the patient as a boy. The real perception of my disability was connected selectively by the patient with the "heart attack," the two events being connected by means of an analogy: the surprise of the mother's "attack" was linked to the surprise of seeing me use a cane after having seen me walk and cycle normally. In the sessions following the one presented, the patient's associations focused on his overwhelming fear of death, a fear that had troubled him since age 8.

The intervention I offered relating my disability to the mother's "heart attack" and to the patient's perfectionistic strivings thus set the stage for the patient's production of a selected fact, the latter serving to organize the material in a novel manner and to link elements of the material that had been defensively kept apart. Langs (1979, 1982) has shown how the production of such a selected fact by the patient is one criterion for the validation of an interpretation in psychotherapy.

Still, the interventive strategy I have outlined is incomplete. There is no reference in the intervention to the patient's associations concerning rape of women joggers. Nor is there any reference to why the "heart attack" incident is brought up at this point. One speculation is that the patient wanted me to contain the fear of death, which was "too powerful for his personality to contain, the idea being that if they [the fearful ideas] were allowed to repose there [within me] long enough they would undergo modification by my psyche and could then be safely reintrojected" (Bion 1959, p. 312).

Another speculation, more convincing if only because of the multiple functions implied, is that the patient speaks of the fear of death in order to frighten me into realizing the effect of my disability on him and in stimulating his fantasies. This would explain the association to the mother's "heart attack." The latter incident, although traumatic, may have been brought into his associations to reassure me and himself that the disability (like the "heart attack") was after all not real. The desire to frighten and harm me (and the mother) is thus placed side by side with the wish to deny my disability and save the loved object. The ambivalence revealed by this explanation is very much evidenced in the patient's overall neurotic style. My having missed this ambivalence in my intervention was undoubtedly a function of my fear of death as connected with the disability, as was my omission of the patient's dream about his recently deceased friend. In this case the adaptive context of my disability is the day residue and latent stimulus for the manifest dream content (Langs 1971).

Another missed formulation concerns the patient's reference to the other jogger who had been mugged and his association to women being raped by men who pretend to be fellow joggers. I missed in this association the patient's emasculation of me, his putting me in the position of the helpless, disabled woman whom he could rape. The role reversal with the mother who pretended to be his friend and then "raped" him with the surprise "heart attack" is obvious in retrospect. Such an interpretation would have been very much in keeping with this man's view of women. My shame and embarrassment as well as my own concerns that my disability was emasculating served as a countertransference basis for the missed intervention.

Thus, in this case my disability was an example of a real disturbance in the therapist's life that led to a countertransference avoidance of interpretations based on the patient's veridical perception of the disability. Such interpretations could have led to various genetic and dynamic formulations, and ultimately to the repressed instinctual forces.

The emotional investment on the part of the analyst in producing validated interpretations sometimes yields to the emotional investment in guarding against the lack of control, inner turmoil, and feelings of interpersonal weakness occasioned by having to view one's disability consistently as an adaptive context. The disability will not always be the major adaptive context in the interactional sphere and thus the focal point for one's interventions. Still, the disability must be kept in mind as a background adaptive context and as such may be connected unconsciously at any moment to the patient's derivative communications. In such a case, the patient's veridical unconscious perceptions must be acknowledged and interpreted before the connection to distorted, unconscious fantasies, memories and introjects (transference) can be made.

When the therapist is unwilling to deal with the role the disability plays as a veridical unconscious perception on the part of the patient, three interventive mistakes are commonly made. (1) As in the vignette presented, interpretations may be missed. This is true not only of the interpretation per se, but also of the listening and formulating process as a whole, even before the interpretation is offered verbally to the patient. The second vignette will also illustrate missed interpretations and derivative communications in the patient's subsequent material that allude to them. (2) Effects of the analyst's countertransferential ignorance of the adaptive context besides the missing of interpretations are illustrated in the papers by Little, Farber, and Singer that I have discussed. In Farber's and Little's papers there is a focus on connecting the patient's associations to genetic material rather than to the patient's veridical perception of the analyst's disabilities. The effect is a premature genetic interpretation of presumably unconscious and distorted fantasies, memories, and introjects and an ignoring of patients' veridical perceptions of the psychotherapeutic setting in general and the analyst in particular. (3) In Singer's paper countertransference is displayed in a focus on the manifest content of associations to the adaptive context of the analyst's disability (or, rather, his absence because of the illness of his wife). In this case the adaptive context is recognized by the analyst (Singer), but the unconscious derivatives related to that adaptive context are ignored. A focus on the manifest content helpfulness of the patient to the distressed analyst is the only result of the analyst's consideration of the adaptive context. Unconscious instinctual drive derivatives elicited by the nature of the analyst–analysand interaction are not considered.

Patient 2

The second vignette illustrates my missing of interpretations as a result of countertransferential fears of the patient's valid perceptions of my disability. In this case the missed interpretation is even more obvious, in that my response to the patient's derivative communication is silence.

The patient was a young, white Jewish man who had lived with a Puerto Rican woman, to his parents' chagrin, until one month after entering treatment. This vignette consists of patient communications in a session involving a break in the therapeutic frame, in which I agreed to change the patient's regular hour because of a job commitment he could not alter:

Well, I ended up going to visit my family after all. [The patient had committed himself to not visiting his family on this occasion but felt blackmailed into doing so by his mother's crying. This may be a response to my being blackmailed by the patient to change his hour or a perception of being "blackmailed" into a makeup visit by my separation anxiety.] It was good in a way. I got together with some old friends. But my friends and my mother and father kept making racial slurs. [This is the first allusion in the session to the financially deprived girlfriend, whom the patient's parents do not want him to see. The parents have also expressed their opinion that their son does not really need to see me.] "Spic" this and "Spic" that, and I felt very bad about it. [The patient is unaware that he is looking down to the side of my chair, where my cane is.] My father was watching a ball game and when one of the players caught the ball, he yelled, "Run, Rican, run!" [This may be an allusion to my not being able to run. It may also be an expression of anger toward me.] My parents fought. It began with an argument between me and my mother, and it ended up with me in the middle and my parents fighting. And my mother, she just cooked and cooked. She couldn't stop feeding me. [Perhaps this is a reference to my "feeding" him with a substitute session, which is a break in the frame of our agreement; if so, it might well be a perception of me as feeding him in response to sensing his anger or distress.] And she's so superstitious. They were out of the house for a while to pick up my sister, who is pregnant, so I moved the television into another room. When they got back, my sister stepped over the TV cord and my mother got hysterical. "Don't step over the cord! The baby will come out twisted and deformed." [This is undoubtedly a perception of me and a fantasy of how I got disabled.] I can't stand it. It's like the story about my grandmother when she was pregnant with my aunt and this big Puerto Rican woman threw a piece of brown bread at her and it hit my grandmother in the thigh and my aunt has a mole on her leg just where the bread hit my grandmother. How can she believe that? And I have this wedding to go to where they live. I don't really want to go. By the way, I went back with my [Puerto Rican] girlfriend, and I didn't tell my parents. [This is perhaps the connecting link in the fantasy of me and his girlfriend as damaged selves.] My mother would just cry. Anyway, I have this wedding to go to and I don't want to go, mainly as a form of self-assertion, but I guess also because I don't really have a suit to wear or the money for a gift. [Here is the connection to his damaged self.] And my mother, she's such a slave to my father. She has a bad heart, but she runs and runs [!] to wait on him. I don't understand it. It's not her job.

One can listen to this patient's words and hear reference to his ambivalent love of his parents, his feelings of guilt when he disobeys them, and his feelings of entrapment. Although all these feelings undeniably are represented, the use of my disability as an adaptive context or stimulus for the patient's associations provides deeper interpretive possibilities and permits the acknowledgment of the patient's real, albeit unconscious, perception of the analyst and the latter's contribution to the patient's associations. The distorted transference-based and projective aspects of the patient's associations can then be seen more clearly as elaborations of his nontransference-based perceptions.

We hear a great deal in this vignette about social slurs leveled against minorities. The patient's reference to his girlfriend, and the fact that they had broken up just after the patient began to see me (and with a very moderate response from him to this break-up, the prospect of which had frightened him terribly and served as his initial reason for entering therapy), suggest that I may have replaced this minority girlfriend as a maligned external representation of his defective self-image (note the reference to the wedding he does not want to attend because he has no suit and no money for a gift). Although the references to his mother's feeding him and to the gift also refer to the adaptive context or stimulus of my "gift" of a substitute session, other derivatives point more strongly to my disability. In two places the patient refers to people who are maligned (the Hispanic ball player and the mother-as-slave) and to running, an obvious derivative allusion to my disability and an attempt at its undoing.

These derivatives indicate how I, as the disabled person, serve as an external representation of his own damaged self-esteem and how, in two derivatives dealing with the mother's superstitious beliefs, the patient's primitive fantasies concerning the cause of the self–other damage is expressed. The pregnant sister, by stepping over the television cord, will produce a twisted baby, and the Puerto Rican woman who throws a piece of bread at the grandmother's leg produces a mole on the aunt's thigh. These associations not only reveal the primitive fantasies underlying the patient's view of my physical disability and his damaged self-esteem, but also may be seen as a working through process in which the patient, in unconsciously identifying with me, strives to work through his inadequate self-image by exploring it through associations to me.

Langs (1978, 1979, 1982) has identified this simultaneous reference of patients to themselves and to the therapist as the "me–not me" interface, and it may serve as one explanation for patients' staying in therapy with what they might consider a damaged container. This damaged container—especially if it proves capable of metabolizing and returning to the patient his or her projections and projective identifications in a new and/or better form—may provide a health-promoting introject for the patient. When the therapist's contribution is acknowledged, there is then an opportunity to explore and resolve the patient's conflict-ridden self-perspective.

Unfortunately, I was not ready at this point to serve in this capacity for this patient. Being frightened by his unconscious derivative communications to me as the disabled therapist, I remained silent, missing the appropriate interpretations that would have connected my disability (adaptive context) to the patient's disturbed self-perceptions (indicators) via his unconscious derivative allusions to the adaptive context.

As Raney (1981) has pointed out, the newcomer to the Langsian method, aware that the patient's associations often refer to his or her veridical (nondistorted, unconscious) perceptions of the analyst, frequently remains silent so as to avoid the narcissistic injury of being "discovered" by the patient. The therapist's silence does not, however, put the matter to rest in the patient's mind. Eventually, when it is appropriate, the patient will communicate his or her perception that an interpretation has been missed.

The patient described in the preceding vignette missed the next session and on his return spoke of how he could never communicate with his father, who was always too shallow or too afraid to try to understand him. My silence had been, in effect, unconsciously interpreted by the patient—as seen in his unconscious derivative communications—as a disability, a weakness. The attempt to defend myself against the narcissistic injury of the patient's perception of my disability proved to be an indication to the patient that I was disabled not only physically, but also in my failure to understand his communications.

The patient's absence, a gross behavioral resistance to treatment, is his first response to the missed interpretation. This man, an extremely passive-dependent character with a rather evident false self-organization, according to Winnicott (1956) requires an analytic setting that provides an opportunity to relive in the present the maladaptive early environment so as to be able to transcend it. Winnicott observes that the resistance in such an analysis indicates that the analyst has made a mistake. Resistance may thus be viewed as a product of the therapeutic interaction and as the patient's response to the therapist's countertransference.

Thus, the role of countertransference is of crucial importance here. If the analyst defends himself or herself against the mistake, the patient "misses the opportunity for being angry about a past failure just where anger was becoming possible for the first time" (Winnicott 1956, p. 388). In the second vignette, my missing the interpretation of the patient's unconscious perception of me as disabled physically led to his viewing me as, like his childhood father, disabled in my ability to relate to him. His absence may thus be seen as a resistance to facing the early traumatic disability of his infantile environment as it is repeated on some level by me in the counter-transference.

Any attempt to help the patient through this past environmental failure requires its correction in the present analytic setting. One possible manner of doing this, and consequently of permitting the patient's anger to be expressed in the analysis, is to interpret his valid unconscious perceptions and reactions to the disability and to my manner of dealing with it, as displayed, for example, in my silence on the subject. When I failed to interpret my silence as the stimulus for the patient's subsequent absence, I created a situation in which the patient could perceive me as disabled not simply physically, but also therapeutically. This left the patient to choose between terminating his treatment because it did not provide an environment good enough to contain his projective identifications and, perhaps more disastrous, continuing the treatment with the analyst serving as the early not-good-enough mother who forces him to deny his veridical perceptions in order to keep the analyst–mother alive and to maintain a false self.

SUMMARY

Factors in the personal life of the analyst, such as a physical disability, serve as stimuli or adaptive contexts for unconscious derivative communications based on veridical unconscious perceptions by the patient. The analyst's narcissistic defensiveness in relation to these adaptive contexts may result in at least one of the following countertransference-based errors in interpretation: (1) the failure to interpret, as illustrated in the two vignettes presented; (2) premature interpretation, focusing on constructions of distorted fantasies, memories, and introjects (transferences) to the exclusion of the patient's veridical unconscious perceptions; and (3) a focus on manifest content and the exclusion of unconscious derivative communications.

The patient inevitably will relate to the therapist his or her perception of the therapist's errors via additional unconscious derivatives. When these derivatives are not recognized and interpreted, there is likely to be a major resistance to—if not outright termination of—the treatment. An alternate patient response is to form a collusive bond with the therapist that repeats the early maladaptive environmental interaction, strengthening the hold of pathological introjects and promoting the maintenance of a false self-organization in both patient and therapist.

POSTSCRIPT

After the completion of this chapter, two psychoanalytic contributions appeared on serious illness in the analyst (Abend 1982, Dewald 1982). The major issue addressed by both authors concerns the amount of information that the (formerly or presently) ill analyst should share with patients when his or her absence from analytic sessions cannot be avoided.

Dewald addresses the effects of reality on the transference-based reactions of the patient. Patients, he states, require different amounts of factual information, depending on the severity of their pathology and the stage of their treatment. Although he mentions nontransference responses by patients to the analyst's illness, Dewald studies these reactions on a manifest level. Unconscious, derivative communications—i.e., reactions based on perceptions of the specific adaptive contexts—are not considered. Dewald considers only underlying fantasy formations, and these on a manifest content basis.

Dewald studies how patients "use the fact of illness to rationalize their avoidance of transference experience and interaction," based on "multiple and rigid defenses against manifest dependency or affective therapeutic involvement" (p. 358). Dewald's patients, however, were notified of his illness by a third party to the treatment—his secretary—and a further break in analytic anonymity occurred when his wife responded to the get-well cards sent to him by his patients. Thus, one might explain his patients' "avoidance of transference experience and interaction" not as "rationalizations" based on unconscious fantasies but as valid and justifiable responses to perceptions of breaks in confidentiality stimulated by the intrusion of third parties into the analyst–analysand relationship.

Abend differs from Dewald in his belief that "optimal analytic technique is more likely to suffer from an analyst's explicit focus, in conjunction with the analysand, on the reality relationship than it will by the analyst's insistence on attending to its unconscious meanings instead" (p. 367). Abend also declares that it is not merely the content of the analyst's revelation to the patient but also the fact of the revelation itself that is significant.[1] He concludes that modifying analytic abstinence when ill is not an advisable procedure because the "inescapable influence of countertransference factors operates precisely against the very objectivity on which we are accustomed to rely in reaching clinical decisions" (p. 378).

It has been my experience that deviation from standard analytic technique is not advisable, and I therefore agree with the position taken by Abend. It is in the area of methodology, however, that we differ. Although he states clearly "that we sorely lack reliable data to guide us in making assessments and decisions in managing these situations," the clinical basis for the conclusions that both he and Dewald reach is insubstantial. Neither the degree of deviation from the standard technique nor the specific unconscious derivative reactions from the patient to these deviations are stated in these

---

[1]To cite a related observation, there have been instances of my alluding to my illness before it was represented in the patient's own material. Without exception, this produced negative reactions—emotionally, cognitively, and interpersonally.

papers or considered in these analyses. Specific excerpts from the sessions in question are required to raise Abend's and Dewald's opinions to the level of empirically verifiable and replicable conclusions. It is with the latter intention in mind that I have offered detailed data in my own presentation. It is on the basis of studying the patient's unconscious derivative responses to the analyst's deviations from standard technique (adaptive contexts) that questions concerning the optimal level of adherence to standard technique can be answered.

REFERENCES

ABEND, S. M. (1982). Serious illness in the analyst: countertransference considerations. *Journal of the American Psychoanalytic Association* 30:365–379.

BION, W. R. (1959). Attacks on linking. *International Journal of Psycho-Analysis* 40:308–315.

———— (1962). Learning from experience. In W. R. Bion, *Seven Servants*, pp. 1–111. New York: Jason Aronson, 1977.

BREUER, J., and FREUD, S., (1893–1895). Studies on hysteria. *Standard Edition 2.*

DEWALD, P. (1982). Serious illness in the analyst: transference, countertransference and reality response. *Journal of the American Psychoanalytic Association* 30:347–363.

FARBER, D. J. (1953). Written communication in psychotherapy. *Psychiatry* 16:365–374.

GLOVER, E. (1955). The therapeutic effect of inexact interpretation: a contribution to the theory of suggestion. In E. Glover, *The Technique of Psychoanalysis*, pp. 353–366. New York: International Universities Press.

GROTJAHN, M. (1964). On being a sick physician. *New Dimensions in Psychosomatic Medicine*, ed. C. Wahl, pp. 117–127. Boston: Little, Brown.

HANNETT, F. (1967). Discussant in Little (1967).

JONES, E. (1957). *The Life and Work of Sigmund Freud.* Vol. 3. New York: Basic Books.

LANGS, R. (1971). Day residues, recall residues, and dreams: reality and psyche. *Journal of the American Psychoanalytic Association* 19:499–523.

———— (1975a). Therapeutic misalliances. *International Journal of Psychoanalytic Psychotherapy* 4:77–105.

———— (1975b). The therapeutic relationship and deviations in technique. *International Journal of Psychoanalytic Psychotherapy* 4:106–141.

———— (1976a). *The Bipersonal Field.* New York: Jason Aronson.

———— (1976b). *The Therapeutic Interaction*, Vol. 2: *A Critical Overview and Synthesis.* New York: Jason Aronson.

———— (1978). *The Listening Process.* New York: Jason Aronson.

———— (1979). *The Supervisory Experience.* New York: Jason Aronson.

———— (1980). *Interactions: The Realm of Transference and Countertransference.* New York: Jason Aronson.

———— (1982). *Psychotherapy: A Basic Text.* New York: Jason Aronson.

LITTLE, R. (1967). Transference, countertransference and survival reactions following an analyst's heart attack. *Psychoanalytic Forum* 2:107–113.

RANEY, J. (1981). Clinical article: narcissistic defensiveness and the interactional approach. *Newsletter of the Society for Psychoanalytic Psychotherapy* 1(2):4–9.

SEARLES, H. (1975). The patient as therapist to his analyst. In *Tactics and Techniques in Psychoanalytic Therapy*, Vol. 2: *Countertransference*, ed. P. L. Giovacchini, pp. 95–151. New York: Jason Aronson.

SINGER, E. (1970). The patient aids the analyst: some clinical and theoretical observations. In *In the Name of Life: Essays in Honor of Erich Fromm*, ed. B. Landis and E. Tauber, pp. 56–68. New York: Holt, Rinehart and Winston.

TOWER, L. E. (1967). Discussant in Little (1967).

WAHL, C. W. (1967). Discussant in Little (1967).

WINNICOTT, D. W. (1956). Symposium: on transference. *International Journal of Psycho-Analysis* 37:386–388.

CHAPTER 4

The Technique of Questioning

Theodore L. Dorpat, M.D.

This chapter examines and discusses the technique of questioning in psycho-analysis and psychoanalytic psychotherapy. A presentation of the author's clinical studies on questioning follows a review of the relevant literature.

REVIEW OF THE LITERATURE

Aside from articles by Olinick (1954, 1957, 1980) and some brief comments by Eissler (1953), Greenson (1967), and others, few analysts have studied or written about the use of questions in psychoanalysis. In the field of psychoanalytic psychotherapy, Langs (1979a, 1979b, 1980) is one of the few who have performed clinical studies on questioning.

With the exception of the work of Langs (1976, 1978, 1979a, 1979b, 1980) and Olinick (1954, 1957, 1980), recent writings on questions simply have reiterated earlier commentaries. Few authors have provided clinical evidence to support their conclusions and recommendations regarding questioning in either psychoanalysis or psychoanalytic psychotherapy. The reader gains the unmistakable impression that contemporary writers on this subject merely have passed on to the present generation what they learned from past generations of analysts.

Eissler (1953) considered the question to be a basic and indispensable tool of analysis and one that is essentially different from interpretation. He accurately observed that the task of questioning has been taken for granted and that the "psychology of questions" has not yet been written. Greenson (1967) recommended the use of questions in psychoanalysis, but he provided little comment on the indications or contraindications for their use. He subscribed to the classical view that all analytic techniques are subordinate to interpretation, and he included questions, as well as clarification and confrontation, as acceptable techniques preparatory to interpretation. In a section on the pursuit of the transference trigger, he gave examples of questioning, such as "If a patient tells me I am disgusting, I ask what is disgusting about me" (p. 308). Other presented examples of questions include: "Where did you have this feeling or impulse before?" "What occurs to you if you let your thoughts drift with these feelings and impulses?" (p. 311), and "Towards whom did you feel this way in the past?" (p. 313).

Glover (1955) sent a questionnaire on psychoanalytic technique to 29 practicing analysts in England, and he received replies from 24. One item in the questionnaire was "Do you ask direct questions: (a) about matters of fact, e.g., family history; (b) about matters of phantasy; (c) about emotional reactions?" A majority of the respondents said they asked questions freely; others occasionally did. Some said they never asked questions in the early stages of analysis.

Glover commented that it seems quite natural to ask questions about matters of fact about which one is in doubt. Some patients are put at ease by being asked questions. Many family situations, he posited, would be grasped much more quickly by the analyst who did not hesitate to ask about some detail instead of waiting. He warned against any use of "history-taking" procedures, because they tend to stultify free association.

In their book on psychoanalytic technique, Menninger and Holzman (1973) devote only one paragraph to questions. They state that it is often important in the early stages of analysis to ask questions about details or other matters of fact and to inquire as to the patient's feelings about a particular matter. Standard questions, in their view, include: "What occurs to you about that?" "What associations do you have to that?" and "What do you think?"

What Olinick said in 1954 still holds true: "Of the behavioral interventions available to the psychoanalyst, perhaps none has been more taken for granted and less subjected to careful scrutiny than has questioning" (p. 57). He claimed that the use of questions by the analyst is more frequent in the early phase of treatment. Olinick (1954) also argued that the discrepancies, misinformation, and omissions of the patient reflect a need on the part of the patient for a guideline, an orienting pattern, toward which the analyst by tactful questions may "nudge" the patient. He noted that the act of questioning may be predicated on the reluctance or passivity of the person questioned or on the impatience or curiosity of the questioner. He recommended questioning when preinterpretive validation requires an inquiry into external and internal circumstances.

Olinick (1954) listed the conditions, such as anxiety or resistance of the patient, that permit a question to be asked. Other conditions included are special situations, such as when one is confronted with an inarticulate, borderline, or psychotic patient. His guidelines and indications for questioning are too general; they cast too large a net to serve as suitable and specific guides for questioning. Except for a brief clinical vignette, Olinick did not provide clinical evidence to support his claims for the conditions for questioning. His vignette does not give sufficient data for the reader to draw his or her own inferences or conclusions about the merits of the questioning used with the case presented.

Olinick (1954) warned about the misuse of questions, and he cautioned that questions may become an intrusion into the patient's freedom of choice. Eissler (1953) viewed questions as part of the basic model of analytic technique. Olinick, in contrast, considered questioning a deviation from the basic model. He claimed that questions should be self-eliminating, but he did not say how they can be self-eliminating. He recommended that analysts look to their countertransference to determine if they are using questioning in an antitherapeutic manner—for example, to enforce a sadomasochistic relationship.

Another article by Olinick (1957) concerns the general psychology of the question and is not concerned specifically with the use of questioning in psychoanalytic technique. He wrote of the unconscious motives and fantasies of the questioner, and he described the question as a device for the expression of aggression and active mastery. He emphasized the intrusive, acquisitive, and aggressive aspects of questioning.

Hollender (1965) discussed the reasons for asking questions in psycho-analytic psychotherapy, including: (1) to clarify a point (he does not state whether the clarification is made for the patient's sake or for the therapist's); (2) to elicit additional information "which might be helpful in substantiating or excluding one or another hypothesis being considered as the basis for an interpretation" (p. 87); and (3) "to encourage the patient to explore a subject mentioned in passing" (p. 87). He proscribed questions designed to satisfy the therapist's personal curiosity.

There have been no systematic studies of the frequency with which questioning is used in either psychoanalysis or psychoanalytic psychotherapy. My impression from reading the relevant literature and from my work as a supervisor is that questioning is the most common mode of intervention used in both psychoanalysis and psychoanalytic psychotherapy. In the type of psychoanalytically oriented therapy called "sector therapy" by Deutsch and Murphy (1955), questions are used extensively. An examination of their two-volume work indicates that questions made up the preponderance of the therapists' interventions. My study of Dewald's report (1972) of an entire analysis revealed that questioning was the most frequent type of intervention. Dewald used questions an average of 8.7 times per session, and 70.5 percent of all of his interventions were questions.

In his earlier writings Langs (1973, 1974) approved of the use of questions, but in his later writings he considers it antitherapeutic and recommends discarding it. He states that "active questioning can shift a patient capable of symbolic communication toward projective identification or intense defensiveness. It moves the patient toward the surface of his thoughts, stresses manifest content, and is inimical to communication of Type Two derivatives" (1979a, p. 213). In his books that report seminars in which residents presented psychotherapy patients, he demonstrates that questions tend to generate resistances and defensive activity (1976, 1979a, 1980).

Instead of the overt questioning of the patient, Langs (1979a) recommends the use of "silent questions" that arise in the mind of the therapist as he or she listens to the patient. Such silent questions can be used to construct hypotheses that can be validated by the patient's response to the therapist's interventions.

The following vignette of Langs (1979a) illustrates the defensive and countertransference aspects of questions. A male patient remarked, "By the way, I met a woman that you know." The therapist responded, "Who is she?" According to Langs, the question reflects considerable anxiety on the part of the therapist, and the intervention is a type of projective identification. The question reflects the therapist's difficulty in managing his own curiosity, and it places into the patient the therapist's sense of anxiety: his poor controls and his defensiveness. The therapist's presentation of what happened after this incident confirms Langs's prediction that the patient unconsciously would introject the therapist's lack of a sense of patience and management.

Langs offers the following formulation about the persistent questioning of this therapist: The therapist's active inquiries unconsciously are designed to restrict the patient's communications about his dating an acquaintance of the therapist. The questioning interventions constrict the communicative field and protect the therapist from the communication of unconscious derivatives relating to the patient's date with the therapist's acquaintance. Whereas the conscious communication is "Tell me more," the unconscious communication is "Tell me nothing more."

In another case study of Langs (1979a), a therapist uses repetitive and often irrelevant questions to create a Type C form of communication. Reality-oriented questions unconsciously are designed as impenetrable defenses and barriers against open symbolic communication.

In Langs's more recent writings, various commonly used interventions are studied from a communicative perspective in which the unconscious qualities and functions of such interventions become the subject of extensive investigation. Langs (1978) recommends discarding questions and such other previously employed interventions as clarification and confrontation. His position is based on repeated tests of the unconscious functions, communications, and meanings conveyed in the interaction between the patient and therapist or analyst by each of the interventions mentioned (1978). Each instance of the use of such interventions was taken as an adaptive context, and the patient's responses were evaluated for Type Two derivatives and studied as commentaries in terms of both meanings and validity.

Langs (1978) claims that questions and clarifications are used largely because of confusion as to the nature of the neurotic communications and the best means of obtaining derivatives from patients. Rather than recognizing that silence and a secure frame offer conditions that best facilitate the patient's self-expression in derivative and analyzable form, some analysts mistakenly believe that pertinent questions and confrontations foster such expression.

There has been little other systematic study of the use of questioning. With the exception of the papers by Olinick and Langs, the subject of questions has gone unexamined and unquestioned.

CLINICAL INVESTIGATIONS OF QUESTIONING

The findings and conclusions of my clinical studies on the use of questioning in psychoanalysis and psychoanalytic psychotherapy apply equally to both types of treatment. The methods used in this study owe much to Langs's communicative approach: I have attempted to study the unconscious interactions that take place in the question-and-answer form of communication in the analytic situation, as well as the unconscious meanings and functions of such communication. Because my use of questions has declined markedly in the past ten years, I have little recent clinical data from my own work in analysis or psychotherapy. With the exception of the next section of this chapter, the clinical data presented are taken from supervisory work with candidates, analysts, and psychotherapists.

Countertransference and Questioning

As part of this study on questioning, I reviewed some progress notes made over ten years ago during the analysis of a case reported previously (Dorpat 1978). The notes cover the second year of a seven-year successful analysis of a 32-year-old woman who began treatment with symptoms of depression and fears of her suicidal impulses.

One of the principle concerns in this period of her analysis was her unstable capacity for object constancy. Whenever she could maintain an image of the analyst outside of analytic hours, her symptoms disappeared. When she could not remember my "presence" (her word) or recall my talking and listening to her, her symptoms would reappear. My explanatory formulations about these changes followed classical dynamic concepts about unconscious conflicts over aggression. In brief, I thought that the patient's anxiety over unconscious angry feelings toward the analyst prevented her from recalling the image of the analyst.

A systematic study of the process notes demonstrated convincingly that a number of related untoward responses (such as depression, withdrawal, verbal expressions concerning her inability to "find you," and fears of being alone) followed my questioning and were reactions to the questions.

Repeated study of the process notes of 60 sessions revealed a consistent interactional pattern. Active questioning was followed regularly by the patient's communication of feeling distant and detached from the analyst and sometimes by the recrudescence of her depressive symptoms. In one session she said, "I had a dream last night. In the dream I am with you. We were talking together. It was very nice. You left. I was all alone. I felt lost. I could not find you." After a moment's pause she continued in a sarcastic tone, "I suppose you will ask me 'How does the dream apply to your life?' I don't know and I guess I don't care."

Her sarcastic remark refers to my questioning the previous day and to the question ("How do you think your dream applies to your life?") I had asked her at that time after she had told me about a dream. Her dream about my leaving her replicates and symbolizes the effects of my intrusive and intellectualizing questions.

In one session I made an interpretation that she had a need to prevent herself from maintaining an image of me because of her fear that she would feel angry toward me. At the onset of the next session she said "I was so pleased to find I could be angry and still have an encounter with someone. I would not have to withdraw when I became angry. I was so pleased—but I tried to hide it—like a squirrel who finds a nut and then tries to hide it."

"What was the need to hide your pleasure?" I asked. She answered in an anguished voice, "I don't know." After a few moments' silence she went on talking, discussing a trip she had taken with her family the previous weekend. While on the trip she had tried to think of me. She explained that when she was anxious she tried to imagine my listening to her. "If you are there, I don't feel so afraid. But sometimes I can't find you. I know why now. It's because I misunderstood trusting you. I never realized that trust was an emotional thing. It's not intellectual! You have to feel it!"

In this interaction she again becomes depressed following my questioning. Her remarks about trust being an "emotional" and not an "intellectual" matter unconsciously refer to the analyst's intellectualizing questions. Unconsciously the patient's comments roughly mean: "Don't worry about not immediately knowing something about me. Your questions are pushing me away!" Her statements about not being able "to find" the analyst unconsciously refer to the interpersonal distance and disrupted communication brought about by my questioning.

As is typical of depressive patients, she took full responsibility for what occurred between us and tended to absolve the analyst for any disruptions in the relationship. She perceived herself as the sole cause of the difficulties she had in experiencing or recalling the "presence" of the therapist. Reviewing my process notes has convinced me that my frequent questioning significantly contributed to her difficulty in experiencing the "presence" of the analyst both within and outside of analytic hours.

In the next hour she told of feeling angry at me since the previous session. She said, "I can relate to nature, to trees and animals, and to the desert but not to people." She seemed about to cry, and she spoke with a tone of dread and despair about the "faceless people." People she had been with lately had seemed "faceless" to her. I asked her what "faceless people" meant. With considerable anger she replied, "Oh, so you don't know! That's just too bad. You mean, I'm supposed to tell you so you can know?" Her statements and her question constituted a confrontation and an unconscious quasi-interpretation about my countertransference-based questioning. Translated, her communication contained the meaning, "Your intrusive questions are part of your problem. You are not asking them to help me to understand me but to satisfy your own compulsion to know."

As I discussed extensively in previous writings, the patient when in regressed states often used nature terms, such as "sun," "moon," "meadows," and "flowers," as metaphors for affective states and personal relationships that she could not talk about in more ordinary language (Dorpat 1978–1979). Frequently these nature symbols represented some aspect of her self-object transference to the analyst. When she experienced the analyst's interventions as indicating emotional warmth toward her, she used the symbol of the sun. At other times, when she felt she could use the analytic situation as a kind of holding environment, she used the metaphor "meadows." In my impatience to understand these frequently obscure symbols, I asked questions about them. The following vignette illustrates how such questions were counterproductive and forestalled understanding for both the patient and the analyst.

She entered one session feeling depressed, and she spoke about wanting to stop the analysis. Then she told of growing tired of "looking," "hearing," and "asking why." She described a fantasy of a vulture perched on her shoulder waiting to eat someone. While she was associating to the vulture fantasy in a somewhat depressed way, I too began thinking about what it could mean. At first I thought of her mother, who had been extremely possessive and demanding and who had, in a sense, attempted to "eat" her daughter.

I rejected my impulse to interpet the vulture symbol as a representation of her mother because such an extra-analytic interpretation would go against a rule I had developed in the analysis with this patient: to look first at disruptions in the patient–analyst relationship to account for any disturbances in the patient. Because any return of her symptoms usually stemmed from some rupture in either the idealizing self-object transference or the nontransference aspects of the patient–analyst relationship, I gradually had learned to attend first to events of the analytic hour in my search for the meaning of her regressive lapses. Then I recalled that I had felt impatient with her during the previous hour and had asked several questions. I made the interpretation, "You fear that the image you have of me asking 'Why?' will envelop you until there is nothing left of you. The vulture stands for your fear of being enveloped."

She replied that she recalled having felt tense in the previous hour and having been withdrawn after my questioning. Her further remarks concerned fears of being close to the analyst and of her anxiety over being "swallowed up" by the analyst, as she had felt in her relationship with her mother.

My interpretation here implicitly acknowledges that my questions have disturbed her, and this acknowledgment leads to the restoration of the therapeutic alliance and to the alleviation of her depressive symptoms. The vulture symbol in her fantasy correctly identifies the unconscious aggressive wishes in my questioning and my voracious need to know.

The realization that the vulture symbol revealed a countertransference problem shocked me, and eventually (along with other efforts toward self-analysis) it induced me to question my previous attitude toward questioning. Whereas before I had taken pride in being able to construct searching questions, I now viewed them with dismay, not only because repeated observations of this patient and others had shown me their detrimental effects, but because I began to be aware of the aggressive need to control patients that previously had energized my questioning technique. Relevant here are my earlier comments about Olinick's emphasis on unconscious aggressive and acquisitive wishes expressed in questioning (1957).

The vignettes presented are only a few of the many instances in which questioning disrupted the patient's free communicative interaction and retarded therapeutic progress. A review of 60 sessions discovered at least 40 instances of questioning having this negative effect. And I found not a single instance in which questioning facilitated the analytic process—for example, questions did not lead to validation through Type Two derivatives.

Repeated and emotionally painful self-analysis revealed other unconscious sources of the countertransference-based questions. Some countertransference elements were similar to those described by Kohut (1971) as typical responses to the idealizing transference. The patient's idealizations sometimes led me to feel uncomfortable with the grandiose contents projected onto me. Initially what most threatened me was the patient's regressive and temporary dissolution of self and object boundaries and the concomitant fusion and confusion over who was doing what and to whom in the analytic relationship. Months of the analysis went by before I understood the therapeutic necessity of the patient's regression to early symbiotic modes of relating. Questioning the patient was an unconscious device to attain affective control of myself and the patient and to reverse the therapeutic regression taking place within the patient and (through temporary, trial identifications with the patient) within myself. Through questioning I unconsciously tried to block the patient's disturbing mode of communication and to substitute for both of us a more rational mode of discourse that would support my defenses and provide emotional equilibrium.

Interactional Aspects of Questioning

The question-and-answer pattern of communication is a mode of interaction that both partners contribute to and participate in. This perspective is akin to that of the bipersonal field concept (Baranger and Baranger 1966, Langs 1976), which holds that every interaction between the two parties to the analytic situation, and every experience within either, is a product of the field and, as such, receives contributions from both its members.

In question-and-answer transactions, each participant partially shapes the responses of the other. Many patients unconsciously evoke questions on the part of the therapist, and the therapist's questioning tends to contribute to the nature and content of the patient's answers. The transactions in question-and-answer interactions may be studied from the point of view of introjection and projection. Some of the more common contents introjected and projected in question-and-answer interactions include the polarities of independence–dependence, power–helplessness, and sadism–masochism. In these interactions the questioner assumes the role of the active agent for both parties and projects onto the person being questioned what the questioner feels to be the less desired quality—e.g., dependence, helplessness, masochism. Then the patient introjects the role of the one acted upon and projects the more active role onto the therapist. These are pathological symbiotic relations in which emotionally important contents and functions of the more passive partner are projected onto the therapist, who, in turn, introjects these contents and functions and acts upon them in questioning. In the following vignette the question-and-answer mode of interaction involves primarily the independence–dependence polarity.

A resident in supervision with me saw a married graduate student in twice-a-week psychotherapy. The student was accompanied to her initial interviews by her overprotective husband, and her presenting symptoms were those of feeling depressed and of being phobic about social situations. In the first interview and decreasingly thereafter, she related to the resident in a helpless and dependent fashion. She was often silent, and she communicated both consciously and unconsciously her wish for the psychiatrist to be directive and to lead the interviews. Over the nine months of supervision, I attempted with some success to assist him in understanding and inhibiting his need to direct and to question the patient. Gradually he decreased his questioning, and he became able to understand and to interpret the unconscious defensive and transferential meanings of the patient's behavior.

As the therapist increasingly adopted an interpretive rather than a directive approach, the patient improved. Because the resident's duties then required him to leave town, it was necessary for him to terminate both the treatment and the supervision. He was troubled by the patient's apparent unresponsiveness to the impending termination: she had said nothing about it during the several sessions prior to the last one. During the last therapy hour she seemed to regress toward the dependent and passively quiet attitude she had shown at the onset of treatment. Feeling frustrated, the therapist reverted to his defensive need for questions by asking, "What are your feelings over the termination?" Her answer was flat and conforming. Still frustrated, he asked another question: "What do you want to work on when you continue your treatment with another resident?"

Again the patient responded in a compliant and matter-of-fact manner. Then she added in a more lively way, "I'm sorry I don't have any strong emotion for you. But I have made headway on my problems of treating people as stereotypes." She went on to explain how the treatment had helped her to be more flexible and free with other people. The short remaining time in the therapy hour went well, and the resident told the supervisor that both the patient and he had said goodbye with tears in their eyes.

In the supervisory hour the resident, with some assistance from me, learned how and why both he and the patient temporarily had reverted to the sterile question-and-answer pattern of interaction. He understood that his regression had been triggered by his anxieties over terminating both the treatment with the patient and his supervision. Also, he appreciated how kind the patient had been toward him in reassuring him that she had benefited from the therapy. She probably unconsciously had perceived that anxiety had prompted his need to question her. This was my last supervisory hour with the resident, and when he left he thanked me by saying, "You taught me how to shut up and listen."

The following case vignette from supervision describes the use of the question-and-answer form of interaction unconsciously to act out the patient's childhood traumatic relationship with her father.

The patient was a 41-year-old married nurse who had been in analysis for five months and whose diagnosis was hysterical character disorder. The patient began a session by telling about having had one of her repetitive "box" dreams during the previous night. In these dreams she anxiously viewed herself as being alone in a box or a room. The analyst became impatient with the vague and hesitant manner in which the patient was talking about the dream, and he pressured her with questions about the details of the dream.

In response to his questions the patient described the dream as one in which the moving walls seemed as if they were about to collapse. She had awakened frightened, and she had had a premonition of something bad happening to her father. She described having called her father on the telephone anxiously in the middle of the night to make sure that he was all right. She told the analyst about a picture book her father had put together about her when she had her first date and attended a prom at age 13. Again she was vague and circumstantial, and again the analyst "took the bait" (as he later said about himself). He impatiently confronted the patient with her vagueness and again asked for details, this time about the picture book.

Prompted by the analyst's questioning, the patient with much embarrassment told the analyst of how her father had taken pictures of her preparations for the prom. He had taken photos of her taking off her panties, of her stepping into the shower, and of her dressing. The patient continued with other accounts of her father's seductiveness and intrusiveness. Often he would "leer" at the patient, and he would touch her in ways and places that were acutely disturbing to her. She exclaimed that many times she had felt like telling her father, "Keep your flabby hands off me!"

At this point in the analysis, I became aware in the supervisory hour that *both* the patient and the analyst were unconsciously repeating the trauma she sustained in the relationship with her seductive and voyeuristic father. I explained to the supervisee that the patient's angry warning "Keep your flabby hands off me!" referred to the analyst as well as to the father. Her statement was an unconscious commentary on the analyst's persistent questioning and probing, which was unconsciously acting out the role of the intrusive father. He was dismayed by my confrontation of what he was doing, and he recalled that his questioning had also been prompted by his anxiety that the patient was forming an oedipal transference neurosis "too soon."

It had become evident that the crucial issue, as the patient's dreams of moving and collapsing walls suggested, concerned both the patient's personal boundaries between herself and others and the boundaries of the patient–analyst relationship. Traumatic relations with her father had compromised the patient's boundaries, and the analyst's impatient and intrusive questioning constituted a symbolic and unconscious reenactment of that trauma.

My recommendation to the supervisee was to cease his questioning and probing and to explore ways of restoring and maintaining the psychoanalytic frame. The integrity of the patient–analyst boundaries was a necessary condition for the patient to work through in the analysis traumas and unconscious conflicts stemming from her experiences with her father. I predicted that an important adaptive context for the next hour would be the analyst's active questioning and that the patient unconsciously would continue to struggle with the issue of boundaries. This prediction was confirmed when, at the beginning of the next session, the patient told of being angry at a pharmacist who was acting like a doctor, countermanding her work as a nurse, and who imposed his unsolicited advice on a patient of hers. Her remarks about the pharmacist may be viewed as a disguised and unconscious commentary on the analyst's tendency in previous hours to overstep the boundaries of their relationship by his impatient and intrusive questioning.

In this case, the patient evoked active questioning behaviors in the therapist by her hesitant and vague way of talking. Her attitude of helplessness served as a defense against unconscious rage toward both the analyst and her father. In behaving helplessly in relation to the analyst, the patient was unconsciously projecting onto the analyst the role of one who would lead and direct her. The analyst introjected what had been projected onto him, and he in turn assumed an active role in his questions that guided and directed what she attended to and talked about. In so doing, he was also projecting onto the patient the passive and helpless parts of himself.

Questioning and Unconscious Communication

Questioning tends to evoke in the patient a mode of thinking and communication that is opposed to the methods and goals of analysis. As Langs (1978) noted, questioning usually shifts the patient's communication away from derivative communication and toward communication that is more literal and superficial.

The supervision of a psychiatrist's psychotherapy cases shows how the use of questioning blocks symbolic or derivative communication. In my supervision of the psychiatrist's therapy of four woman patients, I noted a common interactional pattern connected with his use of questions. Therapy with these patients began well, and the patients reported improvement. Then the treatments stalemated, and I observed that his active and repeated questioning played a role in the therapeutic stalemates. Whenever he felt frustrated over events in the therapy, he would try to take control of the situation by questioning. His patients responded to his questioning by becoming more literal, defensively compliant, and matter-of-fact. Their associations became reality oriented, and symbolic or derivative communication dropped off sharply. The communication of both participants shifted toward what Langs (1979b) calls Type C communication.

The therapist was unaware of the unconscious sadism and need for control that was being acted out in his repetitive questioning. Over time I was able to demonstrate to him how his questioning was evoking passive compliant behavior from his patients and how the questions tended to stultify communication. Partly as a result of these confrontations and explanations, he was able to gain some insights into his own unconscious conflicts regarding aggression toward women and to seek psychoanalysis for himself.

Hollender (1965) provided a clinical vignette in which questioning unconsciously is used to attack and to demean the patient.

The patient arrived seven minutes late and, after apologizing for being late, she was silent for eight minutes. Breaking the silence, the therapist asked, "I wonder why you are silent today?" The patient replied that she didn't know why she was late. "I've been silent before, you know. . . . My mind is just a blank." Then the therapist remarked that he wondered if her mind's being blank had anything to do with her being late. With a trace of petulance, the patient responded, "Well, I got up on time today. I dressed slower than usual. I was too involved, I guess, and the next thing I knew, the clock said ten of nine, and I realized I was going to be late. (*A silence of ten minutes.*) I was just thinking about an upsetting incident at work the other day. My boss is really something. He is so full of nervous energy—he's got to know what's going on all the time, is interested in everybody's affairs, expects everybody to be perfect." She went on to tell how her boss assumed everyone to be dishonest, and she told of a quarrel between the boss and another woman employee.

Then the therapist asked her why she had gone into accounting. First she discussed her conscious reasons for entering the field and then said, "I've often thought, in this field the women do the dirty work and the men get the gravy." The therapist responded with still another question containing an unconscious accusatory and critical message, "Are you saying, in a way, it's sort of a man's field?"

In this vignette, questions unconsciously are used to criticize and to control the patient and to displace the patient's unconscious commentaries on the therapist's sadistic behavior onto other, less charged topics. The patient displaces her anger about the initial questions to her discussion about the intrusive and accusatory boss who harasses women. Her statements about the boss are an unconscious commentary on the therapist's dominance toward the patient and his intrusive and attacking questions. Unconsciously the therapist perceives the patient's communication about his destructiveness that is contained in her remarks about the intrusive boss. He unconsciously retaliates with another question, asking her why she went into accounting. This question, I believe, unconsciously is prompted by his defensive need to change the topic and to lead the patient. She responds with another unconscious commentary about his sadistic behavior, saying that "women do the dirty work and the men get the gravy." He returns with an attacking and demeaning question about her entering a man's field.

Clearly the therapist-patient relationship is marked by an ongoing struggle, one in which both persons appear to view the man–woman relationship as a struggle for dominance. Although Hollender (1965) notes the therapist's need to dominate the patient in this and previous sessions, the interpretations just presented about unconscious communications are my own.

The unconsciously attacking and critical questions of the therapist may be evaluated in terms of both their aggressive and their defensive functions and meanings. He unconsciously responds to the patient's hurt feelings and resentment toward him through his hostile questions, and simultaneously he defends himself from hearing what she is saying about him by displacing the manifest content of his questions to matters outside the patient–therapist relationship. The manifest content of all four of his questions includes no mention of the patient–therapist relationship. Although his attacking questions indicate that he unconsciously is responsive to the patient's resentment toward men, the manifest content of his questions shows that consciously he is not hearing or responding to the disturbing feelings his questions have engendered in the patient. In other words, from the point of view of consciousness, he does not hear her or respond to her. Unconsciously he does perceive her resentment, and he responds with attacks upon her that are camouflaged as questions.

In another psychotherapy case a psychotherapist, through his questions, unconsciously communicates to the patient his wish for her to surrender her autonomy, to fuse herself with him, and to follow his direction.

The patient was a 30-year-old single nurse who was being seen in twice-a-week psychotherapy. The therapist complained to the supervisor about the patient's tendency to fall asleep during therapy sessions, and he described his fruitless efforts to deal with her resistance by interpretations. In one session she came late, apologized for sleeping in previous sessions, and said that she was considering terminating her therapy. The therapist made lengthy interpretation, indicating that the sleepiness stemmed from the patient's need to defend herself against her conflicts over anger at her sister. The patient responded by saying that she could not remember anything about getting angry. Then the therapist interjected, "Don't you remember about how angry you got at your sister and how you would work it out on a punching bag?"

Immediately following his question she fell asleep. Several minutes later, when she awoke, the therapist told her that her falling asleep was a kind of communication to him that she still wanted therapy. The patient replied, "Okay, I guess I must be angry at my sister." She continued, telling how much difficulty she had in remembering her anger. Then the therapist said, "Some of the anger you have about your sister is displaced from your mother, and you really feel angry with your mother." Again the patient fell asleep for about five minutes. When she awoke, the therapist asked her what had happened. The patient said she did not remember. After the therapist said, "We were talking about your anger toward your mother," the patient promptly fell asleep again.

Interactions in which the patient fell asleep occurred five more times. Each time the patient awoke, the therapist attempted by means of questions and other interventions to induce the patient to talk about her anger toward her mother.

Throughout this session, the therapist attempts to lead and to control the patient with questions and interpretations. Nearly all his interventions, including his questions, are covert directives in which he tells the patient what she should think and talk about. In so doing, he is enacting the role transferred onto him: that of the powerful, dominating mother. His directive interventions discount or ignore what the patient is doing and saying, and his comments to her are not responsive to what she is trying to communicate to him. His questions can also be viewed as projective identifications, unconscious attempts to evoke in the patient his repudiated feelings of anger, frustration, and helplessness. The patient responds to his directive and controlling behavior by falling asleep. Evidently, going to sleep is the only autonomous activity she can initiate and use to escape both from her internal conflicts and the therapist's coercive control.

Her sleeping during the hour also represents her introjection of the therapist's projection onto her of being a person who cannot initiate or contribute to the communicative interaction. His interventions persistently ignore on a manifest level what she is communicating and attempt to pressure her to follow his lead and agree with his perspective of what is happening to her. His interpretations and questions communicate the message, "Follow me because you are not capable of thinking for yourself or regulating your own life." Her sleeping in the session symbolizes and expresses both her introjection of this demeaning view of herself and her passive-aggressive defiance of it.

This emphasis on the therapist's unconscious communications and their crucial role in the psychogenesis of the patient's sleeping does not imply that there are not also symbolized in the patient's sleeping important unconscious transference components involving conflicts over anger toward her sister and mother. The therapist's transference interpretations in this regard are unproductive and actually counterproductive, however, because he is involved actively, though unconsciously, in interactions with the patient that repeat what she has experienced with her dominating mother.

One of the major reasons why questioning in analysis and therapy is so prevalent and why the value of questioning has not been challenged or investigated is that therapists tend to consider only the conscious communications in questioning. Questioning, like other interventions, always carries with it unconscious meanings and messages in addition to its manifest content. Often the unconscious communication contradicts the consciously intended message of the questioner. Here the conscious aim of the therapist is to convey the implicit message "It would be useful for you to talk about X." This message is contradicted by the unconscious message "I don't want you to talk about X."

DISCUSSION

A skeptical reader might object that this chapter uses only examples of the misuse or abuse of questions by therapists whose questioning actions toward their patients were strongly and adversely influenced by such factors as countertransference, inexperience, and inadequate training. One could argue that I have ignored the positive and constructive communications and effects of questioning. My rebuttal is that in nearly ten years of studying the use of questions, I have not found one instance in which the validity and value of questioning can be confirmed by the patient's responses to the questioning.

Hollender (1965) held that the wording of a question determines whether the question opens up or closes off some area for exploration and discussion. Although I agree with Hollender that the wording influences the patient–analyst interactions, I hold that all questions tend to have a stultifying effect on the patient's capacities for free association and symbolic communication. Irrespective of the manifest content or the unconscious communications, there is an intrinsic aspect of questioning that is antithetical to open and therapeutic communication. Questioning shifts the patient's attention from whatever he or she has been attending to toward that which the therapist asks about. Thus, questioning serves as a convenient means by which the therapist can exert some control over the experience, communication, and responses of the patient.

There is another quality of the type of questioning most commonly used in the analytic situation that often has untoward effects. It is an aspect of questioning that is almost unique to the analytic situation. Most questioning in the analytic situation consciously is intended for the patient's benefit. The act of questioning directs the attention of the patient to some topic the analyst believes the patient should think and talk about. This is the type of question that is designed to open up areas for exploration and that is supposed to prepare the way for interpretations. Usually analysts communicate directly or indirectly that the question is consciously intended for the patient's benefit.

In contrast, in everyday life the questioner seeks something more selfish, namely, information. There is no presumption that the one who answers will gain by answering. The presumption that answering a question is somehow useful to the patient and his or her analysis puts an additional pressure on the patient. This interpersonal pressure can be perceived variously as an obligation, a duty, an invitation, a promise, etcetera. It is a powerful inducement to a pathological symbiotic mode of relating in which the patient endows the therapist with idealized powers, such as the ability to know how the patient should regulate his or her thinking and behavior.

Another disadvantage of this kind of questioning is that it often contains contradictory communications disruptive to the patient. The implicit message "I'm doing something *good* for you in asking about X, because it would help you to think and talk about X" is contradicted by the unconscious destructive messages (previously described in this chapter) that are *not good* for the patient.

One common subtype in this large category of questions designed to prepare for interpretation are "why" questions. "Why" questions are used consciously to induce the patient to search for reasons and motives for his or her behavior. Several authors, such as Hollender (1965) and Menninger and Holzman (1973), have recommended caution in the use of "why" questions. Hollender (1965) observed that patients frequently interpret "why" questions as criticisms. Menninger and Holzman (1973) recommend the judicious use of "why" questions. They believe that "why" questions can have a stimulating effect but also can easily be overworked and often can evoke rationalizations and false reasoning. I have not observed a single instance in which a "why" question has had a beneficial effect on the patient or on the analytic process.

Another type of question that is used frequently in psychoanalysis and psychotherapy is the restating in an interrogative form the last word, phrase, or sentence uttered by the patient. Although this type of question is recommended by a number of analysts, none of them has provided any investigation of the effects of this type of questioning or of the indications or contraindications for its use (Deutsch 1939, Hollender 1965, Olinick 1954).

We return now to a brief consideration of the type of questioning that is done solely in order to elicit information. It is my impression that this type of questioning occurs much less frequently than the type of questioning performed ostensibly for the patient's benefit. My observations on questioning have been confined to the latter type, and I have not systematically examined the effects of queries done for the sake of information. Although such questioning customarily is carried out in the initial consultation sessions, some analysts, such as Glover (1955), have recommended its limited use after the initial interviews. Langs (1979a) disagrees with the practice of asking questions, during the initial interview or afterward. He maintains that a question-and-answer format in the classical first interview creates "a particular type of bipersonal field in which symbolic communication and illusion are impaired" (p. 113).

What kinds of techniques are preferable to questions and can be used instead of questions? Usually, silence is the method most efficacious in situations in which analysts or therapists use questioning. Sometimes a question can be rephrased into a statement, an interpretation. A Gestalt therapist who was aware of the harmful effects of questioning suggested to me the simple expedient of transforming questions into statements. I do not believe that his suggestion should apply to all or even most situations in which questions are used, because interventions in the declarative form can be as manipulative and antitherapeutic as questions are. Questions can be rephrased as interpretations when the treatment situation is such that the correct conditions and criteria for effective interpretation have been met. Whenever these conditions do not obtain, silence is nearly always preferable.

The attitudes and beliefs about questioning commonly held by analysts and therapists are contrary to the conclusions I reached from the findings of this investigation. Most analysts believe that: (1) Questions are useful and necessary investigative tools for the exploration of unconscious transference and resistance reactions; they are a part of the basic model of analytic technique. (2) Questions, like clarifications and confrontations, are technical adjuncts to interpretation, and they effectively prepare the way for interpretation. Here the assumption is that questions, by drawing the patient's attention to something deemed important by the analyst, can lead the way toward effective interpretation (Dewald 1972). (3) Aside from their cognitive effects of directing the patient's attention to something and their longer-range effects of facilitating interpretation, questions have little or no effect on the patient or on the analytic process.

CONCLUSIONS

As generally employed in both psychoanalysis and psychoanalytic psychotherapy, questions are seldom if ever useful in opening up unconscious resistances and transferences. Questions rarely prepare the way for interpretation, and they do not assist the analysand toward the attainment of insight. Frequently, the asking and answering of questions imposes an interactional resistance. Questions tend to shift communication away from derivative communication and toward communication that is matter-of-fact and superficial. Questions often create or maintain pathological symbiotic relations and interactions in which the analyst holds a directive and controlling position.

A prime component of most questions is some type of pathological countertransference. Often questions are used as projective identifications, communications unconsciously designed to evoke in the patient the therapist's unwanted affects and ideas.

Far from being a neutral or innocuous technique, questioning can and often does have powerful and far-reaching effects on the patient, on the nature of analyst–analysand transactions and communication, and on the analytic process. Contemporary attitudes and assumptions about questioning overlook the role of unconscious communication in questioning. The clinical vignettes presented in this chapter illustrate some of the unconscious and antitherapeutic messages and projections that can be conveyed by questioning. The findings from this study of questioning indicate that questioning rarely if ever has beneficial effects and that it often is detrimental.

REFERENCES

BARANGER, W., AND BARANGER, M. (1966). Insight in the analytic situation. In *Psychoanalysis in the Americas*, ed. R. E. Litman, pp. 56–72. New York: International Universities Press.

DEUTSCH, F. (1939). The associative anamnesis. *Psychoanalytic Quarterly* 8:354–381.

DEUTSCH, F., AND MURPHY, W. F. (1955). *The Clinical Interview*. Vols. 1 and 2. New York: International Universities Press.

DEWALD, P. A. (1972). *The Psychoanalytic Process*. New York: Basic Books.

DORPAT, T. L. (1978). Introjection and idealizing transference. *International Journal of Psychoanalytic Psychotherapy* 7:23–53.

EISSLER, K. R. (1953). The effect of the structure of the ego on psychoanalytic technique. *Journal of the American Psychoanalytic Association* 1:109–143.

GLOVER, E. (1955). *The Technique of Psychoanalysis*. New York: International Universities Press, 1968.

GREENSON, R. R. (1967). *The Technique and Practice of Psychoanalysis*. New York: International Universities Press.

HOLLENDER, M. H. (1965). *The Practice of Psychoanalytic Psychotherapy*. New York: Grune & Stratton.

KOHUT, H. (1971). *The Analysis of the Self*. New York: International Universities Press.

LANGS, R. (1973). *The Technique of Psychoanalytic Psychotherapy*. Vol. 1. New York: Jason Aronson.

——— (1974). *The Technique of Psychoanalytic Psychotherapy*. Vol. 2. New York: Jason Aronson.

——— (1976). *The Bipersonal Field*. New York: Jason Aronson.

——— (1978). *Technique in Transition*. New York: Jason Aronson.

——— (1979a). *The Supervisory Experience*. New York: Jason Aronson.

——— (1979b). *The Therapeutic Environment*. New York: Jason Aronson.

——— (1980). *Interactions: The Realm of Transference and Countertransference*. New York: Jason Aronson.

MENNINGER, K. A., AND HOLZMAN, P.S. (1973). *Theory of Psychoanalytic Technique*. 2nd ed. New York: Basic Books.

OLINICK, S. L. (1954). Some considerations on the use of questioning as a psychoanalytic technique. *Journal of the American Psychoanalytic Association* 2:57–66.

——— (1957). Questioning and pain, truth and negation. *Journal of the American Psychoanalytic Association* 5:302–304.

——— (1980). *The Psychotherapeutic Instrument*. New York: Jason Aronson.

CHAPTER 5

The Langsian Approach to Acting Out

A. Gerry Hodges, M.D.

In the psychotherapeutic environment, where "only talking" occurs, events often take place that are the intrapsychic equivalent of marital triangles, sexual assaults, alcoholic binges, sexual liaisons, and violent attacks. How is this possible? Two recent clinical findings are crucial to answering this question.

First, Robert Langs (1973, 1976, 1978a, 1978b, 1979) and Harold Searles (1965, 1975) recognized independently the vast array of unconscious communication that occurs between patient and therapist during therapy. Each came to this recognition immediately after beginning to appreciate clinically the well-known phenomenon of unconscious perception: the fact that universally an individual's unconscious mind accurately observes far more than is apparent consciously. Langs and Searles then observed that the unconscious mind actively attempts to communicate its perceptions.

The second crucial discovery, indirectly related to the first, is Langs's observation (1973) that the unconscious mind is always reacting to an immediate (real) stimulus and unconsciously communicates detailed information about the stimulus. In other words, the mind functions in the here and now, even when appearing to be working over the past. Clinically, this means that most sessions are unconsciously organized by the patient around one or two reality events, a finding previously unappreciated by most clinicians.

Langs refers to an event or a stimulus as the adaptive context (or the organizer). His clinical work consistently reveals that the stimulus is invariably something immediate occurring within the therapy or directly linked to the therapy. The heart of the psychotherapeutic process then becomes the observation and interpretation of the patient's unconscious reactions to these various stimuli, including their extensions into the past, over a period of time.

This recognition of the consistent stimulus–response nature of the mind allows us to define specifically the patient's unconscious expressions at a given moment, because we now know the exact stimulus (outside of conscious awareness) to which the unconscious is reacting. Observation of the unconscious then becomes analogous to the process of discovery in chemistry, in which the properties of an unknown agent are defined as the substance interacts with a known agent. Thus, the recognition of the adaptive context (the "known agent") permits clear observation of the unconscious mind (the "unknown agent") as it functions at a particular moment. The discovery of the adaptive context itself can be likened to the invention of the microscope, which for the first time enabled us to get a precise look at a hidden world.

Because these two discoveries (unconscious communication and adaptive context) clearly extend and define the function of Freud's original concept (1900) of the unconscious, they are the most important clinical observations in psychoanalysis since Freud's. To expand, we can infer from clinical data regarding unconscious perception that patients, at every moment during therapy (just as individuals do in everyday life), make many accurate unconscious observations about themselves and about the therapists with whom they interact. The patient's unconscious mind communicates its awareness through a symbolic code, repeating the same idea (always in response to a stimulus) over and over in disguised variations occurring amidst seemingly random thoughts.

This coded language, the language of the unconscious, is probably the least understood aspect of the communicative approach, largely because therapists have been inconsistent in their work and have confused conscious and unconscious. The unconscious mind can communicate only indirectly; otherwise, it would by definition be conscious and therefore direct. This subliminal ability of the mind to perceive and to communicate its perceptions indirectly means that now we have a *valuable* (unconscious) *observer* who can serve as a guide to the therapy. Going one step further, we now have a methodology that does not depend totally on the subjectivity of the therapist.

These observations can be applied particularly to the problem of acting out when it occurs during the course of therapy. It has long been appreciated that it is possible for acting out to originate exclusively from the patient (as he or she attempts to disguise pathology in actions). The adaptive context or communicative approach has revealed that crucial contributions by the therapist to the patient's acting out often have gone unrecognized and that many instances of acting out by both patient and therapist have been overlooked.

When the patient and/or the therapist is acting out, each is by definition consciously unaware of his or her own acting out. Because of the existence of unconscious perception (of self and of others), however, the patient (as well as the therapist) is unconsciously observing the acting out and often describes it indirectly in a surprisingly precise, encoded way. In this manner, patients have taught us much about the overlooked incidences, the source, the subtlety, and the function of acting out.

Thus, there are two possibilities when considering acting out within psychotherapy: that the therapist has not participated in the acting out in any way, that the therapist has participated in and perhaps even exclusively originated the acting out. The distinction is important, because different management is indicated in each case.

When solely patient-originated acting out occurs, the therapist's task is threefold: (1) the therapist should not join the patient in acting out; (2) the therapist should wait for the patient to reveal his or her unconscious awareness and the unconscious meaning of his or her actions; and (3) the therapist should interpret this awareness and meaning. Here interpretation (along with ongoing containment) is the primary technique.

If, however, the therapist discovers that he or she has participated in acting out, the immediate responsibility to the patient is to rectify the situation. The therapist must first cease acting out and then interpret the patient's unconscious perception of the therapist's participation in the acting out, as the derivative material permits. In this case, both rectification and interpretation are indicated. Three examples of patients and therapists acting out during the course of therapy will be presented to demonstrate these principles as well as the phenomenon of unconscious perception and communication.

CLINICAL MATERIAL

Patient 1: Mr. P.

A 28-year-old single male with a passive-aggressive personality disorder had complaints of depression, drug abuse, poor social adjustment, and behavioral problems that had resulted in several charges of driving while intoxicated. For the first two months of therapy, he continued to abuse drugs.

In a session prior to the one I shall describe, the patient related that he was still using drugs. He also mentioned repeated images both of disturbing threesomes and of things that needed to be fixed. The therapist, listening to this imagery as a commentary on the patient's unconscious perception of the therapeutic interaction, became aware that a possible threesome now existed in therapy. He recalled having previously accepted a check from the patient's parents as payment for treatment.

Because the patient had not made a manifest reference to the acceptance of the check, the therapist did not mention it directly, but instead alluded to it in his intervention. He pointed out to the patient that in some way these recurring images of threesomes and deficiencies must be linked to his continuing drug abuse and also to the therapy, although the patient had not as yet mentioned anything that might have triggered a sense of a threesome in treatment. (Langs calls this playing back the derivatives. It is an intervention that alludes to but leaves out the adaptive context.) The patient did not speak of threesomes again in this session; he seemingly rambled and was intermittently silent for the rest of the hour. At the end of the session, the patient paid the therapist with another check from his parents.

Hypothesizing that a third-party payment was most likely affecting the therapy in a significant way, the therapist left the check out on the table at the beginning of the following session. To pick up the interaction at that point:

P: (*in noting the check*) Why is the check out? Did it bounce?

T: Let's see what comes to mind.

P: I don't understand. (*Period of brief silence.*) I'm still using drugs, and I'm going to have to lay off them entirely if I want to be in control. This week I tried smoking just one joint on two different occasions, but both times afterward I went on a binge of smoking pot, drinking alcohol, and using Quaaludes and could not even remember all that I had done. I hate to admit it, but I am a bum. I have gone nowhere with my life. At times, and I haven't told you this, I come to the sessions stoned.

My parents often bail me out of jams with money, which only makes things worse. They pay my creditors for me, but I feel like they are taking over for me and actually intruding into my life. I had to borrow my father's car to come to the session today, because mine wasn't working. Actually, I wrecked it. I am really a destructive person. Actually, I should get a second job to pay my own way and repair the car myself. I could even use the money to pay for surgery on my shoulder, which troubles me off and on.

I know an attorney in this building who is a friend of one of my good friends. I recently saw this attorney in the courthouse, and he ignored me. (*Intermittent silence.*)

I have this boss at work who keeps offering me beer during work to relieve the pressure on us. At times we have also smoked a joint together.

I got a letter from an ex-girlfriend I used to live with. When we were living together she used to get government checks because of her father's death, and I think the financial support was bad for both of us because it encouraged us not to work. I don't feel like things are getting any better for me at all. I'm still puzzled why that check is there.

T: You are again referring to the check and seem to be saying, through the images that are coming to mind, that when I accepted your parents' money, it meant that both you and I were dependent on an outside financial source, as you and your girlfriend were when living off government checks. This is causing you to view me and yourself as dependent, incapable, and of gratifying ourselves at your parents' expense. This causes you to view me as someone like your boss, who gratifies himself with drugs and encourages you to handle your problems likewise. That must explain one of the reasons you have continued to abuse drugs.

However, you are also suggesting another way of controlling problems, through abstinence and self-control. All of this must mean that for you to see me and yourself in a different way and for therapy to be meaningful to you, that somehow you are going to have to manage the financial responsibilities of therapy by yourself.

P: I've been very nervous since I've been here today and keep having this recurring thought about an experience I had with a friend one time when we got high together on drugs. Something homosexual took place, but I can't remember all of what happened. I don't know how I could pay for therapy. Maybe my parents could pay for some of the bills, or maybe I could get a second job. (*At the end of the session, the therapist returned the check.*) I'll have to see what I can do. I would like to continue therapy.

In the following session the patient paid the therapist with his own check and reported a marked improvement in his self-control, having been able to abstain from drugs during that week. Throughout the session there were numerous images of understanding and helpful people, for example, "My boss is really patient and hasn't once asked me to drink with him lately" and "My father has been particularly understanding." Apparently because of the new conditions of therapy, in which the therapist and patient were seen as independent and which served to create a private and secure image of the therapist, the patient's drug abuse continued to remain under control.

In retrospect, the patient was engaged in a form of acting out: he had brought his parents into the therapy by using their money. The therapist initially participated in this action by accepting the check. Immediately the patient unconsciously recognized that a threesome had been created and indirectly communicated this recognition through repeated negative images of threesomes (the patient, his family, his creditors; the patient, his girlfriend, the third-party supporter; the patient, his friend, the attorney). These were Type Two derivative images occurring in response to the adaptive context of the therapist's acceptance of the patient's check.

In contrast to Type One derivatives, in which the stimulus is ignored completely, Type Two derivatives are linked specifically to a known stimulus from the therapist (Langs 1978b). They reveal unconscious or intrapsychic reality (perceptions and fantasies) as it exists at a particular moment in response to a particular stimulus. Through Type Two derivative communication, we develop an understanding of the difference between conscious and unconscious reality. We observe the vastly different perceptions (or fantasies) the "two minds" have of the same event. For example, the parents' check was to the conscious mind an innocuous event and yet was, as derivative communication reveals, the intrapsychic or unconscious equivalent of an aggressive, damaging act, a traumatic intrusion, and a sexualized gratification.

Thus, Type Two derivative listening reveals that therapists have the same unconscious propensities toward acting out as do patients. Therapists unconsciously act out primarily by allowing or creating breaks, often supposedly minor ones, in the fixed frame. These breaks express hidden wishes (or fears) of the therapist, and therefore, not surprisingly, the significance of these deviations has remained overlooked for years. The idea of unconscious acting out by the therapist has a long history in psychoanalysis, although detailed attention to it has been lacking. Johnson and Szurek's (1952) elaboration of the concept of "superego lacunae" serves as a reminder of the powerful unconscious tendencies therapists have to act out through their patients.

In the case of Mr. P., Type Two derivative formulations are essential to understanding the effects that the action of accepting third-party payment had on the therapeutic frame, the relatedness between patient and therapist (object relations), the type of cure, the mode of communication, and the immediately observable psychodynamics. Proper understanding of Type Two derivative communication should enable us to determine whether the patient or the therapist is in the forefront of therapy at a particular point—in essence, whether transference or countertransference is primary (Langs 1982).

Derivative communication makes clear that the use of the parents' money had many powerful intrapsychic meanings. First, as always, we note the effect of the action on the frame. This third-party payment became the intrapsychic equivalent (or unconscious perception) of an intrusion and a destructive act that damaged the therapeutic frame and modified its boundaries, as reflected in the images of damaging a car and of intruding into a financial agreement.

The boundary modification directly affected the image of the therapist. The threesome created a poorly defined relationship reflected in the images of people using drugs together or living together. The third-party payment also introduced a gratification into the relatedness between patient and therapist. This was indicated to be unconsciously perceived by the patient as both a homosexual and a drug-related gratification when he spoke of a homosexual experience in conjunction with using drugs. Thus, a clear picture of indefinite ego boundaries and fusion emerges, and the relationship between patient and therapist is now defined by indulgence and incomplete separation—i.e., pathological symbiosis. At the same time, the condensed image of drugs in the context of relating interpersonally paradoxically suggests interpersonal withdrawal into a drug state—i.e., pathological autism. This is a form of relatedness in which a person in various ways demonstrates interpersonal withdrawal as a form of self-protection from specific inter-personal vulnerability. It can be contrasted with healthy autism, exemplified by appropriate therapist silence (Langs 1982).

This deviation of third-party payment also led to an unconscious percep-tion by the patient about the type of cure that existed in therapy—immediate gratification, the equivalent of smoking marijuana to relieve pressure. As frequently happens, the patient accepted the situation consciously, but he protested unconsciously against the deviant cure, revealing his dividedness by holding up a derivative model of abstinence and self-control. The thera-pist made good use of this model of rectification when intervening.

The acting out affected the communication within the bipersonal field in several ways. Primarily, it encouraged the continued use of action dis-charge, a communicative style that Langs (1978b) refers to as Type B communication. The hallmark of a Type B field is action and projective identification—such emotionally charged and nonverbal communications as failures to pay for treatment, abrupt and early departures from sessions, and prolonged outbursts of crying. The goal is immediate relief and catharsis, not insight and adaptive symptom resolution. In the vignette from Mr. P.'s treatment, action discharge is reflected in the patient's continued use of drugs inside and outside therapy, and by his silence in the sessions.

Acting out also fostered a Type C communicative mode, which is one of false communication—one that often appears to convey meaning but that actually is aimed at destroying communication. The patient's silences and ramblings are examples of this communicative mode. The patient's un-conscious recognition that a Type C field has been created seems apparent in his derivative communication about a drug-induced state that affects his memory and that implies obscured or destroyed communication.

The Type A communicative mode also existed. Such a mode is ex-emplified by meaningful, symbolic communication through Type Two derivatives in response to a known adaptive context.

Psychodynamically, the significance of the acting out in this case was its goal of creating a symbiotic homosexual relationship. This goal is visible in the extension of the private, contained, one-to-one therapy to include the parents. Therefore, as Type Two derivatives reveal in the patient's mind and in actuality, the therapist and patient were now living off the parents, a form of pathological gratification. Although the gratification was introduced by the patient and thus reflected the patient's pathology, as long as the therapist had the parents' check, he was indicating his wish to act out just as the patient did. Hence, as derivative communication reveals, the patient was justified in perceiving the therapist as intrusive, destructive, self-indulgent, and unable to maintain proper boundaries. The validity of these perceptions seems confirmed not only by the organization of the negative images around the deviation, but also by the absence of any other satisfactory explanation for the three distinct derivative models of rectification (the images of abstention from drugs, of parents staying out of their children's financial affairs, and of someone getting a second job to pay his or her own way). Langs (1979) has noted repeatedly that models of rectification occur in the face of the deviation by the therapist.

These valid nontransference perceptions of the therapist resulted in his own dynamics being more in the forefront for the moment than the patient's. Because the therapist is the primary identificatory source of health (i.e., nondeviance) in the therapeutic relationship, just as the parent is in the parent–child relationship, the therapist's pathology creates a need inside the patient for correction of this deviation (Langs 1976). Therefore, rectification was the therapist's first job, of necessity preceding any meaningful work.

This vignette demonstrates several important principles in regard to the management of acting out. First, the therapist must wait for the patient to represent in Type Two derivatives his or her unconscious perception of what is being acted out. Here, after making the patient aware that he (the patient) was upset by a threesome, the therapist waited for the patient to provide the stimulus (the missing adaptive context) for this sense of disturbance.

Next, as he listened to the unsettling material, the therapist considered any contribution he might have made, particularly as it affected the basic therapeutic frame. When he realized that he had joined in the acting out, he was prepared to rectify the deviation as soon as possible, and thereby to eliminate further acting out on his part. He did this in the following session by leaving the check out and eventually returning it to the patient.

In his first verbal intervention, in the verbatim session, the therapist intervened around the now clearly represented adaptive context of the deviation (the third-party payment), utilizing the patient's Type Two derivatives as unconscious perceptions to reveal to the patient that he (the patient) was experiencing the third-party payment in an unconsciously deviant way. The therapist also made good use of the models of correction in the patient's derivatives and indicated that rectification was essential for therapy to be meaningful. As always after intervening, the therapist waited for Type Two derivative validation: either new material or indirect references to healthy functioning in others (positive introjects), usually implying an improvement in self-containment and symptom relief (Langs 1978a).

Here we note that all three indirect criteria previously set forth by Langs have been met. The patient immediately related new material that elaborated on the meaning of the frame break: he had been thinking of a homosexual experience. Then, in the following sessions, the patient mentioned several positive images of others (a boss who demonstrated self-control, a father who was understanding) and then further confirmed the therapist's rectification of the poorly defined boundaries of therapy by demonstrating increasing ability to manage his own boundaries, thereby avoiding drugs.

This vignette presents an example of a nontransference reaction on the part of the patient with eventual rectification by the therapist. This patient, like most, attempted on entering therapy to create a pathological environment and therefore a pathological role for his therapist. The therapist in this vignette temporarily accepted the role by participating in the acting out, thus permitting concealment of the patient's pathology. The adaptive side should not be overlooked, however, as the patient with his action has "staged a play" to demonstrate who he is. In his attempts to manipulate the various elements in the therapeutic environment, he has revealed much of himself.

When the therapist, by participating in the acting out, accepted the pathological role the patient offered, the patient immediately revealed his dividedness through derivative communication by calling for rectification. Patients, just like therapists, are divided; they want the therapist to be pathological and nonpathological—i.e., they want both a deviant frame and an intact frame.

Patient 2: Mr. C.

A 39-year-old man initially complained of impotence. He used the couch in his once-a-week therapy. Sessions had been characterized by massive fears of the treatment situation and marked behavioral resistance. The patient had a frequent desire to fuse pathologically with the therapist, (evidenced, for example, by requests for personal information, guidance, and advice). He was also silent and late to sessions, and missed hours.

I shall summarize first the session after he had missed one session. He had been in therapy for one month. The patient spoke of being anxious when alone with another person in a car. He had been experiencing a great deal of anxiety lately and wanted either to terminate therapy or to modify it so that he could arbitrarily change the time of his appointments, each week if necessary.

The therapist intervened and pointed out that the patient's image of being alone with another person in an enclosed space and becoming anxious had to do with what he was experiencing in the present treatment situation, an enclosed threatening environment. This was causing the patient much anxiety and was prompting him to want to escape that environment entirely, by terminating, or to modify it into an indefinite space by coming at different times.

This intervention seemingly was validated by the revelation from the patient that the previous week, on the day of the missed session, he had masturbated and then feared becoming the compulsive gambler and overeater that he had been in the past. The patient also made references to being uncomfortable on the couch.

The therapist then intervened again, selecting as his adaptive context the separation from the therapist caused by using the couch and losing eye contact. He suggested that this separation was prompting frightening impulses—sexual impulses as well as impulses like those in compulsive gambling and overeating.

The patient then spoke of his private club's having moved to a new building and mentioned that, sadly, the deceased members who had worked so hard on the project had not lived to see this new facility. At the end of the session, he expressed a desire to continue therapy. He commented to the therapist that because he had intended to terminate therapy, he had already written the therapist's check for the previous month and also for the present session, which was the first session of the new month. He gave the check to the therapist, who accepted it. It occurred to the therapist that he had collaborated in modifying the original agreement that payment be made once a month at the first of the new month. He wondered about the significance of this alteration.

The next session is presented in detail.

P: (*Upon entering the room, the patient sits in a chair.*) Is it all right if I do not use the couch today?

T: Let's see what comes to mind.

P: I actually looked forward to coming to therapy this week. In a conversation with my wife, she had tried to blame me for our marital problems, but I was able to contain myself, and we were able to talk. Several times during the week, I thought about masturbating so that I would have a reason not to need therapy. One night I attempted to have intercourse with my wife, and she became upset and told me she did not want to be my guinea pig. I told her that I needed understanding and that I did not know if I could make love.

I chose a medical doctor for my therapist because I thought he might give me a physical examination to determine if there were physical causes for my impotence. I had an argument with my wife this week, but I did not take the blame as I usually do, and I did not defend her; she needs to learn to express herself and understand herself, as I have learned in therapy. Money has been somewhat of a problem. The expense of therapy has probably been a subconscious stress on our marriage. I had a dream last night. Dr. Tarnower, of the

Scarsdale Diet, whom I first felt was you, was in the dream. I was in a room with this doctor kind of lying on a couch, and I was very frightened of this doctor until he lay down beside me on the couch. When the dream ended, I felt much more comfortable with this doctor.

I've been thinking since I've been in therapy about some homosexual experiences I had in the past. Once a man performed fellatio on me, but when he attempted sodomy it scared me. He gave me twenty dollars. One other time I had performed fellatio on another man. On another occasion, I once tried to get a friend to go along.

Before we got married, I forced my wife into having sex, and she got pregnant. I do not think that she would have married me if she had known she was pregnant at the time we married. Prior to meeting my wife, I used to try to have sex with girls to build up my self-esteem, but often when I had the opportunity I could not perform. That was really a poor way of enhancing my self-image.

T: You mention that you had a dream in which you were in a room lying on a couch and you were frightened of a doctor who was there and who reminded you of me. Now, in today's session, you are actually foregoing the use of the couch. This must be your way of telling us that to be alone with me in the confined situation prompts fears that I might harm you. This must be why you wanted a therapy where a doctor would perform a physical examination on you. You fear being harmed and you want to feel close to me instead of feeling endangered. This need for closeness seemingly prompts homosexual impulses, as you have mentioned several times today, and perhaps you moved away from the couch fearing that if you stayed in that vulnerable place, these homosexual impulses would surface. You also link the image of money to homosexual involvement and spoke of money having a hidden negative effect on a relationship.

P: I once stole some money from my father and then lied about it, trying to make him think that the money had been lost. Another time I stole some money from an employer. I should have given the money back to both of them. One time I did that, when I stole $300 from a man and later paid him back. [The patient had paid the therapist $300 the previous week.]

T: You're talking a good deal about money, precisely the amount of $300, and about someone having another person's money, along with the idea that this money should be returned. Something specifically must have prompted these thoughts about money, and must surely be linked to therapy, as you suggested earlier when you connected money to the therapeutic situation here.

P: I was never able to talk to my father about the money or in any way tell my father that I had taken the money from him. (*This session then ended.*)

We note again that one seemingly minor act, accepting a check that included a prepayment of only one session, has had major effects on the therapeutic frame and hence on the relatedness between patient and therapist, the type of cure then being offered, the communicative field, and the psychodynamics of the interaction.

The therapist had modified the therapeutic frame by accepting an early payment from the patient. The patient unconsciously made clear in the following session that this had created an enormous gratification, as revealed in the images of masturbation, homosexual contacts, heterosexual intercourse, and a therapist lying down with the patient on the couch.

A sadistic, exploitative, pathologically symbiotic, and parasitic relationship had been immediately created by the therapist's deviation. It was quite instinctualized and was further sexualized by the patient. As the Type Two derivative formulations reflect, the gratification involved was experienced intrapsychically as the equivalent of fellatio, sodomy, intercourse, and stealing. The image of masturbation also suggests that the gratification created a pathologically autistic form of relatedness.

The frame break resulted in an action-discharge or avoidance type of cure, immediately apparent in the patient's behavior when he sat up to avoid anxiety. The action-discharge cure was also noted repeatedly in derivative communication: a therapist in a dream lying down with the patient to immediately alleviate anxiety; thoughts of masturbating to relieve anxiety; a wife crying instead of talking; someone stealing. In the same hour the patient once again unconsciously recognized the deficiency of this method of cure and made two other specific recommendations in derivative form: return the money (rectification) and try to understand (interpretation). The dividedness of this patient is clear: he wants to break the frame, and he wants to secure the frame. This tension between acting out—i.e., breaking the frame—and tolerating a secure therapy (thus enhancing verbalization) exists in all psychotherapies.

The acting out by the therapist affected the communicative properties of the bipersonal field in three ways, creating a mixed Type A, B, and C field. First, it created a Type C field, or a so-called lie barrier; a major falsification has taken place that has created a deviant therapy and thereby a significant degree of impaired or misleading communication. As Langs (1980) observed, often the image of a lie appears when an event has occurred that falsifies therapy and, thereby, communication. In this case, a Type C field was recognized unconsciously by the patient when he spoke of lying to his father about stealing money, thereby clearly linking the image of the lie to the adaptive context (the money) that was the source of the lie.

Although a second type of communication, an incomplete Type A field, has been created around the therapist deviation, the image of a lie serves to remind us that by getting the therapist to participate in a deviation and shifting the focus to him, the patient then was able to conceal his pathology. This pattern is the essence of a Type C field. Hence, there is a

Type A field around the therapist's deviation but a partial Type C field around the patient's pathology. Even the Type A field around the therapists' acceptance of early payment is not complete and contains a major Type C field element, a communicative resistance: that patient withheld the adaptive context, in that he made no direct mention of the check he had given the therapist during the previous session. Unconsciously the patient recognized this resistance when in derivative form he spoke of withholding information from his father.

There is also to some degree a Type A field around the patient's participation in the deviation, to the extent that he described someone who gets others to deviate (images of the patient coercing his wife and other women into sexual relations; images of men coercing one another into sexual relations). However, these derivatives must also be interpreted transversally —that is, taken also as perceptions of the therapist as one who, by accepting the deviation, coerced the patient.

A Type B mode of communication is apparent in the patient's sitting up and was described clearly and unconsciously in derivative communication via the image in the dream of the therapist lying down with the patient. Therefore, all three forms of communication have resulted from the frame break.

The patient, through the frame modification, was offering (and, as his derivative suggests, forcing) a pathological homosexual gratification that the therapist accepted. The Type Two derivatives reveal that permitting this gratification led to the patient's unconscious perceptions of the therapist as someone who was dominated (like someone being forced to have sex), passive (like the therapist who lies down with the patient and gives up his therapeutic role), inappropriately feminine (like a woman who allows herself to be used by a man for inappropriate sexual gratification), homosexual (like a man who performs fellatio or receives fellatio from another man), and corrupt (like someone who steals or uses someone sexually for money). On another level, because the therapist was gratified by the early payment, the patient views himself as the passive one who was offering the gratification and the therapist as the active, dominant one who took it.

In retrospect, it is clear that the patient first intended to create a certain role (passive, dominated, homosexual) for the therapist that permitted concealment of the patient's pathology within the therapist. This manipulation is reminiscent of Mark Twain's often remarked-upon idea of the town drunk being an elected office, a concept identical to that in Johnson and Szurek's discussion of acting out (1952), in which one person is noted to encourage a role involving certain behavior (action) in another. Of all Mr. C.'s derivatives, the dream taken as a whole is the one that most clearly reflects this maneuver and can be referred to as a pivotal (Type Two) derivative—an exceptionally condensed derivative that uniquely elaborates the effect of the adaptive context on the therapeutic interaction. In one derivative the patient has described how things were before and after an event.

Here the therapist, initially unknown and frightening, is transformed by one act—a gratification (lying on the couch with the patient)—into a non-threatening person. He then becomes identical to the patient: they are both now on the couch. (Certainly the gratification referred to in the derivative of lying on the couch with the patient is the equivalent of the actual gratification of allowing early payment.) The image of a therapist lying on a couch with the patient also suggests an unconscious perception of the therapist, a perception that now, of the two people in the interaction, the therapist is the one behaving inappropriately. The shift has worked. The therapist has become the pathological one.

This vignette presents an example of both transference- and nontransference-related acting out. It demonstrates a shift from transference to nontransference and illuminates one of the primary tactics of the patient's unconscious efforts in the service of resistance: to render the therapist ineffective. It appears that in the first part of the summarized sessions, in response to an intact therapeutic environment, the patient was acting out, massively demonstrating various gross behavioral resistances: coming late, missing sessions, wanting to terminate, and attempting to fuse and be gratified pathologically. The acting out at this point was transference based, as the derivatives (being alone in a car with an unknown person; being alone in a room with an unknown therapist) indicate. The moment the therapist accepted early payment, the gratification was obtained: the therapist joined the patient in acting out. From this point on, further acting out (for example, avoiding the couch and sitting up in the chair) was nontransference based. This whole sequence is once again clearly portrayed in the exceptionally condensed dream. First, when the patient is alone with the therapist, the therapist is an unknown, dangerous, and nongratifying person, a clear representation of the intact frame and the transference object. Then, by gratifying the patient (lying down with him), the therapist becomes nonthreatening to him, although his actions clearly represent acting out and are inappropriate.

In the first summarized session, the therapist intervention around the adaptive context of the offer of a secure frame was confirmed by the revelation of new material, a marked fear of regression. The second intervention in that session was not confirmed, as the images of death and of people not being able to see suggest. In the next session, the therapist's first intervention, around the adaptive context of the secure frame, was a clear error in the face of the primary issue: the frame gratification and deviation. The therapist had briefly alluded in his intervention to this adaptive context. The patient responded with unconscious recognition that the gratification involving money was central by elaborating in Type Two derivatives.

The therapist's second intervention in that session was a playback of the images, an attempt to point toward the missing adaptive context. Because the patient did not mention the adaptive context directly, the therapist also could only allude to it in his intervention based on the feeling that the patient was resistant at that point. More important, the patient not only unconsciously perceived himself as reluctant to remedy the deviation, but saw the therapist as reticent as well. This perception is reflected in the derivative of not being able to talk to his father about the money issue, which must be interpreted transversally, as a perception of both patient and therapist. The therapist's reluctance was evidenced by his failure to hold the check and to leave it out at the beginning of the following session. The derivative of returning stolen money supports the idea that leaving the check out would have been a technically correct intervention. It would have conveyed clearly to the patient the therapist's intention to rectify the deviation.

Hence, there are two sources of acting out in this psychotherapy. The first stems entirely from the patient and occurs in response to the therapist's securing of the frame; it is clearly transference based. The second source of acting out stems from the therapist, when he breaks the frame and thus directly encourages further acting out, which from that moment on is nontransference based.

In these two forms of acting out (transference and nontransference based), there are separate and distinct ways of managing a situation. In the first reported session, at which time the therapist had not deviated and the acting out stemmed from the patient, the therapist's sole job was interpretation of the patient's acting out. In the second session, because the therapist had participated in the acting out, he had two responsibilities when intervening: rectification and interpretation.

Patient 3: Mrs. S.

A 60-year-old divorced woman sought therapy for chronic psychosomatic diarrhea and, secondarily, for depression. Significant history included a stroke two years before that had been followed immediately by two days of confusion and disorientation. The patient had recovered completely physically. She was seen in psychotherapy once a week.

Therapy was characterized by the patient's making many assaults on the therapeutic environment. The numerous examples of gross behavioral resistance included wanting to extend her hours, touching the therapist on the arm when going out the door, missing appointments, being silent, and appearing one hour early for her appointment (thus being there when the preceding patient arrived).

In one session, two months into the therapy, the patient described improvement in her somatic complaints. She talked about her stroke two years before and about her grandson, who was seeking gratification through drugs. At one point she made a direct request for the therapist to talk with her. Throughout the session there were long intervals of silence. The therapist was silent for the entire session.

The following session is presented in detail.

P: My diarrhea is much better and enables me to leave the house more comfortably, and I feel much less depressed. This week I saw my medical doctor, who gave me medication to help me sleep on those occasional nights I have difficulty sleeping. I've been thinking about stopping therapy. It's a long drive to the sessions and dangerous. I'm afraid that somebody on the highway might hit me or that I might get anxious myself and run into someone else. One time I lost control of my car and ran into a neighbor's yard and over the mailbox. I have thought of asking my grandson to drive me, but that might be even more dangerous.

He and his friends often sit around and use drugs to escape their problems. He does not seem to face up to his responsibility, and he avoids uncomfortable situations that are really necessary for his own development. My grandson seems to always upset others, probably because he's trying to make others feel what he feels inside. He has a lot of problems, but it's not my place to tell him what to do. It's like when I was teaching school; often the only thing I could do for the kids was to listen and help them understand themselves.

I get frightened living alone at home, and at times I wish that my grandson would come live with me, but I'm not sure that I could trust him because he might leave the stove on or smoke in bed and burn the house down. It's still dangerous to live alone. There's always the fear of somebody breaking into the house. On the other hand, if you make the house too secure, you won't be able to get out in case of a fire.

I have been taking walks with a friend every day. I've also been visiting with a lot of my friends, as usual, have continued to help out at church, and went to a dinner party the other night. Even with all my activities, I still do not like living alone, particularly since my stroke. I wonder why you haven't said anything. (*Silence for several minutes.*)

T: You've been talking about the danger of being in an enclosed space with another person, in the house with your grandson, or in the car with your grandson. You connected that situation to me when you talked about driving to the sessions. This must mean that you have the idea that to be alone with me in the confined setting of this room prompts fears that you will be harmed or that you might lose control over your own aggression and become destructive, as you suggested in the image of someone burning up in a fire when the door was locked.

You also talked about someone who upsets others and makes them feel what they themselves feel. Maybe when you came early, before the other patient, you wanted him to feel that his space here was endangered just as you yourself feel endangered. This must be why you want to stop therapy, which would perhaps be like your grandson, who moves away from difficult circumstances. At the same time you are clearly stating the value of someone facing his or her difficulty. All these modifications that you are making in the therapy, including involving another doctor indirectly, obtaining drugs for relief, must be related to these anxieties about being harmed or harming someone else. Also you mention your stroke—this suggests you have anxieties over you health which also relate to this idea of being damaged.

P: The drive to the session on that highway really makes me uncomfortable. (*The patient is intermittently silent.*) I've been thinking about your office set-up and how strange it is for a doctor's office to have no one else there but the doctor. Other doctors are not like that. If you only had a receptionist, I would feel much more comfortable about coming here. If I only had a friend who could drive with me and sit in the waiting room, I might continue therapy.

T: You're telling us even more clearly how anxious you are here alone with me. Just being here alone with me creates such a dread that you feel you need literally a third party here to keep things from getting out of control. (*This session then ended.*)

After missing the next session, the patient terminated therapy by telephone, once again stating that she would like to continue if only the drive were not uncomfortable and the circumstances of therapy were different. She related she just did not want to be here alone.

This vignette differs from the first two, in that the patient's acting out appears to have originated primarily from the patient. She had obtained psychotropic drugs from another source, and she desired even more directly to introduce a third party into the therapeutic environment by asking a friend to come to the session with her. These are assaults on the therapeutic environment. Within the adaptive context of an intact frame (reflected in the images of private, secure spaces—a house, car, the neighbor's yard), the Type Two derivatives reveal that the patient's actions were an attempt to destroy the therapeutic space (like intruding into a neighbor's private space and damaging property) and an attempt to modify the threatening, defined boundaries of therapy into less threatening, indefinite ones within which pathological gratification occurs (like friends using drugs together).

Because the frame is affected, the unconscious meaning of these actions in terms of relatedness is an attempt to create either an intrusive, pathological, symbiotic relationship or an autistic one. Autism is reflected in the wish to stop therapy, the intrapsychic equivalent of avoiding difficult situations (like the grandson did) and of locking oneself away from others.

It becomes clear now that the patient was seeking two types of cure. The first one is an avoidance cure, as evidenced by her wish to stop therapy and by her obtaining medication. Interestingly, the patient unconsciously perceived her own actions and described them in derivative form when she spoke of her grandson, who avoids difficult situations and who uses drugs to escape problems. She also quickly offered a healthier model of listening and understanding when she spoke of the attributes of a good teacher. The second type of cure the patient was seeking is action discharge. By a supposedly "simple" action she attempted to put into the preceding patient her own sense of chaos and potential destruction. She did this by coming early to the appointment, at the other patient's time, so as to create within that patient confusion, uncertainty, and the threat of losing his space. Once again, the patient unconsciously perceived the function of her actions when she described the grandson as someone who by his actions made others feel what he felt.

This derivative about the grandson's external management of his feelings also describes perfectly a Type B communicative mode, which is present when action discharge is prominent. In such cases the therapist will usually subjectively experience a great deal of the projected identification.

Another communicative style, Type C, is also clearly implied, in that all of the patient's gross behavioral resistances were aimed at destroying meaningful Type Two derivative communication and creating an impenetrable barrier allowing no access to unconscious material. This resistance was represented in the Type Two derivative of someone being excessively locked up and protected inside a house. Type A communication existed in this vignette only when the patient's unconscious mind revealed her unconscious perceptions and self-interpretations of the many resistances.

Dynamically, the patient's desperate attempts to modify the frame revealed the magnitude of her phobic and paranoid anxieties in a secure frame. These anxieties were represented in Type Two derivative form when the patient expressed fears about riding on the highway, and paranoid fears of her house being broken into or her grandson burning the house down. Because these derivatives were organized around the clearly represented adaptive context of an intact frame, they reflect the transferential nature of this reaction, a situation different from that in the first two vignettes. There is an encoded message continually repeated in the images of danger associated with being in a secure space (a car, a house, a yard): a secure therapy (where boundaries are maintained, i.e., where no acting out by the therapist occurs) is the transference-based intrapsychic equivalent of being alone in an inescapable, confined environment threatened by immediate harm from the other party (the therapist) in the environment. This message was also observed in the case of Mr. C., as the dream made particularly clear. When the patient was alone with the unknown therapist in a private space, the patient clearly viewed this therapist as dangerous. Langs (1982), in other clinical findings, has noted this same phenomenon regarding the patients' reactions to the secure frame.

These clinical data suggest that the phobic paranoid anxiety is universal and therefore give new insight into why patients resist the secure frame so strongly. An attempt to destroy the frame usually can be expected, because of the massive anxiety a secure frame mobilizes. Acting out is the only method of destruction.

Securing the frame is therefore the central cause of interpretable transference anxieties. Although the patient dreads the secure frame, it simultaneously becomes a powerful model of containment with which the patient identifies. This identification explains why even in the face of massive resistance, Mrs. S. improved symptomatically. She had incorporated the definitive containment the therapy offered, thus significantly relieving her diarrhea and depression.

An analysis of the therapist's interventions indicates that he seems to have intervened correctly. He maintained the frame consistently. He waited for the patient to provide the material and thus reveal her unconscious perceptions and fantasies. His silence in the summarized session seems validated indirectly in the following session by new information, i.e., improved communication, with the partial development of a Type A field. Along with this validation, there was also the mention of a positive image directly related to the therapist's silence: a good teacher who sat back and listened.

In the verbatim session, the therapist intervened correctly as he persistently interpreted around the adaptive context of the secure frame. The first interpretation of the verbatim session was confirmed by the surfacing of new material that gave further meaning: the patient was so anxious she wanted a literal third party in the immediate environment. The second intervention seems accurate: using this new material to interpret the behavioral resistance. The impetus to terminate therapy at this point seems to have come from the patient's overwhelming anxiety, stemming from two sources. First, external reality (her health problems, advancing age, and, in essence, her "impending death") was an extremely powerful adaptive context. Second, the secure frame was in many ways an identical experience to this external reality, thus mobilizing the same anxieties, bringing them more clearly into focus, and, in a real way, doubling the patient's already massive anxiety. This patient's abandonment of therapy suggests that when these two unconsciously related adaptive contexts (a secure frame and eventual death) are simultaneously paramount, few patients can tolerate the truth of their fears at that moment. In retrospect, we can see that the patient predicted through derivative communication the premature termination of therapy when she spoke of her grandson, one who avoids difficult situations. Additionally, discussion of her psychiatric symptoms with another professional and obtaining another form of therapy (medication) were actions that similarly foreshadowed termination.

SUMMARY

The therapeutic environment, because of its many elements and because of the difference between conscious and unconscious "reality," is a highly translatable space. Emotions may be subtly converted or translated into actions by manipulating this environment. The degree to which acting out takes place depends significantly on the therapist's management of the environment and the patient's own tendencies. Invariably, acting out by the patient (and often by the therapist) can be expected to occur in every psychotherapy, particularly at crucial moments, and the therapist's proper understanding and response will be the key to the successful outcome of therapy.

We have seen two clinical examples in which apparently minor modifications, such as accepting payment from a third party instead of the patient and accepting early payment for only one session, were translated intrapsychically into major sexualized gratifications. The third patient, Mrs. S., quietly translated the environment into massive destructiveness by obtaining medication from another source, attempting to bring third parties into the therapy, intruding into another patient's space, and finally, destroying the therapeutic space entirely by terminating therapy.

These three episodes illustrate the vast potential of the therapeutic environment for antitherapeutic manipulation by both patient and therapist. For example, there are many possible third-party involvements in the therapy (and consequent damages to the frame): the involvement of a spouse or a general physician, a letter to an attorney, a letter to a college for enrollment purposes, a letter to the government for security reasons, communication with insurance companies, the presence of a secretary, the intrusion of another patient, running overtime with one patient into another patient's time, relaying a telephone message to the patient from an outside source.

Consider the manifold opportunities for immediate gratification: a patient requesting to use the therapist's telephone, private restroom, or pen (to write a check); a patient asking for an extra session, an extended session, medication, a professional card, advice, a tissue, a referral to another doctor, the loan of a magazine, or time after the session just to write the therapist a check, or asking the therapist to fill in his or her name on the check. Many of these events, if they occurred, would significantly affect the frame and thus have numerous ramifications.

For these reasons, in the ideal therapeutic environment, the therapist diligently maintains the frame in its entirety and does not allow the patient (or the therapist) to use the environment for the purpose of translating emotions into actions. The therapist's goal is to foster translation of actions into words, and the therapist's primary tool is the secure frame.

As seen in two of the examples, the properly maintained secure therapeutic environment translates intrapsychically into a frighteningly confined space with no outlets. Because the definitions of the "space" or frame prevent any escape from the interaction between patient and therapist, the patient's most primitive fears and impulses are mobilized toward the therapist (and vice versa). Within the frame, the therapist then becomes the dreaded transference object. Almost without exception, patients can be expected not to rest with this alarming and distorted intrapsychic reality, but to attempt to translate this environment through manipulation into a less threatening one, or else to try to escape from it totally. The method they use for translation always involves manipulation—an action or an attempted action.

The communicative approach underscores again that there is an inordinate amount of anxiety that must be tolerated in psychotherapy. Nevertheless, this approach offers definite principles for managing acting out and, possibly, new hope for certain patients with ingrained acting-out patterns (such as Mr. P.).

The maintenance of a fixed therapeutic environment is the foundation of a sound approach to acting out. The stability of this environment determines the strength of the holding or containing quality (Langs 1976) of the therapy. The fundamental aspects of a good holding environment are the therapist's direct demonstration of the self-containment of his or her own emotions and the provision of a stable therapeutic environment through the provision of consistent ground rules. Both these aspects prevent acting out by holding up to the patient constant models of containment with which to identify.

When the therapist acted out in the first two vignettes by accepting a gratification that involved the basic frame, he diminished the containing function of the therapy. At those moments he was uncontained and thus fostered acting out on the patients' part, as evidenced by the patients' continued drug abuse, moving away from the couch, and so forth.

In contrast, in the case of Mr. P., when the therapist rectified the therapeutic environment and reestablished solid boundaries, there was a noted increase in the holding function of therapy and a marked decrease in the acting out, evidenced in the obvious improvement in the patient's drug abuse.

The symptom relief that occurs in a secure therapy often serves to reinforce the value of therapy for the patient. This is particularly true when the patient is in a confused state, making the transition to a more verbal way of operating, and does not as yet understand much of the language of his or her mind, however clear it may be objectively.

Maintaining the frame often results in an initial increase in acting out on the part of the patient, as occurred in the third example, when Mrs. S. massively assaulted the environment by obtaining medication, bringing in third parties, and so forth. The crucial distinction, however, is the source of the acting out—patient or therapist—and, at several key points in most psychotherapies, the therapist determines this source. If the therapist maintains the frame, the acting out will be transference based. If the therapist modifies the frame, the acting out will be nontransference based.

The management of acting out is clear cut. It depends entirely on the source. The therapist who has participated in the acting out must both rectify and interpret. Acting out exclusively on the patient's part simplifies the therapist's task, because now rectification is not required.

Besides offering a more defined methodology for intervention than previous psychoanalytic models, the communicative approach provides another advantage, particularly with acting out: it offers patients the chance to hear "in their own words" (images) what they are doing and what is prompting the action and, additionally, to perceive that they are divided about their actions. This method of interpretation is more specific and intrapsychically more powerful, because the therapist uses patients' own unconscious communications. The therapist introduces none of his or her own ideas, but serves strictly as an interpreter.

It is as though patients, through their derivatives, are revealing exactly what they want to hear about themselves, and what they can hear. Therefore, a therapist who stays within the limits of these derivatives is respecting patient defenses and not going beyond what a patient can tolerate. This method serves to foster protection of patients, protection that has two primary advantages: it creates a positive introject, and it diminishes acting out because patients are not overwhelmed.

The communicative approach clarifies that the therapeutic environment itself, depending upon the therapist's management, is much more easily translated by a simple action (by patient or therapist) into one of violence, gratification, and fear than previously understood, that is, that the potential for acting out is much greater than has been realized. Recognition of the difference between conscious reality and intrapsychic reality leads to a correct understanding of acting out as well as of the function and management of the therapeutic environment in containing the acting out.

REFERENCES

FREUD, S. (1900). The interpretation of dreams. *Standard Edition* 4/5.

JOHNSON, A. AND SZUREK, S. (1952). The genesis of antisocial acting out in children and adults. *Psychoanalytic Quarterly* 21:323–343.

LANGS, R. (1973). *The Technique of Psychoanalytic Psychotherapy*. Vol. 1. New York: Jason Aronson.

——— (1976). *The Bipersonal Field*. New York: Jason Aronson.

——— (1978a). *The Listening Process*. New York: Jason Aronson.

——— (1978b). Some communicative properties of the bipersonal field. *International Journal of Psychoanalytic Psychotherapy* 7:87–135.

——— (1979). *The Therapeutic Environment*. New York: Jason Aronson.

——— (1980). Truth therapy/lie therapy. *International Journal of Psychoanalytic Psychotherapy* 8:3–35.

——— (1982). *Psychotherapy: A Basic Text*. New York: Jason Aronson.

SEARLES, H. (1965). *Collected Papers on Schizophrenia and Related Subjects*. New York: International Universities Press.

——— (1975). The patient as therapist to his analyst. In *Tactics and Techniques in Psychoanalytic Therapy*, Vol. 2: *Countertransference*, ed. P. L. Giovacchini, pp. 95–151. New York: Jason Aronson.

CHAPTER 6

Langsian Theory and Countertransference

Eugene A. Silverstein, M.D.

Langsian theory holds great power not only to illuminate clinical material but, particularly, to make countertransference reactions highly visible and to provide specific means to deal with them. This chapter will outline certain essential differences between this approach, as described in the prolific writings of Robert Langs (1973–1981), and the more traditional viewpoint. The latter scrutinizes the patient's behaviors and communications for inferences about the patient's unconscious pathology. These inferences are presented to the patient in the form of interpretations about his or her developmental difficulties and the pathological state of his or her psychic structures and processes. In contrast, the adaptational, or communicative, viewpoint considers the material produced by the patient to be generated by specific ongoing stimuli provided by the therapist's management of the ground rules and verbal interventions. It is emphasized that material can be understood in adequate depth only when viewed in relationship to the stimulus that produced it. This relevance of the eliciting stimulus is parallel to the importance of the day residue as a key to understanding the dream.

Once the specific stimulus—the *adaptive context*, as Langs calls it—is identified, the clinical material is organized around it and analyzed for disguised valid perceptions and commentary as well as for distortions and pathological adaptational efforts, all prompted by the specific adaptive context involved. Interpretations generated by this method of organizing the material tend to make evident to patients the immediate stimuli causing their reactions, the nature and implications of their valid but unconscious perceptions of the stimuli, and the distortions and pathological adaptational efforts they have mobilized to deal with the stress of each adaptive context. Such interpretations will serve as new stimuli, or adaptive contexts, that patients then can unconsciously work over.

The communicative therapist expects that the unfolding of therapy will be influenced by deviations from ideal performance by both patient and therapist, each according to his or her own pathology as influenced by the other's pressures. Each will respond to the other's expression of pathology, with communications designed to bring the relevant pathology to consciousness and resolution when a therapeutic alliance exists, or with communications directed toward exploiting the pathology when misalliance predominates (Langs 1975a).

The use of free association is common to both traditional and communicative therapy. Because patients are invited not to organize their thoughts in any particular conscious fashion, there is a greater tendency for their associations and behaviors to be responsive to ambient stimuli. As a result, patients will be more likely to offer unconsciously those of their perceptions, reactions, and commentary that have been stimulated by the therapist's behavior. These communications will be in the form of convoluted derivatives that have been condensed, displaced, and made concrete so that they emerge in disguised forms: a description of a scene in a movie the patient saw or of something that happened on the way to the office, for example. These derivatives acquire their full meaning only when organized around the relevant adaptive context. The term *adaptive context* derives from the fact that the therapist's interventions create pressures to which the patient must adapt. Each new intervention provides an adaptive context that offers a basis for understanding the patient's subsequent behavior.

When the therapist's interventions are organized around prevailing adaptive contexts, the patient is helped to become aware of his or her unconscious reactions to events in the therapy at the time they occur, when they are available for observation. This patient awareness specifically antagonizes the neurotic process in which the link between the perception of the adaptive context and the pathological response is repressed. It also helps counter the therapist's defensive tendencies to avoid facing the implications of his or her interventions and the patient's reactions to them.

The adaptational-interactional (communicative) therapist tends to intervene only when the patient indicates a need for intervention. Patients can express such needs in many ways. They may develop symptoms. They may respond to a troubling intervention with derivatives describing the problem analogously. Patients can demonstrate such creativity in weaving these derivatives into their associations that latent content is invisible until the derivatives are organized around the correct adaptive context.

If the patient gives no indication of needing help, silence is felt to be the best response. Thus, the therapist who intervenes without an indication of need from the patient must be motivated by his or her own need. Such interventions are often experienced by patients as requests for help and thereby shift the therapeutic properties of the bipersonal field toward the therapist's problems and cause the patient to feel exploited rather than helped (Langs 1976a).

In a further attempt to minimize their pathological intrusions, therapists using the communicative approach tend to avoid including their own associations and fantasies in their interventions. They rely instead on what the patient has mentioned during the session. The therapist's own ideas and associations are avoided unless they are clearly represented in the patient's associations. Even a reference to a comment the patient made in a previous hour is discouraged. This technique gives the patient considerable control in regulating the therapist and limiting him or her to what the patient is ready to hear.

The same philosophy that encourages the patient's unconscious leadership in the therapy explains the communicative therapist's avoidance of questions. Usually considered the most benign intervention, the question appears on the surface to be a simple request for information or clarification. Questions are used widely by other therapists, often without consideration of their implications or communicative properties.

By implying a particular interest in one area, a question conveys a lack of neutrality toward the material. Questions stop and redirect the flow of the patient's associations and therefore can be used manipulatively. They can provide the therapist with a means of deflecting the patient who begins to communicate unconsciously perceptions of the therapist's pathology. Questions about the manifest content of the patient's communications direct attention away from the latent meanings, which are often more disturbing to both patient and therapist. When the therapist questions the patient about people he or she has mentioned, the questions not only seal off latent content, but also deny links to the therapy and discourage the patient from providing such links. They say, in effect, "I don't want to hear what you are saying as a reference to what is happening here in the consultation room."

Because questions lack neutrality, focus on manifest content, manipulate the flow of associations, and obscure links to significant adaptive contexts, they are not considered correct interventions by communicative therapists. It may be argued that they can be valuable in mobilizing a silent patient. Although some silent patients will respond to questions, what they say will reveal more about the therapist who decides what to ask than about the patient who decides what to answer (see Jones 1953).

Silence is uncomfortable for therapists as well as patients. If the therapist is more comfortable than the patient, the patient will experience the greater pressure to talk. A therapist who instead asks a question in response to such tensions reveals to the patient his or her own difficulties with separation and dependency. The patient is then tempted to continue to be silent to elicit more pathology from the therapist. By reversing roles with the therapist, patients avoid their own pathology and reduce the amount of anxiety they are forced to experience.

An appropriate therapist silence provides a basic hold and indicates attention and willingness to hear more and let the patient decide the course that the material will follow. Silence is a powerful adaptive context that will stimulate the patient to produce derivatives or interactional pressures related to the patient's dependency conflicts. Because the therapist has not asked questions, these derivatives can be better interpreted as responses to the therapist's silence.

The setting and management of the ground rules represents one of the most powerful of adaptive contexts. As one might anticipate, the adaptational attitude about the management of the ground rules or frame of the therapy reflects determination to keep the therapist's pathology out of the field and to avoid infantilizing the patient.

By listening to derivative communication in his own clinical and supervisory work, Langs (1979) has derived a definition of the ideal or standard frame: There must be reserved appointments, with the therapist committed to maintaining the time except for legal holidays and a vacation. There are no makeup sessions. The patient must be responsible for paying a set fee for all reserved times without exception; the patient, not an insurance company or third party, must pay. There is absolute confidentiality. The therapist must not have a secretary or any other third party to the therapy. Nothing is to be exchanged except the fee and the therapy. Thus, the therapist cannot accept a referral from a patient or permit the patient to use the therapist's pen to write a check or to use the therapist's bathroom. The therapist's anonymity and neutrality are also considered part of the frame.

Frame deviations by the therapist represent a failure to maintain appropriate boundaries and replicate past failures by the patient's parents to maintain boundaries. Unlike others who advocate the use of frame deviations only for patients who are very disturbed (Eissler 1953), Langs maintains that patients who have not had the experience of properly maintained boundaries in the past need most of all a therapist who can maintain them in spite of the patient's pressure. The more the patient has been gratified before, the more he or she will attempt to gain inappropriate gratification in the therapy. The sine qua non in such cases is the establishment and maintenance of the standard frame.

The concept of the frame did not originate with Langs. The importance of the analytic contract was recognized by Freud and those who followed him, but the tendency to deviate can be found in Freud's work (Langs, 1978a) and has continued since. The training analysis itself, the model for all analysts, is characterized by a frame damaged in the area of confidentiality. The effect of the policy for training analysts to consult with the analysand's teachers has not been studied adequately. It seems probable that students' assocations in their analyses are affected by the reality that the analyst has the power to influence their progress at the institute. A good deal of agreement between patient and analyst on the manifest level seems likely, along with derivatives that are well disguised and embedded and refer to the deviant frame. For example, a training analysand might complain frequently about the conditions at the clinic where he handles his practice cases: he might dwell on the thinness of the walls and the dangers of being overheard.

In addition to silence and the establishment and management of the ground rules, there are two other basic interventions that are considered appropriate by communicative therapists. These are the interpretation and the playing back of derivatives.

The interpretation is considered to be the preferred verbal intervention by both groups who see it as an attempt to make the unconscious conscious. The difference between these groups is in their conceptions of what the therapist is trying to make conscious for the patient. It has already been stated that communicative therapists build their interpretations around adaptive contexts related to their previous interventions and are therefore trying to make patients aware of unconscious reactions to the events of therapy. Interpretations by traditional therapists are not typically organized around specific acts of the therapist. Interpretations related to the therapy are considered transference interpretations and are usually directed toward making the patient aware of some distortion in his or her perception of the therapist or the therapy. Interpretations by traditional therapists not related to the therapy tend to point out to the patient the unconscious reasons for his or her behavior with others or their behavior with the patient. Interpretations may also attempt to illuminate for the patient the effects of the pathogenic past. These genetic interpretations, like the others, are made without conscious consideration of specific adaptive contexts in the therapy. They thus seal off the patient's unconscious perception of specific events of the therapy and make the therapist appear defensive. The communicative therapist refers to the genetic past only as it pertains to the ongoing therapy. For example, such a therapist may point out to the patient that something that the therapist did has reminded the patient of a particular kind of interaction with a parent, which is evident in the patient's associations.

Because the communicative therapist prefers not to introduce something in an intervention that the patient has not provided in his or her associations, a technical problem develops when the patient does not mention the adaptive context in manifest associations. Such an omission is considered a communicative resistance that the therapist must not bypass by bringing up the adaptive context independently. If the patient's need for intervention is great and the adaptive context is known to the therapist but not represented directly by the patient, a playback of derivatives is indicated.

The key difference in the way the playback is used by communicative therapists and the way it is used by others centers on the adaptive context. Others tend to play back derivatives without selection or organization as a way of prompting the patient to say more or perhaps to fill an uncomfortable silence. Communicative therapists abstract the derivatives and then organize them around known but repressed adaptive contexts to create pressure on the patient to become aware of and verbalize the adaptive contexts. This technique eliminates resistance so that a full interpretation can be made.

Because this concept is somewhat complicated, a fictitious example may help: A patient is permitted to remain for five minutes after the end of his session. At the next session he presents a dream in which someone is moving a fence. He thinks of a teacher he once had who was very seductive. He mentions his son who got sick the night before after eating too much ice cream, and he takes himself to task for being unable to say no to the boy. He speaks of his doubt that he will ever be free of therapy. He says that he feels depressed. He does not refer to the extra time he got in the previous hour.

Playing back the derivatives around that missing adaptive context, the therapist might say, "Something has happened that you represent in your dreams as a modification of a boundary. Like your son, you feel that you have gotten something more than you should have, and that has made you feel depressed and dependent on therapy. It has brought to mind thoughts of a teacher who was seductive." This kind of organized playback creates pressures on the patient to recall the adaptive context. It demonstrates to the patient that the therapist is open to exploring what the therapist has done.

Let us now turn to the important matter of validation. The communicative therapist begins the validating process before making an intervention. The process is begun with the formulation of a silent hypothesis. The therapist continues to listen to the material for confirmation and elaboration of the hypothesis. After the intervention, he or she continues to listen to the material for derivative commentary. Simple agreement or disagreement on the manifest level is not highly valued; validation is found on the latent level. Validation of a playback occurs when the patient presents the related adaptive context. Validation of an interpretation may occur in the form of derivative commentary organized around the adaptive context of the intervention or in the form of introjects of the therapist based on the patient's perception of the interpretation. Validation may also appear as modification of a symptom or of a resistance, but the concept of resistance is not being used here to apply to the quantity or flow of material. A copious flow of material does not validate an intervention. There are forms of resistance besides the patient's refusal to provide material.

Langsian theory defines resistance in terms of the ideal communicative field, which (1) contains meaningful derivatives that (2) coalesce around significant adaptive contexts that (3) are represented by the patient in the manifest context. The absence of any of these three components represents a resistance. For example, a patient may represent extremely clear derivatives but completely omit any reference, even disguised, to the adaptive context, thus preventing the therapist from acting effectively. Or the adaptive context may be clearly represented but the derivative complex poor. Typical non-validating responses that indicate resistance include rumination, symptom formation, and derivatives of negative introjects and of efforts to help the therapist see the basis of his or her error. The patient may even include genetic interpretations of surprising accuracy.

Validating responses include the revelation of new, unexpected information that confirms and elaborates the therapist's intervention. Derivatives related to positive introjects of the therapist's healthy function, perhaps displaced onto third parties and frequently offered as references to the patient, are also validating responses. Symptom removal is considered a very unreliable measure of a validation. Consider the fine line between a symptom removal and positive introjection in the example of the patient who describes herself in response to the therapist's appropriate silence as recently quite able to manage inner tension. Instances that combine symptom removal and positive introjects based on the adaptive context are particularly gratifying validations.

Predictive methodological principles such as these use derivatives of the patient's specific unconscious perceptions to decide the validity of the intervention and limit the influence of the subjective opinions of the therapist, who is likely to be biased. The validation or nonvalidation of an intervention can be determined only from the material that follows it sequentially.

Unfortunately, there is no generally accepted form of presentation for clinical material in the classical literature, certainly none requiring the presentation of the sequential material that follows an intervention. Highly condensed summaries covering months of therapy are nearly impossible to validate by the methods just described. Detailed information concerning the frame is often omitted, further obscuring the therapist's contribution to the therapeutic process. This omission may well reflect the same defensiveness found in the emphasis on transference and projection and away from valid perception and introjection that I have mentioned.

CLINICAL MATERIAL

Patient 1

The first clinical example is taken from material originally discussed during a seminar on dream interpretation presented before candidates at a psychoanalytic institute (Sloane 1979, pp. 127–130). It has been chosen because it depicts attitudes and techniques representative of the non-Langsian psychoanalytic viewpoint. The material is unusually detailed and retains enough sequence to permit us to attempt to apply the preceding principles of validation and to compare the results with the author's observations.

A social worker had the following dream:

I called up my hairdresser and asked to have Ann get breakfast or lunch ready when I come, or perhaps it's something in between, like brunch.

Associations. At her hairdresser's, customers frequently ordered lunch while they were waiting to be taken care of. Ann was the girl who took the orders. The patient felt that Ann was a sour, bitchy kind of person who did not like her and always served her reluctantly. She thought that she herself might have been responsible for Ann's attitude because she never tipped her well.

Calling on the phone was a way of making sure that the food would be delivered by the time the patient arrived for her appointment. The phone could also refer to the analysis (in that one hears the doctor without seeing him). When she woke up in the morning, she felt fresh and on the go. She had felt good after the last two sessions, because she had just accepted a new position and was impatient to get started on it.

I pointed out that she had seemed more friendly toward me lately, after having resented my criticism of one of her friends, who seemed to be interested in her welfare but who had later let her down. I suggested that it resembled her resentment against me once when she thought I was being critical of her mother. This could be a projection of her own anger against her mother. In addition, I had observed that lately she was more punctual in coming for her appointments. Did she possibly regard me as being interested in her welfare, since I had advised her to select a particular area of endeavor and not flit from one thing to another? In this respect I could be Ann, a mother substitute, who provided her with food.

She replied that she herself was not really a good mother. Her children often said, "Why don't you be a mother and prepare breakfast for us?" She had recently given a party but let her husband take over and make all the preparations. At the time I had re-marked that she seemed to expect everything to be done for her by mother figures.

Even though I was "sour and bitchy" in refusing to satisfy her need for plaudits, I might still be a good mother, since I was concerned that she be successful in her career. This ended the hour. (Sloane 1979, p. 127)

The first and most important step in the analysis of any material is the identification of the adaptive context. Recalling our definition of the adaptive context as something that the therapist has done to which the patient is reacting, we look for the intervention that comes earliest in this sequence. Although it is not immediately clear in the material what this might be, the patient and the therapist work together to bring it into focus. The patient alludes to it by speaking of her impatience to get started in a new position. The therapist elaborates that this remark is a reference to advice "to select a particular area of endeavor and not flit from one thing to another" given by the therapist in sessions preceding the dream. This direct advice is the adaptive context of the dream. On the surface the advice appears to be a well-meant offer of help, but there are other implications. The patient could have inferred, for instance, that the therapist wishes to give to her and on a still deeper level that he seeks to polarize the relationship so that he is the one who knows and is wise, whereas she is infantilized and must depend on him and take the direction from him: he orders, she obeys.

Although Langs has found from clinical experience that direct advice is a serious breach of neutrality and therefore a frame violation, what does this patient say? She tells us that she is happy and eager to follow the advice on the manifest level—but she also tells us of a dream about someone who takes orders from others with compliance on the surface but resentment within.

Note that when the adaptive context and the derivative response are abstracted and stated in sequence, the disguise effected by the patient's concretization and displacement is reversed and the meaning becomes obvious. How does the therapist react to this unconscious expression of resentment? It may be that he is unconsciously aware of it and that his emphasis on the identification of *himself* with Ann, the one who is resentful, is a response to this awareness. This response supresses allusions to the patient's resentment. The therapist also attempts to impede any further expression of the patient's anger by suggesting that she is really angry at her mother and telling her that his advice has caused her to view him as interested in her welfare. In effect, the therapist is instructing the patient to displace negative perceptions of him onto objects outside the therapy and maintain an idealized image of him.

The patient tries to correct the therapist. She challenges his identification with Ann and suggests that Ann is a representation of herself by pointing out that she herself is not really a good mother. She offers further help by reminding the therapist that he had said that it was wrong for the patient to want "everything to be done for her by mother figures," thus implying that the therapist's offer of advice was equivalent to a maternal overprotection and inconsistent with his previous stance. This inconsistency is reflected in the dream, in which the one who orders isn't sure if she wants breakfast, lunch, or something in between. The patient is trying to bring the adaptive context back into focus, but, under the influence of significant countertransference, the therapist is resistant to this help. How will the patient react? We now look at more material.

The day after reporting the dream, the patient had difficulty in starting to talk. She then said, "It's not that I am depressed," which immediately suggested that she was depressed. She then went on to say that shortly after leaving the previous session she suddenly felt ravenously hungry. She went to a restaurant and ate a conglomeration of foods which she afterwards vomited up. She also stole a pair of sunglasses at the hairdresser's, justifying herself by saying that Ann was a bitch anyway. Following this she had an intense desire to sleep, and took a fifteen-minute nap in her car. She realized that her behavior was infantile. I suggested that in eating ravenously she seemed for some reason to have a need to regress to feeding at her mother's breast. Her response was negative, as if to say that I was talking nonsense and that she didn't see how that helped her in any way. I pointed out that she was apparently hostile to me and wondered why, particularly in view of the fact that on the previous day she felt I had been so helpful. She replied that as she walked out of my office she saw an attractive young woman sitting in the waiting room. She thought I would naturally be more attracted to the latter than to her, but then comforted herself by thinking she was preparing herself for more important things by becoming seriously involved in her work. Although she felt that she had dealt with the episode in a mature way, it was shortly thereafter that she felt the desire to eat. She recalled a dream of the previous night in which it turned out that a semipsychotic boy, who was one of her clients, had an organic brain disease. She [free associating] had been reading about a boy who had stuffed himself into a trash can and was sent to the acute ward of a mental hospital. It later turned out that he had witnessed a policeman club a woman, who screamed out that he had kicked her in the stomach and killed her unborn child. The boy identified himself with the policeman. He felt he was responsible for the death of his foster mother several weeks earlier, because he had disobeyed her. The patient thought he was punishing himself by treating himself as a piece of trash. I said this might be true, but why did he choose to do it in just this way? In view of the subject we were discussing, I suggested that by getting into a closed container he could be making atonement by returning to his mother's womb, in addition to proving himself unworthy. The patient, in effect, had confirmed my interpretation of the meaning of her sudden hunger after having dismissed it. This happens not infrequently (Freud, 1937, p. 263). I remarked that if the boy of whom she dreamt and who was causing her much frustration turned out to have an organic brain syndrome, he could not be held accountable for his continued misbehavior. Could the boy represent herself? We knew from the past that she could not tolerate success, because she felt guilty for surpassing her mother. She would thus allow her mother to defeat her in tennis even though she was the better player. The day before she had said how well she felt about finally being settled on the proper course in life. Upon leaving the session she automatically assumed that I would prefer the other patient to her, and to make sure that I would consider her unworthy, she proceeded to behave regressively. She did not reject the interpretation but instead recalled that when she became depressed at times she insisted that her condition was organic in nature and she reproached me [at those times] for not prescribing medication for her.

Comment. We seem to have wandered from the original dream and taken up a number of side issues. In a sense, however, the entire discussion may be regarded as a whole. The patient was ambivalent toward me because, although I was helpful, I was also "sour and bitchy" like Ann. This presumably referred to the fact that I did not join others in giving her accolades, but insisted that she be realistic. When she made a serious choice in life she had then to regress. The dream seemed to express a desire to be taken care of by a mother figure, instead of becoming self-sufficient. In other words, out of guilt she could not tolerate the rarefied atmosphere of being successful and had to punish herself by appearing infantile and therefore unworthy in my eyes.

By means of the dream we were able to clarify many aspects of the transference which threw light upon much of the patient's behavior throughout life. (Sloane 1979, p. 128)

The patient begins this session with both an overt resistance and an expression of depression in the form of a denial: "It's not that I'm depressed." These initial responses do not validate the therapist's interventions. Instead, they indicate that his unconscious pressure on the patient to repress anger has produced an iatrogenic depression. This reaction could have been avoided had the therapist geared his interpretive efforts to helping the patient become aware of her reactions to his advice: "In response to my advice, you dream of someone who takes orders resentfully."

The next derivatives are also nonvalidating. There is a reference to taking something in, getting sick, and vomiting it up. Someone has an infantile need to sleep and a need to steal sunglasses. These derivatives are good examples of negative introjects of the therapist and are evidence of nonvalidation of his previous interventions. In that context they imply that the patient unconsciously sees the therapist as someone who needs to protect himself from the glaring truth instead of waking up to it.

The therapist tells the patient that the eating and vomiting represent a wish to feed at the breast. The implication is that it is the patient, not the therapist, who is infantile. This intervention goes beyond the material presented by the patient and ignores any link with an adaptive context. It breaks two fundamental rules established by Langs for intervening and invites the patient on the latent level to contain all the infantile characteristics in the field.

The patient disagrees, implying that the therapist is talking nonsense. Struggling perhaps with his unconscious anger at the patient for refusing to contain his infantile feelings (so that he can remain the adult giver of advice), the therapist attempts to place the anger back into the patient by suggesting that she is hostile toward him. There is the implication that the patient could be rejecting his interpretations for no other reason.

Freely translating the latent content from the manifest material that follows, including that about the woman in the waiting room, we perceive the therapist to be saying, "You were willing to accept a positive image of me in the previous sessions, so why all this resistance now?" The patient replies, "My willingness to repress anger and criticism was based on wishes to be loved, but the serious work of the therapy is more important."

On a more pragmatic level, it seems that the therapist has become less gratifying in recent sessions. This change may have upset a previously stable misalliance based on the patient's need for gratification and love and the therapist's need for the patient as a container into which he can projectively identify disavowed parts of his own psyche and as a source of an idealized image of himself. This hypothesis illuminates the patient's comment that it was her fault that Ann was resentful about taking orders because she did not tip. In other words, she would take the therapist's order to arrange her life if he would give her something extra in return. Perhaps he is attempting to do just this when he challenges her belief that he is more attracted to the patient in the waiting room than he is to her. Does this not imply that he is more attracted to the patient and that she is the favored one? The intervention in which he offers himself as the one interested in her welfare has similar properties.

We turn now to the dream introduced in this session. It is becoming natural to anticipate that the day residue for the dream will be the session preceding it and that the dream will contain the patient's supervisory commentary. The dream refers to a semipsychotic boy with a need to punish himself. There is someone, an authority figure, who has mistreated someone and killed something inside her. These images seem to reflect the patient's perception of the therapist as assaulting her with destructive interpretations because of countertransference (endogenous brain disease).

The therapist focuses narrowly on the image of the trash can, which he associates idiosyncratically with the womb, and uses it as validation of his interpretation that the patient needed to regress to an infantile state. This kind of validation is not based on any consistent methodology and is unlikely to help identify countertransference.

The therapist goes on to suggest that the semipsychotic boy in the dream be identified with the patient (not with himself). One implication in his extraneous comment about organic brain syndrome is that he cannot be held accountable for his destructive interventions and will therefore continue. He goes on to remind her of her guilt toward her mother and her resulting need to let her mother win. On the latent level these interventions may be a request by the therapist that he be allowed to avoid the connection between himself and the boy in the dream and that the patient again repress her anger at him and idealize him, as she did with her mother. He mentions her comment about feeling so well after accepting his advice and after settling on a proper course in life as a way of underlining this request.

The patient seems to acquiesce but points out that when she insists that her problem is organic (i.e., not caused by outside forces), she expects him to give her medication. On the latent level this comment suggests that if she cooperates in helping the therapist avoid perception of his errors and the harmful effects they have on her, she expects him to compensate her.

This material demonstrates how interventions not organized around the available adaptive contexts imply many latent meanings and make possible a dialogue between patient and therapist that is totally outside their awareness but that is accomplished with purpose and creativity nevertheless.

Patient 2

The second clinical example is from my own supervisory work.

The patient, a 35-year-old accountant, obtained the therapist's name from the telephone book. The first session began on time. Although most patients close the doors behind them because of the design of the consultation room (double door with a hallway, which makes it awkward for the therapist to go around the patient to close them), this patient left them open. The therapist motioned and said, "You want to get the door?" The patient closed the doors. After a moment of silence the therapist said, "How can I help you?"

Interspersed with short silences, which the therapist did not interrupt, the following history was given by the patient: He had been psychiatrically hospitalized three years before for symptoms of vomiting, weight loss, and depression. He felt that the hospitalization had been instigated by his parents, who had conferred with the former doctor by telephone from another state. Recently, the patient's mother had pressured him to return home. When he had resisted, he had been threatened with rehospitalization. He had yielded resentfully and moved into his parents' home, where everything was done for him. His brother insisted on driving him everywhere and advised him about everything. He felt unable to stand up to them and was bitter that they could still control him. As a child he had been fed before he could get hungry. He had studied psychology, and he knew that "retroflexed anger" could cause depression. His other therapists (there had been several) had advocated exercises to relieve anger, and he had tried beating on the wall and occasionally had hurt himself. He had been given books to read, but nothing had helped. He felt that he had been manipulated his whole life, but he suspected he invited manipulation. He was afraid to be alone.

The therapist responded that there did seem to be a need for therapy and he believed he could help if the patient could agree on the conditions for therapy. He then outlined the ground rules: reserved time (once a week), fifty dollar fee, no insurance, the patient fully responsible, no excused sessions except legal holidays, no third parties, and total confidentiality. The patient agreed, and a time was set. With fifteen minutes left in the session, the therapist, after about three minutes of silence, said, "We'll proceed by your saying whatever thought comes to mind."

The patient was silent, and then complained about not knowing what to say. He wanted the therapist to ask questions and said he doubted his own ability to communicate. All of this caused the therapist to feel pressured to help or reassure the patient, but he remained silent until the end of the hour.

Let us begin our analysis of this material by identifying the significant adaptive contexts. Because this is an initial interview, we can be fairly certain that coming to a new therapist will be a strong adaptive context and one that will be colored by the patient's previous experience. The patient's description of his parents as creating an environment that was overgratifying and infantilizing is also a reference to the previous therapists' efforts and to expectations of what the new therapist may do. The patient's tone carries a warning to the therapist to resist any efforts from the patient to elicit infantilizing treatment from the therapist, for example, being told to close doors. The patient's comments suggest that the directive to close the door was experienced as "pressure" and "advice" to which he "yielded resentfully." As a result, he feels "bitter about being controlled." Although he feels manipulated, he invited it (by not closing the door himself).

The therapist's interventions made after the patient gave the initial history provide additional adaptive contexts for the material that follows. The first interventions are the establishment of the therapeutic contract, or frame; there was then some silence, and then the therapist mentioned the fundamental rule of free association. Although it seems reasonable to instruct the patient in the fundamental rule, this unusually sensitive patient may have experienced the intervention, because it interrupted the silence, as the therapist's attempt at projective identification of his own dependency and intolerance of being alone. In that adaptive context, the patient's subsequent helpless behavior and expressed doubts about his ability to communicate can be described as a mixture of exploitative role evocations and introjective identifications. In other words, the patient is accepting an invitation to serve as a container for the therapist's helpless feeling and to reserve for the therapist the role of authoritarian helper. There is a clue in this material to the unconscious maternal needs the patient had been required to fill as a child.

Based on these considerations, the therapist's decision not to respond to the patient's pressures for further direction seems correct.

The second session began with the patient's leaving the doors open, requiring the therapist to gesture at them again before the patient closed them. The patient immediately began asking questions: "Where does this door lead to?" "Is this the bathroom?" After trying silence, which elicited even more pressure in the patient, the therapist invited the patient to see what came to mind about the questions. The patient said he felt criticized for asking questions. He went on about how he never said the right things and how he was hesitant to talk now, because it seemed that he could not say the right thing. He continued to plead for direction for awhile, with little variation in the material. The therapist intervened again by suggesting that the patient was inviting him to manipulate and control the patient as others had been reported to have done in the past. The patient replied that he again felt criticized. He always worried about how well he would perform. His mother could never be pleased. Often he would do things almost right, but never completely right. He was afraid of doing the wrong thing in therapy. He then looked accusingly at the therapist and said, "And you! You can just sit back and tell me what it all means in the last ten minutes."

The therapist intervened. "Although you have been talking about your own apprehensions about performing and being criticized, you have now gotten around to some thoughts about my performance. It seems that some of your questions, like about the bathroom, for example, are intended to pressure me to perform and to let me feel what it is like to be criticized. After all, you did not seem to like the way that I responded to your questions. (*The patient smiled.*) Now when you talk about my telling you what it all means in the last ten minutes, I suspect you may be trying to see how I deal with being pressured and put on the spot."

The patient nodded, and paused for about thirty seconds. He then said that this was possible, because he knew he did react quite critically to people who worked for him. As a matter of fact, he felt that he was often quite successful in manipulating his mother. By being sick or well, by gaining or losing weight, he could evoke from her all kinds of efforts on his behalf. He then observed that he was having less difficulty talking now and guessed that he would be able to do okay if he did not worry if what he said was right or wrong and took a more relaxed attitude. The time was up and the therapist ended the session.

The second session contains examples of both validation and nonvalidation as well as the patient's use of the introjective mode to communicate his awareness of certain conflicts within the therapist. As before, we will begin organizing our impressions by identifying the prevailing adaptive contexts. To do so, we must recall the previous hour and the therapist's interventions, particularly their implications or latent contents. The offer of help and the presentation of the ground rules remain important adaptive contexts, but the patient seems to be reacting mainly to the therapist's offer of instructions on how to proceed, perhaps because the patient feels that this interruption of silence is in part countertransference-based and reflects the therapist's unconscious needs to place helpless and dependent feelings into the patient. In that context, the patient's initial pressure in the form of questions is, on the surface, an exaggerated acceptance of the role of the helpless one. On a deeper level the patient is attempting to evacuate feelings of helplessness and place them into the therapist by responding negatively to the therapist's efforts to manage the questions. Because this negativism is occurring in response to the therapist's previous intervention, which had a similar effect on the patient, it is termed a projective counteridentification (Grinberg, 1962).

The therapist reported in supervision that he felt caught off guard by the patient's question about the bathroom. He felt unsure of himself and unable to manage the situation without anxiety, indicating that the patient had touched on an area of vulnerability. The therapist's initial intervention, suggesting that the patient was trying to evoke parental behavior, was off the mark. In retrospect, the therapist felt that he had repressed awareness of the patient's more hostile intent in order to avoid becoming angry. He had done so by inverting the perception that the patient was manipulating his feelings in a hurtful way into the perception that the effort was to get the therapist to manipulate the patient. Supervision focused on the omission of the therapist's instructions about the door as a critical adaptive context.

The therapist's failure to perceive the truth has revealed his pathology to the patient and shifted the therapeutic interaction of the bipersonal field toward the therapist. In the light of these dynamics, the patient's comments about his own concerns about performance can be seen as perceptions of the therapist that have been introjected. The patient's comment about getting things almost right but not quite is a critical commentary on the intervention. The remark about being unable to please his mother may even represent an attempt at a genetic interpretation of the source of the therapist's difficulty. These kind of responses are nonvalidating and can be compared with the patient's validating response to the second intervention. The latter contains new material that confirms the interpretation of the patient's manipulatory wishes by illustrating the operation of such wishes in the patient's relationship with his mother. References to having less difficulty talking and to doing better communicate the patient's awareness of the therapist's improved function, as reflected in the latter's ability to intervene more appropriately. In effect, the patient skillfully has placed his conflict about performance and vulnerability to manipulation into the therapist and then has attempted to cure the therapist with an interpretation disguised as a self-reference. The "cured" therapist then has been reintrojected by the patient. As we have stated, new confirmatory material and positive introjects indicate validation.

In the third session, the patient shut the doors without prompting. He spoke immediately and without difficulty. I will condense considerably. He gave much detail of the manipulatory aspects of his relationship with his mother and sister. He went on to say that his sister had recently said that all the manipulation must stop. He had talked to his mother, who said how much better he seemed and how much that pleased her. He hated it when his mother got all excited when he did well. It made him want to be sick again. Rewards were just manipulations. His doctor in California had been so anxious that he gain weight that he had offered all kinds of inducements. The patient pointed out that another person's wish to manipulate him could be used to turn the tables in a way that allowed him to be the manipulator. He would like to get away from all that, but he did not want to be alone.

The patient continued in that vein without reference to the therapist's previous interventions. He then spoke of some work he was doing. He tended to be frustrated and easily disappointed if he did not get immediate results. With five minutes left in the session, he fell silent.

Feeling inappropriately pressured by the threat of the patient's disappointment, the therapist said that the patient was used to manipulation and felt more comfortable when he could turn the tables and manipulate the manipulator. The patient nodded but remained silent for the remainder of the session.

The adaptive context for this material is the therapist's intervention from the previous hour, in which the patient's manipulatory efforts at projective identification are interpreted. The patient represents this adaptive context only in the latent content of his comment that someone has told him that there will be no more manipulation. This representation implies that he experienced the intervention as an instruction to stop, and his compliance can be inferred from the absence of direct pressure on the therapist in the subsequent material. The reference to improvement and the patient's emerging ability to speak without prompting indicate that the intervention has had a positive effect.

In the last minutes of the session, the pressure on the therapist returns on a latent level in the form of the patient's expression of the frustration and disappointment he feels when he does not get immediate results for his efforts. The therapist responds with a comment that is probably factually correct, but there are several problems with it. It is made in spite of the communicative resistance in the field manifested by the patient's omission of direct reference to the adaptive context. It consists of a replay of the patient's comments and is not organized around the adaptive context, so that it tends to focus on manifest contents. Finally, it is made in the absence of any real indication that the patient needs help.

The patient's references to frustration and disappointment represent further manipulatory pressure on the therapist to reward the patient for talking freely. The patient's comment about his negative reaction to his mother's efforts to reward him with praise for his improvement is a clear supervisory warning to the therapist to respond to the coming pressure with silence. It is a test that the therapist fails by giving the patient a reward for his work in the form of an unnecessary intervention. The supervisory prediction was for trouble in the next hour.

The fourth session began on time. It was the first session of the new month—the agreed-upon time for payment. The patient handed the therapist a check that was too large by the amount of one session. The therapist took the check and placed it on the table between them but made no comment. The patient began relating how depressed he had been all week. He had gone to work, but his mother had been very discouraging. She had said that he only needed to work part time and had warned him not to overdo it. The patient was also very angry about some money that he had had to withdraw from the bank the other day. He had needed it to pay off a loan, but the payment was more than he felt it should have been. He had been thinking a great deal about reward and punishment and how much they influenced his life. He could see this influence in his dealings with his mother and even his sister. He really did not think he could work at all, because he felt so depressed. He continued to ruminate about how depressed he felt but did not refer in any way to the therapy or the therapist's comment in the previous hour.

With ten minutes left in the session, the therapist intervened: "You are reacting to something with feelings of discouragement and depression. You feel you have been treated in a way that tells you not to work and encourages you to act as though you are not up to it. You say that you are too much into reward and punishment and feel that you are spending more money than you should and you have given me more money than we agreed upon."

The patient looked stunned. Finally he said that the check included payment for today's session, which he considered part of the previous month. The therapist pointed out that the date on the check was for the new month. The patient angrily picked up the check and put it in his pocket. He wrote a new check for the correct amount and gave it to the therapist. He spent the remaining few minutes of the hour fuming, talking about how nothing he did was taken at face value and contesting the idea that his writing the check to include today's session had to mean something deep and mysterious.

The adaptive context for the fourth session is the intervention at the end of the third session. It had been uncalled for, and the prediction had been made that it would cause trouble. The patient's commentary, given in disguised derivatives, is that the intervention had been equivalent to an instruction not to work and to be dependent. It had been a manipulatory attempt to reward the patient for working and had caused him to feel depressed. The patient's offer of a check for extra money is a parody of the therapist's behavior. Note how well these derivatives coalesce around the adaptive context, and how the patient demonstrates a communicative resistance by omitting any direct reference to the adaptive context of the therapist's previous intervention.

Any intervention linking the patient's negative reaction during the week with his mother's behavior would have been extremely defensive and bound to have negative results. The intervention actually made repeats and organizes the patient's derivatives around the known but omitted adaptive context. This playback technique avoids bypassing the resistance. Because the intervention contains no conclusions and accuses the patient of nothing, the patient's need to deny any deeper meaning in the incorrect check can be viewed, very tentatively, as a confirmation through denial.

The next hour began with silence, the patient looking away. Eventually he began to complain that he felt like an object in the consultation room. After more silence he said that the atmosphere was so sterile and so unemotional that he did not feel like a person with feelings. Another silence followed. The patient then said that he felt like the object of some mathematical problem. With some heat he said he resented that his check had been rejected. Why was it necessary to analyze everything? It was so frustrating.

After ten minutes of silence, the therapist said, "You are frustrated that I treat you professionally instead of emotionally and invite you to explore instead of accepting your check."

The patient said that in his family everyone reacted emotionally. His older sister always offered help when he did not need it. But his younger sister was different. She was special. Maybe she had been treated in a special way as a child. She was actually able to confront their mother and get away with it. She could split away from the family and did not seem to be affected by their attempts to control her. He continued to talk about how he admired his sister's independence and how he wished that he were more like her until the end of the hour.

In this hour the patient does not omit the adaptive context; rather, he represents it directly in the manifest content by referring to the therapist's giving back the check. The intervention is organized around the adaptive context and has as a justification the patient's sense of negativity and frustration, although with this patient, who is exquisitely sensitive to too much help, silence might have been a better response. Taking this intervention and the one from the previous hour as the adaptive contexts for the material that follows, we see that the patient has a mixed image of the therapist. He is both the sister who induces weakness by offering too much help and the sister who offers a good model by demonstrating freedom from susceptibility to manipulatory pressure and the ability to confront. These are both valid perceptions and illustrate how patients can provide helpful navigational beacons for therapists who can detect such supervisory commentary woven into the patients' responses to their interventions.

Patient 3

The last clinical example, like the first, is taken from the psychoanalytic literature (Giovacchini 1979, p. 96). The material is condensed and lacks the detail and sequential organization found in the second example. Information about the frame is incomplete. Nevertheless, this description, like most of Giovacchini's clinical vignettes, is richer and more detailed than the usual psychoanalytic case report.

An 18-year-old man came to therapy through the efforts of his parents, who were disturbed by his "vegetating." He had always been quiet, pensive, and moody and since puberty had shown no interest in anything around him. He had no friends, never spoke to anyone unless spoken to first, seemed totally inept and gauche, and appeared stupid, although he did well on psychometric exams. His mood was apathetic. In the referral process the parents went to a psychiatrist who encouraged them to send the patient to

Dr. Giovacchini, who gives the following account of the early phase of therapy:

When I first saw him he seemed markedly withdrawn and was completely indifferent to treatment. He saw no purpose in anything and kept his appointments only because his parents insisted. Nothing mattered, nothing would ever change, there was absolutely no hope for him. It was useless to try to change him, he was worthless and one should not waste time trying to help him. He was beyond help.

I did not get the impression that he reviled himself with either anguish or anxiety. He simply felt there was no hope for him, and to some extent, he had been able to accept the situation. The problem was that others would not accept, particularly his parents. They would not leave him alone which was all he wanted. They had ambitions for him but he knew that he was incapable of ever living up to their goals.

He informed me immediately that all my efforts would be futile. Not that he would fight me; I simply would not have anything to work with, and besides, he really had no interest in improving himself anyway. He repeated that all he wanted was to be left alone, but to keep peace, that is, to stop his parents from pushing him, he would not oppose coming to see me. I told him during the first session that since he was here part of him had some wish to be here and to be analyzed. He did not reply. He looked at me as if he did not understand a word I had said.

He had no objection to the frequency of appointments which began with four appointments a week and later was increased to five. He kept them regularly and punctually. I asked him to lie on the couch at the beginning of the second hour and he did so without protest or difficulty. He lay quietly and for the first three months said practically nothing. In fact, during some of these early sessions, he said absolutely nothing. (Giovacchini, 1979, p. 97)

Dr. Giovacchini goes on to report that he did not feel a need to do anything or pursue the patient. From this statement we can only infer that Dr. Giovacchini was silent, but he does not explicitly state so, and we do not know if Dr. Giovacchini said little or said absolutely nothing.

As always, we begin our analysis of this opening segment by trying to identify the important adaptive contexts. Certainly the beginning of therapy must be a major adaptive context, and the circumstances of this beginning will definitely color the patient's reactions. Some of the circumstances are made explicit. We are told, for example, of the patient's great reluctance to enter therapy and that all arrangements preliminary to the therapy had been made by third parties. We know that the therapist had contact with the parents or the referring physician. But there is no direct mention of many frame issues, which suggests that, in contrast to the Langsian point of view, they are considered here of minimal importance.

It seems fair to infer from the material that the fee is paid by the parents and that the patient has no responsibility to the therapist. We do not know the policy for missed sessions, and we do not know if the therapist has any contact with the parents, although we can assume that they receive his bill. There is no indication that the therapist has mentioned any of this to the patient.

If we take as the adaptive context all the deviations we have discussed from the standard frame, the patient's comments about hopelessness take on depth and interactional significance. He says, "[So long as you are a party to the attempts of others to manipulate me, control my life, and make me dependent], I will come only to keep peace with my parents; I will not actively cooperate, and the situation will be hopeless." Note that this is the same passive defense, equivalent to a sit-down strike, that the patient has adopted at home.

This analysis of the chief complaint is interactional and implies that the symptom is a result of an active battle, conducted purposefully but unconsciously by both the patient and his parents. The motivations are, respectively, the wish to be free and the wish to keep a slave. On this basis we can understand rather easily what the patient will be working over with this therapist.

The therapist's analysis of the material focuses on intrapsychic damage from early stages of development and conceives of the patient as very ill. Interpersonal dynamics are not referred to.

The Langsian intervention would begin with the adaptive context: "Because I have been party to arrangements for therapy made by others and not according to your wish, you see me as one of many who are trying to manipulate and control you; after all, your view of the main problem is that others won't leave you alone. You plan to protect yourself here as you have at home by doing nothing." This explication should be followed by an offer of help and an explanation of the ground rules with full rectification of the deviations.

The actual intervention focuses exclusively on the patient's intrapsychic state. The therapist tells the patient that, contrary to what the patient has said, he actually wishes for therapy. The patient's presence is not, in my opinion, adequate proof that the patient wishes for therapy under these conditions (although I believe that the wish to give and receive therapy is present in almost everyone). The patient's noncomprehending response to this intervention is consistent with a wish to convey to the therapist that the intervention has been out of contact with the patient's communications. The perception of the therapist's failure to comprehend is expressed by the patient in the introjected mode.

Another major intervention, mentioned in the text rather offhandedly, is the increase in frequency of sessions from four to five per week. Although this is a major frame intervention that has many implications in light of the interactional dynamics we have suggested, we are not given the sequence in which the change fits. We know neither what prompts it nor what the patient's specific derivative response to it is, so we cannot evaluate its effect.

The therapist's relative silence and decision to allow the patient to be silent without interference deserve special mention. According to the hypothesis that has been developed, this nonmanipulatory, freedom-promoting stance is exactly correct and should bring about therapeutic movement— probably in the form of further testing, because the different interventions must give the patient a very mixed image of the therapist. Let us turn to more material.

Gradually this young man began making offhand comments which seemed trivial. To give an example of the fervor his remarks created and of our interchange, he once told me of a slight change in the schedule of the train he used for transportation to my office. This change in no way inconvenienced him. He was not complaining but he went into detailed particulars about the time changes. I found myself intensely interested in every minute detail of the changed schedule. I asked him many questions about it. (Giovacchini, 1979, p. 98)

The therapist goes on to talk generally about "relationships conducted in subtle symbols [with] neither patient nor therapist aware of what is going on at the time."

This short segment shows a focus on manifest content that is encouraged by the therapist's interest and questions. Such a focus creates pressures that repress latent meaning. For example, in the context of the patient's mention of a "change in schedule," the therapist's intensive questioning and focus on the manifest level of meaning may have been experienced by the patient as an attempt to block the introduction of increase to five days a week as a topic for discussion. The therapist alludes to "relationships conducted in subtle symbols [with] neither patient nor therapist aware of what is going on at the time" but does not connect the idea with the interactions with the patient he has just reported. Instead he states, "Our intensive conversation over apparent trivia was meaningful certainly not because of its content, but because it meant some type of relationship had been established" (p. 100). Is this a denial of the therapist's unconscious knowledge that the patient was referring to the schedule change?

Let us take the therapist's decision to become intensely involved in asking questions as the next adaptive context. Langsian methodology requires us to look at the subsequent material for validation or nonvalidation. We will look for therapeutic introjects, supervisory comments, new material, and the like, all organized around the adaptive context.

Gradually, the patient's material developed a theme. Although he seemed to be jumping from one topic to another without evident rhyme or reason, he was referring to his inability either to understand what was happening to him in the external world or to know how to react to various situations that would have been simple and pedestrian to his contemporaries. He had cast me in a role of an educator. He asked me innumerable questions, again about subjects that seemed trivial or where answers to his questions were particularly self-evident. He concentrated on clothes, how to dress for a particular occasion. He even wondered what type of shoes he should wear to the movies in contrast to what he should wear if he went to a baseball game, although he never went to either movies or baseball games. [The therapist's response] was to give, whenever possible, the information he sought. (Giovacchini 1979, p. 100)

If we take these observations the patient makes about himself as introjects of the therapist prompted by the intense questioning, the patient seems to be saying that such questioning reflects an inability on the part of the therapist to understand what is happening to the patient in the therapy and a lack of theoretical knowledge of how to respond to him. The patient feels that the principles involved are simple and that he will educate the therapist by asking ridiculous questions that the therapist must eventually stop answering.

The therapist, in response to these latent communications from the patient (which can be seen as critical and narcissistically injurious to him), answers all the patient's questions, thus accepting the role of the educator who knows all and implicitly inviting the patient to occupy the complementary position of the student who knows nothing and is very dependent on the educator. By asking questions to which the answers are obvious, the patient tries to communicate that he does not need the therapist to answer. In his discussion the therapist characterizes the patient's questioning and acceptance of advice as indicating that the patient is "trying to incorporate integrative processes" and is "accepting a certain sector of the external world" that the therapist represents.

At this point the therapist took an extended vacation. His commentary indicates that he feels the timing was unfortunate and that he might have considered postponing the vacation had he realized the full importance he had for the patient. He points out that postponing the vacation might well have caused him to feel resentful toward the patient, causing countertransference reactions. Note the use of the term *countertransference* to indicate a justifiable negative attitude on the part of the therapist, rather than to denote distortions in his therapeutic judgment based on his unconscious pathological reactions to the patient. Note also the implied philosophy of not frustrating the patient and not confronting him with reality. The danger of fostering dependency by taking over the patient's reality-testing function is not discussed.

When the therapist returned from vacation, he found that the patient had been hospitalized. The patient had indicated that he did not want the therapist notified. The parents reported that the patient had become a "complete vegetable," a term they seemed to use often when referring to the son. The patient was mute and oblivious to everyone. After the therapist visited the patient three times in the hospital, the patient was discharged and resumed analysis in response to his parents' pressure. The therapist formulated at this point the hypothesis that the patient needed a constant object and felt betrayed by the therapist's absence.

At no time does the therapist try to understand the patient's decompensation and hospitalization in the context of the therapist's previous interventions, the giving of answers to questions. In this context the feeling of betrayal can be seen as justified. After all, someone who encourages another to become totally dependent, even to the point of needing to be told what to wear, has an obligation always to be available. The focus on the patient's intrapsychic defects obscures a probably more relevant exploration of the patient's dependency. No doubt this dependency conflict originated in the interaction with his parents, who seemed to have a need to take over. The patient's questions can be described as role evocations.

After describing further interactions, the therapist relates the patient's report of a dream: "He dreamed of being fed and eating" (p. 111). Someone vaguely outlined was feeding him apples. He was pleased. As a curious aside, he then told the therapist that he could never eat apples, and although he liked their flavor, he was never able to digest them. He would vomit whenever he tried to eat them.

Whereas the therapist here speculates in his discussion that the apples may symbolize the breast, the communicative therapist would look to the therapeutic interaction for the adaptive context. Unfortunately, we are given no information about the interventions immediately preceding the dream. Abstracting the dream "someone feeds me something I like but something that makes me sick," however, provides hints that the patient is referring to what he is getting from the therapist and invites the speculation that the patient is saying that being allowed unlimited dependency gratification and protection from realistic frustration feels good but is bad for him. In that light, the dream becomes a negative commentary on the therapeutic interaction.

The therapist's view of the interaction at this stage is that it was "most striking and gratifying that he seemed to be able to talk to me as if I were a person and not someone threateningly hovering whom he had to fend off"

(Giovacchini 1979, p. 111). The therapist told the patient that "he was able to put himself in a position where he felt he was receiving something from me, that he now seemed capable of taking in some parts of me which he experienced as nourishing. His response and attitude were accepting and he became tranquil and comfortably dependent. Spontaneously he recalled conversations from the beginning of treatment. He referred to much of the advice he provoked me into giving. The patient praised analysis and the therapist."

The therapist's intervention seems to be a suggestion to be dependent and a refutation of the dream's latent content. In essence, the patient is being told how he feels. Communicative technique, in contrast, would advocate frustration of all attempts to elicit dependency gratification from the therapist, silence in response to questions, and then an exploration of the patient's subsequent associations for his response to this frustration. The goals would be (1) to create therapeutic pressure on the patient to bring the derivatives of the dependency conflict to the surface for analysis and (2) to offer the therapist as a model for introjection of someone who does not need to be a participant in overly dependent relationships.

The patient's response to the therapist's suggestion is to accept it and to become "comfortably dependent." His associations indicate, however, that he sees the present situation as reminiscent of the early phase of therapy, which ended in disaster when the therapist went on vacation and was not available to feed him.

To continue Giovacchini's presentation: The "blissful" state was short-lived, and the patient once again became agitated and frightened. On one occasion he arrived and sat down, only to say he was leaving. The therapist intervened, saying he thought it was rather silly for him to have made the trip and then to depart at once. Perhaps they could discuss what was going on, because the therapist had no idea what was making the patient so anxious. Nevertheless, the patient left. He later said that since becoming able to follow the therapist's advice, he no longer hallucinated the therapist, and he felt distressed over the loss. He wanted the hallucinations back. He kept saying, "I have bitten off more than I can chew." He revealed that he was frightened because he had gone too far in the direction of autonomy. He believed that following the therapist's advice on a few occasions was getting him involved in areas that were over his head. He could meet a situation with techniques the therapist had taught him, but the therapist could not equip him for all the unexpected contingencies he might have to face.

The therapist describes this material as vague, because it focuses on problems in the outside world. It is all very nebulous, and the therapist concludes that the material deals with "intrapsychic events."

Analyzing the material, we find the adaptive context of the advice now represented clearly in the manifest content. The view of the therapist biting off more than he can chew by inviting the patient to be dependent is expressed in the introjective mode. The patient's need to leave the session early represents his defenses against the invitation. The therapist first views these thoughts as relating to the outside world, displacing them away from the interaction, but finds they make no sense. He then decides that the associations relate to processes inside the patient. They reflect "intrapsychic events." The patient's wish to leave early is dismissed as "silly" instead of being explored.

The communicative therapist might have intervened in a manner something like this: "You have experienced the advice I have given you as dangerous because it undermines your autonomy and interferes with your ability to think for yourself. You seem afraid of the effects of separation under such circumstances of dependency and are trying to protect yourself by leaving early." (Note the use of the adaptive context as an organizer for the derivatives, which then illuminate the patient's wish to leave early.)

As the therapy continued, the patient gradually became angry. He accused the therapist of causing his problems. He became "paranoid" and thought the therapist was plotting with his parents to have him put away and locked up for the rest of his life. In letters, the patient accused the therapist of not wanting him to have a will of his own and wanting to use him for the therapist's own nefarious purposes. The therapist indicates his view that the patient was undergoing a paranoid psychosis.

Our previous analysis of the latent content indicates, in contrast, that these "paranoid" ideas of the patient actually contain a good deal of valid perception of the therapist's unconscious pressures and processes, mixed with distortion and exaggeration. More specifically, the patient is implying that the therapist is undermining his autonomy because of the therapist's need to be in a position of omnipotence, with others dependent on him. The patient expresses a delusion that his parents and therapist are plotting together against him. But the delusional core is the patient's valid perception of the latent meaning of the frame deviation concerning the fee arrangement. Had the therapist offered a secure frame and scrupulously avoided any intervention that would have fostered dependency, he properly could have viewed the patient's accusation that the therapist was using him and did not want him to have a will of his own as a transference-based paranoid delusion. The patient clearly links these thoughts with the adaptive context of the advice, but the therapist omits the link. This omission is fostered by the intrapsychic view and the concept of transference, because these perspectives encourage avoidance of the needed scrutiny of the interaction and the vital search for prevailing adaptive contexts.

CONCLUSION

There are two major conclusions that can be advanced on the basis of the foregoing analyses:

1. The use of the adaptive context as an organizer for listening to the patient's material can reveal meaning not found by traditional methods, which omit its use.
2. Countertransference error in technique is more likely to be exposed and analyzed through communicative approaches to listening than through approaches that do not begin with the adaptive context. This conclusion follows from the fact that the adaptive context, by definition, focuses on the therapist's interventions, particularly their latent implications. The therapist who listens with an adaptive context in mind is compelled to review his or her actions constantly and to consider the patient's unconscious commentary.

Although there are many merits to the adaptational-interactional (communicative) approach, the technique is also a constant burden. It is intellectually difficult to keep a number of derivatives in mind, abstract them, and build an intervention. It is almost impossible when there is anxiety. Then, too, one has to listen to frequent criticism that is often pointed and painful. But the most serious problem, I believe, is the sacrifice of comfort and niceties (such as a secretary) and money, perhaps a great deal of money.

The loss of money occurs in two ways. First, it is impossible to permit the use of insurance. One soon learns that insurance provides the patient with too much opportunity to avoid the therapy. It destroys the frame. Second, one learns from patients that the best technique is generally to withhold overt signs of approval or affection as well as disapproval. Overt expression of affection begets images of prostitution in the patient's associations. It should not be surprising that many patients want nothing but palliation, usually in the form of an illicit gratification. If they don't get it, they quit, and the fee is lost.

It is even possible that high-frequency therapy—i.e., treatment more than once a week—is too fraught with side effects and countertransference needs to be correct. But it would be difficult to prove that to an audience that stands to lose half its income or more if it adopts this position.

Unpopular conclusions are more difficult to arrive at than popular ones. Perhaps that is why over 70 years elapsed between the first critical discovery of the day residue as an organizer for dream contents and what I see as the second critical discovery of psychoanalysis: the adaptive context.

REFERENCES

EISSLER, K. R. (1953). The effect of the structure of the ego on psychoanalytic technique. *Journal of the American Psychoanalytic Association* 1:104–143.

FREUD, S. (1937). Constructions in analysis. *Standard Edition* 23.

GIOVACCHINI, P. (1979). *Treatment of Primitive Mental States*. New York: Jason Aronson.

GRINBERG, L. (1962). On a specific aspect of countertransference to the patient's projective identification. *International Journal of Psycho-Analysis* 43:436–440.

JONES, E. (1953). *The Life and Work of Sigmund Freud*. Vol. 1 New York: Basic Books.

LANGS, R. (1973). *The Technique of Psychoanalytic Psychotherapy*. Vol. 1. New York: Jason Aronson.

———— (1974). *The Technique of Psychoanalytic Psychotherapy*. Vol. 2. New York: Jason Aronson.

———— (1975a). Therapeutic misalliances. *International Journal of Psychoanalytic Psychotherapy* 4:77–105.

———— (1975b). The therapeutic relationship and deviations in technique. *International Journal of Psychoanalytic Psychotherapy* 4:106–141.

———— (1976a). *The Bipersonal Field*. New York: Jason Aronson.

———— (1976b). On becoming a psychiatrist: discussion of "Empathy and Intuition on Becoming a Psychiatrist," by Ronald J. Blank. *International Journal of Psychoanalytic Psychotherapy* 5:255–280.

———— (1976c). *The Therapeutic Interaction*. 2 vols. New York: Jason Aronson.

———— (1978a). The adaptational-interactional dimension of countertransference. In R. Langs, *Technique in Transition* pp. 501–535. New York: Jason Aronson.

———— (1978b). Interventions in the bipersonal field. In R. Langs, *Technique in Transition*, pp. 627–678. New York: Jason Aronson.

———— (1978c). *The Listening Process*. New York: Jason Aronson.

———— (1978d). Validation and the framework of the therapeutic situation: thoughts prompted by Hans H. Strupp's "Suffering and Psychotherapy." *Contemporary Psychoanalysis* 14:98–104.

———— (1979). *The Therapeutic Environment*. New York: Jason Aronson.

———— (1980a). *Interactions: The Realm of Transference and Countertransference*. New York: Jason Aronson.

———— (1980b). On the properties of an interpretation. *Contemporary Psychoanalysis* 16:460–478.

———— (1980c). Some interactional and communicative aspects of resistance. *Contemporary Psychoanalysis* 16:16–52.

———— (1981). Modes of "cure" in psychoanalysis and psychoanalytic psychotherapy. *International Journal of Psycho-Analysis* 62:199–214.

SLOANE, P. (1979). *Psychoanalytic Understanding of the Dream*. New York: Jason Aronson.

CHAPTER 7

The Reflective Potential of the Patient as Mirror to the Therapist

Patrick Casement, M.A.

The bipersonal perspective highlights many interactional elements of the patient-therapist exchanges in psychotherapy. There is thus an increased need to be able to look closely at *both* sides of this relationship, to expose both the therapist and the patient to close scrutiny of every aspect of their interaction.

The literature provides views of the patient-therapist interaction from the perspective of the supervisor (Langs 1976, 1978, 1979a, 1979b, 1980, 1981). It has not provided an opportunity to follow this interaction from the viewpoint of a therapist using the bipersonal approach with a patient, or beginning to use it. Therefore, this chapter will discuss the functioning, and failures to function, of the therapist's *internal supervisor* (Casement 1973). Two clinical presentations will be provided. In the first, an experienced therapist learns from the patient to listen from an interactional viewpoint. As a result, he is awakened out of a period of professional laxity. This awakening arises from a willingness to reflect on the patient's *unconscious supervisory efforts* (Langs 1978), which leads to the therapist's eventual recognition of what is being played back to him in the derivative communications from this patient. The second presentation is an account of my own reflective use of the patient's supervisory efforts. We shall see how this kind of listening to the patient's communications can help alert us to the ways in which recent and current breaks in the frame are being perceived by the patient and are being reflected back to us. Only after adequate rectification of the frame is it possible to attend to the transference rather than the current reality in the patient-therapist relationship (Langs 1980).

Langs acknowledges his debt to the British school of psychoanalysis, whose members have long been familiar with the interactional aspects of the

127

analytic relationship. A tradition of recognizing the implications of there being two persons involved and more than one unconscious operating in this relationship preceded the extensive work of Langs, as did a tradition of looking at the various aspects of the analyst's responsiveness to the patient, distinguishing between a "self-corrective" awareness of countertransference as pathology in the analyst and a "diagnostic" awareness of countertransference as offering "an instrument of research into the patient's unconscious" (Heimann 1950, 1960).[1]

Most analysts in the British school, and not just the Kleinians, use the concepts of *projective identification* and *the container and the contained* (Bion 1977, Klein 1946). We also use Winnicott's concept of analytic *holding* (Winnicott 1954). The interactional aspects of the analytic relationship are implicit throughout the writings of Winnicott (1949–1970) and Balint (1952) and often are explicit, although the language is not the same. It was Marion Milner (1952) who provided the concept of the analytic frame: "The frame marks off the different kind of reality that is within it from that which is outside it; but a temporal spatial frame also marks off the special kind of reality of a psycho-analytic session." More recently, Sandler (1976) highlighted a further aspect of the interactional dimension in the analytic relationship in his paper "Countertransference and Role-Responsiveness."

The bipersonal approach to listening to the patient-therapist interaction is illustrated in the case presentations that follow. In the first case we see the patient unconsciously battering the therapist until he recovers his therapeutic role. We can see the patient's unconscious supervisory efforts in abundance, particularly when we listen to what the patient is presenting as referring to herself at one level and at another level to the therapist.[2] We thus come to find powerful images of the patient's introjection of the therapist perceived as a damaging object, the patient reproducing in herself enactments of the therapist's own failures toward her and their impact on her. In the second case, which is chosen from an analytic treatment in order to provide some contrast to a case in therapy, we see the analyst also using the interactional viewpoint in his listening to the patient and in his own *silent running commen-*

---

[1]See also Little (1951), to whom I owe the notion of the "patient as mirror to the analyst."

[2]A paper on the work of Matte-Blanco (1976) presented on November 5, 1980, to the British Psychoanalytical Society by Eric Rayner has stimulated me to apply Matte-Blanco's concept of the 'symmetrical logic' of primary processs thinking to the question of listening. I believe it is necessary to use a *symmetry of listening* that allows us to listen to any statement by the patient as referring potentially to the patient/the analyst/any other simultaneously. I prefer the notion of *listening for symmetry* to Langs's concept of listening to the me/not me interface, even though I think we are speaking of the same thing.

tary or (as I call it) the *work of the internal supervisor.* There are examples of several breaks in the *analytic frame*, which these cases clearly show are not the monopoly of therapists in training. By listening to the patient's material around these breaks, which are *primary adaptive contexts* of the session, the analyst is able to recognize the patient's allusions to these various breaks in the frame, and gradually these breaks are rectified. When the analytic frame is restored, the patient offers her own symbolic imagery to convey her acknowledgment of this restoration. She then uses this recovered security in the analytic hold to reexperience a very early trauma, aspects of which had been reenacted dramatically by the analyst in the cumulative effect of the specific series of failures that are described. Several different ways of understanding this particular sequence are offered in the concluding discussion.

In the first case I offer supervisory comments alongside the therapist's own record, in which we can see that he is beginning to adopt an interactional viewpoint in his listening. The main focus here is on a single session set in the context of a prolonged period of unrectified breaks in the therapeutic frame.

CASE 1: MRS. A.

Background to the Session

Mrs. A. was in her sixties when she entered once-a-week therapy.[3] She was referred for severe anxiety attacks with a history of manic-depressive mood swings. Therapy initially had failed to contain the patient, and she was hospitalized. Lithium carbonate therapy was begun by the psychiatrist, who took over her treatment. Later, at the request of Mrs. A., her therapist was asked to resume her insight therapy while she was still hospitalized. Therapy began to be more meaningful to Mrs. A., and she was discharged from the hospital. Not long afterwards, her wish for the medication to be discontinued was also agreed to.

The therapist again resumed responsibility for the treatment, and Mrs. A. began to make significant progress in many areas of her life. The anxiety attacks ceased over a period of two years, and there was no recurrence of the earlier uncontrollable mood swings. Both patient and therapist felt that the therapy was going well. This situation, however, led to a more relaxed relationship, with patient and therapist "soft-pedaling" during a period that seemed a prelude to ending therapy. The therapist was letting himself be influenced to shift from the professional relationship, seen as detached, toward a more realistic and mutual relationship by the not uncommon

---

[3]The background material has been compiled from the therapist's notes. The description of the session is the therapist's verbatim account as written after the session.

rationale that this change enables the transference relationship to be worked through and relinquished more easily.[4]

What remained unknown to the therapist at this time was that the patient was approaching a crisis in her marriage. Stresses had been developing at home because her husband had been used to his wife's readiness to avoid potential conflict by dutiful compliance to his wishes and demands. During her therapy Mrs. A. had discovered that she could disagree with her husband and defend her positions even if doing so led to conflict, but this growth in her was causing pressure for change in the marriage. There had been hints of this problem in the past, but a more direct presentation of these stresses in the marriage was postponed during the period of professional laxity described.

Recent Breaks in the Therapeutic Frame

About two months prior to the session to be quoted, Mrs. A. had been singing praises of her dentist (Dr. X.). Even though it meant traveling a long distance to see him, she had been treated by this same man for years, as he had always been careful and thorough in his work. She recently had been able to combine her weekly visits to her therapist with visits to the dentist, whose office was just down the road from the therapist's consulting rooms. She wished her husband and children would take the same trouble to travel in to see Dr. X., because they probably would be far better off than if they stayed with their local dentist, but they preferred to retain their prior arrangements.

[Comment] We can see here some derivative references to the unchanging state of things in the family and, more obliquely, to the therapy and to the therapist's having begun to overlook the issue of change. We can also see the patient's unconscious rebuke of the therapist for not being as careful and thorough in his recent work as he had been earlier. Mrs. A. points out that she comes as far to see the therapist as to see the dentist down the road. She may be wondering what she is getting in return for her effort. The dentist is at least always careful and thorough—unlike the therapist.

The therapist here fell into a countertransference gratification as a result of his own need for a good dentist near his consulting rooms.[5] He felt tantalized by this unsolicited testimonial for such a dentist. Rationalizing that it might not affect the therapy, particularly as the treatment seemed to be nearing closure, he asked the patient if she would mind giving him the name of her dentist, because he was looking for someone reliable nearby. Mrs. A. was outwardly pleased to supply it and said she was glad to be of help. She hoped the therapist would find Dr. X. as good as she always had.

[4]This reasoning is also sometimes used on the grounds that the treatment is psychotherapy and not analysis.

[5]The therapist was not in supervision. What we will see in this clinical sequence is a lapse in the therapist's self-supervision, and his subsequent recovery of it.

[Comment] We can see in this reply the patient's unconscious hope that the therapist will find the help he is indicating he needs if he is to recover from the present lapse and reversal of roles. We will see later a typical split between the conscious pleasure at being able to be of help and the unconscious resentment at the implications of this request for the patient's "therapy." What follows illustrates Langs's dictum that "one exception begets another." The sequence shows that this statement can apply equally to therapist and patient. Here it is the therapist whose inappropriate demands have been met once, and it is he who initiates a further breach in the professional relationship, and the therapeutic frame, by asking for more.

Two sessions before the one to be presented, the therapist asked the patient for another favor. Mrs. A. had been speaking of her occasional difficulty in getting to sleep and of the usefulness to her of a relaxation tape. The tape was so effective for her that she had yet to hear the end of the tape, because she was always asleep by that time. The therapist said he would be interested in hearing the tape she found so effective. Mrs. A. replied by saying that she could tell him where he could get the tape. Then she correctly assessed that he was hinting at borrowing *her* tape, so she said that perhaps he would prefer to hear it before making the commitment of buying a copy for himself. She offered to bring the tape with her the next week to lend it to him. Her husband could make her a copy in case she needed to use it while the therapist had the original.

[Comment] The therapist's listening has veered completely away from the patient. As with the earlier reference to her good dentist, the therapist is responding like an envious child. Each time Mrs. A. indicates that she has something good, the therapist wants some of it for himself and asks the patient to provide it for him. The patient is unlikely to miss the unconscious implications here concerning the therapist's present difficulties in managing his own state of mind. She may validly be wondering whether he is telling her that he too has sleeping problems, and he seems to be asking her obliquely to be his therapist. Certainly the therapist's countertransference gratification is openly visible here. Mrs. A. indicates her insecurity at this point by turning to her husband to meet her needs in the event that her therapist continues to be unable to attend to them appropriately.

The therapist thanked Mrs. A. and accepted her offer. She brought the tape the next week, and her last words in that session were, "I don't know why, but today doesn't seem to have been as helpful as I had hoped."

[Comment] The therapist has not yet responded to the patient's unconscious efforts to alert him to his role reversal and his need to attend to whatever it is in his own pathology that has led to the various unresolved lapses in his work with her. That the therapist has accepted the loan of the tape even after having had a week to reflect on the implications of this action confirms the patient's fear that he has not yet recognized the need to rectify the frame. We can hear a reference to her disappointment about this in her closing words. Not only has she not been helped in the session as much as she had hoped, but neither has the therapist. Having failed to attend to the frame issues indicated, the therapist is unable to give the patient the help for which she comes. This time, however, the therapist *does* reflect on her unconscious supervisory efforts and is able to make use of his reflection in the following session.

The Session

Mrs. A. came in and sat down.[6] The therapist handed back the tape and thanked her for letting him listen to it. He made no further reference to it, not wanting to lead into an intellectualized discussion of this, and neither did she. She put the tape down on the table between them and left it there throughout the session. (There is a low side table between the two chairs in the consulting room. This patient has always used the chair.)

[Comment] The patient leaves the tape between herself and the therapist as if to give an even clearer cue that it remains an issue that still has to be attended to.

Mrs. A. proceeded to show the therapist a new Bible that her husband had given to her as a wedding anniversary present. Her husband knew that it was just what she wanted. The therapist looked at it briefly and handed it back to her, saying that it was certainly a very beautiful Bible.

[Comment] The therapist is still caught in the quasi-social relationship which he himself had initiated earlier. The patient demonstrates the usual split response. She uses the same kind of break in the frame, asking something of the therapist such as he had earlier asked of her; at the same time, by repeating the therapist's crossing of this particular boundary, she unconsciously alerts him to what has been happening. We may also speculate that Mrs. A. has become concerned about the seductiveness of the therapist in his neglect of the usual professional boundaries and that this is why she is bringing her husband in. She is drawing the therapist's attention pointedly to the fact that she is a married woman.

Mrs. A. said she had had a terrible week and couldn't think why. Nevertheless, she had been able to sleep every night except the last. She had been using the copy of the relaxation tape that her husband had made for her, but the previous night she had not used it, because she was afraid she might not wake up in time and might miss her session.

[Comment] The patient is rebuking the therapist for having caused her to sleep badly. There is also some wish to miss the session expressed in her

[6]These passages were taken from the therapist's written account of the session.

anxiety about oversleeping. She may in addition be anxious about what she will meet in her therapist this week and whether he has benefited from the help she unconsciously has been trying to offer him.

Mrs. A. said she couldn't remember what had happened during the last session. She went on to say that she had had a fall during the week. She had thought for a moment that there might be something wrong with her, that she could have had a blackout, but she then realized this wasn't what had happened. She had tripped over a badly laid paving stone. "It was very uneven and dangerous. It really is not safe leaving the pavements in that condition. So many people fall over them, and some get seriously hurt, but the authorities always find ways to shelve the blame. They still don't do anything to put it right."

[Comment] The patient is presenting a richly meaningful and relevant commentary on the therapist's recent behavior. She has introjected the therapist's own tripping up, and when this came to be enacted in her own falling, she wondered at first whether it might have been her fault. She states that she then realized that it was not something wrong with *her* but was due to the unevenness of the surface she had been walking on, an unconscious reference to the unevenness of the therapist's behavior and his failure to maintain a sufficiently secure basis for the therapeutic frame. This uneven-ness, she says pointedly, could be very dangerous. How many other people (patients) might be hurt in the hands of a therapist who shows such a careless disregard for the ground rules of therapy? She drives this point home by saying that the authorities usually shelve the blame—pass things off as not their responsibility—and do nothing about them. The patient has not given up in her *unconscious curative efforts* toward the therapist, but at this point she is not hopeful of much being done about the problem.

Mrs. A. continued by saying that over the weekend she had suddenly developed a terrible abscess under the root of a front tooth that resulted in the worst pain she had ever experienced. She had phoned Dr. X. (the dentist), and he had told her to come right over. She went to see him on that Monday. He examined her carefully and said that she certainly had an abscess but that there was nothing wrong with her tooth, so she must be run down or something. She couldn't think why this should be so. True, she said, she had gone away to "St. Mary's Rest Home" recently, hoping to come away feeling much better, but she had left there feeling just the same.

The therapist's record here continues.

P: I'll say this for Dr. X.: he did something they don't often seem to do nowadays. When there's poison there underneath I think it is better to lance it, or in some other way to help the poison to come out, and that is exactly what he did. He removed a filling, which allowed the abscess to drain out, and it feels much better now. He gave me penicillin too, which probably helps, but it always makes me feel terribly exhausted. Usually people just give you a pill or whatever and expect that to disperse the infection, or to deal with the problem, without doing anything more about it.

The patient is eloquent in her continuing commentary here. She is very explicit about the abscess at the root, the poison that needed to be dealt with directly, the thoroughness of the dentist compared with other more casual ways of dealing with patients. It is not surprising that some therapists shrink from recognizing themselves reflected by the patient in ways like this. The therapist here deserves rough treatment from this patient and gets it, and it is a measure of the patient's persistent efforts toward adequate rectification that she elaborates so perceptively and directly. The therapist is fortunate that the patient has not turned more of her aggression toward herself than she has. It remains obliquely directed against him. She reports having fallen, and then developing this abscess, but she continues to look for proper treatment—if not from this therapist, then from someone else. It is also worth noting that an earlier break in the frame, concerning the dentist, had been left to fester and to infect the subsequent course of this therapy. The abscess refers back to this, and possibly it is significant that it erupted over the weekend after the latest letdown by the therapist, when he had revealed himself as more her patient than her therapist. It is natural that she thinks of another treatment setting where she can be treated more carefully, alluding at some level to thoughts of terminating treatment with this therapist if these frame issues are not attended to adequately.

> T: I believe you are pointing out to me some of what was wrong about your recent sessions. Last week you had come expecting something that was troubling you to be attended to properly. You left feeling that the session had not been helpful.

The therapist is playing back derivatives here around the adaptive context of the frame issues that he is beginning to recognize as urgently needing attention.

> P: I didn't think I was criticizing *you* in what I was saying, but I suppose it is possible that I was. I don't claim to be much good at understanding these things.

The patient is prepared to consider that she could be expressing criticism of the therapist. She speaks of herself as not claiming to be much good at understanding these things. This may be a further introjective reference to the therapist, who does claim to understand these things but lately has been failing to do so.

> P: I've got *some* good news to tell you. Although John [her husband] and Anne [her 25-year-old daughter] are both being rather difficult still, James [her 19-year-old son] has been a great help. An old lady's electric kettle has not been working. She had taken it to the Electricity Board repair desk, where she was told it needed a new heating element and this would cost 10 dollars if someone else could fit it for her or 25 dollars if she left it at the desk.[7] She couldn't afford that, so she had instead offered it to Anne for her annual charity bring-and-buy sale. James offered to look at the kettle and shortly afterward came back with it mended. He'd seen that the cord was all rotten and needed renewing, and the plug was also cracked in two places. He'd replaced the cord and the plug, and it was working perfectly. James now plans to go to see what other electrical things this old lady has that might have dangerous cords or plugs, and he will be checking everything over for her. It could have been lethal. Fancy someone at the Electricity Board not seeing that this was wrong and handing it back in that condition! They, of all people, should have known better. I suppose nowadays there are lots of people who don't do a proper job. They just sit back and take the money, and don't bother about the consequences.

The themes remain the same—jobs not done properly, faults that are left and that could be lethal—and there are references to more than a single fault being revealed upon proper inspection. We also hear of people who should know better failing to recognize what is wrong. The patient is driving home the point that there is more than one frame issue that needs to be rectified. James has dealt with the faults he has found so far, but there might be more. The cord and the plug can be seen as derivative references to the relationship between the patient and the therapist—those things that link them—and to the fact that this is not as it should be: it is worn out and cracked in ways that could be lethal. It certainly could be lethal to the treatment, and just possibly this last comment could be a veiled suicide thought. We also hear that the kettle that had seemed to be beyond repair had been given away. This may be a further allusion to thoughts of termination if this therapist continues to fail to do a proper job, if he fails to see what is urgently in need of rectification.

> T: You are giving me more examples of jobs not being done properly, because people don't bother to see what is wrong, compared with James's taking the trouble to look properly into what was wrong and putting right those faults that [if left] could have been seriously dangerous or even lethal. I think you

[7]The patient's fee was also 25 dollars.

are still wondering whether I am bothering to do a proper job here, or am I just sitting back and taking the money without adequately dealing with what is wrong. [This session was the last session of the month, so the patient would have been expecting to receive the monthly bill at the end of the session].

The therapist is beginning to acknowledge that there could be a basis in reality for the patient's perception of him as recently having been sitting back in the therapy.

P: Well, now that you come to point this out, I have been wondering about the way in which you work. For instance, it is like a machine, let's say a tape recorder (*and she looks at the tape on the side table*), where something is wrong so that only some of what is being said is recorded. When you play it back, there are bits that are so faint you can't hear it properly. Now, take things like my visits to St. Mary's. I know you know, at least I assume you know, that that is something important to me, and yet you don't ask me about it. I might go on for a whole session to see if you will, but you don't. So when you don't I'm not sure if you really care. But on the other hand, I have assumed it must be because you want to leave me room to say what else may be on my mind. But you do sometimes ask, for instance, you always asked about my leg injury and would offer me the footstool when I was having to keep my leg up as much as possible.

The patient now reveals that she has been following the therapist's way of working very closely and has been trying to understand why he works in this way. In particular, she is trying to understand why he is inconsistent. She indicates the tape as a part of what is wrong. She goes on from there to give an example of a listening machine that is not functioning properly. There are therefore bits which you can't hear properly when played back. We can see references here to the therapist's lapses in attention, his failures to listen adequately, and how these are made evident in the playback to the patient by the unconscious communications about himself he has conveyed in his behavior in recent sessions. The patient goes on to wonder whether he cares. In her example she refers to a time when the therapist had been functioning more appropriately, leaving her space to say what was on her mind, but she concludes with a further reference to his inconsistency. The offering of the footstool is also a move away from the formal therapeutic relationship, and this is brought in here too in the patient's playback to the therapist.[8] She offers fewer breaks in her listening, and in her playback, than does the therapist.

[8]Any exception to the established norm of treatment of the patient is likely to be noted by the patient. The footstool, I think, is seen here as one of several exceptions, but I would regard this as a matter of good manners rather than as a break in the frame as such. Langs might disagree.

T: I think that the key to this is that you have experienced a confusing degree of inconsistency in the way I have been working with you. Part of you would like me to offer a more social kind of relationship, and when I do you may be consciously glad of that—as with the stool. But you actually need me to remain consistently a therapist in this relationship. When I have been more clearly a therapist, you have been able to understand the reasons for this, so long as there was a consistency. What has been confusing to you has been when I have shifted between being therapist at one moment and being more social with you at another, thereby entering into superficial exchanges with you that in the end result in my not listening or attending to the underlying problems. My borrowing of the tape is an example of this and it has become a further source of confusion to you.

P: I must admit I was very surprised when you said you would be interested in hearing that tape, but I thought it was nice to see you being human and to be of use to you. After all, you have been a great help to me in the past.

The patient feels free to acknowledge her surprise at the therapist's behavior now that he indicates that he can look at this himself. She softens this, nevertheless, in order not to hurt the therapist, as she now probably cannot be sure how much he can take. The reference to past help may be partly valid, but we should not overlook the considerable unconscious help that the patient has been offering to the therapist recently from which he is beginning to show some benefit.

T: But I was not helpful to you on this occasion, as you pointed out to me at the end of the last session. You had, after all, told me where I could obtain a copy of this tape without involving you, but instead I took the shortcut of borrowing it from you. That was a break in the usual relationship here, and this has been threatening to be harmful to your therapy unless it is recognized and adequately dealt with. Otherwise, as with the tooth abscess, it could fester.

P: There was one other occasion: when I was surprised that you said Dr. X. must be a very good dentist for me to travel all this way to see him, and you then asked me for his name. It was so unlike you to ask, but again I felt it was nice to be able to be helpful to you.

The patient at least is determined to drain the "abscess" thoroughly. She points to each occasion on which she feels her therapist has stepped out of role. She expresses a rationalized pleasure along with her surprise. The way in which she explains her pleasure includes an unconscious recognition of the therapist's having turned her into his helper, his unacknowledged therapist.

T: So we have more than just one occasion when I can be regarded as reversing roles with you, whereby you find yourself put into the position of having your needs overlooked while you are asked to attend to requests of mine. It may seem reassuring to find that I am human, and that you can be of help to me, but as far as your therapy is concerned, this is certainly not attending adequately to what you need to be dealt with. I believe this is why you have been pointing out to me the contrast between people who do their jobs thoroughly and those who don't. When you pay me it is for me to do my job as therapist, and to do that carefully and attentively, not to have me sitting back and being social with you.

The therapist hands her the bill, which she accepts with a knowing smile—showing that she understands what he has just been saying to her. This marks the end of the session.

The next session will not be given here except to say that the patient returned feeling much relieved by the work done in the session just quoted. She began by presenting the state of her marriage and stresses in the family that had been alluded to briefly in earlier sessions, and in the last session, but that she had not felt able then to discuss in depth. Mrs. A. also confessed that she had come very close to thinking that there was no point in her continuing with her therapy but she was now relieved to find it felt all right to go on. She was beginning to feel positive about her therapy again.

Discussion

Mrs. A. demonstrates a degree of unconscious awareness of the therapist's state of mind that can be quite disconcerting. We might wish to regard it as unusual, but it is probably typical of the majority of our patients, without our realization. The unconscious of more than one person is operating in the relationship between the patient and the therapist, however well analyzed the therapist may have been, and a patient will monitor the therapist either quite consciously (as some patients will occasionally tell us) or unconsciously. Mrs. A. has an intuitive grasp of what constitutes a secure therapeutic frame. She notes every occasion on which this therapist has crossed the boundaries necessary for insight-promoting psychotherapy, she unconsciously recognizes the countertransference implications of these transgressions, and, in the interests of her own therapy, she contributes persistent unconscious supervisory efforts toward rectification (see Langs 1978). At the point in this clinical sequence when the therapist is sliding into a state of countertransference neurosis (see Racker 1968), the patient shifts into the role of unconscious therapist to her therapist (see Searles 1975). Only when the therapist begins to recognize the outstanding frame issues does he start to listen around these as a primary adaptive context. It is this process that prompts his subsequent listening to be focused on the derivative rather than the manifest levels of the patient's communications, and that leads him eventually toward the necessary efforts at rectification. With the therapist becoming able to recover his role as therapist, the patient begins to feel safe enough to point out other departures from the more usual therapeutic frame. She does not miss a single item of which we are aware. Thus, and only thus, is her therapy rescued from the termination of treatment that at one point seemed almost inevitable. The patient is able to resume meaningful therapy.

Many of the interactional dynamics illustrated in this case have been documented extensively with supervisees in the published work of Langs (1976, 1978, 1979a, 1979b, 1980, 1981). It is timely to discover that findings similar to Langs's with his supervisees emerge when we too listen to the patient's communications from an interactional point of view. We thus learn some painful lessons from the patient. Being friendly, being human, may seem to be nice. It also may seem to be reassuring. But the patient makes abundantly clear in the derivative communications around these issues that at a deeper level such behavior can be extremely destructive to the patient and to the patient's therapy. All deviations are precipitated to some extent, and here to a considerable extent, by the therapist's countertransference being uncontained. The case of Mrs. A. documents this principle in definite terms, and it is a salutary lesson.

CASE 2: MRS. B.

Clinical material from the sessions of one week of an analysis will now be presented. Of necessity, this material has been condensed, but as far as possible the sequence and essential detail have been preserved. In addition to the usual presentation of each session, some indications of the work of self-supervision are included.[9] This work grows out of the interplay between the silent reflection of the internal supervisor that takes place in the session, aided as it is by the patient's unconscious supervisory efforts, and such hindsight as we may have when we are not caught up in the interaction of being with the patient. We may arrive at hindsight either on our own or with the help of a colleague, such as a supervisor. The following account is therefore an attempt to indicate these different levels of listening to the patient. This difference depends to a great extent on whether we are inside or outside the session. It also depends on our degree of readiness to be open to our patients' unconscious efforts to reflect back to us how they are perceiving us. What we then see in the patient, as mirror to the therapist/analyst, can be a painfully accurate image of ourselves. It is largely for this reason that we may be reluctant to look closely at this often uncomplimentary reflection of ourselves.

[9]I was not being supervised in this case.

Of necessity, much has been left out of this account, but it is hoped that it will prove to be of more value to have shared as much as is shared than not to have shared the material at all.

Background to the Week of Sessions

Mrs. B. was in the third year of her analysis. She had been about 30 when she started treatment, at which time she had not been married long. She had given birth to a son, here called Peter, six months before the week that follows. Before Peter's birth the analysis had focused mainly on an accident that had occurred when Mrs. B. was 11 months old. She had pulled a pot of boiling water onto herself while her mother was busy elsewhere, and she had been severely burned. This experience had been worked over repeatedly during the analysis, in dreams and in many sessions, but it was still greatly feared as a "memory" never to be remembered.

After her son's birth Mrs. B. became healthily preoccupied with being a mother, and the accident shifted largely into the background of the analysis. Having begun to feel much better, Mrs. B. suggested dropping her Friday sessions as a move toward being less dependent on her analysis. Her baby was beginning to wean himself and, as it seemed, so was she. Mrs. B. told me that she was offering flexibility to Peter to enable him to move away from her but be able to find her still there when he needed her. I felt I was being cued to do the same. [10] Therefore, when she showed anxiety about losing her fifth session indefinitely if she were to experiment with her feeling that she might be ready to do without it, I offered her a compromise arrangement. I said that I would be able to keep her usual Friday time available for her for at least a month or two, during which time she could see how it felt to be coming only four times per week. When Mrs. B. showed concern about my possibly wanting to use that time for another patient, I mistakenly told her that I was quite happy to keep this time free, because I would be using it in the meantime for myself—for reading. Mrs. B. seemed pleased and grateful for this offer, but as soon as she began to come only four times per week, she became increasingly anxious. The week that will now be presented is the fourth week of four sessions per week, the Friday time still being kept

---

[10] Up to this point, the analysis had been carefully conducted without recourse to deviations from classic technique. Here a factor is introduced that deflected the analytic process until its implications had been recognized, analyzed, and dealt with adequately. Use of the interactional point of view helped highlight cues from the patient that pointed toward the necessary rectification. The ongoing analysis could then be resumed, but only once it had been freed from the temporary preoccupation with the analyst's errors. This preoccupation too became an interference and a deflection of the analytic process, as the patient herself came to indicate (see hindsight on the Thursday session).

available for her. It is necessary to know that at the time of these sessions, a nephew and niece were staying with the B. family.

[Hindsight] We can see that I have compromised myself and the analytic frame in a number of ways. I actively present myself in the role of the "good" mother, offering flexible weaning that gratifies the patient and in some ways gratifies me too, rather than analyzing the unresolved anxiety about the change in frequency of sessions. The patient then cues me further with fresh anxiety about the flexible arrangement. She is indicating the inappropriateness of the arrangement, but I fail to recognize her cue. Instead I try to rationalize my offer by getting involved in yet further modifications in the analytic frame. By explaining how I plan to use the Friday time, I am giving the patient valid grounds for perceiving me as wanting a rest from seeing her so often.

The Clinical Sequence

Monday. The patient began the session by saying she had had a mixed weekend. She felt that it was possible she was not yet ready to drop her Friday sessions. (*Pause.*) She had had two dreams. In the first a girl was looking after a cat that had had a kitten. She had helped this cat deliver the kitten, which was lying in a pool of blood. The kitten was too weak to survive, and died. In her associations Mrs. B. told me that she had a friend whose daughter had the same name as the girl in the dream. (I will call her Emma.) "Emma has a white kitten. This kitten has a scratch that won't heal." On saying this, Mrs. B. became very distressed. (*Pause.*)

[Internal supervision] The patient seems to identify herself with the kitten in the dream. I note the references to "too weak to survive" and "the scratch that won't heal." I also note that the adaptive context seems to have been announced at the beginning of the session in "not yet ready to drop the Friday sessions." I therefore choose to interpret with this issue as my focus.

[Hindsight] I may be intervening prematurely, however. It would have been better to formulate a silent hypothesis at this point and to wait for further validation before intervening.

I said that I had the impression that she was anxious about dropping the fifth sessions, partly because she was afraid that she might not be inwardly strong enough to cope with the change; also, she could be afraid that I might assume from such a change that the emotional scars had healed more than perhaps they had. The patient agreed with this interpretation and then told me the other dream: she had been swimming very slowly in a pool. She had no associations.

[Internal supervision] I feel that this dream is offered as confirmation of her need to go slowly, and I prepare to acknowledge that I have heard this.

[Hindsight] There is a selectivity in my playback of the patient's own words that has avoided any reference to the pool of blood or to there having been a birth and a death. The patient now offers a second dream, in which she is swimming in a pool. We can't be sure whether this is a confirmation of the interpretation offered, as I am assuming, or whether it is an indication by the patient that I have been going too fast. She also gives no associations, as if to highlight that I had interpreted, almost on my own, that I didn't seem to want or need her associations to the earlier dream.

I said that I thought this second dream stressed her need to go at her own pace. She replied that she was actually "crawling" (doing the crawl) in the dream and she added that her baby, Peter, was also now actively experimenting with crawling.

[Internal supervision] I feel that these comments are added confirmation of my interpretation that she needed to go at her own pace.

[Hindsight] I am too quick to hear confirmation of this interpretation. The adaptive context of the flexible arrangement is not being confronted directly in this session, and I fail to notice this omission. I am still caught up in my rationalization that this flexibility is what the patient needs, so I am deaf to any indications to the contrary.

What followed in the session was Mrs. B.'s showing the desire to explore the question of the Friday sessions further. I suggested to her that she could do one of two things with regard to these sessions. She either could use the Friday time on a demand-feeding basis, asking for the extra session on a Friday during those weeks when she felt the need for it, or could go back to five sessions for as long as needed. I said she could let me know which way she would like to arrange the Friday sessions when she felt ready to decide.

[Hindsight] There has been a shift away from an analytic approach to the unresolved issue of the Friday sessions, which here represents the various frame issues needing attention. Instead, superficial details of alternate arrangements are suggested to her. The patient is likely to perceive this as my retreat from the deeper issues that exist in this session as threatening to me. We need also note that there has been a shift into a manipulative mode. I am directive, making suggestions, offering "solutions" to the patient rather than allowing her to be free to find her own. By intervening prematurely here, I cut across the patient's continuing with whatever is more important in her mind in the session. I am inviting her to sidestep onto other issues that are being presented to her by me. This is a defensive maneuver on my part, motivated by some countertransference anxiety, and is likely to be correctly perceived as such by the patient.

Toward the end of this session, I introduced an issue, saying that I felt it might be related to the matter at hand but wasn't sure. I wondered aloud to the patient whether she had needed to emphasize the importance for her of being allowed to go at her own pace. She had, for instance, made sure that she did not direct my attention from the baby part of herself by either bringing her actual baby to show me or bringing a photograph of him.

[Hindsight] The fact that there might be some significance in Mrs. B.'s never having volunteered to bring her baby to a session had been suggested to me some months earlier when I had attended a clinical presentation by an analyst who was talking specifically about her experience with patients who had been pregnant during analysis. She had quoted eight such cases, in all of which the mother had at some stage brought the baby to a session. It had been put to me that my experience with Mrs. B. might be atypical and that perhaps I had been blocking her from feeling able to show me her baby. I had not thought so at the time, and I had felt no need to bring this issue up with her until now. For some reason I choose this occasion to raise the issue, even though it is quite irrelevant and far removed from the issues that are much more in evidence in the session.

[Hindsight] I am still blocking the analytic process by remaining in a manipulative mode of functioning. I say that I am not sure whether this further issue, which I introduce here, relates to the matter at hand. My introduction of this issue has more to do with my countertransference (i.e., with my unrecognized need to direct the patient away from what is disturbing the present state of the analytic relationship) than with anything else. The patient needs me not to be diverted from her inner needs, but it is I who initiated exactly this kind of diversion in the name of trying to avoid it. I am also inviting her to bring a third party into the session, indicating through this that there may be some unresolved feelings in me concerning this patient from which I am suggesting she protect me by bringing her baby to a session. Indications of the countertransference operating here are present in the manipulative quality of this intervention (and this is not the first such manipulation in this session) and in the implied pressure upon the patient to feel that she "should" bring either her baby or a photograph of him to show me. The patient's autonomy is being intruded upon in a massive way.

Mrs. B. replied to this by saying that she hadn't felt that I needed to see the baby, or a photograph of him, because she had assumed that I knew him so well anyway through her. (This was the end of the session.)

[Internal supervision] I feel reprimanded by the patient. In her response she had pointed out that I should not need to see her baby, or a photograph of him, at least not for the purposes of the analysis. She indicates that she had assumed that I knew him well through her, but now she may be wondering whether I do. Her use of the word "need" alerts me to the fact that she is picking up some countertransference need being expressed here by me. Because this was the end of the session, this issue was not dealt with. Having allowed my internal supervision to lapse in this session, I would have to be much more alert in the future. The unresolved issues are likely to appear as primary adaptive contexts in the next session(s).

Tuesday. The patient arrived six minutes late. (This was most unusual for her.) She started the session standing and offered two photographs to me while I was also still standing.

[Internal supervision] The patient is acting out her awareness that the photographs do not properly belong to the analysis. She does this by standing, and she alerts me to there being something amiss by coming unusually late.

[Hindsight] We can also see that there is a silent protest here along with the patient's compliance, but I fail to use any awareness of this fact in the current session.

One photo was of Mrs. B. with her baby when he was a few weeks old, and the other was a more recent photograph of him with both parents. I responded to these by saying, "They are lovely," and handing the photos back to her. She then lay down on the couch. After a pause, she repeated what she had said at the end of the previous day's session, that she had felt that I already knew the baby and her husband intimately without seeing the photographs, but outwardly she seemed pleased that I had seen what they look like.

[Hindsight] We can note her repetition that I should not have needed to see the photographs. Even though initially I had been alert to this as a frame issue, I fail to deal with it in this session, possibly because there are so many current frame issues to be dealt with.

The patient continued by saying that she was still not sure about the fifth sessions. She did not know whether it should be on a demand-feeding basis or not, as she might end up wanting her session on every Friday.

[Internal supervision] This structure issue remains unresolved, and the patient continues to be anxious about it. The idea of demand feeding had been introduced by me, not by her. The effect of this is to make her feel she would be greedy if she were to ask for a full return to five sessions per week.

Mrs. B. went on to say that she didn't want me to assume that too many of the Friday times would be available to me for my reading.

[Internal supervision] More errors come home to roost! Mrs. B. specifically picks up the unconscious implications of my earlier self-revelation with regard to the reading. She shows here quite clearly how she is reacting to these implications, that she is anxious that I might want the Friday time for myself when she could be needing this same time for herself. The offer of a demand-feeding arrangement is not turning out to be as reassuring as it was meant to be; it is instead making the patient feel criticized as being demanding if she should need her Friday time back. The patient is being used here as a "pathological container" (Langs 1976) for some unacknowledged greediness of my own.

I said that I felt it had been unhelpful to her that I had told her how I planned to use *her* time while keeping it available to her. The effect of her knowing this fact was that she saw me now as the mother who wants to be allowed to get on with her own things now that the child is beginning to grow up. I was aware of the implications of this for her because her accident had occurred at a time when her mother was busy elsewhere—and at that time she herself had just recently begun to walk.

[Hindsight] There is an attempt here to acknowledge the reality perception before referring to any childhood precedent to it. It is probable, however, that I am being too quick to pass on from the uncomfortable reality in the present to the past. I am in effect directing the patient's attention away from my own failure in attention to that of her mother. This may be perceived by her as a further indication of my sense of discomfort at the recent lapses in the analysis. I don't leave her free to elaborate on this issue in her own way and in her own time. I preempt her by doing this for her.

Mrs. B. replied to this by remembering in some detail how her mother always seemed to be putting housework and cooking before spending time with the children. Her mother always wanted to have the house cleaned and a good meal prepared, as if all they needed was to be housed and fed, whereas Mrs. B. would have preferred a simple lunch and more time with her mother.

[Internal supervision] The patient seems to be playing back her perception of me as having been too preoccupied with getting the recent mess in the analysis cleared up, and myself reinstated as the good mother ready with a good meal, whereas she would have preferred me to have allowed her to have had more time in the session—for her to have used it in her own way.

Mrs. B. then went on to tell me about her nephew and niece. Her niece had been away for the weekend. She had a favorite cookbook that she had brought with her for her stay, and she had also taken it away with her for this weekend so that her brother would not use it while she was away. Mrs. B. had let her nephew use one of her own recipes so that he could do some cooking with her, which he wanted to do. Halfway through making something in the kitchen with her, he complained to her that she was not letting him do the cooking, she was doing too much of it for him.

[Internal supervision] I regard this as unconscious supervision on the part of the patient. I reflect on this and feel that she is alerting me to my having done too much for her in her recent sessions, in relation either to the frequency of the sessions or to the issue of the photographs, or both. I prepare to explore each of these in turn.

[Hindsight] What I do not recognize here is the theme of two people wanting the same thing. The niece wants to keep her cookbook for herself to prevent her brother's using it when she is away. The patient may be alluding to my earlier statement that I would use her time on Fridays for myself when she is away. She could feel that I am wanting that time for myself, not wanting her to have it.

I commented that I felt she needed to confirm that she was being allowed enough freedom for her decision about Fridays to be really her own. Mrs. B. replied to this by saying that she didn't feel that I was interfering in any way with that. There was then a silence.

[Internal supervision] I note the word "interfering," and again I feel rebuked by the patient. I sense that this might be related more directly to the photographs.

[Hindsight] I also have still not recognized that the patient is troubled by the issue of flexibility, so I am missing the point here. The degree of countertransference resistance to seeing this probably stems from the fact that my mistaken offer of flexibility had come from a wish in me to be the "perfect" mother, so I continue to resist seeing that this had been an error. I am still investing in this as an "imaginative" offer on my part.

I said to Mrs. B. that I felt that perhaps the missing freedom had more to do with the fact that I and not she had raised the issue of the photographs. Although she had complied with my comments, apparently quite happily, I felt that she may have had more reservations about doing so than she had been showing. She picked this idea up quite readily and said that although she was pleased that I had seen the photographs, she was aware of being anxious that I might assume from them that everything was well. Everyone looked so well and happy in the photos. She was afraid I might overlook the fact that inside herself she is still having to deal with things that cause her more distress than she feels able to cope with in four sessions per week.

[Internal supervision] The patient is elaborating on her anxiety related to showing me the photos, and she inserts a further reference to the still-unresolved question of frequency. I see that I must attend to this now.

I said that she was clearly still anxious about the question of the Friday sessions. She said she was and asked if she could at least come this week on Friday. This was agreed to.

[Hindsight] The issue of the structure is resolved only partly. It was not until after this week that the patient made an unreserved request for a return to five times per week on a regular basis, which was then how the analysis continued.

Mrs. B. continued by telling me a dream, in which she was holding something that was a container with something valuable in it. There were other people around, and they seemed to want their share of what was in the container. She felt as if they had robbed a bank, or something, and that she was now carrying the loot for all of them. They were sent to prison, but there was a friendly prison officer who saw to it that she was put into a cell on her own for her protection. She finished her sentence before the others. When she was conducted across the yard toward the gate to freedom, the others set upon her and kicked her head in. She lay dead on the ground. Mrs. B.'s subsequent associations referred to the analysis, although it is not possible to recall them in detail here.

[Internal supervision] I feel flooded by this dream and the associations. I am abstracting the themes in the dream while listening to what the patient is saying. I choose to play back those themes that I can recognize as relating to the analysis and to the current issues regarding it.

[Hindsight] There is a further reference to the theme of other people wanting what she has, what she is holding in the container, but I miss this and therefore still do not deal with the issue of the Friday sessions being no longer clearly her time. What is also omitted here in the internal work of reflection upon this dream is any consideration of why the patient introduced the dream at this point in the session. There is no recognition of a specific adaptive context from within this session in terms of the timing of telling the dream, without which the attempt to interpret it is rather diffuse and "wild."

I said that the patient was trying to preserve her analysis, as the container with something valuable in it, from whatever was threatening to take it from her. She needed me to be a protector of it, allowing her to have space to herself, particularly as she may have felt that I intruded on her space by my reference to her bringing her baby or a photograph of him. Maybe she saw me as being jealous of her special relationship with her baby, wanting some of it for me too.

[Hindsight] We can see that this attempt at interpretation is too long. Also, I refer rather ambiguously to two kinds of intrusion by me: (1) into the analytic space and (2) into her space with her baby. We can also see that I have selected what can be regarded as positive references to the analysis, and to myself, omitting the negative. In this selectivity I have left out any reference to the violence, in any of its several forms in the dream, as if it did not also allude to how she is currently perceiving me. She is likely to react to this avoidance by me as an indication that I am finding these themes threatening.

Mrs. B. agreed with what I had said (an agreement too easy to be convincing) and added that she thought her reason for not bringing her baby to show me was that she wanted to be allowed to have something all to herself.

[Internal supervision] She picks up what makes most sense to her from what I have been saying and adopts the same ambiguity in her response, "something to herself," as I had used. This phrase can refer either to the analytic relationship, which she doesn't want shared with any third party, an important aspect of the analytic frame, or to her relationship with her baby, which she doesn't want me trying to intrude on. It almost certainly refers to both, but I chose to pick up first the issue of the analytic frame.

I replied that this comment is particularly true of her wish to have her analysis to herself, without having other people intrude on her being allowed to use her sessions in her own way.

[Hindsight] I have stopped hiding behind the ambiguity and have acknowledged that the analytic frame requires privacy and a freedom to use the sessions in her own way, that is, without being subjected to suggestion or directives from the analyst.

She said that this was true. She then began to relax in the session for the first time; until now in this session, she had been noticeably tense. She remained calm until the end of the session a few minutes later, without talking.

[Internal supervision] During the silence I begin to realize that the attack on the patient in the dream has not been referred to by her or by me. She may be seeing that I have selected only those themes in which I can see myself reflected in a positive light. Because I have ducked the negative references to me, she may be taking her cue from *me* here, seeing me as not yet ready to tolerate this more painful perception of me.

Wednesday.   Mrs. B. arrived eight minutes late. Still standing (again), before moving to the couch she asked me if she had left the smaller photograph anywhere in my room the previous day. I told her that I had not seen it.

[Internal supervision] She is using the same defense of isolation as before, standing rather than using the couch. She is also late again. I recognize that something is still interfering with the analytic space, and I seek to deal with it.

[Hindsight] I am probably motivated once again by anxiety to intervene immediately rather than wait for the patient to continue with the session in her own way. My level of activity remains high, along with my anxiety at having made so many mistakes recently—one leading to another.

Mrs. B. told me she was late because the car wouldn't start. "There was no light in the battery," and it was only the second time that this had happened with this car. She had then taken her husband's car but had to look for the keys, which was why she was late. She hadn't looked in her own car for the missing photo.

[Internal supervision] I hear of something that has been lost, something to do with her having brought the photos the previous day. I listen to this around the current frame issues related to the photos. I try to find a bridge to deal with this.

[Hindsight] "No light in the battery" is a strange way of referring to a flat battery. English is not the patient's original language, but as she is fluent, this expression stands out as unusual for her. There may be a reference to the fact that I should have been more enlightened than I had been in my recent handling of her sessions. I have become like the car that is not working properly.

I said that she may have needed to feel that the photo had been lost, for the purposes of this session, so that we could look at the implications of this for her. She could feel, for instance, with some justification that she wouldn't have lost this photo if I hadn't mentioned that she might bring it in. She agreed with this interpretation. She then wanted to refer back to the previous day's dream.

[Internal supervision] Again her agreement is too quick. I am left feeling unsure whether this is confirmation. I then note the patient's indication that there is something we have not looked at left over from the previous day's dream.

Mrs. B. pointed out to me her passivity in relation to the people threatening her in the dream. She saw them as people from her past. She commented that she couldn't gain anything if she merely sought protection from them rather than facing them.

[Internal supervision] The patient picks up one of the aspects of the dream that I had bypassed in my selective playback of themes from the dream. She also immediately offers me a deflection from me onto people from her past. I consider this to be her way of protecting me from what she feels I may find threatening. For instance, she may see me as having avoided the negative references to me in the dream, and here she expresses her perception of me as needing to be protected from her more negative feelings. I note her passivity in relation to my comment about the photographs.

[Hindsight] We can also see how the patient parallels my defensive maneuver in the previous session, when I deflected too quickly from my own failure onto the failure of her mother, a further indication to her that I might have been feeling unable to cope with the critical allusions to me in her dream.

I said it seemed to me that I appeared in two forms in this dream, as the prison officer who is seen as friendly and who is putting her into protective custody, but I might also be represented in the dream by the people threatening her.

[Internal supervision] This is a clumsy attempt to bring the patient back to the present reality that she is offering to avoid by flight into the past.

[Hindsight] I am interpreting without giving the patient time to present me with the material for an interpretation. I am therefore still responding from my countertransference anxiety.

Mrs. B. seemed puzzled by the second part of my interpretation and asked me how I had arrived at it.

[Internal supervision] The patient points out that I have picked my "interpretation" out of thin air. Certainly she hasn't given me the grounds for this intervention in the course of this session, so naturally she can't see where I have got it from. I am still trying too impulsively to rectify the recent errors. I therefore try to remedy this situation by playing back some of the missing ingredients from the dream, hoping to provide a bridge to my interpretation.

[Hindsight] It would have been better to remain silent and let the patient lead.

I said that I felt we should see how the dream had started. She had been carrying something valuable in a container that she was trying to protect from the other people in the dream, who were seen as wanting to have their share of it. She had also told me that she had had some reluctance about showing me her baby. Nevertheless, she had brought the photos, and then she had had this dream the following night. At the end of the dream her head is kicked in, possibly a reference to her feeling that she had not been allowed to think for herself. She reflected on this and partly agreed with it. She then added that she had not been conscious of any wish not to bring the photographs; it had merely not crossed her mind to do so.

[Internal supervision] It had not crossed her mind—in other words, it wasn't her own thinking. I see this as some degree of confirmation and feel that perhaps we can now look at the transference elaboration of this experience.

[Hindsight] It is evident that I am impatient to move away from the present reality. I am therefore being too active. The patient is not given time to continue from here on her own. I am still threatening her space while acknowledging her need for me not to do so. This is a familiar contradiction in this presentation.

I said that it was possible I had come to represent a bit of her past experience with her mother in which she had not felt able to stand up to her, or in this instance to me. Instead it appeared that she had felt a need to please me by bringing the photographs, but perhaps this apparent need was caused by her seeing me at the time as the mother who needed to be pleased. Mrs. B. was nodding as I was making the last part of this interpretation. She then went on to tell me about something that happened "on Friday—no, Thursday night" of the previous week.

[Internal supervision] The slip seems obvious. I see this as a reference to the missing Friday sessions.

[Hindsight] The Friday issue is dealt with only temporarily here. It is not until after this week that the Fridays are reinstated on a regular basis, so in that sense the Fridays are still missing, and this fact is being missed by me at this point too.

Mrs. B. continued by stating that that Thursday evening her husband had been away, so she had invited herself to supper with friends. She then told me in detail about a rich, sweet dish that she had taken with her to supper, how she had eaten too much and had then felt sick. In the night she had been afraid that she might be ill the following day and unable to feed

Peter, who was still being breast-fed. She therefore made herself vomit, and by the morning she was feeling better and more able to cope.

[Internal supervision] I note the themes: husband absent; feeding herself; making herself feel sick by eating too much; fear of having to interrupt her baby's feeding. I decide to offer a bridge to deal with some of this.

[Hindsight] We can see allusions to my having given her too much, having tried too hard to feed her, with the result that she makes herself vomit. This account is offered during a session in which I have been particularly overactive and can be regarded as having overfed her.[11] My anxiety about the several errors is leading me to try to rid myself of my own unmanageable feelings about them. I am therefore using the patient as a *pathological container* for feelings that I am currently failing adequately to contain within myself. She then feels filled with unmanageable feelings, of which in turn she has tried to rid herself by making herself vomit. She may also be hoping that I, like her, may now be more able to cope.

As my offer of a bridge to interpretation, I pointed out to Mrs. B. the timing of this experience, prior to the Friday morning when she would not be having her usual session. She agreed that it was probably because she was feeling deprived of that session that she had allowed herself to eat too much.

[Internal supervision] She gets to this on her own. I do not need to overfeed her.

She also pointed out that she was aware of having had a choice: either to remain feeling ill and helpless or to do something about it in order not to have to interrupt her present feeding pattern with her baby.

[Internal supervision] She highlights the theme of interruption, which I see as alluding to interruptions of various kinds. I decide not to interrupt her.

She went on to say that it would not necessarily have meant having to wean Peter abruptly, but she certainly thought it would have meant an unwarranted interruption of the feeding pattern.

[Internal supervision] I note the words "unwarranted interruption." The issue I feel she is highlighting here with her reference to feeding is the recent one of the Friday sessions, one of which was the previous Friday just referred to.

I said to her that she had come to experience the recent interruption of her Friday sessions as unwarranted, and on the Monday after the sequence she had just described, she had started the session by indicating that she wanted to review the decision to drop Friday sessions. She agreed. It was then the end of the session.

[11]This comment I owe to Dr. Langs, who pointed this out to me when I showed him this material personally. With this one exception I have confined my use of hindsight to what I arrived at through reflecting upon the material on my own, with the aid of my knowledge of the interactional viewpoint as published by Langs.

[Internal supervision] I think that it became possible for Mrs. B. to refer to her dropping of her Friday sessions as an unwarranted interruption only once it had been agreed that she could come back to her Friday session—at least this week. The long-term arrangement has still not been settled.

Thursday. Mrs. B. started the session by telling me about Emma's mother. This mother had said, in front of the child, that Emma should stay the night with Mrs. B. and her niece. Emma's mother had then said, also in front of Emma, "It would be so nice—for me." Mrs. B. had felt terrible about this, feeling very sorry for Emma and feeling that she should have been given a chance to say what *she* wanted. Mrs. B. went on to say that it seemed wrong to push Emma out of her own home in this way to please the mother.

[Internal supervision] I seem to be hearing about a self-interested mother. Listening first for any reality aspects being alluded to here, I wonder if this incident is being told to me as a further unconscious supervision of me by the patient. I decide to explore this.

I said to Mrs. B. that here we have an example of a child's being separated from her mother because of wishes of the mother rather than of the child, and the child had not been given a chance to say what she felt about it. Mrs. B. agreed and then fell into a distressed silence. After a while she told me that during the previous night she had awakened, thinking that she heard a child calling "Mummy." Her nephew and niece were both soundly asleep. She had gone to see Peter and realized that of course he could not talk yet. Then she noticed that the voice had been saying "Mummee," which was how a child would call for a mother in her own childhood language. She lapsed into silence and was clearly more distressed.

[Internal supervision] There is ample confirmation here of the theme of the absent mother. I feel that she needs some acknowledgment by me that I am aware of the meaning of her distress, rather than having me leave her too long in the silence in which I also could be seen as the mother who cannot hear.

I said, "So it was the child in you calling out for your childhood mother." She agreed and heaved a sigh of relief. She then added that she couldn't count on her mother to hear. She went on to ask why it was that she still went on and on with the same problems, and again became silent.

[Internal supervision] I reflect that the patient needs help to deal with her feelings about the absent mother, and I realize that she is alerting me to my recent "absence" (my lapses of analytic attention), which triggered this material. I look for a current focus to this theme of inattention, a place where I have been failing her in a way similar to that of the mother she is criticizing (Emma's mother and her own).

After a fairly long silence, I said that what set this off again in her might have been her uncertainty as to whether I had been offering her flexibility, with regard to the sessions, to meet *her* needs, or whether I was really wanting to get on with my own business. (I was silently bearing in mind that I had told her I would be using her time for myself.) Mrs. B. said that consciously she had been glad that I had explained to her about the reading.

[Internal supervision] I note her emphasis on "consciously," so I wonder about the unconscious aspect.

I said I felt that to her unconscious, my having told her about my wish to have time for reading had given her room to develop the perception of me as being too much like her mother, wanting to have time to get on with her own things, and like Emma's mother, who had behaved in a similar way. Mrs. B. said that the child part of her would probably latch onto anything of that kind to feel anxious about. She then said that she was wondering whether her need to go back to five times per week had stemmed from a need to be sure that her Friday times would really still be there for her.

[Internal supervision] I see some of this as confirmatory material, but I find myself wondering about the original dropping of the Friday sessions, whether the arrangement had been such as to allow this to happen too readily.

I said I felt that perhaps she had become unsure where she stood with me once I had offered to let the structure of her sessions become flexible, and that she might have accepted this change partly because it had been made to appear seductively easy, rather than her having been given a chance to work it through, to have her own say on it, to the point of being sufficiently clear in herself to take this step on her own.

[Internal supervision] I am beginning to get hold of the point that I had missed until now, that it could have been the flexibility that had made things so difficult for the patient. The analytic frame had begun to suffer further breaks from that point on.

Mrs. B. replied that she didn't know about this; but shortly afterward she said that she had suddenly developed a splitting headache, and it was most unlike her to have headaches.

[Internal supervision] She is telling me there is still a painful conflict around this issue. I listen for further cues.

After a silence Mrs. B. began to tell me about feeding Peter. He had a great appetite and at this time happily ate solids during the day but continued to be breast-fed in the mornings and the evenings. Until recently she had felt that she needed to be very careful about what she herself ate, in order to be sure she had an adequate supply of milk and a proper balance in the milk for the baby. She had since discovered that she really didn't need to be so "ultra careful," and the baby had continued to be perfectly all right.

[Internal supervision] I hear more unconscious supervision here. I have been too careful with her in thinking she needs flexibility, so my attempts to hold her particularly carefully around the time of "weaning" in the analysis actually have made her more anxious and insecure, not less so. As a result, I have lost my balance as analyst, and I am still in the process of having to recover this.

I said that perhaps she had experienced me as being overly careful with her, offering her such a gradual change from five time per week to four times that she felt I was thinking of her as more fragile in this respect than she actually was. Mrs. B. replied with surprise that her headache was gone now.

[Internal supervision] I take this as confirmation of my interpretation, and so does she. I then listen around my countertransference attempts to be the overprotective mother, in preparation for my next interpretation.

I said that there had been a painful conflict in her. She had been anxious for me to be sensitive to her child needs, in order that my behavior did not appear too similar to the insensitivities she had experienced in her mother. She also needed me to acknowledge her adult strengths, however. She agreed that she would feel that I was letting her down either way: if I responded only to the child in her or only to the adult. Then, as the session was ending and she was about to leave, the patient added that she wondered whether she had pointed out to me that she still had the negative of the photograph that had been lost. She had noted to herself that still having the negative meant that she could re-create the positive. I replied that I felt she had needed me to learn from her, to recognize what had been a negative experience in the past few sessions, so that we could reestablish the positive, which during that time had been lost. She nodded and smiled her agreement as she left at the end of the session.

[Internal supervision] The analytic holding seems to have been recovered. The patient has found her own symbolic way of letting me know this.

[Hindsight] My recent preoccupation with the frame issues (although necessary as a step toward resuming the analytic process) also has been presenting a degree of interference. This concern over mistakes may be a hazard in the bipersonal approach. This concern is here being pointed out by the patient as my still being "ultra careful." I had been giving her a pain in the head. Even though I do not acknowledge this in the current session, her headache lifts when I show that I recognize that there had been too much carefulness somewhere and, by implication, that I am ready to relax and to allow the analytic process to be resumed.

Friday. The patient arrived slightly late. She then referred to the previous Wednesday night, when she had had a dream that she had forgotten until that morning.

[Internal supervision] The patient had supposedly forgotten this dream. Maybe she could not let herself remember it while we were still caught up in the frame issues. She is also late, so there may be something still holding her back.

In the dream there was a river. The patient was lying beside this river, the sides of which were in springtime, with new growth all around. She was either very small or was lying on her front, as the water seemed to be at eye level. It had then begun boiling and threatened to destroy everything around. She felt the boiling water was coming straight at her. She wanted to turn away because she was so frightened, but instead she looked at the water and it became an ordinary river again. The patient paused in her recounting of the dream and said with amazement, "I was able to stop it boiling."

[Internal supervision] I note the themes in this dream: springtime and new growth; the patient is very small or lying on her front; there is eye-level water; the water begins to boil; it threatens to destroy; it seems to be coming straight at her. I sense that I am being presented with a traumatic memory or a dream reconstruction of the accident. The boiling water is at eye level. It had been the patient's front that had been so badly burned. She also seems to indicate a readiness to look at the water. Possibly she is letting me know that the "memory" that was too terrible ever to remember is close to being remembered (consciously). Just possibly she is feeling more secure now that we have worked all week on reestablishing the analytic sense of holding. I decide to explore this issue with her.

I commented that the river had stopped boiling once she was able to look at it. I also noted that she had "forgotten" this dream until she felt safe enough with me to look at it. She replied that she hadn't realized until telling me the dream that it so clearly referred to the accident. She then became very distressed and began to experience the accident as happening to her in the session. It was as if the boiling water were pouring onto her and burning her. She cried out loudly in extreme pain. She then sat up, saying that it was because when she was lying down, "It won't stop coming at me." She then sobbed for a long time, holding her head in her hands.

[Internal supervision] Her holding of her head in her hands makes me feel that she needs to feel held. I recall that earlier in the analysis she told me that after the accident the only times that she felt the pain to be tolerable were when she was being carried by her mother. She had then felt as if she were able to put her pain into her mother; but when her mother put her down again, it had been as if the pain were too much for her mother, as if the mother were putting it back into the patient. I cannot but feel under enormous stress from the patient during this experience. It is excruciating to witness. I feel a very powerful wish to stop this experience in any way possible, by trying to reassure the patient, by trying to divert her; anything seems preferable to remaining witness to her pain. Alongside this impulse to protect myself is the realization that this had been Mrs. B.'s perception of her mother's response. For her sake, therefore, I know I must find some way of staying with her through this experience without trying to bypass it.

I said to the patient that I felt she was holding her head in her hands as her way of telling me that she needed to be "held" through this experience. Still crying, she replied, "My mother couldn't bear it—she had to turn away from it—I couldn't face it alone."

[Internal supervision] I recall that the mother had in effect caused the accident by not being in the room where this now mobile child was and where there was water boiling. After the accident the mother (as Mrs. B. recalled it) had not been able to look at the results of the accident. She is remembered as dressing the wounds while trying to turn her face away from them. I feel I am being tested by the patient to see if I can bear to see her in such pain. She is telling me that she can't face this alone.

I said to her, "You need me to be able to stay with you in your pain— and not to have to turn away from it." She looked me straight in the eye (she was still sitting on the couch) and said, "Can you?" I answered, "I know that you need me to bear it with you." After this she lay down, saying, "Let me see if it has stopped now. Before, the boiling water kept coming at me. I couldn't bear the pain. It is better now." After a while she added, "I never believed I could bear to remember it, but now I have."

[Internal supervision] This is a quite different level of experience from all the earlier allusions to the accident. Mrs. B. has dreamed of the accident a number of times, but it has always been more disguised. For instance, the boiling water often has been represented by its opposite, by ice. In one dream it was the movement of the water that was frozen as it began to fall toward her—as in a photograph. I note the progression.

I said to Mrs. B. that this was the first time she had let herself experience the accident undisguised. She replied, "This time I let it flow over me, and, even though it burned me, I now find that I am all right." At the end of the session she again looked straight at me and said, "Thank you for staying with me."

Aftermath of the Sequence

The following week Mrs. B. reported that she had found herself singing over the weekend, singing to herself. This was something quite new, and it reminded her of her mother singing to her. She then recalled prodding her mother to get her to go on singing when she stopped. This was the first remembered link between a good mother from before the accident and a good mother still there after it.

The work done in the week reported needs to be put into context. What followed shortly after the reported sequence was the patient's hating me most intensely, as the mother who had allowed the accident to happen to her and as the analyst who had allowed it to be repeated in the analysis. She also had to test me extensively as to whether I could continue to "hold" her analytically. She expected me to become the mother who couldn't bear being in touch with her pain, or who might retaliate if my being in touch with her pain became unbearable to me. She expected to be left to fall forever. It took an additional year before she could begin to find real peace from the unspeakable dread of the anxieties that had come to be so closely associated with her experience of such intensely regressed dependence on her mother after the accident, and on me as analyst after she had reexperienced the accident in the analysis. Much else, of course, occurred during the next year of treatment, but the experience of the week reported here remained a basic foundation to most of the subsequent progress made in the analysis.

Discussion

The case of Mrs. B. is presented for several reasons. First, the presentation shows us again how closely a patient monitors the analyst, not only for his conscious interventions and other expressions of himself, but also for the unconscious implications of the analyst's behavior, his intrusions, his deflections, his timing of interventions or failures to intervene, the selectivity of his choice in what he refers to, his capacity or unreadiness to cope with what the patient needs to be able to present to him. By a series of cues offered to the analyst, this patient was able to help considerably in the reestablishment of a secure analytic frame, without which she could not have reenacted in the analysis the memory that she had felt she might not survive remembering.

A second reason for this presentation is that it gives us a chance to follow the different levels of supervisory activity, the unconscious contributions from the patient as mirror to the analyst, and the use of the interactional viewpoint as a significant aid to the process of internal supervision and the work of hindsight. I regard the work of formal supervision per se as supplementary to the work of hindsight. Earlier presentations of the bipersonal approach have been limited mostly to the supervisor's use of the interactional viewpoint (see Langs's volumes). I believe that we should have an opportunity to watch an analyst beginning to use this viewpoint as a part of his own process of self-supervision.

A third reason for presenting the case of Mrs. B. is that it illustrates a wider perspective on the bipersonal approach than that which has usually been regarded to be the viewpoint of that approach. If we were to look at the interaction only up close, which is the "focal length" of earlier presentations of Langs's published work, we could conclude that the patient's Friday session was little more than a dramatic commentary on some destructiveness of the analyst to which the patient had been subjected during the sequence described. There certainly had been elements of unjustifiable countertransferential mishandling of the sessions before that Friday, the analytic frame being disrupted in a number of ways, and the analyst undoubtedly had become traumatically like the destructively inattentive mother. We could say that it is not surprising that the patient again felt traumatized in the analysis. We could then hypothesize on how the analysis might have proceeded if the analyst had been more careful and had not fallen into these countertransference errors. I do not think that such a formulation offers an adequate explanation of the full sequence. Once we step back from the close-up view, we also can begin to take into account the more long-term view of the analysis of which this week was just a part.

ERRORS OF MANAGEMENT AND ROLE-RESPONSIVENESS

Because the subtext of this chapter concerns errors of management, I wish to offer another way of looking at the build-up of mistakes in the second case. What had been noticeable in the analysis prior to the reported sequence was that the patient had made me so aware of the nearly lethal consequences that she had suffered from her mother's absence, and from her lack of alertness to the danger to which the child was exposed, that I had found myself being overly careful. I had felt it necessary not to challenge too quickly the patient's defensive need to control her analysis. Only very gradually had I felt it possible to establish myself as outside the patient's control and therefore a separate person. The reported breaks in the frame grew out of a residual overcaution, and what emerged despite that caution was a sequence that was surprising and at first bewildering in the proliferation of errors. It is possible that some countertransferential destructiveness was operating, escaping as it would from a reaction formation of overcaution. But what followed requires further explanation.

Sandler (1976) has illustrated how a patient's unconscious speaks to the unconscious responsiveness in the analyst that is an important aspect of countertransference. Not all of the countertransference response is patho-logical, a view that has been familiar to us since the work of Heimann (1950) and Little (1951). The elements of role-responsiveness here are so remarkably parallel to the circumstances of the original trauma that it cannot be merely accidental. The patient was beginning to experiment with a new sense of confidence, feeling ready for a degree of lesser dependence on the analysis. At 11 months of age, she had been beginning to walk and to explore. Because of her increased mobility, she had needed increased vigilance from her mother. Instead her mother had been catastrophically less vigilant and concerned with her own business, and the child had then pulled the boiling water onto herself. I had fallen into offering an unusual arrangement, a measure that passed beyond the "unavoidable minimum" criterion advocated by Eissler (1953). The flexible change of frequency was a residue of the overcaution from earlier in the analysis. Then, as part of my attempt at rationalizing this error, and mistakenly thinking that it might allay the patient's anxiety about the arrangement being offered, I revealed my private plans to use her time for my own business. The parallels then were clearly all there. At this point I temporarily deflected the patient by diverting her attention, and my own, onto her 6-month-old baby. The frame thereafter became chaotic, and the patient was unable to attend to the reenactment of the accident in the analysis until the frame had been adequately secured. But as a result of my becoming more able to respond to the patient's supervisory cues at this point, I also became more attuned to her and less like her own mother. Then, and not before then, she became free to use me again as a transferential object—able to use my failures as representing the original accident.

Winnicott (1949) speaks of the details from early traumatic events being "catalogued." He describes how the infant ego defends itself against specific environmental failure by a "freezing of this failure situation." He continues: "Along with this goes an unconscious assumption (which can become a conscious hope) that opportunity will occur at a later date for a renewed experience in which the failure situation will be able to be unfrozen and re-experienced, with the individual in a regressed state, in an environment that is making adequate adaptation" (1954). Then, in his article entitled "Fear of Breakdown" (1970), he says, "There is no end [to this fear of breakdown] unless the bottom of the trough has been reached, unless the thing feared has been experienced." Elsewhere he says:

> Corrective provision is never enough. What is it that may be enough for some of our patients to get well? In the end the patient uses the analyst's failures, often quite small ones, perhaps manoeuvred by the patient . . . and we have to put up with being in a limited context misunderstood. The operative factor is that the patient now hates the analyst for the failure that originally came as an environmental factor, outside the infant's area of omnipotent control, but that is *now* staged in the transference. So in the end we succeed by failing—failing the patient's way. This is a long distance from the simple theory of cure by corrective experience. (Winnicott 1963, p. 258)

Types of Failure

We can now begin to compare the different kinds of failure that have been illustrated in the two cases presented and the function of the patient's efforts at rectification in each case.

With Mrs. A., the therapist's failures cannot be understood in any terms other than those of the therapist's countertransference. He was using the patient blatantly to meet needs of his own and was indicating these needs at a manifest as well as a latent level. The patient plays back to her therapist the fact that he has made serious errors, and she indicates her perception of his unconscious reasons for behaving in this way. We can see how accurately she monitors the implications of the therapist's errors, and it is important for us to be aware of our patients' potential for following our state of mind as it is revealed in our management of the treatment setting and frame and our handling or mishandling of the treatment process. The patient's efforts here were almost solely toward rectification, or testing to see if her therapist could make the recovery of the therapeutic frame without which her treatment with this therapist would have been effectively at an end. In this case I have focused on the frame issues because they are so prevalent, but we should not assume that the bipersonal approach is preoccupied exclusively with frame issues. It is also an invaluable aid in following a patient's conscious and unconscious monitoring of our handling of the treatment. This monitoring is always present, even when the frame is being maintained adequately. We continue to reveal ourselves unwittingly to our patients in the ways in which we intervene, and when, and in every intervention we make or fail to make. It is primarily this point that I have wished to illustrate in the second case.

With Mrs. B., there were certainly frame issues too, but I do not believe that these are the most important elements in this sequence. There is a different kind of failure being enacted that is far more complex than the simple failures of professional laxity shown in the first case. We can see how with Mrs. B. I had unknowingly fallen into an attempt to offer a kind of "corrective experience," such as Winnicott speaks of, that does not help. In trying to be so careful to be the "better mother," I became inattentive as analyst. I had been offering myself too actively as the "good object" when the patient was needing to be free to use me transferentially as a "bad object." As such, I was unconsciously communicating some doubts of my own as to whether I could yet tolerate being used as the destructively experienced "bad object" of this patient's childhood trauma. I came to repeat details of the patient's experience of the inattentive mother because I had become—however briefly—the inattentive analyst. I became a poor analyst by trying too hard to be the better mother, and this "corrective experience" was not what the patient needed, nor was it what she unconsciously was looking for. Through a complex process of interaction and unconscious responsiveness, I came to fail this patient in ways determined by her history (Winnicott 1963). She could then hate me for a real experience of failure in her analysis, by which the trauma of her accident had been reenacted between her and me. It is here that she found what Winnicott speaks of: the original failure situation unfrozen and reexperienced in the present, with the patient in a regressed state and in an environment that was making adequate adaptation (Winnicott 1954). This is so much more than a simple matter of making mistakes. It is also more than the patient's elaborating upon the analyst's mistakes in terms of her history. The details of the analyst's failure were essential to the patient's need to find in the present an actual failure for which she could hate the analyst, who stood for the mother of childhood in relation to the original trauma, the details of which had been catalogued.[12]

What I have been saying about this kind of failure applies only to a treatment experience like that of Mrs. B., where what is being dealt with is the experience of actual catastrophic environmental failure in early childhood. Paradoxically the patient needed the analyst both to fail and to be able to recover a capacity to listen responsively to her. It is here that bipersonal listening to the patient enabled the analyst to recognize and respond to the patient's corrective cues. It is here that we again begin to find the environment making adequate adaptation alongside the actual experience of the analyst's failure. Only then could the patient feel secure enough to recognize the significance to her of this particular sequence of failure. Only then could she begin to use the analyst's failures as that real, present experience of the original failure that she needed to find, that she could not find alone, and that I alone never could have "provided" for her.

POSTSCRIPT

What Winnicott says about the patient's need to use the analyst's failures should in no way be used to justify our errors. We cannot and should not retreat behind a simplistic formulation that whenever we make mistakes, the patient has always needed us to fail or has made us fail. Nor can we consciously offer our failures to the patient as a "corrective experience" any more helpfully than, as it was once thought, we can offer ourselves helpfully to the patient as the better object. The kind of failure that Winnicott speaks of is only valid to the patient when it is that real kind that occurs *in the context of our working to our own best limits and still failing*. It is here that we can see the most obvious difference between the casual failing of the therapist in the first case and the failing in the second despite every effort and care not to do so.

A few words about hindsight can be added. It is easy to be wise after the event and even easier when it is someone else's work that we are looking at. It is also comparatively easy to present one's own work for public scrutiny when it shows us in a favorable light. In contrast, these two clinical examples have focused on lapses in the professional relationship and analytic attention,

---

[12]Of this, Winnicott (1949) said, "This cataloguing type of mental functioning acts like a foreign body," a foreign body that continues to threaten the ego as a fear of something still in the future. Only when the ego has been able to encompass the reenactment of this forgotten memory in the *present* can the experience begin to become something that is *past* (see Winnicott 1970).

on blind spots and other errors. I have tried to be true to my belief that we should be at least as tough on ourselves, in our reflection and hindsight upon our own work, as we would be with others. I have tried to be as objective as I can, even though it is not easy to be so when one is being exposed to public comment. Naturally, here I am inclined to feel defensive, but as far as possible I have not allowed this defensiveness to cause me to alter anything in what I have presented. As an exercise in objectivity, I chose to comment on the therapist's work in the first case as if it were the work of someone else (and who would not wish that to be so with such a degree of error involved!), but I was in fact the therapist concerned. This device in presentation made it easier for me to step outside the interaction for the sake of self-supervisory reflection and comment. It also allowed me to feel that the degree of self-exposure could be mitigated temporarily until I had shown myself working differently, albeit still making mistakes, in the second case.

Having revealed so many levels of myself in relation to each case, I realize that much more can be said about what I did, or failed to do, about what I have indicated that I was aware of, and about much else on which I have remained silent.

I have learned much from these patients. I trust that they will not suffer from this attempt to share something of my own difficulties in learning to become a better therapist/analyst, to which they and my other patients each have contributed richly. If other therapists are stimulated to recognize those many occasions on which they too could learn from their patients, by being able to see themselves reflected in their patients as mirror to the therapist, then this sharing of my own learning from my patients will bring more benefit than loss to our profession and to the patients we aim to serve.

REFERENCES

BALINT, M. (1952). *Primary Love and Psycho-Analytic Technique.* London: Tavistock.

BION, W. R. (1977). *Seven Servants.* New York: Jason Aronson.

CASEMENT, P. J. (1973). The supervisory viewpoint. In *Family Therapy in Social Work,* ed. W. H. Finn, pp. 40–45. London: Family Welfare Association.

EISSLER, K. R. (1953). The effect of the structure of the ego on psychoanalytic technique. *Journal of the American Psychoanalytic Association* 1:104–143.

HEIMANN, P. (1950). On counter-transference. *International Journal of Psycho-Analysis* 31:81–84.

——— (1960). Counter-transference. *British Journal of Medical Psychology* 33:9–15.

KLEIN, M. (1946). Notes on some schizoid mechanisms. In *The Writings of Melanie Klein,* Vol. 3, pp. 1–24. London: Hogarth, 1975.

LANGS, R. (1976). *The Bipersonal Field.* New York: Jason Aronson.

—— (1978). *The Listening Process.* New York: Jason Aronson.

—— (1979a). *The Supervisory Experience.* New York: Jason Aronson.

—— (1979b). *The Therapeutic Environment.* New York: Jason Aronson.

—— (1980). *Interactions: The Realm of Transference and Countertransference.* New York: Jason Aronson.

—— (1981). *Resistances and Interventions: The Nature of Therapeutic Work.* New York: Jason Aronson.

LITTLE, M. (1951). Countertransference and the patient's response to it. *International Journal of Psycho-Analysis* 32:32–40.

MATTE-BLANCO, I. (1976). *The Unconscious as Infinite Sets.* Atlantic Highlands, N.J.: Humanities.

MILNER, M. (1952). Aspects of symbolism in comprehension of the not-self. *International Journal of Psycho-Analysis* 33:181–195.

RACKER, H. (1968). *Transference and Countertransference.* New York: International Universities Press.

SANDLER, J. (1976). Countertransference and role-responsiveness. *International Review of Psycho-Analysis* 3:43–47.

SEARLES, H. (1975). The patient as therapist to his analyst. In *Tactics and Techniques in Psychoanalytic Therapy*, Vol. 2: *Countertransference*, ed. P. L. Giovacchini, pp. 95–151. New York: Jason Aronson.

WINNICOTT, D. W. (1949). Mind and its relation to emotional development. In D. W. Winnicott, *Collected Papers: Through Paediatrics to Psycho-Analysis*. London: Tavistock, 1958.

—— (1954). Metapsychological and clinical aspects of regression within the psycho-analytical set-up. In D. W. Winnicott, *Collected Papers: Through Paediatrics to Psycho-Analysis*. London: Tavistock, 1958.

—— (1958). *Collected Papers: Through Paediatrics to Psycho-Analysis*. London: Tavistock.

—— (1963). Dependence in infant-care, in child-care, and in the psycho-analytical setting. In D. W. Winnicott, *Maturational Processes and the Facilitating Environment*. New York: International Universities Press, 1965.

—— (1965). *The Maturational Processes and the Facilitating Environment*. New York: International Universities Press.

—— (1970). Fear of breakdown. *International Review of Psycho-Analysis* 1:103–107, 1974.

CHAPTER 8

Empathy and the Therapeutic Interaction

James Beatrice, Ph.D.

Empathy is the capacity to identify transiently with the psychological state of another. In the psychotherapeutic literature, empathy is considered a clinically useful process occurring within the therapist, but theoretical and technical claims are usually made without the support of sufficient, detailed clinical data. Empathy is one of the prerequisites for establishing a therapeutic relationship and formulating interventions and is therefore a pivotal concept that needs detailed empirical examination.

This chapter illustrates with detailed clinical data the process and usefulness of empathy in the psychotherapeutic relationship. Langs's adaptational-interactional constructs (1976a, 1978) will be used as the conceptual framework for understanding the clinical data. Empathy will be shown to be an interactional occurrence initiated by the patient's projection identifications, which elicit transient identifications by the therapist that must be validated by the patient's ongoing communications.

LITERATURE REVIEW

Since Freud (1912, 1921), empathy has been defined consistently as neutralized trial identifications with aspects of the patient's ego or objects (Deutsch 1926, Fleiss 1942). This transient identification can be utilized in a noncognitive sharing in and comprehending of the psychological contents of the patient (Heimann 1950, Little 1951, Schafer 1959, Weigert 1954). It is emphasized that therapists must subject their empathic reactions to self-analysis in order to understand their patients' unconscious communications and thereby avoid the countertransference difficulties resulting from reacting impulsively (Beres and Arlow 1974, Heimann 1950, Little 1951, Olinick 1969, Reich 1960, 1966, Schafer 1959, Weigert, 1954). With the exception of Greenson (1960), Beres and Arlow (1974), and Langs (1976a, 1976b), authors describe empathy as an intrapsychic process within the analyst, without sufficiently considering the interaction of the patient's contributions and the analyst's response. Empathy is generally considered to be an aspect of countertransference, but a clear differentiation between the conflicted and the nonconflicted—the countertransference and the noncountertransference —reactions of the analyst has not been made. And although many authors advocate validating empathic responses by listening to the patient's communications, claims of empathy may be defensive and serve to rationalize errors in technique (Shapiro 1974), may lack validation in the patient's responses (Kanzer 1975), or may actively constitute the therapist's pathological projections, introjective identifications, and projective identifications (Langs 1976b). Kohut (1971, 1977) has used empathic responsiveness as the cornerstone of major theoretical and technical innovations. This position has been criticized for elevating the role of empathy at the expense of the interpretation of conflict and defense (Kernberg 1980).

Langs's concept (1976a) of the bipersonal field and the validating process provides a new opportunity to study the role of empathy within the therapeutic interaction. According to Langs's theory, the communications of both the patient and the therapist are composed of both conscious and unconscious components and must be evaluated in a specific way. The first consideration is the relatively nonconflicted portion of the patient's functioning. This nontransference component contains perceptions and commentaries regarding the therapeutic interaction that may be largely unconscious and therefore expressed in derivative form. The second factor is the noncountertransference component of the therapist, which represents his or her realistic, nonconflicted responses to the patient. The next component is transference, that is, the patient's pathological fantasies, memories, and introject, which are the distorted, conflicted responses to the therapist. Last is the countertransference component, which consists of the therapist's pathological and distorted responses to the patient. The key is to evaluate first the adaptive responses to the specific realities of the interaction, and then the elaboration of the specific realities resulting from the participants' character structure.

The therapist, by securing and maintaining the therapeutic frame (Langs 1976a, 1978), establishes a specific therapeutic ambience that permits the patient to projectively identify his or her psychic elements into the bipersonal field. By accepting and containing the patient's projective identifications, the therapist transiently identifies with the patient's material and experiences a variety of affects, fantasies, memories, introjects, and role assignments. Before the therapist reacts, these subjective responses must be distinguished as noncountertransference or countertransference components via the validating process. First, the adaptive context is identified. Like the day residue in the dream, the adaptive context is the stimulus that evokes a psychological response around which the patient's associations are meaningfully clustered. The adaptive context may involve the therapist's management of the ground rules for therapy or the therapist's interventions. Next, the patient's associations are seen to be meaningfully organized around the adaptive context. This focus leads to analyzable derivatives of unconscious perception, fantasy, memories, and introjects. The therapist, by containing the patient's material, becomes able to scrutinize his or her own subjective reactions to it and to use the patient's unfolding associations to formulate a silent hypothesis regarding the material. By noting his or her silent, personal, idiosyncratic responses to the patient's material and simultaneously subjecting these reactions to a determination of their fit with the patient's ongoing conscious and unconscious communication, the therapist becomes able to distinguish countertransference and noncountertransference responses.

If the adaptive context has not been identified, the therapist, by listening to the patient's manifest associations, isolating their distinct segments, and assigning to each an unconscious meaning, can formulate inferences of latent content. These inferences are on one level of latent meaning and are without reference to the adaptive context. Because the adaptive context is unknown, on this level of organization the patient's associations are perceived to be derivative of unconscious perception of the therapeutic relationship. Such associations are termed Type One derivatives and represent one of the last stages in the sequence of evaluating the therapeutic interaction (Langs 1978). If the adaptive context has been identified, the patient's associations are seen to be organized meaningfully around the adaptive context and permit access to the most meaningful derivative expression of the patient's pathology and unconscious fantasy and perception, as well as the dynamic and genetic components of these characteristics. This mode of relating and interacting is based on Type Two derivatives, which permit full recognition of the unconscious ramifications of the therapist's interventions (Langs 1978).

As the patient's associations confirm the therapist's silent hypothesis, an interpretation can be formulated and introduced. It may take the form of a Type One or a Type Two level of intervening. The interpretation then becomes the next adaptive context, and so the process unfolds. Validation is expressed in derivatives that refer to positive introjects and in a new reworking and understanding of the material. Nonvalidation of interventions appears in derivatives of negative introjects, in misunderstandings, and in attempts to direct the therapist to reformulate (Langs 1978).

The incorporation of the patient's projective identifications, in the context of a secure frame, evokes identificatory processes within the therapist. The therapist should, as a result, experience empathic reactions to what is contained. These empathic reactions can take the form of affects, fantasies, memories, or behaviors that are harmonious with the patient's self-representation or object representation. Empathic reactions cannot be viewed as immediate, organized insights into the unconscious processes of the patient. Instead, empathic reactions necessitate a determination of their source: either noncountertransference containment of the patient's material or countertransference-based needs that may impel the therapist to intervene incorrectly. Thus, empathic reactions alert the therapist to the importance of holding these reactions in abeyance while seeking from the patient's ongoing associations confirmation and validation of their usefulness. Such reactions require the therapist, before intervening, to attend to the total therapeutic interaction to determine what belongs to the patient, what to the therapist, and what to their interaction.

CLINICAL MATERIAL

The validating process will be illustrated by clinical vignettes portraying empathic responses, the distinguishing of countertransference from noncountertransference functioning, and the formulation of a silent hypothesis, with its alteration, its refutation or confirmation in the patient's material, and the resultant interpretation. The vignettes, written after each session, describe the therapist's empathic reactions, which are represented by personal affective responses connected to the recollection of personal memories. The process by which these empathic reactions were experienced, metabolized, identified, and validated within the context of the patient's communications will be described. Finally, a countertransference-based reaction that disrupted my containing function, leading to frame breaks concerning neutrality and anonymity, will be described. This description will permit a contrasting of and differentiation between the noncountertransference functioning of empathy and countertransference, with its loss of containing and empathic reactions. The following clinical vignettes will illustrate the concepts outlined to this point and their usefulness in assessing empathy as a therapeutic tool.

Empathy and Suicidal Ideation

Miss R. had been seen three times a week for about two months.

She began the session by describing fears about a "new man" she recently had "become involved with." She was "fearful, anxious, and nauseous all the time" when with him. She was fearful that he would make a "sexual advance." She stated that if he became "physical with me I'd be frightened and give in sexually, but if he were verbal I could argue." She stated, "I would have him sexually just to keep him there with me." She would, however, "go numb as a way to get rid of my feelings." She then said, "This is all absurd, like a fairy tale. . . . I play a game, being provocative, yet I test to see if a man really sees my needs; usually they don't and I feel frustrated and resentful." She perceived two aspects of herself: "aggressive and in control or weak and insecure." She then expressed feeling "hateful of men; they're intensely mistrustful; I never know when I'm being deceived or pacified." Foremost were feelings of not being able to leave this man, a belief that she would feel abandoned if he were to leave her, and a sense of emptiness when he departed after they had been together, of anxiety that he would never come back or that he did not think of her when they were apart. She needed him for the closeness, yet was fearful of being hurt and being used. If she expressed her "bad side," she feared, he would leave her. In response to an inquiry about her "bad side," she said she enjoyed yet was fearful of her anger and hostility. Her subsequent associations led her to comment on how difficult it was to look at me. She preferred to make me only a voice. "I don't want to see you as a man; that's a code word that sends me whirling. I see men as impulsive animals that can't be controlled; I date men only to avoid the criticism of being suspected as a gay. I want to be like a cloud or a vapor so I can voice resentments and not be seen." She then became despondent, expressing fears that resentments had to be "backed away from," and described playing "so many roles I don't have any idea what I mean when I say 'I'."

Throughout I thought her fears of passive submission and her resentment of men as "uncontrolled" sexual beings who are manipulative and insensitive were references to and defenses against sexual feelings toward me. Intense hatred was defended against by splitting, depersonalization, and identity diffusion. Homosexual anxieties stemmed from her acute ambivalence regarding symbiosis. She rushed into heterosexual relationships to avoid regressive needs. Perceiving me as a threatening, overpowering man whom she both desired to possess and wanted to attack to avoid passively being attacked, I conjectured, was a cause of her considerable anxiety.

Based on these assessments, I interpreted that she felt many feelings toward men, and perhaps she was describing what terrible difficulty these presented in sitting and talking to me. She sensed the importance of this relationship, yet she was terrified of the feelings it evoked. I inferred that she perceived herself as "bad" when she expressed feelings of closeness and understanding through sexuality, and that she felt hateful because she felt exploited by men. I interpreted her desire to be a cloud as a wish to protect herself from the fear that I would harm her and be like all other men.

She replied by "really wishing to break down and cry," yet she could not do so in my presence. If she cried she would feel "weak and dependent." She stated that she cried at home after the sessions. She was fearful of saying how she felt. She recollected a time in her childhood when she "stared into space and would not move for hours." Her mother had been unable to tolerate this and had begun hitting her with a small broom. When she did not cry, her mother had asked, "Don't you care?" Still she had refused to cry. This report was followed by recollections of not being permitted to be sick or injured as a child; "it wasn't allowed." She recalled sitting in her mother's lap and being burned by coffee. The scar on her forearm, from skin grafts to heal the wound, remained. It was a symbol of "being different, not a perfect little doll but flawed and in error."

From these associations, I concluded that Miss R. had experienced tremendous conflict and deprivation, as a result of which closeness had become fused with pain and physical harm. In my next intervention, I stated that her recollections seemed to indicate that relationships were so painful to her that she felt damaged by them. I stated that she perhaps had many feelings regarding these incidents that she found difficult to share. After this intervention she said nothing, but I noted she stiffened physically and pushed herself slightly deeper into the chair. This was the end of the session.

She began the following session matter-of-factly, describing her conviction to kill herself. She had devised a plan to take an overdose of pills, and had set a deadline. She had made arrangements to settle her financial affairs, had put her household in order, and had written a letter to her parents. She would not be coming to the next session, which would indicate that she was gone. She felt empty, alone, and despondent. She described the suicide as "within me; I feel like a terminal cancer case; the malignancy is forever growing. I can't control it, so why not speed up the process?" She had debated whether to kill herself and was "scared to do it." She was convinced that if she did not follow through, she would feel she had lied and would be "worthless."

I felt acute anxiety. Her bland tone, the firmness of her conviction, and the depth of worthlessness she perceived within herself disturbed me. I was aware of an urgent need to act, to flee from her, because I felt burdened by her impending deadline. I felt pressed, hemmed in, and trapped. My realization that she came to say good-bye and might be hoping to give me her distress so I could defuse it and make it manageable enabled me to contain my reactions and not act on them. I was utterly confused about the precipitant for the suicidal planning. Therefore, I chose to listen to her as if I were she, viewing her perception of our relationship. This is the first step of Langs's method: organizing the material as Type One derivatives concerning the therapeutic relationship.

She continued, stating she felt "pressured from parents and my new man." She felt a failure at "being normal, because I can't prove how serious my pain and desperation are." She described having "unreal feelings" for this man: "I need the closeness, but I need to tell him when to leave." She felt despair about this dilemma and stated emphatically, "Men are always after me; they won't let go." She then described feeling "numbness which spreads from my chest to my shoulders and arms, and I can't move." She mentioned "telling my landlord about suicide among young adults and wondering what was the quickest method, where was the jugular, and if people get sick from an overdose." The landlord responded by mentioning knowing of someone who committed suicide and by commenting "that people who do it are stupid." She felt she was not listened to and that words were deceiving: "There's only truth in action." Suicide would be an action with which no one would interfere. "I can be alone in my room, free, and no one can stop me."

As she spoke, my anxiety continued. I recalled the previous session, in which she had described painful, dominating, and intrusive relationships. To be autonomous and free from such destructive relationships would be my foremost desire if I were she. My desire to flee her burdening me with suicide led me to think that suicide was the only way she could feel autonomous and beyond the conflicts of relationships. I reformulated my assessment and decided she might have experienced my interventions of the previous session as intrusive and deceiving. This hypothesis was supported by her stiffening posture and depersonalization when abused by mother, which had been echoed in her response to my interventions. With my intervention as the adaptive context, these actions and the associations in today's session could be heard as commentary on my intervention and the fears it evoked. Her intense ambivalence in wanting to share her feelings yet fearing that if she did so she would be reprehensible, abused, and dominated led me to this discovery: as I allowed myself to experience her suicidal determination, I was confronted by a desperate sense within myself of wanting help yet fearing being controlled and put away. Her suicidal planning seemed to communicate an attempt to be autonomous, as well as an extreme provocation whose purpose was to determine if I would react impulsively and control her. Now I could reorganize the data as a request to me that I understand her, not with intrusion or dismissal, but with acceptance.

I interpreted that the feelings she had expressed in the last session concerning men presented difficulties, and that when I inferred that these difficulties also related to our relationship, she had perceived me as threatening and deceiving. I stated that my comments had focused on areas of her difficulties that were quite frightening. The confusion regarding her combining sexuality with needs for closeness and understanding, and her hatred of feeling exploited, left her feeling that I would be deceitful and would harm her. To avoid this confusion, she had concocted her suicide plan, which was a punishment for sharing what she considered her "bad side." It was also an assertion that she was independent and separate even though she wished to be understood by me and feared my control and abuse.

Her mood changed after this intervention. "You do understand that I'm afraid of being normal. It's unknown to me, this idea of you helping me. I'm afraid of what this relationship means to me. The suicide is my way of controlling being dependent; then I know I have total control of this relationship. I try to avoid you as often as I can. If you talk, you make contact, but I don't know what's real, unreal, deceiving, or what. When you're quiet, I feel abandoned. I just want you to be a voice." She then expressed fears that being normal meant "coming to your side; see, I want the suicide, you don't. If I come to your side, do I lose me, whatever 'me' is?" As the session ended, she said she would return because she had moved her planned suicide to a later date. The following sessions unfolded material related to maternal abuse and deprivation.

The intense anxiety I had experienced had been a result of the patient's interactional pressure, which, I later realized, was a projective identification. The patient had wanted to evoke adaptive responses within me to assist her in managing her suicidal ideation. In containing these psychic elements, I had made them my own in a transient identification. I had focused my observing ego on my experiencing ego, a process that culminated in a split between my identification with the patient and my objectivity in thinking about these reactions. By containing, metabolizing, and understanding her material, and then seeking confirmation of my silent hypothesis in it, I then became able to offer an interpretation. My ability to contain her suicidal planning seemed to result from my working to avoid being perceived as her intrusive mother, my feeling that she desired to unburden herself and seek my help, and my new-found ability to hear her material as derivative of unconscious perceptions that could be organized around an adaptive context. Although her material included erotic transference material as well as genetic links to her masochistic relationships, in the first session the interventions had been aimed primarily at her primitive defenses for and against relating and expressing herself to me. The direction of these interventions accords with Kernberg's formulations (1980) of intervention with borderline personality organization. These interventions thus were based on Type One derivative inferences. A potentially tragic situation was averted by my containing her projective identifications, searching for the adaptive context, holding in abeyance my empathic reactions until her material confirmed their usefulness, and offering an interpretation based now on Type Two derivative inferences. This interpretation dealt first with her perception of my intervention as intrusive and painful and her need to defend via suicide to maintain autonomy in relation to me. I believe her material following this intervention confirmed my empathic reactions.

Empathy via Personal Memory

Miss M. had been in treatment for two-and-a-half years with twice-weekly sessions. Unfortunately, I had to terminate the therapy prematurely because I was relocating.[1] The adaptive context for the vignette is the announcement of termination.

The patient began the hour talking of incidental events. She felt tired and wanted to go home and rest. She did not wish to talk of my leaving. She became sad and then cried. She was "surprised, shocked, and hurt" that I would leave. "Others come and go, but I felt secure in thinking you would stay. To say good-bye to you is painfully hard; I never imagined doing it or needing to." She expressed not knowing how to say good-bye.

Throughout, I experienced her crying as a futile lament. Her cry had a grasping, imploring quality, to which I reacted with sadness. This reaction stemmed from guilt at leaving prematurely, from my difficulties in saying good-bye and accepting the ending of relationships. These feelings stemmed from personal intrapsychic conflicts that bore some affinity to those of the patient. The connection between noncountertranference and countertransference was prominent.

The patient went on to state that when people leave, "things change and we would never know each other the same again." She recalled that when, as a child, she would protest her mother's leaving, her crying was ignored or met by taunting. When her mother would return from an evening with a man, Miss M. would appeal to the man to like her in the hope that he and the mother would stay with her. Despite her attempts to be "cute and seductive," the mother and her male friend would leave. The patient cried as she expressed the "loneliness and coldness" of being left and the indifference of her mother to her pleas for comfort. She could not talk further. She did not want to feel the pain of my being gone and her world "coming to an end."

After this material was presented, I experienced feelings of abandonment and recurrently felt like a small child, alone and frightened. I recalled when, as a child, I had been hospitalized by my parents for what I presumed was to be only a routine physical examination. I had been told that I was to stay overnight, and I recalled my futile, crying protests at being left. As I listened to my patient, I reexperienced the futility of appealing to adults whom I could not influence. I had learned while in the hospital, to my shock and disbelief, that I was to have a surgical procedure, and I had felt that I was being punished for my outburst of temper and was vaguely responsible for being hospitalized and for my parents leaving me. I realized at this point in

---

[1]The effects of premature termination on the therapeutic interaction has been reported elsewhere (Beatrice 1982).

the session that the reactions I was experiencing were a consequence of my containing and identifying with the patient's psychic contents and were associated with a specific personal conflict having the same theme of separation, anger, and guilt. I could distinguish the countertransference and non-countertransference components of my empathic responses. I therefore held these manifest themes in abeyance, listened to Miss M.'s associations as organized around my leaving, and waited to ascertain how she would attempt to manage them in relation to me and to past significant losses.

She repeated her "shock" and bafflement at my leaving. "I know for certain it isn't my fault, that I'm in the clear on that one." She spoke of her boyfriend and expressed feeling "stupid" because she believed he wanted her only because she was attractive. She voiced regret about being a "pretty face" when "looks don't really matter." She felt uncertain about her need to "save" the boyfriend. Because of her "intense involvement," she felt an inability to "examine, listen, and see" how he mistreated her. She felt confused, because "he says the right words of affection, yet now he's lately not been calling and isn't available." This constellation of feelings paralleled her defending her father when her mother ridiculed him for their divorce. She could not really recall her father, because the divorce had occurred when she was two-and-a-half years old. She knew her boyfriend's faults, yet she had to "defend and save him." She worried that she was not seeing her father and the boyfriend for "what they really are, but hoping for them to be something they're not." She hoped that through her caring and tolerance of their faults they would come to see her loyalty and to appreciate how worthy of their love she genuinely was.

I interpreted that my leaving was evoking recollections of her helplessness regarding her parents' divorce. She was attempting to defend against the loss, helplessness, and anger she felt by emphasizing her physical appearance. I stated that she now felt betrayed and perceived herself as stupid, because her concern with her appearance had not kept me, her boyfriend, or her father with her. I suggested that her remark about "being in the clear" indicated her realization that she was not responsible for my leaving, just as she had not been responsible for the divorce. I interpreted that she felt guilt because the seductiveness not only revealed her intense need to obtain her father's and mother's love, but also contained a hostile component that she felt drove people away. I said that her need to save me, her boyfriend, and her father was her attempt to ward off her hostility at feeling abandoned and mistreated and was also an expression of not wanting to see herself as aligning with mother against father.

Miss M. responded that now she saw why she dated men she knew were unattainable. Although she had no memory to support her conviction, she believed she had been her father's favorite child. She recalled sleeping in a rather ornate bedroom while her sister slept in less appealing surroundings. After an argument she and her sister had once had, her father, as she recalled, had punished her sister. Her mother had described how Miss M. physically resembled her father. Her mother and sister had been hostilely opposed to the father, whereas the patient would rush to his defense. In the following sessions, further material unfolded regarding the sexual fantasies toward the father and the prominence of masochistic trends in her heterosexual relationships, an attempt to avoid loss of lovers.

What was not in this interaction was that the patient had worked on similar themes of separation and loss, defended by seductive and masochistic object relationships, quite frequently in prior sessions. In this session, my empathy with her abandonment, which elicited personal associations to separation, loss, and subsequent feelings of guilt, gave my interpretations a direction that appeared to be validated: she proceeded to offer rich, new material concerning her fantasies toward her father, which idealized his image and defended against her resentment, disappointment, and anger at not being able to control him. These feelings were elaborated on in later sessions through her expression of anger at me for abandoning her and the unfolding of mourning over this loss.

Countertransference and Loss of Empathy

Miss B. had been in twice-weekly treatment for approximately four years.

The patient began the session with an expression of intense sadness "at not wanting to be so split; of being tired of standing next to myself; of having no one to talk to; of not being able to get my soul." She particularly wanted my ability to assemble her thoughts and feelings into an intelligible form. She wanted to "incorporate" this ability yet despaired of a hoped-for rebirth. She shifted at this point from despair to hostility. She wanted to take this ability from me and was angry that I seemed to be purposely denying it to her.

I experienced a burdensome helplessness and felt worthless and pained at not being able to fulfill her request or ease her distress. I thought of myself as an abject failure. I remembered a painful adolescent rejection that had been compounded by my mother's disappointment and criticism. When I linked this recollection to the patient's despondency, I must have appeared pained and saddened. I became aware of the patient's noticing these feelings when she stopped talking and looked at me with a shocked facial expression. Again, instead of reacting, I evaluated the sequence and concluded that my sadness at having failed maternal expectations was displayed for a reparative purpose. I may have been beseeching the patient as a countertransference maternal object to forgive me for my perceived failings.

The patient said she was perplexed about why I allowed myself to feel. She speculated that this was a way of demonstrating my caring, yet she wondered if my caring about her and sharing my feeling meant that she was inflicting pain. "Is that sharing or it is destructive?" She wondered whether I was a martyr: "I feel it's like a punishment where I hurt you, you get some satisfaction, and because I'm causing you pain, you feel better about not giving me the how to interpret!" She continued, stating, "When I was hurting, I didn't see it as sadistic, yet what was your need to take it in?"

This material represented the patient's conscious perception of and commentary about an expression of a manifest countertransference reaction. Her psychic contents had surpassed my containing ability and had re-created a personal feeling of worthlessness, associated with a memory of a punitive and unforgiving mother, that I had projected onto my patient. As a result, I apparently displayed sadness and a need for forgiveness. She introjectively identified with me, thus translating the perception into a perception of herself as destructive and sadistic for expressing despair and hostility. This sequence was necessary because she was aware, at an unconscious level, that my break in neutrality was destructive. I needed to rectify this error and to use the creation of this specific object relationship as the basis for an interpretation.

Her associations then depicted hostile interactions between her parents, in which each belittled the other. The patient experienced these "sharings" as always destructive and could not differentiate shadings of constructive affects. She was convinced that arguments, as well as other exchanges of feelings, were inevitably hurtful. She wondered when to allow herself to be vulnerable to another's feelings and when to defend against them. As a child she had once inadvertently found her father alone and crying. She had been moved, and he had shared his remorse and helplessness regarding his marital problems. When she tried to comfort him, he had realized his vulnerability and become harsh and abusive, sending her away. She had been left feeling confused yet loving toward him. This recounting echoed her confusion over when to be vulnerable and when to attack. If she were in my position, she said, the pain and despair would create a need to defend and attack. She did not trust my vulnerability and preferred that I repulse and leave her rather than feel and accept her pain and mine. She could not understand my motivation in accepting and expressing pain.

She then associated to her lover and expressed the thought that the reason for his verbal attacks on her when she was vulnerable might be his love for her. "He's vulnerable to me so he attacks." He needed to deny vulnerability with verbal abuse to retain a façade of masculinity. Because she was such a danger to men, why did I not reject and leave her, as others did, when my feelings became too painful?

I interpreted to the patient that her feelings of despair regarding improvement gave way to hostility when she perceived me as depriving and withholding. I then elaborated that seeing my sadness caused her to feel sadistic, thus re-creating the experience with her father. Fulfilling her wish that I attack and repulse her would ensure that I would be rejecting and depriving and therefore hurtful, just as she experienced her father and her boyfriend to be. Her need for my understanding and support left her feeling vulnerably open to sharing her feelings, and seeing me as rejecting and abusive would then leave her feeling despondent and hostile and not able to understand why her relationships were so unhappy. In doing so, however, she would not be able to get her soul.

In this intervention I addressed her perception of my countertransference expression as the adaptive context. Then I interpreted the derivatives of this perception and attempted to show how she had worked it over. The image of her father as first showing his feelings and confiding in her and then rejecting her was a disguised representation of the almost uncanny unconscious perception of my emotional display and the destructive element it introduced into the treatment. Her father's rejection was the symbol for my losing my empathic, therapeutic function for her, just as her father had lost his fathering function in the interaction she remembered.

She responded that seeing my pain made her realize there were alternatives regarding sharing. She believed that my way of handling my feelings and hers had had a beneficial effect. "Seeing how you handled your feelings and mine made you real and allowed me to be myself." Sharing was now seen as "time spent together without rejection or hurting abuse." She recollected meaningful talks she had had as a child with her grandmother. In the following sessions she talked about her motivations for engaging in destructive and hostile affairs with men as opposed to having relationships with men who related meaningfully to their feelings and hers.

A potentially destructive therapeutic impasse caused by my loss of the capacity to contain the patient's projective identifications was averted by rectification. The intervention, which included discussion of the adaptive context, my break in neutrality, led to a reestablishment of the therapeutic alliance and further elaboration of pathological object relationships elicited by my error. My subjective associations clarified the elements of rejection, despondency, and hostility against which the patient was struggling to defend. My inability to remain neutral and to contain the role assignment she had attempted to create led to her pathological introjection of my sadness. By feeling sadistic, she assumed a role assignment based in my countertransference projections. Her associations aptly described the pathological consequences of my burdensome demand to seek her forgiveness, a demand that left her confused about her belief that feelings were always hostile and destructive.

DISCUSSION

These examples demonstrate that empathy, studied from the adaptational-interactional perspective, is a process initiated by the patient's projective identifications. The well-functioning therapist takes in, incorporates, and contains the patient's communications. When securely contained, these psychic contents elicit a variety of subjective responses within the therapist. Among these responses are those noncountertransference reactions that result from containing and transiently identifying with particular aspects of the patient's ego or objects.

Within this framework, empathic reactions are not to be understood as providing immediate access to the patient's unconscious. The perspective, instead, calls for holding these reactions in abeyance and employing the validating process. This method of assessing and understanding the therapeutic interaction is essential to a determination of what belongs to the patient, what to the therapist, and what to their interaction. The processing, metabolizing, and integrating of these empathic reactions must be checked against the patient's ongoing material in order to confirm their validity and potential usefulness of the empathic reactions in formulating an intervention.

The first two clinical examples demonstrate how noncountertransference functioning and the use of the validating process in formulating interventions can be based in empathic reactions. The first step in these therapeutic interactions was a transient identification with the patient's self-representation. Then these reactions were checked against the patient's associations to ascertain their goodness of fit. Here the Type One level of derivative listening permitted the emergence of specific themes. Once these themes were identified, they were organized as unconscious perceptions of the therapeutic relationship. This organization led to a search for the adaptive context involving my management of the ground rules and the prior interventions.

By focusing on specific realities within the therapeutic interaction—my first intervention with Miss R. and my leaving of Miss M.—I became able to discern the patients' unconscious perceptions and commentaries and the elaboration of their respective character pathologies through the expression of dynamic and genetic components in derivative form. This assessment represents a move from the Type One level of listening to the Type Two level. Once the intervention has been formulated and evidence supporting its validity has been found within the patient's associations, the intervention can be offered and then becomes the new adaptive context.

The vignette involving Miss B. shows how a countertransference response to empathy can, because of breaks in neutrality, be detrimental. The evidence of this negative effect consisted of the patient's unconscious perception of my self-disclosure, the negative introjective identification it promoted, and the patient's subsequent attempts to elicit adaptive responses in me to rectify the error.

In not all cases could the level of intervention progress from Type One to Type Two in its strictest sense, that is, the full unfolding and interpreting of genetic or transference material. Miss R., suffering a borderline personality organization, primarily used splitting defenses in her intense struggles to relate to me solely as a part-object. She persistently desired me to be only a voice. Therefore, the genetic components of her material were not fully utilized in my interventions, because of her severe core structural damage and the need to establish a therapeutic alliance. Only after an interpretation of her terrors of relating to me, did it become possible to analyze securely the roots of her pathology.

The overlapping of Type One and Type Two interventions enabled Miss M. to reestablish a therapeutic alliance. With this security provided, her following sessions unfolded new material regarding her sexual fantasies toward her father and me.

It thus can be inferred that empathic reactions involve primarily a Type One level of derivative listening, which, when confirmed, organized around an adaptive context, and offered as an intervention, enables new material to surface and moves the work to a consideration of Type Two derivatives. Particularly, previously vague dynamic and genetic components are uncovered. For instance, Miss R. began detailing the deprivation of her early childhood; Miss M. elaborated her sexual fantasies; Miss B. struggled with the roots of her masochistic object relationships. Empathic reactions, when used in the manner presented, solidify the therapeutic alliance, foster the transference into previously unexplored areas, and uncover further derivatives of unconscious fantasies, memories, introjects, and perceptions.

At the same time, empathy may stimulate conflicted or countertransference memories and motives for action. The first two vignettes depict the potential for serious breaks in the therapeutic alliance. Miss R. was suicidal, and Miss M. was struggling to work over, integrate, and understand my eventual departure. Consequently, my capacity for empathy may have been heightened by my countertransference wishes to avoid loss and by guilt, with the resulting need to make reparations. The impetus to organize my empathic responses stemmed from my awareness that only a continued therapeutic relationship would relieve the patients of distresses that I had induced.

Finally, my empathy with the patients' self-representations elicited recollections of myself under similar affective circumstances. Empathy therefore represented reexperiencing and recollecting a past personal trauma. With my patients, I attempted to be a positive object representation, in contrast with the negative and painful ones I recollected and with which the patients were contending. By empathizing with the patients, I was able to avoid perpetuating and being a pathological object. The vignette concerning Miss B. illustrates the failures of empathy that result when the therapist has not integrated and mastered an object relationship reminiscent of a past interaction that is re-created in the therapy situation.

REFERENCES

BEATRICE, J. (1982). Premature termination: a therapist leaving. *International Journal of Psychoanalytic Psychotherapy.* 9:313–336.

BERES, D., AND ARLOW, J. (1974). Fantasy and identification in empathy. *Psychoanalytic Quarterly* 43:26–50.

DEUTSCH, H. (1926). Occult processes occurring during psychoanalysis. In *Psychoanalysis and the Occult*, ed. G. Devereux, pp. 133–146. New York: International Universities Press, 1970.

FLEISS, R. (1942). The metapsychology of the analyst. *Psychoanalytic Quarterly* 11:211–227.

FREUD, S. (1912). Recommendations for physicians on the psychoanalytic method of treatment. *Standard Edition* 12.

―――― (1921). Group psychology and the analysis of the ego. *Standard Edition* 18.

GREENSON, R. (1960). Empathy and its vicissitudes. In R. Greenson, *Explorations in Psychoanalysis*, pp. 147–161. New York: International Universities Press, 1978.

HEIMANN, P. (1950). On countertransference. *International Journal of Psycho-Analysis* 31:81–84.

KANZER, M. (1975). The therapeutic and working alliances. *International Journal of Psychoanalytic Psychotherapy* 4:48–68.

KERNBERG, O. (1980). *Internal World and External Reality.* New York: Jason Aronson.

KOHUT, H. (1971). *The Analysis of the Self.* New York: International Universities Press.

―――― (1977). *The Restoration of the Self.* New York: International Universities Press.

LANGS, R. (1976a). *The Bipersonal Field.* New York: Jason Aronson.

―――― (1976b). On becoming a psychiatrist: discussion of "Empathy and Intuition in Becoming a Psychiatrist," by Ronald J. Blank. *International Journal of Psychoanalytic Psychotherapy* 5:255–280.

―――― (1978). *The Listening Process.* New York: Jason Aronson.

LITTLE, M. (1951). Countertransference and the patient's response to it. *International Journal of Psycho-Analysis* 32:32–40.

OLINICK, S. (1969). On empathy and regression in the service of the other. *British Journal of Medical Psychology* 42:41–49.

REICH, A. (1960). Further remarks on countertransference. *International Journal of Psycho-Analysis* 41:389–395.

——— (1966). Empathy and countertransference. In A. Reich, *Annie Reich: Psychoanalytic Contributions*, pp. 344–360. New York: International Universities Press, 1973.

SCHAFER, R. (1959). Generative empathy in the treatment situation. *Psychoanalytic Quarterly* 28:342–373.

SHAPIRO, T. (1974). The development and distortion of empathy. *Psychoanalytic Quarterly* 43:4–25.

WEIGERT, E. (1954). Countertransference and self-analysis of the psychoanalyst. *International Journal of Psycho-Analysis* 35:242–246.

Part II

The Ground Rules

CHAPTER 9

Negotiating the Impossible

M. Masud R. Khan, M.A.

> At an early stage I had accepted the *bon mot* which lays it down that there
> are three impossible professions—educating, healing and governing—and I
> was already fully occupied with the second of them.
>
> *Freud 1925, p. 273*

> If analysis, as Freud (1937) said, is one of the impossible professions,
> then the analytic relationship is virtually impossible to master in one's
> writings or in one's clinical work.
>
> *Langs and Stone 1980, p. 4*

Fundamental to the approach of this chapter is the use of the verb
"negotiating" (rather than the noun "role"), and the use of the word
"method" instead of James Strachey's preferential choice of "procedure" in
his 1953 translation of Freud's "Die Freudische Psychoanalytische Methode"
(1904) into "Freud's Psycho-Analytic Procedure." In Freud's lifetime the
English translation, by J. Bernays in 1924, was "The Psychoanalytic Method."
Strachey does not say why he decided to change "method" to "procedure."
"Method" is, perhaps more Cartesian in its connotations, and hence dogmatic,
whereas "procedure" in English has the more empirical referents, in law and
scientific investigation. These issues may seem obscure, but my arguments
will clarify my reasons for raising them.

The reader should be cautioned on another count. He should not expect
a reasoned argument from my contribution to this volume. I am offering a
sort of dialogue with Robert Langs's written work. But, as I am sure the
volume's bibliography of Langs's writings over the past decade will show,
Langs is as prolific and erudite a reader as he is a copious writer. He
combines his own views with generous selection and presentation of others'
thinking and writings. As a result, individuals must restrict their frames
stringently to focus on what is personally important in Langs's contributions.

I have already stated my bias by my choice of the opening quotation
from him, and I shall be restricting myself almost exclusively to Langs's

"Clinical Dialogues" with Harold Searles (1980) and Leo Stone (1980). In these dialogues all three analysts are concerned with what happens in the analytic situation and process between two persons, one styled as "analyst," the other tagged as "patient." They question this classic division of labor and roles advocated by Freud. They find that the roles become reversed (Searles) or that the frame of the analytic setting must be extended to encompass the total psychic reality of the patient as a person. This is why they emphasize as much the role played by the patient's conscious and unconscious intrapsychic structures and affectivity (through transference) as those of the analyst (through countertransference). But at a crucial point, all three analysts seem to sweep under the carpet the concept of countertransference, experiences (clinical and social) that I believe are inherent to Freud's psychoanalytic method, which he never spelled out with any thoroughness.

As one reads Freud, one notices that the character and style of his case presentation in "Studies on Hysteria" (1895) is very different in its aims and language from the case histories after "The Interpretation of Dreams" (1900)—that is, after his "self-analysis." To put it crudely, the emphasis shifts from clinical narrative about a "person" with symptoms to the "patient" with *problems* that the analyst can decode with his concepts. This widening scope of analysis led to great new contributions by Freud and, especially after World War II, by his followers. Yet the concept of the "patient" had led in his metapsychological thinking to a dissociation between the "patient" and the "person" who is given that designation. This issue was to become the central theme of research and debate among such analysts as Glover and Brierley (1940), Fairbairn (1952), Guntrip (1964), Winnicott (1971b), and Milner (1969) in England and Menninger (Menninger and Holzman 1958), Greenson (1978), Searles (1979), and Stone (1961) in America.

I wish to examine afresh what constitutes Freud's psychoanalytic method. I differentiate five basic components of the total method:

1. The person as a "patient."
2. The analyst who undertakes to work with this patient. This phrasing is deliberate; I want to emphasize the analyst's responsibility to himself and to the patient in his therapeutic undertaking.
3. A framed space that is going to stay basically the same during the treatment, called the "consultation room," the "analytic setting," etcetera.
4. A temporal commitment to which in its frequency and duration both the patient and the analyst agree. It is dictated largely by two factors: the analyst's *demand* from "knowing" what is required by the patient's ailment, and the patient's means and capacity to meet it, both fiscally and in his sociofamilial circumstances (Main 1957).

5. The analytic process, the knowledge of which is most unequally distributed between the analyst and the patient. The approach of the latter ranges from misapprehension to benign trust to magical expectancies, even though he does not know *how* the process works. All the printed theories and clinical data, as well as the vulgarization of analytic and clinical practices by the mass media, have not changed this imbalance radically. Even in the so-called didactic or training analyses, this imbalance is qualitatively the same.

Freud did not invent the analytic setting and method in one burst of inspiration and insight. It took him years to arrive at a basic clinical frame and the necessary tools (concepts) with which to function in it. If one reads the cases reported by Freud in "Studies on Hysteria" (1895), one is struck by how readily Freud *accommodates* to the patient's wishes and demands. In the case of Frau Emmy Von N (1889), he reports: "She then said in a definitely grumbling tone that I was not to keep on asking her where this and that came from, but to let her tell me what she had to say. I fell in with this . . ." (p. 63).

Freud's narrative is so casual in its drift for two reasons: First he was searching to find and establish his method in these years and with these cases. He visited the patients; he went to interview the mother of Fraulein Elisabeth Von R: "I begged her mother from that time forward to tell Elisabeth everything she needed to know" (pp. 158–159). And when she was "indignant with me for betraying her secret" and stopped her treatment, he states: "I heard she was going to a private ball for which I was able to get an invitation, and I did not allow the opportunity to escape me of seeing my former patient whirl past in a lively swirl." How many analysts would risk stating all this, even if they happily do it for a patient? Only Greenson and Winnicott have. There is little wonder that Freud, in his discussion of this case, somewhat ruefully remarks: "It still strikes me as strange that the case-histories I write should read like short stories and that, as one might say, they lack the serious stamp of science. . . ."

The second reason for Freud's casualness, I think, is that his "language of psychoanalysis," as Laplanche and Pontalis (1967) aptly christen it, was still in the making. After 1900 Freud's whole style changed, because he had established his method in all its essentials and his "vocabulary" was rapidly growing in scope. Hence all the case histories after this time are *illustrating* some theoretical point, rather than giving a picture of the analysis in the round, from Dora to the Wolf Man. This conceptual mode of showing the clinical experience was to become very arid in the hands of his followers, who lacked both Freud's humanism and his literary style. And it is against this mode that Little (1980), Searles, Milner, and Winnicott, among others, have rebelled. Winnicott (1971b), at the end of his life, stated his attitude very emphatically:

> Dogmatic interpretation leaves the child with only two alternatives, an *acceptance* of what I have said as propaganda or a *rejection* of the interpretation and of me and of the whole set-up. I think and hope that children in this relationship with me feel that they have the right to reject what I say or the way I take something. Actually I do claim that it is a fact that these interviews are dominated by the child and not by me. (p. 10)

I believe that Langs, by focusing on the "interactional aspects of therapy," is pursuing a similar clinical undertaking; hence his statement (1980) that in the analytic relationship all we can hope to achieve is "relative mastery." I would add: both for the patient and for ourselves.

In spite of, or perhaps because of, the mammoth literature that exists around Freud's method, one simple fact has never been singled out for discussion: namely, Freud's extraordinary *demands* on the patient. In no society, primitive or industrialized, did any shaman or physician before Freud ever demand that a patient come for a limited time of sixty minutes a day, six times a week, for an unpredictable length of time, according to the healer's assessment of the patient's *need* for the particular type of therapy (which was to be, for all intents and purposes, exclusively psychoanalytic). It may seem banal and rather fatuous to emphasize this, but its implications are monumental and revolutionary. Since the origins of human civilization, culture, and society, insofar as we know them, a person "presented" himself to a shaman, physician, or any type of self-styled healer through his "symptoms." Pouillon (1970), the French anthropologist, has discussed this very thoughtfully (see Khan 1970). It is exactly how Freud encountered his patients in "Studies on Hysteria" (1895). And once the "symptoms" cleared up or refused to be "charmed" away (in the dual sense of magic and fascination), the "treatment" would stop. It was all done on a demand basis; there was no undertaking or commitment beyond that on either side. The last paragraph of "Studies on Hysteria" leaves one in no doubt about this even though Freud is already looking ahead toward the revolution he was to launch:

> When I have promised my patients help or improvement by means of a cathartic treatment I have often been faced by this objection: "Why, you tell me yourself that my illness is probably connected with my circumstances and the events of my

life. You cannot alter these in any way. How do you propose to help me, then?"
And I have been able to make this reply: "No doubt fate would find it easier than
I do to relieve you of your illness. But you will be able to convince yourself that
much will be gained if we succeed in transforming your hysterical misery into
common unhappiness. With a mental life that has been restored to health you will
be better armed against that unhappiness." (p. 305)

In a footnote on the same page, Strachey tells us that until 1925 the
German original of this quotation read "nervous system" and not "mental
life." What I wish to draw attention to is Freud's use of the verb phrases
"promised," "restored to health," and "armed against" and the noun "unhappiness," which is not a symptom but an inescapable vicissitude of a human's
past and present living. At this point and in this context, I do not want to
discuss Freud's use of the noun "health" (a mysterious state, much talked of
but never defined).

As the opening quotation from Freud (1925) indicates, Freud considered
"educating, healing, governing" the "three impossible professions." He
admits having been "occupied" with the second one, healing, for a long
time. But I do not think Freud fully realized to what extent the other two
"impossible professions" were to become necessary components of his
therapeutic undertaking and the psychoanalytic method. In the course of
time, these two components, teaching and governing, were to play an
increasingly predominant role in the analyses of the so-called analysands
(persons in training to become psychoanalysts). Furthermore, in most if not
all of the splits and defections in the International Association, these two
factors play an important part. Throughout his life, Freud maintained a
wryly cynical attitude toward politics, but it is interesting that each of the
two thinkers of the nineteenth century who were to condition the progress
of civilizations and cultures in the century to follow launched an International Association: Karl Marx the "First International" in 1864 in London,
and Freud the "International Association" in Vienna in 1910 (see Jones
1955, Clark 1980). And the two International Associations, in spite of their
idealistic aspirations, have had matching records of acrid defections, splinter
groups, expulsions, and other disharmonies. Marx was committing himself
and others to alleviating the "unhappiness" of the human individual in his or
her socioeconomic context, just as Freud (1904) was to undertake the same
task four decades later in the psychic context of the individual and his
family. Holland (1978) discusses this parallel most pertinently in his book,
Self and Social Context.

I am well aware of Freud's distaste for *furor therapeuticus.* As one of his
analysands recounts:

In his [Freud's] personality the particular impulse which would incline a man towards being a healer was not so strongly developed as his impulse to knowledge. He had nothing of the *furor therapeuticus* that so many doctors display. (Reik 1942, p. 18)

Another analysand comments from his own analysis with Freud:

I once asked Freud what he thought of himself as an analyst. "I'm glad you ask, because, frankly, I have no great interest in therapeutic problems. I am much too impatient now. I have several handicaps that disqualify me as a great analyst. One of them is that I am too much the father. Second, I am much too much occupied with theoretical problems all the time, so that whenever I get occasion, I am working on my own theoretical problems, rather than paying attention to the therapeutic problems. Third, I have no patience in keeping people for a long time. I tire of them, and I want to spread my influence," which is probably why he kept many people for only short periods of time. (Kardiner 1977, pp. 68–69)

Whatever the veracity of this recall years later, it sounds true to Freud, who had himself told his audience (imaginary this time!) in 1932:

As you know, psycho-analysis originated as a method of treatment; it has far outgrown this, but it has not abandoned its homeground and it is still linked to its contact with patients for increasing its depth and for its further development. . . . You are perhaps aware I have never been a therapeutic enthusiast. . . . Psycho-analysis is a method of treatment like others. . . . Psycho-analytic activity is arduous and exacting; it cannot be handled like a pair of glasses that one puts on for reading and takes off when one goes for a walk. As a rule psycho-analysis possesses a doctor entirely or not at all. . . .

I have told you that psycho-analysis began as a method of treatment; but I did not want to commend it to your interest as a method of treatment but on account of the truths it contains, on account of the information it gives us about what concerns human beings most of all—their own nature—and on account of the connections it discloses between the most different of their activities. As a method of treatment it is one among many, though, to be sure, *primus inter pares*. If it was without therapeutic value it would not have been discovered, as it was, in connection with sick people and would not have gone on developing for more than thirty years. (Freud 1933, pp. 151–152)

I have quoted at length because it shows us Freud's commitment to his self-elected task, without earnest bristling to cure or to know too much, as a story from Strachey's analysis indicates:

It had been a critical week in her analysis, which resulted in her having a significant dream. She recounted her dream to the Professor and they worked around it. Then the Professor gave an interpretation, at the end of which he got up to fetch a cigar for himself, saying: "Such insights need celebrating." Alix Strachey mildly protested that she had not yet told the whole dream, to which the Professor replied: "Don't be greedy, that is enough insight for a week." (Khan 1973, p. 370)

Freud (1904) explicitly states: "The session thus proceeds like a conversation between two people equally awake."

What makes the discussion of changes in Freud's psychotherapeutic aims and ambitions difficult is the fact that he himself never spelled out the theme with any consistency. His papers on technique are more in the nature of cautionary admonitions than precepts to be obeyed rigorously. One can, all the same, chart the changing aims of psychotherapy, from "transforming hysterical misery into common unhappiness" (Freud 1895) to the idea that "the aim of the treatment will never be anything but the *practical* recovery of the patient, the restoration of his ability to lead an active life and his capacity for enjoyment" (Freud 1904). His "method" at this stage he states as "an art of interpretation": "The task of the treatment is to remove amnesia, and the task consists in making the unconscious accessible to consciousness, which is done by overcoming the resistances." He makes a definitive statement:

> Nevertheless it may be admitted that the therapeutic efforts of psycho-analysis have chosen a similar line of approach. Its intention is, indeed, to strengthen the ego, to make it more independent of the super-ego, to widen its field of perception and enlarge its organization, so that it can appropriate fresh portions of the id. Where id was, there ego shall be. It is a work of culture—not unlike the draining of the Zuider Zee. (Freud 1933, p. 80)

All this in no way biases my contention that Freud's *method*, spoken of by him variously in terms of "conquering," "mastery," and so forth, seeks a commitment that involves both parties, unequally. This commitment entails, furthermore, a two-way demand: a *demand on* the patient and a *demand by* the patient. Freud's method *instructs* both demands. The demand on the patient is regulated through analysis of the analysand, an apprenticeship that inevitably teaches *the how*, if not the what (which still remains vague and allusive, if not illusive), of making the demand. The demand by the patient is initiated by proferring him a setting and a possibility of "intimacy" to the character and function of which the person as a patient at the beginning has not many clues, but that will soon engulf the patient and analyst in utterly unpredicated amplitudes of relating and refusing to relate (each in his or her own style). The difference is that the style of the analyst is considered "normal" and that of the patient, conditioned by his childhood experiences and unconscious fantasies, is considered sexual and aggressive. Gradually, the supposedly mutual undertaking labeled the "therapeutic alliance," etcetera, takes on the climate and character of a contest! When this contest is benign, it allows for playing, healing, and recovery (see Winnicott 1971a); when it goes sour, it is damaging to both participants, and there is no remedy. It is my deliberate choice to write in a colloquial manner, because all these issues linguistically have been petrified by our metapsychology, especially in its clinical formulations. It is in this area that Langs's fervor for debate and questioning strikes me as both refreshing and purposeful in a creative, sharing way (see Langs 1976).

Because I have undertaken to examine the implications of Freud's use of certain verbs and nouns, I should explain my utilization of the verbs "negotiating" and "relating" and the adjective "impossible," which I borrow from Freud but use in a different context and with different connotations. Freud's method calls for a sort of "programmed intimacy" and a *contest*. The analyst has *some* knowledge, or so he or she believes and is rigorously *educated* to believe, of what this "programmed intimacy" would entail. The understanding of the patient's contribution, masked by his symptoms, if he has the facility to "speak" thus, will constitute most of the relating between patient and analyst, and their discourse. By using the verb "negotiating," I am trying to indicate and emphasize the highly precarious and tentative character of the *commitment* that the analyst offers/imposes and to which the patient becomes an unknowing accomplice, only in due course to turn the tables and make the analyst *accomplice* to the patient's complicity. This double bind, or paradox, is the very essence of the *relating*, which must not grow into a "relationship" because that would be an *enacted* intimacy, and which must not lose impetus through the *lacking* relationship or the game is over.

Hence my use of the adjective "impossible." Both the analyst and the patient bring to this relating in the analytic situation their individuated styles of "self-cure." Only the analyst's "self-cure" is sanctified by personal belief and professional accrediting; the patient's is in question, by both the patient and the analyst. As the dialogues between Langs and Searles (1980) and Langs and Stone (1980) demonstrate eloquently and, fortunately, with humor and good will on each side, this distribution of roles in the "programmed intimacy" and contest undergoes devastating vicissitudes, not only of "material" (as it is called) but of the roles themselves (see Khan 1981). In Gerard Manley Hopkins's verse, it is rendered thus:

> O the mind, mind has mountains; cliffs of fall
> Frightful, sheer, no-man-fathomed. Hold them cheap
> May who ne'er hung there. Nor does long our small
> Durance deal with that steep or deep.

REFERENCES

CLARK, R. (1980). *Freud: The Man and the Cause.* New York: Random House.

FAIRBAIRN, W. R. D. (1952). *Psychoanalytic Studies of the Personality.* Boston: Routledge and Kegan, 1966.

FREUD, S. (1895). Studies on hysteria. *Standard Edition* 2.

—— (1900). Interpretation of dreams. *Standard Edition* 3/4.

—— (1904). Freud's Psycho-analytic procedure. *Standard Edition* 7.

—— (1925). Preface to Aichhorn's *Wayward Youth. Standard Edition* 19.

—— (1933[1932]). New introductory lectures. *Standard Edition* 22.

GLOVER, E., AND BRIERLEY, M. (1940). An investigation of the technique of psychoanalysis. In E. Glover, *The Technique of Psychoanalysis.* New York: International Universities Press, 1968.

GREENSON, R. (1978). *Explorations in Psychoanalysis.* New York: International Universities Press.

GUNTRIP, H. (1964). *Personality Structure and Human Interaction.* New York: International Universities Press.

HOLLAND, R. (1978). *Self and Social Context.* New York: St. Martin's.

HOPKINS, G. M. (1876–1889). No worst, there is none. In *The Poems of Gerard Manley Hopkins,* 4th ed., ed. W. H. Gardiner and N. H. MacKenzie. New York: Oxford University Press, 1967.

JONES, E. (1955). *The Life and Works of Sigmund Freud,* Vol. 2: *Years of Maturity, 1901–1919.* New York: Basic Books.

KARDINER, A. (1977). *My Analysis with Freud: Reminiscences.* New York: Norton.

KAHN, M. M. R. (1970). On Freud's provision of the therapeutic frame. In M. M. R. Khan, *The Privacy of the Self.* New York: International Universities Press, 1974.

—— (1973). The obituary of Alix Strachey (1892–1973). *International Journal of Psycho-Analysis* 54:370.

—— (1981). Le combat. *Nouvelle Revue de Psychanalyse* 24.

LANGS, R. (1976). *The Therapeutic Interaction: A Synthesis.* New York: Jason Aronson.

LANGS, R., AND SEARLES, H. F. (1980). *Intrapsychic and Interpersonal Dimensions of Treatment: A Clinical Dialogue.* New York: Jason Aronson.

LANGS, R., AND STONE, L. (1980). *The Therapeutic Experience and Its Setting: A Clinical Dialogue.* New York: Jason Aronson.

LAPLANCHE, J., AND PONTALIS, J-B. (1967). *The Language of Psychoanalysis.* New York: Norton, 1974.

LITTLE, M. (1980). *Transference Neurosis and Transference Psychosis: Toward Basic Unity.* New York: Jason Aronson.

MAIN, D. F. (1957). The ailment. *British Journal of Medical Psychology* 30.

MENNINGER, K., AND HOLZMAN, P. S. (1958). *Theory of Psychoanalytic Technique.* 2nd ed. New York: Basic Books, 1973.

MILNER, M. (1969). *The Hands of the Living God: An Account of a Psychoanalytic Treatment.* New York: International Universities Press.

POUILLON, J. (1970). Doctor and patient: same and/or the other? Some ethnological remarks. In *Psychoanalytic Study of Society*, Vol. 5, ed. Werner Muensterberger, et al. New Haven, Conn.: Yale University Press, 1972.

REIK, T. (1942). *From Thirty Years with Freud*. Westport, Conn.: Greenwood, 1975.

SEARLES, H. (1979). *Countertransference and Related Subjects: Selected Papers*. New York: International Universities Press.

STONE, L. (1961). *The Psychoanalytic Situation: An Examination of Its Development and Essential Nature*. New York: International Universities Press.

WINNICOTT, W. (1971a). *Playing and Reality*. New York: Basic Books.

—— (1971b). *Therapeutic Consultations in Child Psychiatry*. New York: Basic Books.

CHAPTER 10

Technical Errors in Supervised Analyses

Theodore L. Dorpat, M.D.

This chapter reports a study of technical errors made by 16 candidates supervised by the author. Technical errors were classified into two groups, *interpretive errors* and *frame errors*. Frame errors are those technical mistakes of the analyst that either disrupt the psychoanalytic frame or prevent frame development. The types of frame errors are:

1. Failure of the analyst to maintain set fee, hours, and length of sessions
2. Breaks in confidentiality
3. Use of deviations
   a. Directives
   b. Advice
   c. Limit setting
   d. Reassurance
   e. Educative techniques
   f. Other interpersonal manipulations
4. Nonadherence to neutrality rules
   a. Rule of abstinence
   b. Rule of anonymity
   c. Rule of respecting patient's autonomy
5. Failure to provide a "holding environment" (e.g., excessive inactivity, detachment, and lack of affective communication)

Interpretive errors include inaccurate interpretations, untimely interpretations, and interpretations that bypass the patient's resistance.

The psychoanalytic literature, as Langs (1975b) indicated, has tended to treat the establishment and maintenance of the boundaries and ground rules of analysis—the frame—as separate from the therapeutic interaction. Except in the writings of Bleger (1967), Green (1975), Langs (1975a, 1976a, 1976b, 1979b), Milner (1952), Modell (1976), and a few others, there has been little recognition that the analyst's way of managing the analytic framework is as significant therapeutically as the analyst's interpretations.

SAMPLE AND METHODS

The present study is based primarily on my supervisory interviews with 16 candidates over the past nine years. Because 5 of the 16 candidates each had two control cases in supervision with me, the total number of supervised cases was 21. All the candidates initially were seen once a week. Less frequent supervision was carried out for several candidates, especially advanced candidates, after one or two years of once-a-week supervision.

In making the evaluations for this study, I reviewed my own files on each candidate and the records of the Seattle Psychoanalytic Institute. Information about the performance of the candidates also was gained through my membership over the past seven years on the institute's Candidate Progression Committee.

After reviewing this information, I judged whether the most serious technical errors made by each candidate in his or her supervised case were frame errors or interpretive errors. These judgments for each supervised case are listed as the "Technical Errors" in Table 1. For the purposes of this study, frame errors included only noninterpretive interventions. The distinction between frame errors and interpretive errors is admittedly an arbitrary one, because interpretive errors such as inaccurate or untimely interpretations may disrupt the psychoanalytic frame. A later section of this chapter discusses some comparisons of the frame errors and the interpretive errors made by this sample of candidates.

In each of the 21 control cases, an evaluation was made of whether analytic progress had occurred while the candidate was supervised (see Table 1). The criteria used for this determination included the attainment of insight, symptom relief, and evidence of structural changes. This was not an analytic outcome study, and no attempt was made to assess the final results of the control analyses. Supervision was ended in some cases before the control analysis had ended, because the candidate had either graduated or resigned from the institute.

Each of the 16 candidates was rated by the author as to his or her overall competence in or aptitude for conducting analysis. The two most important factors in this assessment were the candidate's ability to make accurate and timely interpretations and to develop and maintain a psychoanalytic frame. Although these judgments were made solely by me, they largely agree with the judgments made by the other three members of the institute's Progression Committee. The judgments were based on observations concerning the candidate's performance on the one or two control cases I supervised. Three classifications were used: the "good" classification covered the range from above average to superior, the "satisfactory" classification ranged from passable performance to reasonable competence, and the "unsatisfactory"

Table 10-1

CLASSIFICATION OF TECHNICAL ERRORS, EVALUATION OF ANALYTIC
PROGRESS, AND EVALUATION OF CANDIDATES IN 21
CONTROL ANALYSES

CANDIDATE	TECHNICAL ERRORS	ANALYTIC PROGRESS	EVALUATION OF CANDIDATE
1	Interpretive	Yes	Good
2	Interpretive	Yes	Good
3	Frame (case 1)	No	Satisfactory
	Interpretive (case 2)	Yes	
4	Frame	Yes	Satisfactory
5	Frame	No	Unsatisfactory
6	Frame	No	Unsatisfactory
7	Frame	No	Unsatisfactory
8	Frame (case 1)	No	Satisfactory
	Interpretive (case 2)	Yes	
9	Frame (case 1)	Yes	Satisfactory
	Interpretive (case 2)	Yes	
10	Interpretive	Yes	Satisfactory
11	Frame	Yes	Satisfactory
12	Frame	No	Unsatisfactory
13	Frame (case 1)	No	Unsatisfactory
	Frame (case 2)	No	
14	Frame (case 1)	No	Unsatisfactory
	Frame (case 2)	No	
15	Frame	Yes	Satisfactory
16	Frame	No	Unsatisfactory
Totals	Frame errors: 15	Yes: 10	Good: 2
	Interpretive errors: 6	No: 11	Satisfactory: 7
			Unsatisfactory: 7

grade was given to those candidates who performed poorly and who showed a persistent inability to do competent analytic work. Case vignettes in later sections of this chapter have been written in a way that conceals the identities of both the patients and the candidates. For example, all candidates are referred to as "he," when in fact four of them were women.

The data from this study strongly suggest that the most repetitive and damaging errors committed by candidates are frame errors. As indicated in

Table 1, the major technical errors in 15 of the control analyses were frame errors, and in 6 control analyses the major errors were interpretive errors. In 10 of the control cases, there was evidence of some analytic progress; in 11 cases no progress was evident. Ten of the 21 patients unilaterally and prematurely terminated their analyses before 18 months of treatment. Only 1 of the 10 cases that ended in premature termination demonstrated clinical evidence of analytic progress. Two candidates were rated good, seven were rated satisfactory, and seven were considered unsatisfactory.

RELATIONSHIP OF TYPE OF TECHNICAL ERROR TO ANALYTIC PROGRESS

Frame errors tended to have a more detrimental effect on analytic progress than did interpretive errors. In all of the 6 control cases in which the predominant errors were interpretive, analytic progress was evident. A different situation obtained in the cases in which the major errors were frame errors. In 11 of the 15 cases, there was no analytic progress. Thus, in all 11 of the cases in which there was no analytic progress, the errors were predominantly frame errors.

The first control case of each of the five candidates who had two cases in supervision with me ended in premature termination and was marked by a predominance of frame errors. (The label "first control case" refers to the first supervised case analyzed by the candidate during his or her psychoanalytic training.) Three of the five candidates were able to understand and correct their frame errors and did not repeat them in the second control cases I supervised. My experience with these three candidates and with other candidates seen over an extended period indicates that the candidates' inexperience partially accounted for the frame errors. Seven out of the eight *first* control cases in this study were marked by a predominance of frame errors.

There is a tendency among the candidates and the faculty of the institute to attribute analytic failure and premature termination of a control case to the "unanalyzability" or severe pathology of the analysand. My assessment of the 11 cases in which no analytic progress was made indicates that repeated frame errors made by the candidate were a more important cause of treatment failure in the majority of the cases than was the patient's psychopathology. In 8 of the 11 cases, the candidate's frame errors were, in my judgment, the most decisive factor in the lack of analytic progress. Previously undiagnosed borderline pathology played a major role in analytic failure in 3 of the 11 cases.

The failure of the candidate to develop and maintain a psychoanalytic frame in each of the 8 cases made it impossible to determine whether the analysis could have succeeded. The analytic method did not fail in these 8 cases. Rather, the analytic method was not used.

RELATIONSHIP OF TYPE OF TECHNICAL ERROR TO ANALYTIC COMPETENCE

The findings of this study strongly suggest that there is an inverse relationship between analytic competence and the prevalence of frame errors. The two candidates rated good did not commit many serious or repeated frame errors, whereas the seven candidates rated unsatisfactory made serious and continuing frame errors. The major technical errors committed by candidates rated unsatisfactory were frame errors. In the nine analyses I supervised with these seven candidates, the analysands received little or no therapeutic benefit, and all nine terminated prematurely. Five of the seven candidates have resigned from the institute, and it seems unlikely that the remaining two candidates will be able to complete their psychoanalytic training. Although these seven candidates also had serious difficulties in making accurate and timely interpretations, their frame errors were, in my judgment, a more decisive factor in their lack of analytic competence. Their extensive employment of unanalytic and antianalytic methods, their inability to maintain a neutral attitude, and their disruptive interventions prevented the establishment of a psychoanalytic frame and a psychoanalytic situation.

Frame errors predominated over interpretive errors in the seven candidates rated satisfactory. Six of their control analyses were characterized mainly by frame errors, and four by interpretive errors. In contrast to the candidates rated unsatisfactory, the candidates rated satisfactory were usually able to use their own analyses and their supervisory interviews to understand and correct their frame errors.

These findings and others reported later in this chapter warrant the following generalizations about the relationship between analytic competence in the candidates and the commission of frame errors. "Good" candidates were those candidates who had an aptitude for creating and maintaining a psychoanalytic frame. They were capable of fostering therapeutic progress through their adherence to the ground rules of analysis and their avoidance of antitherapeutic technical modifications and deviations. "Satisfactory" candidates initially had serious difficulties in frame management and made extensive use of non-neutral and noninterpretive interventions. With the assistance of their supervisors, they became capable, to varying degrees, of learning and effectively using the principles of frame management. "Unsatisfactory" candidates were not capable of establishing or maintaining a psychoanalytic frame. They frequently broke the ground rules of analysis, and they repeatedly used technical deviations. Their psychoanalytic training, including most notably their supervisory experiences, did not assist them in understanding or using the principles of frame management.

FRAME ERRORS AND PHASES OF ANALYSIS

Issues concerning the disruptions, development, and maintenance of the psychoanalytic frame were most prominent in the early phases of the control analyses. In nearly all the analyses, including those that progressed satisfactorily and were not terminated prematurely, there were serious problems in the development and management of the frame during roughly the first year of treatment. Disruptions in the frame were less frequent and less severe after an enduring therapeutic alliance had been established and after there had been some working through of the patient's central transference configurations. In the analyses that progressed reasonably well, the psychoanalytic frame issues gradually receded after about the first year of the analysis. In these analyses there was abundant clinical evidence that the analyst and analysand had firmly established a relatively stable and secure frame.

The relative diminution of frame disruptions and problems in the middle and late stages of the analyses does not mean that the frame became unimportant. Quite the contrary; the analysand's sense of safety, his or her capacity for a controlled regression, and the therapeutic ambience of the analytic situation are founded on the maintenance of the psychoanalytic frame throughout the analysis (Dorpat 1978, Langs 1976b). The frame deserves equal stature with interpretation as a criterion for assessing the therapeutic aspects of psychoanalytic treatment (Langs 1976b, 1980).

TYPES OF FRAME ERRORS

The different types of frame errors will be discussed and illustrated with case vignettes in the following sections. The frame errors outlined on page 195 are mistakes most authorities consider unacceptable deviations and modifications of psychoanalytic technique. Current concepts about what constitutes acceptable psychoanalytic technique have not changed significantly since Freud (1912a, 1912b, 1913, 1914, 1915) in his basic papers on technique first described the fundamental principles and rules regarding the psychoanalytic method.

Breaks in the Boundaries of the Frame

Some candidates seemed oblivious to the overriding importance of monitoring and safeguarding the boundaries of the psychoanalytic frame.

A candidate was frequently late for his first interview at 7:30 A.M. When the patient protested, the candidate interpreted the transference aspects of her mounting frustration and anger. At no time did his interventions indicate to her some recognition of the reality aspects of her complaints about him and his lateness. His continued tardiness and his exclusive focusing on the transference aspects of the patient's anger led to the eventual collapse of the analysis.

Another candidate had recurring problems in his control cases about fees and appointment times.

In a consultation hour preceding the analysis, a fee was established. Later, after the analysis had started, the candidate increased the fee without discussing the issue with the patient. When he announced the fee increase, he implied that the increase would be retroactive for several previous sessions. The candidate's arbitrary and unilateral action aroused confusion and mistrust in the analysand. Explanations by the supervisor helped the candidate understand his mistake and its effects on the analysis. In the next two weeks of analysis, the candidate was able to rectify his mistake and to restore a therapeutic frame. He implicitly acknowledged that his arbitrary and unilateral action had caused the patient to feel mistrustful of him. He rescinded the fee increase, and later, when the frame was made secure, he negotiated with the patient a new contract concerning fees.

In this and most other instances of frame errors, the candidate was unaware not only that he had committed a frame error but also that the patient's reactions, such as mistrust, clearly demonstrated the adverse effects of the frame disruption on the analysand and the analytic process. My supervisory strategy concerning frame errors has been to point out the errors and to enlist the candidate's collaboration in evaluating the analysand's responses to it. As Langs (1979a) recommends, supervisees are encouraged to use the validating process to confirm, disconfirm, or modify formulations made by the supervisor. Through the validating process some candidates have learned to use the patient's responses to the candidate's interventions to identify frame errors that otherwise would remain undetected.

Infractions of the confidentiality rule were rare in this sample. All the candidates were in private practice. Reports by Langs (1979a, 1979b) strongly suggest that breakdowns in the confidentiality rule are both serious and frequent among psychotherapists who work in clinic settings.

Nonadherence to the Rules of Neutrality

Abstinence. The rules of abstinence and anonymity and the analyst's respect for the patient's autonomy are the principal distinctly psychoanalytic meanings of neutrality (Dorpat 1977). The rule of abstinence applies to both extra-analytic gratifications and the gratifications of the patient's transference wishes. Extra-analytic gratifications, which extend beyond the boundaries of the analyst–analysand relationship, are detrimental to the psychoanalytic frame and to the patient's strivings for constructive change.

Freud (1919) indicated that the abstinence rule referred not simply to sexual abstinence but to the denial of transference gratification generally.

Adherence to the rule of abstinence is required to preserve the psychoanalytic frame and to permit the interpretation and mastery of transferences, as illustrated in the following vignette.

A depressed woman unconsciously had transferred on to the analyst the image of her controlling father. One day she grew silent and embarrassed when she became aware of her dependent wishes for the analyst. In a demanding tone of voice, the candidate said, "Why aren't you sharing your thoughts with me?" Disturbed by the analyst's question, the patient talked of leaving the hour, and she said that she felt as if she were being "pushed." The candidate believed that the patient's feeling of being pushed was an expression of her intolerant superego.

After reviewing this incident and other similar interactions involving the candidate's use of questions, the supervisor was able to demonstrate to the candidate that the patient felt pushed because the candidate was indeed pushing her by his demanding mode of questioning. The candidate then could begin to recognize that he was acting out the transference role of the controlling father. His use of "pushing" questions threatened the patient's sense of autonomy, because it occurred in the service of his unconscious need to control and direct the patient.

Anonymity. Freud considered anonymity necessary to the analyst's interventions if the patient is to resolve the transference. "The doctor should be opaque to his patients and, like a mirror, should show them nothing but what is shown to him" (1912b, p. 118). The anonymity rule should not be interpreted to mean that the analyst should be cold, aloof, or indifferent. It does mean that the analyst should not intrude his private life, values, or needs onto the patient. Neutral technique precludes, except in emergencies, any directives, prohibitions, or injunctions.

The use of explicit or implicit directives was one of the most common frame errors committed by the candidates. Directives and limit setting tend to disrupt the psychoanalytic frame and to prevent the emergence and working through of transferences. Both unfortunate consequences occurred in the analysis of a young professional man.

The analysand had a long history of alternating periods of compliance and rebellion toward authority figures, who unconsciously represented his authoritarian father. In the 20th week of his analysis, he spoke of his plan to seek marital therapy for his wife and himself from another therapist. The candidate abruptly forbade the patient to go to a marital therapist, and he interpreted the patient's wish to see another therapist as a defensive need to displace his feelings for the analyst onto someone else. The patient compliantly agreed, and in the following analytic hour he reported a dream in which he was sitting in the front seat of an automobile driven by the analyst. His associations to the dream indicated that the dream image of the analyst driving the car represented his partially realistic fear of being controlled by the analyst. Sitting together in the car symbolized the patient's need for reassuring closeness to defend against his unconscious anger over being controlled by the analyst's directive.

In this interaction, the candidate's limit setting disrupts the psychoanalytic frame and provokes the patient's regression from a therapeutic alliance with the analyst to an attitude of stultifying compliance. A further harmful consequence is that the patient's fearful compliant relation with his father is being repeated rather than remembered and mastered.

Directives and other antianalytic interventions seriously jeopardized the analysis of a young architect.

A fifth weekly hour was added in such a manner that the patient had a feeling (partly realistic) that he had been induced to do something that was not of his own doing. The patient's concerns about this issue were not taken up, interpreted, or resolved. In an obvious show of growing rebellion and independence, the patient decided to take a trip out of town on a Wednesday after his analytic hour. The candidate, in a battle of wills, argued with the patient and insisted that the patient attend his Thursday hour. When the patient returned to his analysis the following week, he was sullen and consciously resistive. Attendance at analytic hours became even more unpredictable than before, and the analysis foundered, largely because the candidate had attempted to direct and manipulate the patient's behavior.

In this instance, the candidate unconsciously reenacts with the patient the patient's childhood struggle with a harsh and untrustworthy mother. By this reenactment, both the transference and nontransference aspects of the patient's transactions with the analyst regarding attendance at the Thursday and Friday hours are made indistinct and noninterpretable.

Failure to Provide a "Holding Environment"

The frame should not be considered simply a set of technical rules and prohibitions. Langs (1976b) considered the frame to be "the fundamental hold through which the analyst provides the patient with the security, trust, stability, tolerance, support, and safeguards he needs both to garner the basic ego strength required for analytic work and to reveal his conscious and unconscious pathological impulses, introjects, and fantasies" (p. 506). In his study of the treatment of narcissistic character disorder, Modell (1976) adopted Winnicott's concept of the *holding environment* (1956) as a metaphor for certain aspects of the analytic situation.

The holding functions of the analytic situation and the analyst–analysand relationship provide the patient with a background of safety and protection. They depend on a bond of affective communication between the analyst and analysand and on the analyst's adherence to the neutral interpretive role. Modell emphasized that the holding function is based on the analyst's

customary activities and the analytic functions of observation and interpretation.

One candidate's failure to provide a holding environment led to the
premature termination of the analysis of a depressed businessman.

During most of the analytic hours, the overly cautious and restrained candidate said
nothing, and his infrequent interventions failed to create a bond of affective communication with the troubled patient. When the emotional atmosphere of the interviews grew increasingly distant and formal, the patient grew more withdrawn and
abruptly stopped the analysis two months after it started.

Here, the candidate's detached attitude does not meet the patient's reasonable and
realistic needs for a sense of the analyst's presence and concern. His lack of empathic
contact with the patient and the excessively formal and austere ambience of the
analytic hours cut short the development of a viable therapeutic alliance and contribute to the premature termination.

When the supervisor confronted the candidate with his aloof attitude and inactivity, the candidate rationalized his behavior as being neutral. He had confused
psychoanalytic neutrality with inactivity and emotional detachment.

Educative Interventions

Attempts to guide or educate the patient are contrary to both the goals
and the methods of psychoanalysis. Freud (1912b) argued against both
"educative ambition" and "therapeutic ambition" in the analyst. The use of
educative interventions was a common frame error in the analyses conducted
by these candidates.

A young patient who was struggling with conflicts over dependence on her mother
told of a recent automobile accident in which the speeding driver of her car narrowly
missed driving off a mountain road. When she arrived home after the accident, her
mother scolded her and warned her against driving on mountain roads. The candidate
told the patient that she was incorrectly perceiving the situation in black-and-white
terms and that she should consider other possibilities open to her besides driving reck-
lessly or not driving at all. The candidate went on in a lecturing manner to describe
other options open to the patient, such as driving carefully on mountain roads. The
patient became disturbed, missed several sessions, and later returned in a troubled state.

In this interaction, the candidate's educative intervention and slightly reproachful
tone replicate the scolding given by the mother. This intervention threatens the
patient's striving toward independence from her mother and disrupts the therapeutic
alliance.

FRAME ERRORS AND UNCONSCIOUS
ANALYST–ANALYSAND INTERACTIONS

The candidates' frame errors most often were products of unconscious
analyst–analysand interactions in which introjection and projection by both
parties contributed to the error. Some of the foregoing vignettes show how

candidates unconsciously acted out transference roles and attitudes attributed to them by their patients. The candidates' serious and repetitive frame errors appeared to occur more often in the analyses of the more disturbed patients, who tended to provoke countertransference-based modifications and deviations from accepted technique. The relationship of the analyst's frame errors to both the degree and the quality of the patient's psychopathology requires further clinical investigation.

The next vignette demonstrates a common kind of frame error made by candidates in the analyses of patients who make extensive use of projective identification.

A young woman's major unconscious resistance was one of hiding herself both from herself and from others by avoiding direct verbal communication of her thoughts and feelings. Her major communicative mode was the Type B mode described by Langs (1978). Through projective identification the patient evoked feelings of frustration, anger, and confusion in the candidate. The patient's major defensive operations included silence and vagueness. Hinting and making veiled allusions substituted for explicit statement. Unconsciously the patient feared that the analyst would intrude upon her and control her, as her mother had done so often. Her pathological communicative behaviors defended against intrusion and at the same time tended to provoke the intrusion of others. She unconsciously instigated a kind of hide-and-seek game in which she provoked the analyst to make queries, to intrude, and to give interpretations based on fragmentary and disguised communications. In one session some of the patient's associations to a dream seemed to touch in a fragmentary way on themes of childbirth and some kind of surgical operation. The candidate hypothesized that the patient's dream stemmed from memories of an abortion, so he asked, "Have you ever had an abortion?" The patient was silent for a moment and then tersely replied, "No." She felt angry and humiliated by the tactless question, and her resistances of vagueness and silence became more intense.

By his rude and disruptive question, the candidate here unconsciously acts out the role of the patient's intrusive mother. My discussion with the candidate revealed that his question was motivated by his defensive need to deal with the frustration and confusion engendered in him by the patient's projective identification. The candidate's frame error resided in his acting out what was projected onto him rather than using his feelings of confusion and frustration to understand his unconscious interaction with the patient.

The candidate in this instance should have focused his attention upon either the transference or the resistance aspects of the patient's pathological mode of communication. The significance of what was occurring in the analysis resided in the unconscious analyst–analysand interactions, particularly the patient's unconscious wishes to evoke confusion and frustration in the analyst. The relevant meaning of Type B communications resides in *how* the patient communicates much more than *what* is expressed in words.

COMPARISONS OF INTERPRETIVE AND
FRAME ERRORS

Because a systematic study of the candidate's interpretive errors is beyond the scope of this chapter, my aims here are to indicate the relative frequency of the major types of interpretive errors and to make some general comparisons of the effects of these errors and the effects of frame errors. The most common interpretive error was the bypassing of resistances; the second most frequent was inaccurate or erroneous interpretation.

The "bypassing of resistances" refers to the analyst's premature interpretation of some unconscious content before the patient has worked through the defenses, painful affects, and other resistances against the awareness of the content. Bypassing resistances usually has the antitherapeutic effects of evoking more intense resistance and of preventing, at least temporarily, the analysand's attainment of insight.

Although bypassing resistances was the most common error committed by candidates, it was not, in my opinion, the most serious or damaging error. Candidates frequently were able to detect and correct this error themselves, or they were able to understand and constructively use supervisory assistance in correcting and avoiding this type of mistake. My review of the 21 control cases revealed only 3 cases in which there were long-lasting and harmful consequences of bypassing resistances and no instances of the analysis failing principally from this type of mistake.

My conclusions about the long-term effects of other kinds of interpretive errors are similar to those concerning bypassing resistances. In comparison with frame errors, interpretive errors, generally speaking, had far less damaging effects on the progress or outcome of the analysis. The majority of candidates usually were aware of their interpretive errors, and they manifested less resistance to understanding these mistakes than they did to understanding their frame errors. In contrast, most candidates initially were unaware of their frame errors and of the effects of these errors on the analytic process. Some had formidable and, in at least five candidates, intractable resistances to understanding their role in the commission of frame errors and in preventing their occurrence.

Compared with frame errors, interpretive errors were for the most part isolated or encapsulated occurrences. Candidates, with or without the help of the supervisor, usually were able to avoid repeating mistakes in what to interpret and when to interpret. The most destructive effects of frame errors came about principally because frame errors usually were unacknowledged, unrectified, and repeated. Reading the vignettes in this chapter may give the mistaken impression that frame errors were isolated or exceptional occurrences. In fact, frame errors tended to be repetitive, and those analyses that did not progress evidenced a fairly consistently disrupted and pathological frame. (For a discussion of the antitherapeutic effects of modifying the frame by deviations from accepted technique, see Langs [1979b, 1980]).

As noted earlier, interpretive errors, as well as frame errors, can cause disruptions in the therapeutic process and alterations in the psychoanalytic frame. One of the major points of this chapter is that frame errors bring about more serious and long-lasting derailments of treatment than do interpretive errors. These conclusions about the relative power of frame errors and interpretive errors to disrupt treatment are in accord with those of Langs (1980), who classified three types of framework deviations in ascending order of their power to disrupt therapy. He termed erroneous interpretations *Grade One* deviations, noninterpretive and non-neutral interventions *Grade Two*, and alterations in the fixed frame *Grade Three*. Within noninterpretive and non-neutral interventions, he included directives, personal opinions, direct reassurances, and the like. "Alterations in the fixed frame" are changes in the ground rules. Langs's classification of Grade One deviations is akin to the category I have called interpretive errors, and his Grade Two and Grade Three groupings correspond to the frame errors in my categorization.

CAUSES OF FRAME ERRORS

Unconscious countertransference problems and conflicts accounted for most, if not all, of the frame errors and for the candidate's unawareness of their mistakes and their consequences. The previous case vignettes and the case vignettes in the writings of Langs clearly demonstrate the overriding significance of countertransference in the genesis of frame errors. Langs (1976b, 1979b) has argued convincingly that modifications in the psychoanalytic frame that are not clearly indicated by the patient's therapeutic needs reflect the analyst's countertransference problems.

We have examined frame errors and frame disruptions through an interactional perspective, taking into account the role of conscious and unconscious communications of both the analyst and the analysand. One can also examine frame errors from the point of view of the therapist's individual psychopathology. There was a strong tendency for nearly all the candidates to repeat the same type or pattern of frame errors with different patients. It seemed that their most serious conflicts and character defects were acted out in their repetitive frame errors.

One candidate early in training did not recognize how often, with different psychoanalytic and psychotherapy patients, he had disrupted the psychoanalytic frame and undermined the therapeutic efficiency of his interventions by delivering them in an authoritarian and imperious tone of voice. His supervisor's tactful but persistent attention to this problem helped him first to attend to and later to understand and inhibit such disturbing communications. A seductive candidate brought about stalemated analyses in several women patients who developed pathological eroticized transferences. An arrogant candidate had three patients who became moderately depressed during their analyses, in part because of the candidate's denigrating interventions.

Another candidate in three control cases (two of which I supervised) was unaware of how frequently he became involved in power struggles with his patients. He typically engaged in destructive interpersonal conflicts with them in which the crucial issues concerned which of the two contestants would control the payment of the fee, the appointment times, and how and when the patient would talk. Despite the efforts of several supervisors to assist him in understanding and preventing these power struggles, the candidate continued to be unaware of their importance or their destructive consequences.

Some supervisees recognized that they were introducing technical modifications, but they mistakenly believed that the modifications could be justified as necessary to the formation of a therapeutic alliance. They claimed that deviations such as supportive comments and educative interventions were needed to attain an affective bond with the patient. Others argued that the use of technical deviations and modifications was required for the analysis of difficult cases. One candidate rationalized that his antianalytic methods were needed to create a therapeutic alliance, and he believed that his patients could be educated, guided, and directed into forming a therapeutic alliance. Actually, his nonanalytic and antianalytic interventions played a major role in disrupting and ultimately destroying the psychoanalytic frame in at least two cases. Deviations used by the candidates never produced discernible therapeutic progress, and in the overwhelming majority of instances, they had untoward effects.

Many candidates in this sample who held that deviations were needed to establish a therapeutic alliance used the writings and opinions of other analysts to support their position. This fallacy is so widespread among both psychoanalytic and psychiatric groups that one could call it a kind of collective or group countertransference. Thus, among the several roots of frame errors, one should also include the pervasive effects of group countertransferences, irrational and unfounded ideas shared by groups of mental health professionals.

A crucially important variable that this study did not examine is the influence of candidates' training analyses on their capacities for therapeutic management of the frame. Perhaps four or five candidates in the present study showed some indirect evidence that their training analyses had helped them significantly in mastering certain initial problems in maintaining or developing a psychoanalytic frame. And in a few instances I gained the impression that the candidates were repeating with their control cases the same kinds of frame errors that they were subjected to in their own training analyses.

SUPERVISION AND FRAME MANAGEMENT

This review of supervised analytic cases and my experience as a psychotherapy supervisor lead me to conclude that supervision can provide far-reaching assistance to some, but not all, candidates and therapists in recognizing, rectifying, and preventing frame errors.

My supervisory efforts to help the seven candidates rated unsatisfactory to manage the frame were mainly ineffective. The two candidates in this study who were considered good did not often make repeated or serious frame errors, and they required comparatively little supervisory assistance in learning and using the principles of frame management. With them, the major focus of supervision was not on frame issues but on understanding and interpreting the patients' resistances and transferences.

Observations made on the remaining group, the seven "satisfactory" candidates, demonstrated that supervision unquestionably helped them to learn effective methods for frame management. All seven initially had serious problems in recognizing and mastering frame errors. After at least one year of once-a-week supervision, all members of the group had made marked progress in learning the principles and techniques necessary for frame management. Their supervision thereafter became more like that of the superior candidates: more attention could be directed toward the so-called intrapsychic resistances and transferences of the patient.

In the first three years of my analytic supervisory experience, I was not aware of either the frequency or the seriousness of frame errors in my own analytic practice and in the work of other analysts and candidates. My initial bias was that errors in interpretive technique were the most common cause of premature terminations and analytic failure.

Both my attitude and my supervisory technique changed through my studies of psychoanalytic neutrality (Dorpat 1977) and the writings of Langs (1976a, 1976b, 1979a, 1979b). When I reviewed the records of the first four candidates I had supervised, I was chagrined to find that I had missed many opportunities for assisting them in developing competence in forming and maintaining a psychoanalytic frame. Perhaps the premature terminations and unsatisfactory results of some of their control cases could have been avoided had I more actively assisted the supervisees in identifying and rectifying frame errors. As Langs (1979a) has argued, ineffective or defective supervision tends to foster frame errors in the supervisee.

My current more extensive experience as a psychotherapy supervisor supports the conclusions implied and stated here about the role of supervision in frame management. Competent supervision seems a training method that is necessary if candidates and psychotherapists are to develop the skills required for the formation and maintenance of the frame.

EFFECTS OF PSYCHIATRIC AND PSYCHOANALYTIC TRAINING

Other factors implicated in the genesis of frame errors are the effects of the candidates' prior psychiatric and psychoanalytic training. Langs (1979b) held that there is always an element of countertransference in any mismanagement of the frame. Although I concur that countertransference is the most important factor, my review of supervised cases indicates that inexperience and lack of adequate training and supervision are also significant reasons for the frequent frame errors made by these candidates and, I think, other psychotherapists and psychoanalysts as well. The candidates' greater awareness of the therapeutic import of the frame and the detrimental consequences of deviation would have prevented frame errors in many instances. Some candidates could have inhibited countertransference-based impulses to use deviations and technical modifications had they been better informed about the fundamental principles of psychoanalytic neutrality and the psychoanalytic frame. Three candidates, for example, were unaware that their use of educative methods was a departure from accepted technique. After I demonstrated from their own case material the antitherapeutic effects of their educative methods, they stopped using them.

A vignette from an institute continuous case seminar illustrates how rarely candidates consider the role of frame errors in bringing about derailments of the analytic process. In the seminar the candidate, using process notes, presented case material of a depressed patient over a three-week period to seven other candidates and an instructor.

On the day of a snowstorm, the patient arrived late at the candidate's office. She waited for ten minutes in his waiting room, and when he did not appear, she left. During the next day's analytic hour, she told the candidate what had happened on the previous day. He said nothing about the incident to her. Thereafter she became more depressed and withdrawn. In the following three weeks of the analysis, her associations made frequent indirect and unconscious reference to the day when the analyst failed to see her. Her dreams were obvious, painful replications of the episode. She dreamed, for example, of being in an empty room waiting for someone. Other dreams and symptoms manifested the prevailing theme of feeling left out and rejected.

None of the eight candidates in the seminar were aware that the major meaning of what was taking place in the three-week period was the patient's unconscious reactions and communications about the frame disruption caused by the analyst's unexpected absence. When this meaning was pointed out by the instructor, all eight candidates readily could interpret the patient's dreams, associations, and symptoms in terms of her unconscious reactions to the analyst's error. Previously they had viewed all the patient's behaviors solely as manifestations of transference and resistance, and they had not even considered the possibility that the patient might be responding to actual events in the analytic relationship. It is clear that candidates have not been trained in the principles of the psychoanalytic frame and of the conscious and unconscious interactions between the analyst and analysand.

Neither the psychiatric nor the psychoanalytic training of any of the 16 candidates in the present study had provided the necessary knowledge about the fundamental concepts concerning frame management. Institute didactic and clinical seminars give scant attention to the technical principles of psychoanalytic neutrality and the frame. In the past 15 years, the majority of candidates have entered psychoanalytic candidacy with major deficiencies in their training in psychodynamics and psychoanalytic psychotherapy. According to the COPER report, there has been a general decline in psychoanalytic instruction in most psychiatric residencies in the past 10 or 15 years (Goodman 1980).

A surprisingly large number of psychiatric residents and candidates have the mistaken notion that therapists and analysts may combine psychoanalytic methods with the methods of psychiatric management in their psychoanalytic psychotherapy or psychoanalysis of patients. These psychiatric management methods include educative techniques, limit setting, reassurance, advice, moral directives, and various kinds of interpersonal manipulations. All of these psychiatric management techniques are antithetical to the goals and methods of psychoanalytic therapy, and their use in psychoanalysis or psychoanalytic psychotherapy impairs or even destroys the psychoanalytic frame.

SUMMARY

The findings of this study of 21 supervised control cases indicate that the major cause of analytic failure is the errors made by the candidates in developing and maintaining a psychoanalytic frame. The major technical errors committed in 15 analyses were frame errors; in only 6 analyses were the predominant errors mistakes of interpretation. Frame errors occurred much more frequently in the inexperienced and incompetent candidates than they did in the more experienced and competent candidates. Frame errors predominated over interpretive errors in the analyses in which there was no analytic progress. Candidates tended to be less aware of their frame errors than of their interpretive errors, and they had stronger resistances to understanding them. The present chapter defined and discussed different types of frame errors and illustrated them with clinical vignettes.

An important and frequent determinant of frame errors was the candidates' unconscious introjection and acting out of the role transferred onto them by the patient. The major cause of frame errors was the unresolved countertransferences of the candidates. Together with countertransference problems, deficiencies in the candidates' prior psychiatric and psychoanalytic training accounted for the prevalence of frame errors. Supervision helped many of the candidates to acquire the skills required for forming and maintaining a therapeutic frame. The lack of attention given to the conceptual and technical issues regarding the frame in psychiatric and psychoanalytic training programs partly accounts for the disturbing prevalence of frame errors in this sample.

REFERENCES

BLEGER, J. (1967). Psycho-analysis of the psycho-analytic frame. *International Journal of Psycho-Analysis* 48:511–519.

GOODMAN, S. (1980). *Psychoanalytic Education and Research.* New York: International Universities Press.

DORPAT, T. L. (1977). On neutrality. *International Journal of Psychoanalytic Psychotherapy* 6:39–64.

——— (1978). Introjection and the idealizing transference. *International Journal of Psychoanalytic Psychotherapy* 7:21–53.

FREUD, S. (1912a). The dynamics of transference. *Standard Edition* 12.

——— (1912b). Recommendations to physicians practising psycho-analysis. *Standard Edition* 12.

——— (1913). On beginning the treatment. *Standard Edition* 12.

——— (1914). Rembering, repeating and working-through. *Standard Edition* 12.

——— (1915). Observations on transference-love. *Standard Edition* 12.

——— (1919). Lines of advance in psycho-analytic therapy. *Standard Edition* 17.

GREEN, A. (1975). The analyst, symbolization and absence in the analytic setting (on changes in analytic practice and analytic experience). *International Journal of Psycho-Analysis* 56:1–22.

LANGS, R. (1975a). Therapeutic misalliances. *International Journal of Psychoanalytic Psychotherapy* 4:77–105.

——— (1975b). The therapeutic relationship and deviations in technique. *International Journal of Psychoanalytic Psychotherapy* 4:106–141.

——— (1976a). *The Bipersonal Field.* New York: Jason Aronson.

———— (1976b). *The Therapeutic Interaction,* Vol. 2: *A Critical Overview and Synthesis.* New York: Jason Aronson.

———— (1978). *Technique in Transition.* New York: Jason Aronson.

———— (1979a). *The Supervisory Experience.* New York: Jason Aronson.

———— (1979b). *The Therapeutic Environment.* New York: Jason Aronson.

———— (1980). *Interactions: The Realm of Transference and Countertransference.* New York: Jason Aronson.

MILNER, M. (1952). Aspects of symbolism in comprehension of the not-self. *International Journal of Psycho-Analysis* 33:181–195.

MODELL, A. H. (1976). "The holding environment" and the therapeutic action of psychoanalysis. *Journal of the American Psychoanalytic Association* 24:285–308.

WINNICOTT, D. W. (1956). Symposium. On transference. *International Journal of Psycho-Analysis* 37:386–388.

CHAPTER 11

Framework Violations in Psychotherapy with Clinic Patients

Lorna Gale Cheifetz, Psy.D.

Mental health clinics created primarily to treat patients of lower socio-economic status often struggle with pervasive problems. Patients often fail to appear for appointments or arrive late or at nonscheduled times. Few remain in psychotherapy for more than a few months. This patient population frequently has been considered unmotivated and unlikely to respond favorably to analytic psychotherapy.

Robert Langs (1979b) suggests that a secure therapeutic setting has a central and significant impact on the patient's motivation for treatment. He defines a secure setting as requiring stable ground rules. These include privacy, a set fee, a set time and length for all sessions, total confidentiality, and therapist anonymity and neutrality. Mental health clinics rarely provide such an environment. They often offer free services with limited privacy and confidentiality; neutrality is often discouraged.

The clinic patient's motivation and receptivity for psychotherapy may be more a response to the therapeutic setting than a function of race or socioeconomic status.

The cases examined for this study were drawn from a number of outpatient mental health clinics. None of the clinics provides what Langs (1979b) describes as a secure therapeutic setting. Charts characteristically are kept in open files in the reception area. Clerical workers often have open charts on their desks while receiving incoming patients. New patients are seen by one or more interviewers, who must complete specific intake forms. Interviews are conducted in a variety of rooms, none with soundproofing and some with only partitions between them. It is not uncommon for interviews to be interrupted by other staff members transferring phone calls or relaying information that may or may not be related to the case. Patients frequently are referred to psychiatrists to be evaluated for medication. They are later notified of their assignment to a staff member for group, family, or individual psychotherapy, diagnostic testing, and/or medication. Usually

---

This chapter is dedicated to the memory of Irene Josselyn.

patients are told that such decisions are reached during staff meetings in which individual cases are discussed.

A significant number of patients do not return after case assignment. Once assigned an individual therapist, the patient usually is seen in a room like those described. In some instances, especially with student therapists, the room changes from week to week. Therapy sessions often are taped. These procedures are considered by administrators and many staff members to be the most expedient means of organizing such clinics, a belief based on a medical model of mental illness as a disease entity. Treatment is often goal directed, focusing on alleviation of physical symptomatology of emotional disorders.

Langs (1975c, 1976a, 1976b, 1978a, 1978b, 1980, 1980a, 1980b, 1981) questions the viability of treatment in settings such as the one described, settings with what he calls pervasive "framework modifications." The ideal therapeutic frame is composed of ground rules that include: (1) total confidentiality; (2) privacy; (3) predictability and consistency, manifested in a set fee, location, time, and length for all sessions; (4) therapist neutrality; and (5) therapist anonymity. By adhering to these rules, the therapist creates a safe "hold" or "container" for the patient's psychopathology and its exploration and resolution.

The study described in this chapter sought to examine how violations of the ground rules may contribute to the low return rates and lack of therapeutic success with lower-class clinic patients. Patients of lower socioeconomic status referred to in this study are from classes IV and V as defined by Hollingshead and Redlich (1958). In class IV the head of the family may not have finished high school and is likely to be employed as a semiskilled factory worker. In class V the family head is usually not educated beyond the elementary level and, if employed, works as an unskilled factory hand or laborer.

This study of framework violations and their impact in a clinic setting is based on an analysis of clinical vignettes. The technique used to evaluate and analyze clinical material involves explicit patient commentaries following the therapist's efforts to create a more secure therapeutic setting. We first will review the relevant literature.

PSYCHOANALYTIC LITERATURE PERTAINING TO THE FRAME

Freud first described the framework and ground rules of psychoanalysis in 1912. Although he acknowledged the difficulties the therapist faces in maintaining neutrality and holding to the rule of abstinence, he stressed that violations of these ground rules make the patient less able to overcome deeper resistances and at times stimulate the patient to try to reverse the situation and analyze the analyst. He suggested that the analyst maintain evenly suspended attention, that self-revelations can serve as suggestions and are not helpful in uncovering the unconscious motivations of the patient. In his 1913 discussion of fees, Freud advised against free treatment, in part because the patient's subsequent obligation to feel grateful would mobilize resistances in the patient.

Freud (1919) was the first of numerous highly esteemed and reputable analysts and psychotherapists (Alexander 1954, Berman 1949, Eissler 1953, Ferenczi 1921, Frank 1956, Freeman 1966, A. Freud 1954, Glover 1955, Greenson 1965, Jacobson 1954, LaForgue 1929, Stern 1948, Stone 1954) to recommend modifications in his own basic tenets. He prophesied that free clinics would someday be built to provide psychotherapy for the poor. "The task will then arise for us to adapt our technique to new conditions. . . . It is very probable, too, that the application of our therapy to numbers will compel us to alloy the pure gold of analysis plentifully with the copper of direct suggestion" (1919, p. 190).

Since Freud's original discussions of ground rules and their deviations, there has been intermittent but relatively consistent debate concerning the significance of these factors. Hans Strupp (1978) considers the deprivations inherent in a secure frame unnecessary and responsible for undue suffering of the analysand. He points out that patients usually enter therapy to reduce their suffering and the therapist is placed in a parental role, setting limits and controls to help their children/patients become independent adults. He advocates so-called benevolent behaviors to protect the patient from such undue suffering.

These conclusions appear to be based on manifest content listening. There is no apparent effort to ascertain through an investigation of unconscious derivative communications the meanings of patient communications based on specific adaptive contexts. Thus, the patient's unconscious perception of such deviations as Strupp advocates, however sensible these measures may appear on the surface, has not been fully and psychoanalytically explored and should remain open to explicit study. The propensity to dismiss such modifications as irrelevant or to avoid a thorough exploration of their implications may stem from the therapist's difficulty in maintaining the framework and in accepting the frustration it entails. Psychotherapists have invoked deviations in technique for countless reasons: to foster the therapeutic alliance, to modify various types of stalemates, to support the patient, to express the psychotherapist's human qualities, and to ensure financial support for the therapist or institution (thereby justifying the completion of insurance forms or charts that modify the confidentiality of the therapeutic situation). Repeatedly, we are given virtually no basis on which to decide whether a suggested modification actually derives from the needs of the patient or from the countertransference difficulties of the therapist. Flexibility, especially in a clinic setting, has become a watchword but does not appear to be based on in-depth examination and validation. Implicit in this attitude is a devaluation of the positive potential contained within the basic ground rules.

One of the first psychoanalysts to demonstrate the influence of the therapist's management of the frame on the patient's conflicts and fantasies was D. W. Winnicott (1954, 1956, 1958, 1960, 1963). He also first acknowledged the inherent therapeutic qualities of the frame and its positive potential for the patient. He suggested that through the patient's experience of the therapist's "hold," via the management of the setting, the patient becomes secure enough to permit the type of dependence in which he or she feels sufficiently safe to regress and to reveal hidden portions of the self. Mismanagement of the ground rules can, according to Winnicott, create periods of stalemate and resistance that cannot be analyzed until the deviation has been rectified.

He suggested as well that resistances have an important interactional component beyond their intrapsychic basis and that they can stem from difficulties in the therapist's management of the setting. The implication is that resolution of certain resistances relies not primarily on an analysis of the patient's intrapsychic conflicts (although they play a role) but on the therapist's ability to recognize his or her own difficulty in managing the frame and to correct it, using the patient's reactions for therapeutic analysis and resolution.

Modell (1976) extended Winnicott's concepts. "Holding" elements are viewed as providing the patient with a sense of restraint and a background of safety and protection. Holding elements stem from the therapist's basic functioning and from a bond of effective communication between patient and therapist.

Milner (1952), Bleger (1967), and Viderman (1974) consider the frame to be a means of creating a viable therapeutic situation, an analyzable interaction and a relationship with the special qualities that permit the unfolding of an analyzable transference syndrome. Any modifications in the frame and its special rules impair the analyzability of the patient's transference distortions by enacting rather than observing and analyzing them. Such disturbances of the frame alter the characteristics that distinguish the therapeutic situation from other relationships and lead to a variety of disruptive consequences. Thus, modifications of the setting are said to influence the nature of the patient's communications.

Haak (1957) explored the countertransference attitudes that he viewed as attempts to bribe or appease the patient, thus avoiding the patient's aggression, and to express the therapist's unanalyzed need to be "human." Specifically, Haak noted these needs as they pertain to fees. He suggested that fees serve to counteract the patient's guilt for aggressive feelings toward the therapist. They help to prevent the analyst from acting out countertransference difficulties and simultaneously compensate the analyst for the suffering to which he or she is exposed.

Tarachow (1962a, 1962b) extended Haak's findings in his discussion of the mutual need of the patient and therapist to experience the other as human. He believed it to be the therapist's task to impose a therapeutic barrier through nonparticipation and interpretation. Only by maintaining neutrality can the therapist free the patient to assign the therapist unconsciously to any role. Arlow and Brenner (1966) make the point that acting out in a "humane fashion" rather than interpreting often both stimulates and obscures transference reactions. Rangell (1969) added that a firm therapeutic alliance is not based on the satisfaction of the patient's fixed infantile needs but on the consistent functioning of the therapist, who interprets the patient's transference neurosis.

Virtually every type of manipulative and supportive intervention has been reported in the course of a case presentation or directly advocated in the psychoanalytic literature. Others view such measures as essentially disruptive of the psychotherapeutic work and outcome. Langs (1973) empirically attempts to elucidate many misconceptions regarding "supportive" interventions, noting that patients usually respond to direct advice and manipulations with mistrust, resistance, disturbances in the therapeutic alliance, rage over the loss of autonomy, fantasies of being intruded upon and penetrated, and a shift toward acting out based on the living out implicit in the offered directive. The patient, Langs has found, sees such measures as seductive and as a cause for mistrust, and responds with fantasies of revenge. The therapist usually resorts to such measures as a result of countertransference reactions stimulated by feelings of confusion and helplessness, and misconceptions about the unconscious meanings of directives. These interventions serve to convey the therapist's belief in the lack of basic integrative capacities in the patient. This viewpoint is said to be unconsciously perceived and introjected by the patient.

Langs (1976a, 1978a, 1978b, 1979b, 1980a, 1981) points out that the bulk of the literature discussing the ground rules and boundaries of analysis and psychotherapy is not based on definitive psychoanalytic investigations of the ramifications of a policy of sound adherence to such rules. Most writers draw on general clinical impressions, years of experience, or a single striking clinical interlude, and most discussions are superficial.

For example, Eissler (1953), in his landmark study of technique, advocated modifications in technique only when the basic technique has been proved to be insufficient and when the impact of the deviations can be resolved fully. He warned that each such modification increases the likelihood that the therapeutic interaction will be falsified. In addition, he was concerned that psychoanalysts might introduce modifications in technique to obscure their inability to use the interpretive method. There is virtually no attempt specifically to investigate the unconscious meanings of a modification in technique for either the patient or the therapist. No distinction is made between those situations in which the patient has been gratified directly and inappropriately or afforded support for resistance through a modification in technique, and those situations in which the reactions are confined to fantasies and wishes that can be analyzed in terms of their specific meanings to the patient. Thus, the implications of frame alterations are neglected, and the thesis that such modifications may have unalterable or difficult-to-resolve influences on the patient, the psychotherapist, their interaction, and the therapeutic qualities of the analytic field is essentially not considered. Seldom is a modification in the setting taken as a definitive adaptive and therapeutic context for the subsequent patient material, and rarely are there clinical data available with which to assess definitively the impact of proposed changes in the frame.

Langs (1975c, 1976a, 1976b, 1978a, 1978b, 1979b, 1980a) proposes three methods of analyzing data psychoanalytically to examine the impact of frame modifications. First, all proposed modifications in the frame should be viewed as adaptive contexts to be analyzed through the patient's associations. Second, if the therapist has participated in a frame modification, the ground rules should be restored and the adaptive context of the frame alterations and rectifications should be analyzed through the patient's associations. A third means of testing hypotheses related to frame alterations is to analyze the patient's associations without first restoring the ground rules. Langs notes, however, that there are significant limits to understanding the ramifications of frame deviations so long as they remain unrectified.

In an effort to explore and establish definitive boundaries of the psychoanalytic relationship, Langs (1973) began the first of a series (1974, 1975a, 1975b, 1975c, 1976a, 1978a, 1979a, 1979b, 1980a, 1981) of clinical studies. His findings confirm that the patient unconsciously sees therapist deviations in the ground rules as a sanction for acting out, that any modification in the frame becomes a central adaptive context. In an exploration of the need for a one-to-one relationship that guarantees confidentiality, he found that the introduction of any third party (charts, forms, or staff collaboration) has disruptive consequences for both patient and therapist. These circumstances seem to provide a wide range of inappropriate gratifications and reinforcements that can seriously damage the patient's ability to be treated; the reality prevails and cannot be interpreted away. As a result, major areas of misalliance between patient and therapist remain unresolved.

Langs has linked the therapist's management of the frame to his or her containing functions (Bion 1962, 1963, 1965, 1970), noting that the therapist is a living part of the frame who actively invites pathological communications and projective identifications from the patient so as to contain and process interpretations. The therapist may create an appropriately interpretive container or may use the patient inappropriately as a pathological container for his or her own inner disturbances. Maintenance of the ground rules provides one means whereby, under pressure from patients, therapists distinguish themselves from past pathogenic objects.

Langs emphasizes that his findings should not be taken as a brief arguing for therapeutic rigidity or for a lack of humanity and concern in the therapist. He suggests, on the contrary, that a sensitive appreciation of the importance of the frame leads to a stance that is most appropriate to the patient's needs and is based largely on the patient's individual qualities. The best means for therapists to express their humanity thus lies in their concerned capacity to manage the frame properly and to interpret to the patient appropriately. Most therapists, according to Langs, underestimate the positive qualities of a secure hold and frame. He is convinced that adherence to his well-documented principles is not a matter of rigidity but a hard-won indication of the therapist's integrative capacities and ability to manage his or her own conflicts, reflecting devotion to the provision of a setting that offers the patient an opportunity for care and understanding.

Historically, the frame has been relegated to the background of the psychotherapeutic process in favor of a focus on the verbal exchanges between patient and therapist. Langs is convinced that virtually every patient is willing to teach his or her therapist the importance of the frame if the therapist is receptive and able to listen and learn.

CLINIC PSYCHOTHERAPY AND THE POOR

Literature examining clinic psychotherapy is quite diverse, but the potential impact of the setting rarely has been acknowledged as a prime factor worthy of exploration. Because there is little literature explicitly addressing the significance of the clinic setting, it was necessary in the present study to rely on the attitudes expressed within the writings discussing mental health treatment for the poor. The literature comparing and contrasting clinics and patient populations was also examined.

Social Class and Treatment Offered

The proposition that the therapeutic treatment a person receives when he or she becomes a psychiatric patient is often a function of his or her social class was first presented in 1954 by Schaffer and Meyers. They found that theoretical orientations, beliefs, interests, and preferred techniques of treatment vary with the population treated. Class I and II patients were treated primarily by psychoanalysts and psychoanalysis, whereas psychiatrists treating class III, IV, and V patients were less experienced and relied primarily on supportive, suggestive, directive, or biological approaches. Clinic records revealed that 60 percent of class IV and 97 percent of class V patients were rejected as psychotherapy patients, and individuals in these classes were less apt to maintain contact with the clinic. Similar findings were reported by Seward and Marmor (1956), Hollingshead and Redlich (1958), and Brill and Storrow (1960). Seward and Marmor specifically noted that medical students, rather than the psychiatrists and residents chosen for higher-status patients, were assigned the few patients of lower socioeconomic status even accepted for treatment. Higher-status patients were considered better therapeutic "risks," and their treatment was often continued for months, in contrast with the very brief therapy offered the poor. Hollingshead and Redlich pointed out that despite the stress placed on diagnosis in psychological theory and practice, there is no overall relationship for neurotic patients between the type of treatment and the specific diagnostic label attached to the patient. Treatment is, however, directly related to both social class and the agency in which the patient is treated. Even when treatment was provided by the same facility, 85 percent of class IV and V patients received directive psychotherapy, whereas 45 percent of class I and II patients received psychoanalysis or analytic psychotherapy.

Balch (1974) found that although evidencing less self-involvement in seeking clinic services, the lower-class patient is no less concerned about his or her problem than is the patient in the middle or upper classes. This finding leads us to consider what factors contribute to the use of mental health services by lower-class persons who are experiencing difficulties concerning their emotional health. Balch suggests that the degree of concern the patient acknowledges regarding his or her problem may be related to the treatment facility in which such services are rendered.

Therapists in several studies (Brill and Storrow 1960, Nir and Cutler 1978, Schaffer and Meyers 1954, Seward and Marmor 1956) have depicted patients of lower socioeconomic status as hostile, suspicious, lacking in insight, unmotivated, incapable of self-observation, and unable to develop meaningful relationships with their therapists. These authors concluded that clinics should reexamine their emphasis on psychotherapy as their preferred mode of treatment. The impact of the setting and quality of care provided was not addressed.

Cole, et al. (1962), in contrast, found an equal acceptance across social classes of patients applying for psychotherapy, with the exception of bias against class V patients. Once accepted, however, the patients in the upper classes remained in treatment longer than those in the lower classes. Upon discharge, those in the upper classes had a greater chance of being listed as socially improved. This study, when compared with others in the literature, demonstrates a marked variability of acceptance from one setting to another.

Special Treatment Modalities for Patients of Lower Socioeconomic Status

The late 1950s and the 1960s were marked by questioning of the feasibility of providing insight-oriented psychotherapy for patients of lower socioeconomic status. Hollingshead and Redlich (1958), Rosenthal and Frank (1958), and Spiegel (1959) began that trend toward developing new modes of treatment for this difficult and supposedly often unmotivated population.

Rosenthal and Frank (1958) were among the first to acknowledge that a patient's course in psychotherapy may be affected by various aspects of his or her experience at the clinic. Their focus and interpretation, however, differ significantly from my own. They do provide a relatively thorough description of their intake procedure, and this is one of the few studies to provide such data.

During the first visit, the patient was interviewed by a psychiatric nurse, was required to provide two different secretaries with a data sheet (indicating age, sex, race, socioeconomic status, education, etcetera), and was seen by a medical student and, finally, a supervising psychiatrist. The clinic utilized dynamic psychotherapy, with the goals of helping patients to function more effectively in their interpersonal transactions and relieving their symptomatic distress through a "trusting, confidential" relationship with the therapist.

Records from this clinic revealed that 35 percent of the patients (with no significant difference in sex, race, or diagnosis) failed to accept individual psychotherapy when it was offered. Patients of lower socioeconomic status were found to be most likely to refuse psychotherapy and to drop out sooner than those in other groups. Black patients were found to drop out most often. Overall, three-quarters of the patients were reported to terminate without the therapist's "consent." Almost half the patients came for five or fewer sessions. Rosenthal and Frank concluded that these findings suggest disappointment or anxiety in these patients regarding their early experience with this form of treatment; these authors noted that the high rate of patient terminations after only a few sessions, especially without prior discussion with the therapist, suggests that the relationship involved relatively little trust and confidence. The authors pointed out that such findings are not unique to their clinic.

Overall and Aronson (1963) report similar findings. They concluded that insight-based psychotherapies seem less effective with psychiatric clinic outpatients than with patients in other settings. Variables contributing to class and racial differences, however, were not explored. It is unclear from the data whether specific clinic arrangements were identical for all patients. It might be useful, for example, to compare the qualifications of the therapists with the race and socioeconomic status of their assigned patients. The professed confidentiality and its blatant violation seemed to pass unnoticed by the authors.

Hunt (1960) supported his colleagues in hypothesizing that psychotherapy is a middle-class form of treatment and in recommending the development of different approaches for the poor. Lief et al. (1961) furthered Hunt's hypothesis. They noted the 6 percent drop-out rate at their psychiatric clinic, contrasted with 50 percent in other psychiatric clinics. The authors attributed their success with their patients to high patient levels of education and social status. They recommended strenuous efforts to find and improve forms of treatment appropriate to lower-class patients, calling it a "wasteful procedure to include the lower classes of patients in clinics where the main emphasis is on teaching insight therapy" (Lief et al. 1961, p. 118). They suggested that greater therapist activity, desensitization, hypnosis, relaxation, suggestion, drugs, or some combination of these techniques has the greatest application with the poor. They did not provide data to support their conclusions but seemed to imply that insight can be "learned" only by the highly intelligent and well educated. These attitudes were again expressed by Nir and Cutler in 1978.

In contrast, Storrow (1962) found that the lower-class neurotic who is treated with psychotherapy in an outpatient clinic is about as successful in therapy as a similarly treated middle-class patient. Current solutions to the problem of providing better care for the lower-class neurotic, according to Storrow, are based on inadequately tested assumptions.

Albronda et al. (1964) successfully duplicated Storrow's findings. They found that when they attempted to provide psychotherapy to all patients applying for treatment, without selection according to models of treatability, the differences among the social classes tended to level out. In comparing three groups of patients on the basis of the number of patients who continued, the number who declined interviews, and the number who dropped out, the authors again found no significant difference according to social class distribution.

Reissman et al. (1964) continued to challenge the widely held assumption that psychotherapy is not the treatment of choice for low-income patients. They stated that diagnoses describing the poor as nonintrospective, desiring direction, and the like ignore qualities that may indicate a positive potential for psychotherapy. They pointed out that the lower-class cultural tendency not to isolate and intellectualize is an extremely important asset for treatment and that, rather than focusing on traits not compatible with insight therapy, attention might better be directed toward the more positively relevant personality traits. They said, "If emotionally corrective experience rather than cognitive insight is the heart of modern psychotherapy—the key to deep behavior modification—then the poor may be far better therapy risks than is generally realized" (p. 229). These findings lead one to wonder why we often approach the poor with cognitive therapies that avoid the emotional components that may be the greatest prognostic strengths of such patients.

A number of writers have acknowledged that the therapist's inadequacies may contribute to the difficulties in working with a lower socioeconomic status clinic population. Seward and Marmor (1956) recommended that the therapist consider his or her own dynamics in choosing patients, and they recommended an avoidance of pigeonholing, or categorical thinking, in the application of therapeutic procedures. Hollingshead and Redlich (1958) suggested that psychotherapists be trained to recognize and deal directly with the differences between themselves and their patients. Spiegel (1959), in a more thorough discussion, recommended "benevolent neutrality" as a therapist goal but noted that it often offends the patient, signifying that the therapist's real feelings remain undeclared behind a concealing mask of condescension. He contended that true neutrality prevents the establishment of positive transference and results in the patient's feeling he or she cannot get the therapist's attention. This result leads to a therapeutic impasse. Spiegel did not recommend interpreting such feelings to the patient; he instead recommended family involvement and other frame modifications, such as departing from the routine of regular office visits, answering personal questions, and revealing one's own value system. He did not indicate how he gathered information regarding patient responses, but he did acknowledge that his approaches were developed neither via trial and error nor through analytic validation but, rather, out of his own theoretical point of view.

The Impact of the Therapist's Attitudes

Rosen and Frank (1962) candidly acknowledged that most people are to some extent racially prejudiced on both conscious and unconscious levels. They noted that these attitudes can and often do result in the therapist's overt rejection of the patient or in a guilt-originated reaction formation in which the therapist is "too nice," thus prohibiting both resolution of the racial issues and effective therapy. They emphasized the need to deal with racial concerns while being receptive to the unique problems of the patient as an individual.

Haas (1963) agreed with Overall and Aronson (1963) that lower-class patients are often disappointed by middle-class professionals. He, however, attributed this disappointment to the therapist's focusing on his or her own needs without recognizing the individual needs of the patient. He concluded that "the lower class patient, just like other patients, needs to be understood in terms of his own needs and his own accustomed way of life."

McMahon (1964), expanding on these ideas, pointed out that many studies characterizing lower-class patients as needing a therapist who is more active, medically oriented, and immediately helpful in relieving somatic distress reinforce the middle-class rationalization of noninvolvement with low-income groups that is based on the belief that they are hard to reach and not amenable to therapy. McMahon acknowledged that although the social, economic, and psychological data in these studies may well be accurate in their characterization of the poor, one must then ask, "How do low income persons become hard to reach, distant or suspicious in the face of honest efforts to help them?" (p. 287). He pointed out that we are quick to label the complaining poor as paranoid, but he considered the frequent accuracy of their complaints to be more disturbing.

Terestman et al. (1974), Gallegos (1975), and Siassi and Messer (1976) found that sociological and psychological stereotypes were not helpful in identifying patients who improved. Such stereotypes, however, may contribute to poor results and to the rationalization that such patients are not amenable to psychotherapy. In addition, these researchers pointed out that lower-class patients are most often assigned to inexperienced therapists and that these therapists are especially prone to countertransference reactions.

The Setting and Ground Rules

Brandt (1966) and Reder and Tyson (1980) noted that specific factors influencing patients' involvement in treatment are often insufficiently delineated. They recommended distinguishing factors stemming from the patients' psychopathology from variables external to the patient. These external variables include the treatment setting, the therapeutic modality, and the specific therapist.

With the development of the Health Maintenance Organization and third-party insurance payments of psychotherapy, researchers began to examine the impact of these circumstances. Goldensohn and Haar (1974), using informal personal observations of manifest patient material, observed that patients at times feel uncomfortable about not paying a fee, because they infer that they are on par with a charity or clinic patient, which is seen as degrading. The patients studied expressed views that the clinic was for second-class patients who received second-class treatment. These authors stated that patients fear being rejected by the therapist because of unlikability, unworthiness, lack of productivity, or other negative qualities. The fears of rejection are aggravated in poor patients, who feel they can neither "bribe" the therapist with financial payment nor "buy" a different therapist. They are said to perceive their acceptance as tenuous and therefore to feel less free to risk criticizing the therapist than do patients of higher economic status. The poor often view the Health Maintenance Organization as a remote, awesome bureaucratic organization that makes them feel alienated, insignificant, and powerless.

Goldensohn and Haar in addition perceived the poor as expressing feelings about the therapeutic setting different from those of middle-class patients. They stated that the poor patients were satisfied with the noisiness, disorder, and inadequate soundproofing, whereas the upper classes objected to the setting. They also admitted, however, that the poor are less willing to express themselves freely. In their discussion of countertransference, these authors acknowledged that the therapist's evaluation of the patient's worth will be perceived by the patient and incorporated into the patient's self-evaluation.

Nash and Cavenar (1976) confirmed many of these findings in a study of five patients in whom significant resistances manifested themselves and were directly tied to the lack of fees. The absolute fee was not found to be a major issue so long as the patient was paying a fee appropriate to his or her financial circumstances. With most patients, fantasies of sexual involvement with the therapist were stimulated by the gift of free service. In a related study examining the effects of third-party insurance reimbursement, Chodoff (1978) found that the required breach of confidentiality resulted in the development of resistances. Both findings have been confirmed repeatedly by Langs (1975c, 1976a, 1976b, 1978a, 1978b, 1979b, 1980, 1980a, 1980b, 1981).

The clinic literature investigating the treatment of patients of lower socioeconomic status is very diverse, with many similar studies showing differing outcomes. The reasons for these differences remain in question. It is hoped that an analysis of the setting and its impact will lead to the inclusion of at least some previously unrecognized variables.

METHOD OF INVESTIGATION

Efforts were made in the present study to create a more secure therapeutic environment. Although the rooms were not soundproofed, efforts were made to avert disruptions by reserving a consistent room for the patient and requesting that other staff members meet and converse elsewhere. When medication was prescribed, the therapist refrained from involvement except to interpret the patient's concerns.

Several frame modifications were not rectified. Clinic policy prohibited the collection of fees, and total confidentiality could not be guaranteed. Regular progress reports were required and available to all clinic personnel.

The sessions of the first patient to be presented were tape-recorded, reflecting a common though rarely analyzed practice in the training of psychotherapists. Modifications in neutrality and anonymity continued to occur as a result of the therapist's countertransference and naiveté.

In an effort to compare the effects of frame modifications that had been rectified with those that had not, the therapist listened for derivatives, viewing each circumstance as an adaptive context. This was not done to the exclusion of other material.

DATA AND DISCUSSION

Most clinic writers advocating frame modifications have claimed that their conclusions are based on intake data and patient continuation. Their data have been collected in a setting reflecting multiple frame modifications, and the psychotherapists are often students in training. It is my assumption that a secure frame is necessary for effective psychotherapy, and that clinics do not usually provide such a frame.

It is doubtful that intake data and clinic records can adequately measure and convey the impact of the setting. Such data leaves much to speculation. When there are many frame modifications inherent in the setting, patient reactions usually are limited to the obscure and embedded derivatives said to be evoked by an unrectified frame. Without multiple transcripts or process notes taken in a secure therapeutic setting in which many modifications have been rectified, it is doubtful that the total impact of the setting will be available for exploration or understanding. Patient data collected in the settings I have described revealed that patients do indeed respond both overtly and through unconscious derivatives to the setting and its communications. Given the opportunity, patients sometimes functioned in a supervisory capacity as they clearly articulated their reactions to the therapist and the setting.

Although most patients commented on the frame through rich unconscious derivatives, limited space precludes the use of much of this material in this chapter. The purpose here is not to provide the reader with a cross section of patient data regarding the framework but rather to stimulate others to further explorations in this area. Most of the data presented thus are taken from the transcripts and process notes of two patients whose explicit framework commentaries were the most valuable for this study. In the material of the first patient presented, existing in addition to and underlying her explicit commentaries is a wealth of derivative communications regarding the adaptive context of tape-recording her therapy sessions. As noted earlier, frame modifications, as long as they are continued, are not fully available for analysis; thus, the impact of the taping could not be resolved fully. The therapist manifestly rationalized taping as the ideal means of accurately collecting data for supervision and analysis. Continuation of the taping implicitly expressed the therapist's needs to do so. It later became apparent, through patient data, that psychotherapy occurs most effectively in a neutral environment, not one in which the patient feels burdened by the therapist's needs.

Case 1: Ms. A.

The first patient presented here is a lower-class black female in her early thirties. She is married and has six children, the oldest of whom is in her early teens. Ms. A. initially presented herself as acutely depressed and fearful of going insane. Several close relatives have been or currently are institutionalized for psychiatric disorders. Before assignment to her psychotherapist, the patient was evaluated through the usual intake procedure, and medication was prescribed. Her treatment began before efforts were directed toward rectification of the frame. At that time many of her associations pertained to her fears of going "crazy," her frustration and rage at others for failing to rescue her or for being patronizing, and her frustration and rage at herself for her own dissatisfaction and inability to manage her own life effectively. During most of the early sessions, Ms. A. spoke of her own flaws and frustrations with others, but aside from questions pertaining to her medication and diagnosis, she did not refer directly to the therapeutic interaction, nor did she express her views about the clinic.

The following transcript segment was drawn from a session approximately one month after the described rectifications (see p. 227). Because material and interventions from the previous hour are no longer available, these specific adaptive contexts cannot be identified. It is my belief that efforts to secure the environment motivated Ms. A. to acknowledge directly the therapeutic relationship and the impact of the setting. Commentaries will follow many of the segments to acknowledge continuing frame deviations and to explore the patient's latent and manifest communications.

Ms. A. entered the session saying she felt mean and hateful and had nothing to say. She said she did not want to talk about her problems, but she wanted concrete results even if it meant that she got angry. Finally she expressed irritation at the therapist's silence. She said that she did not want to play games and expressed concern that this tendency toward dishonesty might be occurring to the detriment of her therapy.

In this conversation, on a manifest level Ms. A. is irritated at the therapist's silence. She is aware that a tendency toward dishonesty and "game playing" is functioning as a barrier to her progress in therapy. Based on the continued breaches in confidentiality (tape-recording, charting), the provision of free services, and the periodic violations in neutrality and anonymity as adaptive contexts, Ms. A.'s response to the silence may be understood more fully. On a latent level, she may be alluding to the prominent frame deviations as interfering with her feeling secure enough to communicate freely and honestly. She may feel that the therapist is "playing games" by creating an environment that is not safe and secure and then expecting her to free associate.

P: I do want to know that I can come in here and say what I want to say, you know, and not feel that your next words to me will be that, possibly you need to see somebody else.

T: Then if you do come in here and you do get angry . . .

P: And show you on my days when I do get angry and act like I do when I'm like this.

T: That I'm somehow going to reject you? [The therapist is responding on a manifest level.]

P: Yeah, reject me and I actually worry like will you reject me because you're too soft and can't take it. . . . You do make me feel like I could be ugly and your next words would be, I've thought about it and I think you should see someone else. I don't want to hurt your feelings. . . . I expect you to have a shield around yourself or I expect that if I told you that I don't like white people that you could take it, that you would say well, you don't like white people.

T: You hope I could take it; sounds like you're not sure.

P: Well, yeah, this is how I want you to be and I want you to convince me that you can take it, say whatever you want, but I look at you and you just look soft to me.

T: All right, so I look pretty fragile.

The therapist here is responding to the manifest content of the patient's viewing her as vulnerable. Based on the adaptive contexts of the continued frame deviations, the patient's commentaries can be understood in more depth. The manifest concern that the therapist may refer the patient elsewhere may reflect the patient's awareness of the pending forced termination. It may also reflect thoughts of terminating the therapy because of an unstable environment. She may see the taping as evidence of the therapist's vulnerability. The taping as well as other deviations could be viewed as the therapist's "shield," preventing development of a healthy therapeutic intimacy.

P: You look like, I don't know how long you've been in school, in years you'll have hardened up but you don't look like it now. . . . I don't expect you to say "throw my recorder out the window" but "you say what you want to say" . . . back to not wanting to play games.

Ms. A. knows that her therapist is a student (a violation of anonymity) and is concerned about the therapist's capacity to "contain" her pathology. The early mismanagement of the setting as well as the subsequent rectifications, which were only partial, initially only raised more doubts about the therapist's capacities. The lack of consistency, the continued violations of confidentiality, and the knowledge that her therapist is a student are all adaptive contexts to which the patient is responding. Her suggestion that the therapist "throw [the] recorder out the window" while encouraging her to "say what you want to say" appears, in this context, to be an effort to supervise her student/therapist; she has on both a manifest and derivative level offered a model of rectification.

T: Sounds like you're not sure whether you should take care of me or yourself.
P: Yeah, that could be true. I want to take care of myself, but I can't take care of me till I'm sure you can take it.
T: Something else I think I picked up is, I suppose there's an appeal to the idea that I care, but if I care then I'm fragile and vulnerable and you could hurt me. [In view of the both derivative and manifest references to the tape recorder, it is unfortunate that the therapist did not recognize or address its impact as an adaptive context.]
P: Yeah, that I can lash out and just say the things I feel without worrying that I'm hurting that person's feeling.
T: And it sounds like you're kind of testing the water right now.
P: Yeah, I am, because I've said more than I ever planned on saying when I came in here and that's the biggest thing when I question whether you and I could continue. I just don't want anybody that I have to, and that's my favorite phrase, play games with. And I think I'm probably feeling the real way I usually feel more today than any time I've ever been in here. And I just . . . there's things I probably could have said. . . . Now, to show you what I mean like, some days I might feel like coming in here and out of perfect hatefulness I don't want to talk. So you wouldn't have to worry about giving me anything. I would just like to sit here and be perfectly contrary and not talk but I feel like I'm supposed to talk in here.

Prior to the partial efforts to create a more secure environment, Ms. A.'s associations were ruminative, circular, and flat. This session marks a transition in Ms. A.'s style of communication. If we view the changes in the setting as an adaptive context, it appears that the more secure setting has lowered her resistances, enabling her to communicate more freely and in more depth. Earlier, her allusions to the therapy were scanty and occurred only in the form of embedded derivatives that did not clearly coalesce. They were not amenable to silent validation prior to interpretation. She now is able to express clearly her concerns on both a latent and a manifest level and to provide the bridge necessary for effective interpretation. The more secure environment has given Ms. A. hope that she can be helped. It has stimulated her to offer supervision to her therapist by identifying those features in the environment that are destructive to her treatment. She especially is emphasizing that the tape recorder makes her want to "be perfectly contrary and not talk."

T: So, not talking is contrary?

P: Well, it is to me, because I feel like I am defeating my purpose. I told you, I've got it in my mind that when I come in here I'm supposed to talk and get something out of it. . . . So if I came in here one day and you asked me a question and I just answered it, and I know there are days that I just feel like that and I just don't feel like saying anything else, I just don't want to talk. Well, why don't you want to talk? (*Patient says to herself.*) I just don't want to. I guess I'm looking for somebody that I can just do that and not have to explain it that day. I might explain it next week, but I don't want to have to give a reason and you can't do that around people, you can't. If I do that at home and don't talk, my husband pesters the hell out of me and asks, you know, are you taking your medicine? And he gets so nice and that gets on my nerves. And I can see the kids looking at me and saying mommy's feeling bad . . . and it just gets on my nerves. It's almost like I want to be in the dumps and stay there, so leave me alone and that's what I need here, and like I said, I haven't made up my mind if I can get that or not. So, that's about where I am today, so busy trying to analyze you I can't figure out my own problems. . . . Could I tell you to shut up without—I wouldn't care if you thought I was rude, or, you know, that doesn't make any difference, because like I said, that's just part of your job in my book. And I am hung up on what I think is part of a person's job. If you're not capable of handling it, then get in a different field. I have to listen to different people at work curse me out, collecting money, and I can't say anything because it's part of my job. So big deal! Well, I don't like . . . I said get in here and be abrasive, but I feel like, you know, if I was going to a private doctor that whatever I wanted to say would come out.

Ms. A.'s comments that her husband "pesters the hell out of me" by asking irritating questions and being "too nice" may well be allusions to the therapist's behaviors. The frequent interventions may be perceived as pestering. They also function as self-revelations about the therapist's own anxieties. The interventions are not linking the adaptive contexts to the derivative communications in the form of valid interpretations; they are instead acknowledgments and questions pertaining to the manifest commentary. Ms. A. in effect feels she is being offered superficial gratifications (free services and medication) in place of valid interventions in a secure setting. The gratifications offered are perceived as "too nice" and do not

help her resolve her problems. She finally confirms that the excessive interventions function as disruptive self-revelations when she admits being so
preoccupied with the therapist that "I can't figure out my own problems."
She finally asks, "Could I tell you to shut up?" She is conveying her need
for a secure holding environment with a therapist who can contain and
metabolize her psychopathology. She needs a stable environment and sound
interpretations and warns, "If you're not capable of handling it then get in a
different field." She is saying that these factors are essential to the therapist's
"job." She is aware that the task is not always pleasant and implies that she
would feel less ambivalence about expressing herself if she were paying a fee.
With a "private doctor" and the fee, she would feel freer to insist on privacy
and total confidentiality (no tape recorder).

> T: So there's a difference between the two; what is it?
> P: Yeah, what would make the difference, well, that goes way back. . . . It's
> like, that would be in comparison to public aid and I would go into the store
> and use food stamps or cash. If I was shopping with cash, you know . . . I'm
> not going to take no flack off the girls behind the counter, but if I'm shopping
> with food stamps . . . just like here, you're food stamps to me.

In addition to her continued manifest discussion of the impact of free
services, Ms. A. addresses in derivative form her need for adherence to the
ground rule of privacy. In her references to a "private doctor" versus
"public aid," she communicated her concerns that as a free clinic patient her
private concerns become a matter of public record.

> T: Okay, in a way I'm somewhat of a special favor just because you're not
> paying. . . .
> P: Yeah, instead of looking at it like I really should . . . instead of looking at it
> like, well, I'm really blessed coming over here and I'm not having to
> pay anything. (*Pause*.) Just food stamps. And that's how my whole life is to
> me.
> T: So you are in one hell of a bind.
> P: Yes.
> T: Because no matter how angry you are at me, you feel like you are supposed to
> be grateful.
> P: Yeah, I guess so, I really guess so. You know I didn't realize that until
> today. . . . All I can see if I got food stamps is I'll be doing what's expected
> of a woman with six kids. Every week when we go grocery shopping we buy
> almost $135 or something like that, and when we got up to the register last
> week and we had about three carts of groceries, the woman rang it up and she
> just looked at me and she said, "Damn, I forgot to ask you, that's food stamps,
> right?" And that just irritated me and I said, "Why?"

This was the end of the session. The therapist made a final acknowledgment of Ms. A.'s fear that the therapist would pigeonhole her in the role of a poor black woman on food stamps, instead of appreciating her complexity.

This one session provides a great deal of both conscious and unconscious derivative material. Despite the several frame rectifications, the tape recorder was still in the foreground as a major adaptive context. Unfortunately, it signified an inconsistency that Ms. A. found confusing. She was trying to figure out the therapist's motives. She wanted to speak freely but was inhibited by the tape recorder, so she offhandedly suggested throwing it out the window. Knowing the therapist was a student, she was uncertain whether the modifications were the result of ignorance or of the therapist's own problems. She was, however, well aware that whatever the reasons for the therapist's behaviors, as long as there was not a secure setting, she would feel impelled to "play games." She had unwittingly provided valuable supervision. Ms. A. wanted to get better and unconsciously told the therapist how she could best help her.

Throughout this hour, the therapist responded only to the manifest material. She was aware of both the tendency for patients to resist direct discussion of many of their most pressing concerns, and the likelihood that the patient would have concerns about the therapist and the treatment. Thus, for the patient to begin to discuss her difficulties directly in the therapeutic relationship was considered a sign of progress. It implied that the patient felt safe enough to acknowledge these concerns.

A patient can also discuss one topic to avoid the mention of another. The value of derivative communication is that it relies on the unconscious, which, like dreams, is more apt to be truthful in expressing conflictual concerns. That Ms. A. discussed the impact of the setting and her relationship with the therapist on both manifest and derivative levels suggests that the setting was indeed a significant concern.

Case 2: Ms. J.

The second patient was seen at a different clinic and under a different circumstance from the first patient. Her therapist was not a student, had not taped any therapy sessions, and was beginning to integrate the communicative technique into her work. Ms. J. is a white female in her twenties of lower socioeconomic status. She is married and has one child. She has a history of psychiatric hospitalizations and previously had been seen at this clinic by a variety of psychotherapists and physicians (the latter for medication). Close relatives have been or currently are in treatment at this same clinic, and others have personal affiliations with individual staff members. Two years prior to beginning with the therapist conducting these sessions, Ms. J. had discontinued all contact with the clinic. Since her return she has taken no psychotropic medication. She said she returned for psychotherapy because of continuing anxiety and depression. She expressed concerns that her problems might interfere with her parenting. Before assignment to her psychotherapist, she was reevaluated through the usual intake procedure.

During her first therapy session, Ms. J.'s new therapist informed her that their next week's appointment would have to be cancelled. The patient's manifest and derivative commentaries reflected her anger at the cancellation and ambivalence about beginning with the new therapist. These concerns were interpreted. The second session occurred two weeks later.

P: I missed you last week. . . . Susie was sick again. Her bed was a mess again this morning. I get so angry. I know she can't help it, but she's been sick so much since birth and it's hard to enjoy her when she's like this. The doctors don't do anything, and she's growing up so quickly. Why is it back again? They're doing a culture to see if it's *Salmonella* again. . . .

I'm really angry at the people here. I've thought of calling her doctor. They're giving my mother all these pills and she's drinking again, a lot, and I don't know if she should be drinking and taking all those pills. And she's giving the pills to all sorts of people. It reminds me of teenagers. She tells everyone, when they come over, to bring the beer and she supplies the pills. And she's giving them to Tom [the patient's husband]. It scares me because she's blacking out a lot. I know because she forgets half of what I tell her. I think of calling here and telling someone—Ms. Ryan, but I know I'm not supposed to talk to anybody else's counselor. I'm not sure what else to do. I'm going to meet with my mother today, for the first time, at 2:00 P.M. I'm kind of scared, but I've decided to show her the house and let her see the baby. I hope it goes okay. (*At this point the chief administrator walked by the therapist's office yelling down the hall to another staff member.*) I hate the director here. I think he's just awful. What kind of an example does he set? He's worse than all the patients that come to the day treatment center. I check him out every time I come here and he looks terrible. His hair sticks out all over the place; he doesn't take care of himself at all. What kind of an example is that? . . . I wonder why I'm talking about him. It must mean something.

Ms. J. begins the session with little resistance and immediately identifies the adaptive context of the missed session. Based in this context, her subsequent comments can be understood in more depth, especially in terms of their unconscious, symbolic meanings. The anger at ineffective doctors who cannot cure a chronic infection that is messy and interfering with her enjoyment may reflect her feelings about and unconscious perceptions of her current therapist. That these feelings have been stimulated by her experiences with the clinic is confirmed by her next association to anger at clinic employees. Although she is not the designated therapist or supervisor, Ms. J. feels unconsciously impelled to function in that capacity. She is "not sure what else to do." She talks about the use of drugs as an inappropriate gratification that causes "blacking out," not insight or cure. Based on her past experiences at the clinic and her recent disappointment with her new therapist's cancelling the past week's session, she may be anticipating that this new therapist will attempt to medicate her or offer other superficial and potentially destructive gratifications. Her allusions to showing her mother her house and her baby reflect her feelings of vulnerability toward the new therapist. As a consequence of the violations of anonymity by the administrator and previous therapists and, most recently, the new therapist's cancellation, Ms. J. has realized that these people, too, have many problems. She views them as "worse" than the most seriously disturbed patients who attend the day treatment center. By asking what kind of an example their behavior sets, she seems to be questioning who is most seriously in need of treatment and whether such disturbed individuals should be therapists and administrators. Her next statement provides another bridge to the present therapeutic context and indicates her readiness for an interpretation.

> T: When you first walked in today, you mentioned missing me last week. Then you spoke of being disappointed in doctors and angry at people here at this clinic for not helping you and not setting a good example. I wonder if some of that is related to my absence last week. [The interpretation appears to be an accurate though muted reflection of the patient's communications.]
>
> P: Well, last Monday I wasn't angry at all, it just seemed like a long time, and I missed you. . . . But as the week wore on, I got very angry and thought of calling here a number of times. I just got angry at the whole place. I hate getting angry. I feel like I should just be able to handle things better and not get so crazy. I'm trying to get away from that part of my life. . . . It's in the past. . . . I don't want to be like my mother. I want to handle things the right way. . . . I don't like people to think I'm like her. . . .
>
> I really do hate the director. What's his name, Mike? He's always so rude to me. I've been coming here for years and I know a lot of the staff pretty well, so when I come in I talk to the reception people. He always tells me they're here to work, not to talk. He tells me I can't go up to the desk and visit because they're working on files and they're confidential. Well, first, the receptionists work in public with the public, so if he doesn't want them to deal with the public, they shouldn't be in a public area. And second, I don't have any interest in looking at anyone else's file. If they don't want anyone to see anyone else's file, then they shouldn't be in a public area. I really don't like that man. My cousin doesn't look as disheveled as he does. He runs one of those clinics for emotionally disturbed teenagers. He's friends with Kevin [another staff member]; I've known him all my life.

The patient provides brief manifest validation of the preceding interpretation but then resumes derivative communication. Her comment to the effect that she should handle things better without getting so "crazy" indicates that she has made an introjective identification with the therapist who "should be able to handle things better and not get so crazy." (A therapist should not begin treatment with a patient only to cancel the second session.) She then communicates that this type of occurrence feels like a reenactment of earlier traumas with her mother. She admonishes her therapist not to "be like my mother . . . to handle things the right way." Ms. J.'s comments about the rude director and to the receptionist working in public with what should be private files appear to be in part a derivative restatement of her veridical perceptions about the "crazy" and contradictory functioning of her therapist. These comments also serve the function of identifying her concerns about confidentiality. Again she offers suggestions for rectification.

> *T*: You expressed a desire not to be linked with your past and mentioned knowing a number of staff members in a number of different contexts here and outside. You've also been talking about the files not being very confidential in a public area. I think you are concerned about your own file and your confidentiality here.
>
> *P*: You know what really got to me was when Joan did the intake on me. She had my file out and it's really thick. I commented to her about fattening up my file. She laughed and told me about this meeting where you all were going to discuss me and decide what to do. . . . God, everything in that file. When I thought of coming back here again, I thought of going back over my past all over again. I didn't want to go through that anymore. I don't like that to be all over the place. When I was going for my apartment they checked into everything. And it's weird knowing people on the outside and here too. I don't know why, but I need it to be separate. I don't like to wonder what someone out there thinks because of what's gone on here. I'm just very uncomfortable with all of it. You know, yesterday I really took the time to think about my feelings. Usually I'm too busy and keep myself from feeling anything. Yesterday I really let myself feel everything. It wasn't very comfortable, but I realized I love Tom in spite of everything. I couldn't tell him, but I at least admitted it to myself.

Here, the patient again provides validation and elaboration of the therapist's interpretation. She then specifically identifies the additional adaptive context of the staff meeting and her concerns about the therapist's "checking" into her past experiences at the clinic. She is concerned that the therapist will be influenced "because of what's gone on here" before. She also seems to say that although the last intervention was incomplete because it failed to address her introjected identification with the therapist, she feels its positive effects "in spite of everything."

T: It seems from what you've said that your confidentiality is very important to you. In order for you to feel comfortable, you need for our relationship to be private, for me not to discuss your case with other staff members. You don't want me to put much information about you in your case file. You need what goes on here to be separate from your relationships outside.

The therapist's intervention does not identify the specific adaptive context. Although the therapist responds to Ms. J.'s general concern about confidentiality, her specific concern about the therapist's checking into her past is neglected. These factors, coupled with the fact that Ms. J. has not yet indicated a need for an interpretation, suggest that the intervention is premature and largely a reflection of the therapist's discomfort about the lack of confidentiality.

P: Gee, that sounds terribly selfish. I know you have to do these things.

T: But it seems like you are saying, for you to feel comfortable and able to express your feelings, you need confidentiality.

P: How did you do that? I was just talking about the people at the front desk and the files. I had no idea it was related to my own feelings. . . .

  You know, it's too bad that so much energy has to be devoted to all the negative things. There are a lot of positive things too. When I was in high school I was good friends with my cousin and they had such a great family. They really taught me a lot about communication. They could communicate. Like when someone went out they said, "I don't care where you go, just leave a note so we'll know not to worry." They were so good to me. I used to idolize my aunt; she was my ideal woman. She was really caring and understanding. I talked to my cousin recently and he says she has cancer of the spine. I want to go see her, but I don't think I'm strong enough. He says she's in bed and can't move. I can't stand to see her that way. She was always so strong. I still need to see her that way. She was very open about things, and I knew that she used to have problems. She used to drink like my mother and Tom. I could never see her that way. I couldn't stand for her to have been like that. When I knew her she'd stopped. She wasn't drinking anymore, and I didn't want to think of her as weak. I really think I should go see her and tell her I love her. I want to thank her for all she did, but I think she'd want me to be strong. (*Long, teary pause.*) I hate to cry, I hate it. I can't stand to let myself cry; I have to hold it back. I really loved my grandfather. When he died I never got to tell him how important he was to me. Now he's gone. I don't want that to happen again. I just don't know if I can take it. I realize I have to let out my positive feelings toward people . . . as well as my negative feelings. I wish I didn't get so caught up in all the stuff with my mother. I call her everyday to make sure she's okay. I still won't give her my phone number, because otherwise she'll call me at all hours. I can't have her doing that. . . . I realize I love Tom even if there are a lot of things about him I don't like. That was a big revelation for me, to realize I could still love him.

He used to always tell me I was hard and I wasn't sure what he meant. But I think I had to be. . . . I can see we're out of time. This was pretty good. I don't like to cry but I said a lot. I wish you could have given me more. (*She stands at the door.*) So how do you like working here? (*The therapist smiles, silently.*) Do you have a private office?

T: (*Pause.*) Yes.

The patient has had a mixed reaction to the therapist's last intervention. She views the therapist's need to intervene prematurely and therefore incorrectly as "selfish." Although part of the interpretation reflected the therapist's own needs, parts of it addressed Ms. J.'s concerns as well. She has expressed concern about the therapist's having access to her previous record. Her description of her aunt may reflect her impressions of the therapist. She seems to view her as a caring and understanding individual who knows a lot about communication. She also sees her as incapacitated by a terminal condition. People who are weak in character are often called "spineless." Ms. J. struggles with this mixed image of the therapist. In some respects she sees her as "ideal," but in others she sees her as weakened and victimized by both the clinic setting and her own reactions to the clinic conditions. The patient feels she has had to be "hard" so as not to be victimized herself. She is aware of potential in the therapeutic relationship but is not sure if its positive components outweigh the negative. Her final comments and questions provide further confirmation that she is aware of the therapist's conflicts with the clinic setting. The therapist's smile and her answer to the question about the private office serve as additional modifications of anonymity.

The following week, Ms. J. arrived 15 minutes early for her appointment. Her therapist had arrived at the clinic a few moments before and was in the reception area. Renée, one of Ms. J.'s previous therapists, rushed up to her current therapist to discuss details of their luncheon plans. Her therapist left the reception area and the previous therapist as quickly as possible. Ms. J.'s appointment began on time.

P: How can you wear only that? It's so cold in here. Actually it's better in here than it was out there. . . . The first thing I have to say is that I was really taken aback to see you and Renée are friends. I was really taken aback. I can't really see that at all. And then, when I was still out there I heard Kevin talking to someone on the phone. Without him saying anything I knew he was talking to my mom. After he got off the phone I asked if he'd talked to my mom lately, and he said that was just her. I guess I'm just very sensitive to those things. I don't know why but I am.

Well, the baby has *Salmonella* again. The nurse came out and said the test they'd done was positive. She wanted to know how she's doing. Well, the doctor had never told me. So I called her Thursday and she was there but she said I could come in on Monday. I am so angry at her. It's a woman doctor and it's going to be a real confrontation. She should have told me. I'm taking a male friend with me. I don't think it should be that way, but it is. Because I'm a woman I don't think they take me seriously or tell me what's going on. I try but it just doesn't work. Here I thought she was having nightmares or throwing tantrums and I was finally going to start some discipline. Now I find out she had good reason. I keep having to put off the discipline because she's always been sick. How long is this going to go on? She's always in pain. How long will it be before she has to start coming here herself?

When that nurse was at the house, she said it smelled like gas. I'd kind of noticed it too, but I hadn't had time to do anything. How can I get my life together and take care of things when the baby is sick? I keep trying but I never get to it. Anyway, I finally called the janitor and he came and looked at the stove and wouldn't tell me anything. I asked him three times and he ignored me. I told him it's my apartment and I have a right to know. I said I was taking it to the management. Then he yelled at me and said I'd lived there a month, why hadn't I called before. I have only lived there two weeks. I don't know why he had to be so rude. All I want is to be treated with a little respect and have them tell me what's going on. I want to pull my life together, but it isn't easy.

Ms. J.'s first comments, "How can you wear only that? It's so cold in here," do reflect the obvious reality. The clinic is unheated, and the indoor temperature may well have been very low when this session occurred. But Ms. J. also is responding to the many violations of anonymity. She knows her therapist is conflicted about the clinic setting. At the end of the last session, the therapist leaked personal information to the patient when she admitted to having a private office. Now, in addition, Ms. J. knows that her present and past therapists interact socially. When she says she "can't really see" the therapist and Renée as friends, she is saying she must not see, because with the violations of anonymity, the therapist has become over-exposed. Ms. J.'s comments about clinic personnel communicating to other members of her family reflect her continuing concerns about being exposed herself. Everyone at the clinic knows her or at least has access to her file. She is particularly concerned about her present therapist's affiliation with her previous therapist. To her, the environment is emotionally cold.

Her allusions to *Salmonella* (a diarrhea-causing infection) that is out of control are derivatives that aptly characterize her feelings about the treatment. The therapy is sick, painful, and out of control. Her comments about the gas leak are an unconscious reference to the personal information revealed during the last hour. She had noticed it before but "hadn't had time to do anything" because the hour had ended and this week there had been more immediate concern (the friendship between the therapist and Renée). She wants to know how long she will have to tolerate these painful confrontations. She asks "how [she] can . . . get [her] life together and take care of things" when she cannot find a healthy and safe holding environment, one with no "gas" leaks. Her expressed anger at the janitor and the baby's doctor reflects her anger at the therapist. There has been no evidence of rectification, and she fears her concerns are not being taken seriously and are being ignored. She is asking how she can pull her life together under such conditions.

T: You're talking about being angry at people for withholding important information. You referred to a janitor and a doctor. You said you want to be treated with respect and know what's going on. You want to pull your life together, but there are impediments. When you came in today you mentioned. . .

P: (*Interrupting*) I know; I mentioned Renée talking to you. I do wonder what you've said to her or whatever about me. I just don't see how you can be friends with her. You are so different. She is into this woman's stuff, being liberated and all. Stand up for your rights. . . . And maybe she had a point . . . as I think about it now. Maybe you think that way too . . . but in a different way. She was so aggressive. She does seem to have changed. She said hello and was nicer than before. She still is so different from you. You're so much more quiet . . . and you listen. Those doctors don't listen to me at all. . . . They talk a lot but, like, I took the baby to the emergency room and told them to give her a culture. They refused until they talked to her doctor. I'm her mother; don't I count for anything? Why talk to her, she never did anything anyway, Susie is still sick. This is very hard for me. It's very contagious. I have to wash everything separately to keep everything from getting infected or contaminated. I should be kept informed. Don't I have any rights? What do you think?

T: You're talking about doctors listening to each other more than you when you're the one most involved. And you mentioned this after your commentary about seeing me with Renée. Maybe you're concerned that I would discuss your case with Renée and that it could influence how I perceive you. It seems to interfere with your talking freely to me. It seems you are telling me that you need me to discuss your case with no one.

These interventions might have had more impact if the derivative significance of her allusions to *Salmonella* as a contagious, contaminating illness had been included in the interpretations. Ms. J.'s commentary again reveals a split image of the therapist. She refers to the good therapist, who knows how to listen and interpret her concerns, and the bad therapist, who is too "aggressive" and "never did anything anyway."

P: Well, I know how doctors are, discussing their cases with each other. Just like the Tuesday meeting Joan told me about. How am I ever going to get to the doctor today? [It was snowing heavily outside.] You need insulation in here.

[The office was not heated.] I don't mind some of that . . . I guess . . . but I don't like the idea of your discussing it with Renée. I don't think I should discuss her with you.

When I came in this time, I told Joan I didn't want no student or someone who doesn't know what they're doing. I went through that before and I checked and I do have certain rights. I told her so and she promised me. I saw her today and told her how pleased I am. I can tell you that. That's why I asked if you had a private office last week. I figured you did. My cousin says these places are the bottom of the barrel. They're no good. The therapists are students or just not very good. They don't know what they're doing . . . or if they do, they leave as soon as they can. You're different from any therapist I've ever had. What kind of therapist are you? Some say psychotherapist. I guess it probably doesn't matter much because I bet a lot of people can say they're the same kind but still be very different. I see you as the type with the couch that people lie on and they talk and talk. I've never seen any who's as quiet as you. I know you're listening. As a matter of fact, that's what's hard for me. I know you're listening, but I don't know what you're thinking. What are you thinking?

T: You mentioned needing insulation in here after mentioning the concern that I could discuss your case with others. Then you mentioned my private office. I think you're saying you need insulation from the cold and from me talking to others. You need privacy to feel safe in here.

Another significant factor neglected in this intervention is the patient's awareness of the therapist's discomfort in the clinic setting and a perception that if her therapist has a private office and knows what she's doing, she will leave the clinic as soon as she can. The patient may now anticipate the therapist's departure and a forced termination. Her feeling that she should not discuss Renée with her current therapist is her acknowledgment that the contaminated environment has resulted in barriers to communication.

P: That's true. I guess I need more than that, though. At this point I have a safe place to live for me and my daughter. We're secure. But now I want a job. I want more for us. That isn't enough. That's why I need her to be healthy. I stayed home with her the whole first year. Now I want to get out some, but I need a baby sitter I can trust. I don't want to spend the rest of my life on welfare. You know, that's the worst part. I have to give up so much for that. They have so many rules and requirements.

This is kind of off the subject. I went to see my mom Sunday. I stayed for two hours and we didn't have a single fight. My husband was there, but he left as soon as I got there. I felt good about it. Maybe I shouldn't have, but I was glad if I could face up to things whether he could or not. I have a right to take my baby to my mother's. It was very nice. When I left I kissed her goodbye. It was the first time I've kissed her because I wanted to in years. I did feel so warm toward her. I checked with her last night. He never went back all night.

Oh, and remember that woman I told you about? The one who was also so sensitive to my needs. She really could listen to me. Anyway, I finally went to see her. I've been visiting her every day. She's alone for twelve hours a day. I go see her and help adjust her position, or fix her water or whatever she needs. She offered to pay me, but I said no. When I mentioned going to the doctor today with the baby, she asked if I had cab fare. I said yes even though I don't have a dime. She gave so much to me. I am glad to finally be able to do something for her. That's hard for me now with the welfare. There are too many things I have to accept. I hope that someday I'll be able to pay all those people who have been so helpful to me, or to do something in return. Well, I can see that I'm out of time. I'll see you next week.

In this final segment, Ms. J. seemed to be indicating both positive wishes to identify with the therapist and a desire for private treatment. She has to "give up so much" for welfare and free treatment. She is feeling warmth and gratitude toward the therapist, who "could listen to" her and whose last intervention was "sensitive to [her] needs." She wants to be able to pay for her therapy and is planning to look for a job. Still, her image of the therapist is mixed. She still needs a "baby sitter" (therapist) she can trust. She needs a healthy therapist so she can "get out" and attend to her own needs. Her description of visiting her sick relative may be an allusion to Ms. J.'s unconscious perception of sometimes serving as the functional therapist.

Although there are indications of positive introjects, these hours demonstrate that even when many of the framework violations found in clinics are interpreted and validated correctly, they continue to exert a negative influence on therapy. The reality of these continued violations persists and cannot be interpreted away.

The sessions presented and the data included in the discussion that follows clearly confirm the importance of a secure therapeutic environment.

DISCUSSION

Fees

Ms. A. confirmed that the absence of fees was disruptive to her treatment. She said, "I have to listen to different people at work curse me out, collecting money, and I can't say anything because it's part of my job." She implied that she could not communicate freely, or "curse" the therapist, because she was not paying a fee and the therapist was not "collecting money." She viewed her acceptance by the therapist as tenuous. To her, the free clinic therapist represented the gift of "food stamps"; necessary for her survival, but a symbol of her identity as a second-class citizen. As a recipient of this "special favor," she felt she had to act grateful, or "play games," even if she wasn't satisfied. She was aware that this stance could impede her progress in therapy and offered an explicit model of rectification through her reference to seeing a private doctor, a situation in which "whatever I wanted to say would come out."

Relative Anonymity

There were many violations of anonymity in Ms. A.'s therapy. She knew her therapist was a student and therefore relatively inexperienced. The early framework deviations as well as the continued deviations (such as tape-recording, free treatment, and frequent noninterpretive interventions) conveyed further information about the therapist. Ms. A. has communicated clearly on both manifest and derivative levels that these deviations were disruptive to her honest communications. The therapist's continuation of these barriers to her treatment revealed the therapist's limited capacity to create the necessary environment for a healthy therapeutic exchange. The result was that Ms. A. did not feel safe confiding in her therapist. She viewed her therapist as "soft" and thus needing the "shield" of the tape recorder and other deviations. She wanted to attend to her own difficulties but needed to be free from the burden of the therapist's problems. That she was able to address these concerns as directly as she did suggests that the efforts to create a more secure environment were somewhat successful. The consistent treatment room, a more private office and waiting area, and elimination of the secretary had given Ms. A. hope that the therapist would be able to respond to some of her needs.

Ms. J. indicated that the violations of anonymity had a powerful effect on her treatment. The knowledge that her past and present therapists were friendly resulted in fears about privacy and confidentiality. The knowledge that her present therapist had a private office was gratifying to her. She was pleased that her therapist was competent, but this competence also meant that the therapist would not want to stay at this "bottom of the barrel" clinic. She worried that the therapist would leave the clinic and terminate her therapy.

Confidentiality

Ms. J.'s preoccupation with confidentiality has been addressed amply in the process notes of her sessions. She did not like the fact that relatives were involved with the clinic and the staff and was not pleased that her current therapist had access to her file and could discuss her case with her previous therapists. Her comment in response to these circumstances, "I don't think I should discuss her [Renée] with you," indicated that there were specific areas of concern that could not be analyzed or resolved.

When Ms. A. entered therapy, she knew there had been a staff meeting at which her case had been discussed. She knew she had been assigned to a therapist, and a psychiatrist had evaluated her and prescribed medication. She did not know how she was viewed by the variety of clinic personnel. She only later expressed concerns that she might be seen as crazy and be hospitalized if she said the wrong thing. She was not certain who heard the tapes of her therapy sessions or who really determined the status of her relationship with the therapist. She had not been informed that the psychiatrist she was seeing for medication was her psychotherapist's direct supervisor.

In nearly all of the early therapy sessions, Ms. A. referred directly to the psychiatrist or to her dissatisfaction with the medication. She felt he had prescribed the medication to keep her from "going crazy." She said she did not like the effects of the medication but was afraid to stop taking it. Ms. A. had reported that whenever she consulted the psychiatrist, he advised her to continue the medication (a violation of neutrality) and reassured her that she still needed it. Such advice implies a lack of faith in the patient's own curative potential. She eventually discontinued the medication and all contacts with the psychiatrist. She initially described this step as probably an attempt on her part to sabotage herself and treatment.

Ms. A. continued to refer to the psychiatrist after ending all her direct involvement with him. Although these references undoubtedly were a derivative commentary on the "bad" aspect of the therapist, the therapist also began to suspect that the patient was aware (at least on an unconscious level) of the psychiatrist's continued involvement with her case. The patient's discontinuing all contact with the psychiatrist could be her demonstration of a model of rectification for the therapist to follow. She too was providing supervision by unconsciously conveying that the therapist should eliminate those elements in the setting (e.g., supervisor and tape recorder) that are supposed to be helpful but are in fact disruptive. Nonetheless, these concerns were not fully interpreted and corrected. Although the therapy continued to be tape-recorded and supervised, the therapist did transfer the supervision of this case to a supervisor who had no personal familiarity with the patient. It is noteworthy that after the transition, Ms. A. never again referred to the psychiatrist.

Extensive record keeping, staff discussions, and supervision all reflect violations of confidentiality. Because these frame violations were never fully rectified, they could not be resolved. Ms. A. and Ms. J. continued to communicate their concerns on both manifest and derivative levels.

Privacy

Related to the need for confidentiality is the need for privacy in the therapy situation. Ms. A.'s sessions revealed that a lack of privacy (e.g., tape recordings, absence of soundproofing, interruptions) may have a greater impact than is usually suspected. Early in the treatment she had been overtly preoccupied with the therapist's diagnosis and assessment of her problem. She had said she wanted to know the diagnosis so she could make the necessary changes to improve her life. She eventually abandoned these preoccupations on a conscious level.

One day, approximately nine months after beginning treatment, Ms. A. entered a session agitated and hostile. She said she wanted feedback, to know if she'd improved. She said she knew the therapist must have some opinion of her and that she wanted a "report card." Because she had not expressed such concerns overtly for quite some time, the therapist searched to find the origin of her preoccupation. Finally, after Ms. A. had made many attempts to pry the information out of the therapist while the therapist struggled to comprehend why this had again become such a pressing concern, Ms. A. explained: "I guess what really brought all this out was while I was in the waiting room area I happened to overhear a conversation in one of the rooms over there. [The door had been open.] I did not call myself eavesdropping, but I did not close my ears. The man was discussing a couple of his patients and he was stating facts. . . . Ms. A. was again confronted with the lack of privacy and confidentiality, and she was justifiably concerned about the therapist's discussing her case and even playing the tapes for others in the presence of other patients. Her concern was not related to improvement but to a fear of who knew about her case.

Violations of privacy and confidentiality can have a profound impact on treatment. In Ms. A., these violations stimulated a wish for directives and superficiality. She did not feel safe exploring and exposing her vulnerabilities in the presence of her therapist and unknown others.

Ms. J. commented extensively on the lack of privacy at the clinic. She was trying to separate from an enmeshed family with parasitic relationships. She too often encountered close relatives and family friends in the reception area. Clerical workers often tried to relay family messages or told relatives of the patient's appointment time so they could locate her. She frequently expressed a desire for private therapy and made concrete efforts to find employment.

Other patients have overtly expressed similar concerns. Many have expressed embarrassment at having to wait in a public area with regular medical patients, often their neighbors, who see them called into the psychiatry section.

CONCLUSIONS

The data presented in this study seem to support the hypothesis that the setting has an impact on the patient's responses to psychotherapy. Prior to efforts to secure the setting, Ms. A.'s comments were vague and ruminative. As the therapeutic environment became more neutral and secure with fewer external impingements, she began to discuss the factors that had hampered her early work. Her evident capacity to discuss these concerns overtly suggested that she no longer felt that she had to hide her thoughts vigorously from the therapist. Her verbal productions became freer and more honestly exploratory. Ms. A. began to improve. Throughout the year she was in therapy, she kept the same job. She reported never before keeping a job for more than a couple of months. Her anxiety and depression lifted. She reported that in the past she had often borrowed money from close relatives to reassure herself of their devotion and to maintain a helpless role. By the time of termination, this behavior had long since ceased. She was openly pursuing means of attending to her own needs. She proved to be motivated, intelligent, and fully capable of achieving insight. Her success and capacity to articulate clearly factors that obstructed her treatment challenge the stereotype of poor clinic patients as unmotivated and incapable of benefitting from a psychodynamic, expressive psychotherapy in a secure setting.

Ms. J.'s therapist was familiar with the communicative approach and was prepared to listen and interpret from the outset. Experience with this patient confirmed that a secure clinic setting is crucial for therapeutic advancement. Ms. J. was preoccupied with and able to communicate her reactions to the violations of the basic ground rules from the beginning. Despite these violations, she improved. Her object relationships became less inflamed and more stable. She was able to find a part-time job. She, too, was motivated, intelligent, and fully capable of achieving insight. She, too, challenges the stereotype of the poor clinic patient as unmotivated and incapable of benefitting from analytic psychotherapy in a secure setting.

That the frame remained mixed, with parts secured and parts left unrectified (e.g., the lack of privacy, confidentiality, and fees; the advice to take medications), has significance. Although such patients show areas of improvement, it has been my experience that they continue throughout the course of their psychotherapy to address the many violations in both manifest and derivative form. Whenever possible, the patients' concerns about the setting have been interpreted. It is my impression that these concerns cannot be resolved through interpretation in a modified setting. There are at times resistances in the form of silences, missed sessions, or material that becomes vague and ruminative. These resistances cannot be attributed solely to a patient's pathology or "lack of motivation" so long as the setting has not been secured. The continued violations communicate to patients that the clinic is most concerned with the needs of the clinic and its personnel and not with the provision of a secure environment that will enhance patients' efforts toward insightful resolution of their problems.

During the course of her therapy, Ms. J. became increasingly aware of her need for private psychotherapy in a secure setting. With her very limited education, she could not find a job that would pay her enough to cover her expenses, including those for quality child care and psychotherapy. At this writing she is still struggling to determine the value of continuing a therapy so limited by the clinic setting.

Although her concerns could not be resolved, the fact that they were subjected to therapeutic analysis is to Ms. J.'s advantage. In the past she had inferred from her therapists' behavior their belief that she was "resistant" to treatment. The clinic realities that had contributed to her difficulties had not been recognized. She had therefore taken interpretations as blame and had terminated treatment, feeling guilt about her inadequacies as a patient and her anger at her therapists for blaming her but not helping her. This was indeed a reenactment of her childhood traumas with a mother who could not create a secure home and care for her adequately. Her mother had been physically abusive and had indicated to her that her problems stemmed from her personal inadequacies. This background could not be distinguished usefully in the similar clinic setting. Interpretations that have included adaptive contexts of the clinic inadequacies and therapist errors appear to have enabled her to appreciate that the difficulties have not been hers alone. She seems to recognize that she needs a secure environment that will allow her wounds to heal. She continues to feel ambivalence toward the clinic and the therapist, because interpretations cannot actively undo the realities. She shows decreasing guilt and an increasing ability to appreciate and attend to her own needs.

In general, certain changes have become apparent in the approximately 40 patients offered a more stable environment. These patients seem less chaotic and confused than in the past. They rarely call or go to the clinics at nonscheduled times. They are rarely in crisis. These patients seem to mirror the more clearly defined and predictable settings in their own increased stability and clarity of communication.

Within the clinic literature, the setting was rarely addressed or considered to have any impact on a patient's course in treatment. Such an oversight, if we may call it that, in the presence of analytic literature clearly linking mismanagement of the setting to countertransferential reactions seems to be of profound significance in removing a potentially significant and antitherapeutic factor from further analysis and study.

The data presented in this chapter, in conjunction with the diverse literature, suggest the need for further studies in this area. The origins of and rationales for these variations in technique should be thoroughly explored, as well as the impact of frame modifications. Storrow (1962) recommended the creation of a clinic solely to explore the differing treatment modalities and their potential benefits to the poor. Should this idea come to fruition, or if other investigators explore this area, I recommend the creation of a secure therapeutic environment as defined by the analytic ground rules. In a clinic setting total confidentiality usually cannot be assured, so no claims should be made to the contrary. Considerable efforts should be devoted to maintaining confidentiality whenever possible, however. Charts should be kept in a locked file away from public scrutiny. Every discussion of a patient should be considered a possible violation of confidentiality and as potentially damaging to the therapeutic relationship. Most important is an awareness that such violations may serve as adaptive contexts to be listened for and understood from the patient's perspective prior to interpretation. All patient responses and requests should be analyzed and interpreted thoroughly prior to any violations of the basic analytic ground rules. Peer review and supervision may enable therapist to recognize, analyze, and resolve countertransferential reactions stimulated by this population.

Further studies would be enhanced by the analysis of complete patient process notes, which would allow enhanced hypothesis formation and confirmation via the analysis of both unconscious and conscious patient communications. We can hope that such reports would enable us to replace vague speculation with concrete patient data.

SUMMARY

The present study indicates that the therapeutic setting may have a powerful impact on the patient's response to psychotherapy. The stereotype of clinic patients from lower socioeconomic levels as unable to benefit from dynamic psychotherapy may be false. The frequently reported high drop-out rate and poor therapeutic response may stem from factors in the clinic setting rather than characteristics of the patient population. More research is necessary to assess further the impact of frame modifications and to determine the origins of and rationales for the frequent modifications in technique.

Acknowledgment

I want to express my deep appreciation and thanks to Dr. Marc Lubin. He created a secure setting as he advised me and supervised my work. He made a profound personal and professional contribution to my development. I want to thank Dr. Robert Langs for his technique, his editorial assistance, and his personal efforts on my behalf.

REFERENCES

ALBRONDA, H. F., DEAN, R. T., AND STARTWEATHER, J. A. (1964). Social class and psychotherapy. *Archives of General Psychiatry* 10:276–283.
ALEXANDER, F. (1954). Some quantitative aspects of psychoanalytic technique.

Abstracted in R. Langs, *The Therapeutic Interaction*, Vol. 1, pp. 109–110. New York: Jason Aronson, 1976.

ARLOW, J. A., AND BRENNER, C. (1966). The psychoanalytic situation. Abstracted in R. Langs, *The Therapeutic Interaction*, Vol. 1, pp. 297–299. New York: Jason Aronson, 1976.

BALCH, P. (1974). Social class and pathways to treatment at a community mental health center. *American Journal of Community Psychology* 2:365–371.

BERMAN, L. (1949). Countertransference and attitudes of the analyst in the therapeutic process. Abstracted in R. Langs, *The Therapeutic Interaction*, Vol. 1, pp. 74–75. New York: Jason Aronson, 1976.

BION, W. R. (1962). Learning from experience. In W. R. Bion, *Seven Servants*, pp. 1–111. New York: Jason Aronson, 1977.

——— (1963). Elements of psycho-analysis. In W. R. Bion, *Seven Servants*, pp. 1–110. New York: Jason Aronson, 1977.

——— (1965). Transformations. In W. R. Bion, *Seven Servants*, pp. 1–183. New York: Jason Aronson, 1977.

——— (1970). Attention and interpretation. In W. R. Bion, *Seven Servants*, pp. 1–136. New York: Jason Aronson, 1977.

BLEGER, J. (1967). Psychoanalysis of the psychoanalytic frame. *International Journal of Psycho-Analysis* 48:511–519.

BRANDT, L. (1966). Studies of dropout patients in psychotherapy. In *Psychotherapy Research*, ed. K. Stollak, A. Gurney, and M. Rothberg, pp. 268–276. Chicago: Rand McNally.

BRILL, N., AND STORROW, H. (1960). Social class and psychiatric treatment. *Archives of General Psychiatry* 3:340–344.

CHODOFF, P. (1978). Psychiatry and the fiscal third party. *American Journal of Psychiatry* 135:1141–1147.

COLE, N. J., BRANCH, C. C. H., AND ALLISON, R. B. (1962). Some relationships between social class and the practice of dynamic psychotherapy. *American Journal of Psychiatry* 118:1004–1012.

EISSLER, K. R. (1953). The effect of the structure of the ego on psychoanalytic technique. *Journal of the American Psychoanalytic Association* 1:104–143.

FERENCZI, S. (1921). The further development of an active therapy in psycho-analysis. Abstracted in R. Langs, *The Therapeutic Interaction*, Vol. 1, pp. 43–44. New York: Jason Aronson, 1976.

FRANK, J. (1956). Indications and contraindications for the application of the "standard techniques." Abstracted in R. Langs, *The Therapeutic Interaction*, Vol. 1, pp. 134–135. New York: Jason Aronson, 1976.

FREEMAN, A. (1966). Countertransference abuse of analytic rules. Abstracted in R. Langs, *The Therapeutic Interaction*, Vol. 1, p. 135. New York: Jason Aronson, 1976.

FREUD, A. (1954). Discussion. The widening scope of indications for psychoanalysis. Abstracted in R. Langs, *The Therapeutic Interaction*, Vol. 1, pp. 119–120. New York: Jason Aronson, 1976.

FREUD, S. (1912). Recommendations to physicians practising psycho-analysis. In *Therapy and Technique*, pp. 117–126. New York: Macmillan, 1963.

—— (1913). On beginning the treatment (further recommendations on the technique of psychoanalysis I). Abstracted in R. Langs, *The Therapeutic Interaction*, Vol. 1, pp. 34–35. New York: Jason Aronson, 1976.

—— (1919). Turnings in the ways of psychoanalytic therapy. In *Therapy and Technique*, pp. 181–190. New York: Macmillan, 1963.

GALLEGOS, J. A. (1975). Psychotherapy and the poor: problems and perspectives II: the poor patient in psychotherapy. *Revista de Neuro-Psiquiatria* 38:74–93.

GLOVER, E. (1955). The technique of psycho-analysis. Abstracted in R. Langs, *The Therapeutic Interaction*, Vol. 1, pp. 128–132. New York: Jason Aronson, 1976.

GOLDENSOHN, S. S., AND HAAR, E. (1974). Transferences and countertransference in a third-party payment system (HMO). *American Journal of Psychiatry* 131: 256–260.

GREENSON, R. R. (1965). The working alliance and the transference neurosis. Abstracted in R. Langs, *The Therapeutic Interaction*, Vol. 1, pp. 281–282. New York: Jason Aronson, 1976.

HAAK, N. (1957). Comments on the analytic situation. Abstracted in R. Langs, *The Therapeutic Interaction*, Vol. 1, pp. 160–161. New York: Jason Aronson, 1976.

HAAS, K. (1963). The middle-class professional and the lower-class patient. *Mental Hygiene* 47:408–410.

HOLLINGSHEAD, A. B., AND REDLICH, F. C. (1958). *Social Class and Mental Illness*. New York: John Wiley.

HUNT, R. G. (1960). Social class and mental illness: some implications for clinical theory and practice. *American Journal of Psychiatry* 116:1065–1069.

JACOBSON, E. (1954). Transference problems in the psychoanalytic treatment of severely depressive patients. Abstracted in R. Langs, *The Therapeutic Interaction*, Vol. 1, pp. 116–117. New York: Jason Aronson, 1976.

LAFORGUE, R. (1929) 'Active' psychoanalytic technique and the will to recovery. Abstracted in R. Langs, *The Therapeutic Interaction*, Vol. 1, p. 47. New York: Jason Aronson, 1976.·

LANGS, R. (1973). *The Technique of Psychoanalytic Psychotherapy*. Vol. 1. New York: Jason Aronson.

—— (1974). *The Technique of Psychoanalytic Psychotherapy*. Vol. 2. New York: Jason Aronson.

—— (1975a). The patient's unconscious perception of the therapist's errors. In R. Langs, *Technique in Transition*, pp. 139–154. New York: Jason Aronson, 1978.

—— (1975b). Therapeutic misalliances. In R. Langs, *Technique in Transition*, pp. 155–188. New York: Jason Aronson, 1978.

—— (1975c). The therapeutic relationship and deviations in technique. In R. Langs, *Technique in Transition*, pp. 189–230. New York: Jason Aronson, 1978.

—— (1976a). *The Bipersonal Field*. New York: Jason Aronson.

—— (1976b). *The Therapeutic Interaction*. 2 Vols. New York: Jason Aronson.

—— (1978a). *The Listening Process*. New York: Jason Aronson.

—— (1978b). Validation and the framework of the therapeutic situation: thoughts prompted by Hans H. Strupp's "Suffering and Psychotherapy." *Contemporary Psychoanalysis* 14:98–124.

——— (1979a). *The Supervisory Experience.* New York: Jason Aronson.

——— (1979b). *The Therapeutic Environment.* New York: Jason Aronson.

——— (1980a). *Interactions: The Realm of Transference and Countertransference.* New York: Jason Aronson.

——— (1980b). Truth therapy/lie therapy. *International Journal of Psychoanalytic Psychotherapy* 8:3–34.

——— (1981). *Resistances and Interventions: The Nature of Therapeutic Work.* New York: Jason Aronson.

LANGS, R., AND STONE, L. (1980). *The Therapeutic Experience and Its Setting: A Clinical Dialogue.* New York: Jason Aronson.

LIEF, H. T., LIEF, V. F., WARREN, C. O., AND HEATH, R. G. (1961). Low dropout rate in a psychiatric clinic. *Archives of General Psychiatry* 5:200–211.

McMAHON, J. T. (1964). The working-class psychiatric patient: a clinical view. In *Mental Health of the Poor*, ed. F. Reissman, J. Cohen, and A. Pearl, pp. 283–302. London: Free Press of Glencoe.

MILNER, M. (1952). Aspects of symbolism in comprehension of the not-self. Abstracted in R. Langs, *The Therapeutic Interaction*, Vol. 1, pp. 94–96. New York: Jason Aronson, 1976.

MODELL, A. H. (1976). The holding environment and the therapeutic action of psychoanalysis. Abstracted in R. Langs, *The Therapeutic Interaction*, Vol. 1, pp. 600–603. New York: Jason Aronson.

NASH, J. L., AND CAVENAR, J. (1976). Free psychotherapy: an inquiry into resistance. *American Journal of Psychiatry* 133:1066–1067.

NIR, Y., AND CUTLER, R. (1978). The unmotivated patient syndrome: survey of therapeutic interventions. *American Journal of Psychiatry* 135:442–447.

OVERALL, B., AND ARONSON, H. (1963). Expectations of psychotherapy in patients of lower socioeconomic class. *American Journal of Orthopsychiatry* 32:421–430.

RANGELL, L. (1969). The intrapsychic process and its analysis: a recent line of thought and its current implications. Abstracted in R. Langs, *The Therapeutic Interaction*, Vol. 1, pp. 412–413. New York: Jason Aronson, 1976.

REDER, P., AND TYSON, R. L. (1980). Patient dropout from individual psychotherapy: a review and discussion. *Bulletin of the Menninger Clinic* 44:229–252.

REISSMAN, F., COHEN, J., AND PEARL, A. (1964). *Mental Health of the Poor: New Treatment and Approaches for Low-Income People.* London: Free Press of Glencoe.

ROSEN, H., AND FRANK, J. D. (1962). Negroes in psychotherapy. *American Journal of Psychiatry* 119:456–460.

ROSENTHAL, D., AND FRANK, J. D. (1958). The fate of psychiatric clinic outpatients assigned to psychotherapy. *Journal of Nervous and Mental Disease* 127:330–343.

SCHAFFER, L., AND MEYERS, J. K. (1954). Psychotherapy and social stratification in a psychiatric outpatient clinic. *Psychiatry* 17:83–93.

SEWARD, G., AND MARMOR, J. (1956). *Psychotherapy and Culture Conflict.* New York: Ronald Press.

SIASSI, I., AND MESSER, S. (1976). Psychotherapy with patients from lower socioeconomic groups. *American Journal of Psychotherapy* 30:29–40.

SPIEGEL, J. P. (1959). Some cultural aspects of transference and countertransference. In *Individual and Family Dynamics*, ed. J. H. Masserman, pp. 160–182. New York: Grune & Stratton.

STERN, A. (1948). Transference and borderline neurosis. Abstracted in R. Langs, *The Therapeutic Interaction*, Vol. 1, p. 74. New York: Jason Aronson, 1976.

STONE, L. (1954). The widening scope of indications for psychoanalysis. Abstracted in R. Langs, *The Therapeutic Interaction*, Vol. 1, pp. 117–119. New York: Jason Aronson, 1976.

STORROW, H. (1962). Psychiatric treatment and the lower-class neurotic patient. *Archives of General Psychiatry* 6:91–95.

STRUPP, H. (1978). Suffering and psychotherapy. *Contemporary Psychoanalysis* 14: 73–97.

TARACHOW, S. (1962a). Interpretation and reality in psychotherapy. Abstracted in R. Langs, *The Therapeutic Interaction*, Vol. 1, p. 259–262. New York: Jason Aronson, 1976.

—— (1962b). The problem of reality and the therapeutic task. Abstracted in R. Langs, *The Therapeutic Interaction*, Vol. 1, pp. 258–259. New York: Jason Aronson, 1976.

TERESTMAN, N., MILLER, D., AND WEBBER, J. (1974). Blue-collar patients at a psychoanalytic clinic. *American Journal of Psychiatry* 131:261–266.

VIDERMAN, S. (1974). Interpretation in the analytic space. Abstracted in R. Langs, *The Therapeutic Interaction*, Vol. 1, pp. 562–564. New York: Jason Aronson, 1976.

WINNICOTT, D. W. (1954). Metapsychological and clinical aspects of regression within the psychoanalytic set-up. Abstracted in R. Langs, *The Therapeutic Interaction*, Vol. 1, pp. 127–128. New York: Jason Aronson, 1976.

—— (1956). Symposium. On Transference. Abstracted in R. Langs, *The Therapeutic Interaction*, Vol. 1, pp. 152–154. Jason Aronson, 1976.

—— (1958) *Collected Papers*. London: Tavistock.

—— (1960). Countertransference: the theory of parent-infant relationships. Abstracted in R. Langs, *The Therapeutic Interaction*, Vol. 1, p. 226. New York: Jason Aronson, 1976.

—— (1963). Psychiatric disorders in terms of infantile maturational process. Abstracted in R. Langs, *The Therapeutic Interaction*, Vol. 1, pp. 272–273. Jason Aronson, 1976.

CHAPTER 12

Community Mental Health, Clients' Rights, and the Therapeutic Frame

Mark Vlosky, Ph.D.

In 1980 there were approximately 600 community mental health centers in the United States and another 100 planned (Kiesler 1980). In 1975 the centers served 1.6 million people and provided 29 percent of all outpatient care (Kiesler 1980). The substantial group of psychotherapy providers working at these centers is under constant pressure to safeguard clients' rights.

Mental health centers receiving federal funds fall under the provisions of the Mental Health Systems Act, which specifies that:

> A person admitted to a program or facility for the purpose of receiving mental health service should be accorded . . . the right to an individualized, written treatment or service plan . . . , the right to be informed of the rights described in this section [and] the right to assert grievances with respect to infringements of the rights described in this section. . . . Each program and facility should post a notice listing [in appropriate language] the rights described in this section. (Mental Health Systems Act 1980, pp. 1598–1601)

Mental health centers not funded by the federal government but receiving funds from states find that state laws modeled after the Mental Health Systems Act similarly require written treatment programs and posted notices of clients' rights (e.g., State of Wyoming 1982). Additionally, professional journal articles champion the client's right to a written treatment contract (Hare-Mustin et al. 1979) as well as to a clients' rights statement and informed consent form (Everstine et al. 1980). If the maintenance and protection of *all* of a client's rights were secured by giving documents at the outset of therapy, there could be no quarrel with such procedures. Paradoxically, however, the very focus on a written clients' rights statement, individualized treatment plan, informed consent form, and the like constitutes a turning away from interactive truth therapy (Langs 1980) and severely

255

compromises the most basic right of all: the client's right to a secure therapeutic frame. The secure frame excludes any intimation that third parties evaluate private consultations.

Interactive psychotherapists experience difficulties in community mental health centers, the greatest being the clinic-induced frame issues discussed by Langs (1979). The American Psychological Association's Division of Community Psychology attempts to follow an exclusively socioecological approach to theory and intervention (American Psychological Association 1980). Technically, such an approach means intervening at an organizational and community level, engaging natural support systems, and targeting special "needy" populations, such as children and the elderly, for intensive outreach efforts. A content analysis of journal articles on community mental health revealed that the authors' conceptualizations largely were guided by the community systems approach but that actual intervention strategies remained at the individual and small group levels (McClure et al. 1980). Thus, business as usual seems to occur in community mental health centers, but with a gap between practice and praxis. The effect has been a downgrading of regard for individual psychotherapy in many centers and the assumption of a crisis intervention stance, with time-limited counseling the only option for every patient.

Regardless of the relative merits of intensive psychotherapy and short-term counseling, many community mental health center clients are deprived of the opportunity for a thorough therapeutic experience. Rural mental health centers serving sparsely populated catchment areas that cannot support a single private practitioner almost invariably restrict or forbid outside private practice by their employees. The Mental Health Systems Act specifies that applicants for funding "will adopt and enforce a policy . . . which prohibits mental health professionals who provide [services] to patients through the applicant from providing such services to such patients except through the applicant" (1980, p. 1592). Many centers, federally funded or not, prohibit any practice outside the center by employees within the catchment area. Consequently, as Graziano (1969) points out, the catchment area concept in community mental health creates local monopolies that may be insensitive to clients' needs. In particular, rural inhabitants desiring or requiring long-term insight psychotherapy are not served.

At the heart of community mental health and the Mental Health Systems Act is the concept of people in need of mental health services. The need concept leads to a presumption that a professional, rather than the client, is the person able to determine the necessity and nature of treatment. From this attitude follow provider subsidies for needs analyses and outreach programs, but the approach is fundamentally incompatible with psychotherapies that regard the client as an active, willing, and responsible participant in therapy

(Buck and Hirschman 1980). For most psychotherapy clients, need is felt to issue from within. And as Langs has shown repeatedly, an intrinsic aspect of felt need is the need for a secure therapeutic frame.

A description of one community mental health center follows. We then present case material illustrating the impact of this setting on clients' felt needs.

THE MENTAL HEALTH CENTER

The community mental health center where all the clients to be presented were seen is a state and locally funded institution. It serves a 7,000-square-mile catchment area in Wyoming with a population of approximately 18,000. Because there are no private practitioners in the area and employees are forbidden to see clients privately, there is no competition within any reasonable distance. The center rents space in an office park away from streets and thus affords some privacy from passing traffic.

The center occupies three offices, each opening directly onto a waiting room dominated by the secretary's desk. File cabinets stand in plain view. The center's outside door opens from the waiting room, so people coming in must either wait in the presence of the secretary or pass her on the way into an office. Visitors of the secretary are sometimes seen by patients. The mailman generally spends a few minutes with her as a break from his rounds. Additionally, some therapist–secretary business is conducted at her desk in the waiting room and can include the mention of patients' names. Efforts have been made to sensitize the staff to this breach of confidentiality, but it cannot always be controlled. In the absence of patients, the waiting room becomes a lounge for the staff. Patients have walked in on such gatherings. The offices are not sufficiently soundproofed.

CASE MATERIAL

Through their manifest and derivative communications in my office at the center, patients have demonstrated keen sensitivity to various framework aspects of the community mental health setting.

Billing Procedures

A 28-year-old laborer began treatment to work through difficulties with his divorce. Months later he was engaged in twice-weekly therapy for neurotic and characterological problems. He came to a session slightly late and proceeded to complain that his ex-wife was still dunning him for household goods through her lawyer. It infuriated him that she didn't ask for what she wanted directly. He was insulted to be thought so cheap as to deny her the iron, ironing board, and other supplies that she wanted. He shifted to describing a water leak in his house, saying a plumber had investigated but failed to locate the problem. Later the patient had fixed the leak himself. He resented the plumber's bill, although he did feel that the plumber was entitled to collect. He went on to speak of damaging machinery at work and being castigated severely for the mistake. He said his nose had really been rubbed in it.

During this session it occurred to me that a billing period had recently closed and that the patient might have received his bill that week. Additionally, I recalled he had missed a session the previous month and probably would be billed for that hour. The bill would have made a clear adaptive context for the derivative complex of a lawyer's dunning on behalf of his ex-wife (the secretary's billing for me), his being charged for work the plumber didn't do (charge for the missed session), and, less clearly, of his having had his nose rubbed into a mistake. Unfortunately I wasn't sure he had been charged for the missed session, or even that his bill had been sent. Consequently I could not interpret the material with confidence. I might have risked an interpretation of his dismay at my using the secretary for billing and his resentment over being charged for the missed session, but I was puzzled at the derivative of his having had his nose rubbed in a mistake. I decided not to intervene along these lines. He left the session with some sourness, undoubtedly resulting from my missed interpretation.

After checking with the secretary, I found a copy of the patient's bill, which indeed had been mailed. The secretary had typed "missed session" beside a date among the others, which accounted for the "having his nose rubbed in it" derivative. Following this episode I arranged for the secretary to stop identifying missed sessions on bills; more important, I began reading the bills and personally handing them to patients. This procedure avoids third-party billing and permits the evaluation of adaptive context functioning of the bills.

Anonymity

Frame breaks caused by breaches in the therapist's anonymity are inevitable in rural and small town settings, but the community systems approach to service delivery fosters and intensifies such breaks. Community mental health centers require their therapists to consult with social service agencies, among whose employees are many candidates for insight psychotherapy.

I was asked to evaluate an apparently psychotic child at a public school and to confer with involved school personnel afterward. A teacher who had been seeing me weekly attended the conference and was visibly uncomfortable throughout. This major frame contamination was not clearly represented in therapy for several weeks. Eventually, the teacher said she had been struggling not to be as perfectionistic as usual and was trying to settle for less in several domains. She had contacted an organization that helped people form self-help groups and was planning to start such a group herself. She said she would stay in treatment with me until the group got going, but if the group seemed helpful she would end therapy and rely on the group. She didn't feel she was making any progress. She said she didn't do enough in the community and felt guilty that she wasn't helping people less fortunate than herself. Several weeks had intervened since our meeting at the school, so that frame contamination did not occur to me as an adaptive context for this material. I credit Robert Langs, my tape supervisor at the time, for the following discussion.

The school conference was represented by the self-help group and by the patient's wish to do more in the community. Accompanying this representation of the break in our therapeutic frame was the patient's statement of being less perfectionistic, of struggling to settle for less. Also, there was dissatisfaction with therapy and a felt lack of progress. Derivatively, the patient was reconciling herself to a less-than-perfect psychotherapy in which the frame contamination was blocking progress. Her desire to start a self-help group was a response to an unconscious perception of me as participating in group contacts. She was saying, "If it's going to be that kind of deviant therapy, I might as well structure it myself."

Presence of a Secretary in the Waiting Room

Patient after patient was starting sessions on a jocular note, with such comments as "Hi, how are you?" and "How's your week been?" This behavior puzzled me, because I generally don't answer such questions. Finally I realized that these people had been greeted that way by the secretary. With some difficulty I convinced her to be more reserved. Thus relieved of a perpetually friendly introject on the threshold of my office, these patients proceeded to start sessions with various affects, including sullenness, which I had rarely seen before. The sullenness, however, may well represent another secretary introject, thus illustrating that a secretary's presence in the waiting room constitutes an intractable frame deviation.

The secretary's presence can influence therapist as well as patient. Near the end of an hour, one patient was sobbing copiously. As the time ended I uncharacteristically asked her to stay a few moments to compose herself. She remained about 30 seconds and then left saying, "Time's up; got to go; there's a limit for everything." Reflection revealed that my offer of time for composure represented a projection on my part of embarrassment lest the patient return to the secretary in tears. Langs (1976) points out that patients often react to countertransference-based frame deviations with unconscious efforts to correct them. In this instance the patient left very quickly, thereby rectifying my secretary-induced break in the frame.

Secretary–Patient Telephone Calls

In many community mental health centers, telephone calls for the purposes of making, changing, and cancelling appointments routinely are handled by the secretary. A woman left a message on the overnight answering machine saying she would miss her next appointment but wanted to reschedule. I instructed the secretary to call her with the message that I would see her the following week at her regular time.

In that next session the patient talked about a date she had had, for which her date had arrived with his parents and another woman in the car. After dinner he had dropped the others off, driven the patient home, and made love to her, and then had told her about other women he took out. He had maintained that she was "number one." The patient cried while telling me this, and it led to rumination about sewing projects and other endeavors that she undertook but then abandoned. She claimed she never finished anything she started.

This material constitutes a derivative complex around the adaptive context of manifold frame deviations. The patient discusses a date with others present and having been made love to while her partner spoke of other women. Symbolically this material represents her view of our therapeutic relationship. When she comes to see me the secretary is there, and often others are sitting in the waiting room. The secretary even gets involved in the private matter of scheduling appointments. Her boyfriend avoids a one-to-one relationship with her, and so do I. At the same time that she sees me wrecking the frame by sending messages through a secretary, the very message I send—that we'll stick to regular hours—claims to maintain a secure therapeutic frame. My contradictory message is represented in the boyfriend's claim that the patient was "number one" at a time he was demonstrating that she wasn't. My mixed message is represented further by the patient's lament that she can't finish anything she starts. I have started to secure the frame by holding to regular hours but have failed to complete the job by not calling the patient myself. These derivative communications indicate the devastating effects of certain framework deviations. The routine procedure of asking my secretary to return this patient's call has evoked in the patient emotions of betrayal and destruction of relationships, and profound despair at an inability to carry projects through.

A further vignette illustrates the extent to which inconsistent framework management can ruin psychotherapy.

Partial Frame Rectification

My office was far from soundproof. The walls were insulated sheetrock, but the door was hollow with a gap at the sill. Upon occupying the office I put weatherstripping around the door, which helped muffle some sounds but failed to exclude voices fully between the waiting room and office. Several patients commented on the noise leak, particularly after sitting in the waiting room while I was talking on the telephone. Derivatively, I never heard the end of patients' complaints about people who gossiped, snooped, and wouldn't leave them any privacy. The situation was intolerable and called for a change. I presented my case to the mental health center's board of directors, who authorized me to install acoustical tiles and a second door. The result was imperfect but satisfactory and represented a vast improvement over what had been. The work was done on a weekend, so patients saw the change as having taken place suddenly.

A patient arriving for her regular appointment entered the office and sat down as I closed the doors. She said, "Wow, you have two doors. That's something new. I'm impressed." She added, "Do you prefer for me to call you Doctor, or can I call you Mark?" Here was a key derivative of the patient's sensitivity to my having rectified an aspect of the frame. She was impressed with the double door manifestly, but then asked derivatively if we were going to have a fully secure treatment frame or if new deviations would arise. This patient had been incestuously victimized by her father throughout her adolescent years, and now at the first moment of privacy she wondered which form of address I preferred. The transference–countertransference question was whether I still want to be called Doctor and conduct therapy despite my double doors, or if I would rather be called Mark in private, illicitly and therefore incestuously. I failed to grasp these ramifications at the moment but responded to her question naively, saying, "It's up to you." She said, "Okay, I'll call you Mark," thus colluding with her unconscious model of me as a potentially incestuous frame breaker.

She went on to ruminate over the vagueness of her problem, saying she didn't know whether she should be in treatment at all. She said, "If we're going to have private therapy, I should know why I'm here." Here, she was stating derivatively that in secure psychotherapy the boundaries must be defined clearly. My contradictory actions of soundproofing the office while allowing her to call me Mark here confused our boundaries to a disturbing extent. The "me–not me" concept was reflected in her indication that I, the therapist, did not know why *I* was there.

For the remainder of that session, she grew increasingly upset, while I continued to miss the cause for her upset—namely, my confusing management/mismanagement of the frame. She quit a few days later by calling the secretary to say she would not be back.

Emergency Services

A minister called me at home one evening to say that a patient of mine was at his house feeling very agitated. There was no mention of suicide, but the woman needed someone to talk to and the minister had to go out. Would I see her?

Only a community mental health worker on call understands the specific force of such pressure. Each community mental health center is organized under a lay board of directors elected from the local community. These boards and their centers are funded for emergency services, which usually are provided by staff on a rotating basis. While on call, one's job can depend on gratifying emergency requests, even if such gratifications do not make good therapeutic sense. I asked if the patient could meet me at my office. No; she didn't have a car. I agreed to see her at the minister's house and drove over. The minister left when I got there and I visited with the patient—there is no other term to describe our interaction—for about 45 minutes until she let me go.

At the next appointment she was furious with my initial silence, which she always had tolerated before. She wasn't comfortable in the chair and had to pace around the office. She finally wound up on the floor. She complained about her husband's unreliability and his never being around when he was needed. She then attacked my technique, saying she wanted a friend, not someone who was distant, as I was. She rejected every effort I made to interpret. Clearly my seeing the patient at her minister's home had been a disruptive encounter that betrayed her need for a secure therapeutic frame. Her unwillingness to settle into the chair and to continue to participate in an interpretive psychotherapy dramatized her perception that I had abandoned my role as a frame manager. The complaints about her husband were further derivatives of her unconscious perception. If I were truly reliable and available as a therapist, I would have respected her non-need that evening and refused to visit at the minister's home. This episode had long-lasting consequences. The patient subsequently called me at home several times to report anxiety. Only slowly did she return to accepting an interpretive approach.

Intake Forms

The mental health center's intake procedure involved asking new patients to read and complete two forms. This business was conducted by the secretary in the waiting room, a logical procedure because she sent bills and maintained patients' files. One intake form was a data sheet, asking for name, age, address, phone number, and employment, income, and family information. The other was a clients' rights statement to be read and signed. No patient ever complained about the forms or mentioned them manifestly, but time and again in first sessions they indicated fears of being talked about, fooled, lied to, and controlled.

I once happened to read the statement of clients' rights, which contained the following provisions:

(1) Communications made to your counselor are private and confidential and will not be revealed to anyone except with your written consent, *or as provided by the statutes of the State* [italics added]. (2) You have the right to discuss and have established a written treatment plan. (3) You cannot be restrained in any manner. (4) You cannot be hospitalized against your will. (5) [Above the area where the patient must sign] I have read the above statement and received a copy for my personal use.

Point 1 is a confusing double message, implying lack of protection rather than protection. Points 2 and 4 are lies, as no one gets a written treatment plan and the law does provide for involuntary hospitalization. Point 3 is a spurious reassurance that infantilizes the reader, and point 5 requires new patients to lie: no one is ever offered a copy of the form. This cornucopia of deceits, hidden threats, and double messages was an obvious adaptive context for the derivative expressions of similar material I so frequently heard in first sessions.

Rather than continuing to allow the secretary to supervise patient intake, I began presenting the forms myself, usually near the end of the first session. My undocumented impression was that the quality of initial sessions became more varied following my change in procedure. One effect of bringing the forms into treatment was the discomfort I always felt when having patients sign the clients' rights statement. I raised the matter at a staff meeting, and we decided to discontinue using that form. Although Wyoming State operating standards for community mental health programs mandate clients' rights statements, our rejection of this measure rested on a clause stating, "Nothing in this chapter shall obligate an individual mental health professional to administer treatment contrary to such professional's clinical judgement" (State of Wyoming 1982, p. 29). Perhaps such clauses appear in similar statutes as well.

CONCLUSIONS

The foregoing examples of derivative responses to frame breaks in therapies conducted in a community mental health center represent typical patient communications. All these patients expressed an unconscious need for a secure psychotherapeutic framework. They all responded to breaks in the frame with a sense of disruption and distress. In contrast with the community systems approach to mental health services delivery, which

264 / MARK VLOSKY

emphasizes natural supports, organizational interventions, and cross communications about patients within a helping network, even patients in this
remote, rural region demanded to be treated in a securely private therapeutic
frame.

The result of this need is that deviations such as third parties in the
waiting room, secretaries making calls and sending bills, noise leakage,
extratherapeutic meetings in the community, non-life-saving "emergency"
interventions, and the presentation of spurious documents in the name of
clients' rights all have a seriously destructive impact on patients' perceptions
of treatment. Langs states that patients are universally sensitive to technical
and framework deviations and invariably react to them (1975). Evidently
this is true.

In order to experience patients' reactions to the treatment setting, one
must apply proper listening, which permits hearing manifest content as
derivative of latent meanings (Langs 1978). This challenging technique is
most difficult when the latent meanings bear on frame issues introduced by
the therapist. For instance, in the described instance in which the patient
complained about never finishing what she started, I failed to hear this
immediately as a "me–not me" reflection of my incomplete efforts to rectify
the frame. It is impossible, for me at least, to hear such unexpected material
correctly without profound chagrin. Technically there are two necessary
responses: truthfully interpret a patient's treatment-induced distress, and
rectify the frame whenever possible.

Unfortunately, rural insight patients and their therapists must work
inside the local monopolies of community mental health. Some centers will
allow employees to perform their own intake, billing, and appointment
procedures, to soundproof their offices, and otherwise to secure treatment
frames. Others will not.

With the help of an interpretive psychotherapist, patients can decide how
long to stay in treatment. One man talked ceaselessly for three sessions
about bookkeeping, audits, filing systems, and the Internal Revenue Service.
He was told that these preoccupations reflected deep concern over the
center's files and a fear of what might happen if they were read. He agreed,
saying he didn't like having his name on file and was unable to confide in
me. In response to the unrectifiable record-keeping system, the patient quit. I
counted his a brief psychotherapy with an insightful ending.

REFERENCES

AMERICAN PSYCHOLOGICAL ASSOCIATION (1980). Division of Community Psychology *Newsletter*, no. 13. Washington, D.C.: American Psychological Association.

BUCK, J. A., AND HIRSCHMAN, R. (1980). Economics and mental health services. *American Psychologist* 35:653–661.

EVERSTINE, L., EVERSTINE, D. S., HEYMANN, G. M., TRUE, R. H., FREY, D. H., JOHNSON, H. G., AND SEIDEN, R. H. (1980). Privacy and confidentiality in psychotherapy. *American Psychologist* 35:828–840.

GRAZIANO, A. (1969). Clinical innovation and the mental health power structure: a social case history. *American Psychologist* 24:10–18.

HARE-MUSTIN, R. T., MARECEK, J. M., KAPLAN, A. G., AND LISS-LEVENSON, N. (1979). Rights of clients, responsibilities of therapists. *American Psycholosist* 34:3–16.

KIESLER, C. A. (1980). Mental health policy as a field of inquiry for psychology. *American Psychologist* 35:1066–1080.

LANGS, R. (1975). The therapeutic relationship and deviations in technique. *International Journal of Psychoanalytic Psychotherapy* 4:106–141.

———— (1976). *The Bipersonal Field.* New York: Jason Aronson.

———— (1978). *The Listening Process.* New York: Jason Aronson.

———— (1979). *The Therapeutic Environment.* New York: Jason Aronson.

———— (1980). Truth therapy/lie therapy. *International Journal of Psychoanalytic Psychotherapy* 8:3–34.

McCLURE, L., CANNON, D., ALLEN, S., BELTON, E., CONNER, R., D'ASCOLI, C., STONE, P., SULLIVAN, B., AND McCLURE, G. (1980). Community psychology concepts and research base. *American Psychologist* 35:1000–1011.

MENTAL HEALTH SYSTEMS ACT (1980). Public Law 96-398.

STATE OF WYOMING (1982). *Standards for the Operation of Community Mental Health and Substance Abuse Programs (Proposed Rules).* Cheyenne, Wyo.: Department of Health and Social Services, Division of Community Programs.

CHAPTER 13

Framework Rectification and Transient Negative Effects

Cynthia Keene, Psy. D.

THE CONCEPT AND COMPONENTS OF THE FRAME

Because the major goal of psychoanalytic treatment is to understand and adaptively alter unconscious processes, the course of treatment and the total environment in which it occurs must be tailored to that purpose. To this end, paramount emphasis must be given to thorough analysis of all manifest data for their latent implications. The framework for psychoanalytic treatment, then, must meet two basic requirements. First, the analytic environment must provide a medium conducive to the expression of the patient's most primitive unconscious processes. This requirement calls for a setting that is perceived as safe and secure, promising that no impulse will find direct expression in reality. The second criterion demands a firm and constant matrix as a background against which the derivatives of unconscious functioning may be compared reliably. Here, the framework serves to limit external contamination that may confound the accurate interpretation of the patient's unconscious material. These twin standards, then, form the basis of the optimal and secure therapeutic framework for psychoanalytic treatment.

The origin of this formulation lies in Freud's discussions of the conduct of treatment (1912, 1913, 1914b, 1915), in which he established the basic ground rules and boundaries of the psychoanalytic method. His crucial observations, however, have often been taught en masse, with the determinants of the analytic setting being relegated to a mere set of rules. As a result, the impact of the framework on the unconscious functioning of both patient and therapist generally has been ignored.

In reviving Freud's cache of insights in this area, Langs (1976a, 1976b) adopted the metaphor of the frame to describe the multiple functions of the analytic environment. This metaphor was based on Milner's analogy (1952) to the frame around a painting, which protects the piece of art and simultaneously sets off the creative reality contained within it. As such, it both demarcates and enhances the "creative illusion" of the painting while acting to protect it. Milner compared this with the process of psychoanalysis, in which the transference is the crucial "creative illusion" of the patient's intrapsychic reality. For the symbolic relationship of the transference to reach full fruition, the unique "temporal spatial frame" of the analytic environment is necessary for "a transcending of that common sense perception which would see a picture as only an attempt at photography, or the analyst as only a present-day person" (Milner 1952, p. 190).

Langs (1979, 1980, 1981) has formulated the totality of the therapeutic framework as being composed of fixed and fluid determinants. The former include the quantifiable aspects of treatment, such as the duration and frequency of sessions, the physical environment and the positioning of patient and therapist, fee arrangements, and the requirement of total confidentiality and privacy. The fluid components are so termed because they are more easily variable according to "the humanness and residual countertransference reflected in the ongoing work of the therapist" (Langs 1979, p. 541). Such fluid elements are the therapist's neutrality, anonymity, accuracy of interpretations, and abstinence, as well as the patient's adherence to the fundamental rule of free association and the need to preanalyze all major decisions. Together, these fixed and fluid determinants constitute the commonly detailed ground rules and boundaries of the ideal analytic frame. Maintenance of this frame is designed specifically for the efficient use of interpretive and reconstructive interventions as the primary instruments for attaining therapeutic resolution of unconscious disturbances.

According to Langs's empirical studies (1981), deviations of the fixed frame are most disturbing to the patient and find ready representation in the communicative network; i.e., they are conveyed in terms of an accessible indicator of disturbance, adaptive context, coalescing derivative complex, and bridge or link to the therapist (Langs 1982). Whenever such full representation is available from the patient, immediate rectification is necessary, along with remediating interpretation. Deviations in the fluid frame are likely to be more highly disguised and convoluted in their communicative representation (Langs 1981, p. 184), especially when they occur in conjunction with more compelling errors, such as deviations in the fixed frame components. Hill (1981) has also found that when a deviation has particular resonance with a major aspect of the patient's neurotic complex, it can serve as a vital instrument for resistance to the analytic process. Therefore, it is difficult to predict the ultimate effect of a particular deviation, and its rectification, on an individual without thorough understanding of his or her pathology and its developmental origins.

When therapists rectify deviations, Langs (1981) observed, there often occurs a marked surfacing of diverse disturbances within the treatment process. This rectified frame reaction (RFR) results when deviations have been corrected at the behest of the patient's material and after derivative validation of the rectification. What follows is an upsurge in paranoid, phobic, and/or hypochondriacal material that may be evidenced on both latent and manifest levels. This development commonly is accompanied by sharp increases in communicative and gross behavioral resistances (Langs 1979) and appears to represent an overall intensification of defensive processes within the more secure frame.

This RFR is similar to and must be distinguished from iatrogenic paranoia (Langs 1974). Although the overt symptomatology can be virtually identical, the iatrogenic syndrome is induced in the patient by treatment conducted in the presence of disruptive deviations. Its appearance, therefore, would not be expected after appropriate rectification. This seeming paradox can be resolved only through careful analysis of etiology within the therapeutic process. Whereas iatrogenic paranoia derives from the patient's efforts to adapt to impinging deviations, the RFR is a response to the removal of the deviation and loss of any attendant neurotic gratification. As such, the RFR evidences a greater proportion of the patient's real pathology as its prime motivating factor.

Ultimately, the RFR must be recognized to be an admixture of both iatrogenic and intrapsychic factors, with the former being carried as a residual product of prior deviations. This admixture presents a continuum for assessing the functional nature of various disturbances in treatment, according to the relative contribution of deviant input from the therapist's management of the overall treatment frame. Such ongoing diagnostic appraisal is crucial in differentiating the patient's actual pathology from that which is an artifact of the treatment.

The appearance of the RFR also raises the issue of the appropriate management and interpretive stance required to facilitate its constructive resolution. This issue is of special concern in the case of those patients who sustain a prolonged and tempestuous RFR that threatens to destroy treatment, often by eventuating in premature termination. Such an extreme situation appears to be a specific form of the broader negative therapeutic reaction in which the patient is unable to tolerate the curative process because of massive resistive needs to maintain his or her pathological status.

LIABILITIES OF THE SECURE FRAME

Careful consideration must be given to the threatening aspects of treatment within the secure analytic frame. Within such a frame, the patient's maladaptive defensive maneuvers progressively are analyzed rather than being pathologically gratified and reinforced. As a result, the patient experiences an increasing sense of neurotic frustration that triggers regression to earlier coping and defensive strategies. The process of cure also entails eventual confrontation with all the trauma and conflict that once threatened to overrun the child's ego and thus had to be exiled from conscious awareness. The psychoanalytic method attempts to reverse that original process of repression, so that the "relatively mature aspects of the patient's ego" can rework these childhood dangers more adaptively (Greenson 1967, p. 29). This process of derepression, however, threatens to resurrect both the content and the affect of the original memories, as well as intensifying the immediate signal anxiety (Freud 1926) that accompanies any potential resurgence of unconscious components. It is this process that begins to account for the patient's subjective experience of threat within the analytic frame as treatment gradually sets about retrieving those elements of danger that the patient has for so long attempted to keep from conscious awareness. Such a phenomenological explanation, however, fails to address the subtle and powerful intricacy of forces mustered within the patient to defend against just such a threat—those factors within treatment that collectively are termed *resistance.*

Resistances

The study of the sources of resistance is particularly pertinent to understanding the etiology of various disturbances within the secure frame, whether these take the form of a mild and transient RFR or the more severely disruptive full-blown negative therapeutic reaction. Freud first recognized resistance as unconscious opposition to treatment in his "Studies on Hysteria" (Breuer and Freud 1893–1895) and went on to establish the analysis of resistances as both a theoretical and a technical fundamental of the psychoanalytic method. Freud (1914a) later determined that the patient's modes of resistance were actually what one might term in vivo demonstrations of the same processes by which the repression of painful and conflicted memories, the basis of neurotic illness, was originally established and subsequently maintained. Analysis of resistance therefore became a key vehicle for immobilizing defenses so that the originating trauma and conflict consciously could be accessed and resolved. Although resistances are an important impediment to the treatment process, Anna Freud (1936) has also pointed out that they provide crucial data for assessment of ego functioning. Because resistances reflect the patient's habitual modes of defense, they demonstrate both the ego's adaptive abilities and its nodes of relative insufficiency (see also Fenichel 1945, Greenson 1967, Langs 1974).

In 1926 Freud developed a basic classification of resistances according to their sources. He first defined repression resistance as stemming from the ways in which the ego customarily defends against the anxiety aroused by both intrapsychic and external danger or conflict situations. This is the most obvious resistance; it occurs in direct response to the threat of derepressing the traumatic origins of the patient's illness. Transference resistances were characterized by Freud as deriving from the patient's need to displace conflicts from past objects onto present ones—i.e., the therapist—"thus re-animating a repression which should only have been recollected" (Freud 1926, p. 160). Although Freud distinguished between these two forms of resistance, Langs (1981) has argued that the immediate interaction of therapist and patient will always impose a communicative vector linking repression and transference resistances within the clinical arena. He states that "this contribution is often critical to the unconscious basis of the primary repression resistance, and unless it is rectified where necessary and the relationship component analyzed, the repression resistance will not be modified" (p. 479).

Freud noted three additional types of resistance, the first being "epinosic gain." This has often been termed the "secondary gain of illness" and occurs when the ego adapts to the neurotic symptom for the sake of the gratification and relief it provides. The next mode of resistance, from the id, pertains to the "compulsion to repeat" and the strength of "psychical inertia from the adhesiveness of the libido" (Freud 1914b). Freud believed that, even when the first three ego resistances have been resolved, "the power of the repetition compulsion—the attraction exerted by the unconscious prototypes upon the repressed instinctual processes—has yet to be overcome" (1926, p. 160). This resistance finds clinical resolution during a period of persistent working through. Last, Freud mentioned a type of resistance generated by the superego, whose punitive tendencies can be fulfilled through the maintenance of the patient's neurotic suffering as atonement for unconscious guilt.

Another source of resistance to treatment can derive from the therapist's errors. Freud (1937) alluded to such resistance in commenting on Ferenczi's paper (1928) on termination in analysis. Ferenczi had emphasized that successful and timely analytic outcome, or appropriate termination, is determined in large part by the therapist's ability to rectify his or her own errors. Freud noted that such factors act in ways similar to the patient's resistances to impede the analytic work, thus prolonging it. Langs (1978, 1980, 1981, 1982) has carried this a vital step further by demonstrating how therapist errors directly increase the patient's resistive operations, a point also made, less emphatically, by Sandler and colleagues (1973) and Greenson (1967). It is therefore of great importance to appreciate that iatrogenic resistance is an appropriate demonstration of defense that differs significantly from those resistances cited previously. Iatrogenic problems are clear demonstrations of the adaptive and self-protecting function of defense within treatment (Stone 1973). Langs (1982) has given careful consideration to this difference and terms the iatrogenic problem an "interactional resistance," because it can be traced back to some type of therapist error in the failure to provide a comprehensively secure frame.

In reviewing the sources of resistance, Sandler and colleagues (1973) included threats to the patient's self-esteem and the character resistances (Reich 1928, 1929) as additional unconscious factors working against the therapeutic process. Of greatest import, however, is the authors' consideration of the more object-relational dimensions of resistance. They noted that the progressive restructuring of the patient's internal object economy demands a collateral realignment of his or her preexisting interpersonal relationships. Such realignment threatens the loss of these relationships, in whole or in part, to the extent to which they have been based on a pathological object-relational substrate now being altered in treatment. Although this formulation calls attention to the reciprocity of function between the internal "representational world" (Sandler and Rosenblatt 1962) and the external object environment, this interface is most crucial within the immediate therapeutic relationship.

Sandler and Sandler (1978) have pointed out that any interpersonal relationship is based on the mutual communication of "very subtle and complicated cues and signs. They are unconscious exchanges of messages, as well as the conscious and unconscious experiencing of all sorts of other interactions" (p. 285). Such a dynamic interplay among conscious and unconscious perceptions and fantasy distortions, based on the functional object-relational substrate, generates specific "need/motivational systems" (Sandler and Joffe 1969, Sandler and Sandler 1978) within the therapy relationship. Because they are active human systems (von Bertalanfy 1968), they emphasize the role of each participant in determining the "vector moment" of the direction of treatment. This thrust may be directed toward either preserving homeostasis, in support of continued neurotic functioning by either or both parties, or effecting more adaptive "systemic change." The option for homeostasis is a prime object-relational and interactional resistance that can be triggered and then perpetuated by the patient, the therapist, or both.

Within the secure frame, where the contribution from the therapist's pathology is curtailed most effectively, the demonstration of object-relational resistance and the consequent interactional pressures exerted on the therapist give clear evidence of the patient's underlying organization of introjects and identifications. They also flag the crucial projective–introjective mechanisms through which the object system has been established and currently is maintained (Meissner 1978, 1981). According to Dorpat (1976), careful clinical attention must be given to the expression of these internalized objects and introjects; they are specifically related to the organization of drives, drive derivatives, and defenses, which cannot be isolated from the object-relational schema.

Meissner (1981) noted that many resistances are rooted primarily in the basic need to support the object economy itself. This point recalls Hartmann's detailing (1964) of the genetic and dynamic relationship between the development of object relationships and defensive operations (see also A. Freud 1949, Kris 1950) and the ways in which the two can find mutual expression within treatment. It also suggests that the immediate object relationship with the therapist can function antagonistically to the maintenance of the patient's introjective configuration when the well-functioning therapist is introjected positively into an internal system based on negative objects. The resultant disequilibrium is highly anxiety provoking and may trigger various reprojective efforts to restore the original internal balance (Langs 1981).

Meissner (1981) also has addressed carefully the process of regression within treatment, and its stimulation of all levels of resistance. He has identified two basic levels of resistance, the first occurring early in treatment with a focus against "the analytic pressures and the technical interventions of the analyst" (p. 156) as the patient adapts to the rigors of the analytic frame. This "extrinsic resistance" eventually gives way to more intrinsic demonstrations of defense against "the internal effects of the activation and the greater availability of the underlying introjective configuration" (p. 157). This shift from a more external to a more internal locus of defense is a crucial factor in the enhanced experience of threat stimulated by the secure frame in its fostering of regression. As Meissner has succinctly stated, "the mobilization of developmental potential through regression is both a source of therapeutic change and a source of increased anxiety and threat" (1981, p. 86). That threat stems not only from a resurgence of infantile dangers and their attendant anxiety, but also from the possibility that the regression will continue unchecked to ever more primitive levels of functioning.

This discussion leads us to consider a last major source of resistance, which has been postulated to derive from the existence of a "universal infantile psychosis" that has its origins in the most primitive stages of self-object experience (Grotstein 1977a, 1977b, 1981). According to Grotstein, this "psychosis" occurs when there is a "lack of background object of safety (a deficient self-object experience) and therefore a failure to transform organismic panic into signal anxiety" (1981, p. 8). For the infant with no capacity to delay, nonimmediate instinctual gratification generates panic that can be dealt with only by the most primitive of defenses, which serve to annihilate both the panic experience and the cognitive and perceptual apparatus that registers it (Bion 1967, Peto 1977). This violently defensive attempt at mindlessness is usually salved by the fairly prompt and adequate ministrations of the maternal figure. The chaotic residual, however, remains deeply buried as a primitive fear of psychotic mindlessness and self-oblivion. This formulation is similar to Balint's concept (1968) of "the basic fault" as a preverbal state of precarious equilibrium between the potentially dangerous primary environment and its life-sustaining primary object. The same "psychotic core," as Langs (1981) has termed it, threatens to reemerge during regression, when habitual defenses have been analyzed progressively and thus stripped of their protective function of keeping such disturbing contents at bay.

Bleger (1967) has specifically addressed the interaction of the analytic frame with the psychoticlike components of what he has called "the patient's ghost-world of the non-ego" (p. 514). According to Bleger, the non-ego is based in the infant's most primitive and undifferentiated symbiosis with the mother's body. As such, it is the nonprocess foundation on which the ego begins differentiation: "The non-ego is the background or the frame of the organized ego; the 'background' and 'figure' of a unique Gestalt" (Bleger 1967, p. 515). Each patient will bring his or her own frame to treatment, a reflection of this non-ego, and often will seek to modify the therapist's frame accordingly. When the therapist resists such efforts, the non-ego is brought to the fore, along with all the psychotic remnants of earliest personality formation. Langs (1981) notes that the extent to which this "psychotic core" is expressed in treatment depends on each patient's level of mastery over such primitive anxieties. As with higher-order disturbances, the danger of exposing the psychotic core fuels the patient's resistances and often will result in efforts to disrupt the analytic frame as a way to obtain a renewed, and safer, extrinsic focus (Meissner 1981). These efforts often find the therapist in unconscious collusion, as both parties develop protective "bastions" (Baranger and Baranger 1966) or "misalliances" (Langs 1976a, 1976b) against such threatening aspects of treatment within the secure frame.

Any of the foregoing sources of resistance can be activated to the point of stalemating the process of treatment. Many resistances, however, are amenable to appropriate management, which often takes the form of the therapist's secure holding silence that allows the patient to resolve his or her internal resistance (Langs 1981). On occasion, however, some patients will evidence a severely disruptive response to the very best of psychoanalytic technique. This particularly malignant type of response, the "negative therapeutic reaction," stands as the most problematic and ominous example of an intractable RFR.

The Negative Therapeutic Reaction

In 1919 Abraham examined the occurrence of chronic and seemingly immutable resistance to psychoanalytic treatment, which he believed was the result of the patient's narcissism being wounded by appropriate interpretations. This increased destructive envy is then directed toward the wounding therapist in retaliation. This relationship between narcissism and pathological envy later was traced to roots within the oral-sadistic phase of character development (Abraham 1924). Freud (1923, 1924), however, took a different tack in explaining the paradox of the negative therapeutic reaction. He maintained that the exacerbation of symptoms that follows a correct interpretation is caused by a pervasive sense of unconscious guilt that demands atonement through the maintenance of neurotic suffering. This process was regarded as evidence of a sadistic superego operating in tandem with the masochism of the ego to produce a major unconscious need for continued punishment that is disturbed by the therapist's curative efforts. These twin approaches—the punitive superego and the vicissitudes of narcissism—appear to have formed the basis for most later works on the origin and function of the negative therapeutic reaction.

Horney (1933) described the patient's attack on the therapist in much the same way as did Abraham, noting that the good interpretation exposes the patient to some element of his or her defective functioning. The patient is thus provoked to seek revenge on the better-functioning therapist in order to restore the patient's sense of supremacy. Such an attack, however, enhances the patient's anxiety that he or she would be threatened similarly for exhibiting more healthy functioning. Although Horney approached this process on a manifest level, her observations can be translated into the more subtle terms of the unconscious interaction between patient and therapist. On such a level the patient's actions can be seen as attempts at projective identification of his or her own disturbance into the therapist, so that the therapist might detoxify it and then return it to the patient in a more adaptive form.

Riviere (1936) took a quite different approach to the negative therapeutic reaction and first warned against too readily assuming that interpretations are completely correct; he held that therapist error is most likely to produce such a reaction. When the therapist feels sure that such error is not the cause, he or she must carefully reevaluate the status of the patient's inner world of object relations and its narcissistic components in order to gain access to the underlying roots of depression. From this Kleinian perspective, the negative therapeutic reaction was seen to be an expression of manic defense against the depressive confrontation fostered by treatment. Such defenses as omnipotent control and manic contempt lessen the patient's awareness of his or her dependence on destructive internal objects as these internal objects are threatened through the process of treatment. Riviere felt that the negative therapeutic reaction derived from the patient's paramount need to rescue and preserve these objects and thus avoid the depressive position, even at the expense of his or her own freedom from the neurotic suffering such objects may anchor.

Riviere's paper predated Klein's later elaboration (1946, 1957) of the developmental sequence from the paranoid-schizoid to the depressive position proper. In those works Klein described the primitive defenses of splitting, omnipotence, denial, and the need to control all objects as originating in the need to combat the persecutory anxieties of the paranoid-schizoid position. These same defenses can later be activated in more manic form to defend against depression, as Riviere noted. Klein, however, felt that the most severe form of the negative therapeutic reaction is rooted in the earlier phase of development, in which the destructive and envious action of the primitive superego fosters intense persecutory fears and fantasies. The envy itself is strongly defended against through reactivation of primitive defenses and is thus split off from the ego and projected onto the therapist in treatment.

In a further contribution to the study of the negative therapeutic reaction, Olinick (1964) described the patient's efforts to employ the transference regression to enact his or her conflicts between omnipotence and dependent gratification. This attempt occurs not only through intrapsychic projection, but also via a provocation of the therapist to assume the role of both the loved and the hated object. In this way the patient can enact both sides of the sadomasochistic conflict during recurrent negativistic crises in treatment. Loewald (1972) also noted that severe negative therapeutic reactions are likely to be based in preoedipal distortions of instinctual drives and their allied ego mechanisms for defense and control that are expressed in treatment as intractable masochism.

From Asch's perspective (1976), the negative therapeutic reaction was a more multidimensional intrapsychic phenomenon. He outlined three major areas of contributing pathology, likely to be evidenced in combination. The first is a "masochistic ego [that] derives from ego-ideal identification with a martyred maternal love object" (p. 387). The second area consists of disturbances in the separation–individuation phase of early development (Mahler 1968) that generate unconscious guilt for supposed "pre-oedipal crimes." Third, there is likely to be a strong regressive pull toward fusion with an ambivalent and depressed preoedipal love object, and this regression must be defended against.

Vianna (1974, 1975) and Rosenfeld (1975) stressed the role of pathological narcissistic organization in the intensification of envious aggression; Rosenfeld particularly noted the importance of differentiating "the attack by the superego on the ego from the violent, apparently critical attacks derived from the narcissistic omnipotent organization which turns against the infantile dependent part of the self" (p. 227). As Baranger (1974) commented, such intense primitive narcissism and envy are often exercised through massive and violent projective identification into the therapist. This dramatic interactional expression of the negative therapeutic reaction necessitates careful examination of the sequence of object exchanges between therapist and patient.

It is also important to note the observations of other authors who have detailed the patient's efforts to harm the therapist by sabotaging treatment. Bird (1972) made this point quite directly in stating that the patient's self-destructive aims are more likely to be interpreted than are the immediate, although usually unconscious, efforts to devastate the therapist. Cooperman (1979) addressed a similar issue by noting that a highly effective way to attack the therapist is to destroy the treatment that is the therapist's strongest point of investment. Whereas the clinician may well weather personal assaults and criticisms, an attack on the therapist's professional expertise carried out through the patient's decompensation is often an ideal and subtle way for the patient to extract his or her revenge.

Finally, Searles (1959) pointed out that many instances of the patient's unanticipated relapse derive from a need to maintain a pathological symbiosis between patient and therapist—what Langs (1982) has termed a "pathological mode of relatedness." When the process of cure begins to foster more adaptive separation and individuation, either party to treatment can instigate the patient's relapse as a means of maintaining or regaining the jeopardized symbiotic gratifications of the treatment relationship. Although this formulation implicates elements of therapist error that are proscribed within the comprehensively secure frame, it also calls needed attention to various modes of relatedness and the interactional dynamics that govern the unique human habitat of the therapeutic framework.

An Overview

Langs (1982) has summarized the numerous secure frame factors that contribute to the patient's increased experience of threat within such a setting. In general, the secure frame tends to limit the patient's use of habitual defenses, pathological modes of relatedness, and general maladaptive behaviors, because these are subject to constant analysis rather than precipitous gratification. Under such circumstances the patient's current best level of coping with his or her pathology loses its self-protective efficacy because the patient comes under "considerable pressure to experience his or her own psychopathology and maladjustment, and to express internal disturbance and its basis, directly and through derivatives" (Langs 1982, p. 329).

As the focal point of the secure frame, the therapist is the immediate target for raw expressions of disturbance, a situation described by Strachey's comment that ". . . at the moment of interpretation the analyst is in fact deliberately evoking a quantity of the patient's id-energy while it is alive and actual and unambiguous and aimed directly at himself" (1934, p. 126). When the therapist is able to withstand such stressors, contain and detoxify the patient's pathology, and then render a therapeutic intervention in its stead, the therapist becomes a highly powerful and threatening positive introject. It is this positive introjective identification with the well-functioning therapist that throws the patient's internal object economy into disequilibrium, because that original economy is likely to have been based on a need to maintain destructive objects. The ensuing internal conflict threatens the ultimate loss of such maladaptive objects but also generates the fear that the presently "good" therapist eventually will prove no better than the original objects.

The secure frame also facilitates expression of transference-based distortions as the therapist's anonymity and neutrality allow the patient to revivify the aggressive and erotic wishes of the past in the present. This revivification, then, results in increased guilt and fear of punitive response. When such retribution is not externally forthcoming through actual sadistic frame breaking by the therapist, the patient's cruelly primitive superego pathology becomes ever more apparent and threatening. In addition, the well-functioning therapist stimulates the patient's malignant envy and the collateral wish to destroy the therapist and his or her ability to cope with the rigors of the secure frame.

This general picture of the patient's experience of threat within the comprehensively secure analytic frame takes on a somewhat different look when there has been an intervening rectification, as is the case with the RFR. A deviation, whether established at the beginning of treatment or instituted later on, will always provide some measure of pathological gratification. With rectification, even at the full and timely behest of the patient's material, the patient will sustain an increased sense of deprivation at the loss of the deviation. This feeling of deprivation leads to a heightened sense of rage and feelings of intensified persecution. In addition, the deviation–rectification process leaves a split introject of the therapist, who is seen as possibly subject to future deviations. This introject tends to undermine some of the therapeutic benefits of rectification and may well lead to increased attempts by the patient to restore a deviant frame.

CLINICAL MATERIAL

All the foregoing tendencies are shaped and colored by the specific pathological constellation of each patient–therapist pair. Therefore, the dynamics of the RFR can be portrayed most vividly through presentation of actual clinical material. Rather than illustrating an extreme example of an intractable negative response to the securing of the frame, the following case sample will demonstrate the more commonly confronted instance of the transient disturbance seen subsequent to appropriate rectification.

This clinical material extends over five sequential hours that encompass both the rectification process and the subsequent sessions during which the RFR is evident. The data, suitably disguised to protect confidentiality, are taken directly from the therapist's process notes but in part have been summarized for ease of presentation.

The Patient and the Frame

Mr. A. began feeling anxious and depressed during the increasing legal wrangles over his second divorce. His difficulty in sleeping led him to seek medical evaluation, and, when he was found to be in good physical condition, he started to consider psychotherapy as a way to help him manage the stress he was experiencing. One of Mr. A.'s friends, a physician, referred him to a female therapist who had worked with the physician as a consultant to his medical practice. This physician was sensitive to the frame issues in psychoanalytic treatment, and he gave Mr. A. little information about the prospective therapist.

Mr. A. began in private psychotherapy on a once-a-week basis, and most aspects of the fixed frame seemed to be relatively secure at the outset. By the seventh month of treatment, however, several major frame issues had become apparent. First, the patient had discovered independently that the therapist was a regular consultant to his friend, the physician. The patient raised this point in treatment, and his associations revolved around the potential for failed confidentiality along with many oedipally determined fantasies of jealous competition for the female therapist. At the time, these associations were interpreted around the adaptive context of the contaminated referral route and led to a productive period of the analysis of the patient's then primarily transference-based fantasies. This interlude was interrupted by the therapist's relocation of her office about two months later, an incident the patient linked to the childhood trauma of moving to a new home after his parents' divorce. On the heels of this break in the frame, the patient had to miss one session due to a planned business trip. Because the therapist had been informed of the trip well in advance, she did not charge him for the cancellation.

In and of itself, this sequence of breaks in the frame would be sufficient to disturb treatment significantly. The situation was further complicated when, after the patient's return from the trip and prior to his next scheduled session, he saw the therapist having lunch at a restaurant with one of her male colleagues. He announced this occurrence in his following hour and proceeded to associate to his feelings of jealous rage and abandonment when, at the age of seven, he came home from prep school on vacation to find that his parents had divorced, his mother had remarried, and he was expected to live in a new house with a new father. He also recalled his intense competitive rivalry with his friend, the referring physician. During subsequent hours the therapist interpreted this wealth of material around the cumulative adaptive contexts of the change in offices, the missed session, his seeing the therapist at lunch with another man, and the earlier concerns about the referral relationship. These interpretive efforts received adequate manifest and derivative validation and were accompanied by additional new genetic material.

Although the patient appeared to gain a good deal of therapeutic benefit from working over this incident, the therapist still felt some lingering concern about her management of the situation. In supervision it became apparent that the therapist had missed interpreting the unconscious meaning of her failing to charge for the cancelled session as a major contributor to the patient's experienced disturbance. In effect, the therapist had interpreted around unavoidable deviations and ignored her role in breaking the frame. By this time, about three weeks later, the patient's derivatives around the incident had faded and there was no immediately workable representation of the failure to charge for the cancellation. The therapist felt that this might be evidence of the patient's "holding up his end of a misalliance bargain," in that it was the therapist who had failed to maintain the ground rules and who had avoided the pertinent derivatives that would have led to timely rectification.

Rectification

The issue of charging for missed sessions was raised again during the tenth month of treatment, when the patient had to cancel one hour for another business trip. In the session before the cancellation, the patient began to talk about his boss's letting people leave work early when they were trying to track down the solution to an important problem. He then related a rich vignette about how irritated he had been when his car was not repaired on schedule and he had to waste time waiting for the mechanic to finish. He emphasized the repairman's irresponsibility and how he, the patient, should have billed the shop for *his* time. When he commented that the therapist probably had been in similar situations, she began to offer an interpretation, pointing out the possible parallels to his feelings about cancelling appointments and her failure to charge him for that time. Although he manifestly denied this connection on the grounds that he had always given plenty of advance notice before missing a session, he went on to discuss a similar situation at work, in which a business client always wasted a colleague's time and they had decided to bill the client accordingly. Because this material was presented at the very end of the hour, the therapist decided not to force the issue but to wait until the next session, which was scheduled for two weeks later.

Mr. A. began that next hour by stating that he had missed having his appointment the preceding week, and he then recounted some of the events of his business trip. He especially commented on a "spoiled favorite son," and executive who always kept everyone waiting at meetings, and how much the patient admired the way the chairman finally had told the man to keep to the schedule because he was interfering with everyone else's work. At this point, Mr. A. began to discuss a disturbing dream that he had had the night before this session. Because this material is crucial to the rectification sequence, the following interchange is reported directly from the therapist's process notes of the hour.

> P: So that was pretty much the week that was. What I really wanted to talk about was this dream I had last night. It bothered me a lot, but the dream itself was very innocuous—don't understand it. It was Christmastime and there was this immense tree with tons of presents underneath, but I was in this huge house all alone. No big deal, but I woke up in a cold sweat. Don't know why it should bother me so. (*Silence for about two minutes.*)
>
> This huge Christmas celebration, but there's no one there. Like the gifts are worthless somehow. Sad and upsetting, kind of panicky. Doesn't fit because the setting is innocuous, even should be pleasurable. You know, the big beautiful Christmas tree and the excitement of all the presents, like a kid getting all the goodies they've been hoping for.

The patient then went on to talk about spoiling his children, that they always wanted more, and how he wanted them to have things because the other kids in the neighborhood received so much. He said this was especially true the year before his first divorce, "because I knew what lay ahead."

> P: Maybe that's the thing about the house being so empty in the dream. So many gifts, but it's like buying you off for being alone. Goes back to the stuff with my mother. Always had plenty of material stuff but felt pretty much on my own all the time, like I didn't have a place of my own in the new house. Deep down I figured if she got remarried so easily, that she could get rid of us like she got rid of Dad.
>
> T: So spoiling someone with gifts can be a way to make up for leaving them alone—like the panicky feeling in the dream when you're all by yourself with nothing but the presents and the tree, feeling abandoned and displaced. . . .
>
> P: (*interrupting*) Yeah, and how I bought off my kids before the divorce the way my mother did to me.
>
> T: That may be connected to your comments about the business meeting and your irritation with the "favorite son" who wasted everyone's time until the chairman had to tell him to keep to the schedule or get out. Those two themes seem to come together around the way you started out today by saying that you really missed having your appointment here last week.

P: That you'd kick me out if I didn't meet my responsibilities and keep to the schedule? We talked about something like that last time. I figured you'd just fill my time with something else since you knew in advance. (*Pause.*) More like fill my time with some*one* else. I'd lose my place here when someone else came along. So that's all my stuff about good business practices and billing clients.

T: So when I don't charge you for a missed session, it's like a gift of not charging you. It undermines the feeling that this time is really yours and triggers the fear that once again you'd be displaced, like when your mother remarried and even when you had to leave your own kids during your divorce.

P: That was probably there this summer, too, when I got so upset seeing you at the restaurant with that guy. Hadn't put it together with the gifts thing before, though. Like the paying makes a firm contract so I don't keep going through all this paranoid stuff each time, don't keep feeling so insecure.

Funny thing about gifts. (*The patient begins to tell how his stepmother used to make special gifts for him and his brothers, even though his father made a great deal of money.*) One thing she'd make for us was worth ten presents my mother would buy at [an expensive department store]. She put so much time and effort into it, it always meant so much more.

Always been suspicious of people who give you things just to show how nice they are. That's rampant in business and you know it's just a con. (*Pause.*) I think I'm saying that you'd better charge me when I cancel.

T: That will be part of our contract from here on. (*End of session.*)

Analysis of this part of the rectification sequence reveals the unique capacity of the theapeutic framework to serve as a repository for the entire history of an individual's treatment. This function is apparent when, during any frame-related disturbance, all prior frame issues find some form of representation in the patient's associations. Such a phenomenon is demonstrated in the foregoing material as the patient integrates the earlier, primarily transference-based concerns about the referral source with the later frame breaks of the office change and his seeing the therapist at the restaurant. The response to these relatively unavoidable disturbances, however, comes to focus on the therapist's failure to charge for the missed session and is shaped significantly by that major deviation. The patient's cumulative representation of all these frame issues can be understood as a derivative image of the developing therapist introject, determined by the clinician's management of the comprehensive treatment framework. The present relative malleability of this therapist introject is evidenced during the process of rectification when, after the therapist's interpretation of the effects of her failure to charge the patient, the patient goes on to represent the positive object of his stepmother, whose appropriate "gifts" were so cherished. This derivative commentary reflects both an unconscious validation of the interpretation and a partial repair of the therapist as an internalized object.

Another factor that commands attention is the patient's prominent use of genetic material. Langs (1982, p. 514) has pointed out that reference to historical objects must be examined carefully for its "functional capacity" as a representation of the current status of the treatment interaction and the patient–therapist relationship as a whole. All too often, any reference to a genetic figure has been presumed to be transferential and therefore has been considered an unwarranted distortion. In the present example, however, it is clear that both genetic references, to the mother and to the stepmother, reflect the patient's accurate unconscious appraisal of the therapist's behavior. When the therapist compounded the earlier frame instability by failing to charge for the cancellation, she recapitulated the patient's childhood trauma by acting similarly to the original, hurtful maternal object. This connection was confirmed by the therapist in supervision, when she realized her "gift" of not charging had been an unconscious attempt to "buy off" or forestall development of the negative transference. There is here a clear dynamic parallel to the actions of the mother, who bought her son expensive presents in order to placate his rage at her over the divorce. In essence, then, the patient's response in treatment cannot be credited to transference distortion as much as to a precise, unconscious recognition of the therapist's failure to behave differently from the original maternal object. A similar formulation is also applicable to the later positive image of the stepmother that is elicited in response to the therapist's improved functioning after her offer of the appropriate interpretation toward the end of the second hour.

The levels of resistance that are demonstrated by both patient and therapist in this rectification sequence must also be considered. In each session presented, the patient shows few gross behavioral problems and unusually minimal communicative resistances: he develops a full derivative complex that coalesces around the cited adaptive context and also gives a manifest linkage to the treatment situation proper (Langs 1981). The highest level of resistance, in fact, is evidenced by the therapist in the first session, when she is unable to give a complete interpretation that culminates in rectification. This absence of a complete interpretation, in addition to the disturbance of the intervening cancellation, appears to have heightened the patient's unconscious therapeutic efforts to secure the frame in the second session. Following the therapist's accurate interpretation at the end of that hour, the patient actually is able to suggest the rectification himself. This markedly low level of resistance can be credited largely to the patient's strong therapeutic need for a secure treatment framework in order to avoid a real repetition of the trauma and turmoil he experienced as a child. Only if the therapist can maintain some semblance of the comprehensively secure frame, will the patient be able to risk the stressors of regression, having then the implicit assurance that his terrifying neurotic fears and fantasies will not find immediate behavioral expression in reality. Under these conditions the therapist's behavior does not merge with that of the original neurotic object, and thus the two can be "reasonably" differentiated (see Gill 1979, 1982) by the patient during the interpretation of true transference manifestations. In this light, the therapist's closing confirmation of the rectification is crucial to the patient's full experience of securing the framework, because it defines a functional difference between the therapist and the maternal object.

Validation of Rectification

Because the foregoing rectification process generally is adequate from a technical perspective, one might predict that the patient would first show a beneficial response to the better-secured frame and the appropriate gratifications inherent in it. Such a response would be demonstrated through derivatives that reflect positive introjects of more adaptive functioning and a collateral increase in the production of new salient material, i.e., Bion's "selected facts" (1962). Because of this patient's clear need for rectification and the minimal resistance with which he unconsciously pursued it, an early negative reaction would seem less likely.

This prediction was generally borne out in the patient's following hour. He began by saying that he had started to resolve a problem that had been plaguing him for months at work, and he expressed his pleasure at his team's having worked on this resolution all weekend. Although the patient reported this vignette in a generally positive manner, he also mentioned that the problem appeared to stem from the interference of another department. Such an allusion to a disturbance generated by a third party recalls the still unrectified framework issue around the contaminated referral source. The therapist began a silent organization of the patient's material around this last framework problem as a potential adaptive context.

The patient then announced that the legal procedures of his divorce finally had been completed. After the decision had been rendered, he had phoned his now ex-wife, and their conversation had been very pleasant. They both felt the divorce was sad but that it would prove to have been a good decision in the long run. He then commented that his ex-wife had said something that touched him: that maybe they had been too close as husband and wife and might now be able to be better friends. This reminded the patient of his boss and his admiration for the boss's ability to maintain an ideal working distance with his employees. The patient stated that this boss was one of the best models he had ever had. He then said that his friend, the referring physician, was similar, but that they wouldn't be seeing much of each other now, because their schedules had changed. Although the patient said he would miss his friend, he also expressed a sense of relief, stating that "he's just too good for all my competitive urges."

Here the patient has added another rectification by distancing himself from the referral source, and his material coalesces as a clear derivative commentary on how the therapist must also maintain an appropriate "working distance" with no third-party contamination. When the therapist played back these themes around the adaptive context of the referral source and the patient's need for an appropriate distance in his close working relationships, the patient gave further confirmatory associations about experiencing "a loss for a gain" in separating from his wife. He also said this concept could apply to his friendship with the physician, because his feelings of rivalry and competition were so intense. The patient then made manifest reference to treatment as having helped him start making changes, and stated that this help was why therapy was so important to him. At this point the therapist offered the interpretation that the patient's feeling of rivalry toward the referring physician might have infiltrated the therapy relationship, and that the loss in not seeing his friend so often might feel like some gain in terms of a better working distance in treatment.

The patient immediately validated this interpretation, both manifestly and through derivatives concerning the admiration people felt for the physician for never discussing his patients in social situations. He then elaborated on his feeling jealous and competitive, and stated that these feelings had been prominent when he saw the therapist at the restaurant during the summer. The patient manifestly confirmed the therapist's interpretation from the previous hour about his fear of being displaced by another patient because the therapist had not charged for the cancelled session. He also offered new material, stating that when his wife had first asked for a divorce, he had assumed she had been cheating on him. He stated that he felt "very territorial and that extends even to here with you," and he added that he played with the fantasy of being the therapist's only patient "or maybe your best patient." Here, at the end of the hour, the therapist made the interpretation that recent rectifications had made the treatment feel like a more appropriate professional relationship. This interpretation was offered with the hope of making it safer for the patient to explore some of these very fantasies without the fear that they would be realized.

In this final hour of the rectification sequence, the patient evidences a number of constructive reactions to the securing of the framework. His material contains a series of references to positive and better-functioning objects, ranging from his self-representation to the images of his boss, his ex-wife, and the referring physician and friend. Such associations can be taken as general validation of the therapist's interventions, which the patient has positively introjected. More important, these images convey an unconscious directive for the therapist to preserve the newly secured frame in order to maintain an effective working relationship with the patient. This wish is most apparent in the patient's effecting the additional rectification of distancing himself from the contaminated referral source and in his presentation of this separation as "a loss for a gain," an allusion to the process of treatment. Such an action is evidence, unconsciously given, of the ego-enhancing benefits that derive from the secured therapeutic environment as the patient becomes more able to forego the neurotic gratifications attendant to prior deviations. In many ways the first rectification around charging for missed sessions has elicited or facilitated the further rectification concerning the referring physician. This suggests a reverse corollary to Greenacre's warning (1959) about the potentially malignant generativity of deviations; one could also hypothesize that one good rectification helps "beget" further remediation.

Additional validation of rectification is demonstrated by the patient's collateral production of new and salient material. His discussion of his feeling that his wife had been cheating on him prior to the divorce had not been presented prior to this hour. Of even greater consequence, the patient's direct comments about being very "territorial" and his conscious fantasy of being the therapist's only patient or "best patient" indicate a significant upsurge in transferential material, which has followed the therapist's accurately interpreting the contaminating effects of the referral route. In so doing, the therapist has acted as a positive and better-functioning object who, in turn, becomes a safer target for the patient's open expression of predominantly transference-based fantasies and their attendant distortions, fantasies the therapist also attempts to interpret at the end of that hour.

Although that closing intervention is relatively valid, it is somewhat premature and tends to avoid the patient's subtle communication of distress in expressing his predominantly transferential wishes toward the therapist. Here, the therapist's conscious efforts to encourage "the expansion of the transference" (as in Gill 1982) may be experienced as too intrusive; they simultaneously ignore the patient's struggles to adapt to the primary securing of the fixed framework. Such interventions therefore could contribute to the appearance of any RFR-like manifestations in following hours, which accordingly must be distinguished from representations of the RFR proper.

Reaction to the Rectified Frame

Mr. A. began his next session by saying that things had been going fairly well all week, although he was feeling exhausted. He said that he was pleased with the rapid progress being made on the project he was directing at work, but he voiced concern that he and his co-workers might be pushing themselves too hard in trying to get the job done quickly. He said, "But we are a hardy bunch, the work has to be done, and we'll get through it together somehow." This brief opening segment contains not only a derivative reference to the mounting pressure the patient is experiencing within the more secure frame, but also a possible allusion to the therapist's premature "pushing of the transference" at the close of the previous hour. Despite the relatively positive images through which these feelings are conveyed, the therapist is being given an unconscious warning that pacing is of great importance during this phase of treatment.

After a short pause, Mr. A. said he was particularly worried because his stomach kept bothering him, a problem he had reported early in therapy but had not mentioned for several months. He mentioned that he had discussed the problem with his physician during his recent annual check-up, and that he was now "scheduled for a full GI series because he [the physician] is pretty sure it's an ulcer." To continue directly from the therapist's process notes:

> *P*: Hate the thought of going through that. . . . Never had it done before. Feels like my body's betraying me by acting up like this and I can't control what's happening. (*Long silence.*)
>
> Never could understand people who enjoy their ulcers . . . brag about them like status symbols. My father had an ulcer but always kept quiet about it. Like it was a flaw he was ashamed of, so he kept it to himself. Always knew when it was bothering him, but it wasn't something he'd talk about. (*Long silence.*)
>
> Guess I'm just plain scared. . . . Dread the procedure and what they're going to do to me. Shouldn't feel that way because I've known Dr. X. for years and he's the very best; very likable and well-respected all around. I trust him but still don't want to go through it. (*Long silence.*)
>
> (*Faltering here; many pauses.*) This terrible image . . . being held down and at their mercy, like in an operating room. Can't stand that lack of control even if the procedure's easy. It's being so helpless, like a little kid. (*Long silence.*)
>
> *T*: So if there's an ulcer, it's like your body's betraying you from inside. You have no control over what's happening inside yourself. That was something your father was ashamed of, like a flaw you'd best keep to yourself. Then you mentioned being at the doctor's mercy . . . held down and helpless like a kid. Even though you consciously trust Dr. X., the dread is still there.
>
> *P*: It really scares me, and I don't think I want to know why. (*Silent for almost ten minutes.*)
>
> *T*: We have to finish up for today.
>
> *P*: (*as he is leaving*) I'll see you next week.

In comparison with the earlier hours, this session shows a dramatic change in both the tone and the content of the patient's material. This change can be seen first in the heightened levels of resistance that the patient clearly demonstrates. Most apparent is the gross behavioral resistance of silence, which is noted by the therapist throughout the hour and especially at the end. It is accompanied by an increase in communicative resistance, visible in the patient's failure to offer any bridge or link to treatment that would allow the therapist to make a Type Two adaptive context interpretation (see Langs 1978). This resistive change is quite apparent after the therapist attempts to play back selected themes around the suspected adaptive context of the rectification. Here, the patient gives only brief manifest validation of his being scared, but then states, "I don't think I want to know why," a clear statement that he is not ready to go on. This statement is followed by a prolonged silence that lasts until the close of the hour. The therapist's electing to maintain this silence as a quiet "holding" of the patient is appropriate, given the lack of material for a Type Two interpretation at this point and the patient's clear need for time to resolve the resistive difficulties at his own pace.

Also crucial to an analysis of this hour are the derivative images the patient uses to portray the therapist and the intensification of such representation over the course of the session. At first the patient comments on the pressures he and his fellows are experiencing at work, but the situation is given a generally positive cast through references to being "hardy" and able to get through the project at hand by working together. This relatively hopeful image gives way to the more disturbing representation of Dr. X. as a trusted and respected object who nevertheless is seen as the instrument of the patient's distress. This split image leads to the patient's terrifying fantasy of being at the doctor's mercy, as in an operating room, and being helplessly restrained, like a child. Here the patient is offering a derivative portrait of the therapist as a powerful and threatening object who is somehow in control of the patient's internal functioning, whereas he, himself, is not. It is possible that the patient's earlier comment about his "body's betraying" him refers to this fear of the therapist's interpreting/operating on his unconscious functioning by using the derivatives, which he cannot consciously control. The operating room symbol is also a crucial representation of the better-secured framework with its minimal contaminants and necessary deprivations. It recalls Freud's famous analogy (1912) comparing the optimal attitude of the psychoanalytic practitioner with that of the dispassionate surgeon.

Another important part of the content of this hour is the patient's use of genetic material in referring to the way his father dealt with having an ulcer. The paucity of the patient's associations makes it difficult to interpret fully this genetic referent, but it first must be considered a possible representation of countertransference difficulties. Such difficulties are not likely to be a predominant factor here, however, because the therapist's interventions, including the use of silence, in this and the previous session generally have been appropriate. More probable is that such new material surfaces as an important genetic identification with the father around the embarrassment and shame associated with exposing some inner "flaw." The material would then function as the patient's derivative response to the regression fostered by the better-secured frame, i.e., the dread of uncovering the raw origins of his pathology.

Overall, this hour exemplifies development of an RFR, in which resistances substantially increase following appropriate and validated rectification. Such a transformation is likely to stem from the alteration in the relative amounts of pathology contributed by patient and therapist that occurs after securing the frame. Optimally, the predominant "vector of pathology" emanates from the patient, but this is unlikely to be the case when countertransference-based deviations occur. Appropriate rectification, however, markedly decreases the therapist's contribution of pathology and thus creates disequilibrium within the treatment system. As a result, a kind of vacuum is generated within the framework; a vacuum that draws into it a greater expression of the patient's pathology. As the patient unconsciously experiences this enhanced "pathology gradient," the counterforce of resistance is increased in turn.

Settling In

Once the RFR appears, its mode and intensity of expression are determined mainly by three factors: the particulars of the patient's pathology, the ability of the therapist to contain and detoxify this pathology, and the cumulative therapist introject that has been developed over the course of treatment. The last factor has been described previously as a determinant of the extent to which the holding benefits of the secure frame outweigh its threatening potential. It is crucial to emphasize, however, that the therapist is always the ultimate focal point of the treatment frame. Therefore, the patient's unconscious comparative appraisal of the benefits and adverse effects of rectification will depend greatly on this cumulative therapist introject. Thus, a major feature of the settling-in period is the patient's adaptation to the rigors of the better-secured frame and the working over of the split representation of the therapist that has been generated by rectification.

Although this sequence of rectification, reaction, and settling in has been described as fairly discrete stages, in actual clinical practice these phases tend to overlap and can build in a spiraling fashion as one interpretation becomes the adaptive context for the patient's subsequent material. The sequence is also influenced by the omnipresent element of countertransference-based interference as the therapist, too, adjusts to the rectified frame. These features are all evidenced in the next segment of clinical material:

P: (*after arriving two minutes late; he is usually two to three minutes early*) Sorry I'm late—one of those mornings. Had a weird dream last night, but before we get into that, want to ask if I can change appointment times next week. Want to get to the office early because there's a big meeting scheduled for later that morning. Want to be sure everything's set for it. Do you have any time in the afternoon or evening?

T: Let's go on for now and see what comes to mind about it.

P: Things going well in general, but hectic at work. Lots of changes to adjust to. My new assistant is terrific, very competent. We work real well together . . . knew we would. First time there's someone I can trust to stay on top of all the details so I can attend to the bigger problems.

Funny, though, because it's hard to give up being right down in the nitty-gritty of things. Gives me a sense of control to hold all the reins. So I'm trying real hard to let him just do his job and not bug him. After all, it's what I hired him to do in the first place. But that's hard for me. . . . I need to feel in charge.

That's like the dream I had last night. Was driving through the mountains and it was just beautiful, real idyllic. Then I realized there were no brakes and the car starts hurtling down these steep curves. Here I am fighting to stay in control, and it's just going faster and faster. Scared the hell out of me so I was glad to wake up.

T: First you mentioned how hard it is to turn some control over to your assistant, even though you hired him for the job. You linked that to the dream where suddenly you were battling for control over a runaway car. Seems like this might all be related to how you came in today and asked for a change in appointments. Maybe that's a way to hold onto the reins here. Feel that you're more in control of both you and me.

P: Maybe, but I was more thinking about getting ready for the meeting. (*Pause.*) But, actually, we'd probably be all set to go by then anyway. T. [the assistant] is arranging all of it and he's excellent at that kind of thing. It's why I hired him. Guess checking all the details over is my way of handling the anxiety. It *is* an important meeting, but I know we're ready for it. (*Long pause.*)

I guess it's like when I was a kid. I'd reorganize my whole room when I got really upset. Helped me keep my emotions under control. So maybe that is what I was doing here, too.

Like last week with the ulcer thing. I was really scared they'd find something awful. Turned out to be a small thing that should go away by itself if I'm careful. And as worried as I was, the doctors were great. I felt kind of silly telling you about it last week.

Somtimes I get the feeling that you know what I'm saying even before I do. So it's hard to let my guard down at times. It's a little spooky, but nice, too. Kind of protected and taken care of, but I'm afraid to get too dependent on that. With my mother, I'd just start to count on her and something would happen.

T: Seems you're saying two things about letting your guard down here with me:

that it can feel nice to be protected and taken care of, but you couldn't count on your mother to be consistent for that and there's the fear that I won't be either. Then there's the other part that's spooky: that I might find something awful inside you, worse than an ulcer, even before you could realize it.

P: (*after a pause*) Yeah, I'd agree with all of that. Like, I remember back in college . . . I smashed my leg in football right before Thanksgiving. When I came home, my stepmother was wonderful. Felt like she really cared and was helpful and concerned. Didn't feel like it was an act or that I'd have to reciprocate somehow. Just that she wanted me to take it easy and heal the leg. She's always been like that, which is pretty different from my real mother. (*End of session.*)

In comparison with the previous session, this hour shows a major change in the patient's expression of resistance. First, he has foregone the gross behavioral tack of silence in favor of the two fixed frame disturbances of arriving late and requesting a change in appointment times. Although these latter resistances are highly significant, they are more amenable to therapeutic intervention than is his earlier use of silence. Second, the patient's level of communicative resistance is lowered: he refers manifestly to the immediate indicators of late arrival and the request for changed hours. These manifest references are the required link to the immediate treatment situation and afford the therapist all the necessary ingredients for an appropriate Type Two interpretation, because the accompanying derivative complex is coalescing. An additional indicator for intervention is quite apparent in the disturbing dream. Thus, the patient's overall level of resistance has subsided almost to the prerectification intensity, although there is the noted variation in the form of resistance expressed.

There is still evidence of counterresistance on the therapist's part in her failure to address the late arrival as an indicator of disturbance. This counterresistance reflects the therapist's own postrectification settling-in process, during which the anxiety of managing the rectified frame interfered with her ability to give manifest expression to all the latent meaning of the patient's material. The interpretations that are offered appear to receive adequate validation in the patient's subsequent material, through both generally positive object representations and the development of new, pertinent information.

The patient's use of the dream material in this hour is also of particular significance, because it symbolically portrays the suddenly enhanced experience of threat that commonly attends framework rectification. This dream continues to express the theme of loss of control that the patient began to reveal in the previous hour in the derivative of being "helpless and at the doctor's mercy" because of the possible ulcer. The derivative disguise appears to have been insufficient and too close a parallel to the immediate treatment situation, thus aggravating the patient's already heightened resistance. In the present session, however, the more disguised dream material facilitates development of the patient's unconscious response to and working through of the effects of rectification. The dream evidences transformation of the earlier passive self-representation of "held down and helpless" into the more ego-syntonic dream element of the patient "battling for control" over the runaway car. The therapist's first interpretation of this material and the ego-enhancing benefits of the secure frame enable the patient to connect the dream to the more terrifying content of the prior hour as a representation of his overall reaction to rectification.

The settling-in period is also characterized by the patient's beginning struggle with the split representation of the therapist that results from the rectification process. For Mr. A. this dichotomy is elegantly expressed in this hour in terms of the actual genetic split between his two maternal objects, the mother and the stepmother. The latter is characterized as reliable, appropriately nurturing, and able to provide an environment conducive to the patient's own "healing" efforts. He contrasts her with his real mother, described as generally inadequate and functioning with much autistic self-preoccupation. A major part of the patient's fearful response to rectification stems from the anticipation that the now better-functioning therapist will lapse back into prior errors and thus recapitulate the mother's pattern of eliciting Mr. A.'s dependence and then not sustaining him. After the therapist's interpretation of this connection, the patient offers the image of the good and "therapeutic" stepmother. This image both validates the interpretation and provides an unconsciously accurate model of the reliable functioning on the part of the therapist that the patient will require if he is to risk further therapeutic regression.

The patient's next hours continued at the reduced level of communicative resistance with minimal gross behavioral problems. In addition, the patient reported several signs of symptom alleviation: improvement of his stomach condition, successes at work and in social encounters, more positive dream elements, and a lessening of anxiety in general. This stage of settling in then gradually gave way to the treatment period of "lying fallow" (Langs 1981, 1982) in which both the patient and the therapist generated few adaptive contexts that would necessitate any active Type Two interpretive efforts.

DISCUSSION

When psychoanalytic treatment is conducted in the presense of major deviations from the optimal therapeutic framework, many patients evidence an iatrogenic distress syndrome through which they unconsciously communicate the disturbing and disruptive effects of the deviant framework.

The process of rectification employs such accurate derivative perceptions of countertransference-based errors as the foundation for therapeutic remediation of these pathogenic deviations. The result is the securing of a safer and more reliable holding environment (framework) in which the patient is better able to risk exploration of the deeper levels of his or her neurotic functioning. Initially many patients show a positive response to rectification because they have introjected the better-functioning therapist object and have derived the ego-enhancing benefits from the more secure framework.

Despite such initial gains, rectification also carries with it an increased experience of threat for both parties to the treatment interaction and involves a number of structural and object-relational dynamics. Many of these are enhanced by the sharp curtailment in the efficacy of habitual defenses and pathological modes of relatedness that follows rectification. The appearance of the RFR defines a period of general disequilibrium during which the loss of defensive adequacy is exacerbated by the decrease in pathological input from the therapist. This disequilibrium generates an increased pathology gradient that acts on the patient to elicit greater expression of underlying neurotic disturbance. There are fewer external (i.e., countertransference-based) contaminants through which the patient can avoid or disguise his or her own pathological trends, and as a result resistances are heightened.

The increase in resistance in conjunction with an upsurge of deeper pathological elements is not unusual following accurate interpretive efforts. It has often been noted in the continual cycle of regression, resistance, and interpretation (Greenson 1967, Meissner 1981) and is explained by the basic analytic paradigm that the patient will naturally resist many therapeutic efforts to derepress and then work through the essentials of his or her pathology. This paradigm is echoed in the general explanation of the negative therapeutic reaction: proper technique generates adverse effects because of relatively intransigent patient pathology.

Study of the RFR, however, demonstrates that analytic technique is composed of both interpretive and managerial functions, either of which can generate a negative response in the patient. Management of the treatment framework rarely has been identified as a specific therapeutic intervention in the classical analytic literature. In clinical practice, rectification requires both corrective management and remediating interpretation. These two components—framework management and interpretation—may occur simultaneously or, depending on the specifics of the patient's communicative sequence, develop one from the other. In either case, they are complementary interventions that constitute the necessary technical ingredients for conducting the overall process of rectification.

The existing literature is also seriously remiss in its almost exclusive focus on the role of the patient's pathology in the development of heightened resistances and the negative therapeutic reaction. This focus has generated the subtle and seductive presupposition that therapists generally provide optimal treatment, and it carries the corollary that any negative reactions must stem primarily from the patient's dysfunction. Despite the obvious counterresistive forces at work here, there is also the pragmatic issue of the absence of sound clinical methodology by which to test empirical data for the propriety of therapist interventions. The literature abounds, then, with plausible hypotheses that must be tested for their reliability and validity. Langs (1978, 1982) has tackled this task directly and has devised the first precise clinical system for the assessment of *both* therapist and patient functioning. With this methodology now in hand, earlier hypotheses can be reevaluated for their predictive validity and ultimate clinical utility.

As a case in point, examination of the RFR sharply delineates the rigid dichotomy of therapist/health versus patient/pathology. Here, the intervening therapist error must be carefully assessed in its role as a major confounding variable that bears significantly on the aftermath of the validated intervention of rectification. The various dynamic, structural, and object-relational explanations of resistance and the negative therapeutic reaction, as offered in the literature, are only partially applicable to the RFR because of the iatrogenic components that must be taken into account in weighing the patient's overall response to the process of rectification.

After rectification, the patient not only is faced with a loss of the neurotic gratifications and discharge available through frame faults but also must adapt to the now better-functioning therapist. The communicative approach to psychoanalytic treatment places great emphasis on the integrity of the frame, in large part because it serves as a primary representation of the therapist's own functioning. Countertransference-based errors, as exemplified by framework deviations, become negative, or contratherapeutic, introjects. In the same way, appropriate interventions during rectification are internalized as positive therapist representations. Rectification necessarily involves both kinds of introjects and thus leaves the patient with a disturbing split representation of the therapist as object. The patient's subsequent ability to cope with this disparity will be determined largely by the overall status of his or her internal object economy, as well as the developmental and interactional levels of object relatedness in general.

The above factors become crucial in the specific object relationship that has been developed within the immediate treatment situation. It must be recognized that the internalized therapist object begins to form on the patient's first contact with the prospective therapist. A fuller object representation of the therapist gradually is built on the basis of the patient's day-to-day experience of the efficacy of the therapist's managerial and interpretive efforts. When the therapist has acted with general consistency and presented relatively appropriate interventions, the overall object representation is likely to be a positive one despite irregular countertransference lapses. This positive representation facilitates adaptive resolution of any later split introjects resulting from therapist errors and their subsequent rectification. In other words, a positively toned cumulative therapist introject is a vital aspect of the holding benefits of the secure frame and helps to outweigh its more threatening determinants. This, then, aids in limiting the intensity of the RFR and advances the process of settling in.

Because of the crucial importance of this therapist introject over the course of treatment, some comment is necessary about the problems that can occur when the therapist is ambivalent about rectification. This ambivalence can derive from any number of counterresistive forces that readily become apparent in the face of the patient's full communicative representation of the therapeutic need for rectification. If the therapist attempts rectification with a great deal of reticence, the patient will introject the ambivalence, and this introjection may well lead to an exacerbation of the initial split representation that derives from rectification proper. In addition, the patient's evidenced resistances may demonstrate the therapist's own problematic functioning and result in a particularly tempestuous and, to a great extent, a more iatrogenic RFR. At such junctures, rigorous self-analysis and, possibly, supplementary consultation become mandatory.

A variation of this issue is that concerning the ease with which the therapist's RFR can be used as a countertransferential rationale for abandoning the rigors of the comprehensively secure therapeutic framework. All the secure frame stressors operating on the patient also exert tremendous pressure on the therapist. Not only must the therapist contain and detoxify the patient's upsurge of pathology, which includes reactive attempts to restore prior pathosupportive deviations, he or she must also contend with an intensification of parallel or complementary processes within him- or herself. These processes can result in the premature sacrifice of the better-secured frame with the rationale that "the patient's RFR was too destructive," when it may have been the therapist who was unable to tolerate the rigors of providing treatment within such a setting.

Perhaps the most important factor in adaptive management of the entire rectification sequence is the therapist's sensitive monitoring of all the patient's communications for their immediate applicability to the treatment relationship and especially for their accurate unconscious appraisal of the therapist's functioning. When such derivatives are attended by the remaining complement of a full communicative network, Type Two interpretations must be offered along with any indicated framework management interventions. Should the patient's resistances significantly curtail the full development of the communicative network, the therapeutic use of attentive silence is a potent intervention that often will provide the patient with a vital aspect of the secure hold. With the use of such silences, many resistances will resolve of their own accord. Here, the therapist is providing the essential and facilitating "background of safety" (Sandler 1960) that, in and of itself, is one of the greatest assets of the rectified and secure therapeutic framework.

FURTHER CONSIDERATIONS: THE SEVERE RFR

This chapter has attempted to examine the various determinants of the development and adaptive resolution of common negative reactions following therapeutic rectification of the treatment framework. A major issue, however, is how to deal with those patients who, despite the best frame management and therapeutic approach, develop a full-blown and intransigent negative therapeutic reaction. Such patients offer massive resistances that derive from deep intrapsychic and object-relational pathologies and are directed at the total subversion of the psychoanalytic process. The specifics of the pathological constellation typifying these pervasively resistive patients have been outlined previously, but the immediate interactional dynamics of such patients in treatment deserve further examination.

These patients usually are what Langs (1978, 1980, 1982) has termed Type C communicators. Such patients, because of the particulars of their basic pathology, make extensive use of derivative lie barriers to treatment. The patient tends to create a communicative field in which ". . . the essential links between patient and therapist are broken and ruptured, and in which verbalization and apparent efforts at communication are actually designed to destroy meaning, generate falsifications, and to create impenetrable barriers to underlying catastrophic truths" (Langs 1980, p. 547). In the rectification process, the Type C patient is unlikely to provide full communicative representation of the disruptive effects of frame deviations. Therefore, the formulation of complete Type Two interpretations directed toward rectification is extremely difficult. This situation can often leave the therapist with clear indications of the therapeutic necessity of rectification, but without the communicative essentials on which to base subsequent remediating interpretations and managerial efforts. In such instances, attempts to rectify may receive some initial derivative validation, only to be quickly annihilated by the patient's pathological need to devastate meaning within the treatment process.

It is the patient with strong Type C tendencies, aggravated by the frequent use of action-discharge modes of functioning (Type B), whose responses most closely approximate the classical model of the negative therapeutic reaction. Here, the very best of therapeutic interventions is likely to be met with significantly adverse effects, because the patient's pathological constellation necessitates a paradoxical response to appropriate treatment. This kind of reaction is evidenced in the RFR when, following validated rectification, the patient is unable to tolerate the better-secured frame and, perhaps, precipitously terminates treatment. A similar response is not precluded in predominantly Type A patients, although effective management and interpretation stand a better chance of resolving the negative reaction when the communicative field is less impaired than it is with Type C-B individuals.

The problem of the severe and protracted RFR is likely to leave the therapist with the dilemma of having to choose between the patient's expressions of the unconscious therapeutic need for maintenance of the secure framework and concurrent, powerful indicators that the patient may be unable to tolerate provision of the secure hold. This dilemma is aggravated when it is clinically apparent that the patient desperately needs treatment but is likely to flee the firm management and interpretive efforts that the communicative therapist feels obliged to provide. Such an impossible choice—whether to redeviate in order to preserve the treatment relationship or risk the threatened termination—is a major ethical conflict for the therapist. When the therapist is aware of the unconsciously destructive potential of allowing deviations to remain, then to redeviate invites a multitude of countertransference difficulties that can only exacerbate the original problems in treatment.

The resolution of this plight is complicated further by the present lack of detailed clinical data that would permit more comprehensive study of both the severe RFR and the broader negative therapeutic reaction from the unique perspective of the communicative approach to psychoanalytic treatment. This is an area that demands further investigation, especially to determine the best possible therapeutic management techniques for this range of patients. During this uncomfortable interim period, the clinician who is dedicated to working with the truth of his or her patient's unconscious messages and interactions might best be guided by Freud's caveat:

> . . . The psychoanalytic treatment is founded on truthfulness. A great part of its educative effect and its ethical value lies in this very fact. It is dangerous to depart from this sure foundation. When a man's life has become bound up with the analytic technique, he finds himself at a loss altogether for the lies and the guile which are otherwise so indispensable to a physician, and if for once with the best of intentions he attempts to use them he is likely to betray himself (1915, p. 163).

REFERENCES

ABRAHAM, K. (1919). A particular form of neurotic resistance against the psychoanalytic method. In K. Abraham, *Selected Papers on Psychoanalysis*, pp. 303–311. London: Hogarth Press, 1948.

―――― (1924). A short study of the development of the libido. In K. Abraham, *Selected Papers on Psychoanalysis*, pp. 418–501. London: Hogarth Press, 1948.

ASCH, S. (1976). Varieties of negative therapeutic reaction and problems of technique. *Journal of the American Psychoanalytic Association* 24:383–408.

BALINT, M. (1968). *The Basic Fault: Therapeutic Aspects of Regression*. London: Tavistock.

BARANGER, W. (1974). Discussion. In Vianna, H., A peculiar form of resistance to psychoanalytic treatment. *International Journal of Psycho-Analysis* 55:445–447.

BARANGER, M., AND BARANGER, W. (1966). Insight in the analytic situation. In *Psychoanalysis in the Americas*, ed. R. Litman, pp. 56–72. New York: International Universities Press.

BION, W. R. (1962). Learning from experience. In W. R. Bion, *Seven Servants*, pp. 1–111. New York: Jason Aronson, 1977.

―――― (1967). Attacks on linking. In W. R. Bion, *Second Thoughts: Selected Papers on Psychoanalysis*. New York: Jason Aronson.

BIRD, B. (1972). Notes on transference: universal phenomenon and the hardest part of analysis. *Journal of the American Psychoanalytic Association* 20:267–301.

BLEGER, J. (1967). Psychoanalysis of the psychoanalytic frame. *International Journal of Psycho-Analysis* 48:511–519.

BREUER, J., AND FREUD, S. (1893–1895). Studies on hysteria. *Standard Edition* 2.

COOPERMAN, M. (1979). A possible development in psychoanalytic psychotherapy, and some caveats. Paper presented at the Southeastern Conference of the National Association of Private Psychiatric Hospitals, Atlanta, March.

DORPAT, T. (1976). Structural conflict and object-relations conflict. *Journal of the American Psychoanalytic Association* 24:855–874.

FENICHEL, O. (1945). *Psychoanalytic Theory of Neurosis*. New York: Norton.

FERENCZI, S. (1928). The elasticity of psychoanalytic technique. In S. Ferenczi, *Final Contributions to the Problems and Methods of Psychoanalysis*, pp. 87–101. New York: Basic Books, 1955.

FREUD, A. (1936). *The Ego and Mechanisms of Defense*. New York: International Universities Press, 1966.

―――― (1949). Aggression in relation to emotional development: normal and pathological. *Psychoanalytic Study of the Child* 3–4:37–42.

FREUD, S. (1912). Recommendations to physicians practising psycho-analysis. *Standard Edition* 12.

―――― (1913). On beginning the treatment (further recommendations on the technique of psychoanalysis I). *Standard Edition* 12.

―――― (1914a). On the history of the psychoanalytic movement. *Standard Edition* 14.

―――― (1914b). Remembering, repeating, and working through (further recommendations on the technique of psychoanalysis II). *Standard Edition* 12.

―――― (1915). Observations on transference-love (further recommendations on the technique of psychoanalysis III). *Standard Edition* 12.

―― (1923). The ego and the id. *Standard Edition* 19.

―― (1924). The dissolution of the oedipus complex. *Standard Edition* 19.

―― (1926). Inhibitions, symptoms, and anxiety. *Standard Edition* 20.

―― (1937). Analysis terminable and interminable. *Standard Edition* 23.

GILL, M. (1979). The analysis of the transference. *Journal of the American Psychoanalytic Association* 27:263-288.

―― (1982). *Analysis of Transference*, Vol. 1: *Theory and Technique*. New York: International Universities Press.

GREENACRE, P. (1959). Certain technical problems in the transference relationship. *Journal of the American Psychoanalytic Association* 7:484-502.

GREENSON, R. (1967). *The Technique and Practice of Psychoanalysis*. New York: International Universities Press.

GROTSTEIN, J. S. (1977a). The psychoanalytic concept of schizophrenia. I. The dilemma. *International Journal of Psycho-Analysis* 58:403-425.

―― (1977b). The psychoanalytic concept of schizophrenia. II. Reconciliation. *International Journal of Psycho-Analysis* 58:427-452.

―― (1981). *Splitting and Projective Identification*. New York: Jason Aronson.

HARTMANN, H. (1964). *Essays on Ego Psychology*. New York: International Universities Press.

HILL, B. (1981). The role of framework rectification vs. nonrectification as related to the achievement of symptom relief. Clinical Research Project, Illinois School of Professional Psychology.

HORNEY, K. (1933). The problem of negative therapeutic reaction. *Psychoanalytic Quarterly* 5:29-44.

KLEIN, M. (1946). Notes on some schizoid mechanisms. In M. Klein, *Envy and Gratitude and Other Works 1946-1963*, pp. 1-24. New York: Delta Publishing, 1977.

―― (1957). *Envy and Gratitude*. London: Tavistock.

KRIS, E. (1950). Notes on the development and on some current problems of psychoanalytic child psychology. *Psychoanalytic Study of the Child* 5:24-46.

LANGS, R. (1974). *The Technique of Psychoanalytic Psychotherapy*. 2 vols. New York: Jason Aronson.

―― (1976a). *The Bipersonal Field*. New York: Jason Aronson.

―― (1976b). *The Therapeutic Interaction*. 2 vols. New York: Jason Aronson.

―― (1978). *The Listening Process*. New York: Jason Aronson.

―― (1979). *The Therapeutic Environment*. New York: Jason Aronson.

―― (1980). *Interactions: The Realm of Transference and Countertransference*. New York: Jason Aronson.

―― (1981). *Resistances and Interventions: The Nature of Therapeutic Work*. New York: Jason Aronson.

―― (1982). *Psychotherapy: A Basic Text*. New York: Jason Aronson.

LOEWALD, H. (1972). Freud's conception of the negative therapeutic reaction, with comments on instinct theory. *Journal of the American Psychoanalytic Association* 20:235-245.

MAHLER, M. (1968). *On Human Symbiosis and the Vicissitudes of Individuation*. New York: International Universities Press.

MEISSNER, W. (1978). *The Paranoid Process*. New York: Jason Aronson.

—— (1981). *Internalization in Psychoanalysis.* New York: International Universities Press.

MILNER, M. (1952). Aspects of symbolism in comprehension of the not-self. *International Journal of Psycho-Analysis* 33:181–195.

OLINICK, S. (1964). The negative therapeutic reaction. *International Journal of Psycho-Analysis* 45:540–548.

PETO, A. (1977). A model of archaic thinking based on two formulations of Freud. *International Journal of Psycho-Analysis* 58:333–344.

REICH, W. (1928). On character analysis. In *The Psychoanalytic Reader*, ed. R. Fleiss, pp. 129–147. New York: International Universities Press, 1948.

—— (1929). The genital character and the neurotic character. In *The Psychoanalytic Reader*, ed. R. Fleiss, pp. 148–169. New York: International Universities Press, 1948.

RIVIERE, J. (1936). A contribution to the analysis of the negative therapeutic reaction. *International Journal of Psycho-Analysis* 17:304–320.

ROSENFELD, H. (1975). Negative therapeutic reaction. In *Tactics and Techniques in Psychoanalytic Psychotherapy*, Vol. 2: *Countertransference*, ed. P. L. Giovacchini, pp. 217–228. New York: Jason Aronson.

SANDLER, J. (1960). On the concept of the superego. *Psychoanalytic Study of the Child* 15:128–162.

SANDLER, J., DARE, C., AND HOLDER, A. (1973). *The Patient and the Analyst: The Basis of the Psychoanalytic Process.* New York: International Universities Press.

SANDLER, J., AND JOFFE, W. (1969). Toward a basic psychoanalytic model. *International Journal of Psycho-Analysis* 50:79–90.

SANDLER, J., AND ROSENBLATT, B. (1962). The concept of the representational world. *Psychoanalytic Study of the Child* 17:128–148.

SANDLER, J., AND SANDLER, A. (1978). On the development of object-relationships and affects. *International Journal of Psycho-Analysis* 49:285–296.

SEARLES, H. (1959). The effort to drive the other person crazy: an element in the aetiology and psychotherapy of schizophrenia. *British Journal of Medical Pathology* 32:1–18.

STONE, L. (1973). On resistance to the psychoanalytic process: some thoughts on its nature and motivations. In *Psychoanalysis and Contemporary Science*, Vol. 2, ed. B. Rubinstein, pp. 42–73. New York: Macmillan.

STRACHEY, J. (1934). The nature of the therapeutic action of psychoanalysis. *International Journal of Psycho-Analysis* 15:117–126.

VIANNA, H. (1974). A peculiar form of resistance to psychoanalytic treatment. *International Journal of Psycho-Analysis* 55:439-444.

—— (1975). Author's response to Willy Baranger's discussion. *International Journal of Psycho-Analysis* 55:439-444.

VON BERTALANFY, L. (1968). *General Systems Theory.* New York: Braziller.

Part III
Communicative Fields

CHAPTER 14

Psycholinguistic Phenomena of the Bipersonal Field

Richard M. Billow, Ph.D., and
Jill Grant Lovett, M.A.

Psychoanalytic psychotherapy assumes that speech enhances emotional development and that emotional maturity contributes to the capacity for well-chosen speech. But this mutually beneficial relationship between words and emotions is more an ideal than a reality. Speakers strain to put previously unnamed experience into coherent words. And it is the compromise with one's imperfect ability to find adequate words, and the struggle to understand verbal symbols despite their limitations, that is enhancing. At times the tension among experience, words, and the speaker becomes too great, causing ruptures in symbolic processes, in object relationships, and in the ability to perceive reality. In emphasizing the radically different modes of communication in psychotherapy, Langs (1978, 1980) stimulates further consideration of the ways in which the use of words between patient and therapist can enhance or derail emotional growth.

In this chapter we relate an object relations theory of linguistic symbol formation to Langs's theory of communicative fields (1978). From this description emerges a model for empirical research. We also refer to psycholinguistic studies of clinical interviews that may be interpreted as supportive of our model.

Langs (1978) delineates three styles of communication in psychotherapy (Types A, B, and C communicative fields). In the Type A field, language provides a means to organize, think about, and communicate conscious and unconscious experience. The speaker appreciates, at least unconsciously, the symbolic function of language. By "symbolic," we mean the capacity of a word to represent many dimensions of meaning simultaneously, such as conscious and unconscious meaning, or imagistic and abstract meaning.

In the Type B field, language is used primarily to discharge tensions and affects. The speaker unconsciously (and often consciously) does not respect language as a device that conveys meaning, much less multidimensional meaning. The Type B communicator relies on primitive modes of communication, such as projective identification and introjection. He or she uses language as a vehicle in these primitive modes to discharge affect, establish emotional contact, and evoke responses in the listener.

In the Type C field, language obscures and blocks meaning by substituting static and evasive verbal maneuvers for truth-seeking communication. The speaker exhibits unconscious contempt for the power of language to symbolize experience through ideational or even a discharge-evocation mode of communication. At the same time, such communicators may appear to themselves and to listeners as verbally sophisticated and sincere.

What often emerges in the Types B and C fields are perverse uses of language. Like a snake that consumes its own tail, language may ultimately destroy its capacities to create and communicate meaning by turning on itself destructively. From its festering remains, pathological verbal organisms rise to spread catastrophe.

THE TYPE A FIELD

Meaning is generated in the Type A field by the continuous exploration of inner and outer experience through symbol formation, and symbols are formed through this same experience. The symbols become linked to the transference and, as Langs (1978) has emphasized, to the boundaries and adaptive context of the treatment. Symbols generated in the therapy are enlarged; they are filled with multiple meanings of varying richness and depth. In this fashion verbal symbols take on metaphoric properties, referring as they do to the transference and other aspects of the bipersonal field as well as to manifest content, including events outside the therapy situation.

The participant's expanding self-awareness may lead to new appreciation of the metaphorical properties of language, and he or she may attempt to understand the multileveled nature of his or her communications. The participant may feel and think about the symbolic possibilities of language as well as about language's literal references. Thus, the participant grows not only as a symbolizer but as a symbol interpreter as well. Realizing the tentativeness of any one layer of meaning, the symbolizer may also grow more able to tolerate ambiguity and momentary meaninglessness. In the Type A field, the discovery of meaning becomes an oscillating process, the very absence of meaning reflecting back on the thinker to create anxiety and the possibility of new meaning and new reality.

Developmental Perspective on Type A Functioning

The ability to use linguistic symbols to process and communicate internal and external reality develops in conjunction with the growing sense of separation from the mother (Bion 1967, Klein 1930, 1940, Segal 1957, 1964). At this phase of development the infant has reached a critical choice point: he or she may evade the frustrating quality of the absent other by continued hallucination or may modify frustration through precursory symbol formation (Freud 1911).

The modification of frustration through symbol formation has a developmental sequence. Sensory experience is initially sorted by the mental apparatus into "good" and "bad." Primitive meaning is dependent largely on action. "Good" is experienced as the physical presence of the satisfying object and/or the evacuation of the frustrating, anxiety-producing object. "Bad" is experienced as any physical or emotional discomfort. The mother's administering actions (in response to the infant's constitutional contribution) at first "contain" (Bion 1962) the somato-psychological experience of bad. She transforms bad meaningfully into good by removing unbearable or toxic physical and psychological stimuli and by supplying digestible psychological experience. For example, the mother who feeds the child not only removes the "badness" of hunger, but also removes the "badness" of meaningless suffering by supplying the infant with a model of regularity between absence and presence, hunger and its satisfaction.

Good and bad sensations co-occur in relationship to the present, evacuated, or absent object. At first the simultaneous occurrences of satisfying and frustrating sensations are felt as disruptive and disorganizing—multiple stimuli impinging on an apparatus ill equipped to organize the experience. Hence, sensations are often ejected. With normal mental maturation the infant begins to bind the disparate sense elements into nascent images. Such kinesthetic–physiological–visual images seem to be the earliest precursors of symbol formation. The images are linked to the primitive experience itself. No distinction is made between the imaged representation and the object or thing being represented.

The mother–child interchange remains crucial to the growth of symbolic thought. The infant fantasizes that developing images, along with the parts of the self (also a fantasy image), can be projected into the mother. As she did initially with somato-psychological experience, the mother contributes meaning and potential coherence to developing images by modifying their anxious or bad aspects. She returns to the infant its projected images integrated and made benevolent.

The infant's image-making capacity matures during the second stage of symbol formation, that of symbolic equations (Segal 1957) or ideographic (imagistic) representations (Money-Kyrle 1968). The infant generates images of physical objects that are not at the moment present to the senses. But the infant does not yet fully accept absence, in that he or she equates the imagistic symbol with the absent object. There is partial separation from the mother, because her actual presence is not needed to construct her imaged representation. Easily overloaded with anxious experience, however, the imagistic symbol remains partially dependent on the mother's physical availability. It is a fragile construction that must rely on the availability of a more stable construction of meaning from another to reinforce its boundaries and remove potentially fragmenting elements. The vitality of the mother–infant interchange contributes to the infant's reparative efforts to construct and maintain a whole and loving yet realistic image of mother in her absence.

The third phase of symbol formation, that of nascent verbal representation, is reached when symbolic representation is maintained without the mother's physical presence, imagistic representation, or frequent reappearance. The infant tolerates the absence of the object by naming it rather than merely imaging it. (The verbal name is not at first formed into grammatical words, but probably exists as a sound and then as a phoneme.) Symbol formation is dependent on separation from the mother. Reciprocally, symbol formation contributes to toleration of separation. The mother's constant presence is not necessary, because she exists internally, represented by a name. Tolerance of separation from others is based on the meaningful processing of the absence of a once present object.

Developmental psychologists describe similar stages of development. For example, Werner (1948, p. 266) describes how a thing gets to have a name: (a) At first the name is a material property of the thing. (b) Gradually the name becomes a physiognomic "picture" of the thing. "Picture" here does not refer solely to a visual image. Rather, a name is linked to its referent via symbolic processes composing "affective, interceptive, postural, [visually] imaginal elements" (Werner and Kaplan 1963, p. 18). (c) During a later stage the name becomes an algebraic symbol, or sign, of the concept. The sensuous character of the representation seemingly can be lost. Should the linking process be interrupted, however, word meaning lapses (Werner and Kaplan 1963, p. 30).[1]

[1]Whereas Werner and Kaplan's time sequence of hypothetical stages of mental maturation is close to that proposed here, Piaget's timetable (1969) differs greatly. He describes the sensory-motor stage (the first 18 months of life) as one in which mental operations depend on the physical presence of objects to be manipulated. Once the mental image is constructed (at about 18 months of age), dependence on real objects is lessened. Eventually the image-dominated thinking of the preoperational or "intuitive" stage gives way to stages of increasingly representational thought (concrete operational and formal operational stages). The role of the image, and the distinction between object and person permanence, are discussed by Decarie (1962), Fraiberg (1969), Greenspan (1979), and Wolff (1967).

To the extent that a word functions as a symbol, a concrete linkage remains after processing reaches the naming stage. The symbol simultaneously denotes and abstracts from sense experience. But a word, as opposed to the more concretely linked imagistic symbol, supplies greater flexibility for mental manipulation and is prerequisite for more advanced thought processes.

Separation from previously established meaning is crucial to the development of advanced thought, as separation from the real object initially was crucial to the establishment of primitive representational thought. Not only do objects alternate between presence and absence, but meaning also alternates. Vital symbolic language oscillates between presence and absence, abstraction and concretization, and meaning and its lack. Certain particulars are abandoned to reach an abstraction; and abstraction is abandoned to see new particulars. The security of any one clear idea is sacrificed to the forging of new meaning.

Symbolic Language in the Type A Field

A person capable of constructing depth of verbal meaning develops an ever-deepening capacity to feel and think about experience. Words serve both to organize and explain experience, and to discover it. Merleau-Ponty (1964, p. 88) captures this process when he writes, "My spoken words surprise me and teach me my thoughts." To be surprised in something spoken suggests finding something of the self in the words that previously was unsymbolized. An unknown part of the self is put into the symbol and is discovered there. The secure ability to learn through verbal expression is the essential linguistic feature of the Type A field.

Metaphor is the consummate verbal symbol for psychological learning. It condenses multiple levels of potential meaning into one expression, and parallels in its form the process of oscillation essential to the growth of thought. Metaphor makes an implicit or explicit comparison via its syntactic structure, creating a tension between levels of experience.[2] Not only is sense experience replaced by a name, but one name also is replaced by another.

[2] Ortony (1979a) differentiates two types of similarity statements that constitute the bases of metaphor. In *attribute-promoting* statements the matching attributes that link the terms being compared exist in both terms. In *attribute-introducing* statements attributes of one term of the comparison are not normally associated with the other term. The person must take some of the salient attributes of one term and build them into the other term, creating a similarity link. To the extent that a metaphor works because of its attribute-introducing qualities, absence must be tolerated. When a match for similarity between compared objects fails, "it is not possible to conclude that the attribute in question cannot be applied, but only that it is not already present" (p. 173). In attribute-introducing metaphor, the toleration of absence allows for meaning building; "either the existing value of a variable is changed or value is provided where previously there was only a variable" (p. 173).

The replacement has a paradoxical effect. One is first struck by an absence of meaning. For the figurative nature of the expression to be meaningful, concrete or sensory experience first is evoked and literal meaning considered. Imagery and literalness are then partially or fully denied as the interpreter forms an abstraction through analogical reasoning. The present literal reference must be partially removed to create the absent metaphorical comparison. The meaningfulness of a metaphor lies neither in its concrete nor in its abstract qualities, but rather in the process of vital interchange between concrete and abstract thought and meaning and its lack.[3]

The oscillation between presence and absence in metaphor recapitulates early experiences of fusion and separation.[4] To understand a metaphor, however, indicates psychological maturity. Metaphor requires toleration of and conjecture into the relativity and tentativeness of conclusions based on one's thoughts. The metaphor interpreter extends the self into the metaphor with evoked emotion, sense experience, and hypotheses on meaning. The newly understood metaphor further stabilizes emergent meaning for the interpreter (compare Wright 1976). If this interchange succeeds, depth of meaning accrues, both to the metaphor and to the self. As is essential to understanding metaphor, the Type A communicator bears the pain and anxiety of generating new meaning within the self and the symbol.

Linguistic Characteristics of the Type A Field

The Type A field is characterized by the use of *metaphor, contextual metaphor*, and *thematic variability*.

Metaphor. The hallmark of Type A communication is abstract language that also conveys vital sensory, affective, and imagistic references. Because of the ability of metaphor to condense many meanings into one expression, genuinely figurative language should characterize the Type A field. The burgeoning literature on figurative language (see Billow 1977, 1981, Honeck

[3]In psychoses there are losses both in concrete and in abstract representations of objects, as well as a lack of differentiation between the two. Searles (1965, p. 561) observes that just as "the schizophrenic is unable to think in effective, consensually validated metaphor, so too is he unable to think in terms which are *genuinely* concrete, free from an animistic kind of so-called metaphorical overlay" (emphasis in original).

[4]Searles refers to the elements of fusion and separation in metaphor:

. . . perhaps the reason why so many metaphors have a peculiarly poignant beauty is because each of them kindles in us momentarily a dim memory of the time when we lost the outer world—when we first realized that the outer world is outside, and we are unbridgeably apart from it, and alone. Further, the mutual sharing of such metaphorical experience would seem, thus, to be about as intimate a psychological contact as adult human beings can have with one another. (1965, p. 583)

and Hoffman 1980, Ortony 1979b, Pollio et al. 1977) distinguishes vital metaphor from cliché or dead metaphor. We argue that it is vital, not dead, metaphor that signifies the Type A field. In contrast, dead or clichéd metaphor has a particular use in the Type C field to devitalize or obscure communication.

Contextual Metaphor. Because language is multicontextual in the Type A communicative field, referring to manifest as well as to latent content, to the past and to the transference, and so forth, nonfigurative verbalizations will also reveal themselves to be metaphoric (i.e., to have multiple meanings and to make unconscious comparisons) when examined empirically in the context of the total communication. We predict, then, that the field also will be distinguished by *contextual metaphor*, language that emerges as metaphoric upon analysis of the semantic context.

Thematic Variability. Because of the multilayering of meaning, we predict that a greater variety of meaningfully elaborated content themes will emerge upon statistical analysis of verbalizations in the Type A field than in the other communicative fields.

Empirical Findings

Findings on Metaphor in Psychotherapy Communication. Barlow (1973, reported in Pollio et al. 1977) studied the relationship of live and dead metaphor to insight by analyzing five psychoanalytic sessions with one patient. We are assuming here that segments containing genuine insight contain features of the Type A field. Clinical judges defined *insight* according to their individual criteria. Segments of therapy sessions rated by at least three out of four judges as demonstrating insight were studied. Figurative language was defined as 15 specific types of figures of speech (e.g., metaphor, simile), each rated as novel or frozen (clichéd). Barlow found that insight appeared either concurrently or conjunctively with the use of novel figurative language. Although insight segments did not always coincide with high rates of novel figurative production, the contiguity led the author to conclude that the process of using language to make implicit knowledge (expressed in figurative language) explicit (literalization of the figure) is an important component of what is judged to be insight in psychotherapy. Barlow's findings suggest that in the Type A communicative field, where insightful meaning is established through verbal activity, figurative language appears with frequency and may contribute to the communicative process.

Findings on Contextual Metaphor in Psychotherapy Communication and in Clinical Interviews. The underlying metaphoric quality of seemingly everyday words, phrases, and/or semantic categories has been empirically supported by computerized statistical analyses of speech samples (Dahl 1972, 1974, Spence et al. 1978, Spence 1980). Repetition in a speech sample of the same or similar words, or the use of words that are different but are in the same semantic category, establishes and conveys the underlying concerns of the speaker in an organized manner. These concerns, experienced subtly in the context of language, may evade both the speaker and the audience. The computer becomes a most sensitive clinician as it reveals "hidden" metaphoric messages awaiting discovery and exploration.

Dahl (1972) factor analyzed the verbatim texts of 363 sessions of one patient in psychoanalysis. A *work* factor designated periods in which conflicts and content were discussed. A *resistance* factor designated periods of seeming avoidance of conflictual themes. Ten *work* hours, ten *resistance* hours, and five middle hours were searched for frequency of words from categories in the Harvard Psychosociological III Dictionary (Stone et al. 1966). The dictionary contains 3,200 words assigned to one of 55 denotative categories and to one or more of 28 connotative categories. The words in 17 connotative and denotative categories appeared significantly more often in the *work* hours, whereas only 3 word categories were related to the *resistance* hours. If indeed the *work* hours share features of the Type A field, Dahl's findings suggest some confirmation for our hypothesis that in this field meaningful verbalizations appear with more thematic variability than in Type B and C fields.

Dahl (1974) found also that 47 words occurred more frequently in the *work* than in the *resistance* hours. When factor analyzed, these words fell into semantic categories that seemed to represent unconscious metaphoric themes. For example, a category that included such words as "ashamed," "guilt," "father," "baby," "intercourse," and "into" suggested an oedipal theme. That more words clustered thematically in *work* than in *resistance* hours tends to support our hypotheses that more verbally symbolic material appears in a Type A field than in the other fields.

A similar computer analysis was applied to transcripts of interviews, with equally striking results (Spence et al. 1978, Spence 1980). Sixty-two women were interviewed after having biopsies for cervical cancer. To assess the relationship of word choice to biopsy outcome, the patients' texts were analyzed for frequency of words connoting hope and hopelessness. The *hope* group consisted of words such as "want," "yearn," and "wish." The *hopeless* group consisted of words such as "fail," "grief," and "fear."

The patients were rated by clinical judges and divided into two groups, *Defended* and *Concerned*. The former tended to deny any danger of disease; the latter expressed open concern about cancer. How openly the women discussed their fears was related to whether their word choice revealed unconscious knowledge of the absence or presence of disease. Both the *hope* and *hopeless* clusters were significantly correlated with eventual diagnostic status (no cancer and cancer, respectively) for the *Concerned* group, but neither word cluster was significantly related to biopsy outcome in the *Defended* group. The *Concerned* patients illustrate essential communicative qualities of the Type A field. Given the adaptive context (Langs 1978) of the interviews, i.e., the threat of cancer, the women "admitted" rather than evaded painful experience and put it into words. Besides openly naming their fears of cancer, these women also conveyed unconscious knowledge of presence or absence of the disease. They chose everyday words that clustered meaningfully into underlying metaphoric themes of hope and hopelessness.

DEVELOPMENT OF PATHOLOGICAL
SYMBOL FORMATION: THE TYPE B AND C FIELDS

When anxiety is not adequately contained in the mother–infant dyad, it becomes overwhelming and persecutory to the infant. Given lengthy periods of unmanageable anxiety, the infant does not develop a tolerance for absence of the mother and concurrent symbolic processes, and instead resorts to evacuation and/or hallucination. If these solutions are used excessively, the mother's attempts to restore a thought-producing projective–introjective interchange may be experienced as persecutory. The mother's very presence becomes intolerable, and a state of mindlessness is preferred to experiencing presence, absence, or their alternation. This sequence contributes to reliance in verbal maturity on a Type B or Type C communicative style. The essential feature shared by these fields is the distrust and avoidance of a thoughtful interchange expressed in meaningful language.

THE TYPE B FIELD

The Type B communicator discharges anxieties and affects through action and projective identification. Speech is employed as an action to eject disturbing inner stimuli and also to evoke verbal or action responses in the listener. The Type B speaker simultaneously attacks and ejects symbolic meaning and strives for containment in the listener. Ideas, events, the transference, and the multiple meanings of words are destructively disregarded under the pressing need for discharge and evocation. Langs (1978) has identified two distinct uses of Type B communication, designated Types B-A and B-C. In Type B-A, projective identification and discharge are employed immaturely and excessively in an attempt to communicate. The speaker values the meaningful processing of experience, but the task of forming complete symbolic thought is projected into the listener. Given a listener who is sufficiently available to metabolize and return the projected aspects, the speaker may eventually tolerate absence and produce symbolic thought in its place. In Type B-C communications, projective identification and action are employed pathologically and perversely to defeat communication and destroy knowledge. The speaker attacks and fragments both his or her own and the listener's efforts to understand and to speak clearly. The Type B-C speaker forcefully communicates distrust of and contempt for symbol formation and the contact that would lead to its growth, but simultaneously uses affective discharge to maintain control.

Developmental Perspective on Type B Functioning

The developmental process leading to Type B communication has three progressively deteriorated stages: (1) fixation at the level of ideographic symbols, with an excessive reliance on projective and introjective identification; (2) an imbalance of projection and splitting over introjection; and (3) fragmentation of self and symbol through violent projections and perverse communications.

As mentioned earlier (in the section on the development of Type A functioning), dependence on projective identification to communicate reflects a normal maturational stage in which separation of self from object, and image from referent, is incomplete. Partial failures in symbol formation co-occur and interrelate with partial failures in internalizing object relationships. The self remains concretely linked to the symbol and the signified; the symbol and signified are also partially identified or fused with each other. The infant uses these concrete symbols both to eject and to represent anxiety. As imagistic symbols, they momentarily organize experience but also discharge affect and evoke caretaking. The infant remains dependent on the mother's empathy and thinking to further his or her own thinking.

An infant will grow to rely on Type B communication to the extent that he or she remains fixated at the precursory or ideographic level of symbol formation. When this kind of thinking persists beyond its appropriate developmental phase, pathological modes of communicating develop concurrently with normal verbal modes. The infant continues to deposit ideographic symbols, as well as unsymbolized experience, into the mother via projective identification. The interchange, however, fails to return to the child his or her experience adequately relieved of its overwhelming anxious components, and further symbolized. The infant remains anxious and intolerant of the separation from the real object that adequate internalization of the symbol-forming process would entail. Thought of the absent mother, the basis of mature symbol formation, would bring with it intolerable anxieties of separation, of loss, and of ultimate self-dissolution. As development proceeds, the infant strives to represent experience and to use the other constructively to modify anxiety and to further symbol formation. Simultaneously, the infant evades completion of symbol formation because of intense underlying fear that thinking will be emotionally unbearable. For the Type B communicator, discharge of thoughts and feelings predominates over thinking about thoughts and feelings. Projection into and introjection of the external object remain excessive, immature, and insufficiently supplemented and supplanted by independent verbal thought.

If the imbalance between the infant's needs and the mother's capacity to fulfill them is extreme, the infant painfully reintrojects his or her inadequately symbolized, anxious experience. The interchange does not return a distressed child to comfort; instead, the fear and anxiety intensify. The infant reintrojects an ideograph, concretely linking separation to painful sensations of persecutory absence. With extended periods of such a failed interaction, the infant associates precursory symbolic interchange with pain and disorganization. The projective-introjective mode of communication becomes pathologically imbalanced. Excessive projection replaces the gradual predomination of normal introjection as the infant attempts to evade feared symbolized interaction.

If this pattern persists, projection may become pathologically forceful and violent. The outer and inner world become pervasively influenced by violent projective identifications. Precursory symbols are ejected with great force, leaving the infant frustrated and empty, yet fearful of further introjection. The violence of the projection fragments the impoverished self, the ideographic symbol, and the object (Bion 1962, 1963, 1970; Grotstein 1978, 1980; Meltzer 1975).

Excessive and violent projection perverts the infant's efforts toward cohesion, particularly those efforts directed toward integrated symbol formation. The mother's presence, as well as her absence, become represented by pathological symbols constructed perversely from the melding of fragmented bits. These perverse, ideographic links among self, symbol, and object are feared and hated. The mother's attempts at communication now are experienced not as inadequate but as attacks. The infant employs projection and fragmentation to destroy a dreaded bad object and a perverse interchange.

Language in the Type B Field

In the Type B field, anxiety remains insufficiently contained by symbols and the symbol-forming process. Verbal symbols become overloaded with affects and break down, losing depth of meaning. Words serve as vehicles for discharge and relief, rather than for verbal symbolic communication. Symbols that in normal development are immature and in need of maternal processing become, in pathological development, deformed symbolic structures that contribute to at least three characteristic modes of verbal disarticulation. In *affective* language or *ruptured* language, the verbal symbol forms a leaky container of meaning. Its disintegrating boundaries become overburdened with anxiety-laden contents seeking discharge. An *amalgamation* tautly contains impact contents that overload appropriate boundaries to deform verbal structure. These modes of verbal disarticulation obfuscate, but in their obfuscation also convey conflict and affect. An empathic listener may be able to construct a clarified symbol from the primitive and/or distorted linguistic elements of affective and ruptured language and amalgamations.

In the Type B-A field, excessive projection is used to communicate; in the Type B-C field, it is used to attack meaning. Each of the three characteristic modes may be employed primarily to communicate or to abort communication, depending on the clarity and interpretability of the language. The violence and intensity of the projective identification can be perceived in the degree of deterioration represented in the particular vocalization. As language becomes more primitively and excessively affective, more minutely ruptured and fragmented, and more bizarrely amalgamated, the speaker or listener has greater difficulty reconstructing meaning from linguistic disaster.

Linguistic Characteristics of the Type B Field

The Type B field is characterized by a disportionate use of affective language (primitive onomatopoeia), ruptured language, and amalgamations.

Affective Language. Even if speech is perfectly coherent, the primary meaning of the communication may be conveyed by the affective tone, independent of the semantic meanings of the words. When used in this way as vehicles to evacuate anxiety, words discharge the raw elements of sense impressions and/or emotions. Sharpe (1940, p. 157) detailed how, at times, speech functions as a muscular mode of bodily discharge and language expresses "pure feeling without thought." Such affective language may be understood as a primitive form of onomatopoeic expression insofar as the vocalizations serve to express and discharge feeling through sound. When used excessively, affective language signifies a disrespect for and rejection of verbal meaning. Examples of affective language with minimal linguistic structure include "Wow," "Ugh," "Oh." These semilinguistic elements, along with excessive laughs, sighs, grunts, and groans, may be particularly pervasive in the Type B field.

Ruptured Speech. Unmediated affect intrudes upon the structure of words and sentences, creating ruptured speech. Such ruptures include stutters and excessive repetition of syllables, words, or phrases. The symbolizer may seek to discharge affects directly, breaking down words and sentences into semiarticulate elements of speech. Ruptured speech signifies both a need for psychic relief and an attack on meaning. It represents the fragmenting effects of intense anxiety and aggression on efforts at symbol formation. Composed of deteriorating elements of thoughts and language, ruptured speech is frustrating for speaker and listener and may motivate further ejection and fragmentation rather than symbol formation.

Amalgamations. In amalgamated speech, semantic elements are fragmented and then recombined. Amalgamations include parapraxes such as misnomers, spoonerisms and neologisms, and pathological metaphor, in which concrete and abstract levels of meaning are fused and confused (see Billow 1977, Billow and associates also are presently observing metaphor comprehension and production in schizophrenia and borderline states [in progress]). The symbol's consensually valid properties as a signifier may be obscured. Part of the listener's job is to differentiate or unscramble the various denotative and connotative properties of the amalgamated symbol, to relate specific aspects of the verbal communication to specific referents. Amalgamations both convey information to the listener and serve as a barrier to communication by virtue of being impacted rather than compact verbal symbols. They evidence fragmentation and recombination of fragments in a simultaneous effort to create and to evade meanings.

Empirical Findings

Mahl (1956, 1961, 1963, 1981) has researched extensively disturbances in verbal fluency. He groups speech disturbances empirically as follows: "'ah,' sentence change, repetition, omission, stutter, tongue-slip, sentence incompletion, and intruding incoherent sounds" (Mahl 1963, p. 81). He has found speech disturbances to be related to several other indices of emotional variability but to be independent of manifest verbal expression of affects. For example, speech disturbance (other than "ah") correlated with the speaker's anxiety level as measured by a number of criteria, including independent clinical judgment, sweat response, heart rate, galvanic skin potential level, number of galvanic responses, and skin temperature, but did not correlate with manifest verbal expression of anxiety.

Mahl's findings support our hypothetical model of psycholinguistic phenomena in the Type B field. Verbal expression of anxiety signifies the translation of inner experience into words, the essential criterion of the Type A field. In the Type B field, anxiety overburdens the symbolic container so that words no longer adequately hold semantic meaning. The speaker fragments thinking and language and ejects these elements, along with anxious affects, in the form of speech disturbances. Stuttering, for example, serves to attack the semantic content of words as well as the syntactic container (Bion 1967). At the same time, stuttering conveys the speaker's anxiety to the listener and evokes impatience and action, such as the caretaking response of completing the verbalization for the speaker.

A Case Example of Type B Patient Communication

A case example from Mahl (1963) provides empirical support for our hypothesis that speech disturbances represent an attack on meaning to protect the self from unbearable anxiety. In an interview a patient's speech disturbance rate rose while discussing the event precipitating chronic headaches. He associated a recent hunting trip with a previous one on which he saw his cousin shoot himself in the head. Speech disturbance did not coincide with any report of anxiety or fear but did coincide with expressions of negativity, such as "I don't know" and "I can't," used in various contexts.

Mahl interpreted these expressions as representing denial and repression in the service of maintaining ignorance. The patient not only symbolized a wish not to know by expressing the wish meaningfully in words, he also acted it out by rupturing speech. Therefore, speech disturbances suggest to us a failure of repression, rather than the operation of repression. Anxiety breaks through, overwhelming the repression barrier that contributes to self-integration and symbol formation. The patient ruptures the semantic units of language, splitting, ejecting, and projecting phonetic and syllabic speech fragments.

THE TYPE C FIELD

In the Type C field, anxiety and aggression are heightened, but psychic withdrawal rather than discharge results. Verbal symbols are at times not attacked directly but rather are used effectively to attack meaning by "clearly" presenting lies and falsity. Words create barriers between patient and therapist, between past and present, between external events and transference, and between themes within the narrative, while masquerading as a mode of communicative connection. Material is repetitive and pointless and reveals an emotional stance of noncooperation and a lack of self-reflection. Themes that seem important are abandoned or repeated rather than elaborated. The speaker may appear to be communicating in a symbolically imaginative and engaging manner. The material fails to organize around an adaptive context, however, and eventually reveals itself to be shallow (Langs 1978).

The lack of meaningful expression in the Type C field is itself the symbolization of an effort to seal off an internal world of impending or actual chaos, psychosis, and dissolution. In that the speaker may evoke such understanding and the appropriate "holding" response (Langs 1978, 1980), the Type C field remains a field of potential communication and interaction. The intense negation of meaning in the communications makes such recognition difficult and the effort of adequate holding and eventual containment arduous. The Type C communicator threatened with understanding may redouble his or her efforts to deny meaning through further withdrawal of projective identifications and the institution of lies.

Developmental Perspective on Type C Functioning

If during development, projection and fragmentation become excessive and violent (as described earlier in the section on the development of Type B functioning), the infant may be unable to maintain an emotional relationship to the mother and to the mother's ministrations. The emotional relationship becomes increasingly persecutory to the infant. A cycle of projection, fragmentation, reamalgamation, and reprojection develops. The infant may attempt to end the painful intrusion of persecutory and fragmented communications by withdrawing from the projective and introjective process (see Klein 1975, p. 144ff.). Rather than continue the painful and perverse interchange, the infant evades contact. The fantasy is established that the part of the self vulnerable to pain has been "successfully" ejected along with anxiety. The infant presents a facade of a "good baby" (Bion 1973) who interacts as expected, but the exchange is empty. What does remain alive in the baby is hidden from both child and mother, preserved behind a barrier of conventionality. Personality develops as a protective yet empty shell.

Language in the Type C Field

Symbolic language development in the Type C communicator is seemingly similar to the normal progression. Words are learned and are used conventionally. But meaningful language is used to create meaninglessness. The expected effect of language—to deepen emotional and intellectual awareness—does not occur. Words, like the developing self, become empty shells that may appear appropriate. They are used "as if" they conveyed meaning, whereas in fact they are drained of emotional vitality and hence are left without truth value. The conventional meanings of words are not necessarily negated; in fact, at times *only* the conventional meanings are employed. Unintended meaning is rigidly excluded from consideration, so that neither speaker nor listener is ever surprised by language. Ambiguity is appreciated not to stimulate thinking, but to hide, obfuscate, bore, or sadistically mislead.

The Type C field evidences a preponderance of static symbol formation. Language, although seemingly multidimensional in its representational qualities and coherent, is on closer examination flat, one-dimensional, intellectually deadening, and often confusing. The static symbol, in contrast to the normal symbol, does not mask or hide conflictual meaning while partially expressing meaning along with underlying impulses (see Jones 1916). A mask presents itself to be uncovered. But when the mask is worn by the Type C speaker, the person behind the mask may have disappeared, along with the meaning expressed in the symbol.

Linguistic Characteristics of the Type C Field

Three prevalent forms of perverse communications we believe to characterize the Type C field are *static metaphor*, *cliché*, and *referential vagueness* (e.g., pronouns without clear antecedents).

Static Metaphor.   In the static use of metaphor, the metaphoric quality of oscillation between concretization and abstraction, meaning and no-meaning, is halted. Rather than confuse and distort the play among levels of meaning as in a Type B-C use of amalgamated metaphor, the speaker rigidly isolates different levels of meaning from one another. The speaker may seem indirect and overabstract. At other times he or she may become incongruously obtuse, suddenly failing to grasp the abstract level of a metaphoric communication. The speaker evades or circumvents the relevant emotional and semantic dimensions of the expression by maintaining stubborn disinclination to move from literal or sensuous to abstract meaning. Metaphorlike communications may be offered when literal messages are expected, but the metaphor may be responded to in a literal manner. This failure to allow play among levels of meaning results in a subtle missing of the point on which the metaphor, and hence the communication, turn.

Cliché.   Clichéd language, of which dead or frozen metaphor is one type, also is utilized to establish a static field of no-meaning. Although cliché functions as a well-used coin of language because it communicates familiar truths, familiar truths may deaden the communicative field so that fresh truths are no longer sought. Cliché exists in the place where truth once was vital. It functions as if it were a live symbol but may provide nothing nutritive that will lead to learning and growth in the speaker or listener. Filling the internal mental space as well as the space between participants with empty contents, cliché may lead the listener to dullness, exhaustion, and defensive withdrawal. He or she may institute countercliché.

Referential Vagueness.   Vagueness creates, as do static metaphor and cliché, an expectation in the listener of eventual understanding and communicative contact. Vagueness frustrates the listener, however, by failing to provide clear references that would "name" experience so that further meaning may be constructed. The listener is not given clear referential boundaries with which to organize figure and ground and create multiple perspectives. The listener becomes trapped in a vague referential field and may quickly lose any sense of cognitive boundaries. Feeling confused, stupid, and useless, the listener may withdraw in defeat.

Empirical Findings

The use of language to block psychotherapy communication has been studied empirically only indirectly. In an investigation cited earlier (in the section discussing empirical findings on the Type A field), Barlow (1973, in Pollio et al. 1977) found a lack of correspondence or a negative correlation between insight segments and frequency of frozen figurative language. In contrast, positive relationships between metaphor and insight were found. Perhaps clichés more likely than metaphor may be used to create a static field (like the Type C field) that therefore would not strike judges as containing insight.

Further tentative support for our hypotheses is offered by Dahl's findings (1972) concerning word usage in *resistance* hours (discussed earlier). One of the word categories that distinguished the *resistance* hours consisted of nonspecific object references, e.g., "anything," "everything," "it," "that," "they." These words lend themselves to vagueness of referent and could be employed to obscure meaning, as in a Type C field.

SUMMARY

We have called attention to parallel symbolic phenomena in the bipersonal field, intrapsychic experience, and language. In the Type A field, simultaneous absence and presence is tolerated in all three spheres. In the bipersonal field, the speaker acknowledges through adherence to the frame the "illusion" quality (Khan 1973) of the other's being and not being many transference objects. Intrapsychically, the speaker feels his or her feelings as real, and simultaneously abstracts meaning by thinking about his or her feelings while putting them into words. Such a speaker does not cling rigidly to words. One level of word meaning may be replaced by another. The prevalence of verbal symbols calls attention to the capacity of language to generate undiscovered meaning by a consideration of ambiguity. The dyad, introspection, and language function as dynamic processes through which the capacity to bear and learn from experience is enlarged.

In the Type B field, discharge and evocation prevail. In each of the dynamic spheres—the dyad, the self, and language—the speaker's capacity to tolerate the development of meaning is fragile and needs the constant presence of the symbolizing other. The illusion quality of the transference is lost. The speaker discharges feelings with the belief that the other is in reality the transference figure. Conflicts are not tolerated; rather, one set of feelings, ideas, and fantasies seems present and real, while a conflicting set is split off and denied. Again, it remains for the symbolizing other to retrieve what is absent to create meaningful cohesion. Finally, verbal symbols reflect the fragile and limited capacity for complexity. In the face of anxiety, language loses depth, breaks down, and directly conveys affect. Language also may be attacked, fragmented, and pathologically amalgamated to destroy meaning and the communicating couple. The listener's task becomes one of transformation and/or repair, of returning projected aspects of the self transformed into verbal symbols.

In the Type C field, the painful problems of the development of meaning and of communication are evaded. A vacuous, absent quality exists and masquerades as vital presence. The evasion of a genuine exploration of presence and absence is not obvious. Rather, it is carried out insidiously through behaviors that mock the dynamic processes in the dyadic interchange, in self-exploration, and in symbol formation. Communicative barriers may engender subtle but pervasive feelings of chaos and confusion in the listener. The frame of the relationship may be respected scrupulously, but the relationship is just as scrupulously avoided by the speaker's underlying emotional withdrawal. The speaker acts as if engaged in a task of self-exploration but in actuality behaves to avoid collaboration or self-exploration that might lead to meaning and consequent painful feelings. Verbal symbols similarly appear functional, but the appearance deceives. In the absence of interchange with emotion, with the experiencing self, or with the other, potential meaning decomposes. The deteriorated verbal symbol contributes to the stagnant communicative Type C field.

REFERENCES

BARLOW, J. (1973). Metaphor and insight in psychotherapy. Unpublished doctoral dissertation, University of Tennessee, Knoxville.

BILLOW, R. M. (1977). Metaphor: a review of the psychological literature. *Psychological Bulletin* 84:81–92.

——— (1981). Observing spontaneous metaphor in children. *Journal of Experimental Child Psychology* 31:430–445.

BION, W. R. (1962). Learning from experience. In W. R. Bion, *Seven Servants*, pp. 1–111. New York: Jason Aronson, 1977.

——— (1963). Elements of psycho-analysis. In W. R. Bion, *Seven Servants*, pp. 1–110. New York: Jason Aronson, 1977.

——— (1967). *Second Thoughts: Selected Papers on Psychoanalysis.* New York: Jason Aronson.

——— (1970). Attention and interpretation. In W. R. Bion, *Seven Servants*, pp. 1–136. New York: Jason Aronson, 1977.

——— (1973). *Bion's Brazilian Lectures.* Vol. 1. Rio de Janeiro, Brazil: Imago Editora.

DAHL, H. (1972). A quantitative study of psychoanalysis. In *Psychoanalysis and Contemporary Science*, Vol. 1, ed. R. Holt and E. Peterfreund, pp. 237–257. New York: Macmillan.

―――― (1974). The measurement of meaning in psychoanalysis by computer analysis of verbal contents. *Journal of the American Psychoanalytic Association* 22:37–57.

DECARIE, T. (1962). *Intelligence and Affectivity in Early Childhood.* New York: International Universities Press.

FRAIBERG, S. (1969). Libidinal object constancy and mental representation. *Psychoanalytic Study of the Child* 24:9–47.

FREUD, S. (1911). Formulations regarding the two principles in mental functioning. *Standard Edition* 12.

GREENSPAN, S. (1979). *Intelligence and Adaptation: An Integration of Psychoanalytic and Piagetian Developmental Psychology.* New York: International Universities Press.

GROTSTEIN, J. S. (1978). Gradients of analyzability. *International Journal of Psychoanalytic Psychotherapy* 7:137–151.

―――― (1980). A proposed revision of the psychoanalytic concept of primitive mental states: part 1. *Contemporary Psychoanalysis* 16:479–546.

HONECK, R., AND HOFFMAN, R., ed. (1980). *Cognition and Figurative Language.* Hillsdale, N.J.: Lawrence Erlbaum.

JONES, E. (1916). On symbolism. In *Papers on Psycho-analysis.* London: Bailliere, Tindall & Cox.

KHAN, M. M. R. (1973). The role of illusion in the analytic space and process. In M. M R. Khan, *The Privacy of the Self.* New York: International Universities Presss, 1974.

KLEIN, M. (1930). The importance of symbol-formation in the development of the ego. *International Journal of Psycho-Analysis* 11:24–39.

―――― (1940). Mourning and its relationship to manic-depressive states. *International Journal of Psycho-Analysis* 21:125–153.

―――― (1975). *Psycho-analysis of Children.* London: Hogarth.

LANGS, R. (1978). Some communicative properties of the bipersonal field. *International Journal of Psychoanalytic Psychotherapy* 7:87–135.

―――― (1980). Truth therapy/lie therapy. *International Journal of Psychoanalytic Psychotherapy* 8:3–35.

MAHL, G. (1956). Disturbances and silences in the patient's speech in psychotherapy. *Journal of Abnormal and Social Psychology* 53:1–15.

―――― (1961). Measures of two expressive aspects of a patient's speech in two psychotherapy 1961 interviews. In *Comparative Psycholinguistic Analysis of Two Psychotherapeutic Interviews*, ed. L. Gottschalk, pp. 91–138. New York: International Universities Press, 1963.

―――― (1963). The lexical and linguistic levels in the expression of the emotions. In *The Expression of Emotions in Man*, ed. P. Knapp, pp. 77–105. New York: International Universities Press.

―――― (1981). Normal disturbances of speech. In *Spoken Interaction in Psychotherapy: Strategies of Discovery*, ed. R. Russell. New York: Irvington Publishers.

MELTZER, D. (1975). *Explorations in Autism.* Perthshire, Eng.: Clunie Press.

MERLEAU-PONTY, M. (1964). On the phenomenon of language. In *Signs.* Evanston, Ill.: Northwestern University Press.

MONEY-KYRLE, R. (1968). Cognitive development. *International Journal of Psycho-Analysis* 49:691-698.

ORTONY, A. (1979a). Beyond literal similarity. *Psychological Review* 86:161-181.

——— (1979b). *Metaphor and Thought.* New York: Cambridge University Press.

PIAGET, J. (1969). *The Language and Thought of the Child.* Cleveland: Meridian Books.

POLLIO, H., BARLOW, J., FINE, H., AND POLLIO, M. (1977). *Psychology and the Poetics of Growth.* Hillsdale, N.J.: Lawrence Erlbaum.

SEARLES, H. (1965). The differentiation between concrete and metaphorical thinking in the recovering schizophrenic patient. In H. Searles, *Collected Papers on Schizophrenia*, pp. 560-583. New York: International Universities Press.

SEGAL, H. (1957). Notes on symbol formation. *International Journal of Psycho-Analysis* 38:391-397.

——— (1964). *Introduction to the Work of Melanie Klein.* New York: Basic Books.

SHARPE, E. (1940). Psycho-physical problems revealed in language: an examination of metaphor. In *Collected Papers on Psychoanalysis by Ella Freeman Sharpe*, ed. M. Brierly, pp. 155-169. New York: Brunner/Mazel, 1978.

SPENCE, D., SCARBOROUGH, H., AND GINSBERG, E. (1978). Lexical correlates to cervi-*American Psychoanalytic Association* 28:115-132.

SPENCE, D., SCARBOROUGH H., AND GINSBERG, E. (1978). Lexical correlates to cervical cancer. *Social Science and Medicine* 12:141-145.

STONE, P., DUNPHY, P., SMITH, M., AND OGLIVIE, D. (1966). *The General Inquirer: A Computer Approach to Content Analysis.* Cambridge, Mass.: MIT Press.

WERNER, H. (1948). *Comparative Psychology of Mental Development.* New York: International Universities Press.

WERNER, H., AND KAPLAN, B. (1963). *Symbol Formation.* New York: Wiley.

WOLFF, P. (1967). Cognitive considerations for a psychoanalytic theory of language acquisition. In *Motives and Thought: Psychoanalytic Essays in Honor of David Rapaport*, ed. R. Holt, pp. 299-343. New York: International Universities Press.

WRIGHT, K. (1976). Metaphor and symptom: a study of integration and its failures. *International Review of Psycho-Analysis* 3:97-109.

CHAPTER 15

The Development
of Communicative Modes
in the Mother–Child Relationship

Joan Balogh Erdheim, Ph.D.

Robert Langs has been a pioneer, exploring and developing a multitude of original concepts pertaining to the patient–therapist relationship. Langsian interactional explorations have led to an increased focus on unconscious communications in the bipersonal field. *The Bipersonal Field* (1976), *The Listening Process* (1978), *Interactions: The Realm of Transference and Counter-transference* (1980), and *Resistances and Interventions* (1981) have developed Langs adaptational-interactional point of view, enhancing the serious clinician's appreciation for and understanding of psychotherapeutic communications. Langs has illuminated the crucial stimulus as well as synthesis potential of every communication, be it an emotional expression of the patient, an interpretive intervention of the therapist, or, on a more latent and probably more significant level, the communication conveyed by the therapist's management of the ground rules and basic therapeutic environment. Langs recognizes that each crucial communication directly provokes the response that immediately follows and also contributes to the "spiraling conscious and unconscious communicative interaction" (Langs 1980).

The categorizations of the communicative styles in the clinical situation that Langs has formulated (Type A, Type B, and Type C styles, or fields) that may result from the patient–therapist interactional relationship are distinct in nature and function.

This chapter will begin by reviewing the three fields, or communicative styles, and then will suggest that the separation–individuation process and its forerunners not only permit the emergence of the intrapsychic self-object world, as Mahler et al. (1975) and Jacobson (1964) suggest, but also are responsible for the full development of an interpersonal communicative style.

This assumption will be discussed in terms of the following hypotheses:

1. The mother's communicative style and her utilization of it is a crucial determinant of the baby's communicative style.
2. Separation–individuation for the baby can be understood as a communicative developmental process in which Type B and C fields are passed through before the child achieves the Type A communicative style.
3. The rapprochement subphase presents a crucial communicative challenge: the opportunity for the Type A communicative capacity.
4. The Type B and Type C communicative styles can be understood as communicative fixation or regression phenomena.
5. The child's communicative modality is apparent by the late rapprochement subphase.

THE THREE COMMUNICATIVE STYLES

The Type A communicative field, as depicted by Langs, is characterized by the analyst's facilitation of a play space or transitional space wherein the patient metaphorically communicates analyzable derivatives of his or her unconscious fantasies, memories, introjects, and perceptions (Langs 1978). The therapist in turn demonstrates the capacity for appreciating symbolic communication via appropriately processing the manifest material, relating it to the crucial provoking stimulus, and then imparting these understandings through valid interpretations. The essence of the Type A field is contained in reliable boundaries, illusory representation, insight intentionality, and integration as well as differentiation of reality and fantasy.

Winnicott and Khan emphasized in their discussions of transitional space the reality–fantasy juxtaposition as well as the self–object existence therein. These ideas anticipated Langs Type A field. By extending his transitional object concept, Winnicott (1951) likened the analytic field, in which reality and fantasy exist side by side and patient and therapist interrelate, to the baby's special blanket, which is real, yet symbolic; associated with mother, yet the baby's creation. Khan (1974) conceived of the analytic situation as a transitional space in which new experiences are initiated to be affirmed or negated. He implied a creative individuation process as well as a "particularizing" and "validating" function, the latter to which Langs refers (1978, p. 12). Indeed, in the Type A field, reality perceptions become differentiated from fantasy projections, and patients contributions from those of the therapist. Yet at the same time fantasy and reality can mutually enrich each other, as can the self and the object (or patient and therapist). For example, Langs emphasizes the importance of the adaptive context, a reality event that stimulates the patient's fantasy contributions. The adaptive context is likened to the day residue of the dream (Langs 1971). Both are crucial, real occurrences that pave the way to latent understandings.

According to Freud (1900), the latent dream wish could never be actualized without the entrepreneurial "know-how" of the reality-based day residue. According to Langs, in-depth Type A understanding could not occur if the scattered Type Two derivatives, the metaphorical representations of the patient's intrapsychic and interpersonal conflicts, were not integrated with the activated adaptive context.

The self and object are mutually enriched in the Type A communicative field. According to Langs's communicative object-relations point of view, either the commensal mode of relatedness or the healthy symbiosis typically exists. In the commensal object relationship each participant satisfies the healthy needs of the other and receives in turn a full measure of appropriate satisfaction of his or her own, whereas the healthy symbiotic relationship is skewed toward the gratification of one of the members of the relationship dyad. (In the Type A communicative field, this is the patient.)

The Type A analyst is capable of managing and maintaining a secure frame that he or she recognizes as communicating the holding function. This analyst avoids interventions that encourage pathological symbioses, introduce barriers, or move the patient from latent to manifest material. Rather, he or she listens to the patient's Type Two derivative responses as a commentary on the preceding intervention (the validation process) and discovers that interpretations, the playing back of selected derivatives, and silence seem to suggest to the patient an interest in truly listening and a capacity to understand and integrate patient material. Questions, confrontations, and clarifications, however, might communicate controlling and surface preoccupations.

What about the Type A communicative patient? The Type A patient presents acute symptomatology yet genuine motivation to search for and to express derivatives to obtain understanding. The patient's interpersonal and intrapsychic resistances reveal some need for protective concealment but also a quest for truth, however threatening. Although the Type A patient may initially try to modify the frame, his or her individuality will be nurtured if the secure hold is maintained, for this patient can tolerate the interpersonal barriers and the frustration of his or her pathological symbiotic needs. The stable, secure therapeutic environment serves to catalyze this patient's growth.

The Type B communicative field is replete with projective identifications, with interactional pressures, and with demands serving the discharge need. This is an action-oriented, impulse-ridden field in which "dumping" (Langs, 1980) typically takes precedence over insight. The Type B communicative mode is highly interactionally provocative; thus, pathological symbioses or therapeutic misalliances (Langs 1975) are likely results. The agitations expressed are aimed at securing merger or fusion while avoiding the self-containment or the distance that the Type B communicator cannot tolerate.

Bion (1977) would say such impulse-ridden individuals, because their alpha-function is poorly developed, have difficulty in pursuing truth and knowledge. The classical psychoanalyst might view such action-discharge as manifestations of intrapsychic sexuality and/or aggression that has been insufficiently neutralized and repressed.

Langs (1981) has delineated two Type B communicative styles. Because one is more akin to Type A communication, it has been termed the B-A mode. In the B-A mode, projective identification is utilized in the service of understanding and contains derivative meaning. Also evident in the B-A patient's latent material is an unconscious wish for the more healthy symbiosis (that is, for a merger that will enable individuation of a "true self").

In the other B mode, the Type B-C, projective identifications are major obstructions to communication. Any degree of separation or distance between self and object is experienced as dangerous, because one is left totally helpless with the inner turmoil that is so desperately defended against. The Type B-C communicator thus adheres to a pathological merged state, a pathological symbiosis or object relationship in which the obligatory relatedness is stultifying.

How do Type B (B-A or B-C) patients present themselves? In the opening phase of treatment, Type B patients will critically challenge the frame. B-A patients concomitantly communicate a wish for containment (for a healthy symbiosis), which may be evidenced in comfort and growth manifestations when the therapeutic boundaries are adhered to. The Type B-C patients, however, demonstrate primarily a wish for pathological merger. B-C patients want the therapist to accommodate to their own impulsive and chaotic needs, and if the therapist does not do so, they will often terminate prematurely (Langs 1981).

The "good enough" therapist communicates with Type B patients as a good receiver—as Bion (1977) would say, a receptive container—because he or she is relatively unperturbed by closeness demands and by intrusions. Thus, the therapist metabolizes the patient's interactional devices toward cognitive understanding. The positive introjects and insights based on the therapist's capacity to communicate appropriate reverie and interpretations can become integrated, thus enabling these patients to tolerate violent disturbances within (Langs 1981). An analyst with a Type A style could assume the task and possibly achieve the results described. So could a B-A analyst, who offers sensitive and meaningful understanding intermixed with release of his or her own tensions or utilizes projective and introjective identifications so as to gain understanding. If handled as described, the

Type B patient will be more prone to Type B-A than Type B-C communications.

Type B patients, however, can provoke the analyst to communicate in the same Type B mode that they do. (Langs believes that the Type B-C patient is the most difficult to work with.) The beleaguered therapist may break the frame (i.e., cancel an appointment, be late) or make chaotic, intrusive interventions. Such behavior suggests that the therapist's need to discharge inner tension has superseded his or her responsibility to listen and to understand. The therapist has been seduced into a pathologically fused interrelationship.

Searles (1961) talks of the difficulty therapists often have in waiting, particularly when working with regressed patients. In such treatment relationships, it is not easy to resist the lure into a pathological symbiosis, in which the patient and therapist share defenses. As Langs has explained, a therapeutic misalliance has resulted.

If a Type A communicative patient suddenly begins to cancel appointments or talks of quitting a job because his or her supervisors' expectations are unpredictable and arbitrary, or perhaps speaks of plans to marry someone he or she recently met who is an alcoholic, it is possible that the patient has introjected impulsivities and symbiotic needs from the therapist. The "good enough" therapist (the Type A or B-A) should examine his or her own behavior (handling of the frame, overall therapeutic environment, and interventions) for Type B communicative elements. Winnicott, who has given us the "good enough" mother concept (1971), acknowledges that it took years for him to realize that many of his interventions were for his own comfort. "If we can only wait the patient will grow to trust the analytic technique and setting and understanding will come creatively and with immense joy," Winnicott has concluded (1971, p. 102).

In contrast to the Type A field, with its communicative aims of insight and understanding, and the Type B field, with its activity and merged quality, stands the Type C communicative field. The Type C field is static and distant. Langs states that it is a field in which the essential links between patient and therapist are broken and in which verbalization and apparent efforts at communication serve rather as impenetrable barriers. Meaning may lie hidden behind those massive barriers that pervade and predominate the field, but Langs (1978), as well as Bion, believes that meaning does not exist in this field. The purpose of the field, in their opinion, is destruction of meaning through the use of lie barriers (Langs 1980); underlying truths are characteristically sealed off.

Although all human beings need distance at times, need self-involvement, an opportunity to make use of a "flexible lie barrier system," or a lying-fallow stage of treatment (Langs 1981). Type C patients persistently seal off rather than reveal. They typically associate in a flat, empty manner and have prolonged silences and somatic symptomatology. An absence of instinctual drive derivatives is the rule.

According to Langs, the Type C patient may be the "overt liar" or, as Burland (1980–1981) has discussed, the psychopath who needs to actualize infantile grandiosities because accepting reality relatedness is too frustrating. Burland has likened Langs's Type C "mindless patient" to one characterologically fixated in the normal autistic phase of development: a fragmented, asocial individual who presents lies because he or she has never known a truthful, caring, consistent relationship.

On probably a higher developmental level is the "lie narrator," whom Burland sees as "the narcissistically vulnerable child entertaining mommy" only to bask in her approval. The lie narrator is a perpetual performer and practicer rather than an interactor.

According to Langs, Type C patients usually begin treatment because of environmental pressure. They accept the frame as they do the recommendation for treatment, but they have difficulty in going further. Occasionally their voids will be metaphorically represented by tombs or vaults, in which case the need to deaden feeling, to lock up valid ideas, can be interpreted. But too often there are merely flat tales told with diminished relatedness and no meaning.

To work well with Type C patients, the therapist must be capable of dealing with voids, with destruction of meaning and relatedness; he or she must be able to understand enduring silence. Most important, he or she must focus on the unconscious function of the patient's lie barriers and be truthful, reliably related, and communicative. Such therapists must themselves resist autistic behavior or communications; they must not fail to intervene when necessary. They must ensure that their interventions do not themselves communicate too great an investment in barriers (for example, discussions of genetics when threatening interpersonal dynamics exist). They must refrain from the hollow, the unintegrated message, the "analytic cliché" that is not individualized to the particular patient or the particular moment and thus serves only to reinforce nonrelatedness.

COMMUNICATIVE FIELD THEORY FROM A PSYCHOANALYTIC-DEVELOPMENTAL POINT OF VIEW

The Mother's Communicative Style and Her Utilization of It as a Crucial Determinant of the Baby's Communicative Style

What communicative capacities should the mother demonstrate in order to facilitate the Type A communicative potential in her offspring? First, mother should be appropriately in touch with her Type B and Type C communicative nature. She must be comfortable with receiving and responding to her baby's merger, or Type B, needs as well as the infant's autonomous distancing Type C drives. The subordination of the Type B and the Type C communicative nature to the Type A communicative function is a developmental-communicative description of Winnicott's "good enough" mother. She is the mother who within the context of a secure holding environment and by reading her baby's latent expressions allows for a healthy symbiosis as well as adaptive autism.

At certain developmental stages one communicative modality is called forth, whereas at other periods another communicative style is suggested. In the early autistic stage as well as the later practicing separation–individuation subphase, the Type C communicative capacity is subordinated to the Type A style if mother communicates the capacity to tolerate, allow for, and perhaps at times encourage her child's necessary self-absorption and distance. Mother demonstrates an ability to subordinate her Type C communicative capacity to the Type A if she judiciously avoids intrusions when baby rests or, later, when the toddler joyfully takes exploratory strides away from her. When her baby sleeps, mother might allow herself some respite, some private self-indulgent moments. Later, with her practicing-age toddler, she might begin to demonstrate some of the pleasures of self-preoccupations: reading, painting, exercising, and so forth. Thus mother can communicate tolerance of and appreciation for, as well as herself model, "healthy autism" (Langs 1981) and thereby encourage such behavior in her youngster.

The normal symbiotic stage especially calls for the mother's adaptive utilization of the Type B communicative mode, or the subordination of the Type B to the Type A communicative style. The maternally preoccupied state (Winnicott 1956b) enables mother to derive comfort from the fused, symbiotic state, that is, from the baby's need to spit out affects and utilize mother as the container. Winnicott (1960) describes the "good enough" mother as one who meets the omnipotence of the infant and makes sense of it. The mother who is not "good enough" is not able to implement the infant's omnipotence; she repeatedly fails to meet the infant's gesture and instead substitutes her own. At this stage the mother's Type C mode or expression of her "differentiation" is not helpful to the very needy baby.

The concept of projective identification in the service of empathy must be employed by the mother at this symbiotic stage to move the child on to the Type A mode of relatedness. This neutralized or sublimated (Hartmann 1955) implementation of projective identification results from a mature libidinal investment in the offspring. The mother's feelings are put into her child not for riddance or battle needs but to understand more intimately what her youngster is experiencing and to know better how to intervene. Related to this process is Bion's reverie concept, in which the mother (or analyst) receives projective identifications from the infant (or patient), appropriately metabolizes them, and returns them to the other in a relatively detoxified form.

Grotstein (1981) views projective identification as a primitive mechanism of communication that exists first between preverbal infants and their mothers but also in adult life as a form of affective communication. He too believes that in its more positive sense, projective identification is responsible for vicarious introspection, and in its most sublimated form, for empathy.

The communicative challenges to mother during rapprochement are greater than at other phases, because this is an intensely ambivalent stage. Making sense of the child's vacillating and conflictual messages regarding closeness or the child's need for simultaneous dependence and independence is not easy for the mother. For example, one mother, Mrs. A., described rapprochement as "baffling." During the first few months of her daughter Robin's life, Mrs. A. understood her child's need for closeness and nurturance. She could appreciate Robin's wishes to be distant during the practicing stage (the period from about 9 through 14 months in which the exploration of the environment and the practicing of locomotor skills are highly libidinally invested [Mahler et al. 1975]). But how was she to make sense of and to contend with the demands of rapprochement?

Mrs. A. described them as follows:

Robin has a big vocabulary: "No, No, No, No," and "No. . . ." She broke an antique table the other day. She knew she wasn't supposed to go into that area of the room. When my husband hit her I felt like we had damaged the child's self-esteem for life. . . . I feel as though I'm always saying no to her. . . . She's so clingy, more so than ever, and it's so confusing as she's also so angry and independent and wants her space. I really don't know what she wants: security? attention? to be left alone? I feel guilty if I get angry. I know I need some space, some rest from her demands, but I worry about leaving her now, because I know she needs my reassurance. I feel she needs me to be around and to understand. . . . It's not easy.

The "good enough" rapprochement mother needs to be comfortable with both closeness and distance and with dependence–independence issues. She also has to be able to tolerate ambiguous and fluctuating communications. She needs to be at once comfortable with the Type B and Type C communicative modalities, and she furthermore needs strong Type A functioning to be able to negotiate appropriately the two fields. If mother can appreciate and read the baby's metaphoric communications, she can more easily employ the Type B or the Type C communicative style as her child requires it. If Mrs. A. could read the metaphor, she might discover the following: Robin is communicating the wish to break away from her antique self; to table some of her infantile claims and seek more the adult valuables existing in mother's private spaces and places. But with these wishes comes the clinginess, which is a result of the accompanying fears; thus the "No, No, No, Yes? No."

Although the Type A communicative capacity is now very much called for, it is tempting for a mother to view the child's increased clinginess (brought about by the child's awareness of his or her own vulnerabilities) as a regression. Darting-away behavior can be equally perplexing. It is not easy for mother to understand a deep longing for yet fear of symbiotic merger concomitant with a fervent need to assert a new little intense self, because such needs seem paradoxical. Furthermore, the mother's parallel needs can be stirred either to use her toddler as a vehicle for projective identification or to remove herself from a difficult, confusing scene. She is pulled toward the more primitive, the less integrated communicative modalities, the Type B and Type C fields that exist in us all.

Separation–Individuation as a Communicative Field Developmental Process

The first two weeks of the infant's life have been termed the primary autistic stage by Mahler et al. (1975) because the infant spends most of the day in a half-sleeping, half-waking state and lacks awareness of a mothering agent. Using Freud's metaphor (1911), the newborn's state is analogous to that of a bird's egg. In both we see a neat example of a physical system shut off from the stimuli of the external world. The "good enough" mother at this period participates in this Type C field, I believe, by protecting her neonate from external overstimulation. If the mother moved into her own self-absorbed world, unrelated to her infant, she would pave the way for her baby to become a serious Type C adult communicator, but she does respect the baby's need for withdrawal, i.e., for a great deal of sleep. A mother appropriately in touch with her Type C communicative predisposition but who has subordinated it to a Type A style is protective of her baby's space. She recognizes that although interacting is necessary to invite the baby into his or her new world, too much communication might be impinging. And mother herself is provided by this beginning stage with unusual opportunities to go off into her own world, to read, to write, to think her own thoughts while her little one sleeps. Thus the normal interactional pattern in this first psychoanalytic object-relations (or per-object relations) stage can be likened to Langs's Type C field.

In the stage that follows, the symbiotic one, the baby becomes aware of mother but believes her to be a part of the self. Given the average expectable environment, the baby feels able to discharge uncomfortable stimuli into mother, a process that leaves baby feeling grand. According to Freud's purified pleasure ego concept (1915), the infant at this time divides the external world into a part that is pleasurable, which it incorporates into itself, and the remainder, which is extraneous. The baby then separates a part of his or her own self, which is then projected into the external world. Jacobson (1964) has added her belief that at this time self and object representations are typically fused and confused.

The "good enough" mother at this symbiotic stage is able to use adaptively her Type B communicative potential. She projectively identifies into her baby, but her intent is to facilitate empathy rather than to dump or discharge unacceptable affects. Harris (1960) explains that projection need not be restricted to the process of getting rid of an undesirable ego-alien component; it can include the externalizing of desirable ego-syntonic components, a process that contributes to healthy identification. Projective identification, he continues, need not be deleterious to the child. Furthermore, when introjection and projection are refined and sublimated, Harris states, the libidinal cathexis of parent (and analyst) is likely, as is the resultant emotional growth of child (and patient).

The healthy, phase-adaptive utilization of projective identification, which is crucial at this symbiotic stage, requires that the Type B communicative mode be subordinated to an overall Type A communicative style. The mother who maintains a healthy symbiosis functions as a receptive container; in addition, she metabolizes her own contributions. She does not merge only to satisfy her own needs for contact or discharge. The process of using projection and introjection to become more familiar with the baby enables the mother to become exquisitely atuned to her offspring's needs, even to anticipate them.

There are, however, mothers who are not comfortable with this fused state, in which it is incumbent on the mother to contain tensions, and read and metabolize preverbal communications. Some mothers have difficulty with the containing function, because they themselves have tendencies toward discharge (as do some intrusive therapists). A Type B communicative mother would have particular difficulties with the intense interpersonal and interactional closeness of this stage. Mother's tensions, as exacerbated by baby's projections, would be reprojected into the child. In contrast, a Type C communicative mother might seriously detach herself from the necessary task of fine interactional attunement. Either of these situations presents potential communicative problems for the child and, later, for the adult communicator. Either pathological symbiosis or withdrawal—interpersonal retreat—might be the encouraged communicative modality.

During the practicing subphase of separation–individuation (the subphase that follows beginning differentiation), the incipient toddler becomes self-invested and absorbed in his or her new-found autonomous capacities. According to Mahler et al. (1975), there is a such preoccupation with walking and climbing and with exploring and discovering an expanded world that attention to mother's whereabouts is minimal. The chief characteristic of this practicing period is the child's great narcissistic investment in the functions of his or her own body and love affair with the world. Differentiation has, for the time, taken the toddler so much away from mother that there is negligible communication between them. One is reminded of Langs's lying fallow or normal autistic stage of therapy (1981), in which the patient typically works over internally a multitude of intrapsychic conflicts yet offers no bridge to therapy or the interpersonal relationship.

The sensitive mother, as well as the sensitive therapist, is appropriately in touch with the Type C nature in us all. (As Langs states, no one can tolerate too great or too extended exposure to emotional, interactional truth.)

Rapprochement: The Subphase Presenting the Opportunity for the Type A Communicative Capacity

The rapprochement subphase of the separation–individuation process is the most crucial (Lax et al. 1980) for the achievement of whole and integrated self and object intrapsychic representations. It is in addition the significant subphase for the development of the Type A communicative style. At this time interactional grandiose demands, the hallmark of the Type B mode, become tempered by realistic expectations; conflictual communicative drives toward and away from mother (the closeness–distance polarity) become reconciled; and the cognitive symbolic function (Piaget), which is the characteristic of the Type A mode, emerges.

During the normal rapprochement the more senior toddler rediscovers the human need for the "other." These children, having experienced their smallness, the fact that they cannot conquer the world no matter how hard they practice, are stimulated to develop their grandiose self views and idealized object-relations expectations. From an intrapsychic point of view, more realistic self and object representations emerge. From an interactional, communicative point of view, the toddler can be described as emerging from the Type C communicative self-absorbed world in search of a significant interpersonal relationship. The child may be tempted to return to the primitive symbiotic Type B communicative style, in which mother contains and compensates for unacceptable parts. Indeed, the child now is often seen clinging to and shadowing mother; yet he or she now knows the truth about their separateness. There is also investment in Type C expression of independent functioning. The toddler communicates this via darting-away behavior. Consolidating ambivalences, closeness with distance needs, fantasy wishes with reality expectations—the crucial and unique task of this subphase—is not easy for the rapprochement toddler. Yet resolution can occur, as can the emergence of the Type A communicative capacity: the capacity to express fantasies but only as related to and integrated with reality events, to be appropriately (i.e., whole self to whole object) interpersonally involved, and to appreciate and be capable of symbolic expression.

The time is right for the toddler to develop the ability to communicate symbolically, in that the crucial symbolic functions of play and language begin to emerge at the rapprochement stage of approximately 1 1/2 to 2 years. At this age, Piaget claims, the symbolic function, as evidenced in children's games, supersedes the earlier sensorimotor type of play, in which games are nothing more than exercises. One could say that there is progression from the Type C to the Type A communicative mode. Games become a play of fiction, a vehicle for representing something by means of something else. Winnicott (1971) has likened the psychoanalytic process to a game or to play, attesting that psychoanalysis has been developed as a highly specialized form of play in the service of communication with oneself and with others. Galenson (1971) has suggested a line of development leading from early nonverbal thought, as manifested in play, toward either sublimation (the general capacity for symbolic communication) or acting-out behavior in adulthood. Acting out would imply a tendency toward Type B communication.

Fixation at or Regression to the Type B or Type C Communicative Style

A communicative modality that suggests the wish for a pathological symbiosis (the Type B style) or the need for an autistic noncommunicative state (the Type C style) can indicate a faulty rapprochement resolution. The Type B or Type C communicative style, however, might also signify communicative style fixation or developmental arrest. Whereas communicative style regression characterizes the individual who is able to function in a higher communicative mode (i.e., A or B-A) but who under stress regresses to the more primitive Type B or Type C style, communicative fixation implies more serious interactional difficulties. It suggests that interactional experiences in the early developmental communicative modes were so disturbed that progress to higher communicative levels did not occur. Thus, the attainment of the integrative or the symbolic function (the Type A communicative capacity) is not clinically evident. Such patients are those who evidence the chronic character disorders; they are individuals who have never progressed to the rapprochement subphase and are probably the Type C or B-C communicators. When regression, rather than fixation, is operative, the Type B or Type C mode is utilized temporarily, when the individual is under stress. This acute (versus chronic) C or B-C communicative patient is clearly more treatable.

Burland (1980) gives credence to the notion of viewing certain pathological communicative styles as evidencing rapprochement subphase regressions and others, characterological communicative fixations. His developmental description of Langs's "mindless patient" suggests fixation at the Type C communicative style. These are severely maternally deprived children of all ages who as a result of grossly inadequate mothering, have failed to establish the libidinal object. Thus their behavior looks as if the child were characterologically fixated in the normal autistic phase of development. They have a scattered and fragmented quality, are asocial and narcissistically infantile.

Burland regards the "frame changer" as an individual who has failed to cope effectively with the rapprochement discovery of separateness. This apparent Type B communicative patient who seeks pathological merger behaves like Aladdin with his magic lamp. The lamp must be constantly carried and controlled by Aladdin, because the omnipotent genie within is relied upon for enlightenment.

Examples of potential rapprochement pitfalls that encourage more primitive communicative modalities are the mother's communication during rapprochement of too great a need to have her child back (possibly stimulating regression to the Type B mode) and the mother's overencouragement of the child's darting-away behavior. If the mother has too great an investment in her child's autonomy, the Type C communicative mode, a mode that defies interpersonal links, may very well result.

These regressions are all the more likely when the mother has serious difficulty in appreciating and facilitating the symbolic function vitally emerging at this time. Mother must provide a good audience for her toddler's important creative productions. If mother can use regression in the service of ego functioning (Kris 1950), she can allow herself to participate in the child's play. The incipient Type A communicative style would certainly be supported by such a maternal capacity. Mothers who have difficulty with the playing process, with appreciating the sanctity of the playground environment, encourage communicative regression via the discharge or the self-involved, noncommunicative route. Sensorimotor behavior might prevail in lieu of the development of more mature symbolic expression.

The Three Communicative Styles in Interactions with Mothers and Their Rapprochement-age Toddlers

Mrs. M. and Jane. Mrs. M. and Jane were observed several times in their home. The environment was dark and drab, with a marked absence of natural light, bright coloring, and pictures or other decoration. Both Mrs. M.

and Jane were reserved and quiet people, often dreamy. Neither was very communicative with the interviewer or with the other. At various moments both mother and child appeared preoccupied with distant thoughts. Mrs. M. and Jane typically were involved in noninteractive pursuits (mother would read the newspaper; Jane would ride her toy motorcycle). Jane would travel away from her mother and the interviewer into her room, where she seemed content to remain. Mother seemed likewise to be content with the distance; she rarely called out to Jane.

At one point, while Mrs. M. was gazing at her newspaper, Jane rode away on the toy motorcycle and collided with a wall. After the collision (which might be seen as a significant adaptive context), the nonchalance of both mother and daughter was striking. Jane did not cry for soothing, nor did mother rush to comfort her. Instead there was a bipersonal, "walled-off," detached quality that a collision into a wall made all the more pronounced. An imperviousness to communicating feelings about collisions, resultant hurts, and possibly joys as well demonstrated a Type C communicative style. This style corresponded to the field exemplified by the home environment.

Mrs. W. and Melissa. Mrs. W. and Melissa were observed each week in a mother-and-toddler group for a period of five months. Mrs. W. presented herself as a very well-groomed, proper-looking woman. She would wear stylish silk blouses and often complained that it was upsetting when her daughter Melissa put her dirty hands on them. Mrs. W. would often state that Melissa's messes and general emotional discharges made it hard to have her around. Mother hired a full-time babysitter, because Melissa's "grunting demands" gave her a headache. "She can sound like a savage and be hard to read even if she tells me what's wrong." In the group situation Mrs. W. appeared to distance herself from and seemed awkward toward Melissa.

Melissa was quite provocative and seemed especially to express her frustrations with mother in terms of her relationships with children, by pulling their hair and taking away their toys. She would attempt to connect with others by coercing and dragging them over to her play space.

It seemed that Mrs. W.'s reserved quality and problems with involvement made it difficult to tackle the regressions of rapprochement. These qualities were evidence of a Type C communicative style. In response, Melissa intensified her communicative activity, aimed at reaching, touching, and possessing, albeit via discharge and fusion. In doing so, she reflected the B-A communicative style.

Mrs. K. and Amanda. Mrs. K. and her daughter Amanda were observed three times in their home when Amanda was between 20 and 25 months of age. The K.'s home was large and sunny yet extremely disorganized. Not only were children's toys strewn about, but dirty dishes and dirty laundry were evident.

Mrs. K. introduced me to her daughter when I arrived for a first visit and then immediately pointed out her 7-month-old baby Amon. Amanda, who had been sitting at the dining room table eating her lunch, jumped off her chair and screeched again her identity: "My name is Amanda!" She proceeded to point out all the toys in all areas of the room that were hers. "That's mine; that's mine," she said as she pointed to the numerous toy animals. Mrs. K. timidly asked that Amanda return to the table to finish her lunch. Amanda screamed a defiant "No!" Amanda's "tough-little-guy" style, her blue-jean attire, deep loud voice, and rough and surly manner, contrasted with her long blonde hair, blue eyes, and refined features.

My discussion with Mrs. K. was disturbed by Amanda's charging about on her tricycle. In contrast to Jane (in the first illustration), who rode away from others, Amanda rode into others. She rode into her mother and brother. I asked Amanda if she felt "left out of our conversation," to which mother promptly replied, "No, it's just her way to become destructive and interfering." Mother continued, "I admire her stamina and self-assertive drive, though."

At this point Amanda veered toward a large unlocked window that opened onto a narrow porch area (the apartment was on the 14th floor). Mother exclaimed, "Stop!" and dove toward the porch to block Amanda. Amanda screamed and the two wrestled.

During a later interview, mother and Amanda were interacting around a book with a picture of a ghost and children. Amanda was shouting, "Get away ghosts, go away from me!" She threw the book at her mother. Mother attempted to reassure her but was not effective in quieting Amanda's activity.

Discharging ghosts (discharging haunting affects into mother and others) seemed characteristic of Amanda's communicative style. Mother's containing function, her capacity for creation of and preservation of some boundaries and order in the home environment (a reliable, safe, secure frame), was impaired. The environmental chaos, occasional critical comments, and latent encouragement of impulsivity suggest a possible Type B communicative style. Mrs. K.'s encouragement of Amanda's defiant behavior, a projective identification mechanism, served to steer Amanda toward the Type B communicative style. The mother's problems in receiving and processing Type B communications indicated an absence of a Type A communicative mode (especially the containing function). This absence made it difficult for Amanda to give up the Type B, the action-discharge, communicative mode.

Mrs. R. and Caroline.   Mrs. R. and her daughter Caroline were also observed weekly in a group for five months. Mrs. R. is a basic-looking woman with a sardonic sense of humor. A former kindergarten teacher, she had taught large classes of hyperactive youngsters in an inner-city school where she had felt it was necessary to take a firm disciplinarian posture. After many years of trying unsuccessfully to conceive a child, she and her husband adopted a little girl. The child had an eye problem that required her to endure some stressful surgical procedures.

When her daughter was 20 months old and becoming very self-assertive, Mrs. R., to her surprise, became pregnant. She was attending a mother–toddler developmental education group at this time, and it was noted that her behavior toward Caroline was becoming increasingly critical and punitive. She often seemed to be reprimanding Caroline. The girl's entanglements with other children caused Mrs. R. to jump up and become critical of her daughter. She would exclaim, "When you're wrong others will hit you back." In group meetings in which the children were discussed, Mrs. R. seemed more and more to bring up her daughter's intransigences, which ranged from talking too much when there was company to biting another child in the park or having "an accident" with bowels or bladder.

Caroline was previously affectionate toward her mother, very much seeking her approval by snuggling close to her and showing Mrs. R. her accomplishments. She now presented a different picture. In the play situation she often hit her doll and said, "Bad," and she pulled the hair of other little girls. With her mother, Caroline now manifested highly negativistic and oppositional behavior. It seemed that Caroline had projectively identified her angry feelings into her mother and playmates as she had felt her mother to be doing (especially since Mrs. R. had discovered her own pregnancy, a significant and surprising occurrence with apparent new pressures). Mother had thus skewed Caroline's rapprochement negotiation with her projective identification defense, perhaps predisposing her to the Type B communicative style.

Mrs. L. and Tanya.   Mrs. L. and Tanya are another mother–toddler dyad who were interviewed and observed in their home. The birth of a second child during the period of observation allowed Mrs. L. to return to a discussion of Tanya's infancy and her own motherhood initiation process. She talked enthusiastically and seemed to describe a capacity to change yet remain consistent when necessary.

Mrs. L. remembered that when she was first pregnant she had read a good deal and spoken to a range of types of new mothers. Her readings had also had a wide range, spanning a spectrum "from the superradical women's literature to the traditional child development books." She had spoken to friends and people with whom she worked and eventually had decided that although curtailing her work hours was not financially or professionally possible, she could work out a way that Tanya might accompany her to her job. To do this, she had put much effort into finding a capable and flexible child care assistant. Mrs. L. felt she had made an excellent choice in Susan, a creative and zestful child psychology student. Mrs. L. claimed that the situation she had been able to arrange at work enabled her to continue to feel fulfilled professionally as well as to spend important time with her little one when her flexible schedule allowed it. Tanya seemed to thrive: she was cheerful and curious and related well to others.

A big move and potential adjustment was under way, however, because Mr. L. wanted to pursue an extremely promising job opportunity in another part of the country. The family had explored the new environment and had attempted to work on the real losses and separation. Mrs. L. talked of the change for herself in terms of a mourning process yet a welcome adventure, and she projected this reality–fantasy stance to Tanya. She discussed games played and stories made up regarding saying good-bye to old places, dolls, and toys and hello to new ones. She encouraged fantasy elaboration with Tanya around her new anticipated environment ("What would you like your new room to be like?") yet attempted to reassure her that some important old standards could be brought along ("Of course Pookie [a favorite doll] would come").

When I met Tanya and Mrs. L., the family was in the moving process. Cartons were about, yet Tanya's drawings were still on the walls. Tanya would at times cling to her mother's shirt, which Mrs. L. accepted, adding, "It must not be easy to lose the special only-child status as well as your familiar home." Yet Tanya was also able to venture forth, away from mother and interviewer, to draw and creatively express her conflict.

She drew three circles and two lines and explained that the three circles were Mommy, Tanya, and the new baby, whose name was "Poopoo." Tanya explained that Mommy and Tanya are making dinner for the baby in the new house but "they forget something in their old house so they have to go back to get it."

Mrs. L.'s comfort with receiving and participating in symbolic communication as well as her capacity to be both in touch with and a creative integrator of sameness and difference (old and new) permitted the development of the Type A communicative style in Tanya.

Mrs. T. and Jeremy. This mother–toddler pair in the developmental education group illustrates another Type A mother–child field. Mrs. T. is a warm and witty woman who seemed able to empathize with others' struggles and to make colorful jokes about the commonly shared difficulties. She'd say of the rapprochement stage, "You feel like you're on a roller coaster, but it's certainly not boring." Neither her son Jeremy's negativism, nor his clinginess, nor the intermittent fluctuations of both terribly upset Mrs. T. She would make a game of her son's comings and goings. She would bid farewell to Jeremy, her "little explorer," as he ran out of the room, then welcome him back with inquiries into what he had discovered during his investigations outside.

Jeremy himself demonstrated the ability to be both assertive and tender, distant and close, and was especially creative with others in his play. He enjoyed playing train and involving the other children. He would suggest that someone be an engine, another a caboose. They would travel around the room and in and out of it; typically the final stop, the "station," would be mother.

Here again, mother's flexibility and comfort with symbolic communication seemed to exemplify and permit the development of the Type A communicative field and style.

Discussion

In the illustrations presented we were able to witness the mother's crucial role in encouraging a communicative style in her child. We could also recognize the communicative challenge and opportunity associated with the rapprochement subphase. We were able to discover mothers and toddlers manifesting distinct communicative fields and styles, particularly illuminated by a significant stimulus, or adaptive context (a pregnancy, a move, a collision). There are parallels to the various patient–therapist communicative interrelationships.

Mrs. M. and Mrs. W. both used the Type C communicative style. These Type C communicative mothers tended to detach and distance themselves from intense communicative discharging (Langs 1980) that is so characteristic of the rapprochement toddler. Jane also exhibited a walled-off modality of interacting or noninteracting, which became especially clear after her collision. Jane's collision should be recognized as an activated adaptive context, and her response to it—withdrawal—is communicatively significant. From a developmental-communicative point of view, we might arrive at the following formulation: Mrs. M., a Type C communicator, was most comfortable and effective in receiving her child's communications during the practicing subphase. She could allow for Jane's self-absorption and explorations because these behaviors corresponded to her own walled-off communicative style. Mrs. M. probably overencouraged Jane's independent pursuits, thus creating a communicative fixation at this mode and subphase. Regression to this Type C mode might have occurred later to avoid the dependency needs that were reactivated during rapprochement. By walling herself off from interpersonal needs, Jane might have been creating a false, self-contained, or characterological "lying-fallow" state.

Melissa had a different reaction to her mother's aloof Type C communicative style. Rather than representing a denial of interpersonal neediness, her communicative style conveyed a message concerning the nature of the unmet needs. Although the message was expressed via projective identification of Melissa's dirty, angry discharges into mother and playmates, the need for a healthy symbiosis was evident. Melissa's expressions also contained a wish to cure the other, i.e., mother. Perhaps the therapeutic plea reads: Tolerate these affects that have been reactivated during rapprochement that were not tolerated earlier during our symbiosis. It could be good for both of us!

Mrs. K. manifested problems maintaining a secure home environment. She can be likened to the therapist who has difficulty maintaining a secure frame and therapeutic setting. An impulsive, chaotic Type B communicative mode was thus projectively identified into Amanda. The failure to provide a safe holding environment contributed to Amanda's difficulty in establishing the Type A communicative capacity. The delay of instinctual activity permits metaphoric expression.

Mrs. R. was observed to be discharging her own angers and frustrations into her child. These affects of mother's were exacerbated during Caroline's rapprochement subphase because of new environmental pressures (an unexpected pregnancy). The effect on Caroline was evidenced in her regression to a more aggressive "dumping" (Langs 1975), a communicative modality like the Type B, a modality toward which Caroline possibly was predisposed.

The last two mothers and children, Mrs. L. and Tanya and Mrs. T. and Jeremy, best demonstrate the Type A field and communicative style. Each of these mothers maintained constancy amid change yet seemed very aware of the impact of change on her child. Each seemed to have a concept of the adaptive context, a crucial stimulus, be it environmental or developmental, and enjoyed and encouraged symbolic play. In addition, both Mrs. L. and Mrs. T. showed a capacity to feel equally comfortable with the fused and the autistic communicative states (the Type B and Type C communicative styles), which vacillate but require integration during rapprochement.

SUMMARY

This chapter has reviewed and amplified developmental aspects of Langs's communicative field theory. The study has shown the usefulness of the Langsian depiction of the Type A, Type B, and Type C fields and communicative modalities as a diagnostic and research instrument.

My work is part of a new interest in interrelating the communicative and adaptational-interactional thinking of Langs with object relations theory.

My primary thesis, that the separation–individuation process and its fore-runners are responsible for the full development and solidification of an interpersonal communicative style, has suggested a specific relationship between communicative field theory and the mother–child developmental process.

I have more specifically discussed:

1. The normal autistic stage and the normal practicing separation–individuation subphase as contributing to adaptive or maladaptive Type C communications later on (autonomous expressions versus distancing devices).

2. The symbiotic phase in which the functioning of mother and child is fused as being the origin of the Type B communicative field (a field associated with merger demands for containment or self-completion) or as contributing to mature empathy and healthy identification.

3. The rapprochement subphase of the separation–individuation process as significant in its presentation of complex communicative challenges (integration of the Type B and Type C modes) and facilitation of the symbolic communicative capacity (the Type A style).

4. The mother's role (like the therapist's) as being extremely important in facilitating Type A development in the child (and the Type A communicative capacity in the patient). The "good enough" or Type A mother (or therapist) should be appropriately in touch with Type B and Type C communicative functioning, thus allowing for the healthy symbiosis and for inevitable self-preoccupation. In addition, there must be appreciation for symbolic, metaphoric expression.

REFERENCES

BION, W. R. (1977). *Seven Servants*. New York: Jason Aronson.

BURLAND, A. (1980). Developmental perspectives on the bipersonal field. *International Journal of Psychoanalytic Psychotherapy* 8:35–43.

FREUD, S. (1900). The interpretation of dreams. *Standard Edition* 4.

—— (1911). Formulations on the two principles of mental functioning. *Standard Edition* 12.

—— (1915). Instincts and their vicissitudes. *Standard Edition* 14.

GALENSON, E. (1971). A consideration of the nature of thought in childhood play. In *Separation-Individuation*, ed. J. B. McDevitt and C. F. Settlage, pp. 41–59. New York: International Universities Press.

GROTSTEIN, J. S. (1981). *Splitting and Projective Identification.* New York: Jason Aronson.

HARRIS, I. (1960). Unconscious factors common to parents and analysts. *International Journal of Psycho-Analysis* 41:123–129.

HARTMANN, H. (1955). Notes on the theory of sublimation. In H. Hartmann, *Essays on Ego Psychology,* pp. 215–240. New York: International Universities Press, 1964.

JACOBSON, E. (1964). *The Self and the Object World.* New York: International Universities Press.

KHAN, M. R. (1974). *The Privacy of the Self.* New York: International Universities Press.

KRIS, E. (1950). On preconscious mental processes. *Psychoanalytic Quarterly* 19:540–560.

LANGS, R. (1971). Day residues, recall residues, and dreams: reality and the psyche. *Journal of the American Psychoanalytic Association* 19:499–523.

——— (1975). Therapeutic misalliances. *International Journal of Psychoanalytic Psychotherapy* 4:77–105.

——— (1976). *The Bipersonal Field.* New York: Jason Aronson.

——— (1978). *The Listening Process.* New York: Jason Aronson.

——— (1980). *Interactions: The Realm of Transference and Countertransference.* New York: Jason Aronson.

——— (1981). *Resistances and Interventions: The Nature of Therapeutic Work.* New York: Jason Aronson.

LAX, R., BACH, S., AND BURLAND, J., ed. (1980). *Rapprochement: The Critical Subphase of Separation-Individuation.* New York: Jason Aronson.

MAHLER, M. (1972). Rapprochement subphase of the separation-individuation process. In M. Mahler, *The Selected Papers of Margaret S. Mahler,* Vol. 2: *Separation-Individuation,* pp. 131–148. New York: Jason Aronson, 1979.

MAHLER, M., PINE, F., AND BERGMAN, A. (1975). *The Psychological Birth of the Human Infant.* New York: Basic Books.

SEARLES, H. (1961). Phases of patient-therapist interaction in the psychotherapy of chronic schizophrenia. In H. Searles, *Collected Papers on Schizophrenia and Related Subjects,* pp. 521–559. New York: International Universities Press, 1965.

WINNICOTT, D. W. (1951). Transitional objects and transitional phenomena. In D. W. Winnicott, *Playing and Reality,* pp. 1–30. Middlesex, Engl.: Penguin Books, 1971.

——— (1954). Withdrawal and regression. In D. W. Winnicott, *Through Paediatrics to Psychoanalysis: The Collected Papers of D. W. Winnicott,* pp. 255–261. New York: Basic Books, 1975.

——— (1960). The theory of the parent-infant relationship. In D. W. Winnicott, *The Maturational Processes and the Facilitating Environment,* pp. 37–55. New York: International Universities Press, 1965.

——— (1971). Playing: a theoretical statement. In D. W. Winnicott, *Playing and Reality,* pp. 44–61. Middlesex, Engl.: Penguin Books.

CHAPTER 16

Psychoanalytic Psychotherapy of the Nonsymbolic Communicator

Martin Greene, D.S.W.

Recently Robert Langs (1978a) introduced a classification of communicative fields that illuminates aspects of the therapeutic situation from a new vantage point, providing a means of extending the scope of psychoanalytic psychotherapy to patients previously viewed as untreatable. This chapter is concerned primarily with furthering our understanding of one of the fields identified by Langs, the Type C field, characterized by an excessive preoccupation with the minutiae of external events and an absence of symbolic forms of communication. Because it is through symbolic forms of expression that the unconscious is known (Segal 1978, p. 315), the absence of such forms of expression poses a formidable obstacle to the success of either psychoanalysis or psychoanalytic psychotherapy.

Because this chapter is concerned primarily with psychoanalytic psychotherapy and its application, it is necessary to define what is meant by the term. Psychoanalytic psychotherapy, like psychoanalysis, emphasizes the resolution of unconscious conflicts within the transference, with the therapist maintaining a position of anonymity and neutrality while structural change is achieved through interpretations. Freud (1912, 1913) discovered the fundamental rules that Langs (1978b) has conceptualized as the frame, or the requisite therapeutic environment.

Thus, psychoanalytic psychotherapy requires an interpretive stance that utilizes the therapeutic relationship, both transference and nontransference, as the primary locus of the therapeutic action. Unconscious conflicts and primitive internalized object relationships are mobilized in vivo, with immediacy, at "the point of urgency," in accordance with Strachey's concept (1934) of the "mutative interpretation." Strupp (1977, p. 17), an eclectic, research-oriented psychologist, arrived at much the same conclusion in discussing the central ingredient of therapeutic change. Psychoanalytic psychotherapy is easily differentiated from psychoanalytically oriented psychotherapy, which, although drawing on psychoanalytic principles and developmental theory, disregards such fundamentals of psychoanalytic technique as the basic rules characterized by the frame and the primacy of interpretations made within the transference. It is more difficult to differentiate psychoanalysis and psychoanalytic psychotherapy. Kernberg (1978, pp. 77–80) has attempted such a differentiation, emphasizing a distinction based on quantitative rather than qualitative factors. In his "expressive psychotherapy" technical neutrality and an interpretive stance are maintained, but the transference is not interpreted as fully or as systematically as it is in psychoanalysis.

Langs has emphasized repeatedly the similarity of the spiraling, unconscious interactions that occur in psychoanalysis and psychotherapy. Psychoanalysis and psychoanalytic psychotherapy are more alike than they are different (Paolino 1981, pp. 12–24). Both require a rigorous adherence to a psychoanalytic posture that recognizes the primacy of unconscious processes as they are expressed within the transference. Both differ markedly from psychoanalytically oriented psychotherapies, which are characterized more by deviations from than by adherence to a psychoanalytic stance. For some time there has been considerable interest in expanding the scope of psychoanalytic treatment. Stone (1954), Eissler (1953), and Kohut (1971) are among those who have made outstanding contributions to this effort. But, like many psychoanalytic writers, these authors limit their discussion to psychoanalysis, disregarding the implications for psychotherapy. Others, such as Searles (1979), Winnicott (1971), and Kernberg (1978), have formulated their findings in a manner applicable to both psychoanalysis and psychoanalytic psychotherapy. The ideas to be developed in this chapter apply to psychoanalysis as well as to psychoanalytic psychotherapy, with the view that both require a rigorous adherence to basic principles and technical procedures.

COMMUNICATIVE PROPERTIES OF THE BIPERSONAL FIELD

After reviewing his experience as a therapist and analyst, Langs (1978a, pp. 87–96) expressed puzzlement over the realization that most patients seem to conform neither to the image of the patient considered most suitable for psychoanalysis nor to the patient image generally presented in the literature. He pointed out that most analysts seem to assume that a specific communicative patient style is a prerequisite for psychoanalytic treatment. He noted:

> The type of communicative field which these analysts accepted and found workable can be characterized as one in which the patient readily and verbally free associates, conveys analyzable derivatives of his inner mental world—his uncon-

scious fantasies, memories, introjects, self-representation, and the like—and in which the analyst in response interprets relevant contents, defenses, and dynamic constellations as they have a bearing on the patient's intrapsychic conflicts and psychopathology. (pp. 88–89)

Although such a field exists, at least fleetingly, it may not be the norm. Frustrating as it is likely to be, despite the therapist's level of competence and devotion to the analytic task, most therapeutic situations do not conform to the ideal model just described.

Frustrated by an inability to interact with the patient in accordance with the ideal model, the therapist is likely to abandon an analytic position in favor of whatever seems to work. Frequently, major deviations are introduced. Alternately, unable to treat difficult patients within a rigorous psychoanalytic psychotherapy model, therapists propose new treatment models, such as those introduced by the proponents of the psychology of the self (Kohut 1971) or showing the Mahlerian emphasis of the Blancks (1974). Our comprehension of such diagnostic categories as borderline and narcissistic personality organizations has expanded the scope of psychoanalytic psychotherapy by introducing concepts that can be used in comprehending and treating patients previously deemed untreatable. At the same time, as reflected in the controversies concerning the implications of this knowledge, there are as yet no clear solutions concerning the choice of appropriate treatment techniques.

The concept of communicative fields emphasizes that the psychoanalytic situation is influenced by the communicative styles of both participants. Although each patient and therapist has a distinctive communicative style, the psychoanalytic situation is dyadic, and the interactions of the two participants create a specific communicative field. Individual communicative styles are not synonymous with forms of pathology, although it is possible that some complex relationship between style and pathology exists. Although the literature suggests that the ideal style is the prerogative of neurotic personalities, this is an assumption not supported by any empirical data. Clinical experience suggests that many neurotic patients fail to conform to the ideal style, whereas some more deeply disturbed individuals provide a rich network of analyzable derivative material. Langs's Type A field, generally viewed as the ideal, is characterized by symbolic forms of communication, with intense, analyzable unconscious derivatives that can be organized around specific adaptive contexts (similar to day residues) that emerge directly from within the therapeutic interaction. The field is similar to what Winnicott (1971) has termed the "analytic space," an area of play and illusion, a form of transitional phenomenon open to imagination and creativity, similar to the "potential space" that exists between mother and infant.

In contrast to the "as-if," illusory, mentally imaginative, and verbal quality of the Type A field, the Type B field is an action-oriented field in which dumping of emotions and projective identification predominate. Intense, volatile, often disruptive emotional states are experienced by both participants. Although there may be a paucity of verbal material with few analyzable derivatives embedded in the content of oral discourse, conflicts, resistances, unconscious fantasies, unconscious perceptions, and interactional phenomena may be revealed through actions, gestures, emotional overtones, and the induced emotions of both participants. The impact of such volatile emotional states on the cognitive processes of the participants makes this a difficult field to manage, but when such states are contained, metabolized, and understood, the latent meanings of the interactional phenomena can be interpreted, structural changes do occur, and relatively ambitious therapeutic goals are achievable. Whereas many patients who communicate via a Type B style participate in constructive therapeutic alliances, however, others are involved primarily in extruding their inner contents and destroying the therapeutic potential of the psychoanalytic situation (Langs 1980a, pp. 31–33).

Within the Type C field, communication is on a manifest level; there is a pervasive absence of derivative meaning, and when there are rare moments with unconscious implications, associations fail to organize around a viable adaptive context. Langs (1978a), in discussing the functions of the Type C mode, states:

> In delineating this static, noncommunicative field I would stress at the outset that while the Type A and [most] Type B fields reflect modes of positive communication and are designed to convey derivatives of inner mental states, contents, and mechanisms, the Type C field is designed for noncommunication, for the destruction of meaning, and for the absence of derivative expression. . . . Typically, these patients ruminate emptily for long periods of time or tend to report detailed, extended narratives in a form that renders their possible unconscious meanings undecipherable. (pp. 106–107)

Thus, according to Langs, Type C communications are designed to seal off meaningful content and stalemate the treatment as a consequence of a fear of inner chaos, psychic upheaval, and excessive psychic pain that frequently covers over a basically psychotic core (1978a, pp. 116–119). In the presence of such a patient (or of a Type C therapist), there is an experience of intense boredom, frustration, and despair. To escape from the static, monotonous interaction, therapists and patients are often driven to extreme measures in their attempts to enliven the field.

Langs suggests that Type C patients require "holding" by a Type A therapist over extended periods of time. The therapist remains patient, maintains a listening attitude, and adheres to the basic frame. He or she maintains an analytic stance, alert to the patient's expression of metaphors that can be used to determine the form of defensive barriers as well as to suggest the nature of the dreaded inner experience and the link to the prevailing adaptive context. Although Langs is not explicit about the nature of the change anticipated, presumably it is possible to achieve the modest goals of modifying defensive barriers, increasing the capacity to acknowledge and deal with inner conflicts, and, in turn, fostering ego strengths and furthering development.

Langs's conceptualization of the communicative properties of the bi-personal field provides a new perspective that enriches our understanding of clinical phenomena. The implications of his perspective generate a fertile realm for further study. In reviewing the literature, I have discovered that other theorists have described and developed treatment approaches to patients similar to Langs's Type C patient. Tending to view the communicative style as something intrinsic to the patient, they, unlike Langs, have not considered that the therapist may make a significant contribution toward creating a Type C field. A summary of some of these points of view, divided into descriptions of the phenomena, ideas on causation, and approaches to treatment, follows. In the interest of achieving further understanding of the Type C field, I compare and contrast these viewpoints with Langs's perspective.

OTHER DESCRIPTIONS OF NONSYMBOLIC COMMUNICATORS

In a paper written in 1930, Klein, describing her work with a 4-year-old boy, discussed patients who are deficient in their capacity for symbol formation and unconscious fantasy. She postulated that in the absence of symbolization, the whole development of the ego is arrested. Similarly, Klein's followers Segal (1957) and Bion (1953) presented cases that demonstrated deficiencies in symbolization. In these patients the primary deficiency was the inability to differentiate a symbol and its referent, a form of concrete thinking associated with the psychotic personality.

From another perspective, Marty and de M'Uzan (1963) observed psychosomatic patients characterized by their preoccupation with trivial, mundane, superficial details and the minutiae of external reality. These patients evidenced a marked impairment in the use of imagination and fantasy, and they were unaware of their feelings and unable to express them. De M'Uzan noted, "The patient's language is poor, flat and banal, glued to the present or only producing facts stated chronologically" (1974, p. 462). Marty and de M'Uzan designated this style of thinking as the *pensée opératoire* ("operatory thought"). Nemiah (1975) and Sifneos (1974, 1975) have written extensively of psychosomatic patients with similar characteristics. They view these patients as lifeless, colorless, and dull, lacking any of the quality of resonance that usually develops in a relationship over time. Sifneos (1975, p. 67) coined the term *alexithymia* to denote a condition characterized by a lack of words and emotions. Krystal (1979) added substance-dependent patients as well as those suffering from severe posttraumatic states to the alexithymic category.

McDougall (1978), a member of the French psychoanalytic group, noted the lack of neurotic symptoms in these patients and emphasized that the content of their associations remains strictly at the manifest level, devoid of latent meaning and of any mingling of dream imagery, fantasy, and conscious thought. She stated that in these patients, "the unconscious theatre never reveals itself" (p. 216). Because their style seemed so totally antithetical to the psychoanalytic process, she dubbed them "anti-analysands" and also used the descriptive term "robot analysands" to refer to their mechanistic, lifeless mode of interaction (p. 215).

The descriptions of these patients, who seem to cut across traditional diagnostic entities, are remarkably similar, despite the variety of perspectives represented. Although compiled from differing vantage points, considerable evidence thus exists that supports Langs's conceptualization of the Type C field and indicates that such patients are not at all rare.

CAUSES OF NONSYMBOLIC COMMUNICATIVE STYLES

The deficit in symbol formation and the consequent paucity of symbolic forms of communication, both within the self and with others, is believed to be the basic cause of these patients' difficulties. In 1916 Jones drew a distinction between the use of the term *symbol* in psychoanalysis and its use in other systems. For Jones, only the repressed is symbolized. In his view, when a wish is repressed, the object of that wish may then be replaced by a symbol. Segal (1957) emphasized the failure to distinguish between the symbol and the object symbolized. According to the Kleinian view, fully formed symbols are created during the depressive position, when it becomes possible to invest the whole object and experience loss and mourning; then the object may be re-created within the psyche as a true symbol. The depressive position is believed to ensue at about 3 months of age, a time analogous to the beginnings of Mahler's separation–individuation phase (Mahler et al. 1975), although, in Mahler's scheme, the capacity to internalize a whole object takes considerably longer to be achieved. Although Jones is concerned with only those symbols that are derivatives of the unconscious and Segal includes the stuff of metaphor and conscious fantasies, both equate the development of symbol formation with the capacity to experience the loss of an object. From this perspective some degree of self-object differentiation and the capacity to endure mental pain and to internalize functions of external objects would seem to be prerequisites for using symbols to refer to things previously external. Thus, deficiencies in these capacities, or defenses that militate against the use of such capacities, would interfere with the development of symbolization.

Bion (1962a, 1962b) sought to conceptualize the nature of the mental apparatus that produces the incapacity to use symbolic processes. Building upon Kleinian theory, he emphasized the role that frustration and the capacity to bear frustration play in the development of "thinking," a process generally considered synonymous with both conscious and unconscious symbolic processes. Thought for Bion, as for Jones and Segal, involves the capacity for delay, which Bion views as a tolerance of frustration. For example, when an expectation of a breast is associated with the realization that a breast is not available for satisfaction, there is an internal experience of an "absent breast" or a "no-breast." If the frustration can be tolerated, then the "no-breast" becomes a thought, and thoughts in turn make frustrations more tolerable. If, however, the bad object, which is a concrete thing rather than a representation, cannot be symbolized, the inner world retains a frightening and bizarre quality (Bion 1962a, pp. 8–37).

Bion postulates that in the mental apparatus there is a function, which he designates as "alpha," that is responsible for producing alpha-elements that are suitable for "storage" and for "dreaming," that is, for thinking and for unconscious fantasy. Without alpha-functioning, there is a loss of the "contact barrier" that creates differentiation between that which is conscious and that which is unconscious. Unable to think or to dream, that is, incapable of symbolic communication, an individual cannot contain experience, which instead is discharged and excreted. Fundamental to Bion's point of view is the role the mother's lack of "reverie" plays in creating the deficit. If the mother lacks the capacity to contain, metabolize, and return what the child puts into her in a more benign form, then what Bion calls "beta-elements," the raw emotions, "things in themselves," and "bizarre objects," retain their primitive, raw, and terrifying form. Under such conditions, a vicious cycle ensues, in which the terror of inner experience, coupled with the incapacity to deal with external experience, reinforces and further intensifies the deficiencies in symbolization. Unable to learn from experience and terrified of inner chaos and turmoil, the patient uses communication primarily to avoid frustration and to inhibit thought and fantasy, filling the space with empty ideas intended to keep out thoughts and symbols that more accurately reflect the individual's experience but that are also likely to evoke such terrifying mental states as chaos, pain, and thoughts of death and destruction. Thus, the patients Bion describes seem more intent on noncommunicating than on communicating and seek to destroy the therapeutic setting rather than to use it to discover anything meaningful.

Nemiah and Sifneos (1970), Sifneos (1974, 1975) and Nemiah (1975) speculate that there is a multiplicity of causes of alexithymia, including biophysiological, familial, social, and intrapsychic factors. Their emphasis, however, is on the possible existence of some inherent deficit that underlies developmental failures and current interpersonal difficulties, a neurophysiological deficit that resides in the limbic system and leads to a disturbance in its connections with the neocortex. Thus, in their view it is not that the feelings and fantasies of these patients are rendered unconscious by defense mechanisms, but rather that their brains are structurally and functionally incapable of processing their feelings and of thinking in symbolic terms. Contrary to the psychoanalytic emphasis, that such deficits are the consequence of conflicts and defenses, they conclude that the condition of alexithymia itself may be responsible for exacerbating emotional conflicts: structural deficiencies within the brain interfere with these patients' capacities to deal with their emotions when physiological reactions to stress are mobilized (Sifneos 1975, p. 68).

Krystal (1979) disagrees with the neurophysiological explanation of Sifneos and Nemiah and instead emphasizes early interpersonal difficulties that interfere with the development of an adequate inner representational world. Stressing affect development, he posits that these patients fail to achieve affect differentiation, desomatization, and the capacity to verbalize affective states and therefore can express emotions only along physiological channels. The primary deficit is viewed as one of self-representation. Self-caring functions reside in external objects or the external world and one's own functions are a part of that world; the alexithymic patient hypercathects the external world and fails to develop an inner representational sphere capable of sustaining symbolization.

In a fascinating paper on the impact of trauma on affect development, Krystal (1978) further illuminates the origins of the Type C personality. He notes that although the prior state of psychic development is an intervening variable, catastrophic trauma inevitably involves reality events of an unusually compelling nature. Terrible things have actually been experienced. Krystal states that above all, the traumatic state is experienced in an overwhelming sense of helplessness. I believe that most Type C patients have experienced infantile traumatic states or near-traumatic states. When catastrophic external events can no longer be warded off by characteristic coping mechanisms, a state of being overwhelmed, helpless, and paralyzed may ensue. According to Krystal, the greatest threat is to surrender to the inevitability of the peril and helplessly submit. Emotions and associated fantasies become the medium through which the trauma is experienced, a sort of "trauma screen," and hence such emotions and fantasies must be blocked before they make an impact. Among the aftereffects of near-traumatic or traumatic states is the implementation of a "trauma signal," a hyperalertness to phenomena capable of initiating the traumatic state. "What we observe in the direct aftereffects of severe childhood trauma in adults is a lifelong dread of the return of the traumatic state and an expectation of it" (Krystal 1978, p. 98). In a desperate effort to survive, the patient develops a psychic closing off, a form of "walking death" characteristic of Type C patients. Also characteristic is the posttraumatic loss of specificity of emotional response, and an impairment in the capacities for verbalization of emotion and symbolic representation and fantasy formation (pp. 95–98).

McDougall (1978) also emphasizes the role that psychic trauma plays in the formation of the "anti-analysand." In her view, the style of these patients represents a definitive response to the mental pain associated with overwhelming psychic trauma. "They have mummified their internal objects (whether good or bad), and attach themselves predominantly to factual and concrete aspects of interchange with others" (p. 242). Unlike neurotics, they show no evidence of the operation of repressive mechanisms or of the derivative content that seeps through repressive defenses. Instead, there is merely a void, a sterile, empty space that functions to obliterate the existence of internal objects (self and others), thereby permitting these patients to disregard the intolerable mental pain associated with self and object representations and accompanying affect states (pp. 227–228). Their mode of defense is to construct in effect a concrete wall, a process McDougall calls "disavowal." It is expressed as a complete disregard for all objects and represents a split between the desires associated with the past and the indifference felt toward current external objects, among them the therapist.

We can summarize the major points presented in this section as follows:

1. Although there may be predisposing constitutional factors, the failure in symbol formation and affect development is a result of early defenses against childhood trauma and massive psychic pain. This view disagrees with the notion of an inherent neurophysiological deficit.

2. The deficit in symbolic functioning and affective development is a means of assuring that the images and emotions associated with trauma and pain will never be experienced again. It represents a massive defense against pain and psychic catastrophe.

3. The impairment in symbolic functioning and affect development occurs early and has a devastating and spiraling impact on subsequent psychic development. The inner representational world is impoverished,

and there is an absence of adequate internalizations of significant others as well as of the self. The consequence is an ongoing dependence on concrete and external, but superficial and impersonal, sources of care.

TREATMENT OF THE
NONSYMBOLIC COMMUNICATOR

Whereas the Type A patient, characterized by repressive mechanisms, and the Type B patient, characterized by projective mechanisms, both reveal the latent content embedded within their manifest associations and behaviors, the Type C patient is characterized by communications of a concrete, literal, and entirely manifest nature. Although the defensive barriers of the Type C patient are evident, they reveal little about the drives and conflicts being defended against. In essence, the absence of derivative communication, together with the destruction of links to the therapist and to the prevailing adaptive context, poses formidable barriers to interpretive work. Clearly these patients, although they often suffer and lead impoverished emotional lives, pose an enormous challenge to the psychoanalytic psychotherapist.

It would be incorrect to assume that Type C fields are strictly manifestations of the patient's personality organization. Type C therapists also contribute to Type C fields, and in such a situation the therapist may be the one requiring treatment. But let us assume that, even given a Type A therapist, Type C patients will impose their style and create a Type C field. Considering the strain engendered by working with such patients, even the most rigorous of analytic therapists is likely to give in to despair and resort to whatever techniques seem to work.

The intent of this chapter is to describe a viable psychoanalytic approach to the treatment of these patients that continues to adhere to the basic principles of psychoanalytic technique while taking the special needs of such patients into consideration.

Sifneos (1974, 1975) believes that psychoanalytic psychotherapy is contraindicated for alexithymic patients. In his opinion, psychoanalytic psychotherapy, which requires the expression of fantasy and emotion, the very capacities these patients lack, only increases their level of anxiety and frustration and leads to the exacerbation of psychosomatic symptoms. He maintains that whereas psychoanalytic approaches are the treatment of choice for the neurotic, alexithymic patients do best with "anxiety-suppressive" techniques used in conjunction with psychotropic drugs. He concludes that treatment is best done by medical personnel who are able to provide support, with the consultation of a psychiatrist (1975, p. 69). Sifneos fails to provide any detailed clinical material and seems to assume that the term *psychoanalytic* denotes a standardized method dispensed in some uniform manner that disregards the patient's defenses. His own material evidences an emphasis on techniques, such as questions and answers, that prompt manifest responses. He seems unfamiliar with the relevant analytic literature, yet dismisses the psychoanalytic approach.

Freyberger, in a discussion of psychotherapy with psychosomatic patients ("Panel and Plenum Discussion" 1977, pp. 367–368), also advocates a supportive approach, which he rationalizes through references to object relations theory. In his view, the fear of relationships reinforces the pathology. The therapist should mollify this fear by becoming a "good object," and he suggests that this objective could be achieved by having an auxiliary pool of student therapists so that one would always be available. This suggestion reveals Freyberger's lack of familiarity with the ingredients of object constancy. His solution is antithetical to psychoanalytic psychotherapy, which is deeply rooted in the privacy and confidentiality of a one-to-one, primary relationship. Others on the same panel suggest a variety of corrective emotional experiences, including touching and being touched in order to help patients perceive and express bodily feelings.

Although the therapeutic ambitions of these and other writers concerned with finding viable therapeutic approaches to alexithymic patients represent imaginative efforts to work with a difficult group of patients, their emphasis appears to be manipulative and unrelated to the nature of their patients' inner experiences. Their suggestions and techniques imply that the void in object relationships can be filled without first resolving the defenses that impede the capacity to benefit from good experiences with external objects. They suggest placing the therapist in an actual, as opposed to a fantasized, maternal role, and ignore the unconscious implications of their own activities. Their reports also lack explicit data drawn from the clinical exchange and therefore fail to provide evidence that validates their assumptions.

Krystal (1979) views the alexithymic patient as having a specific disturbance that can be treated with modified psychotherapeutic procedures. His technique also differs markedly from that of psychoanalytic psychotherapy. Because, in his view, the primary problem of such patients is the fear of being overwhelmed by their affects, the therapist's primary tasks are to educate such patients as to the nature of their affects and to help them develop the ability to use affects as emotional signals. Krystal emphasizes a direct, reassuring emotional exchange, with the therapist's role analogous to that of the mother who permits the child to experience the full range and intensity of emotions but protects the child from being overwhelmed and traumatized by them. Krystal does not believe that transference phenomena should be dealt with before considerable preparatory work is done, and he does not provide any evidence that his work goes beyond this preparatory phase.

In contrast to the ideas just cited, Taylor's view (1977) is that the feelings of alexithymic patients are neither absent nor denied but are deeply buried and experienced as highly dangerous and potentially ego disruptive. Through the use of projective identification, these patients attempt to rid themselves of their threatening inner contents. Creative use of the countertransference—that is, the feelings induced—gives the therapist access to the patient's archaic inner world. In his clinical example, interventions emphasize that the aggressive, hopeless feelings Taylor is experiencing are reflections of what the patient is projecting into him. As a means of promoting symbolic activity, he directs a patient to transform her physical symptoms into "violent dreams." Through these maneuvers, he reports, "access to childhood memories and feelings were gained, and the patient began to express feelings and fantasies associated with the therapeutic relationship (p 145).

Although Taylor's emphasis on the use of induced feelings is of interest, problems emerge in his interpretation of the clinical material. Nonsymbolic communicators do induce uncomfortable feelings in therapists, but it may be erroneous to conclude that the therapist's feeling state reflects the patient's inner state. Because in the case presented Taylor took a rather aggressive and somewhat assaultive stance in provoking the patient to react, it is possible that the violent childhood memories and fantasies evoked were primarily unconscious perceptions of the intrusive nature of the therapist's interventions, rather than transference material.

McDougall (1978) also makes extensive use of her countertransference responses, but, unlike Taylor, she does not assume that her feelings are based upon projective identifications. With one patient, after trying almost every possible technique, she asks herself, "Should I throw away the structured analytic situation? Invite him for a drink? Have him sit up and face me? Anything to shake him up" (1978a). But she realizes that if she were to act on such wishes, she too would besome an "anti-analysand." "Thus I resist the temptation to throw away the analytic relationship—But what next? I must also resist the temptation to fall asleep!" (1978, p. 219).

Her emphasis is on detecting and interpreting the impact of the trauma as expressed in a preverbal, unconscious form through the analysand's manner of being and speaking. These patients do not use language as a means of symbolically communicating ideas and affects, but rather as an action that wards off the reemergence of the traumatic state. "Rather than seeking to communicate ideas, moods, and free associations, the patient seems to aim at making the analyst feel something, or stimulating him to do something. This something is incapable of being named, and the patient himself is totally unaware of the aim" (1978, p. 256). The words in themselves express emotional states apart from the content that is being recounted (1978, pp. 274–275). The primary intent, rather than to inform, is to make contact, or to convey emotional states to, or arouse them in, others. With these patients, to focus on the word is to hear nothing; there is no symbolic meaning in the form of derivatives embedded within the manifest content.

What is the attitude that the therapist must convey in working with such patients? In McDougall's view, it is an attitude different from that required by other types of patients. "The attitude of 'expectant silence' which to the neurotic spells hope, and opens a psychic space wherein long-buried desires may once more come to light, offers little but desolation and death to [such patients]. Their need to feel they exist in other people's eyes, to feel truly alive to a large extent dominates all other wishes and invades almost totally the territory of desire" (1978, pp. 297–298). Thus, McDougall advocates the therapist's adoption of an attitude more active and emotionally expressive than that generally required of the psychoanalytic psychotherapist, one that differs from Langs's emphasis on "holding" and interpreting defensive barriers. But in her emphasis on her patients' use of words as actions that stimulate the therapist to respond, McDougall makes these patients seem more like Langs's Type B, or at least a combination of the C and B Types.

Taylor's and McDougall's view, that there is meaning intended in non-symbolic communication, contradicts Langs's and Bion's opinion that such communications are intended to obliterate meaning. Is it possible that both views are valid? Or are these two differing perspectives based on experiences with different types of patients? As has been noted, and as stated by Langs, the communications of patients who use projective identifications can be translated and used to facilitate the therapeutic process. Type C communicators, in contrast, generally present little that can be processed and used to promote understanding.

Aside from Sifneos, most writers agree that the adaptations of these patients represent defensive responses to early traumatic experiences and object relationships. Unlike those therapists who prescribe some form of corrective emotional experience based on the assumption of the role of the good mother, the psychoanalytic psychotherapist, exemplified by Langs and McDougall, although assuming that the therapeutic relationship provides inherently corrective introjects, seeks to discover what the patient is actually experiencing, to resolve resistances and defenses, and to understand what is being communicated within the therapeutic relationship. Sifneos, Nemiah, and Krystal seem either to ignore or to attempt to circumvent the patient's defensive barriers. Taylor uses countertransference responses to confront the patient's defenses and stirs up derivative material in the form of unconscious perceptions. McDougall uses induced feelings to reconstruct early traumatic experiences and offers a relationship characterized by activity and emotional responsiveness. Langs emphasizes the firm entrenchment and impenetrability of these defenses, but also respects the patient's need for them in light of the underlying chaos they serve to contain.

Although a number of writers believe they have discovered a key to treating the nonsymbolic communicator, one is left wondering to what extent their findings are applicable to the Type C patient.

CLINICAL MATERIAL

Miss A., 26 years old, had been seen in once-a-week, face-to-face psychotherapy for two years. She had sought help when she became frightened by suicidal thoughts and sleeping problems. She had also complained of feelings of isolation, of an inability to maintain relationships, and of worsening peptic ulcers. She had been abandoned by her mother when she was 2½ years old. Her distraught father had later attempted to kill himself and his daughter by jumping off a boat at sea. At the last moment, both had been rescued by the crew of a passing ship. Her deeply disturbed father had become something of a recluse and had attempted to bind his daughter to him by confining her to the house. Yearning for a son, he had often dressed the patient as a boy. He had also taunted her sexually, walking around scantily clad and touching her genitals. She had gained some love and consistency in her relationship with an aunt. Proficient at her work, she was liked by people but fled from them when they started to get close. She had had several affairs, each of which had ended when a commitment had had to be made. She had strong doubts about her own femininity, and homosexual anxieties.

In treatment, after an initial period of distrust, she had initiated an affable, friendly, somewhat social relationship. During each session, however, she became increasingly anxious and lapsed into a silent, withdrawn state, punctuated by brief communicative moments. For some time the therapist had maintained a relatively silent, expectant, listening attitude, there being little pressure from the patient to intervene. Initially the patient had had no idea what she was feeling but frequently talked of the horrors of her childhood, with little affect but with increasing vividness and detail. Until the recent sessions to be presented, she had communicated in a concrete, literal manner. Over the course of treatment, her affect had become at times increasingly appropriate and intense. She could not free associate, and when there were prolonged silences, she failed to report what she had been thinking. At first, even if asked, she had no idea what she had been thinking, but in time she began to report some fleeting thoughts. She never shared conscious fantasies, nor did she report dreams until a recent session (to be presented). Each session was completely isolated from the others, with no direct or indirect reference to anything that had transpired between patient and therapist. Since the beginning of treatment, she frequently had been late or absent. At times she missed several consecutive sessions. Initially she would call after the missed session to give some excuse; later she stopped calling. Once she had missed four consecutive sessions and had not called, which had convinced the therapist that she would not return. The following week she had called to say that the therapist should be sure to be there for the next session, because she planned to come in. By that time, rather than making excuses, she was able to say that she stayed away because she was frightened.

Every impending holiday or vacation activated intense, near-delusional responses. At times an exacerbation of her ulcer was precipitated. For example, after being informed of the dates of the therapist's vacation with ample advance notice, she had revised what she had been told and in the next session had expressed her understanding that the therapist had told her she was doing so well that they would plan to terminate before the vacation. She continued to respond to separations by missing sessions. After the therapist repeatedly connected her missed sessions with the holidays and vacations, Miss A. began to describe increasingly vivid memories of early trauma with much more emotion. Because her memories of drowning or of being abandoned appeared to be fully conscious or preconscious, images of the early traumas seem not to have been repressed, and derivative and symbolic content was absent. She defended herself through withdrawal, denial, and disavowal of her attachment to the therapist. She did not provide metaphors descriptive of her defenses. The only material that conveyed meaning was the fact of the missed sessions. It seemed futile to wait for derivatives to coalesce around a current adaptive context. Feeling that it was not sufficient merely to listen in silence, the therapist chose to maintain emotional contact and presence through occasional reflective comments and by encouraging her to share her conscious, though suppressed, thoughts.

From the beginning, although the material presented was flat and strictly manifest, the therapist experienced a wide range of countertransference responses. He sympathized with the pain and anguish Miss A. had experienced, and he identified with her struggle to overcome the crippling effects of her childhood. At the same time, he felt frustrated by her absences and bored by her literal style and the absence of derivative communication. All his own conflicts about loss and his abandonment fantasies were activated when he waited in vain for a patient who did not arrive. Were these manifestations of his own unresolved difficulties, or were they induced feelings that support McDougall's thesis that there is communicative value in these patients' material that has to be inferred by reference to the therapist's own responses? If the latter, what was being communicated and how are such communications to be interpreted? Throughout, with never a question, Miss A. paid for all missed sessions, and it was clear that she viewed the set time as her time whether she came or not.

Following the summer vacation break, Miss A. missed three sessions. In the first session she attended she greeted the therapist with her characteristic warm smile and a handshake. He responded in kind. After saying she was sorry but that it had been too difficult to come for the prior sessions, she recounted the horrors of the last month. Her father had been ill, and she had taken care of him despite her anger toward him. A friend had been murdered. Her ulcers had acted up. Following a long period of withdrawn silence, perhaps ten minutes, she mentioned that the therapist had been away and said, without affect, "I felt helpless, like my hands were tied behind my back and I was thrown in the ocean. I was terrified and felt paralyzed by fear, but there are no words that can really describe it. It reminded me of when I was a child, drowning, with the water coming into me, and I could see and hear my father screaming and crying. I didn't have words to describe it, but I sure did know what was happening. Last month, I had the feeling that I was the last person left on this earth." (Silence.) The therapist replied: "Your father was ill, your friend murdered, and I had abandoned you, leaving you with the feeling that you were the last person left on this earth with no hope of relief and the horrible sense it would go on forever and ever. Since I had caused you such pain, you avoided seeing me again so as not to have to experience such pain again." She started to cry, remained silent for a time, and then said, "Yes, and I hated you for leaving me." She then remained silent for about five minutes, until the session ended.

The following week, she neither came nor called. The week after, she again did not appear, but she called to say that she would be in the next week. The therapist would have been there even if she had not called. On arriving, she announced that it had been difficult to come. She was frightened. She had seen her mother, who as usual seemed cold and disinterested. Relatives had told her that her mother, who had remarried, and at this time saw the patient from time to time, wished to see Miss A. more often, but according to Miss A. her mother never acted as if she wanted to see her. "I'm building a high wall between myself and everybody else, a wall that will keep all of my feelings in. I don't want to allow what happened—my mother leaving me without a word of warning—to ever happen again. He tried to kill me. My own father. God, can you believe it." She wept profusely. After a period of silence, the therapist said, "Perhaps you were frightened by the feelings evoked when we last met. By staying away and not calling, you leave me waiting and you are letting me know how horrible it is to sit and wait for a mother or a therapist who goes away. You are frightened by the anger this evokes in you, and so you need to build a wall to protect us from hurting each other. Also, you believe if you let down the wall here, you will experience the same horrible feelings all over again." After another silence, Miss A. said, "Yes, I hate the way you sometimes just sit there and look at me as if, like my mother, you have no feelings about me. I really feel that it will all happen again, and the angry feelings frighten me. I know it's not the same now as it was then, but that doesn't matter. I feel it will happen anyway. I feel that I am enclosed behind a wall and can't get out. It's like a living death, like being a zombie. After all, I didn't imagine it. All of those horrible things really did happen." After a brief silence, the therapist nodded in empathic agreement. "Yes, all of those horrible things really did happen." She said, "I thought things would get easier, but they just seem to get harder and more painful."

Miss A. arrived for the next session. She said she had been afraid to come but had decided to do so anyway. She was up for evaluation for promotion at work and feared that the way she reacted to our sessions might interfere with her capacity to work effectively. For the first time she reported a dream: she was with a male prostitute who rejected her and forced her to take off her clothing and walk through the streets nude. After telling the dream, she remained silent for about ten minutes, then said she found it a waste of time just to sit there. The therapist waited to see if she would go on, and when she again remained silent, he commented, "You have told me a dream but have nothing to say about it. Perhaps you are afraid to think about it." After a few minutes' silence, she said, "The male prostitute reminds me of my father, who stripped me and threw me into the sea unprotected." She recalled that the prostitute was blind and wondered what the therapist had to say about that. The therapist thought about the images in the dream and particularly about the blind prostitute. For the first time there appeared to be derivative material. Was the image of being made to walk through the streets nude Miss A.'s unconscious perception of the nature of his prior intervention? Was she responding to some failure on his part or still to his absence during the vacation? After thinking of these possibilities, he said, "You fear that the work here is not effective—that I will strip you of what you need to protect yourself, leaving you unable to function. Perhaps you believe that I, like the prostitute, am blind to the horror of your predicament." Miss A. replied, "I have to make it on this job. I'm terrified that I won't be able to bear up to all this stuff, that I'll just fall apart and screw everything up."

She did not appear for the following session. She came the week after and told of feeling nauseated, of having headaches, of her ulcer acting up, and of having been terrified of coming to the present session. She mentioned the fright she had felt when a friend had shared personal intimacies and had gotten close to her. After ten minutes of silence, the therapist related her symptoms and fears to the close and intimate feelings that had been discussed during their last session together. She agreed that she had such fears and then proceeded to talk of her fear of sex. Once people had gossiped about her and an older man she had been friendly with, but it actually had been only a platonic relationship. The therapist wondered if in talking of a fear of sex, she was indicating that she perceived him as forcing her into greater intimacy, and perhaps she had some reason to fear that what transpired in the sessions would be talked about. She remained silent for awhile, then recalled that she had once seen the therapist entering the elevator in the building in which she worked.

She came for the next session and told of having had a horrible experience a couple of days before. "I was standing in the street, and all of a sudden I felt I was frozen to that spot and couldn't move. I was thinking about therapy when it happened. I had no energy whatsoever. My sense of helplessness was terrifying. There was absolutely nothing I could do about it. I felt that I was no longer on this earth. After awhile I was able to walk again, got back to my apartment, thought further about our sessions, and felt better. I noticed that my ulcer didn't bother me anymore. I thought about how my father had tried to kill me and had ridiculed me whenever I expressed emotions, telling me that I should be strong like a boy. I had to put up a wall, a thick stone wall that nothing could get in or out of. I've been seeing you awhile, and I have a lot of warm, loving feelings for you, but I'm terrified of letting them out." After a period of silence, the therapist responded, "You're terrified that if you continue to let down that wall with me, you'll have no means of protecting yourself, that I would destroy you as your father and mother had done, and that in turn you would destroy me." Miss A. replied, "Yes, I'm terrified that I'll be crushed, destroyed, that I will die and that I would kill you, and there would be absolutely nothing that could prevent it. I feel I'd be completely helpless. I don't ever want to feel those horrible feelings again. I prefer being a zombie to that." Crying convulsively for a period of minutes, she added, "Can you imagine if I feel this way now, what it must have felt like then—unable to do a single thing to help myself, paralyzed with terror, suffocating and waiting to die? It's too horrible to describe. It was such a horrible feeling." The therapist nodded, agreeing it was horrible. It was time to stop, and Miss A. gave the therapist an intense, seemingly caring look on leaving.

After these sessions, the therapy continued along similar lines and seemed to go further into the terrors that were associated with her childhood traumas but that were repeated in the immediacy of her current relationship with the therapist. When the summer vacation again approached, the pattern of missing sessions reappeared.

Discussion

Miss A.'s personality organization and communicative style were shaped by her early catastrophic traumas. Devastating and overwhelming realities flooded her immature ego with affects that rendered her helpless and resulted in arrested emotional development and deficiencies in symbolization. The continued curtailment of her affective and symbolic development served as a defensive assurance that the state of trauma would never have to be experienced again. The therapeutic situation, although providing the hope of a new solution, became an arena that contained the terrifying potential of reawakening and, through the resolution of defenses, fostering the reexperiencing of the early traumas that the patient had spent much of her energy avoiding.

Perhaps the fact that catastrophic traumas are realities that are cruelly forced upon the immature ego of the child leaves little room for illusion and fantasy and explains in part why patients such as Miss A. focus on the minute details of their everyday existence. After all, it is strictly these externally induced catastrophic events that have deprived them of a normal existence and have led to their being flooded by overwhelming affects. This fact may also explain why the details of these traumatic events seem, at least in the case of Miss A., to be clearly remembered rather than repressed.

Is it possible that Miss A.'s fears were triggered by her unconscious perception of the therapist's countertransference struggles (e.g., his anxieties about separation and loss) or by his intervening, perhaps precipitously, because of the intensity of Miss A.'s difficulties in the sessions presented? Was the association to a fear of not being able to get the work done an introjection of the therapist's concern? Was Miss A.'s dream of the prostitute who rejected her and forced her to walk through the streets nude primarily an evocation of memories of her father, who used her by attempting to force her to accompany him in death and subsequently taunted her sexually? Or was it a perception of the therapist's prior interventions, his stating that she wanted him to know what it was like to be left waiting and his references to her fear of hurting and being hurt, which, together with his empathic nodding, were experienced by Miss A. as alternatively stripping her of her defenses and being seductive? These are difficult questions involving the interplay between the past and current realities, between the patient's tendency to misperceive the present in terms of the past and the extent to which the therapist's activities actually repeat the past.

Countertransference is inevitable, and, according to Langs (1980b), there is an element of countertransference in every intervention. Countertransference is also necessary, because it supplies that bit of reality that triggers unconscious fantasies and traumatic memories. There is an interplay between unconscious processes—fantasies, memories, and perceptions—that intrude on conscious processes and distort and color perceptions of current realities, and current experiences that trigger memories and fantasies of the traumatic past (Arlow 1969, p. 8). In this case the current experiences, Miss A.'s interactions with her therapist, were unconsciously interpreted as corresponding to her earlier traumatic experiences. Similarly, in this case the symptom formation, Miss A.'s experience of being unable to move and of being the last person on earth, was precipitated by the sense that, once again, she was in a situation from which there was no escape from overwhelmingly horrifying affects. These patterns help us understand why the adaptive context, the current reality that stimulates fantasies, memories, and attempts to cope, is of such significance. Because countertransference is inevitable and necessary, as is transference, and both involve a mixture of reality and distortion, the major concern is to be able to maintain a minimal degree of countertransference in order to activate the conflicts, memories, and defenses that underlie and perpetuate developmental deficiencies and arrests. The danger is that countertransference will be maximal and only create new traumas on top of the old.

Although Miss A.'s initial communications were in the Type C mode—literal, flat, and cliché ridden—as treatment progressed she began gradually to use the Type B mode as well. For example, the intensity of the material that followed her return from vacation induced strong emotional responses in the therapist that required great effort to manage. Her missed sessions were both protective and informative, a form of projective identification that forced the therapist to experience and cope with the threat of being abandoned and of being forced to wait for a loved person who may never return. This material raises the issue of whether Miss A. is a typical Type C communicator or is, rather, more of a B-C communicator, even, as in the dream of the prostitute, capable of using the Type A mode at times. One might also consider the extent to which the nature of the therapist's interventions influenced Miss A.'s communicative mode.

Initially the therapist seemed to have no meaning to Miss A. His presence or absence were met by a wall of indifference. The patient's communications consisted primarily of a repetitious recitation of the events of the past, disassociated from her current life. With repeated interpretations of the connections between the exacerbation of her symptoms and the theapist's absences, she began to become aware of and to acknowledge the extent to which conscious memories of the early traumas were being relived in her current relationship with the therapist. As she acknowledged the intensity of her attachment to the therapist, she could at times experience the pain and terror associated with his loss without resorting to her usual defenses of withdrawal and disavowal. As she became better able to tolerate her affects, she began to miss fewer sessions.

For some time after he began seeing Miss A., the therapist maintained an empathic, relatively silent but attentive listening stance, providing a holding environment by maintaining consistency and dependability. Symbolic content and adaptive contexts were never represented either directly or indirectly in the material. In time Miss A. began to express metaphors, such as references to herself as a "zombie," a "robot," and "one of the living dead," which served to characterize her affectless and nonsymbolic communicative style. The therapist used such references to acquaint Miss A. with the nature of her defenses as well as with the underlying dread of annihilation and her murderous rage.

The material was sparse, with long, empty silences and superficial, concrete statements, leaving little to the imagination or to the process of interpretation. Meanwhile, the therapist struggled to maintain his analytic posture: anonymity, neutrality, and the set time as well as the patient's responsibility for the sessions. For example, when Miss A., after missing two sessions, arrived a half hour late, the therapist ended the session on time despite his wish to see her for a longer period. But it seemed essential to provide Miss A. with more than consistency, dependability, and interpretations. The concreteness of the material, together with the therapist's silent, listening stance, did not seem to be experienced by Miss A. as an adequate holding environment: instead, it seemed to create an arid and sterile atmosphere that only deepened Miss A.'s sense of detachment and emptiness. It was crucial to breathe some life into the exchange, to let Miss A. know that she existed in the eyes of the therapist (McDougall 1978, pp. 297–298) and that he truly empathized with the traumatic experiences she had described. Thus, he mirrored her smile on entering, communicated his capacity to feel her pain and terror, and expressed his understanding of her need to miss sessions in order to survive.

The term *presence* (Nacht 1958) best describes the additional dimension required. This view modifies and amplifies my belief, expressed earlier (Greene 1982), that the therapist's silent, holding stance must be stressed in the treatment of patients who have experienced early object loss. Patients like Miss A., who have experienced early psychic traumas, struggle to maintain whatever precarious sense of self persists, terrified that this sense will be destroyed should they once again experience the traumatic state. These patients require that the actuality of their experience be acknowledged and confirmed. The therapist must confirm the reality of the catastrophic experiences they have endured, even when such realities are presented on a strictly manifest level. In addition—and this is even more crucial and difficult to accomplish—the therapist must acknowledge the full extent to which his or her interventions contribute to the patient's current difficulties and serve as triggers that resemble or activate the traumas of the past.

In this case, the therapist agreed with Miss A. that the experience of being nearly drowned by her father was indeed horrible, and that "all of those horrible things really did happen." In saying this, he confirmed that what she had experienced was not merely a figment of a wild imagination (and he had enough evidence to know that Miss A.'s memories had the ring of historical truth). Thus, although such crucial dimensions of the frame as consistency, privacy, empathy, anonymity, neutrality, and valid interpretations provide the essential core of the therapist's activities, something more—presence, expressions of compassion, and affirmation of historical reality—is required when working with nonsymbolic communicators who have experienced catastrophic traumas.

REFERENCES

ARLOW, J. A. (1969). Unconscious fantasy and disturbances of conscious experience. *Psychoanalytic Quarterly* 38:28–51.

BION, W. R. (1953). Notes on a theory of schizophrenia. In W. R. Bion, *Second Thoughts: Selected Papers on Psychoanalysis*, pp. 23–35. New York: Jason Aronson, 1967.

——— (1962a). Learning from experience. In W. R. Bion, *Seven Servants*, pp. 1–111. New York: Jason Aronson, 1977.

——— (1962b). A theory of thinking. *International Journal of Psycho-Analysis* 43: 306–310.

BLANCK, G., AND BLANCK, R. (1974). *Ego Psychology: Theory and Practice.* New York: Columbia University Press.

DE M'UZAN, M. (1974). Analytical process and the notion of the past. *International Review of Psycho-Analysis* 1:461–480.

EISSLER, K. R. (1953). The effect of the structure of the ego on psychoanalytic technique. *Journal of the American Psychoanalytic Association* 1:104–143.

FREUD, S. (1912). Recommendations to physicians practising psycho-analysis. *Standard Edition* 12.

——— (1913). On beginning the treatment. *Standard Edition* 12.

GREENE, M. (1982). On the silence of the therapist and object loss. *International Journal of Psychoanalytic Psychotherapy* 9:183–200.

JONES, E. (1916). The theory of symbolism. In *Papers on Psycho-analysis*, pp. 87–144. Baltimore: Williams & Wilkins, 1948.

KERNBERG, O. (1978). Contrasting approaches to the psychotherapy of borderline conditions. In *New Perspectives on Psychotherapy of the Borderline Adult*, ed. J. F. Masterson, pp. 77–104. New York: Brunner/Mazel.

KLEIN, M. (1930). The importance of symbol formation in the development of the ego. In *Love, Guilt and Reparation: Contributions to Psycho-analysis 1921-1945*, pp. 219-232. London: Hogarth Press, 1975.

KOHUT, H. (1971). *The Analysis of the Self*. New York: International Universities Press.

KRYSTAL, H. (1978). Trauma and affects. *Psychoanalytic Study of the Child* 33:81-116.

—— (1979). Alexithymia and psychotherapy. *American Journal of Psychotherapy* 33:17-31.

LANGS, R. (1978a). Some communicative properties of the bipersonal field. *International Journal of Psychoanalytic Psychotherapy* 7:87-135.

—— (1978b). Validation and the framework of the therapeutic situation: thoughts prompted by Hans H. Strupp's "Suffering and Psychotherapy." *Contemporary Psychoanalysis* 14:98-104.

—— (1980a). Some interactional and communicative aspects of resistance. *Contemporary Psychoanalysis* 16:16-52.

—— (1980b). *Interactions: The Realm of Transference and Countertransference*. New York: Jason Aronson.

MCDOUGALL, J. (1978). *Plea for a Measure of Abnormality*. New York: International Universities Press, 1980.

MAHLER, M., PINE, F., AND BERGMAN, A. (1975). *The Psychological Birth of the Human Infant*. New York: Basic Books.

MARTY, P., AND DE M'UZAN, M. (1963). La pensée opératoire. *Review France Psychoanalytique* 27:345-356.

NACHT, S. (1958). Variations in technique. *International Journal of Psycho-Analysis* 39:235-237.

NEMIAH, J. C. (1975). Denial revisited. *Psychotherapy and Psychosomatics* 26:140-147.

NEMIAH, J. C., AND SIFNEOS, P. E. (1970). Psychosomatic illness: a problem in communication. *Psychotherapy and Psychosomatics* 18:154-160.

Panel and plenum discussion: psychotherapeutic problems with psychosomatic patients (1977). *Psychotherapy and Psychosomatics* 28:361-375.

PAOLINO, T. J. (1981). *Psychoanalytic Psychotherapy*. New York: Brunner/Mazel.

SEARLES, H. F. (1979). *Countertransference and Related Subjects: Selected Papers*. New York: International Universities Press.

SEGAL, H. (1957). Notes on symbol formation. *International Journal of Psycho-Analysis* 38:391-397.

—— (1978). On symbolism. *International Journal of Psycho-Analysis* 59:315-319.

SIFNEOS, P. E. (1974). A reconsideration of psychodynamic mechanisms in symptom formation in view of recent clinical observations. *Psychotherapy and Psychosomatics* 24:151-155.

—— (1975). Problems of psychotherapy of patients with alexithymic characteristics and physical disease. *Psychotherapy and Psychosomatics* 26:65-70.

STONE, L. (1954). The widening scope of indications for psychoanalysis. *Journal of the American Psychoanalytic Association* 2:567-594.

STRACHEY, J. (1934). The nature of the therapeutic action of psychoanalysis. *International Journal of Psycho-Analysis* 15:117-126.

STRUPP, H. H. (1977). A reformulation of the dynamics of the therapist's contribution. In *Effective Psychotherapy: A Handbook of Research*, eds. A. Gurman and A. M. Razin, pp. 3–22. New York: Pergamon.

TAYLOR, J. G. (1977). Alexithymia and the counter-transference. *Psychotherapy and Psychosomatics* 28:141–147.

WINNICOTT, D. W. (1971). Playing: a theoretical statement. In D. W. Winnicott, *Playing and Reality*, pp. 38–52. New York: Basic Books.

CHAPTER 17

Pinter's Use of Language and Character Interaction Compared with Langs's Theories of Communication

Vera Jiji, Ph. D.

In real life, no psychoanalysis can be exhaustive, given the length and complexity of human existence. In drama, however, the characters have no lives except those seen on stage or provided by the playwright. This circumstance allows us to conduct an exceptionally lucid investigation of the interaction and structure of dramatic characters, as long as we remember that we are dealing with analogies since fictional characters do not exist. They have no real lives. Within this limitation, the availability, unity, and wholeness of drama provide so many advantages that we profitably may study these characters as we might study the case histories of real people. In addition, the work of gifted writers has a richness, depth, and complexity of texture not often present in "real-life" interactions. Thus, a study of a playwright's work is often of exceptional value in making accessible the wide range of human emotion. This point was appreciated by Freud, whose graceful tribute to the world's great writers—his statement that they intuitively had anticipated his discoveries—seems applicable to the work of the gifted contemporary British playwright, Harold Pinter. In this chapter I attempt to show how his plays illustrate the insights into psychological processes that Robert Langs also has developed, quite independently.

I want to emphasize Pinter's use of "realistic" dialogues that illustrate very effectively the kinds of language used by many contemporary analysands. As Pinter (1964) says,

> A thing is not necessarily either true or false; it can be both true and false. A character on the stage who can present no convincing argument or information as to his past experience, his present behavior or his aspirations, nor give a comprehensive analysis of his motives is as legitimate and as worthy of attention as one

who, alarmingly, can do all these things. The more acute the experience the less articulate the expression. (p. 576)

I also want to illustrate how on-stage interactions encode unconscious fantasies while also dealing with the adaptive context. Because the Pinter dialogues are not between therapist and patient, we postulate the following analogy: in real life, a person's unconscious fantasies and perceptions relate to his or her previous and present existence outside the therapeutic framework. Within the therapeutic environment, the patient's unconscious fantasies and perceptions are organized around the adaptive context as it is created by the therapist and patient together. In any play, the characters' implied unconscious fantasies and perceptions must derive from the character structure as defined and developed by the playwright. Nonetheless, we will assume for the purposes of this chapter that these characters have an independent existence to the extent that their actions seem consistent with our understanding of behavior in the real world.

This viewpoint is analogous to that which Robert Langs takes of the functioning of the patient and the therapist within the therapeutic frame. Langs's bipersonal approach treats the therapy participants as largely independent, at least for therapeutic or interpretive purposes, of their life outside the therapeutic frame, the adaptive context providing the structure to which the patient's behavior refers, directly or indirectly.

In dramatic theory the framing structure is provided by the precipitating event or change that begins the play. (Here we are assuming that the audience understands the playwright's societal world view, use of dramatic conventions, and given character-defining structures, just as the therapist must be attuned to the patient's world view.) In some plays the precipitating event is difficult to find. In Samuel Beckett's *Not I*, for example, the event is the focusing of the stage light on the monologist's mouth, which motivates her to speak, just as the beginning of the therapeutic hour causes the patient to speak. But in most plays the precipitating event is more obvious. In *Macbeth*, for example, it is Macbeth's elevation by Duncan to Thane of Cawdor, accompanied by the witches' predictions of further glories. In Chekov's *Cherry Orchard* the precipitating event is the imminent auction of Mme. Ranevskaya's estate. In every play some such occurrence triggers the action and governs its unfolding. We will compare that precipitating event to the adaptive context provided by the therapeutic framework, and we will see how it governs the action in Pinter's play just as the management of the frame governs the progress of the analysis.

Before we begin study of a particular play, it may be helpful to set Pinter's development of character structure and motivation briefly into a historical context. What the playwright assumes the audience understands without explanation and what the audience finds interesting changes over time. Thus in Renaissance drama (late 16th and early 17th centuries), we are given explicit motives for characters' actions, often in the form of soliloquies to the audience. (That is one reason for critics' bedevilment by Iago's "motiveless malignancy," because the motives he articulates are both too numerous and too weak for credibility.) Restoration drama (late 17th century) relies instead on a set of conventional motives, such as the search for sexual partners or money, or the attempt to reconcile the conflicting demands of selfish motives and honor. The so-called modern period in drama (late 19th to mid-20th centuries) focuses primarily on middle- or lower-class characters whose ordinary lives are "realistically" drawn and whose psychological motivations are carefully delineated. (One thinks of plays by Ibsen, Chekov, O'Neill, Miller, and Williams as examples.)

Pinter's style derives from the post-Freudian contemporary school of drama known as Absurdism, a type defined by Camus (1942) as originating in "a universe . . . suddenly deprived of illusions and of light [in which] man feels a stranger . . . deprived of memories of a lost homeland . . . lack-[ing] the hope of a promised land to come. This divorce between a man and his life, the actor and his setting, truly constitutes the feeling of Absurdity" (p. 18).

Like other absurdist playwrights, Pinter does not provide the explicit detailing of family history, character structure, and introspection that would enable audiences to reconstruct the reasons for the characters' behavior. It is in part this absence of specific motivation that sets these writers' works apart from those of such earlier dramatists as Williams and Miller, who provide, say, a limp for Laura in *The Glass Menagerie* or a false set of values for Willy Loman in *Death of a Salesman*. The postmodernist dramatists assume a degree of psychological sophistication on the part of the audience, expecting the audience to interpret elliptical, encoded messages. Pinter takes this dramatic form one step further by illustrating humanity's alienation from the "lost homeland" of bourgeois ideals of happiness through his skillful use of language and situation. He plays off his characters' behavior against bourgeois ideals, which are still brought into the theater as audience expectations.

Pinter's statements about the relationship between his characters and the language they use should be very striking to analysts and therapists interested in Langs's discussion of patient–therapist dialogues, especially regarding the Type C personality. As Langs (1978) explains, "The Type C field is . . . a very interesting field, in that noncommunication is the medium. Language is used in order not to communicate. . . . In a Type C field, all language is used as a barrier. . . . The destruction of meaning and of interpersonal links, and the creation of massive impenetrable barriers . . . constitute an attempt to seal off a psychotic core, an inner catastrophe, intense psychic pain" (pp. 124–125). That description can be compared with Pinter's (1964) comments in an interview he gave when his plays were first startling audiences. He said:

> We have heard many times that tired, grimy phrase: "Failure of communication" . . . and this phrase has been fixed to my work quite consistently. I believe the contrary. I think that we communicate only too well, in our silence, in what is unsaid, and that what takes place is a continual evasion, desperate rear guard attempts to keep ourselves to ourselves. Communication is too alarming. To enter into someone else's life is too frightening. To disclose to others the poverty within us is too fearsome a possibility. (p. 579)

This understanding of the use of language to attempt to hide, rather than to communicate, is emphasized by Langs. Pinter's understanding of *how* language is used to hide is articulated in the same interview, as he adds,

> There are two silences. One when no word is spoken. The other when perhaps a torrent of language is being employed. This speech is speaking of a language locked beneath it. That is its continual reference. The speech we hear is an indication of that which we don't hear. . . . One way of looking at speech is to say that it is a constant stratagem to cover nakedness. (p. 578)

This statement is again analogous to Langs's (1978) description of Type C communication which "generate[s] extended narratives without a relevant adaptive context" (p. 593).

These statements show Pinter's sophisticated, subtle use of stage language, a use that is very similar to Langs's communicative approach. Pinter's plays resemble therapeutic situations further in that almost all of them are created from very limited elements: a room, people in it who "own" the room, while others invade or enter. A struggle for the territory (either the room itself, or sexual possession of those in it, or their defined status or positions) ensues. At the play's end the "invaders" often have won possession of the territory by using language as a weapon (although sometimes they lose and are ejected), and it is left to the audience to ascertain the motives that have determined the progress of the battle. John Russell Brown (1963), a prominent drama critic, explains that the "basic concern of a Pinter play" is the "progressive disclosure of antagonisms, desires or appetites which were hidden at the beginning" (p. 251). Again, that description might serve equally well for an analysis.

Pinter's work is unique in that his characters' *primary* source of power lies in their ability to use language to control or mystify others. Such characters often resemble Langs's Type B and Type C patients. We see these types illustrated, respectively, in Lenny and Teddy, major characters in *The Homecoming*. I would like to use that play to illustrate Pinter's use of language, partly because it is probably the one of Pinter's works best known to American audiences, and partly because I believe it to be Pinter's best-balanced play aesthetically, although for reasons not germane to this discussion.

The play begins with the fairly banal situation of a man bringing his wife home to meet the family. The man, Teddy, is the oldest son of Max and Jessie. Max lives with his bachelor brother, Sam, and Teddy's two unmarried brothers, Joey and Lenny. Their house in London has been unchanged since the death of Jessie, except that they have enlarged the living room by taking out a wall that had created a separate hallway. The resulting large living room, in which the entire play takes place, is cold, gray, and quite depersonalized. Six years before, Teddy had married Ruth and taken her off to live in America (where he is a professor of philosophy at an unnamed college) without notifying his family of the marriage or introducing Ruth to them. Now he brings her to London on a surprise visit.

We meet the all-male household before the couple arrives, and hear a great deal about their lives and relationships. We hear that Max, a retired butcher, now the household cook, was a terror in his youth, dominating his neighborhood with his friend Mac. We hear his reminiscences about his wife (Pinter 1965), "a charming woman,"[1] according to Sam. "Mind you, she wasn't such a bad woman," says Max, "even though it made me sick just to look at her rotten stinking face" (p. 9). The father–son relationship is equally loving. Lenny calls his father a "daft prat" (p. 7); Max warns his son, "I'll chop your spine off . . . ." (p. 9), and summarizes: "Look at what I'm lumbered with. One cast-iron bunch of crap after another. One flow of stinking pus after another" (p. 19).

Teddy and Ruth arrive after the others have gone to bed. When Ruth goes out "for a breath of air" (p. 24), Lenny reenters the room, and he and Teddy chat before Teddy retires, without either having mentioned Ruth. Upon Ruth's return, she and Lenny chat. She then retires. Max awakens, wondering to whom Lenny's been talking. Again, Lenny doesn't tell Max about the couple's arrival. They have a short but telling conversation before the scene ends. In the morning Max and the London family are at their usual back biting, Max now insulting Sam, calling him useless and a "tit" (p. 40), when the couple comes downstairs in their dressing gowns. Furious at having had his son there overnight without his knowledge, Max asks Teddy, "Who asked you to bring dirty tarts into this house?" (p. 41).

---

[1]All subsequent references to this text will be from the Grove Press edition and will be cited in the text. Because Pinter often indicates short pauses in the text by three dots, any ellipses in the quotations will be indicated by four dots. Where three dots are used, the text is complete as given.

Despite Teddy's explanation that Ruth is his wife, Max protests, "I've never had a whore under this roof before. Ever since your mother died" (p. 42). During this scene Max hits both Joey and Sam before finally "greeting" Teddy with a grotesque parody of love. Act I ends.

Act II begins pleasantly, with after-dinner cigars after Max's cooking has been consumed by all. During this scene the London brothers, Lenny in the lead, make increasingly overt advances to Ruth, who accepts them all as if nothing could be more natural. After kissing Joey and rolling on the floor with him, she goes upstairs with him for two hours. When Joey returns, reporting that he didn't "go the whole hog" but "you can be happy . . . . and not go the whole hog" (p. 68), Max thinks they might invite Ruth to stay with them.

We suddenly realize that Lenny is a pimp as he suggests that he "put her on the game." Ruth drives a hard bargain, insisting on three rooms and a written contract, but they soon agree, and Teddy returns alone to America.

When the play was first produced in 1965, it aroused a good deal of discussion, because the motivation was puzzling to audiences and yet simultaneously felt quite "right," somehow. One scholarly article was succinctly entitled "Why the Lady Does It" (Walker 1975). And certainly some explanation was required of Ruth's motivation in choosing the life of a prostitute in London, living with a bunch of rotters, over the life of a professor's wife in America. A reading of the entire play, which I strongly recommend, would clarify Ruth's choice. Langs (1978) points out that in dealing with a Type C patient, the analyst "must master his dread of being attacked and even annihilated by the patient's noncommunication and negative projective identifications, which create a void in which his capacity to think, formulate, and organize—to function meaningfully and relatedly—are being destroyed" (p. 584). With this point in mind, we can understand why Ruth, in her need to remain sane, abandons Teddy, a Type C communicator, to remain with the Londoners, whose need for her becomes achingly evident. This chapter will illuminate Ruth's shift of loyalties by examining selected key passages from the play.

Pinter's characters often build their lives around what has been called a "game," which Pinter (1967) has elsewhere described as:

two people in one room having a battle of an unspecified nature, in which the question was one of who was dominant at what point and how they were going to be dominant and what tools they would use to achieve dominance and how they would try to undermine the other person's dominance. A threat is constantly there: it's got to do with this question of being in the uppermost position, or attempting to be . . . . it's a very common, everyday thing . . . . a repeated theme in my plays. (pp. 362–363)

This communicative style illustrates Langs's Type B projective communicative field. These characters interact chiefly by insulting one another and not appearing to let the insults get under their skins. What the dialogue presents us with is a provocation followed by a lack of response to the provocation followed by a new provocation from the character who refused to be visibly disturbed by the first.

Teddy gives indirect evidence of a desire to escape from the game in every conceivable fashion. Although he married Ruth in England, he never told his family about her. He took a job overseas. He chose to become a professor, that is, one whose work sets him apart from the ordinary concerns of most work-a-day lives, and a professor of philosophy at that, a domain that is supposed to inspire the greatest degree of distance from ordinary problems. Teddy's refusal to become emotionally involved with the others is also tested during the play. He remains calm through his father's initial insults to his wife and himself. Later, he refuses to get involved in an abstract philosophical discussion with Lenny, claiming that the subject of "the known and the unknown" is not in his province. When one of Ruth's remarks reveals to Teddy that he will have trouble with her, he deals with it very indirectly (see p. 387, this chapter). When Teddy sees his brothers and Ruth in passionate embraces, he does nothing to stop them. It is after this climactic scene that Ruth asks, "Have your family read your critical works?" and he replies:

> You wouldn't understand my works. You wouldn't have the faintest idea of what they were about. You wouldn't appreciate the points of reference. You're way behind. All of you. There's no point in my sending you my works. You'd be lost. It's nothing to do with the question of intelligence. It's a way of being able to look at the world. It's a question of how far you can operate on things and not in things. I mean it's a question of your capacity to ally the two, to relate the two. To see, to be able to see! I'm the one who can see. That's why I can write my critical works. Might do you good . . . have a look at them . . . see how certain people can view . . . things . . . how certain people can maintain . . . intellectual equilibrium. Intellectual equilibrium. You're just objects. You just . . . move about. I can observe it. I can see what you do. It's the same as I do. But you're lost in it. You won't get me being . . . I won't be lost in it. (pp. 61–62)[2]

This speech of Teddy's, which comes closest to revealing his personality, clearly exemplifies the Type C style. We can see how vague the speech is, how clichéd. Because we've been exposed to this scene, we can understand how powerful his need is to feel superior to the others, to reduce them to

[2]See footnote 1. This speech is quoted as it appears in the original. All ellipses are as given in the text.

objects, whereas he, the intellectual, "prefers" merely to observe and to remain the only one "who can see." Most amazing in the speech is its total avoidance of the subject of the family's sexual exploitation of his wife (the relevant adaptive context).

To a literary critic familiar with Western drama from the classical Greek to the post-modern period, Teddy's repeated references to being "able to see" would evoke Oedipus, who was spiritually blind when he could see, and who blinded himself as a punishment when he "saw" the nature of his oedipal crime. Teddy, too, has taken the mother for himself, because Ruth is portrayed with increasing explicitness throughout the play as Jessie's replacement, her second incarnation. Although Teddy does not suddenly go blind in this play, as several of Pinter's characters do in his other works (Rose in *The Room*, Disson in *Tea Party*, Edward in *A Slight Ache*), his behavior demonstrates that he may as well be blind for all he communicates of his understanding of his wife's and family's motives. Finally, at play's end, he is exiled back to America, as Oedipus was exiled after his crime was uncovered. Ruth's last words to Teddy have always puzzled critics. As he goes to the front door, Ruth calls, "Eddie." Teddy turns, and there is a pause. Ruth says, "Don't become a stranger." Teddy leaves without replying to her, shutting the door (p. 80). Perhaps Ruth is calling him not by a pet name, but by a shortened form of Oedipus.

But comparisons to previous playwrights do not describe Pinter's unique qualities at all adequately. The adjective "Pinteresque" has been added to the critical vocabulary, because no existing word or phrase describes the combination of a sense of line-by-line realism in the dialogue with the mystery in motivation, menace in tone, and power in effect that he manages. The critic Katherine Burkman (1971), for example, reminds us not to attempt to explain Pinter's work by reference to the Oedipus complex. "Pinter's plays are most definitely not case histories. . . . If the mysterious emerges and takes over in Pinter's drama, it is never completely explained" (pp. 92, 5).

Even without references to the Oedipus complex or the cultural traditions of Western drama, we can read the encoded message in this key speech of Teddy's. His reduction of the others to "objects" serves to reduce his pain. His references to "intellectual equilibrium" serve to remind him of the nature of his acquired character structure. His repetitions, abstractions, broken diction, and repeated assertions of noninvolvement show how Teddy's apparent imperviousness to emotional involvement serves as his defense mechanism. For example, without being asked, Teddy takes on the job of suggesting to Ruth that she may, if she wishes, stay on with his family, earning her way by becoming a professional whore. Teddy's only violation of the rules of polite behavior in the play comes when he eats a "cheese roll" that Lenny has made for himself. The equation of a cheese roll with a wife is very amusing, because although Lenny carries on about the lost cheese roll, Teddy says absolutely nothing about the loss of his wife. Teddy's refusal to be provoked, his saying as little as possible no matter how extreme the provocation, illustrates the flat, affectless quality of a Type C Langsian patient.

In contrast, although Lenny's view of women is certainly warped, he is very much involved with them and quite loquacious. Let us examine the dialogue that develops during Lenny's first meeting with Ruth, for it is their two scenes together that motivate the family's offer to Ruth. As I have written elsewhere (Jiji 1974), in this play the basic precipitating cultural event is the bringing of the bride home to meet the family. In the normal situation, although the wedding celebrates a sexual event, every attempt is made by the family of in-laws to be circumspect, to avoid any discussion of the bride's sexuality. We might go so far as to say that a Type C communication style is an acceptable norm in many situations involving in-laws. But here it is Ruth whose homecoming the play celebrates, although she is the alien (Pinter may have intended the Biblical reference). Thus we see that in this play, all our ritual expectations of proper behavior are systematically violated, just as, in an analysis, the recalcitrant patient systematically attempts to disrupt every aspect of the frame, testing the therapist's resolve to adhere to the rules of treatment at every opportunity.

If we wished to "explain" Lenny's motivation in terms of family history, it would be easy enough. If his mother had been something of a whore (and evidence for this develops gradually throughout the play), if the men simultaneously had been dependent on and contemptuous of her (and that becomes clear), then they would wish to reduce Ruth to a similar stereotypical figure in their eyes. And this is precisely what they proceed to do. Pinter has made it even easier by increasing the parallels between the women. Ruth, like Jessie, has had three sons, and it is in response to her initiatives, her sexual invitations and veiled confession of previous sexual irregularities, that the men make the offer. To explain the play's events in terms of a particular family pathology, however, is to do injustice to Pinter's reach. The play takes on universal symbolic implications, reminding us more, perhaps, of Freud's hypotheses about the tribal beginnings of "civilization" in his *Totem and Taboo* than of one of Freud's case histories.

Before Lenny and Ruth's first scene together, we are meant to realize that Lenny has overheard Ruth and Teddy's first conversation, which has revealed that they are husband and wife and that this wife does what she wants to, not what her husband says she should. (In the film version, there is a cut to Lenny's room showing him listening to their chatting.) Yet when Ruth reenters the house after her late-night stroll, Lenny, like the characteristic Type B or C communication patient in the presence of an obvious adaptive context, acts as if he knows none of this information. The scene begins:

> (*Lenny comes back into the room, goes to the window and looks out. He leaves the window and turns on a lamp. He is holding a small clock. He sits, places the clock in front of him, lights a cigarette and sits. Ruth comes in the front door. She stands still. Lenny turns his head, smiles. She walks slowly into the room.*)

  1. Lenny: Good evening.

  2. Ruth: Morning, I think.

  3A. Lenny: You're right there. (*Pause.*)

  3B. My name's Lenny. What's yours?

  4. Ruth: Ruth. (*She sits, puts her coat collar around her.*)

  5. Lenny: Cold?

  6. Ruth: No.

  7A. Lenny: It's been a wonderful summer, hasn't it? Remarkable. (*Pause.*)

  7B. Would you like something? Refreshment of some kind? An aperitif, anything like that?

  8. Ruth: No thanks.

  9A. Lenny: I'm glad you said that. We haven't got a drink in the house. Mind you, I'd soon get some in, if we had a party or something like that. Some kind of celebration . . . you know. (*Pause.*)

  9B. You must be connected with my brother in some way. The one who's been abroad.

  10. Ruth: I'm his wife.

  11A. Lenny: Eh, listen, I wonder if you can advise me. I've been having a bit of a rough time with this clock. The tick's been keeping up. The trouble is I'm not all that convinced it was the clock. I mean there are lots of things which tick in the night, don't you find that? All sorts of objects, which, in the day, you wouldn't call anything else but commonplace. They give you no trouble. But in the night any given one of a number of them is liable to start letting out a bit of a tick. Whereas you look at these objects in the day and they're just commonplace. They're as quiet as mice during the daytime. So . . . all things being equal . . . this question of me saying it was the clock that woke me up, well, that could very easily prove something of a false hypothesis. (*He goes to the sideboard, pours from a jug into a glass, takes the glass to Ruth.*)

  11B. Here you are. I bet you could do with this.

  12. Ruth: What is it?

13A. Lenny: Water. (*She takes it, sips, places the glass on a small table by her chair. Lenny watches her.*)

13B. Isn't it funny? I've got my pyjamas on and you're fully dressed? (*He goes to the sideboard and pours another glass of water.*)

13C. Mind if I have one? Yes, it's funny seeing my old brother again after all these years. It's just the sort of tonic my Dad needs, you know. He'll be chuffed to his bollocks in the morning, when he sees his eldest son. I was surprised myself when I saw Teddy, you know. Old Ted. I thought he was in America.

14. Ruth: We're on a visit to Europe.

15. Lenny: What, both of you?

16. Ruth: Yes.

17. Lenny: What, you sort of live with him over there, do you?

18. Ruth: We're married.

19. Lenny: On a visit to Europe, eh? Seen much of it?

20. Ruth: We've just come from Italy.

21. Lenny: Oh, you went to Italy first, did you? And then he brought you over here to meet the family, did he? Well, the old man'll be pleased to see you, I can tell you.

22. Ruth: Good.

23. Lenny: What did you say?

24. Ruth: Good (*Pause.*)

25. Lenny: Where'd you go to in Italy?

26. Ruth: Venice.

27. Lenny: Not dear old Venice? Eh? That's funny. You know, I've always had a feeling that if I'd been a soldier in the last war—say in the Italian campaign—I'd probably have found myself in Venice. I've always had that feeling. The trouble was I was too young to serve, you see. I was only a child, I was too small, otherwise I've got a pretty shrewd idea I'd probably have gone through Venice. Yes, I'd almost certainly have gone through Venice. Yes, I'd almost certainly have gone through it with my battalion. Do you mind if I hold your hand?

28. Ruth: Why?

29A. Lenny: Just a touch. (*He stands and goes to her.*)

29B. Just a tickle.

30. Ruth: Why?

30A. Lenny: (*He looks down at her.*) I'll tell you why. (*Slight pause.*)

30B. One night, not too long ago, one night down by the docks, I was standing alone under an arch, watching all the men jibbing the boom, out in the harbour, and playing about with the yardarm, when a certain lady came up to me and made me a certain proposal. This lady had been searching for me for days. She'd lost track of my whereabouts. However, the fact was she eventually caught up with me, and when she caught up with me she made me this certain proposal. Well, this proposal wasn't entirely out of order and normally I would have subscribed to it. I mean I would have subscribed to it in the normal course of events. The only trouble was she was falling apart with the pox. So I turned it down. Well, this lady was very insistent and started taking liberties with me down under this arch, liberties which by any criterion I couldn't be expected to tolerate, the facts being what they were, so I clumped her one. It was on my mind at the time to do away with her, you know, to kill her, and the fact is, that as killings go, it would have been a simple matter, nothing to it. Her chauffeur, who had located me for her, he'd popped round the corner to have a drink, which just left this lady and myself, you see, alone, standing underneath this arch, watching all the steamers steaming up, no one about, all quiet on the Western Front, and there she was up against this wall—well, just sliding down the wall, following the blow I'd given her. Well, to sum up, everything was in my favour, for a killing. Don't worry about the chauffeur. The chauffeur would never have spoken. He was an old friend of the family. But . . . in the end I thought . . . Aaah, why go to all the bother . . . you know, getting rid of the corpse and all that, getting yourself into a state of tension. So I just gave her another belt in the nose and a couple of turns of the boot and sort of left it at that.

31. Ruth: How did you know she was diseased?
32A. Lenny: How did I know? (*Pause.*)
32B. I decided she was. (*Silence.*)
32C. You and my brother are newly-weds, are you? [Pinter 1965, pp. 27–31]

Lenny's first remark is already "wrong," because it's too short. Either he should go on, "I understand you're my brother's wife. I'm glad to meet you," or, if he wishes to pretend he doesn't know who she is, he might continue, "May I ask what you are doing in my house in the middle of the night?" His speaking first is correct, because it establishes that, even though the house is his territory, he will welcome her verbally into it. But he is, like most Pinter characters, trying to say or reveal as little as possible. One of the unwritten rules of Pinter dialogue is that any known yet undivulged information is like an ace in the hand. Thus his first remark is already somewhat ambiguous. Instead of offering a reply that will explain her presence, Ruth counters with, "Morning, I think," establishing early her willingness to contradict her unknown host, to stand up for what she sees as correct, even in a small matter with which most people would not have bothered. But Ruth, having lived with Teddy for six years, knows the rules of the game. She must fight back immediately, to demonstrate that she will fight and expects to conquer this territory.

Lenny's agreeable reply, "You're right there," preserves the civilized façade he intends to convey; his pause is his counterthrust. He is waiting for her to become nervous, perhaps to feel a need to explain her presence. As in an analytic hour, pauses in Pinter serve many purposes. Here, the audience, having heard Lenny's nasty earlier conversations with his father, uncle, and brother, may also be wondering just how he will greet Ruth. Thus the audience is tense with concern at the potential battle between these two characters.

Ruth does not feel a need to explain her presence. We will learn during the play that she never gets nervous at other people's silences, or says more than she has intended to. (This moment can be contrasted, for example, with the dialogue between Lenny and Teddy preceding this one. Here Lenny waits for Teddy to speak first, although Lenny has walked into the room where Teddy has been standing, and the ordinary rules of courtesy would dictate that the visitor be greeted. Moreover, Lenny asks nothing about Teddy's previous whereabouts and the like, and whenever he allows the conversation to lapse, it is Teddy who gets nervous enough to speak next. Thus it is Teddy who is the first to ask "How are you?" Teddy who volunteers, "I've . . . just come back for a few days," without having been asked, Teddy who says, "I've been keeping well," again without having been asked.) As Ruth outwaits Lenny, he continues, starting in line 3B, offering his name, meaningless small talk about the weather, an "aperitif," so she will hear his precise and elegant diction. Upon her refusal, he undercuts the offer, letting her know that it was no more real than the other courtesies he's proffered. "Some kind of celebration" in line 9A, followed by a pause, again gives her a chance to initiate a new subject, to offer an explanation of her presence, such as, "As a matter of fact, you might look at this visit as sufficient cause—you see, I'm your brother's wife." Again Ruth refuses the gambit. Lenny yields almost enough to phrase a question, and gets the answer in line 10. But now, instead of responding to the information (because a response would indicate that she has something over him, i.e., the ability to command a response), he goes off on something superficially unrelated to her remark, a torrent of language about "things which tick in the night" and "give you . . . . trouble." These are likely to be sexual "things," related, especially in the case of a periodic object, to women. The encoded message, which is related to Lenny's underlying views toward women and the adaptive context of Ruth's arrival in the household, might well be, "So the old boy married, did he? And are you giving him trouble, just as my thoughts about women give me trouble?" This flood of language, with its reliance on logical jargon—"all things being equal . . . . that could very easily prove something of a false hypothesis"—is intended as a smoke-screen, because there is a great deal of emotion connected with the subject for Lenny.

His giving Ruth water seems a bit odd. After all, we might expect something a little more fancy. Water, however, is a basic need. When Ruth later drains the glass and says, "Oh, I was thirsty" (p. 35), it is as if she has played a good joke on Lenny, getting something she wanted and needed from him when he thought he was giving her nothing of value. In the film version the clear glass of water is focused on repeatedly. It becomes symbolic of the dialogue, which is simultaneously very easy to understand, i.e., transparent, and yet difficult to fathom as to its meaning, i.e., as lacking in information as water is lacking in features.

Line 13B articulates a basic motif in the play: if Ruth is dressed while Lenny is in pajamas, she must be his mother. We will see this theme reappear later in this scene. Line 13C plays with linguistic styles: "Mind if I have one?" and "chuffed to his bollocks" are equally funny in their inappropriateness.

Lines 18 and 19 repeat the action of lines 10 and 11: Lenny again refuses to react to being told that Ruth is Teddy's wife. Ruth, by being composed enough to repeat the information without getting angry, is being characterized further. She is a Type C communicator at this point, like her husband, and not easily provoked. (Her first offensive move, as we will see, occurs in line 51. Rather than merely rebuffing Lenny, she initiates a new line of thought and action there.)

Lenny's line 27 is an interesting one. Again it demonstrates the image he wants to project—debonair and somehow above it all. Here we see him weaving a conscious fantasy about having been in Venice, a fantasy that Ruth will echo later when her alliance has shifted from Teddy to Lenny. "Do you mind if I hold your hand?" is a more direct attack. When it fails to disturb Ruth's calm demeanor, he suddenly assaults her much more strongly, in line 30B. This long story reveals his sadism, contempt for women, and obsession with sex no less for being an invention. Ruth's response is, significantly, not to the horror or inappropriateness of the story. "How did you know she was diseased?" punctures his story by focusing on his logical powers: here is a fact he could not possibly have known. Thus she challenges him, showing that he has not frightened her, and frustrates his attempt to bully her with a projective fantasy (what Langs terms a Type B communication) by not responding, and thus not "accepting" the surface meaning of his communication. (She will use a similar device for deflating Max's boasting after he has drawn an idyllic picture of his past life with Jessie, when he promised to buy her "a dress in pale corded blue silk, heavily encrusted in pearls and for casual wear, a pair of pantaloons in lilac flowered taffeta" after he had planned to "negotiat[e] with a top-class group of butchers with continental connections . . . . going into association with them" (p. 46). Ruth then asks, "What happened to the group of butchers?" Max replies, "The group? They turned out to be a bunch of criminals like everyone else" (p. 47), and abruptly changes the subject. Again we see that the more elaborate the diction, the less likely the memory.)

Lenny's reply to Ruth's question, "I decided she was," acknowledges that the story was something he "decided" on, thus demonstrating the insignificance of objective facts in fantasy life. It is unimportant not only whether the woman was diseased, but also whether she was his mother, as elements in the story imply (e.g., we know that Sam, the chauffeur, used to drive Jessie around). It is even unimportant that the obviously Freudian incident did not actually occur, because it is a product, rather, of Lenny's interior life: his fear of women with their sexuality and their power to infect him with their "diseases." Lenny's purpose in telling Ruth the story is to frighten, not to inform her. This response to the adaptive context of greeting a sister-in-law allows Lenny to vent his feelings. Only then can Lenny finally acknowledge, in line 32C, that he has heard that Ruth is Teddy's wife.

The subject of Lenny's disturbance at his mother's sexuality, the subject of the anecdote in this dialogue, is reinforced in his second long story, this one about "an old lady" who makes him feel emasculated by asking him to move a "mangle" for her from her front room into her back room. Lenny's inability to lift the mangle puts him in "a good mind to give her a workover there and then," but he contents himself with a "short-arm jab to the belly and jump[s] on a bus outside" (p. 33). These two anecdotes reveal the threat from woman as both sexual object and mother.

As we might expect from a Type B communicator (one who projects and acts out on the basis of his feelings rather than trying to communicate them to the therapist), Lenny acts to deprive Ruth of the comforts usually provided for a guest. After the second long story, he goes on without a pause to ask, "Excuse me, shall I take this ashtray out of your way?" Despite Ruth's assurance that it is not in her way, he removes it. The dialogue continues:

40B. Lenny: And now perhaps I'll relieve you of your glass.
 41. Ruth: I haven't quite finished.

42. Lenny: You've consumed quite enough, in my opinion.
43. Ruth: No, I haven't.
44. Lenny: Quite sufficient, in my opinion.
45. Ruth: Not in mine, Leonard. (*Pause.*)
46. Lenny: Don't call me that, please.
47. Ruth: Why not?
48A. Lenny: That's the name my mother gave me. (*Pause.*)
48B. Just give me the glass.
49. Ruth: No. (*Pause.*)
50. Lenny: I'll take it, then.
51. Ruth: If you take the glass . . . I'll take you. (*Pause.*)
52. Lenny: How about me taking the glass without you taking me?
53. Ruth: Why don't I just take you? (*Pause.*)
54A. Lenny: You're joking. (*Pause.*)
54B. You're in love, anyway, with another man. You've had a secret liaison with another man. His family didn't even know. Then you come here without a word of warning and start to make trouble.
55A. Ruth: (*She picks up the glass and lifts it towards him.*) Have a sip. Go on. Have a sip from my glass. (*He is still.*)
55B. Sit on my lap. Take a long cool sip. (*She pats her lap. Pause. She stands, moves to him with the glass.*)
55C. Put your head back and open your mouth.
56. Lenny: Take that glass away from me.
57. Ruth: Lie on the floor. Go on. I'll pour it down your throat.
58. Lenny: What are you doing, making me some kind of proposal?
59. Ruth: (*She laughs shortly, drains the glass.*) Oh, I was thirsty. (*She smiles at him, puts the glass down, goes into the hall and up the stairs.*)
60. Lenny: (*He follows into the hall and shouts up the stairs.*) What was that supposed to be? Some kind of proposal? (*Silence. He comes back into the room, goes to his own glass, drains it.*) [Pinter 1965, pp. 33–35]

Again, these are derivative communications. Far from being frightened by Lenny's stories of aggression against sexual and threatening women, it seems that Ruth is already, so to speak, feeling at home with Lenny's communicative style. According to Paul Rogers (1971), who played Max in the original production:

She's come home. She knows this area, these people, this behavior—this attitude, to a lesser and greater degree of cruelty, is something which is very much of the Cockney mind. It isn't a strange dramatic form that Pinter elected to use, it is firmly based in reality. . . . In that scene between her and Lenny . . . whenever she does speak she cuts everything straight through. . . . All that stuff he comes out with to try and shock her isn't going to shock her at all. (pp. 162, 165)

Ruth immediately displays her expertise at the Londoners' "game"; Rogers observes that the family "are interdependent not for the ordinary things of life, just for the game they play which is their life. They can't survive without it" (p. 164). Ruth's replies to Lenny indicate that she understands that his aggressive anecdotes are sheer bravado, intended to obscure his complex ambivalent feelings toward women. So her threat to "take" Lenny if he takes her glass is directly responsive to her correct reading of his communication. She has indicated that she is to be a player in the Type B communicative style of the family. She accepts the sexual gambit, even as her reduction of Lenny from sexual mate to victim to child (as she invites him to sit on her lap) and then to baby (as she tells him to lie on the floor) communicates her understanding of his impotence. Were she to pour water down his throat, she literally would choke him. So this dialogue has established her as the winner in this contest. Moreover, the open quality of her sexuality is already strongly indicated in her line, "Go on. Have a sip from my glass." Her repetitions of this threat (lines 55B, 55C, and 57) show that she has succeeded in reprojecting the inner turmoil of the sexual mother. Lenny's weak repetition (lines 58 and 60) and his references to his mother (lines 46 and 48A) show why she is "getting [him] into a state of tension."

(Again, the use of pauses is subtle and interesting. Note that after Lenny's pauses, he must resume speaking, because Ruth never jumps in to fill a silence. The only time she continues after one of her pauses is when she is using a series of threats, building them up from statement to statement.)

After Ruth leaves, Lenny has a most distasteful conversation with Max, asking his father "about the true facts of that particular night—the night [he was] made in the image of those two people *at it*" (p. 36; italics in original). Again, there is an implied challenge to his father. Was Max even there? Later, Sam will blurt out, "MacGregor had Jessie in the back of my cab as I drove them along" (p. 78). Although Max's only comment is that Sam has "a diseased imagination" (p. 79), it is difficult not to believe this assertion, toward which Sam has been building throughout the play.[3] There are a number of strong hints that this family of men is largely impotent (see p. 388, this chapter). Perhaps Lenny is not Max's son. Certainly the tone of contempt in which Lenny habitually addresses Max may well have an origin in Lenny's assumptions about the events of "that night." Lenny's thought association from Ruth's presence to the two women in the anecdotes to his parents having sex is sufficiently clear, although more indirect than would have been the case with a writer before Pinter's time. Lenny's fury at women,

---

[3]Sam has said that he does not mess up his car "like other people." He has also implied that Teddy is MacGregor's son (Pinter 1965, pp. 62–63). Max's question to Teddy after learning that Ruth has three sons—"All yours, Ted?"—further raises the possibility that things have been different in his generation.

his fear of them and desire to control them, are expressed perfectly in his choice of profession. So shaken has Lenny been by meeting a woman who is his equal that he remains silent for the next fifteen minutes of the play, as if he is trying to determine how to get back into the family game on the winner's side. He resumes talking only to tease Teddy on the subject of philosophy, asking him, "What do you make of all this business of being and not-being?"

At that point there is a most interesting development, one that is very surprising to those who have not had the benefit of the kind of dialogue analysis in which we have been engaged. Although we have quoted Pinter on people's desire "to keep ourselves to ourselves," he has also said, "I'm not suggesting that no character in a play can never say what he in fact means. Not at all. I have found that there invariably does come a moment when this happens, where he says something, perhaps, which he has never said before. And where this happens, what he says is irrevocable, and can never be taken back."[4] Now one of those marvelous moments of revelation occurs. Tired, perhaps, of the kind of meaningless intellectual persiflage common in Teddy's Type C world that Lenny's teasing has introduced, Ruth deflects the after-dinner conversation from the metaphysical to the physical level by her general observation addressed to the assembled family:

> Don't be too sure though. You've forgotten something. Look at me. I . . . move my leg. That's all it is. But I wear . . . underwear . . . which moves with me . . . it . . . captures your attention. Perhaps you misinterpret. The action is simple. It's a leg . . . moving. My lips move. Why don't you restrict . . . your observations to that? Perhaps the fact that they move is more significant than the words which come through them. You must bear that . . . possibility . . . in mind. (pp. 52–53)[5]

Here Ruth suddenly says what is on her mind. She allies herself definitively with the Londoners, who, although they obviously are flawed human beings, at least contact one another through the "game." It is now that Teddy tries to get Ruth to agree to leave, aware that he is losing her.

---

[4]Pinter, speech reported in the Sunday *Times* (London), as quoted by John Lahr in his Introduction to *A Casebook on Harold Pinter's The Homecoming* (1971, p. xi). This Introduction, and Lahr's essay in this volume on "Pinter's Language," are very fine.

[5]Analysts as interested in the creative process as I am may be fascinated to learn that Pinter says, "My characters tell me so much and no more, with reference to their experience, their aspirations, their motives, their history. Between my lack of bio-graphical data about them and the ambiguity of what they say there lies a territory which is not only worthy of exploration but which it is compulsory to explore." (In Lahr 1971, p. xi.)

Whereas in their first scene she had suggested that they leave before she'd even met the family, she now resists the idea. Teddy tries to appeal to her:

> You can help me with my lectures when we get back. I'd love that. I'd be so grateful for it, really. We can bathe till October. You know that. Here, there's nowhere to bathe, except the swimming bath down the road. You know what it's like? It's like a urinal. A filthy urinal! (*Pause.*) You liked Venice, didn't you? It was lovely, wasn't it? You had a good week. I mean . . . I took you there. I can speak Italian. (p. 55)

Again, this speech is a beautiful illustration of Pinter's understanding of the ways in which people use language. Teddy gives Ruth five reasons why she should prefer living with him to staying in London: she could help him with his lectures (i.e., engage in a high-status activity), earn his "love" and gratitude, bathe till October, and perhaps (it is implied) look forward to other trips like the one she enjoyed to Venice; and he can speak Italian. Three of the five reasons refer to Teddy's high status and are therefore amusing in their lack of insight: doesn't Teddy know he has offered no inducement to a woman like Ruth? What of value has he offered her? Bathing till October? How important is that? He points out that "Here . . . it's like a urinal." She has already caught him on that point earlier, when he has said that America is cleaner and she asks, "Is it dirty here?" to which he must reply, "No, of course not. But it's cleaner there." But the kind of aseptic cleanliness Teddy has to give Ruth is certainly not what she wants or needs. Teddy's pitifully weak arguments are made more so by the sentence structure, with its primitive declarative sentences, its resort to invective, its repetitions, its running down into the weakest reason of all: "I can speak Italian." Ruth's reply now identifies her with Lenny, whose fantasy she takes on: "But if I'd been a nurse in the Italian campaign I would have been there before." It does not surprise us that Teddy does not respond to this remark. He has appealed to her to the limits of his ability by saying "please" and stating that he would be grateful for her help. Now he merely repeats, "You just rest. I'll go and pack" (p. 55).

But Lenny has also understood that he and Ruth are natural allies. Immediately after Teddy's departure to pack, Lenny returns, and he and Ruth have a second chat alone. Now she reveals that she "was a model for the body. A photographic model for the body." In contrast to America, which she had described as being "all rock. And sand. It stretches . . . so far . . . everywhere you look. And there's lots of insects there" (p. 53), she describes her modeling work in England as having been done near a big house with a lake where they drank and had a "cold buffet" before modeling. To a literary critic, the equation of America with sterility and of her former

English life with fecundity and need satisfaction is as obvious as it is to Lenny. He asks her to dance, kisses her, and the transformation is all but complete.

At that moment, Joey and Max return. Joey has the next line: "Christ, she's wide open. Dad, look at that. (*Pause.*) She's a tart" (p. 59). The ensuing scene is very funny: Max makes heavy puns about Teddy's having married a woman "beneath" him while Ruth is literally lying beneath Joey. When she pushes him off, it is to resume speaking in an entirely new, imperative tone:

Ruth: I'd like something to eat. (*To Lenny.*) I'd like a drink. Did you get any drink?
Lenny: We've got drink.
Ruth: I'd like one, please.
Lenny: What drink?
Ruth: Whisky.
Lenny: I've got it. (*Pause.*)
Ruth: Well, get it. . . .
Lenny: Soda on the side?
Ruth: What's this glass? I can't drink out of this. Haven't you got a tumbler?
Lenny: Yes.
Ruth: Well, put it in the tumbler.
Lenny: (*He takes the glass back, pours whisky into a tumbler, brings it to her.*) On the rocks? Or as it comes? [The implied sexual puns continue.]
Ruth: Rocks? What do you know about rocks?
Lenny: We've got rocks. But they're frozen stiff in the fridge. (*Ruth drinks. Lenny looks round at the others.*) Drinks all round? [pp. 60–61]

This speech too has wider echoes, for by play's end Ruth will have agreed both to staying in the household as Jessie's replacement and to being put "on the game" by Lenny, thus providing drinks "all round" (with some exceptions: Teddy is sent alone to America, and at play's end Max, apparently unsuccessfully, is pleading for a kiss).

The next line is Joey's. Ruth had said she wanted something to eat, and although the other men are too fascinated by what has just happened to think about this request, Joey, the youngest and least corrupt of the bunch, has not lost sight of it. He moves closer to Ruth and asks, "What food do you want?" The implied equation is that if Ruth is to serve the men sexually, she will be served herself, in other ways.

But Ruth, too, is now thinking about other things. Teddy has not said a word since Lenny and Ruth began dancing. Perhaps now to get some sort of reaction from him, any sort at all, or perhaps to ridicule him by referring to the nonsensical stuff he considers so important, Ruth says to Teddy, "Have your family read your critical works?" His reply is the speech discussed earlier in this chapter (p. 375).

Is Ruth a credible human character? Earlier it was pointed out that the credence we give to fictional characters is conditional: we accept them as true to life to the extent that their behavior seems credible to us according to our understanding of human behavior in the "real" world. Pinter gives no background information about Ruth aside from what we have quoted here. Can we say that her character, as portrayed, is merely an exaggerated, simplified version of "realistic" tendencies?

On one hand, her complete lack of interest in her children, her alternations among threatening, mothering, and servicing the men, her intermittent dreamlike compliance with their wishes as well as with their distorted view of her all contribute to a sense that she is much less a realized character from within than a projection outward of the fantasies of Pinter's male characters. Thus, whereas Max calls her "a smelly scrubber" (p. 41; translation: a tart) on first meeting her, he now puns unconsciously, telling her she "could do a bit of cooking here if you wanted to. . . . scrub the place out a bit" (p. 78).

There is other evidence that the play is more concerned with exploring the male characters' relationships to Ruth as a central "earth-mother" figure than with portraying Ruth as an individual. What we see in each of the men is an aspect of the male–female relationship writ large. If Max is the primal father, he is certainly a failure in that role. Instead, he's a partial figure, feminized by his being the family cook; by the implications about Jessie's sexual intimacies with "others," such as his friend Mac; and by his own boasts of his femininity (such as his boast "I gave birth to three grown men! All on my own bat" [p. 40], which have not been quoted because the focus has been on other matters. Lenny's profession, Teddy's coldness, Joey's infantile response to Ruth as mother are all partial, unsuccessful responses to Ruth's open sexuality.

On the other hand, Ruth's behavior may be seen as "realistically" responsive to life with Teddy. She has acquired his style as a Type C communicator, breaking her silence only at a moment of despair, making her almost direct appeal for the family's sexual interest as a last-ditch effort to change her life, now characterized by "rocks" and "insects." Her description of America is also evocative of the Type C communicative field; there are innumerable views of America that Ruth could have chosen to discuss, but she focuses on the images that will communicate most directly her feelings about the sterility of her marriage. (During her second conversation with Lenny, she also says, "That's [i.e., "renewing one's wardrobe"] a good thing to do," and remarks that she can't get "the ones [the kinds of shoes] I want over there" [p. 56].) Langs, too, insists that the patient will choose to describe his or her experiences outside the therapeutic situation in ways much more closely linked to the therapeutic situation itself than to the events, objectively viewed, of the patient's normal life experiences.

Thus we see Pinter's use of metaphor as psychologically very apt. Speech in Pinter does even more than serve as a vehicle for carrying the underlying meaning. Even the male characters' embellishment of their tall tales by a jargon either of advertising ("a dress in pale corded blue silk, heavily encrusted in pearls") or Freudian punning ("I was standing alone under an arch, watching all the men jibbing the boom . . . . and playing about with the yardarm") tells us something about their fantasies: Max's idea of himself as a bourgeois entrepreneur "dolling up" his little woman, Lenny's obsessions with sexual images and ideas. These puns do more than deliver encoded messages. The character's choice of cliché, choice of vocabulary, give us clues as to the probable degree of truth in the assertions. For example, when Lenny says, "He's always been my favorite brother, old Teddy. Do you know that? And my goodness we are proud of him here. I can tell you. Doctor of Philosophy and all that" (p. 31), a literary critic would focus on his choice of words. The empty fillers—"do you know that?" "I can tell you" and "and all that"—show the hollowness of the expressed idea. The banal sentimentality of "old Teddy," the use of "my goodness" as a mild oath (as if Lenny were a Victorian old maid), reveal that he is lying. In one of the passages quoted previously (p. 388), a literary critic would be interested in the ugly imperative style and impoverished vocabulary of the section from "Did you get any drink?" to "Well, get it." We may assume that Lenny's description of the family "rocks" as "frozen stiff in the fridge" depicts the state of the men's sexual anatomy with precision. But the critic would look at the words used. "On the rocks" is apparently an Americanism, because Ruth asks, "What do you know about rocks?" "Quite a bit," Lenny could reply, though not at this point unless he wants to tip his hand.

There are whole areas of word play we have not considered. When Ruth agrees to whore for the family, a long parody of business language, including contracts, business cards, and international terms, ensues. Her professional name is discussed. Max suggests "Spanish Jacky," only to be corrected by Lenny: "No, you've got to be reserved about it, Dad " (p. 74).

Even the physical sounds of words are carefully manipulated by Pinter. When the actor playing Lenny barks out the question asking about the "true facts about that particular night [with] those two people at it," the hammering *t*'s, *p*'s, *f*'s, and *ct*'s create a miniature but very effective explosion.

Ruth, however, aside from her key speech quoted on p. 386, reveals almost nothing of her thoughts, leaving her motives and fantasies subject to various interpretations. Therefore, it is difficult to tell at the play's end just who is using whom. The men seem to believe that they are using Ruth. But just then Max begins to worry, saying, "Listen, I've got a funny idea she'll do the dirty on us, you want to bet? She'll use us, she'll make use of us, I can tell you! I can smell it! You want to bet? (*Pause*) She won't be . . . adaptable!" (p. 81).

Ruth's only answer here is silence. What we have discussed in this chapter is a typically Pinteresque situation. As Austin Quigley (1975) has observed, "In the Pinter world [the battle for dominance] is grounded in the power available in language to promote the responses that the speaker requires and hence the relationship that is desired. . . . Language is not so much a means of referring to structure in personal relationships as a means of creating it" (p. 52).

But beneath all the language lurks the experience to which the language refers. The play's final tableau shows Ruth sitting in Max's chair, with Joey's head in her lap. She strokes his head lightly while Lenny stands behind them and Max, on his knees, implores a kiss. Ruth's enigmatic silence holds all the ambiguities of the complex familial relationships portrayed in the play.

SUMMARY

Through the use of selected passages and quotations from the contemporary British playwright Harold Pinter, this chapter has shown how his *Homecoming* utilizes character development, individual linguistic style, and communicative techniques consonant with Robert Langs's views of the interactional process. Dialogue in the play is shown to be analogous to the therapist–patient dialogue, with the precipitating dramatic event—bringing the bride home to meet the family—being analogous to the adaptive context. Teddy is shown to be a typical Type C character and Lenny a Type B character; Ruth's character, on the surface Type C, is seen to be more readily open to differing interpretations. This chapter describes for the therapeutic community a playwright skilled in portraying the linguistic sparring tricks involved in the fascinating "games" that his characters—and people—play.

REFERENCES

BROWN, J. R. (1963). Mr. Pinter's Shakespeare. *Critical Quarterly* 5:251.

BURKMAN, K. (1971). *The Dramatic World of Harold Pinter: Its Basis in Ritual.* Columbus, Ohio: Ohio State University Press.

CAMUS, A. (1942). *Le Mythe de Sisyphe.* As quoted in *The Theatre of the Absurd*, rev. ed., ed. M. Esslin, p. 5. New York: Doubleday, 1969.

JIJI, V. (1974). Pinter's four-dimensional house: *The Homecoming. Modern Drama* 17:433–442.

LANGS, R. (1978). *The Listening Process.* New York: Jason Aronson.

LAHR, J. (1971). Introduction. In *A Casebook on Harold Pinter's* The Homecoming, ed. J. Lahr, p. xi. New York: Grove Press.

PINTER, H. (1964). Writing for the theatre. In *The New British Drama*, ed. Henry Popkin, pp. 576–579. New York: Grove Press. As quoted in J. R. Hollis, *Harold Pinter: The Poetics of Silence.* Carbondale: Southern Illinois University Press, 1970.

PINTER, H. (1965). *The Homecoming.* New York: Grove Press.

PINTER, H. (1967). Harold Pinter. In *Writers at Work, Third Series*, ed. G. Plimpton, pp. 362–363. New York: Viking Press.

QUIGLEY, A. (1975). *The Pinter Problem.* Princeton, N.J.: Princeton University Press.

ROGERS, P. (1971). An actor's approach. In *A Casebook on Harold Pinter's* The Homecoming, ed. John Lahr, pp. 151–174. New York: Grove Press.

WALKER, A. (1971). Why the lady does it. In *A Casebook on Harold Pinter's* The Homecoming, ed. John Lahr, pp. 117–122. New York: Grove Press.

Part IV

The Langsian Approach in Relation to Others

CHAPTER 18

Robert Langs on Technique: A Critique

Merton M. Gill, M.D.

Beginning with his *Technique of Psychoanalytic Psychotherapy* in 1973, Robert Langs has produced a rich, voluminous, complex, tightly organized system prescribing and defining the technique of psychoanalysis and psychoanalytic psychotherapy. Langs sees his system as psychoanalytic but as a significant improvement over prevailing practice, which he labels *classical analysis*. I will follow Langs's usage, but I believe it is important to make clear my agreement with Lipton (1977a), who has argued that prevailing practice departs significantly from Freud's practice. The latter would seem to be more appropriately called "classical." Although in large part I agree with Langs's main ideas, I also have some serious disagreements with him. I believe the disagreements are a reflection of the extent to which Langs remains a captive of classical—and again I mean prevalent, not Freud's—psychoanalysis. I present my agreements first and then my disagreements. My presentations of my agreements will give a somewhat misleading impression, because they are couched in Langs's terms, whereas a discussion of the central difference in my view from his requires a recasting of his terms. I believe my exposition will be understood more easily if this recasting is delayed until I express my disagreements. I assume some reader familiarity with Langs's writings and therefore do not always explain his idiosyncratic terms. They have become sufficiently numerous and specialized that he appends a glossary to his books.

AGREEMENTS

Langs's major difference from classical psychoanalysis—and in this major respect from Freud's, too—is his insistence that the psychoanalytic situation constitutes a bipersonal field in which the inputs from both participants are a complex compound of appropriate and inappropriate elements, one hopes with a greater preponderance of appropriate over inappropriate on the analyst's part than on the patient's. The classical analyst, to the contrary, sees the input of the therapist as primarily appropriate, with occasional regrettable lapses resulting from a countertransference, whereas the input from the patient is often a neurotic distortion of the real situation, as defined by the analyst. Langs defines the bipersonal field as a metaphor that "suggests that every point in the field—every communication, interaction, structure, and occurrence within and between the two members of the dyad—receives vectors from both participants, albeit in varying proportions" (Langs 1978, p. 558). One might characterize Langs's view as a shift in attitude toward a greater egalitarianism in assessing patient and analyst. The analyst is a participant and always, to a greater or lesser degree, participates pathologically. One might also say Langs is adopting the Sullivanian attitude: the analyst is a participant observer, and we are all much more simply human than otherwise.

Not only is the analytic situation a bipersonal field with appropriate and inappropriate inputs from both participants, but inappropriate inputs, in varying proportions with appropriate inputs, are ubiquitous. One must therefore say that transference and countertransference are continuous rather than occasional, the latter being the classical position.

These transferences and countertransferences are expressed primarily in disguised and allusive form in the patient's associations and the analyst's interventions. These disguised associations and interventions are derivatives of the transferences and countertransferences to which they allude.[1] Because transferences and countertransferences are regarded as occasional in the classical view, the classical analyst fails to give adequate attention to the fact that the associations and interventions are derivatives of such transferences and countertransferences.

Not only because the field is a bipersonal one but also because of the purpose for which it has been established, it is around the relationship between analyst and patient that the associations and interventions are in fact primarily organized. It is this relationship, therefore, that should be the focus of the analyst's interpretations. The analysis of the transference in the here and now should be the primary focus of work in the therapy. In contrast, the classical view, in practice if not in theory, places at least equal emphasis on extratransference interpretation, both contemporary and genetic, whether intrapsychic or interactional.

The analyst's interventions are hypotheses whose correctness or incorrectness can be determined only in terms of the patient's ensuing associations.

---

[1]There is a minor, although sometimes confusing, condensation in Langs's use of the concept *derivative*. The term sometimes refers to the associations and sometimes to the psychic contents to which the associations allegedly allude, that is, to the inferences drawn from the associations. This condensation perhaps points to a failure to distinguish sharply enough in practice, although not in theory, between inferences and their validation, as I will discuss later.

Although at first this may seem a tenet of classical analysis, the difference of Langs's view is his belief that conscious associations bearing on an intervention have little validating relevance to that intervention, and his almost exclusive emphasis on validation by encoded derivatives, as already defined. I believe that although derivatives deserve more attention than they usually receive, conscious associations, as I will amplify later, are important as well.

Desirable change in the patient results not only from insight but also from the experience of a good relationship with the therapist. The classical point of view, with some notable and increasing exceptions, places much less emphasis on the experience of the relationship as a mutative factor, indeed often to the extent of considering change in which the experience plays any significant role as evidence of unresolved transference and, therefore, of the "psychotherapeutic" rather than "psychoanalytic" nature of the process. Langs also holds that the evidence of the beneficent experience is to be found primarily, at least at first, in associations that are derivatives, that is, that in their manifest content refer to a good experience with someone other than the therapist.

In most instances the essentials of the therapeutic process should be the same, regardless of the nature of the disorder, the frequency with which the patient is seen, whether the patient is seen vis-à-vis or lying down, and the experience of the therapist. The essentials should be psychoanalytic, as defined by the principles we have stated. The classical point of view is of course sharply divergent, specifying only analyzable patients, a frequency of at least four times a week, the lying-down position, and a therapist who has been trained in psychoanalysis. Langs's view—with which I agree—is often mistakenly considered an assertion that there is no difference between psychotherapy and psychoanalysis. Rather, it asserts that the range of applicability of psychoanalysis is far wider than generally believed. I hold that the term *psychotherapy* should be reserved for the application of the principles we have described in only truncated, partial ways. It is my belief in the wide applicability of analytic technique that results in my using the terms *analyst* and *therapist* and *analysis* and *therapy* interchangeably in this chapter.

DISAGREEMENTS

The Nature of Interpersonal Reality

In what may at first seem like a rather abstract formulation of a central difference between Langs's view and mine, I suggest that this difference can be described as a divergence in the perception of the nature of an interpersonal reality. I say "interpersonal reality" because I want to avoid, if I can, some of the pitfalls of a philosophical discussion of the nature of reality by confining myself to the reality of how two people relate to each other. I stated earlier that one might characterize Langs's view as a shift in attitude toward a greater egalitarianism in assessing patient and therapist. This change in attitude on Langs's part does not go far enough. The classical analyst is an aristocrat in believing that the analyst is in the privileged position of knowing what the interpersonal reality is, except for those unfortunate lapses into countertransference. Langs believes that at least a modicum of countertransference is always present, but he also believes that by proper attention to his or her own input—which Langs calls the adaptive context—to which the patient reacts, as well as to the derivative nature of the patient's associations, the analyst can distinguish between what is valid and invalid in the patient's reaction, that is, what is a correct perception and what is a distortion of the analyst's input. The true egalitarian takes a perspectival view (Levenson 1972), in which the reality of any particular interpersonal transaction depends on one's point of view. If one takes the point of view into account, the patient's assessment of the transaction may be as plausible as the analyst's, however much they differ.

Do I mean to deny the analyst as expert? No; but analysts must make clear their areas of expertise. They presumably are more aware of how they relate as participants in a therapeutic situation (although not necessarily outside such situations) than the patient is. That is, they are more aware on the whole. In any particular transaction, the analyst may be blind to something the patient can see. And every particular transaction should be approached by the analyst as though it is one of those in which the patient is aware of something of which he or she is not. Even if the analyst is familiar with a range of types of interpersonal transactions and is convinced that the assessment of an interpersonal transaction is indeed not absolute but relative to the subject's point of view, a particular patient may share this familiarity and conviction. The analyst's expertise resides in the fact that, as the therapist rather than the patient, he or she is in an emotional position that permits a degree of distance and objectivity likely to be greater than the patient's—although, as I said, in any particular instance this may not be true.

A series of consequences flows from this central difference between Langs's theories and mine. Langs and I define transference (and countertransference) differently. He sees transference as a distortion, whereas I view it as an experience of the relationship that is at least understandable and perhaps even plausible. He sees countertransference as inappropriate, whereas I say again that it is understandable, if not plausible; just as the patient's experience includes a plausible interpretation of the therapist's behavior, so does the therapist's experience include a plausible interpretation of the patient's behavior. The very stress that Langs places on the continuing projective and introjective identifications on the part of both participants, the degree to which each influences the other actually to behave in ways attributed to him or her by the other, argues for looking at experience as including plausible inferences rather than as being divisible into correct perception and incorrect distortion. Langs's definition of transference is thus different from mine, and transference for me is not the combination of veridical perception and incorrect distortion that for Langs constitutes the totality of the experience of each participant. His conception of the totality implies its divisability into correct and incorrect aspects, whereas mine does not. As Hoffman and I have written (Gill and Hoffman 1982), if there is a distinction to be made in assessing interpersonal attitudes, it is not between correct and incorrect but between attitudes that are rigidly held and unsusceptible to influence and those that are flexible and open to change.

This difference in our views of transference leads Langs to believe (Langs 1980, p. 451) for two reasons that I underestimate the importance of the therapist's contribution to the patient's experience of the relationship. One reason is that Langs sees the patient's point as sometimes a correct reading of the therapist's inappropriate implicit attitudes, whereas I see such an instance as only an understandable or even plausible reading. The second reason is that, because I emphasize more than he that the ultimate purpose of clarifying the therapist's contribution is to clarify the patient's contribution, Langs believes I do not see the "validity" of the patient's experience. Furthermore, because I emphasize that the point of departure for understanding the allusions to the patient's experience of the relationship should be the patient's explicit references to this relationship, Langs (1980, pp. 448–449) believes that I underestimate the expression of the transference in disguised allusive derivatives. I explicitly stated in my discussion of analysis of transference (1979) and my more recent detailed exposition of my views (1982) that, like him, I consider transference to be continuous rather than occasional, and that I believe the analyst is always making a contribution to the patient's experience of the relationship. Furthermore, I described the analyst's contribution as largely to be inferred from derivatives in the patient's associations and as that to which attention must be paid first in the analysis of transference. Where we differ is that I believe the patient's experience is never simply a distortion or simply a correct perception of the analyst's contribution.

It is our differing views of the nature of interpersonal reality that lead Langs, in assessing concrete instances, to distinguish—as does the classical analyst and as I do not—between neurotic and non-neurotic, transference and nontransference, countertransference and noncountertransference, pathological and nonpathological, resistance and nonresistance, counterresistance and noncounterresistance. I believe he knows something is wrong in this dichotomy, because he speaks of "more or less," of "relative" this or that, of "inevitable admixtures" and other qualifying locutions. But he has not cut the Gordian knot and admitted that such assessment depends on one's point of view. The acceptance of this position changes one's attitude. If one is thoroughly persuaded of the relativity of interpersonal reality, one becomes less interested in deciding just what the reality is and more interested in clarifying just what the patient's view of the reality is and what makes that view plausible to the patient even if quite a different one seems plausible to the analyst. The certainty that he or she is right becomes much more difficult for the analyst to sustain.

Another indication that Langs continues to be a captive of the prevailing classical point of view on interpersonal reality is that he labels a great proportion of the work he discusses in his books, both classical work drawn from the analytic literature and that of his relatively inexperienced supervisees, as betraying the analyst's neurotic input. He usually ascribes the therapist's inappropriate behavior to pathology of considerable severity. I mean not so much that he speaks of unconscious homosexuality, sadism, and the like but that he implies that the analyst should be free of such motivations, even if he hedges by using such expressions as "relatively free." I suggest that this means he continues to subscribe to the ideal of the essentially appropriately behaving analyst. To some extent Langs is able to maintain the illusion that the good analyst will behave essentially appropriately by using the work of relatively inexperienced trainees for his clinical demonstrations. He is not willing to submit his own work for examination, on the grounds that to do so would violate the rule of privacy. The obtuseness of beginners can be so gross as to seem to justify the designation "inappropriate." But it is the very frame of reference—the appropriate–inappropriate continuum—that I am calling into question.

Evidence that Langs is at least peripherally aware that he overstates the analyst's ability to distinguish between transference and nontransference as well as between countertransference and noncountertransference is provided by his concept of inevitable countertransference, which he defines as: "a term which implies not only the inescapability of countertransference expressions in the therapist's work, but also its existence as some small element of every attitude, silence, and intervention. This minimal quota of countertransference is a reflection of the ever-present unresolved, though relatively controlled, psychopathology of the therapist" (Langs 1981, p. 725). A great span of the continuum from appropriate to inappropriate can be covered in that formulation. An effort to specify just how much countertransference is inevitable would be bound to fail.

The difference between my view and Langs's might seem to be merely one of degree, but I believe it is, rather, a crucial difference in concept as well as in attitude. What I emphasize about well-functioning analysts is not that they are less likely to be inappropriate than is the patient, but that they continuously concern themselves with trying to understand the transactions between themselves and the patient by taking their respective and differing points of view into account.

Another indication that Langs does recognize peripherally that the dichotomies between transference and nontransference and countertransference and noncountertransference cannot be sustained is his insistence that the analyst should assume not only that some degree of countertransference is always present and may indeed be the primary determinant of the patient's experience of the relationship, but that it is the first thing to look for in examining the import of the patient's associations. This injunction leads to one of Langs's central technical precepts: an interpretation must always be made in the context of what the patient is responding to in the therapist's interventions, whether verbal or behavioral. He calls this the "adaptive context," that is, "the specific reality that evokes an intrapsychic response" (Langs 1981, p. 719).

There are several additional important consequences that flow from the difference between Langs's views and mine on the nature of interpersonal reality. One is the position he takes on the frame. He is correct in saying that the frame plays an important role in the patient's experience of the relationship. It is also true that the way the analyst manages the frame is of vital importance. But he assumes that for some features, such as absolute confidentiality, there is only one correct frame, and that for other features deviations from the frame, once it is set, are universally and inevitably experienced by the patient as harmful, even though, as he says, the patient's manifest reaction to an alteration of the frame may seem positive. Langs insists that flexibility about changing a patient's hour cannot truly be experienced by a patient as a friendly accommodation rather than as, for example, an inability to bear the patient's reaction to a refusal and thus a betrayal of the analyst's ability to "hold" the patient. Langs assumes that all patients want to be "held" in the same way. To argue for flexibility is not necessarily to overlook that a change in the frame may have great significance to the patient, significance that may well be disguised. But a refusal ever to change the frame may be experienced as uncompromising rigidity. I believe that Langs's overall attitude may be experienced this way by some, if not many, of his patients.

This issue emerged clearly in Langs's extended dialogue with Leo Stone (1980). Stone devoted a good part of his earlier monograph on the psychoanalytic situation (1961) to an attack on the rigidity of an unqualifiedly pure attitude toward the frame, as well as toward abstention from interpersonal interaction, emphasizing how these attitudes could produce an iatrogenic regression.

My most general criticism of Langs's attitude toward the frame relates to his view that a particular external situation necessarily has the same meaning to all patients. He believes that the rigid maintenance of the frame is always reassuring to a patient and that deviations from it are always disturbing. Stone (1961), in contrast, believes that the ordinary analytic setting is always frustrating to a patient. It is my view that they are both mistaken in attributing a universal meaning to the setting. As Langs says, the rigid maintenance of the frame may reassure the patient that he or she is being "held," but it can be frustrating as well. Such rigid maintenance may, for example, mean to the patient that the analyst is afraid of breaking rules, as Stone says, or it may fit into the patient's avoidance of the anxiety aroused by interaction with the analyst by keeping the relationship mechanical and stereotyped. Any particular frame, or deviations from it, will have a particular meaning to a particular patient at a particular time. Its meaning has to be investigated. It cannot be inferred from the external situation.

Langs's attitude toward tape-recording for research purposes illustrates his attitude toward the frame. Whereas in general he shows an admirable insistence on empirical evidence for his positions, he appears to have a prior unshakeable conviction that tape-recording is necessarily incompatible with a good therapeutic relationship. It is true that recording may easily be experienced as exploitation. But my experience is that if the therapeutic situation is otherwise good and if attention is paid to the meaning of the recording, a meaning that may vary as the treatment proceeds, it is possible to record without damage. The point is of special importance, in my opinion, because I believe it is very important to have recordings for research in the therapeutic process.

Langs has recognized that his emphasis on the necessity of maintaining the frame inviolate may be a reaction to the frequency with which, he believes, the frame is altered in the work of many classical analysts without recognition of the important repercussions of such alteration. It is noteworthy that nowhere in his writings does one find an instance of associations that he interprets as derivatives of the patient's experience of excessive rigidity in the therapist's maintenance of the frame. In part this is a result of the fact that the data from inexperienced therapists with which he deals so often involve alterations of the frame, and alterations that occur without examination of their meanings to the patient. But I think the lack of such instances is also based in his firm bias that an alteration is always harmful and is always experienced as such by the patient, even if only unconsciously.

Another illustration of Langs's a priori attribution of a universally appropriate significance to a particular therapist behavior, and thus a further indication of the difference in our views of interpersonal reality, is his discussion of the therapist's silence. He considers silence one of the three appropriate interventions, the other two being maintenance of the frame and interpretations. His view contrasts sharply with Lipton's insistence (1977a), with which I agree, that silence should mean only that the analyst is listening, not that he or she is employing it as an intervention. Again, I believe Langs peripherally is aware of this point, as shown by his recognition that silence may be misused. If silence is considered to be an appropriate intervention rather than simply an accompaniment to listening, the analyst will be less ready to consider the patient's reactions to silence to be understandable responses that need further examination, whether the patient complains or is gratified by the sense of conducting his or her own therapy, for example, and whether the response is explicit or to be inferred from an allusion. The analyst will be less likely to recognize that the silence may be the primary adaptive context. Lipton (1983) has argued that a vignette recently described by Kanzer (1981) shows this very blind spot.

The relationship between Langs's emphasis on the maintenance of the frame and the use of silence as an intervention becomes especially noteworthy in his description of the typical course of therapy in the several types of communicative fields he delineates. Major phases of therapy are described as involving no more on the therapist's part than the maintenance of the frame and silence, while the patient works independently, primarily with Type One derivatives and lie-barrier systems of varying degrees of pathology. In other contexts such lie-barrier systems are vigorously decried (Langs 1981, pp. 549-556, 660-663).

In another illustration of the use of silence as an intervention, Langs argues that it is wrong for the therapist to mention the adaptive context if the patient does not. His reasoning is that the patient's failure to mention it is a manifestation of resistance based on a defense or on an effort at pathological drive gratification, and "these should not be bypassed or gratified by the introduction of the missing element by the therapist" (Langs 1981, p. 627). He does not realize that the silence itself may be experienced as some type of bypass or gratification, or both, because it cannot be meaningless to the patient.

Similarly, Langs argues that any effort by the patient to modify the frame should not be met by any immediate direct reaction, thus, in his view, permitting free association that will reveal in derivative form the meaning of the attempt at frame modification. Langs overlooks the fact that the avoidance of any immediate direct reaction will have its own meaning to the patient, so that the ensuing associations may well refer to the avoidance of a reaction rather than to the meaning of the effort to modify the frame.

Langs's view of silence, like his dichotomies between transference and nontransference, countertransference and noncountertransference, seems to betray his continuing adherence to the classical perspective on the nature of the relation between patient and analyst in the analytic situation. This perspective assumes that one can discern a patient's experience of the relationship free from any contribution by the therapist, in effect a version of the analyst as a blank screen or mirror.

Despite Langs's criticism of prevailing psychoanalytic practice for not maintaining the frame with enough circumspection, his attitude concerning the frame puts him in an important sense squarely in the camp of those espousing the prevailing "classical" view. In effect, he sees the relation between patient and analyst as entirely encompassed by technique. He thus stands in opposition to Lipton (1977a), who criticizes prevailing technique on this very ground and argues that there should also be a personal relation between patient and analyst that, although relatively limited, can be neither prescribed nor proscribed in terms of specific behaviors. Lipton describes the coexistence of this personal relationship with the technical one as the method used by Freud, and spells out what he sees as the advantages of such technique, as exemplified in Freud's analysis of the Rat Man. He believes it is not possible to define the exact limits of permissible behavior in this personal relationship, because the character of the relationship will vary from one analyst to another and, indeed, among a particular analyst's relationships with his or her various patients. Lipton furthermore is very clear that although this personal interaction is spontaneous and not undertaken as a matter of technique, it may very well have repercussions affecting the transference that must become the subject of technical examination and intervention.

I agree with Lipton's general position and disagree with Langs (1980), who criticizes Lipton's views (1977b). I also find Langs's description of Lipton's position seriously distorted. Langs writes:

> Adopting an approach confined to manifest content and Type One derivatives, [Lipton] has suggested that the ground rules of psychoanalysis, and the use of noninterpretive interventions and direct gratifications of the patient, are beyond the confines of technique; there are no rules of treatment, he argues, that can be applied to these dimensions. Pointing out that the patient will respond to either gratification or nongratification (though failing to distinguish the important differences in the actual unconscious communications so contained, and their implications and consequences for both patient and therapist), Lipton suggests that either approach is valid. Setting aside the rule of abstinence . . . he counsels analytic work in this area only if the patient introduces the subject. (Langs 1980, pp. 501–502)

Only a reading of Lipton's paper will suffice to show how distorted a view of Lipton's position this is. Lipton does not suggest that "the ground

rules . . . and the use of noninterpretive interventions and direct gratifications . . . are beyond the confines of technique." He suggests only that
there is a restricted but undefinable area of interaction that is not subsumed
by technique, although it may of necessity become the subject of technical
intervention. Nor does he "counsel analytic work in this area only if the
patient introduces the subject." He does not set aside the rule of abstinence
unless one construes that rule as Langs does, that is, to mean that *all* the
analyst's behavior is governed by technique, that *all* the analyst's behavior
must conform to rules, and that these rules must be fixed and inviolate. In
this regard Langs is indeed a captive of contemporary "classical" technique
and at odds with Freud's position.

The Significance of the Patient's Conscious Experience of the Therapeutic Relationship

A second major difference between Langs's views and my own with
important repercussions affecting the therapeutic process concerns the significance of the patient's conscious and manifest experience of the relationship. Langs is justifiably critical of the prevalent readiness to consider such
manifestations in isolation, that is, without examining the adaptive context
in which they are taking place. This criticism is, after all, only another way
of saying that the field is always bipersonal. He is also correct in saying that
when these manifest attitudes are considered in isolation, they are often
regarded as true transference, that is, as distortions of the "real" situation,
and explained away in terms of some genetic or contemporaneous situation
outside the therapeutic one. But again, this is only a way of saying that the
patient's experience is considered to be solely intrapsychically determined
rather than rooted in the therapeutic transaction.

Langs does recognize that a manifest reference to the patient's experience
of the relationship is an important clue to the adaptive context. Indeed, he
recommends that in the absence of such a manifest reference, and even if
fairly clear indications do exist of disguised references to the patient's
experience of the relationship, one should "play back" these indirect allusions in the hope of eliciting a direct reference to the adaptive context. I
agree with him that such a manifest reference may be mentioned only in
passing (Gill and Hoffman 1982).

At the same time, Langs insists that associations that are predominantly
conscious ideas about the relationship, especially if they are repetitive, are
relatively valueless and should be dealt with by silence. I agree that a
stereotyped repetition of such conscious descriptions of the patient's experience of the relationship bespeaks some barrier to useful communication,
but I believe the use of silence as an intervention at such a point may be
unfortunate. The silence may come to be the overriding adaptive context

and as such, especially if it is not recognized, make even more difficult the explication of the original impasse.

An important difference between Langs's position and mine that flows at least in part from the divergence in our attitudes toward conscious associations lies in our attitudes toward the analyst's actively intervening to gain information about the patient's psychic content. If one assumes, as one always should, that there is an adaptive context for a stereotyped attitude, the alternative to waiting for derivative associations that will give one a clue is to assume the possible presence of additional conscious ideas that the patient is reluctant to voice. An effort to gain access to such ideas by questions, clarifications, confrontations, and other such devices may well lead to better results than will a silent wait for encoded derivatives of the patient's experience. The silence is easily experienced as a sullen complaint that the patient is not offering usable material. And although the therapist may set great store by inference from derivatives, the patient's conscious experience carries a certainty that nothing else can. To belittle this experience must be felt by the patient as a belittling of the importance of his or her conscious subjective state.

But questions, clarifications, and confrontations are ruled out by Langs. That the significance of such interventions may itself require examination is surely true, but their rejection seems to me another indication of Langs's preference for indirect evidence. I believe it also bespeaks his blind spot for silence as an adaptive context.

Langs seems to underestimate, on one hand, how commonly the patient resists voicing conscious ideas regarding the relationship and, on the other hand, how often parts of the patient's experience have not acquired verbal representation in his or her mind. Questions, confrontations, and clarifications, as well as interpretations, assuming due attention is paid to the possible repercussions of all interventions on the patient's experience of the relationship, can play an important role in revealing these conscious thoughts and in formulating what has not yet been given verbal shape.

Another consequence of the difference in our evaluation of conscious associations concerns the matter of evaluating the validity of the therapist's interventions by the patient's ensuing associations. I agree with Langs in emphasizing to a far greater extent than is usual in classical technique what he calls the clinical methodology of testing an intervention by the patient's ensuing associations. I also agree with him in his greater emphasis on the derivative nature of many of these ensuing associations. My difference with him lies in what he considers necessary and appropriate for the validation of an intervention. In practice, as one can see in the many illustrations in his books, he is satisfied with the conclusions drawn from the massing of inferences.

Langs underestimates the ingenuity—and his is striking—with which one can make inferences from manifest associations that seem to validate one's conclusions about how the patient is experiencing the therapist's intervention. This is particularly true if the intervention is an interpretation about something other than the patient's experience of the relationship, and the vast majority of the interventions that Langs evaluates in his books manifestly concern something other than this relationship. For example, beginning with a prior conviction of the inevitably harmful effect of any alteration of the frame, Langs accepts inferences from the patient's associations after the frame has been altered as validating his view of how the patient has experienced the alteration. The only direct validation would be the patient's conscious revelation of the experience that has been hypothesized.

I am aware of some of the pitfalls in assessing the patient's conscious experience. Of course, I do not believe that a patient's "yes" or "no" to an intervention, whether to one about the patient's experience of the relationship or to one about something else, validates or invalidates an intervention. I mean, rather, that Langs is too ready to accept indirect evidence, too belittling of conscious direct evidence. A conclusion based on even apparently massed and highly plausible derivatives is still an inference.

A common sequence of associations is that the patient makes a passing reference to his or her experience of the relationship—not merely to the adaptive context, which would refer to what the patient is reacting to and not to what his or her reaction is—and then proceeds to associations that are not manifestly about his or her experience of the relationship. In agreement with Langs, I believe these later associations continue to refer to the patient's experience of the relationship, albeit in derivative form. By inference from these derivatives, and in light of the hypothesis that they represent a continuation and amplification of the passing explicit reference, the therapist interprets the patient's experience of the relationship. The most unequivocal affirmation would be the patient's revelation that this was indeed an experience of which he or she was conscious, but one that had only been alluded to in the passing reference. Validation must of course often fall short of this ideal, and one must base inferences to what was presumably preconscious on derivatives, memories, dreams, and other material.

Even more inferential is the assessment of the response to interpretations that deal with experience that had not achieved verbal form. I am not referring to such experience as preconscious, because the concept of preconsciousness implies ideas already in verbal form. When the analyst casts nonverbal experience into verbal form, he or she inevitably adds something. Should the patient agree to the formulation, he or she is agreeing to something more than had been formulated entirely within the patient.

I believe that, at least to some extent, Langs's contrary views, like his views on the general level of pathology of therapists, stem from the clinical material he describes in his books. His inferences often seem persuasive because he is reporting the gross blunders of inexperienced therapists who are not using the principles he espouses. Because these errors are so gross, and because the inexperienced therapist is often unaware of them, it is easier for Langs to see the patient's reactions to them as valid perceptions of the therapist, and therefore for Langs to believe that as therapist he can distinguish between transference and nontransference and countertransference and noncountertransference. Even to refer to the therapist's "blunders," however, is to risk dichotomizing countertransference and noncountertransference. As I said earlier, just as the patient's experience is an understandable response to the therapist, so is the therapist's experience an understandable response to the patient.

The kind of clinical material with which Langs deals also plays a role in his underemphasis on the importance and value of conscious references to the patient's experience of the relationship and in his related conviction that validation can be obtained from inferences from derivatives alone. The communication between therapist and patient in his material is so prevalently disguised and allusive that one rarely sees the kind of conscious and direct statements of the patient's experience that would lead one to recognize the importance of such statements. The absence of such conscious direct statements seems to leave one perforce with the conclusion that inferences suffice. Even so, Langs comes close to recognizing the weakness of such validation by his frequent admission that his speculations have not been verified, although he attributes such failure not to a real possibility that the inferences are mistaken but to the absence of more clearly validating derivatives. A possible indication that Langs recognizes the uncertainty of validation by inference exists in his reference to his mode of validating as a clinical methodology that does not meet the standards of research (personal communication, 1979). I must emphasize that I am not discussing the general issue of accepting the patient's conscious experience as such, but the particular matter of the correspondence of conscious experience to interpretations in assessing interpretations.

A CLINICAL ILLUSTRATION

Langs's discussion (1980, pp. 502–509) of a clinical vignette by Lipton (1977b) will illustrate a number of the points I have made in this paper.

When the patient, a woman lawyer, came to her session, the analyst at once realized that she was sick. . . . She had malaise, weakness, abdominal pain, and had been vomiting. I thought she had made a mistake in coming to her session and suggested she might better go home but she insisted on continuing. I asked if she had taken her temperature and she said she had not. I asked if she wanted to take it right then. She was surprised and asked if I would really let her use a thermometer. I said I would. However, she said she did not want to. We continued then with the session (Lipton 1977b, p. 468).

The patient came for her next session two days later. She had been ill but had recovered. She had awakened suddenly at four o'clock that morning and "realized" that she had written an order regarding a case of child custody with hopeless incompetence and should be doing some simple menial work. Because her session was at four o'clock, Lipton reasoned that her associations might represent an identification with him, and he suggested she must feel he thought he had made a bad mistake with her and should be in some simpler field. She said it was not the thermometer; his offer of the thermometer "did not bother her a bit." Although she did see it as a minor bit of overprotectiveness and some residue of playing real doctor, she thought that *he* would think his action had been rash, intimate, and irregular and would castigate himself for it.

The offer of the thermometer and the suggestion that she might better go home are, of course, the actions that Langs considers a violation of technique and that Lipton considers personal actions, neither prescribable nor proscribable.

Lipton continues: "Now, with the identification out of the way, the transference configuration which we already knew something about became clear. She wished for and enjoyed these representations of intimacy but she was anxious that I would feel guilty about them and would worry lest I had done her irreparable harm" (p. 469).

Langs is convinced that the analyst had done something wrong and that the patient correctly perceived it as his having done something wrong, instead of the patient's view that *he* would think he had done something wrong (1980, p. 504).

To buttress his point, Langs makes the usual kind of inferences that I have referred to as inadequate for a conclusion. For example, he considers the patient's feeling of hopeless incompetence to be an allusion to the analyst's incompetence and the hopelessness of the analytic situation. He interprets the patient's having said that she should have insisted on more adequate visiting rights for the child's mother, her client, and that she had allowed the opposing lawyer to bully her to be a "commentary" on the analyst's "wish" to send her home, which Langs believed she experienced as an encroachment on her autonomy and as a bullying intrusion. His bias is revealed in his presentation of these ideas in the spirit of facts, not inferences, and in such subtle changes as his referring to what Lipton had called a "suggestion" as a "directive."

Once again, Langs's view that a particular behavior must have a universal meaning is involved. In the service of this bias he describes as a fact what actually he infers: the patient's unconscious perception of the analyst's sexual motivations (1980, p. 505). His bias leads him to refer to the thermometer as Lipton's "personal" thermometer, a designation for which he has no warrant, in his discussion of the same vignette in a later book (1981, p. 489).

In sum, Langs rejects the notion that the patient's conscious experience is a valid statement of her reaction to the event and draws a series of inferences from her associations that in his view validate what he considers to be her true unconscious response.

On the basis of his analysis of the episode, Langs expresses approval of Lipton's recognition of the patient's introjection, but he believes that what was introjected was the analyst's inappropriate behavior rather than the analyst's presumed ascription to himself of inappropriate behavior. He concludes that "analysts such as Lipton" suffer from "a neurotic delusion to the effect that the analyst's behaviors in certain spheres are devoid of conscious and unconscious communications" (1980, p. 505) and from "an overriding need to eventually characterize all the material from the patient as transference-based and to quickly bypass any indications of realistic and perceptive (nontransference) responses" (1980, p. 506). He sees Lipton as interpreting the introjection solely to show how it served as a transference resistance. He describes his own position as considering "*all* manifest and derivative communications from the patient . . . as to some degree introjective" (1980, p. 506).

Langs has a point. It is noteworthy that Lipton did not consider that his offer of the thermometer might have a repercussion on the transference, especially in light of the patient's surprise that he would let her use a thermometer in the session. He explains that he "had not given the interchange special weight because it was perfectly explicit" (1977b, p. 409). He explains in a personal communication (1981) that the patient's surprise at his violations of allegedly correct analytic technique had already been explored in various connections, but that would make all the more surprising his failure to anticipate that there might well be a reaction to his offer of a thermometer.

I believe Langs is correct in his view that analysts often overlook how they are being experienced by the patient as well as the countertransference motivations that play a role in how they are being experienced. I also believe that they do so to spare themselves discomfort. In this particular instance it is not impossible—indeed not unlikely—that there was some seductive motivation in the offer of the thermometer and that Lipton did too quickly get the "identification out of the way" so as to deal with the "transference configuration." But in this instance Langs damages the case for his conviction that such interaction is universally characteristic of analytic work by distorting data, however unwittingly, and by converting inference too readily into facts.

CLOSING REMARKS

There are additional aspects to Langs's view with which I differ, but they do not directly involve technique and I shall therefore only state them. Apparently because of the influence of Kleinian thinking, Langs is convinced that there is a psychotic core to every neurosis. He believes this so strongly that he often states that resistance and counterresistance find their deepest explanation in the fear of exposing this psychotic core in both patient and therapist. It may be that his belief in this psychotic core is related to his distrust of what is conscious and manifest. Langs's writing deals so largely with technique that his views on the nature of the psyche for the most part are only implied. One therefore cannot tell to what extent one agrees or disagrees.

Langs remains true to the classical tradition in the rigidity of his approach. A therapist employing his approach must feel that the channel between Scylla and Charybdis is narrow indeed; there are so many things one can do wrong, such ubiquitous temptations to violate the frame, such unflagging alertness demanded to catch hidden meanings.

My perspective provides a place for spontaneity. My technique overall is considerably more interactive than Langs's. I believe his general stricture against activity is a persisting attempt to make the analyst a blank screen. Because I believe that even the silent analyst is interacting with the patient, I say that what is important is not to be constantly vigilant against one's involvement in an interaction with the patient, but to be ready to see that interaction and incorporate that insight into one's understanding and interpretation of the patient's experience. One should also recognize that inevitably, to a greater or lesser degree, one will play the role that the patient has assigned. Furthermore, the therapist's personal involvement, not designed for its therapeutic effect, provides that spontaneous human interaction without which the therapeutic relationship can seem inhuman indeed.

My position can be misunderstood to mean that "anything goes" as long as its possible repercussions on the patient's experience of the relationship are sought out and made explicit. Rather, I believe that the effects of some actions cannot be annulled by making them explicit. The analyst should remain within a relatively circumscribed range of behavior and affective intensity. But, as I have said, the limits of this range can be neither prescribed nor proscribed.

Despite Langs's reiteration of the inevitability and universality of some degree of countertransference, he conveys the message that almost all therapists, including analysts, are heavily and pathologically subject to countertransference. He leaves no room for inexperience, mistaken conceptions, or a range within which inevitable countertransference has relatively little effect on the elucidation of transference. I agree with him that the therapist is always involved and that it is important to deal first with the basis for the patient's ascription of such involvement to the therapist. I believe his emphasis on these contentions is a major contribution. But I believe he presents his point in a way that seriously interferes with the recognition and acceptance of the sense in which it is valid. This is unfortunate, because I concur that therapists generally play a greater role in their patients' experience than is generally acknowledged and that the recognition of this role would improve significantly the conduct of psychotherapy and psychoanalysis.

REFERENCES

GILL, M. (1979). The analysis of the transference. *Journal of the American Psychoanalytic Association* (Suppl.) 27: 263–288.
———— (1982). *Analysis of Transference*. Vol. I. New York: International Universities Press.
GILL, M., AND HOFFMAN, I. (1982). A method for studying the analysis of resisted aspects of the patient's experience of the relationship in psychoanalysis and psychotherapy. *Journal of the American Psychoanalytic Association* 30:137–167.
KANZER, M. (1981). Freud's "analytic pact": the standard therapeutic alliance. *Journal of the American Psychoanalytic Association* 29:69–88.
LANGS, R. (1973). *The Technique of Psychoanalytic Psychotherapy*. Vol. 1. New York: Jason Aronson.
———— (1974). *The Technique of Psychoanalytic Psychotherapy*. Vol. 2. New York: Jason Aronson.
———— (1978). *The Listening Process*. New York: Jason Aronson.
———— (1980). *Interactions: The Realm of Transference and Countertransference*. New York: Jason Aronson.

——— (1981). *Resistances and Interventions: The Nature of Therapeutic Work.* New York: Jason Aronson.

LANGS, R., AND STONE, L. (1980). *The Therapeutic Experience and Its Setting: A Clinical Dialogue.* New York: Jason Aronson.

LEVENSON, E. (1972). *The Fallacy of Understanding.* New York: Basic Books.

LIPTON, S. (1977a). The advantages of Freud's technique as shown in his analysis of the Rat Man. *International Journal of Psycho-Analysis* 58:255–274.

——— (1977b). Clinical observations on resistance to the transference. *International Journal of Psycho-Analysis* 58:463–472.

——— (1983). A critique of so-called standard psychoanalytic technique. *Contemporary Psychoanalysis* 19:35–46.

STONE, L. (1961). *The Psychoanalytic Situation.* New York: International Universities Press.

CHAPTER 19

Views on Neurosis, Listening, and Cure: A Discussion of Gill's Comment on Langs

Marc Lubin, Ph.D.

As a therapist who is reasonably well acquainted with the therapeutic techniques of both Merton Gill and Robert Langs, I found the previous chapter by Gill on Langs's work to merit further comment. Such a thoughtful and critical review of one analyst's work by another is all too rare, and Gill's efforts to understand and to challenge Langs's work deepen our understanding of the sources of disagreement regarding different approaches to technique. A review of these sources of disagreement and misunderstanding may direct us toward an appreciation of how such differences may develop and may then distort and constrict the emergence of an even more useful dialogue between theorists. Gill's efforts represent a significant movement in this direction, and my response to him is in the spirit of extending and deepening this exchange.

Gill defined his major disagreements with Langs's theory of technique in two areas: the nature of the interpersonal reality within the therapeutic relationship and the significance of the patient's conscious and manifest experience of the relationship. Although these two areas are approached in dramatically different ways by the two writers, Gill has not fully addressed two critical arenas of his difference with Langs's position: their disparate views on neurosis, and their divergent listening and formulating processes.

Gill's problems with Langs's views on transference, the frame, therapeutic technique, and validation derive from the two analysts' basic disagreement about the primacy of unconscious forces in neurosis, and the significance of listening to and encouraging derivative communication of these unconscious forces in the resolution of neurosis.

THE UNCONSCIOUS IN NEUROSIS
AND DERIVATIVE COMMUNICATION

Langs has presented his position many times (1978a, 1978b, 1979, 1980, 1981, 1982). Most recently, however, he has stated that "critical unconscious perceptions and intrapsychic fantasy-memories—the dynamic and genetic basis for Neurosis and emotional disturbance—are expressed by the patient through derivatives. *Derivative communication is therefore the hallmark of Neuroses*" (1982, p. 41; italics in original). If neurosis is then articulated primarily through derivative communication, manifest patient comments about the therapist are not true expressions of the neurosis. Such direct comments, in Langs's terms, are indicators of a disturbance in the patient–therapist relationship, but not full expressions of the unconscious elements promoting that disturbance. Neurosis, in basic analytic terms, is the product of unconscious conflict between instinctual drives and self and object representations. Because of the threat or fear that would be evoked by direct expression of these elements, they are blocked from awareness and expressed indirectly as symptoms or derivatives. Because the neurosis involves the relationship with the therapist, the same principle holds in that situation: unconscious perception of underlying disturbance in the relationship will be, by necessity, expressed in encoded and disguised form.

Therefore, in Langs's system (1978a), the primary focus of the therapist should be on listening to the major carrier of unconscious perceptions and responses: the encoded images and narratives of the patient that derivatively allude to significant disturbing stimuli and their meanings within the therapeutic interaction.

From listening to patients' associations in this way, Langs (1978a, 1978b) has concluded that the patient responds quite powerfully and unconsciously to *specific* stimuli (adaptive contexts) within the therapeutic relationship and will represent both those stimuli and his or her reactions to them in *specific* images and narratives displaced from the therapist. All patient material is, then, reviewed by Langs in terms of these connections between actual therapist interventions and patient derivatives.

By listening in this manner to patient communications, Langs (1980) has evolved his rather dramatic positions regarding transference and nontransference, the positive unconscious meanings of the optimal therapeutic environment, and specific modes of intervention and validation around patient material.

Gill's listening process reflects his basic disagreement with Langs over the primacy of unconscious forces in neurosis and neurotic communication. Although Gill (1979) employs a listening approach that is similar to Langs's in its advocacy of listening for general derivatives related to the transference,

Gill does not endorse the primacy of derivative communication to the extent that Langs does. Encouragement of direct revelation of withheld thoughts and feelings about the therapist following some general interventions around derivative meanings is a major pattern in Gill's therapeutic technique. His greater emphasis on the value of fuller conscious expression of disturbing transference ideas suggests a belief that conscious factors play a more active role in neurotic functioning than do unconscious forces; Langs, in contrast, believes in the primacy of unconscious forces in such functioning.

Gill (1979) also does not organize his analysis of derivatives around the specific types of adaptive contexts that Langs does. Because he does not accept the central and overriding significance of frame arrangements or therapist interventions as primary adaptive contexts (they may or may not be such in Gill's system), Gill's listening for derivatives is not founded on as systematic a search for the appearance of those contexts in disguised form. Derivative interpretations thus may lead to specific adaptive contexts, or they may lead to rather general fantasies or feelings around the therapist. Again, Gill might directly inquire as to the adaptive context of the patient's reaction, whereas Langs would expect it to be presented either in passing or in disguised form. So whereas Langs (1981) has specific "tests" for derivative material, in terms of its fit with known and potentially unknown adaptive contexts, Gill has no such tests or specific contexts by which he organizes derivative material.

These major distinctions in the valuing of unconscious and conscious forces in neurosis and the specific listening–formulating process in Gill's and Langs's systems lead to their extracting different data from the therapeutic exchange. These data influence their conclusions about the therapeutic relationship, the role of the therapeutic frame and the quality of therapist interventions, and the criteria used for assessing the validity of therapist interventions.

It is my contention that these differences in approach, as well as some misunderstanding of Langs's position, lead Gill to distort Langs's contributions significantly by confusing him with the so-called classical analyst.

THE THERAPEUTIC RELATIONSHIP
AND INTERPERSONAL REALITY

Langs's intense study (1978a, 1979, 1980, 1981, 1982) of the therapeutic relationship through his analysis of patient derivatives regarding therapist interventions had led him to conclusions about the "reality" elements in that relationship that are far more definitive than those of Gill. In fact, Gill maintains that there is no interpersonal "reality" between therapist and patient, only "plausible" and "understandable" experiences of the other.

This point of difference again can be traced back to the very different ways in which Gill and Langs listen to patient material. Langs (1978a) develops specific hypotheses related to patient commentary following particular therapist interventions (frame management and interpretations) and then reviews material in the light of those hypotheses. As a result of such reviews, he has concluded that there is some element of predictability in patient responses to certain types of therapist interventions. As a result of such listening, he has developed a basis on which to discriminate between "transference" and "nontransference" reactions in the patient (Langs 1980, 1981, 1982). Again, this basis derives from his extensive study of many patient reactions to particular types of interventions and frame deviations.

Gill (1979), in contrast, does not develop specific hypotheses regarding the frame, therapist behavior, or patient reactivity, nor does he review material as exhaustively in the light of specific adaptive contexts generated by the therapist. He also does not wait for extensive derivative expression of such reactions and contexts, preferring to probe for consciously withheld ideas about the therapist. Although Gill clearly appreciates the significance of therapist behavior to the patient, his approach is unlikely to locate the element of "universal" unconscious reactivity that Langs's approach does.

Gill's listening and intervening approach, which is based on more frequent therapist probing, clarification, and confrontation techniques, thus quite purposefully short-circuits the development of more extensive patient derivative commentary. Such commentary, however, is the basis on which Langs's hypotheses about the meanings of particular adaptive contexts may be validated or rejected. Therefore, the "reality" of the patient–therapist relationship Gill is studying, infused with frequent and probing therapist interventions, is dramatically different from that studied by Langs. In essence, they are not discussing a common body of data. Agreement on a mutual therapeutic "reality" would be impossible given these two very distinct interventive and interpretive systems.

The following analogy illustrates my understanding of this difference: One physician might attempt to assess the extent of patient injuries resulting from a blow to the chest from patient complaints and speculations about what happened to the patient's body (Gill); the second physician might, in addition, examine x-rays of the injured area (Langs) with specific criteria in mind about normal and abnormal structures. The physical analogy might hold further: all individuals would experience a "universal" injury from a blow to the chest (reddening, swelling, and so forth) (nontransference), as well as specific and idiosyncratic reactions based on body structure, age, state of health, and the like (transference). Langs is positing essentially the same "reality" (nontransference) and idiosyncratic (transference) elements in the psychic realm. Without using the same tools to examine the "injury," each physician could reach very different conclusions about the "reality" or "extent" of those injuries.

Gill views Langs's efforts to define the reality and distorted aspects of patient reactions as arbitrary, and merges Langs's conclusions with his depiction of the classical analyst. Gill's concern here is that Langs's approach to and sharp emphasis on transference and nontransference categories has inherent in it an "aristocratic" attitude, one that quite automatically leads to rigidity and lack of deep appreciation of the range of plausible reasons for the patient's experience of the therapist.

Yet in all of Langs's recent writings (1978a, 1979, 1980, 1981, 1982), he actually has developed and presented a listening–formulating and validating approach that has myriad safeguards that keep the therapist from arbitrarily assuming a rigid approach to the patient's experience. In fact, although both Gill and Langs insist that the therapist listen for his or her own contribution to a pathological perception of the patient, Langs in his derivative listening methodology goes much further to search for realistic bases than does Gill. It seems that Langs's search for both realistic and distorted sources of patients' reactivity, although more systematic and unconsciously derived than Gill's search for "plausibilities," hardly necessitates therapist closure, condescension, or rigidity. It actually requires a more extensive and respectful review of therapist actions than does the "plausibility" assumption. In fact, the "plausibility" assumption could be used to defend the therapist against the acknowledgment of the partial truth or validity of the patient's encoded comments. In essence, it seems far less "aristocratic" to assume that the patient may be partly "right" than to assume that the patient may have a "plausible" position.

To address Gill's concerns more specifically: Although he is correct that Langs (1978a) has developed a very clear set of convictions regarding the primacy of meanings of certain therapeutic interventions, Langs has not created such convictions a priori. The convictions have been established from extensive study and review of his own and others' clinical data. Clearly, Langs (1973) did not begin his writings with the same perspectives he holds now (1982). In order to ensure that such convictions are not imposed arbitrarily on the patient, however, Langs (1978a, 1979) has also incorporated a number of checks in the formulating–intervening process that discourage the therapist's becoming totally and immediately enamoured of his or her hypotheses. Procedures such as "silent hypothesizing," assessing material for "coalescence of derivatives" around hypothesized adaptive contexts, and waiting for specific bridges to the therapeutic relationship, as well as the additional injunction, derived from Bion (1967), to "enter each session without desire, memory, or understanding," all clearly reflect Langs's efforts (1978a, 1979, 1982) to ensure that within each hour the arbitrary, narcissistic, and "aristocratic" application of inferences will be held in check. In fact, Langs's use (1978a) of Bion's concept of the "selected fact" again bespeaks an openness to hearing material and adaptive contexts that are not included in preliminary therapist formulations. Although Langs (1980, 1981) is quick to put forth hypotheses regarding patient material in his written supervisory accounts, he stresses restraint and review in the actual interventions of the therapist.

In the connection, Gill's argument that Langs's concept of "veridical perception" and the "divisibility" implicit within it contribute to an ossification of therapist openness is not a strong one. These categories can be useful in allowing the application of different perspectives to the same material. Such options yield the therapist further hypotheses about the various meanings of patient response, ranging from those most dominated by patient factors to those most influenced by therapist interventions. Even a projective test like the Rorschach attempts to consider and rate percepts according to their consensual and idiosyncratic meanings, and to derive hypotheses from such clusterings. In short, such "categories" need not be actualized in such rigid form as Gill expects; indeed, they may allow for a further openness and flexibility in the therapist's work with patients.

Gill seems concerned about the supposed assumption in Langs's categorization of "transference" and "nontransference" elements that a patient's comments would be viewed in toto by a therapist as having only a transference basis, with no "plausible" source in the therapist. In actuality, Langs (1981) argues that at different points a therapist, after fully assessing his or her interventions, frame arrangements, and so forth, would be in a better position to judge the degree of distortion contributed by the patient. In fact, one would expect a clearer judgment of patient inputs and distortion in a therapist who was functioning with fuller control and awareness of countertransference vectors than in one who had no such awareness and no criteria for judgment. Gill offers no system that provides criteria by which to judge these elements except the therapist's subjective impressions of the presence or absence of countertransference. In fact, he counsels against the development of such criteria.

Thus, although Gill suggests that therapist awareness of his or her contributions is helpful in assessing "plausibility," he stops short of suggesting that such efforts are in the service of a greater "objectivity" (whether that be consensual or actual). Gill's less systematized search for patient derivative allusions to the therapist (1979), however, does not contain an exhaustive self-research procedure through which the therapist may scan and validate his or her own real contributions to patient perceptions and images of the therapist. Such an approach could not be expected to yield the type, depth, meaning, or validation of clinical data on the interaction that

Langs's more focused and disciplined hypotheses-generating and checking approach discovers. Again, it would seem that the development of more "objective" standards for the assessment of the clinical interaction is better served by Langs's approach than by Gill's. Thus, although Gill writes that the "expertness" of the therapist resides in his or her greater awareness of possible contributions to the therapeutic relationship, he has misjudged Langs's extensive and systematic reviews of therapist contributions to the therapeutic interaction. I would argue, then, that there is far less of the "aristocrat" in Langs than Gill ascribes, and that Gill's "classicalizing" of Langs is based in Gill's lack of adequate attention to Langs's profound efforts to heighten therapist self-awareness on the patient's behalf.

THE IDEAL THERAPIST AND THE OPTIMAL FRAME

Gill takes issue with Langs's definition of an "appropriate–inappropriate" continuum of therapist behavior and his positing of an "ideal therapist" and "optimal frame." If one listens to patient material in Gill's terms and adopts Gill's view of more conscious determinants of neurotic functioning, one will not be able to support Langs's contentions. If conscious and preconscious patient perception and reactivity are the primary basis of judgment, there will be little validation for Langs's position. Patients are so divided in their wishes to be rid of their neuroses that they will rarely directly demand to be supplied with conditions in which those neuroses will be most safely, and yet most starkly, addressed. And because Gill also does not listen to patient material in terms of derivative expressions of patient *needs* for a secure frame, clearer boundaries, etcetera, or in terms of unconscious patient disappointment when such conditions are not offered, Langs's propositions appear to him to be arbitrary, self-serving, and invalid. Without close listening for derivatives of the extensive and profound unconscious psychological meanings patients attach to deviations and rectifications of the frame (the adaptive contexts), the therapist cannot appreciate the importance of developing a definition of "appropriate" or "ideal" behavior. Although Gill has some sense of these matters, his own theory of neurosis and cure, and his associated listening and formulating process, rule out a fuller appreciation of the deeper unconscious meanings of the therapist's optimal management of the frame. As a consequence of these differences, Gill again interprets Langs's efforts to define optimal therapist frame management and interventions as just another return to the outdated image of the classical, "blank screen" analyst.

Gill also deemphasizes the profound influence of most therapist behaviors, because he believes that the meanings of those behaviors (for the most part) can be altered and resolved by subsequent therapist interventions around the patient's reactions. He indicates, in his agreement with Lipton

(1977), that there is considerably more room for a personal relationship with the patient outside the bounds of "technique," and assumes that a rigid adherence to the frame and proper technique can stimulate the development of a nontherapeutic regression in the patient.

Indeed, Gill goes even further in restricting the potentially positive meanings and therapeutic utility of the model of "optimal" therapist activity and frame management when he defines the well-functioning analyst. He writes, "What I emphasize about well-functioning analysts is not that they are less likely to be inappropriate than is the patient, but that they continuously concern themselves with trying to understand the transactions between themselves and the patient by taking their respective and differing points of view into account" (this volume, p. 400–401). This comment implies that there is essentially less purpose or possible gain in the analyst's efforts to be "more" appropriate (mature, integrated, and so forth) than the patient, since the major role of the analyst is to understand the impact of his or her inappropriateness (a term Gill attempts to dismiss as "inappropriate" as well). It then would seem that Langs's emphasis on the curative and positive meanings to the patient of the therapist's being "less likely to be inappropriate" is a factor Gill clearly considers of secondary or peripheral significance in his understanding of technique, with the implication that such efforts may actually damage the patient.

In Gill's defense, however, one must understand he has not had a Langsian hour for study, nor has he witnessed the quite profound effects of frame rectification and Langsian type interventions. He needs, as do other readers, far more direct acquaintance with how Langs and his students have implemented these observations. Although Langs has included more examples of positive work in *Psychotherapy: A Basic Text* (1982), skeptics need transcripts and accounts of successful treatment to understand more fully what Langs is trying to say. The *Basic Text*, this volume, and future writings and research should help provide critics like Gill with a more extensive acquaintance with Langs's ideas in action. Distortions about his position, one hopes, would be diminished with the availability of such materials. How much of Gill's misunderstandings are caused by his lack of direct familiarity with Langs's clinical work is difficult to say. It is critical, however, that this deficit be redressed.

Gill (this volume, p. 402) has noted that Langs appears blind to derivatives around the frame that suggest a view of the therapist as "rigid." Actually, Langs would attempt to understand such a derivative response to frame issues as he would all others; that is, there would be an effort to identify the specific adaptive context stimulating the patient's perception, and a subsequent effort to locate the transference and nontransference reactions to the perception. Langs is open to the notion that the therapist might have done something around holding the frame that would be perceived by the patient as motivated by the therapist's anxiety or excessive defensiveness. It is obvious that therapists may manage the frame in pathologically rigid ways—or with a full integration of the meanings of its proper functions. After careful listening, Langs (1981) might also conclude that such a derivative commentary was related to the patient's phobic and paranoid fears related to the therapist's hold, fears that indeed can be quite intense.

In short, Langs (1981, 1982) does not assume an unequivocal embracing of the frame by patients, as Gill seems to imply. In fact, in the *Basic Text* (1982), he has elaborated both the patient's and the therapist's anxieties and resistances around establishing and maintaining the ground rules.

What seems most disturbing is Gill's implicit view of the frame as primarily a set of mechanical, depriving, and frustrating rules, applied with rigidity to the patient's behavior. This view contrasts sharply with a fuller perception of the positive unconscious meanings of the frame to the patient: a profound and serious commitment to creating secure and confidential conditions that the therapist believes are optimal for the insightful resolution of neurosis, and to providing a reasonably mature (or maturation-striving) and well-integrated therapist in such a relationship to reinforce the meanings and directions of such work. The frame is, in Langs's terms (1978a), *not* to be thought of as a mechanical and inhuman set of rules, but more as a deeply essential and humanly applied set of guidelines for optimal psychoanalytic work. Gill seems to equate Langs's views on the frame with the older, more classical conception that the primary value of ground rules lies in the provision of a frustrating environment, whereas Langs (and others) have been emphasizing the very positive meanings of the frame in terms of the positive "holding" and individuated introjects of the therapist it affords the patient.

In sum, it is Langs's belief, based on extensive derivative listening to patients' reactions around frame securing and frame deviations, that the constituents of the frame should be applied with a deep appreciation of its both therapeutic and genuinely disturbing implications for patient and therapist alike. The very point of taking the frame so seriously is to enrich and stabilize the treatment, and to make possible the most extensive, insightful resolutions of the patient's neurosis, deepened and reinforced by the patient's identification with a well-functioning, empathic, and integrated therapist.

THERAPIST INTERVENTIONS

Taping

Gill's view that Langs sees tape-recording as incompatible with a "good psychotherapeutic relationship" is only partly correct. The reasons for this incompatibility are complex, however, and recording is not to be understood as simply "damaging" or not damaging the therapeutic relationship.

Langs (1981) has suggested that patients reveal their reactions to taping and to the taping–therapist figure in derivatives. Frequently these derivatives appear *after* taping has been stopped, when the patient may be able to undertake a more extensive review of the unconscious meanings of the recording. Langs (1981) has argued that taping may have neurotically gratifying and disturbing implications for the patient, give a significant unconscious "tilt" to the patient's introject of the therapist, and determine and influence the extensiveness and direction of his or her associations. Again, these meanings could be found only in the therapist's review of the patient's derivative material.

Langs (1982) currently maintains that taping, as well as other impairments of the frame, can be worked with as long as they are considered crucial adaptive contexts and are rectified after a period of working through within the therapeutic relationship.

Gill does raise a valid point in stating the usefulness of taping in the necessary research examination of the therapeutic process. We must, however, separate therapeutic and research goals. Although taping may compromise the treatment relationship, a taped therapy is also required for research, and on that basis it should proceed, albeit with considerable attention to its conscious and unconscious meanings for the patient. Thus, an alertness to the taping as an adaptive context for understanding the patient's derivatives would, one hopes, allow for a more productive treatment even under research conditions. The following research questions might also be addressed (at least in part): Are there distorting effects of taping? What is the nature of the "damage" (if any) to treatment connected with taping? What types of unconscious gratifications does taping afford? These questions, of course, bear on the meanings of the research findings as well. One doctoral research project has addressed these questions (Frick 1982).

Silence

Gill has also equated Langs's conception of silence as an intervention with the classical position and goes on to note how it may, at certain times, have very destructive and disturbing meanings to the client (an "iatrogenic regression" [this volume, p. 401]), with the analyst failing to acknowledge silence as the precipitating factor. Actually, Langs (1982) has devoted considerable space in the *Basic Text* to the different meanings of silence, and strongly believes that silence should always be considered a potential adaptive context because it *is* an intervention by the analyst. In fact, Langs's method of listening allows the silent therapist to hear allusions to the meanings of that silence and to assess its value or destructive meanings for the patient. Perhaps Gill has not understood that although Langs has criticized neophyte therapists for too much activity, he has also been alert to the dangers of missed interventions. In fact, he has developed specific criteria (1981, 1982) that allow the therapist to judge the most appropriate timing for intervening and to use the material that follows an inappropriate therapist silence as commentary on the unconscious meanings of that silence for the patient. His rating of "indicators" is for the explicit purpose of helping the therapist judge the patient's therapeutic need for an intervention in any particular session.

In that context, Gill misrepresents Langs as "overlook[ing] the fact that the avoidance of any immediate direct reaction [to a patient request] will have its own meaning to the patient" (this volume, p. 403). In fact, Langs does not deny that patients have very powerful reactions to therapist non-compliance and that such meanings may be presented derivatively in ensuing associations. He also is aware, however, that the request for a deviation may have even more extensive and critical meanings, and that patient material may also be organized around a hidden adaptive context that has stimulated the patient's request. A review of the derivatives around both adaptive contexts would direct the therapist's focus and intervention.

Although Gill believes Langs is biased toward material around frame deviation requests, Gill himself probably would be quick to listen for the patient's reactions to therapist noncompliance and eager to probe the patient for those reactions (no doubt withheld consciously from the therapist). The difference in emphasis is characteristic of the basic distinctions between Langs's and Gill's approach to material. From my observations of both systems, I believe Gill places higher priority on the immediate and conscious responses of the patient around therapist frame maintenance, whereas Langs gives more prominence to immediate but unconscious reactions to all aspects of frame management, with particular attention to frame deviations, because these tend to have more convoluted meanings to the patient. Again, however, he reviews derivatives before making a final judgment.

Gill views Langs's approach to silence as more evidence that Langs is attempting to re-create the "blank screen" analyst whose goal is essentially to be a noncontributor to the patient's experience of the relationship. Such an attribution, of course, neglects Langs's extensive efforts to note the myriad and subtle ways in which the therapist's conscious and unconscious intentions are expressed to the patient through frame management and interventions. It also neglects Langs's belief that far from being a "blank screen," the therapist is attempting to create a healthy symbiosis with the patient and implicitly to foster extensive positive introjects from the therapist's management of the frame and his or her responses to the patient. This emphasis on the growth-promoting and individuating implications of therapist behavior is a far cry from the view of an inert therapist, present only to accept and interpret projections and transferences from the patient.

This merger of Langs and the classical analyst appears again in Gill's remarks regarding the inefficacy of prescribing or proscribing therapist behavior. Once more, Gill fails to appreciate Langs's awareness that a positively functioning therapist (in Langs's terms) is one who provides a deeply significant relationship to the patient and that it is not only unnecessary but antitherapeutic to offer anything more than that to the patient. Gill believes that a therapist who is "all technique" is, by definition, a cold, rigid, and inhuman figure for the client, one who will not create a climate for growth. Gill would endorse a more spontaneous, but circumscribed, personal relationship with the patient as a means to diminish the depriving qualities of the old "blank screen" analyst. It seems that just as Langs has reacted strongly to the deviation-prone analysts, Gill is reacting to the ritualized, deprivation-prone analysts of the past. Langs is clearly not attempting to re-create such a figure.

Verbal Interventions

Gill's differences with Langs are most dramatic in the area of verbal interventions, and flow most clearly from the divergences in their approaches to neurosis, listening, and cure. Although Gill considers derivative communication a highly significant clue to the patient's experience of the therapist, he also believes it is not the sole mode through which the patient may express neurosis. Preconscious and inhibited conscious ideation are, in Gill's framework, critical elements in uncovering and working through patient disturbance. The freeing of these restrained or vaguely articulated ideas about the therapist has considerable power in Gill's system (1979). On this basis, Gill invites extensive manifest discussion of the patient's experience of the relationship after a bridge to introductory derivatives, hoping to unhinge and bring to awareness and discussion even more obscure and troubling patient thoughts about the therapist for further working through and analysis.

This viewpoint supports Gill's active, probing, and clarifying techniques, which are aimed at bringing to the surface more and more extensive conscious and preconscious observations of, and thoughts and feelings about, the therapist. The surfacing and direct expression of these immediate ideas in the presence of the therapist is part of the positive therapeutic experience of the patient, in Gill's terms. Further analysis of the bases from which the patient developed such ideas is the next task of the therapist and patient. This experience thus allows for abreaction, analysis, and a mutative experience, in Strachey's terms (1934). The patient, by so voicing these threatening preconscious or conscious ideas in the presence of the person toward whom they are directed, will integrate further elements of their experience, as well as exerience the therapist as a figure dramatically different from the "super-ego" image of the therapist formerly held.

Because Langs believes conscious and direct thoughts about the therapist reflect only a small and minimally conflictual portion of the patient's neurosis, he does not believe active pursuit of even consciously withheld ideas reveals any significant information about the core of the patient's pathology. In fact, pursuit of consciously withheld material results only in brief abreaction and extended intellectualization and rumination, in Langs's view. It is not that manifest transference material is suspect, but that it simply can do no more than carry meanings the patient already knows. Encoded image and narra-tive derivatives carry meanings the patient seeks to hide from him or herself and from the therapist, meanings so disturbing they must be encoded to escape detection. Fleeting conscious thoughts about the therapist may indicate a disturbance but in themselves rarely yield significant informa-tion about the patient's more disturbing perceptions of and reactions to the therapist.

As a consequence, Langs (1978a) believes that appropriate silence and implicit encouragement of *indirect* communication permit the patient a fuller opportunity to express unconscious perceptions and fantasy-memory con-stellations through encoded derivatives than do active questioning and efforts at clarification. The latter force the patient to the "surface" and result in little new information about the patient's unconscious reactions.

In short, Gill is working with what Langs (1982) terms "inference" derivatives, intellectualized conclusions based on manifest content, Type One communications from the patient. Such inferences are drawn in the absence of adaptive contexts and generally are based on the patient's intra-psychic and interactional patterns, now evident within the therapeutic inter-action. Langs maintains that deeper and more significant information will be found in patient images and narratives displaced from the therapist but capable of coalescence around adaptive contexts.

It seems evident that Gill's critique of Langs does not indicate a full awareness of these differences. If there were such an awareness, Gill would understand more clearly Langs's reasons for choosing not to pursue manifest reactions, and would see more clearly the role of silence in the treatment.

Gill also seems not to be aware of Langs's efforts (1981) to address the repetitive and intellectualized communicator in ways other than silence. Langs has stated that interventions will develop around understanding the possible adaptive contexts for this empty type of communication and linking those contexts with the patient's wishes to destroy meaningful communica-tion. Gill, however, believes Langs is stating a case for the silent and paralyzed analyst, rather than trying to develop an analyst who is internally quite active and constantly waiting for the optimal moments to intervene in a meaningful way. Unending silence is not espoused by the communicative approach—even with Type C communicators. Langs's answer (1981), however, does not lie in extensive probing and confronting, as does Gill's with such patients.

Gill seems not to appreciate that as the therapist becomes engrossed in the various listening and formulating tasks and grows increasingly convinced of the importance of the frame, he or she is not in a constant state of anxiety or paralysis with respect to "not violating" the frame. One becomes increasingly less ambivalent about such decisions—again, based on the observations of patient derivatives and behavior following such deviations.

Here, too, Gill is at a disadvantage in not having been given the type of available clinical data that would demonstrate the extensive positive effects of these positions. A review of this material would replace the image of the petrified therapist (frequently the image held by therapists beginning the Langs approach) with the image of a more secure, holding therapist, no longer anxiously preoccupied with committing a therapeutic error. Advanced Langs students would, in most cases, report such a secure state of mind.

The aforementioned differences in listening and models of cure are illuminated by Gill's emphasis on validation of therapist interventions through manifest patient commentary and recovery of fleeting conscious thoughts of the therapist, and by Langs's view (1980, 1981, 1982) that validation will occur primarily in encoded form, with some conscious validation, the emergence of "selected facts," and the presence of a positive figure in patient associations following an effective therapist intervention.

This validation model is necessarily strict to ensure that inferences fit the associational material as well as invite further, newer material and some conscious working through. Thus, validation not only indicates that the therapist is in the preeminent area of the patient's activated disturbance, but also should demonstrate that the intervention has had a positive, empathic meaning to the patient (encouraged the positive figure) and create the stimulus to further significant revelations previously inaccessible to the patient.

Gill's greater belief in conscious material and his suspicions about extensive reliance on inference lead him to reject Langs's emphasis on derivative validation. Again, this difference is consistent with these analysts' distinctive views of disturbance, listening processes, and cure. Langs's insistence on the criteria just mentioned, as well as his methodology around "silent hypotheses," represent his efforts to check the self-fulfilling prophecies of the therapist's interventions.

FINAL OBSERVATIONS

Gill is somewhat critical of Langs for limiting himself to student presentations, suggesting Langs's conclusions would be different if the clinical material were drawn from the cases of more experienced clinicians. This criticism seems misplaced, because Gill goes on to discuss Langs's analysis (1980) of Lipton's presented material. Langs has also reviewed hours presented by Freud (Langs 1978b), Searles (Langs and Searles 1980), Stone (Langs and Stone 1980), and the Blancks (Langs 1980)—as such hours have been published. His approach in each instance has yielded findings that he believes support his conclusions concerning beginning therapists. In fact, after Gill criticizes Langs for distorting Lipton's material, Gill himself offers further evidence in partial support of Langs's position.

In his final remarks in this volume, Gill states that he is not advocating an "anything goes" treatment with no guidelines, but simply proposing that the limits of these guidelines "can be neither prescribed nor proscribed" (p. 412). I suggest that a failure to attempt such limitation, and a subsequent failure to observe carefully the consequences of this failure in terms of the patient's derivative responses, leaves psychoanalysis with no consensual data with which to argue these propositions regarding effective technique. Gill and other critics of Langs appear to believe that Langs essentially has created and artfully elaborated what he wants patients to say by inferring what he wishes from derivative material. If an analyst such as Gill would review the same material using derivative commentaries on therapist interventions, perhaps a meaningful dialogue could take place concerning the very critical questions Gill has raised. It is clearly Langs's contention that he has learned the powerful meanings of the frame from patients, not projected his meanings onto them. A common listening process would aid in addressing the question—and would direct psychoanalytic therapists in creating more nearly optimal treatment settings for their patients.

Although I have presented areas of Gill's disagreement with Langs's position, Gill himself notes important areas of common ground in the early pages of his chapter. Yet there is one further area of agreement that Gill fails to mention, an area that he and Langs alone share: a commitment to a *systematic* study of the psychoanalytic interaction. In their efforts to investigate the complex meanings of this interaction, both Gill and Langs have made dramatic contributions to the areas of technique and the training of psychoanalytic psychotherapists.

Their debate should continue, and a more informed dialogue with Langs should be ensured by the provision of clinical documentation of effective and successful applications of the communicative approach. This material should allow Gill and other open-minded analysts to have a fuller conception of the therapeutic and rather dramatic results of Langs's work, and to note more accurately its significant departures from what is commonly viewed as the classical approach.

REFERENCES

BION, W. (1967). Notes on memory and desire. *Psychoanalytic Forum* 2:271–280.

FRICK, E. (1982). Latent and manifest effects of audio recording in psychoanalysis and psychotherapy. Clinical Research Project, Illinois School of Professional Psychology.

GILL, M. (1979). The analysis of the transference. *Journal of the American Psychoanalytic Association* (Suppl.) 27:263–288.

LANGS, R. (1973). *The Technique of Psychoanalytic Psychotherapy*. Vol. 1. New York: Jason Aronson.

——— (1978a). *The Listening Process*. New York: Jason Aronson.

——— (1978b). *Technique in Transition*. New York: Jason Aronson.

——— (1979). *The Therapeutic Environment*. New York: Jason Aronson.

——— (1980). *Interactions: The Realm of Transference and Countertransference*. New York: Jason Aronson.

——— (1981). *Resistances and Interventions: The Nature of Therapeutic Work*. New York: Jason Aronson.

——— (1982). *Psychotherapy: A Basic Text*. New York: Jason Aronson.

LANGS, R., AND SEARLES, H. F. (1980). *Intrapsychic and Interpersonal Dimensions of Treatment: A Clinical Dialogue*. New York: Jason Aronson.

LANGS, R., AND STONE, L. (1980). *The Therapeutic Experience and Its Setting: A Clinical Dialogue*. New York: Jason Aronson.

LIPTON, S. (1977). Clinical observations on resistance to the transference. *International Journal of Psycho-Analysis* 58:463–472.

STRACHEY, J. (1934). The nature of the therapeutic action of psychoanalysis. *International Journal of Psycho-Analysis* 15:117–126.

CHAPTER 20

Communicative Psychotherapy and Object Relations Theory

Maury Neuhaus, Ph.D.

In this chapter, I will demonstrate how the communicative approach to psychotherapy, as described by Langs (1978), has implemented clinically the essence of W. R. D. Fairbairn's theory of object relations (1952). I will clarify specifically how sound, adaptively formulated interventions generate positive internal introjects. Clinical examples will illustrate how, when the framework of therapy is not secure and interventions are not based on the prevailing therapeutic indicators, on an adaptive context, and on the most meaningful aspects of the derivative complex, negative introjects of the therapist will predominate. The most important terms used in this discussion are defined.

FAIRBAIRN'S THEORY OF OBJECT RELATIONS

Fairbairn (1952) believed that the significance of living is in object relationships; only through relationships can our life have meaning, for without object relations the ego cannot develop. The more individuals cut themselves off from relationships in the outer world, the more they are driven back into their fantasied object relations in their inner worlds. The real loss of all objects would be tantamount to psychic death.

A repressed inner world of internalized, bad objects is the result of bad external relations in infancy. The inner psychic world duplicates the original, frustrating one; because the person is tied to bad objects, he or she usually feels angry, guilty, anxious, and frustrated, tempted to project these feelings back onto the external world. The infant internalizes unsatisfying objects in an effort to control them in inner reality, because they cannot be mastered in the outer world.

The developing psyche has six distinct structural aspects. There is one central ego, which is in touch with the outer world and governs the activities of object seeking, and there are two subsidiary egos, the libidinal and the

431

antilibidinal ego. The individual's pristine, natural self is the libidinal ego which, if smothered in the course of development, comprises only the potential for a true self. The antilibidinal ego is basically an internalization of the outer world's repression of the needy self—the demanding infant perceived as a nuisance to be kept quiet. As the psyche develops, these three egos become attached to three different kinds of internalized objects: ideal, exciting, and rejecting. The central ego of the infant idealizes the real parent, and the parent's exciting and rejecting aspects are further split into separate, fantasied objects of the infant's libidinal and antilibidinal egos. The exciting object is attached to and arouses libidinal needs; the rejecting object, which denies libidinal needs, is attached to the antilibidinal ego.

Inevitably, the libidinal ego is hated and persecuted by the antilibidinal ego as well as by the rejecting object, so the infant becomes divided. This situation develops because the antilibidinal ego attempts to deny all feelings related to ego weakness. The part of the ego that has withdrawn from external reality has created an inner world of objects, both exciting and persecuting. Although this inner world results in states of persecutory anxiety, the ego still exists, thus warding off feelings of depersonalization and fragmentation stemming from withdrawal from emotional contact with objects in the real world.

This theoretical description has important implications for the conduct of therapy. Many patients, in order to avoid contact with their inner worlds and the ultimate acceptance of a therapeutic regression, will accept and at times even welcome poor therapeutic practices so that the therapist will be *unconsciously* perceived as persecuting the patient as the antilibidinal ego sadistically attacks the libidinal ego. On a conscious level, however, the therapist usually is perceived as helpful. The essential aim of this defense is the conversion of an original situation in which the child is surrounded by bad objects into a new situation in which the objects are good and the child is bad. Under these conditions, the patient can hide areas of his or her pathology in those of the therapist. In addition, the patient's sadistic, self-directed attacks, abhorrence of his or her own immaturity, and hatred of his or her own weakness, which are attempts to obliterate a perpetual fear of inner weakness, are now reinforced by any errors by the therapist, either in the management of the therapeutic frame or in the interventions offered.

A clinical example will demonstrate how frame mismanagement by a therapist who is attempting to be helpful on a manifest level is perceived unconsciously as inadequate and unhelpful by the patient. This therapist considered her patient to be a borderline personality and therefore felt justified in making major modifications in the therapeutic frame. For example, because the therapist felt that this patient could not function outside the therapy hour without additional contact, the patient was encouraged to call the therapist any time he felt intensely anxious. Whenever the patient's appointment fell on a legal holiday, the therapist would suggest a makeup appointment even though the patient had not requested one. In prior sessions, the patient had spoken frequently of several life situations in which there were themes of inappropriate gratification resulting in emotional attachment and dependence on others. This therapist, because she worked primarily on a manifest level, did not notice the indications that she was encouraging inappropriate dependence in her patient. When, as in this case, the therapist does not manage the frame of the therapy appropriately, the patient unconsciously experiences that no boundaries exist, and often there is a role reversal. Such a situation was illustrated in one session when the patient arrived early, before the therapist. Instead of waiting in the waiting room, he entered the therapist's office and sat in her chair. During the ensuing session, the patient consciously expressed his gratitude to the therapist for allowing him to call her during the week and continued to blame himself for being needy and dependent. Positive images resulting from a seemingly helpful therapist were not represented in the patient's material; instead, virtually all the images were negative and destructive. For example, the patient discussed relationships in which he was emotionally abused and used in a parasitic manner. In formulating the patient's material, the therapist did not consider the possibility that, through displacement, the patient was offering valid unconscious perceptions of the manner in which he was being treated by his therapist. Such negative introjects are unconsciously welcomed by the patient, because this type of relationship supports his or her defenses. Unconsciously, the patient under these conditions remains tied to his or her inner world of bad objects. The therapist's countertransference thus permits the patient to avoid experiencing the therapeutic regression and the accompanying feelings of depersonalization and fragmentation.

Although Fairbairn did not use therapeutic techniques that consistently fostered the generation of positive introjects, this process was an integral part of his theory.

LANGS'S COMMUNICATIVE APPROACH

The communicative approach consistently recognizes the spiraling sequences of adaptive contexts and responses in both patient and therapist. The therapeutic work unfolds according to the actualities in the relationship between the patient and the therapist as they reveal themselves from moment to moment. The therapist continuously monitors the influence of the therapeutic setting, the ground rules and frame, projective and introjective processes within both patient and therapist, and direct and displaced reactions. Every association and behavioral element is examined for unconscious allusions to both patient and therapist, and the patient's material is viewed transversally in terms of both self and not-self, transference and nontransference, perceptiveness and distortion. Both genetic and dynamic aspects are then traced from the central nodal points of the unconscious communicative interaction.

Examining therapy in this manner permits a more accurate distinction to be made between reality and fantasy, in that both the introjective and the projective aspects of the patient's experiences in the therapeutic interaction are included, and fosters understanding of the sources of the patient's neurosis, both the genetic sources and those within the treatment situation. This description is the essence of what Langs (1980) calls truth therapy.

Interactional and cognitive validation of the therapist's interpretations, the major element of truth therapy, links Fairbairn's conception of the crucial importance of the patient's unconscious perception of the therapist as a good object with Langs's therapeutic techniques developed to accomplish this validation. For Langs, interactional validation of the therapist's interpretations occurs through *derivative* representations of positive introjective identifications of the therapist. Cognitive validation is revealed through indirect, surprising, and unique Type Two derivatives. Within a secure frame, the patient's pathology is increasingly represented in the subsequent associations. In response, the therapist is able to interpret these distortions around the prevailing adaptive contexts, unconscious distortions, and fantasy constellations. The patient again responds with Type Two derivative validation, which, as I shall point out, gives evidence of a positive introject.

DISCUSSION AND CLINICAL MATERIAL

The term *lie*, in the sense of unconscious falsification, can be likened to Fairbairn's concept of the patient's need to maintain his or her inner world of bad objects. The lie serves to obliterate expressions of and seal off the truths of the patient's neurosis and his or her valid unconscious perceptions of disturbances in the therapist.

In a similar vein, Fairbairn considered the patient's maintenance of the inner world of bad objects as a closed system to be the greatest source of resistance to be overcome in therapy. The patient clings to the closed inner world because of unconscious identification with the bad, introjected parents. The dissolution of this identification feels like a loss not only of one's parents, but also of a part of one's self. The threat of a therapeutic regression leading to a schizoid withdrawal from object relationships causes patients unconsciously to choose bad objects rather than have no objects at all.

Although he advocated overcoming this situation, the greatest resistance in psychotherapy, Fairbairn's style of listening and intervening undermined his basic intentions. Langs (1978, 1980) states that only when a therapist interprets by using Type Two derivatives within a secure frame will positive introjects be generated. Only under these conditions will a patient tolerate the therapeutic regression. All other methods of listening and intervening offer the patient pathological instinctual drive gratifications; gratify the patient's wish for inappropriate fusion and merger; create barriers against the influence of pathological unconscious fantasies, memories, and introjects; help deny the separateness between patient and therapist and the dreaded anticipations of nonexistence and death; and unconsciously collude with the patient in avoiding the necessary but temporary therapeutic regression that exposes the most primitive parts of his or her personality.

Manifest Content Therapy

Langs avers that most therapeutic listening and intervention take place on a manifest and Type One derivative level. Although Freud and other analysts often emphasize the importance of unconscious fantasy constellations in the development of neuroses, in their clinical work conscious fantasies are often taken at face value and the patient's neurosis is attributed to them.

In one example of clinical work by a manifest content therapist, the patient was a severely disturbed woman, diagnosed as schizophrenic. In the session prior to the one that will be presented, the therapist had been quite active, making so-called supportive interventions that implicitly suggested to the patient that she not quit her job because she needed money desperately. In the session that followed, the patient spoke of getting advice from her brother, whom she felt to be lecturing her and imposing his values on her. Her brother had suggested that she return to living with her husband, from whom she was separated. [She wanted to have her own apartment.] She had been angry with her brother but had not said anything to him. During the week, she had earned more money and felt better. Her boss had been in a better mood. The patient had been promoted to waitress; the other waitress had been fired for being lazy. She stated that she became confused and made mistakes when she felt pressured. She hoped that business would pick up, because she was starting to feel relaxed and at home at the restaurant. She had started by cleaning tables and had been allowed to become a waitress at her own pace. She felt so much calmer that she had stopped taking pills. She was going out to buy clothes even though she didn't need them; buying them made her feel better. She only read the amusement section of the newspaper, avoiding anything that was too serious and disturbing.

In working on a manifest level, the therapist is not able to organize the patient's material in this session as valid unconscious perceptions of the manner in which he had intervened in the previous session (the intervention context). Although consciously the therapist had attempted to be supportive in the previous session, in the following session the patient, through derivative material and through displacement, reveals how she experienced his efforts. The patient represents the therapist's non-neutral, directive style of intervening by mentioning the manner in which her brother had treated her; he had lectured and imposed upon her. Next, the mode of relatedness desired by the therapist and the patient is represented in the material: her brother wanting her to move in again with her husband into a destructive relationship suggests a form of pathological symbiosis and parasitism desired by the therapist, whereas the patient's wish for her own apartment is a desire for separateness and individuation. The patient further expresses her valid unconscious perceptions of the therapist's intervention when she states that she had been angry with her brother but had not said anything to him. She is perceiving both the unconscious anger in the therapist as expressed in his directive, and the further implication that when he intervenes in this manner he is not saying anything meaningful. Later, she comments, through derivatives, on her fear that the therapist's anger will result in his terminating the therapy if she does not comply with his wish for her to keep her job. This fear is expressed through mention of the waitress who was fired for being lazy. Another interpretation of this encoded message is that the patient will terminate her therapy if the therapist continues to intervene in such a lazy manner.

The patient then mentions how well she does when she goes at her own pace, a message to the therapist not to place his anxieties into her. Also, her relaxed feeling seems to be a valid unconscious perception of the therapist in this session; his silence is appropriate, and she senses how much less pressured he is than he had been in the previous session. The mode of cure offered by a manifest content therapist is expressed through derivatives. The patient's earning more money and feeling good, and wanting to buy clothes in order to feel better, are allusions to gaining relief not through insight and understanding, but by action discharge. She does offer the therapist a model of rectification when she mentions being able to stop taking pills; he should cease offering interventions that are equated with the use of medication. Her avoidance of anything disturbing in the newspaper is a commentary on manifest content therapy. This approach tends to deny realities within the unconscious communicative interaction, especially the patient's valid perceptions of the therapist's pathology and poor functioning. The past is virtually always thought of as distorted in the present; that the present can repeat the past in the therapy is not considered. Interventions are offered almost entirely in terms of surface material, with respect to both the therapeutic and outside relationships.

The next example shows that in manifest-level clinical work, there can be significant differences between the therapist's conscious intentions and what the patient unconsciously perceives. In the session, the one before the therapist's vacation, the patient asked if the therapist would be back in two weeks. He had been told previously that this was the case, but the therapist repeated the information. Because this patient had had difficulties during previous separations from his therapist, she thought this reassurance would be beneficial for him and make this impending separation less anxiety producing. He immediately responded by changing the topic, saying that he had been doing pretty well on his new job. He had been there three days. He then wondered if perhaps he was a con artist; his boss has been showing him things that he should be doing, and he had been taking his cues from him. People had been telling him he had been doing well on his new job, but he was still concerned that they really were not sure that he would be able to continue to perform well and not get fired from his job. Manifest content therapists, who do not understand the latent implications of derivative communication, might view the patient's references to doing pretty well on his job as justification for the therapist's offering reassurance about the length of her vacation. They would not consider the possibility that the patient's reference to being a con artist could be interpreted as both a self and an object representation; that the patient was able to con the therapist into giving reassurance and the therapist was unconsciously perceived as a "con artist," attempting to con the patient out of his separation anxiety. Also, the reference to being told he was doing well on his job but believing that those who were offering him this reassurance really did not know if he would be able to sustain his performance and not get fired might be interpreted as an expression of his doubts that this kind of therapeutic approach would have any lasting effects, and as a statement that if his therapist continued to intervene in this manner, he would fire her.

Thus, manifest content therapeutic work keeps the patient tied to his or her inner world of bad objects for two reasons. First, the surface relatedness between the therapist and patient does not generate positive introjects. Second, because only the manifest content is addressed, the underlying catastrophic truths pertinent both to the therapeutic interaction and to the inner world of both patient and therapist are obliterated. Both factors enable the patient to avoid a therapeutic regression.

Type One Derivative Therapy

The next level of listening has been termed by Langs the Type One derivative level. Most psychoanalysts, including Fairbairn, work at this level. On this level of listening, the therapist attributes to the patient some unconscious intention, meaning, or function based primarily on displacements from past relationships and on projections of current intrapsychic fantasies and needs. These inferences focus on the patient's dynamics and their genetic sources.

In a case described by Fairbairn (1952, pp. 197–222), although his level of listening is on a Type One derivative level, his style of intervening can only be inferred from his account, because no interventions are included. That this patient was not analyzed in a secure frame is evidenced by Fairbairn's comment that he had been in contact with her family doctor and, subsequently, with her gynecologist. His contact with her doctors represents a violation of the patient's right to total confidentiality and privacy. Other aspects of the frame, including both fixed components, such as location of the analyst's office, set fee and hours, and length and frequency of sessions, and the human components, such as his capacity to understand and intervene, relative anonymity, use of neutral interventions, and capacity to offer the patient appropriate gratifications, are impossible to determine from the description.

Fairbairn describes this patient's mother as playing an important role in the formation of a strict superego. The first breakthrough in the analysis was the emergence of memories of early childhood connected with the patient's grandfather. Once some preliminary resistance was overcome, these memories poured into consciousness. A change in the patient's behavior was then noted. On the train on the way to the analysis, she began to flirt with men and on a few occasions was hugged and kissed by strangers. Fairbairn attributed these occurrences to the sudden release of pent-up libido that analysis had effected. Subsequently, these experiences produced a sense of shame and embarrassment in the patient, so she avoided contact with men as much as possible.

Fairbairn conceptualizes her analysis as having three stages. During the first stage the analysis did not penetrate beneath a genital level. In the second stage the deeper levels of the unconscious made their presence felt. The presence of a strong anal fixation had been inferred from the beginning because of her passion for cleanliness. In the third stage components of the superego relevant to anal and oral situations began to emerge.

From this case description, it can be surmised that Fairbairn appeared to function as a Type One derivative therapist. All his formulations linked the patient's associations to her intrapsychic dynamics. It must be assumed that his interventions were consistent with these formulations. Fairbairn explained the patient's sexual acting out according to intrapsychic dynamics and did not consider that it might have been a reaction to his management of the frame or to his interventions. That he does not include his interventions suggests that no attention was paid to unconscious perceptions of the therapist or to the continuous therapeutic interaction. He apparently did not consider that his twice violating the patient's confidentiality and privacy led to the formation of negative introjects or otherwise adversely affected the therapy.

The therapist who works on a Type One derivative level does offer an atmosphere of analytic effort but at the same time seals off chaotic truths by interpreting elaborate fictions. The analyst projectively identifies much of his or her own pathology into the patient while consciously denying its influence. This kind of patient–therapist interaction is designed to exclude realizations connected to the spiraling communicative interaction and to deny the inevitable and continuous countertransferences of the therapist. Fairbairn does not acknowledge the possibility or the evidence in his patient's derivative communications of any countertransference.

By working on a Type One derivative level, Fairbairn reinforced the very resistance he attempted to overcome. He states that the only way to dissolve the patient's maintenance of the inner world as a closed system is through the generation of positive introjects. Yet his case study contains derivatives of valid unconscious perceptions of his behavior that suggest, contrary to his claim, that negative introjects were generated, or at least reinforced, and the closed system maintained. Further, because he did not acknowledge the patient's communication and behavior as a reaction to his management of the frame or his interventions, he held the patient responsible for all that had transpired. Working in this manner, he inadvertently re-created the early pathological situation in which the child was blamed for the parents' inadequacies. Negative, rather than positive, introjects were generated under these conditions, and the patient remained tied to her inner world of bad objects.

Type Two Derivative Therapy

Langs's description of the third level of listening and intervening, the Type Two derivative level, seems to achieve most closely Fairbairn's concept of the generation of positive introjects. Type Two derivatives are inferences from the manifest content of the patient's material organized around specific adaptive contexts. The adaptive context is the specific reality that evokes an intrapsychic response. In Type One derivative therapy, the patient is considered sick and distorting and the analyst is viewed as free of disturbance; in contrast, in Type Two derivative therapy, the analyst assumes or soon learns that patients can function quite well most of the time, but on an unconscious level. They are impaired only in that they cannot use these resources in their everyday life. The analyst also tries to be aware of the continuous, inevitable countertransferences.

Langs's communicative approach, utilizing Type Two derivative listening and intervening, is illustrated by the following case material. In the session previous to the one being presented, the patient had requested a change in her appointment time for one of the summer months. She would not be working during that month and thought if she could come at an earlier time during the day, she could then use the remainder of the day to go to the beach or to be with friends. The therapist told the patient that she was asking for a change in the structure of the therapy and perhaps she could continue to say what came to mind so her associations could be used as a basis for making a decision. She then went on to talk about how important having structure was in her life, because it gave her a sense of stability; when she was faced with unneeded changes, she felt fears of going out of control and of going crazy. Later in the session, the therapist interpreted to her that although on a conscious level she wanted to change her appointment time and had offered realistic reasons for this request, her indirect material indicated that she obtained a certain degree of stability from structure and that when it was removed she felt out of control and crazy. She decided to withdraw her request for a change of appointment time.

Working on a Type Two derivative level, the therapist organized his intervention around the adaptive context of the secure frame that he offered the patient and the patient's attempt to break it. Unlike Fairbairn in the previous case, he understood the unconscious implications of a secure frame for the patient. This patient eloquently described, from the derivatives she provided, how a secure frame offers the patient a holding environment that provides the stability, security, and boundaries that permit a therapeutic regression without the need for pathological defenses against the inner turmoil and loss of control.

Proper maintenance of the therapeutic frame provides the patient constructive interactional experiences that lead to positive inner structural changes through incorporative identification with the positive qualities of the therapist. This process is the essence of Fairbairn's theory. The therapist's sound functioning in this session should generate positive introjects for the patient, and her material in the following session should contain positive images and possibly some new, surprising associations.

In the following session she talked of going out with a man she had not seen for a while. When she had met him, years before, she had perceived him as bright and sexually aggressive. Now she realized that he did not want to make a commitment. They used to go out, and have sex, and then she would not hear from him for a while. Now she was not as interested in seeing him as she used to be. They had gone out on the previous Friday night and had a good time, but she felt that she had changed. She then went on to talk about her present boyfriend. This was someone she really liked; he was so much more committed, someone who really cared. Although she had some doubts about her present boyfriend, he far surpassed the other man. She had learned that she was not afraid of commitment; it was the other man who was. She thought it would be better if she did not get involved with the elusive types. Having sex on the previous Friday night, she had felt almost disloyal to her boyfriend. She did not understand why having sex with her boyfriend sometimes hurt. It would hurt when he first penetrated, and there would even be a little blood. She had been able to have sex with the other man on Friday and not lose any enjoyment on Saturday with her boyfriend. This was a significant change. They had even had sex on Sunday. Having sex three days in a row was unusual; she felt that this was progress for her.

In the adaptive context of the therapist's keeping the frame secure in the previous session, the patient introjectively identified with a committed therapist. She then was able to begin to lose interest in relationships with men previously perceived as exciting who were afraid to make a commitment. Her interest and involvement had become centered upon her boyfriend, whose commitment and stability she now valued. This process is quite similar to what Fairbairn stated earlier: the patient can relinquish his or her attachment to bad objects safely only when these internal bad objects are replaced by the positive, introjective aspects of the therapist. When this process occurs, the patient can then tolerate a temporary therapeutic regression. In the session, transference occurred in the patient's allusion to being physically damaged by her boyfriend during sex. This reference is a fantasy related to being damaged through an intimate relationship. The allusion was the beginning of a therapeutic regression. It is beyond the scope of this chapter to delineate the communicative approach to transference, except to state that transference always refers to *unconscious* fantasy constellations and may be conveyed by patients through allusions to outside figures.

CONCLUSION

In this presentation a link has been made between some aspects of Fairbairn's theory of object relations and Langs's communicative approach. Fairbairn believed that the greatest resistance in therapy is the patient's maintenance of the inner world as a closed system. Only by the therapist's generation of positive introjects can the patient relinquish these bad inner objects. If this process does not occur, the therapy is stalemated.

Langs's communicative approach facilitates this process. The therapist's establishment of ground rules and boundaries with the patient fosters healthy relatedness yet separateness. Valid silences and interpretations help to provide a model of someone capable of mature relatedness and a necessary frustrator and interpreter of the patient's pathological symbiotic wishes. Individuation and a strong sense of identity follow such interactions and therapeutic endeavors.

REFERENCES

FAIRBAIRN, W.R.D. (1952). *Psychoanalytic Studies of the Personality*. New York: Basic Books.

LANGS, R. (1978). *The Listening Process*. New York: Jason Aronson.

———— (1980). *Interactions: The Realm of Transference and Countertransference*. New York: Jason Aronson.

CHAPTER 21

Self Psychology and the Dynamics of the Bipersonal Field

Douglas Detrick, Ph.D.

In the postclassical period of psychoanalysis, three general trends in theoretical orientation are discernible. The first, characterized by the attempt to deepen our theoretical knowledge (and, therefore, clinical leverage), relies on the models of the personality that Freud first put forth in "The Ego and the Id" (1923) and subsequently elaborated in "Inhibitions, Symptoms, and Anxiety" (1926). This approach relies exclusively on the so-called structural model (id–ego–superego) of the personality. The Oedipus complex is considered to be at the core of most psychological disturbances, either in the form of the disguised oedipal wishes themselves or through a character structure determined by the defensively motivated regression away from oedipal anxieties (Arlow and Brenner 1964, Brenner 1976).

The second trend is characterized by an elaboration of Freud's structural theory through an emphasis both on preoedipal defensive constellations and on internalized object relations. In the theoretical domain, the work of Otto Kernberg is the best known (1975, 1976); in the clinical–technical domain, Robert Langs's work is in the forefront. In this context Langs has stated that his work *The Bipersonal Field* represents "the integration of the interactional dimension into classical psychoanalytic theory and technique" (Langs 1976, p. 11). Langs's theoretical ideas owe a debt to Melanie Klein and the English object relations school.

The third trend is exemplified in the work of Heinz Kohut and psychoanalytic self psychology. Although within the science of psychoanalysis, self psychology is a theory of personality development essentially different from Freud's. In contrast with Freud, who placed drives and defenses at the motivational core of the personality, Kohut places the self and its aspirations (that is, its ambitions and ideals) at this core. As a result, many see Kohut as the first truly post-Freudian psychoanalyst.

SELF PSYCHOLOGY: AN OVERVIEW

Psychoanalytic self psychology was introduced by Heinz Kohut in his *Restoration of the Self* (1977). In this work he introduced the concept of the bipolar self and the essential role that selfobject relationships play in human development. Kohut describes the bipolar self as comprising the person's ambitions at one pole and ideals at the other. The unique contexts and relationships between the person's ambitions and ideals make up the *nuclear self*, the motivational core of the personality. Between these two poles reside the person's talents and skills, allowing for the realization of the "nuclear program": that program of action intrinsic and essential to the nuclear self. Kohut has stated, "It is psychoanalytic self psychology which has hypothesized the existence of a core self consisting of nuclear ambitions, nuclear skills and talents, and nuclear idealized goals and has thus explained the fact that the human self is poised toward the future. The dynamic tension of the program laid down in our nuclear self strives toward realization and thus gives to each of us a specific destiny that we either fulfill, partially fulfill, or fail to fulfill in the course of our lives" (Kohut 1980, p. 544).

According to Kohut, the bipolar self is the end result of two developmental lines. The first, which results in the adult's ambitions, begins early in life in the infant's needs for confirmation and enthusiastic parental acceptance of the innate feelings of vigor and perfection. As the child matures, phase-appropriate ways of "saying" the same thing to the parent also develop, just as there are phase-appropriate confirming parental responses. The adult's ideals, those internalized values for which we strive, are also the end product of a second developmental process. This developmental line begins in the parent's capacity to soothe the overstimulated or upset infant by allowing the child to "merge" with the adult's calmness and thereby be soothed and regain the feelings of calmness or vitality. Sometime after infancy, although the parental practice of soothing by allowing the child to merge with the parent does not stop, the child also has needs to look up to the parents and believe them to be infallible or perfect.

Complementary and essential to Kohut's concept of the bipolar self is the concept of the selfobject. The two developmental lines that eventually consolidate in the ambitions and ideals are in essence the results of selfobject experiences. Selfobjects "are objects which we experience as a part of ourself; the expected control over them is, therefore, closer to the concept of the control which a grownup expects to have over his own body and mind than to the concept of the control which he expects to have over others" (Kohut and Wolf 1978, p. 414). It is the role of selfobject experiences in human development that is the centerpiece of Kohut's contribution to psychoanalysis as a general psychology. To the clinician, his discovery of the selfobject transferences (referred to in *The Analysis of the Self* as the narcissistic transferences) is of seminal significance. Those selfobject needs for mirroring and idealization that are met less than optimally in the growing child will result in defects in the functioning of the developing self.

Kohut and Wolf (1978) put forward three dimensions in the assessment of the state and organization of the self: (1) *vitality*, ranging from enfeeblement to vigor; (2) *cohesion*, ranging from fragmentation to cohesiveness; and (3) *functional harmony*, ranging from chaos to harmony. Patients with disturbances of the self (self disorders) present a wide variety of clinical symptom complexes and character structures. Tolpin (1978) described three categories of symptomatology associated with disorders of the self in children: First, the deficits may manifest themselves directly and include free-floating anxiety, empty (guiltless) depression, or rageful feelings. Second, self disturbances may be given symbolic expression. Tolpin states that "inner tensions associated with fragmentation, depletion, and narcissistic rage can be expressed symbolically as any of the anxieties associated with the genetic series Freud . . . described—for example, as fears of darkness, noise, annihilation, starvation, helplessness, rejection, desertion, mutilation, illness, poverty, kidnappers, robbers, witches, monsters, animals, insects" (Tolpin 1978, p. 176).

The third possibility is that the deficit in the self may be sexualized. Tolpin states that the child "may attempt to regain cohesion (fill in for the deficits due to frustrated development needs) by reorganizing himself around his own body, especially the erogenous zones and their functions and products" (Tolpin 1978, p. 176). Kohut, in *The Analysis of the Self*, states, "The regressive psychic structures, the patient's perception of them, and his relationship to them, may become sexualized both in the psychoses and in the narcissistic personality disorders" (Kohut 1971, p. 9). He has further specified that perversions such as voyeurism and masochism are correlated with deficits in the developmental line that leads to the ideals, whereas exhibitionistic or sadistic perversions are correlated with deficits in the developmental line that leads to the ambitions (Kohut 1977, pp. 127, 171–172).

It should be stressed that all the sexual and hostile wishes and behaviors that occur as a result of a disruption of a self–selfobject relationship are secondary occurrences. They are not instinctual drives that have in some way evaded ego defenses but rather are disintegration products resulting from an unsupported self that is "breaking apart."

SELF PSYCHOLOGY AND THE TREATMENT PROCESS

Kohut has discussed in considerable detail the psychoanalytic process as it relates to the reactivation and working through of the selfobject transferences. In the empathic environment that characterizes the psychoanalytic situation, the selfobject needs that were present early in life but subsequently were defended against (repressed, disavowed, or both) become reactivated and are directed toward the therapist. In *The Analysis of the Self*, Kohut (1971) calls the therapeutic reactivation of the originally frustrated childhood need for enthusiastic acceptance and confirmation of one's being the *mirror transference*. He terms the therapeutic reactivation of the originally frustrated childhood need for merger with a calming, "omnipotent" other the *idealizing transference*.

About the establishment of the selfobject transference, Kohut states, "The analyst shall acknowledge the presence of all . . . resistances and define them with friendly understanding, but in general he need do nothing further to provide reassurance. He can, on the whole, expect that the pathognomonic regression will establish itself spontaneously if he does not interfere by premature transference interpretations (which the analysand understands as prohibitions or expressions of disapproval) or other deleterious moves" (Kohut 1971, p. 88). This "friendly understanding," or empathy, is central to the psychoanalytic process as conceptualized in self psychology (see also Basch 1981, Wolf 1979). Kohut (1977, p. 88) has discussed this important issue by further elaborating the distinction between the "understanding" and "explaining" aspects of both the overall course of psychotherapy and each separate intervention. He stresses that it is the patient's experience of being understood by the therapist that is essential to movement in the therapy and is the sine qua non for effective "explaining" interpretations.

Because the analyst is *experienced* not as a separate or independent person but as an extension of the patient's own self, "the patient's reactions to the disturbance of his relationship with the narcissistically experienced object . . . occupy a central position of strategic importance that corresponds to the place of the structural conflict in the psychoneuroses" (Kohut 1971, p. 92).

The working-through process of the idealizing transference thus follows this typical sequence of events: "(1) the patient's loss of the narcissistic union with the idealized selfobject; (2) the ensuing disturbance of the narcissistic balance; (3) the subsequent hypercathexis of archaic forms of either (a) the idealized parent imago or (b) the grandiose self; and, fleetingly, (4) the hypercathexis of the (autoerotic) fragmented body-mind-self" (Kohut 1971, p. 74).

> Over and over again will the analysand experience these regressive swings after suffering a disappointment in the idealized analyst. But he will be enabled to return to the basic idealizing transference with the aid of the appropriate interpretation. . . . If the repeated interpretations of the meaning of the separations from the analyst on the level of the idealizing narcissistic libido are not given

mechanically but with the current empathy for the analysand's feelings . . . then there will gradually emerge a host of meaningful memories which concern the dynamic prototypes of the present experience. (Kohut 1971, pp. 97–98)

The back-and-forth process of selfobject transference disruption followed by its reinstitution through an empathic interpretation leads to what Kohut has termed *transmuting internalization.* In the idealizing transference, this is the structure-building process that leads to the increasing resiliency of the personality and the strengthening of the internalized ideals. For this process of structure building to proceed, the primary transference manifestations must represent the reactivation of those early selfobject needs and expectations that were repressed or disavowed. Kohut has termed this the "pathognomonic transference" (see Kohut 1971, p. 24).

The working-through process surrounding the mirror transference is concerned largely with integrating into the mature reality sectors of the personality the archaic repressed or split-off grandiose and exhibitionistic images of the self. Such a task involves a slow and painstaking bringing into consciousness of not only these shame-laden fantasies but also the anxiety-producing aspects of the intense motivation correlated with them. Like the working-through process of the idealizing transference, the central working-through process of the mirror transference involves the analysand's experience of the temporary loss of the selfobject analyst. Again, the essential working-through process of the selfobject transference starts with the patient experiencing an increased sense of well-being and an increased feeling of effectiveness in action. The patient pleasurably experiences himself or herself as "an independent center of initiative, an independent recipient of impression" (Kohut and Wolf 1978, p. 414). In the properly conducted analysis, these feelings are the result of the pathognomonic transference. They are the result of the empathic exploration of the deepening transference and the analysis of the resistances, again from the empathic point of view, that furthers such a process.

THE CASE OF MR. A.:
A SELF-PSYCHOLOGICAL PERSPECTIVE

A case that Langs discusses (Mr. A., Langs 1975, pp. 119–128) will be used here as the focus for further discussion of Langs's theories and those of self psychology. Although the clinical material is Langs's, I will offer alternate interpretations from a self-psychological perspective. Such an endeavor is fraught with difficulty. Although there is no one self-psychological approach, I believe my approach to Langs's case material demonstrates the shifting state of the self (e.g., feelings of well-being, fears of losing control) caused by the vicissitudes of the selfobject relationship with the therapist.

This case was chosen because Langs describes it in considerable detail over the course of 12 sessions.

Langs supervised the therapist who treated Mr. A. Langs describes Mr. A. as "a young man with a severe character disorder, in twice-weekly psychotherapy for a severe depression that followed the suicide of an older sister who had terminated her psychotherapy just weeks before her death. In addition, he was confused about his goals in life, seriously concerned about again becoming a homosexual, and disturbed over his inability to find a suitable marriage partner" (Langs 1975, p. 119). Self psychology adheres to the strictly psychoanalytic perspective: the quality of the transference relationship that the patient establishes yields the most significant information about diagnostic issues such as character structure, the organization of the personality, and the prognosis. To the therapist oriented to self psychology, the most important diagnostic question is whether the patient can establish one of the several varieties of selfobject transferences. Those patients who, no matter how empathic the therapist is, are unable to establish a selfobject transference relationship are either psychotic or borderline patients. Kohut explains them as those who are unable to establish a selfobject transference because the core of the personality, the nuclear self, has never attained sufficient cohesiveness. Different from the overtly psychotic patient, however, the borderline patient is able to function by relying on complex defenses that protect the chaotic core of the personality from manifest disintegration. Those patients who can establish transferences are suffering from either neurotic or selfobject disturbances. The latter category of disturbances includes two separate groups: the narcissistic behavior disorders and the narcissistic personality disorders (see Kohut 1977, pp. 192-193). It is impossible to determine a clear diagnosis for Mr. A. His symptoms, intense affective states, and interpersonal difficulties suggest a borderline character disturbance. Yet it is his capacity to establish a cohesive selfobject transference that is the arbitrator of such diagnostic questions.

Mr. A.'s complaint of being "confused about his goals in life" touches on one aspect of self psychology's approach to depth psychology that is significantly different from what has gone before. As mentioned earlier, the core of personality is a bipolar nuclear self that extends into the future. For one to judge one's life as meaningful, i.e., fulfilling, the nuclear self must be sufficiently cohesive and functional to allow its ambitions and goals to guide the individual's actions. Mr. A.'s confusion about his "goals" therefore suggests a disturbance in the functional harmony of his self.

Mr. A.'s concern "about again becoming a homosexual" suggests the presence of Tolpin's third category, a sexualization of one aspect of Mr. A.'s self structure. As discussed, sexualizations are used as a means to cover defects in the self. In this regard Kohut's definition of perverse sexuality is psychological, whereas Freud's was biological. The drives are not necessarily disintegration products. It is their covering or remedying of a defect in the self (chronic or acute) that is important.

In the second session described, Langs states, "the patient described feeling exceptionally well, although the previous day had been his sister's birthday and he had been quite depressed; he had thought of calling the therapist. He ruminated about fears of becoming dependent on the therapist and about the guilt that the therapist had suggested he had experienced in regard to the death of his sister" (Langs 1975, p. 120). A number of factors could explain the patient's describing himself as feeling much better, "exceptionally well" (e.g., defense of denial, hypomanic stimulation). From the self-psychological point of view, the patient has felt understood, that is, the therapist has empathized accurately with him, and he describes one of the manifestations of a salutary selfobject relationship, an increased sense of well-being.

Several associations later Mr. A. ruminated "about fears of becoming dependent upon the therapist." In the early stages of an analysis in which eventually a pathognomonic selfobject transference will establish itself, it is not uncommon for the patient to indicate concern about becoming dependent. It is as though the patient seeks desperately after an empathic responsiveness, only to find himself fearful once such responsiveness is forthcoming. The fear of dependence is one of a series of events that contains significant information about early pathogenic relationships and a child's eventual but inadequate solution of the problems they cause.

In the next session, the third session in this sequence, Langs describes an incident in which the neophyte therapist asked the patient "how the driving had been" and the patient responded that "it had been pretty bad." In response to this interchange, the patient asked the therapist if he had had difficulty driving to the office (there had been a heavy snowstorm), and the therapist told the patient that he lived within walking distance. In response to this interaction, the patient at first was silent and then said he felt "quite shy." He noted that he had seen his father, mentioned his sister's suicide, and then said that he would not visit his father again; he didn't hate him, but "felt rather sorry for him; he then thought of the snow falling on his sister's grave" (Langs 1975, p. 120). Langs's comment about this interaction is:

> Despite this deviation's human qualities, it was predicted in supervision that it would be experienced by the patient as a homosexual gift and seduction offered as compensation for the therapist's failure adequately to intervene and as an attempt to undo his unresolved hostilities toward Mr. A. . . . As supervisor, I anticipated that it would evoke homosexual longings and anxious suicidal fantasies, and that

the patient would seek out further deviations in order both to gratify his own neurotic unconscious fantasies and needs, and to reinforce the defensive misalliance.

Langs goes on to suggest that the patient would also, "assist the therapist in re-establishing the boundaries of their relationship and in modifying the therapist's unresolved countertransference difficulties" (Langs 1975, p. 121).

Although it is very difficult to arrive at a satisfactory technical definition of "human qualities" as they relate to the responsiveness of the therapist to the patient within the therapeutic situation, Kohut has emphasized that the analytic process will be facilitated if the therapist maintains an expected level of human responsiveness. The self-psychological viewpoint would not emphasize the personal aspects of the therapist's comments in explaining the disruption, but rather the attempt by the therapist to maintain his own inordinate selfobject needs. In other words, the underlying anxiety and need for reassurance that motivated the therapist to involve himself in this interaction was the primary cause of the ensuing disturbance in the patient. A self-psychological viewpoint would be that the patient came to the session anxious and hoping for (expecting) a calming, empathic therapeutic presence, but in fact was confronted with the therapist's own inordinate selfobject needs for a calming selfobject. Langs emphasizes, in his explanation of the results of this therapist's incorrect intervention, the hostility and homosexuality wishes. A self-psychological perspective would certainly take these ideas into account but would emphasize that both the homosexuality longings (or fantasies motivated by them) and the hostility are results of a breakdown in the selfobject relationship, that is, a lack of empathy implied in the therapist's incorrect interventions. In this regard Langs states, "implied here are feelings of rage toward his father who, he felt, had contributed to his sister's suicide, and sense of compassion for him—feelings, in the present adaptive context, that are displaced from the therapist" (Langs 1975, p. 121). At the end of this first series of associations, however, there is the image of snow falling on his sister's grave, perhaps a poignant fantasy reflecting the cold isolation experienced by this man as a result of an unempathic interaction with the hoped-for idealized (selfobject) father.

Langs then describes the next seven sessions, which were characterized by gross empathic errors on the part of the therapist (seemingly motivated by the therapist's need to utilize the patient as a stabilizing selfobject) that resulted in such untoward reactions as fears of losing control—"He could remember wanting to sleep with his mother" (Langs 1975, p. 125)—and rage at the therapist. Although explicable by such concepts as "ego weakness" and "ego defect," such "id" impulses would be emphasized by a self-psychological perspective to be fragmentation products of a disintegrating self. Mr. A.'s "fear of losing control" points to another important contribution by Kohut, the relationship between the ego functions (thought *processes*) and the self. Although Kohut has said they are on different levels of abstraction, it is true that disordered ego functions are the result of a fragmenting (or fragmented) self (see Kohut 1971, p. 132).

In the next-to-last session Langs describes, the patient has returned from having missed two sessions.

> Upon his return the patient began his hour by expressing a fear that the therapist would not be there. He spoke of a movie he had seen while he was away, in which an extremely self-centered man promiscuously made love to many different women. The therapist commented that the patient seemed conflicted about returning and was afraid of getting too close to him, and Mr. A. agreed, saying that he had had an image during his absence of begging the therapist not to seduce him. (Langs 1975, p. 128)

Later in the session the therapist stated that he felt that the patient's sexual feelings toward him "had apparently intensified because of the self-relevations he had made, adding that this seemed to be interfering with his talking in the sessions and with others" (Langs 1975, p. 128). The patient agreed.

In the next session the patient began by reporting that he "felt considerably better and expressed gratitude toward the therapist, stating that for the first time he could see the therapist as a real person who understood him" (Langs 1975, p. 128). A self-psychological perspective would stress that, as a result of the empathic interventions in the previous sessions, the patient was able to develop a more advanced level of functioning and a feeling of well-being. Langs then reports the next associations of the patient: that he "had told his cousin of his homosexual fantasies toward the therapist and this had terrified the cousin, who was afraid of such things. He then went on to describe how he once tried to seduce a very close friend who had refused him, and he then spoke further about the death of his sister" (Langs 1975, p. 128). In regard to these associations, Langs states: "This material begins with a further unconscious perception of the therapist's difficulties and emphasizes the seductive aspects of his deviations in technique. The patient's actual fear of being seduced strongly reflects his own psychopathology, including some degree of difficulty in reality testing and his extensive homosexual conflicts" (Langs 1975, pp. 128–129).

A self-psychological perspective allows for another plausible interpretation of the clinical data. The earlier material strongly suggests that Mr. A. is an exceptionally vulnerable individual in whom the unempathic responsiveness of the therapist, motivated by the therapist's own selfobject needs, has evoked feelings of despair and rage, and wishes for homosexual contact. In the most recently described session, the therapist is uncharacteristically empathic, and Mr. A., at least initially, responds with an increased sense of well-being and gratitude toward the therapist. Mr. A.'s associations, however, move to a description of a conversation about his homosexual feelings with a cousin that led to feelings of terror, and a memory of how he had once tried to seduce a very close friend who had refused him. This line of associations may point to another area in which the structure of Mr. A.'s personality is threatened: the overstimulating and hence fragmentation-producing thoughts of the longed-for empathic contacts with the therapist. It is noteworthy that in this latest series of associations, Mr. A. concludes with the image of his dead sister. Although the issue is somewhat confused in this case because of the countertransferences manifested by the therapist, such sequences of events, in which the empathic resonance felt by the patient produces an overstimulated state that then leads to fears of fragmentation and various defensive structures (e.g., sexualizations) designed to maintain the integrity of the personality, are common in highly vulnerable individuals.

Langs then goes on to say:

> On the other hand, his statement about not wanting another lover—the therapist—but just someone who understands him, is a poignant expression of the specific need of every patient in psychotherapy: inappropriate love repeats past neurotic interactions and reinforces the neurosis, reasonable "love" in the form of concern offers a positive identification, but only insightful understanding leading to interpretations can promote lasting, adaptive, inner change based on conflict resolution. (Langs 1975, p. 129)

Langs and self psychology agree that one of the central dimensions of effective psychoanalytic cure is understanding ("a poignant expression of the specific need of every patient in psychotherapy" [Langs 1975, p. 129]). Mr. A.'s statement about wanting not another lover "but just someone who understands him" must derive from recognition that the sexualization of the defect in his self is at best a remedial action that leads to no genuine solution of his problems.

EMPATHY, "THE PATIENT'S ATTEMPT TO CURE THE THERAPIST," AND THE SELFOBJECT ENVIRONMENT: SOME THEORETICAL CONSIDERATIONS

One of the clinical phenomena that Langs has focused on and discussed is the patient's perception of the therapist's deviations from the correct therapeutic technique and the so-called attempt to cure the therapist. He has adduced data to support the idea that the patient is exquisitely sensitive to any deviation in technique. In this regard Langs states: "Impingements on the therapeutic environments—the ground rules, framework, hold, and setting of the psychotherapeutic and analytic situations—evoke intense but highly predictable responses in patients" (Langs 1979, p. ix). He also contends that the patient subliminally perceives the area of the personality responsible for the countertransference error leading to the deviation and that the patient's associations then communicate both the disturbance in the therapeutic situation and what it is in the therapist that has led to it. For example, in the case of Mr. A., Langs attributes most of the patient's associations to fears about being seduced to the unconscious homosexual wishes residing in the therapist (see Langs 1975, p. 121). The self-psychologically informed clinician would judge that Langs, using different words, is referring to the disruptive impact of an unempathic intervention, i.e., a therapeutic deviation.

A number of issues need to be resolved, the most important of which is the extent to which the patient's associations following a disruption are determined by the subjective experience within the patient rather than those factors in the therapist that led to the disruption. It seems more useful to discuss these issues on a more broadly based theoretical (metapsychological) level than on a clinical plane.

As self psychology has come to focus on the role of selfobject experiences in human interaction, it has also come to focus increasingly on the concept of empathy. This is not surprising, as there is an intrinsic connection between selfobject relationships and the experience of empathy and empathic communication. Fundamental to the understanding of selfobject relationships is the fact that they are *in essence* communications between people. But what kind of communications? At their foundation is *affective* interaction (i.e., communication). Basch has laid the theoretical groundwork for an understanding of the importance of affects in psychoanalysis (Basch 1976, 1983). He puts forward the idea that early in life the infant signals its inner state to the mother via the channel of affective communication. The infant's affective state evokes a similar but modulated reaction in the caretaker, who then, on the basis of this "vicariously introspected" knowledge, is able to undertake actions that attempt to remedy the child's dysphoric state.

Following Tomkins, Basch sees the affective behavior of infants as comprising eight basic reactions, which are manifested primarily by the facial musculature. In discussing the central role affects play in early life, he says, "Dramatic as it is, speech manifests itself relatively late in our individual development, and we tend to overlook the fact that already at birth and for the rest of our lives our ability to communicate through the facial, mimetic musculature is uniquely and highly developed. We are born equipped with the basic requirement for a complex social existence, i.e., an effective, though nonverbal method for communication" (Basch 1976, p. 764). It is this affective "information," the soothing or stimulating affective feedback from the mother, that allows for the eventual (second-year) consolidation of the self, that is, the subjectively based symboling axis around which information processing is oriented (see Basch 1975).

This theoretical position allows for a clearer understanding of the psychoanalytic situation as "container." In the therapy of self disorders (such as that of Mr. A.), the "holding and containing functions of the frame" (Langs 1977, p. 32) are at the center of interpretive focus. It is not that a secure "frame" allows for projection of the core psychopathology (i.e., manifestations of pathogenic conflicts and controls), but rather that the analysis of the disturbances in the selfobject transference—the "analytic container," as it were—is the primary focus of the treatment.

Langs approaches empathy differently: "Empathy involves both affect and cognition, and is based on a relatively nonconflicted interplay of introjective and projective mechanisms, and a variety of forms of unconscious sharing" (Langs 1979, p. 540). By building the concepts of projection and introjection into his definition and not placing affective communication at the center, he no longer is able to explain those clinical findings out of which the fabric of clinical self-psychological theory is woven. For example, he focuses on drive–defense constellations as primary in a clinicotheoretical approach in which there is always self and other (hence the "bipersonal field").

But the fact that selfobject experiences and transferences are in essence communications allows for a theoretical approach to the observations Langs makes regarding the "patient's attempt to cure the therapist." This phenomenon can be explained as the disrupted patient's attempt to signal to the (selfobject) therapist that a disruption, a breakdown in the selfobject relationship, has taken place. The patient's associations in such situations are determined by the subjective experience of the patient and the need to communicate this experience as accurately as possible to the "caretaking" selfobject analyst. This analysis is consistent with the genetically analogous situation in which the disrupted infant sends a distress signal to the caretaking parent.

SUMMARY

Psychoanalytic self psychology and the work of Robert Langs represent two of the more important trends in postclassical psychoanalysis. The two share the view that the analysis of defenses against infantile sexual and aggressive (oedipal) fantasies is not the major focus of the psychoanalytic process. Both are attempts to broaden and deepen the clinical application of classical psychoanalysis. There are many important differences between the two views, however. In the clinical domain, the phenomenon of the self-object transferences of self psychology is perhaps the most significant difference. The selfobject transferences, the discovery of Heinz Kohut, are the centerpiece of self-psychological clinical theory. Many of Langs's clinical observations can be understood through this concept. Whereas Langs has restricted his focus to the clinical situation, self psychology also puts forth a new theory of personality. Rather than placing the drives (id) and the defenses at the motivational core of the personality, as did Freud, self psychology places at the motivational core the nuclear self and its aspirations.

REFERENCES

ARLOW, J., AND BRENNER, C. (1964). *Psychoanalytic Concepts and the Structural Theory*. New York: International Universities Press.

BASCH, M. F. (1975). Toward a theory that encompasses depression: a revision of existing causal hypotheses in psychoanalysis. In *Depression and Human Existence*, ed. E. J. Anthony and T. Benedek, pp. 485–534. Boston: Little, Brown.

—— (1976). The concept of affect: a re-examination. *Journal of the American Psychoanalytic Association* 24:759–777.

—— (1983). Empathic understanding: a review of the concept and some theoretical considerations. *Journal of the American Psychoanalytic Association*. 34:101–126.

BRENNER, C. (1976). *Psychoanalytic Technique and Psychic Conflict*. New York: International Universities Press.

FREUD, S. (1923). The ego and the id. *Standard Edition* 19:3–66.

—— (1926). Inhibitions, symptoms and anxiety. *Standard Edition* 20:77–175.

KERNBERG, O. (1975). *Borderline Conditions and Pathological Narcissism*. New York: Jason Aronson.

—— (1976). *Object Relations Theory and Clinical Psychoanalysis*. New York: Jason Aronson.

KOHUT, H. (1971). *The Analysis of the Self*. New York: International Universities Press.

—— (1977). *The Restoration of the Self*. New York: International Universities Press.

—— (1980). Two letters. In *Advances in Self Psychology*, ed. A. Goldberg, pp. 449–469. New York: International Universities Press.

KOHUT, H., AND WOLF, E. (1978). The disorders of the self and their treatment: an outline. *International Journal of Psycho-Analysis* 59:413–425.

LANGS, R. (1975). The therapeutic relationship and deviations in technique. *International Journal of Psychoanalytic Psychotherapy* 4:106–141.

—— (1976). *The Bipersonal Field*. New York: Jason Aronson.

—— (1977). *The Therapeutic Interaction: A Synthesis*. New York: Jason Aronson.

—— (1979). *The Therapeutic Environment*. New York: Jason Aronson.

Tolpin, M. (1978). Selfobjects and oedipal objects. *Psychoanalytic Study of the Child* 33:167–184.

Wolf, E. (1979). Ambience and abstinence. *Annual of Psychoanalysis* 4:101–115.

CHAPTER 22

A Comparison of Langs's Interactional Frame and Schafer's New Language for Psychoanalysis

Lars Bejerholm, Ph.D., and Gunnar Windahl, Ph.D.

In this chapter we propose that the perspective of Roy Schafer's "action language" provides a useful framework for viewing the transition in technique and clinical theory Robert Langs has charted. We will start with a short presentation of Langs's and Schafer's ideas.

LANGS

Basic to Langs's approach is his conviction that the patient's relationship with the analyst reveals both transference and nontransference elements, and although the former are expressions of his more or less permanent psychopathology, the latter are manifestations mostly of nonpathological curative aspects in his personality. The patient in an unconscious manner works over the communications from the analyst and responds both in terms of valid unconscious perceptions and introjections and in terms of neurotic defensive and distorting elements. The analyst too responds both validly and inappropriately to the patient's communications.

Langs's conception of the analytic interaction includes conscious and unconscious intrapsychic contents and operations of both patient and analyst, as well as the conscious and unconscious interaction and the interactional mechanisms at work. It is a bipersonal field concept within an adaptational–interactional framework. The analytic situation is viewed as a spiraling interaction within the analytic dyad in which the patient's communications become the adaptive context for the therapist's interventions and these interventions in turn become the adaptive context for the patient's responses. Each reaction to the predominant adaptive context (adaptive stimulus) is considered a Type Two derivative, with both realistic and distorted elements, as important commentaries on the unconscious communications, bred in each particular context. Thus the therapeutic relationship is viewed as a continuous communicative interaction, conscious and unconscious, with projective and introjective components that become the central vehicle for therapeutic work. All the patient's communications have some influence on the analytic transactions and experiences, and the therapist is a consistent participant who makes perpetual inputs rooted in both his valid, noncountertransference functioning and in his undetected countertransferences.

Above all, Langs's approach clarifies the confusion between transference and nontransference material. Here he is in the tradition of Strachey (1934) and Little (1951), both of whom underscore the fact that Freud's so-called abstinence rule not only promotes topographic regression in the patient but also serves as a prerequisite for the patient's reality testing, that is, his deciding what comes from his own mind and what has been triggered by the behavior of the therapist (countertransference behavior as technical errors, frame deviations, and so forth).

SCHAFER

Schafer (1976) wants to reformulate the language of classic metapsychology, "this mixed physicochemical and evolutionary biological language." Concepts like cathexis, structure, force, economy, and mechanism imply that there exists a "ghost in the machine" that causes behavior (a homuncular model). To rectify this situation, Schafer would translate this mechanistic model of the mind into an "action language" in which all psychological behaviors, processes, and experiences get an action status, where every action is designated by an active verb, or adverbial locution, stating the mode of the action. Nouns and adjectives are avoided when possible, and no references to quantity, location, movement, direction, and internal processes are to be found in his model of the mind.

What Schafer does is to attack the bad habit of reification and say that we make a mistake to take "mind," "introjects," "self," and "emotion" to refer to things (Ryle 1949). An antinoun language should be preferred (verbal nouns), in which the person (speaker, dreamer, thinker) is responsible for his actions. A phobia is not a phobia but a person's way of thinking anxiously.

Schafer's ideas have received much criticism (Friedman 1976, Barratt 1978, Aufhauser 1979). We have a positive attitude toward Schafer's "new language," and we want to point out that general psychology often favors an "action frame."

Piaget (Piaget and Inhelder 1969) has, for example, shown that action and its structuralization is the core of mentation, that need-gratifying, aim-directed action predates even imaging, and that imaging itself is an activity.

The behaviorist school is another action-prone branch of psychology, even if this school makes the mistake of restricting the definition of behavior (action) to observable or motoric acts.

LANGS'S MODEL AS AN ACTION THEORY

When we confront Langs's key concepts of the adaptational-interactional viewpoint ("a clinical metapsychological approach to the patient and inter-actional processes, conscious and unconscious in both spheres") and the bipersonal field ("a metaphor for the therapeutic situation which stresses the interactional qualities of the field, and postulates that every experience and communication within the field receives vectors from both patient and therapist"), it is evident that the idea of action predominates.

Concepts like interactional symptoms, interactional defenses, and inter-actional projections all underscore action more than anything else. Langs consistently seems to avoid the static language of ego psychology. When, for instance, discussing resistance, he makes no reference to *pure* intra-psychic defense mechanisms, but there is a consistent emphasis on shared responsibility within the active bipersonal field. The patient is never de-scribed as coming into the therapeutic situation with his psychopathological mechanisms and history in a closed suitcase (mental laundry). In this way, Langs always favors the actor, or better, the actors (patient and therapist) before the mechanism or intrapsychic structure.

One of Langs's central concepts is the adaptive context ("the specific reality stimulus that evokes an intrapsychic response"). This concept, analogous to Freud's concept of the day residue, focuses on the patient's most urgent and important mental activity in the therapeutic situation. Besides considering the role the adaptive context plays in preparing for an uncontaminated transference interpretation, we want to point out that the whole therapeutic situation becomes more alive, and by getting an interpre-tation of it by the analyst, the patient receives the message that he is capable of thinking constructively here and now, that he is creative, and that he is permitted to see things. Again, action and aliveness are stressed.

When discussing how to handle manifest communication from the patient in the therapeutic situation, Langs introduces the concept of derivatives. By implication, this concept focuses on modes of organizing the patient's com-munication, or what the therapist makes out of the patient's raw material. Langs avoids here, at least to a certain extent, the pitfall of reification by emphasizing cognitive action in the therapist instead of latent meaning or content located in the patient or his material. Freud's differentiation be-tween the manifest and latent dream content is an example of that "category mistake" (Ryle 1949) one often makes when not considering the act of derivation. There can be only one kind of dream: the manifest dream. The so-called latent dream content is a product of derivation, that is, what the analyst or interpreter infers from the reported dream with the assistance of the dreamer's free associations, the transference situation, and so forth. The latent content is a consequence of cognitive activity of the interpreter and has no isolated location in the mind of the dreamer.

Another of Langs's important theoretical innovations is his classification of communication styles in the bipersonal field. Langs has, for instance, made Bion's notion of "attacks on linking" (1967) quite comprehensible and extends this idea to account for psychotic as well as nonpsychotic communication. Langs calls it Type C communication and shows the patient's and/or therapist's intention to destroy meaning. This leads us to a problem we want to consider at some length: the problem of intentionality.

The concept of intentionality is a stumbling block to many a metapsychological theory. Together with other mental terms such as meaning and interpretation, it has been adopted by various humanistic theories of knowledge as a supposed safeguard against there being too much influence in the realm of psychoanalysis from the methods and outlooks of natural science, positivism, and the like. It seems, though, that no metapsychology hitherto has provided psychoanalysis with an easy way out. To side with natural science to a large extent, as Freud did, creates problems, many of which have been listed by Schafer. To side with more recent, hermeneutic schools of metascience does seem to create other and no less formidable difficulties. It would be philosophically naive to believe that the concepts of intentionality and meaning will protect psychoanalysis from metascientific criticism. These concepts are, alas, problematic in themselves.

Intentionality has a long and rather complex history in the philosophy of psychology. Used to designate actions performed willingly as opposed to human behavior of a more automatic kind, the concept has little or nothing to do with its use inside phenomenology, the school of thought that emphasized this concept in the last century, foremost in the works of Bolzano, Brentano, Husserl, and Frege. In Husserl's *Logische Untersuchungen*, for instance, the concept of intention is introduced to denote entities that are specifically *non*psychological—the intention of a thought designates its definite content, i.e., that it is a thought *about* this or that—and thus intention is nothing that can be studied as such by empirical psychology. In phenomenology the same is true for central concepts like meaning and interpretation; neither of them is a psychological term in the sense of designating properties of human action (Fuller and McMurrin 1955, pp. 532–556). To those who believe that intention might be better defined in terms of meaning, one must point out that Ogden and Richards (1923), in their classic *Meaning* *of Meaning*, suggest that the latter be rendered in terms of the former. One can make better use of these concepts in formulating some principles of Gestalt psychology than in describing the properties of human actions. To regress to a less philosophical and supposedly more common sense use of intention and meaning does not solve problems of metapsychology either; to use them in explaining the process of psychoanalysis is more often than not an example of the fallacy traditionally called *obscurum per obscurius*: to explain the obscure notion by an even more obscure one.

Precisely because these central concepts are blurred, it seems important to look for specific and well-defined situations in which they are being used in what Ryle would have called a paradigmatic way (see Ryle 1953). To those not thoroughly familiar with this way of reasoning, we offer the following elucidation. Suppose you deny that man has free will (whatever that means). A counterargument would be that it makes very good sense to say that "Peter married Mary of his own free will, not forced to do so by his parents, society, and so forth." This would be a *paradigm case* of what we can understand by talking about free will in man, and it would thus be nonsense to deny that man has free will. In Langs's insistence upon the intentional actions of the patient in Type A, B, and C communications, one can find such paradigmatic uses of intention, and these give Schafer's suggestions of how to apply this concept in action language (1976, p. 199 ff.) a defined sense. Thus Langs's systematic description of the activities of the patient and the analyst in the Type A, B, and C communications can be studied as arguments for the use of action language in psychoanalysis that Schafer advocates.

Langs, however, leans heavily on Kleinian theory, the concepts of which very often confound structure and content (Zetzel 1956). The Kleinian objects are reified mental objects and not hypotheses about existing structures. Certainly Schafer would not hesitate to criticize Langs's use of concepts like "supervisory introject," the "psychotic part of personality," the "taking in and processing of projective identification (containing)".

Langs commits the sin of reification and anthropomorphism—one he shares with many a psychoanalytic writer.

ACTION LANGUAGE AND CLINICAL OUTCOMES

The mainstream of philosophy in this century, especially in the Anglo-Saxon world and in Scandinavia, is generally known as *analytical* philosophy. Developed by Russell and Wittgenstein, it has branched out in various directions, some of which give special attention to language. There exists a group of philosophers working in the United States whose interest in semantics is coupled with their efforts in mathematical logic. Another group is often called the linguistic group, or the Oxford school, of which Gilbert Ryle is perhaps best known. One could say that this latter school takes a primary interest in ordinary, daily use of language and looks upon it as an activity rather than as a system of symbols.

In his widely read and very controversial book *The Concept of Mind* (1949), Ryle attacks the so-called Cartesian myth of the ghost in the machine, i.e., the use of nouns to designate mental entities in a misleading way. In ordinary language such nouns often do a good and uncontroversial job. To ask, "What do you have in mind?" usually leads to quite comprehensible responses: you get some kind of answer as to what the other person is thinking about. But if you are beset by a dualistic view of the world, you may well construe the use of such nouns to be proof of the existence of 'MIND', asking and answering all kinds of spurious questions as to its ontological and epistemological status, and so forth. Whereas mental terms cause few, if any, problems in ordinary use of everyday language, they may cause havoc in, for instance, metapsychology (see also J. L. Austin's classic *Other Minds* [1953]). Many a book in psychoanalysis can be viewed as a gallery of pictures of famous mental entities painted by an author who has misunderstood the use of plain English. Hypostases like ego and id may cause the analyst to look in the wrong direction.

According to Ryle, the remedy lies in the rearranging of the syntactical structures of possibly misleading expressions. One way would be to replace nouns with verbs—a main theme of Schafer's. In a sense, linguistic philosophy has a therapeutic side: it reformulates, rearranges, and puts things in a new and different light, thus enabling us to get rid of haunting entities that have been created by our misuse of words. This therapy does not give answers to questions as formulated. Rather, it heals by analyzing linguistic origins and suggesting new outlooks, new ways of formulating fruitful problems.

Schafer makes full use of these notions in his appeal for a new language for psychoanalysis. There is little wonder, then, that he is open to criticism of the same kind as has been launched against linguistic philosophy. Just as a metaphysically inclined philosopher may miss spurious questions like "do universals exist?," so many analysts may have a nostalgic longing to speak in terms of traditional metapsychology. One could ask what difference it really makes whether you formulate the fundamental rule as "Say everything that comes to mind" or in an action language that avoids the noun "mind" (Schafer 1976, p. 143 ff.). In our language, Swedish, there is no literal translation of the first phrase, the rule being automatically formulated in an action language. Does this linguistic fact imply that Swedish patients are less apt to be misled by the words of the analyst into believing themselves to be victims of alien hidden forces, the spurious "mind"? This, an empirical question, should have some verifiable empirical answer. Yet one feels inclined not to engage in empirical research but rather to ask whether this line of reasoning does not overemphasize the fact that different languages have different forms of syntax. The German language is notorious for its tendency to make nouns out of action words, notable, for example, in the philosophy of Heidegger. The fact that Freud wrote in German should not be held against him.

Nevertheless, language as an action preformed by both analyst and patient has such obvious relevance in discussing analysis that it seems prima facie to be of paramount interest to seek reformulations of psychoanalysis in terms of action—or, for that matter, in terms of interaction, in Langs's version. Action is a notion of long and fruitful standing in psychology.

CONCLUSIONS

Langs's views in many instances can be regarded as an argument in favor of Schafer and as an appeal for action language. The possible advantages of such a language for psychoanalysis can be outlined as follows:

1. Action language avoids the reification of functions and therefore eliminates in several instances the possibility of building metapsychological edifices that give false shelter to the analyst and are looked on by the outsider with awe and well-founded mistrust. Action language reduces radically the number of concepts used in analysis and thus applies the classic rule set up by another Oxford philosopher, the 14th-century scholar William of Occam: "Entities are not to be multiplied except as may be necessary." Without being an infallible guarantee against misuse of language and vain speculation, action language nevertheless guards against *some* forms of theorizing that notoriously lead to a cul de sac for metapsychology.

2. Compared with the language that analysis ordinarily uses both in practice and in theory, action language tends to lower the levels of abstraction. To talk about what people do in simple, empirical terms instead of in the terms of a cumbersome jargon of metapsychology can even be seen to have definite advantages in analytical practice. As Langs points out, Type C communication is habitually infested with jargon and clichés used as effective barriers to meaningful communication. Both patient and analyst can find secure hiding places in traditional psychoanalytic verbiage.

3. The relative simplicity of action language can make it easier for the analyst to formulate interpretations. It thus promotes detechnification and makes analysis more comprehensible and alive.

There are, however, several problems involved in an exclusive use of action language for analysis. It is sufficient to point out the necessity for complete translations of all that hitherto has been discovered and valued as essential components of analysis. Whether this material can be reduced to and reformulated in action language is so far an open question; action language has not yet been investigated systematically. Further, the need for demythologizing in analysis must not be an excuse for a conceptual and linguistic purism. The criterion of a new language is its ability to open new avenues of thought and exploration. Insofar as Langs's theories of action within the bipersonal field and Schafer's strong emphasis on action language have contributed to such explorations, they have made a good case for an appeal for action language in the broadest sense of the term.

REFERENCES

AUFHAUSER, M. C. (1979). Review of "A New Language for Psychoanalysis" by Roy Schafer. *Journal of the American Psychoanalytic Association* 27:209–215.

AUSTIN, J. L. (1953). Other minds. In *Logic and Language*, Vol. 2, ed. A. G. Flew. Totowa, N.J.: Biblio, 1973.

BARRATT, B. B. (1978). Critical notes on Schafer's action language. *Annual of Psychoanalysis* 6:287–303.

BION, W. R. (1967). Attacks on linking. In W. R. Bion, *Second Thoughts: Selected Papers on Psychoanalysis*. New York: Jason Aronson.

FRIEDMAN, L. (1976). Problems of an action theory of the mind. *International Review of Psycho-Analysis* 3:129–138.

FULLER, B. A., AND McMURRIN, S. (1955). *A History of Philosophy*. 3rd ed. New York: Holt.

LITTLE, M. (1951). Countertransference and the patient's response to it. *International Journal of Psycho-Analysis* 32:32–40.

OGDEN, C. K., AND RICHARDS, I. A. (1923). *The Meaning of Meaning*. New York: Harcourt Brace Jovanovich, 1959.

PIAGET, J., AND INHELDER, B. (1969). *The Psychology of the Child*. New York: Basic Books.

RYLE, G. (1949). *The Concept of Mind*. New York: Barnes and Noble, 1962.

——— (1953). Ordinary language. *Philosophical Review* 53:1.

SCHAFER, R. (1976). *A New Language for Psychoanalysis*. New Haven: Yale University Press.

STRACHEY, J. (1934). The nature of the therapeutic action in psychoanalysis. *International Journal of Psycho-Analysis* 15:127–159.

ZETZEL, E. (1956). An approach to the relation between concept and content in psychoanalytic theory. *Psychoanalytic Study of the Child* 11:99–121.

CHAPTER 23

Narcissistic Defensiveness
and the Communicative Approach

James Raney, M.D.

> I do not think it is possible, as a scientist, completely to ignore someone's
> work which is believed in and followed by so many of our colleagues. It
> ought to be studied. I do not say believe it or accept it, but study it.
> —Ralph Greenson on Klein (Greenson et al. 1970, p. 150)

Robert Langs has developed an approach to listening, understanding, and
intervening that seems to produce a unique, sometimes extreme, defensiveness in therapists who attempt to apply it in the clinical setting. A similar
attitude is evident in a different sphere—recent psychoanalytic writings—
which contain remarkably few appropriate references to Langs's work. The
omission exists in writings that discuss issues Langs has addressed. It is
especially flagrant when the authors are known to be familiar with Langs's
work.

In clinical practice such defensiveness is manifested by an interlude in
which the therapist is inappropriately silent. Such a lack of intervention by
clinicians new to the communicative approach seems common and has not
been noted previously as a prominent problem of beginning therapists (e.g.,
Halleck and Woods 1962, Holt 1959, Kubie 1971, Mehlman 1974, Merklin
and Little 1967, Sharaf and Levinson 1964). I shall argue in this chapter that
this silent phase is unique to the communicative approach because of the self-
disclosure inherent in the approach. The silence is an attempt to protect
against a potential disturbance of narcissism in the therapist. I suggest that
the silence of writers who have been exposed to Langs's work has a similar
cause.

THE SILENT THERAPIST

Students of the communicative approach, many with considerable experience and training, commonly report lengthy silences in early attempts to
apply the technique clinically. They describe an odd inhibition of speech, an

465

inability to find anything to say. The silences seem to occur when many of the criteria of the communicative approach have been learned and erroneous interventions reduced, but before a full facility with the technique has been acquired. They often occur in the presence of an abundance of interpretable patient material. These silences, sometimes extending for entire therapy hours, contrast with experiences of students using other approaches, who more often err on the side of saying too much (Mehlman 1974).

Langs (1980a, 1982b) has established specific criteria for intervening. These are: (1) the presence of a manifest allusion to a major *indicator*, a reflection of the patient's resistances or "neurosis," which also signifies a need for a therapeutic intervention; (2) a direct or thinly disguised representation of the prevailing *adaptive contexts*, the interventions of the therapist that stimulate the "neurotic" disturbance; and (3) decodable *derivatives* that are organized by the adaptive contexts and that reveal the *unconscious* meanings of the neurotic response.

In contrast to other, less specific approaches, the implication of this approach that intervention not be made until these specific criteria have been met may account for some of this silence. This does not, however, explain therapists' silences for entire therapy hours and the odd, paralysislike sense of having nothing to say. When these hours are reported, supervisors and peers can often hear material quite clearly that meets the criteria for intervention—implications that were overlooked by the therapist.

Often, when a previously unnoticed adaptive context becomes apparent, the patient's material assumes startling clarity. These adaptive contexts may include some aspect of a recent intervention or some implications of an alteration by the therapist of the therapeutic frame—meanings that have been perceived unconsciously by the patient and then expressed through disguised derivatives (Langs 1973, 1982b). Among therapists who are just starting to use the method or those who do not use it at all, these adaptive contexts are usually deviations of the *fixed frame* (i.e., the physical setting, fee, time of sessions, confidentiality, and so forth) or of the *variable frame* (the direct interventions of the therapist) (Langs 1980a, p. 526). The therapist presenting such a case is usually bewildered by the material and describes his or her inhibition of speech as an inability to recognize the context that organizes and provides meaning to the patient's productions. When identified and interpreted, these contexts become convincingly validated as *selected facts* (Bion 1963) that organize and give meaning to the otherwise puzzling material.

The adaptive context seems to be the central and also most disturbing factor in the mastery of this new approach. When confronted with these contexts, which are usually errors and imperfections in technique, beginning therapists often will misconstrue them to be evidence of defects in their personal worth. To some extent, this is a phenomenon common to the learning of any new skill or theory (Lewin 1958). In order to confront and attempt a new idea or skill, students (and, more so, practicing therapists) must disturb their narcissistic stability. Their awkward early efforts as well as confrontation by teachers and others contradict a sense of competence, mastery, and self-perfection. Criticism, because of the narcissistic cathexis or investment of their sense of "self" in the work (Kohut 1966), is equated with an attack on the narcissistic self and self-image.

Irrespective of the approach used, inappropriate therapist silence may consistently signal an anticipated narcissistic threat in the therapist. Gill and Hoffman (1982) note inappropriate therapist silence in their study of audio-recorded analytic treatments. This silence could be a reaction to the inescapable revelation of the analysts' recorded verbalizations. Potentially revealing recorded interventions are not consistently disguised or defended with silence, because non-Langsian supervisors focus on issues other than the validity of the therapist's interventions. With the use of the communicative approach, however, supervision is more consistently narcissistically disturbing, because it focuses on the accuracy of the therapists' interventions as they are reflected in the patient's encoded reactions.

Therapists who use other approaches more often are specifically silent about certain narcissistically invested issues. On one occasion an experienced practicing psychiatrist in his second year of psychoanalytic training presented a patient whom he had evaluated for seven interview hours. He had decided after the first session or two that analysis was feasible for this patient. The patient indicated indirectly, through derivatives, that he perceived the need to begin and expressed disguised bewilderment and impatience over the analyst's delay in setting out the terms and conditions for therapy. The candidate had yet to "defend" his case in mandatory interviews with two supervising analysts. He seemed aware of his anxiety about criticism and possible rejection, and the resultant inordinate need to gather excessive information for the evaluation and presentation. His usual approach permitted questions and other remarks, which constituted most of his activity. In the most important area, however, he was "silent." He had not intervened in any regard about the most critical issue: making the long overdue arrangements for the indicated analysis.

OTHER PERSPECTIVES OF THERAPIST SILENCE

Previous writers have offered reasons for inappropriate therapist silence that differ from those proposed here. Grinberg (1970) cited the extremes of manic and inhibited students as well as those with intermediate attitudes. He suggested that inhibited therapists as a rule make interpretations that are

468 / JAMES RANEY

ambiguous or scanty. Lebovici (1970) described the widespread silence of psychoanalytic students at the beginning of treatment. This attitude, he offered, seems to be related to the inexperience of the therapist, who is overwhelmed by the variety of the patient's inhibitions and resistances. The new analyst, according to Lebovici, also may be tempted to intervene too early and too much. Flournoy (1971) suggested that the silence of the analyst may be used to defend against the impact of the analytic relationship. Franz Alexander (1959), cited by Halleck and Woods (1962), described a psychiatric resident, bound by a pledge to "*not* act as an analyst" by interpreting unconscious material, who was paralyzed and did not interpret even when he knew the meaning of the material.

Brockbank (1970) discussed the effect of the silent analyst on the patient. He postulated that certain transference projections of the patient (perhaps images of absent or unempathic early figures) are introjected and identified with by the analyst, leading to one type of therapist silence. Brockbank seemed to consider this phenomenon a form of countertransference. In other instances, according to Brockbank, the analyst's silence may stem from frustration felt as a result of futile attempts to deal with the patient's negativistic defenses. When these dynamics are considered in the light of Langs's communicative field concept, Brockbank is discovered to have described the basic components of the Type B, projection–introjection, communicative field (Langs 1978b).

The analyst's frustration implies an effort to do something to the patient—cure him or her, remove or defeat his or her resistances and defenses—rather than to interpret the meaning of the encoded material. Interpretations can include explication of resistances but ideally also include all meanings, especially those in the patient's encoded derivatives of unconscious perception of the therapist's interventions and management of the frame. When the therapist either *reacts*, through frustration, or enacts, through his or her identification with some aspect of a projected, unconsciously remembered figure of the patient's past, the Type B, action–discharge communicative field is typified. Both therapist and patient proceed as if their inner tensions and unconsciously related important people can be transferred or passed back and forth between them.

THERAPIST SILENCE AS A SYMPTOM

The key postulate of this chapter is that a therapist silence can be based on the analyst's resistance to interacting with the patient at the Type A, symbolic imagery level. With such a silence, the analyst unconsciously resists acknowledging the patient's symbolic, Type Two images, which are derivatives of the unconscious perceptions and working over of the adaptive contexts of the therapist's interventions and functioning. The concept of inappropriate therapist silence as used here is not the same as Lipton's "silence in spite of having something to say" (1977). Lipton seems to refer to silence used not in order to listen, but as a specific *appropriate* intervention.

The central carriers of meaning, according to communicative theory, are Type Two derivatives (Langs 1974). These symbolic expressions result from the modifying influence of ego defenses (e.g., repression, displacement, symbolism, denial, introjection, projection) and from needs to communicate in response to *adaptive contexts*. In the therapeutic setting, these adaptive contexts are usually the patient's unconscious veridical perceptions of the therapist's actions and interventions. The images are *derived* from the unconscious perceptions that have been modified by the ego.

An Inappropriate Therapist Silence

The following example, taken from supervision and suitably disguised, illustrates an inappropriate therapist silence in the presence of several well-represented adaptive contexts and interpretable derivatives. In the hour just prior to the one to be described, the patient mentioned meeting and discovering the name of another patient in the waiting room, who had apparently arrived an hour early. The patient was quick to point out that he had not revealed his own name. He also mentioned some muffled sounds that emanated from the waiting room while he was in his session. He expressed doubt that the office was soundproof. Other derivatives were expressed in that hour that could have been organized around the stimulus (or *indicator*) (Langs 1980b) of the meeting and the adaptive context of the sound leakage from the waiting room. The therapist made one comment in that session; it did not refer specifically to adaptive contexts or derivatives. She said, "You sound like you are trying to correct something."

During the session to be described, the room was noticeably cooler than usual. The patient was two to three minutes late—very unusual for him—and was silent for five minutes. He then said:

> It is cold. I don't feel well. You never get a cold. . . . Oh, once you did. I don't want to talk. I am bored. Is it okay to be bored? You are mad at me; not really, but I feel you are. I want to do anything I can to get you to talk to me today. I can't remember your comment at the end last time.

The almost complete silence of the therapist in the prior hour and her failure to interpret adequately are the primary adaptive contexts for this session. The patient's unconscious perception of the omission and his conjectures as to the reason for the omission can be discerned in these derivatives.

The patient's introjection and identification with the silent and omitting therapist can be inferred from his lateness, initial silence, and statement "I [you] don't want to talk." The reference to cold may reflect the reality stimulus of the cold room but also convey his perception of the "cold" therapist. The reference to the one cold of the therapist may refer to the one intervention of the last hour, which was an expression not of sound therapeutic functioning, but of countertransference pathology (note the reference to sickness and cold). The terms *pathology* and *pathological* are not used in this chapter in a pejorative sense. They are, rather, *functional* usages that encompass any action or intervention that does not meet the patient's therapeutic needs.

The patient had also forgotten the remark itself, suggesting that some ego work (repression) had been done on it: the interpretation had stimulated rather than resolved some conflict. The patient's conjectures about the reasons for the therapist's silence in the prior hour appeared, via introjective identification with the functionally "ill" therapist in derivative form, in the statements "I don't feel well. You never get a cold. . . ." An even less disguised reference to the relative silence of the prior hour appeared when the patient said that he would do anything, including introjecting the therapist's "pathology," to get the therapist to talk.

In the rest of the hour, the patient's communications ranged over several other derivatives, with similar images of people being irritated and rejecting. His father, for example, had been away for a week. He was amused yet made anxious by his idea that despite several years of sobriety, his father was drunk and shacked up somewhere. The patient said he usually liked to come to his sessions, but on the day of the prior hour, he had hated it. In the last few minutes of this hour, he again mentioned feeling bored, feeling like not speaking, and he finished the hour in silence. The therapist said nothing during this hour.

In reviewing this session the therapist said that she had felt very vulnerable and helpless. Her conception of the secure frame had been disrupted both by her patient's meeting and name discovery in the waiting room and by her concern over the possibly inadequate soundproofing. Earlier she had made a considerable effort to modify her office (e.g., solo office, soundproofing, no secretary, and separate entrance and exit) and felt at a loss to do more. She acknowledged that she was not convinced of the necessity for such changes and was still adjusting to her own deprivations necessitated by the alterations. (In a later hour the same patient offered a very simple solution that she has since employed.) Her helplessness had been compounded when the derivatives of the hour did not seem to organize around the sound leak or the patient contact. She had remained silent, waiting for this specific material to unfold. She was not alert to the possibility that the derivatives might point to another adaptive context. Until supervision, she had not thought of the adaptive context of her silence, her missed interpretation, or the incorrect intervention in the prior hour.

During these two sessions, the therapist had been preoccupied with her new office setup, which turned out to be of less concern to her patient. She had felt torn between her personal uncertainty and her wish to do well with the communicative principles on the one hand, and the immediate expressed needs of her patient on the other. Her comment in the first session seemed to address mainly her own thoughts about correcting her own view of the disturbed frame; it was not an accurate interpretation of her patient's wishes. She also seems to be attempting to repair her own narcissistic dishabille by denying and overlooking the possibility of another narcissistic affront, i.e., a failure to make timely interventions. She had endeavored to listen for clues to what she had considered the adaptive contexts in the derivatives, adhering to the correct procedure by waiting for a sufficiently clear derivative complex and representation of the adaptive context before speaking. She had been unable to search for new adaptive contexts that might have better organized the material of the second hour and led to a useful interpretation.

WHY SILENCE?

The communicative approach, in contrast to all others, seems to promote the specific reaction of silence. Problems arise in other therapies, but anxiety and pain in such instances usually lead to a flight from listening for and interpreting unconscious contents and processes (Kubie 1971) that takes the form of advice, intellectualization, directives, and other actions and frame alterations (Mehlman 1974).

Lewin (1946), for example, suggested that the therapist who intuits the enraged core of the sick patient may feel compelled to act, perhaps to placate the patient by giving something to him or her. Lewin implied that such interventions, when offered intuitively, may be incorrect. Langs, through derivative listening, has confirmed that these interventions in psychotherapy are rarely useful, more often harmful, and therefore he specifically interdicts them. His communicative approach includes the study of both patient and therapist with equal intensity. Other therapies do not acknowledge the patient's communication of derivatives that include valid unconscious perceptions of the activities of the therapist. Greenson (1967) and Blum (1981) express a similar view when they state that gross errors of the analyst may be reflected in the manifest remarks of the patient or in a lack of treatment progress. Langs extends this idea by suggesting that the actions of the therapist are reflected in the more critical unconscious responses of the patient; this is a unique aspect of his concept (Langs 1979).

Because Langs's approach is relatively new, there may be an undue emphasis on the errors of the therapists. Critical writing and supervision to this time have been based largely on data from either unskilled therapists or skilled therapists working with manifest content or Type One derivative listening and interviewing (Langs 1981, 1982a). Incorrect interventions and alterations in the therapeutic frame therefore have been the principal adaptive contexts in these therapies, leading Langs to emphasize unduly the study and scrutiny of the therapist. This focus may continue until more therapists have mastered the skills necessary for sound work in the technique.

The communicative approach recognizes that the patient functions unconsciously as a persistent supervisor who is not easily evaded. The patient constantly monitors the therapist's functioning during the therapy hours. The patient's symbolic derivatives provide information about the therapist that, because it is often valid, may be disturbing if decoded. The information therefore remains disguised and unconscious in both therapist and patient. When the material is presented to peers or to supervisors, however, who have less need to keep the information repressed, the therapist is likely to be confronted with a decoding of the Type Two derivatives of the patient's unconscious perceptions of the adaptive contexts. Such decodings are actively traumatic to the therapist because the adaptive contexts are therapeutically incorrect. Supervisors and peers may offer hypotheses that uncover previously unconscious personal and sensitive material (Langs 1975a). As a result such comments, no matter how well stated and how clearly based on the patient's derivative (or direct) associations, assault the therapist's narcissistic sense of perfection (Rothstein 1980). They disturb the natural inclination of therapists to keep countertransference issues unconscious (Little 1951) and to maintain that one can hide one's faults and errors (T. L. Dorpat, personal communication, 1982).

As demonstrated in the last case example, silence may seem a relatively secure retreat until the therapist discovers, usually through supervision, that patients produce perceptive and telling derivatives in response to inappropriate therapist silences.

SILENCE AS A REACTION TO SUPERVISION

Several writers, although not specifying the approaches used, have commented on the potentially disturbing effects of supervision. Halleck and Woods (1962) suggested that supervision can be a significant contributing factor in the emotional decompensation of the psychiatric resident. Holzman (1976) stated: ". . . the analyst's pride and self esteem are easily wounded when his work—like the performance of an actor or a musician—is carefully scrutinized; and, it is true, we have not learned well enough how to be criticized without feeling condemned" (p. 257).

The therapist faced with these exposures and anxieties also realizes that the supervisory situation lacks the security (e.g., confidentiality, imperviousness of one's career) inherent in a true therapeutic alliance (Halleck and Woods 1962). With other approaches, as Holzman suggested, the supervisor may appear to criticize, and the therapist responds by enlisting the patient as an ally. Peers in a seminar, for example, do not seem as threatening and may provide support (Holt 1959) because of their lack of authority, their frequent directly supportive comments, and their less accurate criticism (Grinberg 1970).

Reactions such as silence that occur in response to the supervisory process, in which the patient's Type Two derivatives are decoded, may indicate that the student therapist has displaced the supervisor and persecutor role to the patient. The patient may appear to be in league with the agent of the real and potential narcissistic injury, the supervisor. Many authors imply that performing psychotherapy necessitates the therapist's personal analysis, which should be carried out under the best conditions possible—that is, within an optimally secure therapeutic frame. Supervision may activate and reveal personal discomforts. Peer groups may make the process more tolerable, but some personal issues in the therapist must be resolved with a personal therapeutic analysis. The personal analyst and analysis must be separate from the educational process (Kairys 1964, McLaughlin 1973, Szasz 1960, Thompson 1958) to enable the therapist to carry through these issues without becoming overwhelmed by the complexities of the process of learning and the temporary adversary qualities of the supervisor and patient.

Many therapists work within deviant frames and use noninterpretive interventions, thus obscuring neurotic elements in both therapist and patient. Such a process may foreclose the therapeutic analysis of the patient as well as dissipate the therapist's impetus for personal analysis (Langs 1982a). Individual variations in the techniques of psychoanalytic therapists are also determined, at least initially, by each therapist's neurotic and character predispositions (Grinberg 1970). Thus, whether resulting from the choice of therapy method or from an individual style within an analytic therapy, disturbances of the therapeutic frame or of the intervention mode serve to protect and pathologically gratify. The therapist's method therefore is motivated and maintained by his or her own transferences. The communicative point of view brings this personal element of the therapist emphatically into focus via the derivative commentaries of the patient.

Another reason for the effect of supervision is the contrast between Type Two derivative listening–relating and other theories. Therapists may have idealized the theories and their exponents (Sharaf and Levinson 1964). Indeed, another considerable barrier may be the differences between the communicative approach and the methods of the therapist's own personal analyst. It is very difficult to break an unconsciously acquired tradition based on idealization of and identification with one's own analyst, especially when the idealization and identification have been determined defensively through what are now known to be erroneous interventions and faulty technique.

For the therapist who has made an original written contribution, the problems with this theory are compounded. Personal investment in his or her own ideas is likely to be great and to be dislodged only with difficulty.

SILENCE IN THE PSYCHOANALYTIC LITERATURE

The absence of reasoned discussion of the communicative approach and the theories of Langs in the psychoanalytic and psychotherapeutic literature is troubling, because this literature is the forum for objective review, debate, and reports of efforts at clinical replication or refutation of theories and approaches. Other than several reviews (e.g., Calef 1979, Casement 1980, Chessick 1981, Comer 1979, Dewald 1978, Firestein 1982, Fordham 1978, Gill 1981b, Jackel 1978, Klumpner 1979, Loeb 1977, Lothane 1980, Meissner 1978, Osman 1981, Rabinovitz 1978, Ross 1978, Solomon 1974), and a few articles (e.g., Uchill 1979, Raney 1982), a search of the literature uncovered very little that discussed or evaluated Langs's ideas.[1] In a recent supplement to a major psychoanalytic journal (Blum 1979), for example, there were many extensively referenced articles on the current theories of therapy and technique but only one brief reference to Langs (Arlow 1979a). More recently, the same journal published several articles about aspects of therapy with no explicit references to Langs's work (Blum 1981, Greenacre 1981, Kanzer 1981, Kaplan 1981, Rangell 1981, Stone 1981).

According to Decker (1977), Freud also had little difficulty getting his work published but received a mixed reception to his ideas (see also Freud 1900, p. 93). Dissemination of his theories via reviews in widely read journals was limited. Freud's emotional reaction, Decker suggested, may have been responsible in some part for retarding dissemination of his views.

The comments of colleagues and therapists in supervision are much more personal and detailed than are the observations of those known only indirectly through their writings. I therefore take some risk in extrapolating from the reactions of the therapists whom I personally have observed and

---

[1]Recently, however, Gill (this volume) and Gill and Hoffman (1982) have begun openly to debate Langs's ideas of veridical unconscious perception.

making assumptions about writers from the evidence in their psychotherapeutic and psychoanalytic articles. Nevertheless, the writers, like the therapists in their consulting rooms, may have for defensive purposes developed an irrational bias against the communicative theories. One of the manifestations, or "symptoms," of this reaction is a resistance that takes the form of a reluctance to write critically and substantively about the approach. Some writers imply rather than overtly acknowledge the existence and influence of Langs's ideas, thereby indicating an awareness of them. The purpose in pointing out several references in which omissions can be found is not to "analyze" the authors but to encourage the needed examination of Langs's theories rather than the *ad hominem* examination of his psyche that has been so common in many of the criticisms both in and out of print.

Some manifest arguments seem to be consistent with the overt omission of references to and lack of direct discussion of Langs's theories. Some critics, for example, argue that the interactional–communicative approach is not pertinent to psychoanalysis. Langs also may have alienated himself from traditional psychoanalysis by suggesting that psychoanalysis and psychotherapy cannot be pragmatically distinguished (1976b) and by challenging analysts to engage him on that (and other) clinical issues (Langs 1981; see also Blanck and Blanck 1982). According to others, Langs has written nothing that is new to the field; he has only applied new terms to old concepts. These ideas are expressed despite Langs's contentions that his theories are founded on traditional and contemporary psychoanalytic sources and solid clinical data.

It is likely that his use of new terms for old concepts is part of focusing and further defining some ideas that have been introduced before but that have not been clarified or systematized. Langs's *misalliance cure*, for example, includes the concept of "transference cure," which is the familiar phenomenon of the relief of symptoms that occurs early in the course of treatment (Langs 1976a, p. 81). The concept, however, involves more than the influence of transference distortions within the patient; it includes the transferences of the therapist. More specifically, the concept involves the shared transference resistances of each party to the therapeutic interaction. These resistances are considered *interactional* because they are contributed to by both therapist and patient; they do not stem solely from the pathology of the latter. Thus, the term *interactional resistances* is a more inclusive concept than is *resistances* (Langs 1976b). New terms are necessary when concepts are expanded and reorganized; they provide tools or bases for new and higher conceptualizations.

Langs's additions to and revisions of basic psychoanalytic clinical concepts seem useful to those who have compared them with other perspectives. They are clearly important enough to argue, test, and discuss in the psychoanalytic literature in the usual scientific fashion. Other controversial and often more superficial approaches find considerable space in the journals. The absence of consideration in the literature of Langs's several revisions of clinical technique is therefore remarkable; it does not seem to be based on adequate objective study and suggests less than objective reasons for avoiding Langs's ideas.

A NEW PARADIGM

Langs's communicative concepts may be sufficiently unusual to constitute a new paradigm of the way clinical data are perceived and organized. Langs and many of his students would say that they are. Others would say that the ideas do not justify that status. If Langs's concepts do indeed constitute a new paradigm in the field of psychoanalysis, the difficulties in acknowledging and applying them may be explained by the ideas of Kuhn (1962), later expanded by Rothstein (1980).

Kuhn (1962) suggested that a new explanation or paradigm reorders existing observations in science and leads to new formulations, more complete explanations, and, ultimately, new observations. Practitioners of existing sciences (theories) are characteristically reluctant to relinquish their old theories. Acceptance of a new theory requires a revolution that is sometimes more political than scientific.

Rothstein (1980) espoused and extended Kuhn's views regarding irrational investment in a theory: "The narcissistically invested theory is perceived (consciously and/or unconsciously) to be perfect. . . . it assuages [one's] sense of vulnerability and helplessness. Armed with the narcissistically invested paradigm, the practitioner can face the uncertainty of the clinical situation" (p. 387). Stone (1975) also discussed resistance to change in analysts. He mentioned their rigid maintenance of a "narcissistically invested fiction of certainty in countering intellectual malaise" and their "hostility toward the malefactor who threatens this defense" (p. 343). Stone also noticed that resistance to change may be expressed in ignoring contributions and attributing them to personal neuroses (1975, p. 345). (Nevertheless, despite his dialogue with Langs [Langs and Stone 1980], he appears manifestly to have ignored Langs in a later paper [Stone 1981].) Bahai (1977) suggested that the resistance to new ideas in psychoanalysis is "to a degree proportionate to the importance and/or validity of the departure." These approaches may partially explain those who have clung to the familiar and ignored the new. Langs's approach initially offers little certainty and creates much turmoil. There seems to be accumulating evidence of its validity, however.

Nonscientifically founded resistance to a new idea or clinical approach is therefore irrational and has properties similar to the resistance or defensiveness seen in patients in psychoanalysis and psychotherapy. In psychotherapy a patient will resist an interpretation that comes very close to an unconsciously held conflicted or dangerous (anxiety-provoking) image or belief but that is made at the wrong time or incorrectly.

Glover first suggested that in analysis, accurate interpretations made "not at the moment of true interpretation" (1931, p. 401) result in a defensiveness not seen in instances of glaringly inaccurate interpretations. "Not at the moment" seems to mean "outside of a good analytic context," for example, before the material has had enough time to unfold, or too early in the development of a safe and trustworthy relationship. Glover called these accurate interpretations made at the wrong time *inexact interpretations*.

In a similar fashion, Langs's ideas may be received as premature or inexact interpretations by the unprepared therapist. Type Two derivatives reveal, often starkly and painfully, the adaptive contexts, which can be errors of technique and contain implications about the countertransferences of the analyst. A psychotherapist who reads one of Langs's books, hears him discuss a case, or presents a case to a supervisor who is working in a Type Two derivative mode, and who does not have peer support and supervisory, classroom, or comparable personal analytic experience, will, like Glover's patients, react defensively, and initially with rejection. In the calmly considered written scientific article, the rejection assumes the form of manifest "silence."

Glover further suggested that the patient's unconscious sadism in particular should not be interpreted out of analytic context. Analogously, because the communicative approach posits a listening method that reveals evidence of the direct, often harmful, effects on the patient of the therapist's technique, supervisory decoding of the derivative evidence of these harmful effects may be heard as interpretation of the unconscious sadism of the therapist. Glover stated that such interpretations with a patient disturb guilt systems; as a result, the patient dramatically may terminate therapy in a negative transference (Glover 1931). With therapists, similar dramatic rejection may occur in response to the interpretation-like supervisory confrontations. Langs (personal communication, 1982) reports students who work conscientiously, present good cases, comprehend derivatives, and then suddenly give up the approach entirely. Decker (1977) reports that several of those who tried Freud's method also abandoned it.

Evidence of the Reaction to Langs's Paradigm

Arlow (1979b), in a discussion of metaphor in psychoanalysis, made no citations to Langs's work in his review of the literature despite acquaintance with Langs and with the central role of metaphor and symbolism in Type A communication in the Type Two derivative concept. In 1980 Arlow described a case vignette and vaguely referred to an "early transference manifestation" (p. 111). Despite his own earlier work on metaphor and the availability of Langs's ideas, he overlooked the derivative possibilities in the material of a patient of one of his students. This patient had fallen in love with a young man who was supervised by a probation officer. Arlow suggested that her falling in love was a defensive "flight into health," with the probation aspect making such an action unacceptable. He did not mention the likelihood that the description of the event was a derivative of her attachment to the supervised ("probationer") analyst. Further, the description may have been the patient's effort to convey her veridical unconscious perception of the analyst's nontherapeutic feelings of love (or possibly, by reversal, frustration and hate) toward her. Arlow seems to have considered the patient's love relationship a defensive flight from "the transference," when the event was, at the very least, an acting out of some aspect of her perception of the therapeutic relationship (which may have included the *therapist's* defensive flight from some aspects of the interaction). Her *telling* of the event, however, conveyed just the opposite. Unlike an action, which deflects or reduces the impetus for analytic work, the telling was an effort to communicate her unconscious perception of a current problem in the analytic interaction. Arlow referred to the "dynamic context of the analytic situation" (1980, p. 131), but this vignette and the other in his essay instead seem to reflect a manifest content and Type One derivative orientation to the material. The patient who falls in love with a supervised probationer and who is in analysis with a supervised candidate provides a Type Two derivative and adaptive context that are hard to miss and that afford a much more understandable supervisory intervention than the one Arlow reported.

Blum, in a 1981 overview of therapeutic theory and technique, mentioned that the patient may correctly and rationally perceive the analyst's ability as well as the analyst's "anxieties, errors, and countertransference reactions" (p. 60). Blum referred to these errors as nontransference and cited Greenson (1971). Blum continues: ". . . the patient's compliant praise of, complaints about, collusion with, or adaptation to the analyst's possible real difficulties cannot be explained only in terms of transference and resistance. . . . Patients, however, react to the analyst's personality and possible problems in terms of their own personality and transference dispositions" (p. 60). This excerpt contains assertions that are very similar to those of Langs. The major and, especially, the recent work of Langs that amplifies these ideas (Langs 1975b, 1975c, 1976a, 1976b) is manifestly ignored.

Leavy (1977) compared some of Jacques Lacan's ideas with those of Sullivan, Erikson, and Schafer (p. 217) but did not seem to notice how Lacan's idea of the "signifier" and the "other" resemble Langs's adaptive context. Leavy's view of Lacanian psychoanalysis as a dialectical process also could have been compared to Langs's concept of the bipersonal interaction.

Lipton (1977) discussed the tendency in modern psychoanalysis to emphasize the behavior of the analyst rather than the analyst's intent or purpose, which seems to have been the emphasis in older practice. This contemporary trend seems important to Lipton, yet despite its crucial importance and central role in Langs's ideas, Langs's work was not cited. Langs emphasizes that communication, conscious and unconscious, is mediated by all the analyst's actions, behavior, and comportment. The analyst's unconscious purposes as well as conscious intentions are expressed only through behavior. This principle was assumed, but not in fact systematically studied or practiced, until the advent of the communicative approach.

Leo Stone's eloquent article (1981) about the function of noninterpretive elements in psychoanalysis is worthy of comment because of its appearance shortly after a dialogue with Langs (Langs and Stone 1980). Stone covers areas of common interest yet makes no direct references to Langs, although he demonstrates a familiarity with the length and breadth of the psychoanalytic literature. He provides a few brief examples of noninterpretive actions but no validation of the actions. Instead he supports his assertions with his own beliefs (1981, pp. 90, 94, 101), his own experience (pp. 92, 94-95), and, with colloquial familiarity, the experience of the reader: "Now the past, we know, may be restored by recollection or by the analyst's constructions" (p. 95). He expresses his position:

> My essential position is directed against the superfluous iatrogenic regressions attendant on superfluous deprivations, regressions whether or not the patient is aware of suffering as such. None of us would wish to court or provoke suffering, but . . . I recognize that it may sometimes be an inevitable accompaniment of benevolently purposive processes. I believe the powerful effects of the basic principle of abstinence are operative, whether or not there is manifest reaction to them by the patient. (p. 113)

Here, he seems to indicate that although some deprivation is inherent in the psychoanalytic process, some is unnecessary and can be avoided by noninterpretive but humane interventions. The last sentence in this excerpt seems to refer to an *unconscious* effect, but Stone does not say how he arrives at his belief.

What may be an implicit reference to Langs appears without citation shortly thereafter: Stone, after implying that he would answer a patient's question about whether he saw patients on Christmas and would wish a patient well prior to a major surgical operation, states, "yet I know that there are others to whom my view is unacceptable" (p. 101). And again: ". . . I do not believe that an arbitrary fixed and tendentious principle would properly be invoked in either instance, except perhaps the general principle of 'minimization' and the commitment to afterinterpretation"

(p. 109). He seems to take issue with "others" who are not cited, an omission that is significant in view of his otherwise extensive citation of those with whom he agrees or disagrees. Each of these nonreferenced views exactly opposes a strongly held view of Langs.

In addition to the Christmas and surgical operation examples, which seem hypothetical, Stone offers another instance of the same type, although one that he terms a commonplace and innocuous example of an ad hoc deprivation. He advises a patient: "Why not see if you can dispense with routine brushing of the couch before you lie down for each hour?" (Stone 1981, p. 104). This is a noninterpretative intervention, but, according to Stone, it seems a deprivation of an entirely different order from those that Stone would have interrupted with his "humane" Christmas response and surgical well wishes. In one instance, the patient is "deprived" of the discharge through action of brushing the couch; in the other, the analyst's good wishes interrupt the "deprivation" of his exclusively interpretive stance. The suggestion to dispense with brushing the couch is offered in lieu of interpretation and seems based on the premise that if the anxiety is not discharged through action, it is more subject to interpretation. The reader is left to accept the assertion without the reason (e.g., interpretation of the couch brushing had not been successful) and without any follow-up evidence supporting the validity of the suggestion.

Stone uses two other examples, neither from the writings of Langs. Stone mentions the herring meal offered by Freud to Rat Man (Freud 1909) and the offer of tissues to a patient by de la Torre (de la Torre 1977). Stone does not describe how each of these actions was either validated or refuted by the patient. Stone mentions that he would not share a meal with a patient or even eat or drink coffee in a patient's presence but does not distinguish these actions from his "humane" interventions (1981, p. 106). He does not mention the many derivatives in the original record of the Rat Man case that seem to be unconscious commentary on the herring meal (Freud 1909, pp. 303, 304, 307, 309, 310, 311), nor does he mention Langs's discussion of the same episode (Langs 1974).

De la Torre's offer of tissues is not a good choice for an illustration because there are insufficient data in the original article. According to de la Torre, the incident was followed by an abreaction of copious sobbing; the analyst then explained what had happened and more material followed (de la Torre 1977). Neither Stone nor de la Torre provides later material that is specific enough to demonstrate the unconscious meanings and derivative validation or refutation of the offer of tissues. Stone seems to ask the reader to accept his assertions on the basis of Stone's experience. He seems to agree with Kohut's view that the "refined empathy of the trained human observer . . . constitutes a potentially adequate instrument" for understanding (Kohut 1977, p. 142). This view is attractive but should be subjected to further psychoanalytic and systematic study and to much-needed validation by Type Two derivative assessment of detailed case material.

Three recent papers of Gill (Gill and Muslin 1976; Gill 1979, 1981a) appear to demonstrate the use of derivatives of patients' unconscious perceptions of the adaptive contexts. Although Gill and his colleagues describe other varieties of interventions in their clinical examples, Gill's discussion implies interventions seemingly very similar to those of Langs. In his 1979 paper, Gill suggests that interpretations should be based largely on what Gill considers transference as it appears in the immediate interaction with the analyst and should include a plausible reference to that interaction. Avoidance of the interaction, he says, and flight into the past can be a relief for the analyst and for the patient (p. 266).

Gill suggests that there are occasions when transference as well as extratransference interpretations are important. According to Gill, the patient's preoccupation with an extratransference event and the existence of insufficient support for transference interpretations would be justification for not making a transference interpretation. He is, however, less specific about what conditions would occasion a nontransference intervention. The essence of this idea is remarkably similar to those advanced by Langs (e.g., 1975a, p. 248; 1978c, p. 639). Langs has allowed for exceptions in one specific circumstance: emergencies, when the adaptive context is very disguised and yet the need for a direct intervention is apparent. The inevitable negative consequences, which one hopes would not outweigh the immediate benefit, would be left for later analysis (Langs 1978c, p. 647; 1982b, pp. 126–143).

There are no clinical examples in Gill's 1979 paper, but a comparison of case vignettes in the 1976 paper and in the expanded version of the 1979 paper (Gill 1981a) seems to show a subtle shift in the focus toward discussion, but not clinical interpretation, that addresses the Type Two derivatives in the case material. An example appended to the 1979 paper (Gill 1981a) is intended to show how transference interpretations can be related plausibly to the interaction. In his written discussion of this vignette, Gill offers three hypotheses (*not* offered by the therapist) that seem consistent with Langs' Type Two derivative mode. Each is followed by what seems to be derivative validation in the case material. The therapist in the example, however, seemed to use active questioning as his predominant intervention mode.

Whereas Blum and Stone seem to argue with Langs in absentia, Gill (1981a and this volume) seems at times to agree with implicitly and to use, at least in his written discussion, the Type Two derivative concept of

Langs. This agreement would indicate that Gill too is unnecessarily silent about Langs's work, especially in regard to the concept of Type Two derivatives.

A VARIATION ON THE "SILENCE" THEME

A recent article by Langs (1981) has produced what seems to be a variation of the defensiveness manifested by "silence" about Langs's contributions. In this article Langs paraphrased a vignette from Blanck and Blanck (1974). He analyzed the vignette and suggested that the patient had been directed away from the therapeutic relationship to conscious thoughts, fantasies, and remembered experiences. According to Langs, the vignette contains no concept of "an unconscious communicative interplay" between patient and therapist.

The Blancks responded with a letter (1982) charging Langs with intentionally misrepresenting their position and slanting the material for his own purposes. The Blancks suggested that Langs should have shown the manuscript to them as the original authors, as they had done with their summaries of the works of various ego psychologists in order to ensure correct representation. Other charges were made about Langs's intentions that seem more conjectural.

A comparison of Langs's paraphrase and the original, very brief vignette shows very little distortion. Langs is more faithful to the Blancks' material than the Blancks are to his. His conclusion seems descriptive and based more on a differing view of how unconscious meanings are expressed than on a misrepresentation of the material. Langs does not appear to have intended to represent the Blancks' view of the unconscious interplay. Rather, he seems to have intended to argue his own.

The Blancks err in their assertion that Langs is wrong. They say that "by definition, every analyst uses unconscious communication as a concept everyday, in every case that he or she treats" (1982, p. 87). Evidence, not definition alone, is necessary in scientific discourse.

The activity of the therapists in the Blancks' examples (1974) seems to hinder the production of understandable derivatives that patients usually provide in response to their therapists' interventions. The method of these therapists includes frequent reconstructions and questions that allow derivative imagery little time or room to develop. This may raise the problem that Lubin (this volume) mentions: the Blancks create a body of data that makes it difficult to identify the kind of material that Langs is writing about.

Other vignettes offered by the Blancks, especially those involving borderline patients, provide more of a sense of an unconscious interplay (e.g., see Blanck and Blanck 1974, p. 333) but no *evidence* that the therapists are working with or considering unconscious communication, at least in respect to derivative expressive imagery. The Blancks' therapists, for example, address comments to the patients' conscious withholdings rather than to their unconscious disguises and derivatives. The importance of the therapist as a stimulus and as an unconscious introject is not considered. If this were just a divergence in theoretical perspectives, the differences could be conceptualized and explained. The heated *ad hominem* conjectures in the Blancks' response suggest a reaction that is displaced into an effort to silence Langs himself.

Partial references or distortions, less heated than the Blancks' but nevertheless suggestive of defensiveness, are found elsewhere in the recent literature. Boyer (1977), for example, cited Langs's misalliance paper (1975b) but overlooked others, especially Langs's discussion of residues (1971), when he stated, "I have come to contemplate each interview as though it might have been a dream and material from recent interviews as part of the day residue" (Boyer 1977, p. 389). Calef and Weinshel (1981) cited Langs and gave ambiguous credit to his term *dumping* (Langs 1976a). Perhaps they had not had sufficient time to read Langs' relevant paper "Some Communicative Properties of the Bipersonal Field" (1978b), in which the Type B and especially the Type C communicative fields are outlined. This particular article of Langs's is hard to miss; it has been published in at least four places (Langs 1978a, 1978b, 1978c; Grotstein 1981). Calef and Weinshel also overlooked McLaughlin's important contribution (1975b) in this same area. McLaughlin did not cite Langs, although at the time of that writing, Langs's ideas may not yet have crystallized.

Another distortion can be found in the writing of Gill and Hoffman (1982). Although some of their comments about their case examples fit the criteria of Type Two derivative hypotheses (see, e.g., p. 200), their one citation of Langs (p. 4, Vol. 2) appears incorrect. I have been unable to find the term *preconscious* in the cited work (Langs 1978c). The predominant reference made in that work and others is to *un*conscious veridical perception and assessment of the meanings of the analyst's interpretations.

CONCLUDING COMMENTS

Therapists avoid a method of listening, considering, and writing about their patients' reactions to their interventions and activities if they unconsciously anticipate an uncomfortable narcissistic disturbance. Similarly, criticisms of Langs's ideas, offered informally and without adequate study, reflect an attitude that is a regression from a scientific position. Such criticism suggests the presence of a major disturbing stimulus that has taxed and defeated advanced ego adaptations. Scientific study is a manifestation of such adaptations.

Because scientific writers consciously aspire to honesty and objectivity, such criticisms and omissions of citations qualify as "symptoms" of a "disorder," at least of our science if not of the practitioners thereof. We are faced with an irrational lacunae (see Spitzer 1980, p. 6). Writers may be more vulnerable than nonwriting colleagues, because their work and product, the written article, has been invested with "narcissistic idealizing libido" (Kohut 1966). The significant omission indicates conflicted unconscious contents and needs. A patient struggles with an unconsciously perceived reality by omitting a reference to it, but then signals its presence through derivatives. Similarly, these papers, by omitting direct citations yet referring indirectly (or incorrectly) to the work of Langs, seem to signal that Langs's communicative theories are a major troublesome "adaptive context" in the current psychoanalytic and psychotherapeutic literature.

In the clinical setting, the therapist takes the analytic step of recognizing the personal inner disturbance in all its forms and disguises (Balter et al. 1980) and remedies it through self-analytic scrutiny. This recognition-resolution process leads the therapist to the awareness that mistakes are inevitable. Further, therapeutic competence is less metapsychological and interpretive virtuosity than it is, at least in part, the ability to respond to the patient's unconscious supervision in a manner advantageous to the therapy. If errors are rectified and the patient's responses interpreted (when necessary and possible), the patient's pathological ego usually improves. Therapist tolerance for and even enjoyment of the shifting, ambiguity, contradiction, and inconsistency that come from not categorically foreclosing relatedness with patients is advantageous (McLaughlin 1978). Patients respond well to the therapist's learning about them and consequently tailoring interventions more closely to their unconscious therapeutic needs. In turn, the therapist develops a new sense of self-competence and narcissistic integrity (Mehlman 1974, p. 137). This sense is based on fresh observations and on the self-analysis, which has been stimulated by the observations and by discomforts raised and successfully resolved in the process (McLaughlin 1975a).

Because this approach necessitates uncomfortable and continuous self-examination, psychoanalytic authors likely will remain "silent" in regard to the approach until they act as students, analyzing and working over some of their own cases using aspects of the communicative approach. Fresh self-analysis will be necessary, as will reexamination of the interventions and frame management of their own analyses.

Quite possibly the Langs paradigm cannot be discussed in calm scientific debate. The communicative paradigm is especially and distinctly disturbing to others in the psychotherapy field because it acknowledges that the patient can be acutely aware of the validity or invalidity of the therapist's technical interventions, thus forcing the student to work over his or her personal neurosis as well as therapeutic technique. If the student relentlessly scrutinizes his or her work in the light of communicative principles or permits scrutiny by others with such a perspective, the meanings revealed either become obvious or evoke defensive operations such as denial, isolation, withdrawal, disavowal, or projection. A new paradigm, such as Langs's, organizes and explains data in such a way that the observer must change. This change leads to new observations and data. The ego of the observer is irrevocably altered by the synthesis of the new meanings and new observations. An awareness of and facility in listening to Type Two derivatives is a "truth" from which there is no turning back.

Perhaps the larger group of psychoanalytic practitioners and creative thinkers needs more time to digest and evaluate Langs's concepts. As Firestein tentatively wrote in a recent review, "Langs' arguments stirred me to think about some of my own attitudes and behaviors, with worthwhile results" (Firestein 1982, p. 148). Much in the communicative perspective could enhance and advance the therapeutic potential of psychoanalytic treatment. The young science of psychoanalysis and psychoanalytic psychotherapy, like other sciences, progresses unevenly. Every advance is based on hard work and meets opposition. Contributions to the advancement of psychotherapy and psychoanalysis that are inherent in most of criticisms of Langs's work remain unrealized until the critics can adopt a more scientific and less personal approach. Increased reasoned consideration of the major elements of the communicative point of view should be stimulating and beneficial to all concerned.

SUMMARY

Langs's communicative theories are of great potential benefit to psychotherapeutic and psychoanalytic technique. Although the approach creates major difficulties because of its inherent exposure of the therapist, this exposure and the consequential technical procedures can be turned to the advantage of both patient and therapist.

Therapists learning this approach progress through stages of activity that seem unique to this approach.[2] One of these stages occurs before the therapist has integrated the elements of the new concepts into an effective style of therapeutic work. Periods of inappropriate therapist silence are

[2]Not discussed in this chapter are the next two stages that seem to occur in learning this approach. These are the tendency of the therapist to confess or unnecessarily reveal his or her own countertransferences (or facsimiles thereof) in the therapy situation, and to adhere excessively stringently to the rules, including zealously searching for adaptive contexts. Each of these tendencies is defensively motivated, does not follow the patients' pace or mode of unfolding, and produces overt or derivative reactions in the patient.

usually reported at some time during this phase. Facility with the method does not seem to be achieved until the narcissistic disturbance that results from the introduction of the technique is analyzed and reintegrated.

The absence of objective discussion and citation of Langs's work in the psychotherapeutic literature is also a manifestation of the defensiveness stimulated by the potential for self-exposure and narcissistic disturbance inherent in the approach. The "silence" of creative writers in the literature appears to be a result of defensiveness, and this defensiveness stems from the disturbance of this narcissism by the self-observing and self-revealing potential of Langs's theories. In addition, his ideas constitute a new paradigm that threatens the narcissistic investment in the theoretical approaches practiced by most therapists. A reworking by these writers of some of their own cases in the light of the communicative approach would considerably advance the science and practice of psychotherapy.

REFERENCES

ALEXANDER, F. (1959). Psychotherapy. Paper presented at the Academy of Psychoanalysis, Philadelphia, April. Cited in Halleck, S. L., and Woods, S. M. (1962). Emotional problems of psychiatric residents. *Psychiatry* 25:339–346.

ARLOW, J. A. (1979a). The genesis of interpretation. *Journal of the American Psychoanalytic Association* 27:193–206.

——— (1979b). Metaphor and the psychoanalytic situation. *Psychoanalytic Quarterly* 48:363–385.

——— (1980). Object concept and object choice. *Psychoanalytic Quarterly* 49:109–133.

BAHAI, A. B. (1977). New theories: their influence and effect on psychoanalytic technique, *International Journal of Psycho-Analysis* 58:345–363.

BALTER, L., LOTHANE, Z., AND SPENCER, J. H., Jr. (1980). On the analyzing instrument. *Psychoanalytic Quarterly* 49:474–504.

BION, W. R. (1963). Elements of psycho-analysis. In W. R. Bion, *Seven Servants*, pp. 1–110. New York: Jason Aronson, 1977.

BLANCK, G., AND BLANCK, R. (1974). *Ego Psychology: Theory and Practice*. New York: Columbia University Press.

——— (1982). Letter to the editor. *International Journal of Psycho-Analysis* 63:87.

BLUM, H. P. (1981). Some current and recurrent problems of psychoanalytic technique. *Journal of the American Psychoanalytic Association* 29:47–68.

———, ed. (1979). Psychoanalytic technique and theory of therapy. *Journal of the American Psychoanalytic Association* (Suppl) 27:1–374.

BOYER, L. B. (1977). Working with a borderline patient. *Psychoanalytic Quarterly* 46:386–424.

BROCKBANK, R. (1970). On the analyst's silence in psychoanalysis: a synthesis of intrapsychic content and interpersonal manifestations. *International Journal of Psycho-Analysis* 51:457–464.

CALEF, V. (1979). Review: *The Bipersonal Field. Journal of the American Psychoanalytic Association* 27:702–705.

CALEF, V., AND WEINSHEL, E. M. (1981). Some clinical consequences of introjection: gaslighting. *Psychoanalytic Quarterly* 50:44–66.

CASEMENT, P. J. (1980). Review: *The Therapeutic Environment. International Review of Psycho-Analysis* 7:525–528.

CHESSICK, R. (1981). Critique: The wild supervisor. Review: *The Therapeutic Environment. American Journal of Psychotherapy* 35:445–448.

COMER, R. J. (1979). Review: *The Listening Process. Contemporary Psychology* 24:647–648.

DECKER, H. S. (1977). *Freud in Germany: Revolution and Reaction in Science 1893–1907.* New York: International Universities Press.

DE LA TORRE, G. (1977). Psychoanalytic neutrality: an overview. *Bulletin of the Menninger Clinic* 41:366–384.

DEWALD, P. (1978). Review: *The Bipersonal Field. Psychoanalytic Quarterly* 47:634–635.

FIRESTEIN, S. (1982). Review: *The Therapeutic Environment. Psychoanalytic Quarterly* 51:145–149.

FLOURNOY, O. (1971). The psychoanalyst and the psychoanalytic process. *International Journal of Psycho-Analysis* 52:127–135.

FORDHAM, M. (1978). Review: *The Therapeutic Interaction. Journal of Analytical Psychology* 23:193–196.

FREUD, S. (1900). The interpretation of dreams. *Standard Edition* 4/5.

—— (1909). Notes upon a case of obsessional neurosis. *Standard Edition* 10.

—— (1912). The dynamics of transference. *Standard Edition* 12.

GILL, M. M. (1979). The analysis of the transference. *Journal of the American Psychoanalytic Association* (Suppl) 27:263–288.

—— (1981a). The analysis of the transference. In *Classics in Psychoanalytic Technique*, ed. Robert Langs, pp. 69–82. New York: Jason Aronson.

—— (1981b). A frame for therapy. Review: *The Therapeutic Environment. Contemporary Psychology* 26:36–37.

GILL, M. M., AND HOFFMAN, I. Z. (1982). *Analysis of Transference.* Vols. 1 and 2. New York: International Universities Press.

GILL, M. M., AND MUSLIN, H. L. (1976). Early interpretation of transference. *Journal of the American Psychoanalytic Association* 24:779–794.

GLOVER, E. (1931). The therapeutic effect of inexact interpretation: a contribution to the theory of suggestion. *International Journal of Psycho-Analysis* 12:397–411.

GREENACRE, P. (1981). Reconstruction: its nature and therapeutic value. *Journal of the American Psychoanalytic Association* 29:27–46.

GREENSON, R. (1967). *Technique and Practice of Psychoanalysis.* New York: International Universities Press.

—— (1971). The "real" relationship between the patient and the psychoanalyst. In *The Unconscious Today*, ed. M. Kanzer. New York: International Universities Press.

GREENSON, R., HEIMANN, P., AND WEXLER, M. (1970). Discussion of "the nontransference relationship in the psychoanalytic situation." *International Journal of Psycho-Analysis* 51:143–150.

GRINBERG, L. (1970). The problems of supervision in the psychoanalytic setting. *International Journal of Psycho-Analysis* 51:371–383.

GROTSTEIN, J. S., ed. (1981). *Do I Dare Disturb the Universe?* Beverly Hills: Caesura Press.

HALLECK, S. L., AND WOODS, S. M. (1962). Emotional problems of psychiatric residents. *Psychiatry* 25:339–346.

HOLT, R. R. (1959). Personality growth in psychiatric residents. *Archives of Neurology and Psychiatry* 81:203–215.

HOLZMAN, P. S. (1976). The future of psychoanalysis and its institutes. *Psychoanalytic Quarterly* 45:250–273.

JACKEL, M. (1978). Review: *The Bipersonal Field*. *International Journal of Psycho-Analysis* 59:537–539.

KAIRYS, D. (1964). The training analysis: a critical review of the literature and a controversial proposal. *Psychoanalytic Quarterly* 33:485–512.

KANZER, M. (1981). Freud's "analytic pact": the standard therapeutic alliance. *Journal of the American Psychoanalytic Association* 29:69–87.

KAPLAN, A. H. (1981). From discovery to validation: a basic challenge to psycho-analysis. *Journal of the American Psychoanalytic Association* 29:3–26.

KLUMPNER, G. H. (1979). Review: *The Therapeutic Interaction*. *Psychoanalytic Quarterly* 48:500–506.

KOHUT, H. (1966). Forms and transformations of narcissism. *Journal of the American Psychoanalytic Association* 14:243–272.

——— (1977). *The Restoration of the Self*. New York: International Universities Press.

KUBIE, L. S. (1971). The retreat from patients. *Archives of General Psychiatry* 24:98–106.

KUHN, T. S. (1962). *The Structure of Scientific Revolutions*. Chicago: University of Chicago Press, 1970.

LANGS, R. (1971). Day residues, recall residues, and dreams: reality and the psyche. *Journal of the American Psychoanalytic Association* 19:499–523.

——— (1973). *The Technique of Psychoanalytic Psychotherapy*. Vol. 1. New York: Jason Aronson.

——— (1974). *The Technique of Psychoanalytic Psychotherapy*. Vol. 2. New York: Jason Aronson.

——— (1975a). The patient's unconscious perception of the therapist's errors. In *Tactics and Techniques in Psychoanalytic Therapy*, Vol. 2: *Countertransference*, ed. P. L. Giovacchini. New York: Jason Aronson.

——— (1975b). Therapeutic misalliances. *International Journal of Psychoanalytic Psychotherapy* 4:77–105.

——— (1975c). The therapeutic relationship and deviations in technique. *International Journal of Psychoanalytic Psychotherapy* 4:106–141.

——— (1976a). *The Bipersonal Field*. New York: Jason Aronson.

——— (1976b). *The Therapeutic Interaction*. 2 Vols. New York: Jason Aronson.

——— (1978a). *The Listening Process*. New York: Jason Aronson.

——— (1978b). Some communicative properties of the bipersonal field. *International Journal of Psychoanalytic Psychotherapy* 7:87–135.

—— (1978c). *Technique in Transition*. New York: Jason Aronson.

—— (1979). *The Therapeutic Environment*. New York: Jason Aronson.

—— (1980a). *Interactions: The Realm of Transference and Countertransference*. New York: Jason Aronson.

—— (1980b). On the properties of an interpretation. *Contemporary Psychoanalysis* 16:460–478.

—— (1981). Modes of "cure" in psychoanalysis and psychoanalytic psychotherapy. *International Journal of Psycho-Analysis* 62:199–214.

—— (1982a). *The Psychotherapeutic Conspiracy*. New York: Jason Aronson.

—— (1982b). *Psychotherapy: A Basic Text*. New York: Jason Aronson.

LANGS, R., AND STONE, L. (1980). *The Therapeutic Experience and Its Setting: A Clinical Dialogue*. New York: Jason Aronson.

LEAVY, S. A. (1977). The significance of Jacques Lacan. *Psychoanalytic Quarterly* 46:201–219.

LEBOVICI, S. (1970). Technical remarks on the supervision in psycho-analytic treatment. *International Journal of Psycho-Analysis* 51:385–392.

LEWIN, B. D. (1946). Countertransference in the technique of medical practice. In *Selected Writings of Bertram D. Lewin*, ed. J. A. Arlow, pp. 449–458. New York: Psychoanalytic Quarterly, 1973.

—— (1958). Education or the quest for omniscience. *Journal of the American Psychoanalytic Association* 6:389–912.

LIPTON, S. D. (1977). The advantages of Freud's technique as shown in his analysis of the Rat Man. *International Journal of Psycho-Analysis* 58:255–273.

LITTLE, M. J. (1951). Counter-transference and the patient's response to it. *International Journal of Psycho-Analysis* 32:32–40.

LOEB, F. F. (1977). Review: *The Bipersonal Field*. *American Journal of Psychiatry* 134:1174–1175.

LOTHANE, Z. (1980). The art of listening: a critique of Robert Langs. Review: *The Listening Process*. *Psychoanalytic Review* 67:353–364.

MCLAUGHLIN, J. T. (1973). The nonreporting training analyst, the analysis, and the institute. *Journal of the American Psychoanalytic Association* 20:697–712.

—— (1975a). Presentation of the Council for Advancement of Psychoanalytic Education, Workshop on Psychoanalysis, New York, December.

—— (1975b). The sleepy analyst: some observations on states of consciousness in the analyst at work. *Journal of the American Psychoanalytic Association* 23:363–382.

—— (1978). Primary and secondary process in the context of cerebral hemispheric specialization. *Psychoanalytic Quarterly* 47:237–266.

MEHLMAN, R. D. (1974). Becoming and being a psychotherapist: the problem of narcissism. *International Journal of Psychoanalytic Psychotherapy* 3:125–141.

MEISSNER, W. W. (1978). Review: *The Technique of Psychoanalytic Psychotherapy*, Vols. 1 and 2. *International Journal of Psycho-Analysis* 59:535–537.

MERKLIN, L., AND LITTLE, R. B. (1967). Beginning psychiatry training syndrome. *American Journal of Psychiatry* 124:193–197.

OSMAN, M. P. (1982). Review: *The Listening Process*. *Journal of the American Academy of Psychoanalysis* 9:319–323.

RABINOVITZ, H. (1978). Review: *The Bipersonal Field*. *Smith College Studies in Social Work* 6:277.

RANEY, J. (1982). The payment of fees for psychotherapy. *International Journal of Psychoanalytic Psychotherapy* 9:147–181.

RANGELL, L. (1981). From insight to change. *Journal of the American Psychoanalytic Association* 29:119–141.

ROSS, J. L. (1978). Review: *The Bipersonal Field. Bulletin of the Menninger Clinic* 42:77–78.

ROTHSTEIN, A. (1980). Psychoanalytic paradigms and their narcissistic investment. *Journal of the American Psychoanalytic Association* 28:385–395.

SHARAF, M. R., AND LEVINSON, D. J. (1964). The quest for omnipotence in professional training. *Psychiatry* 27:135–149.

SOLOMON, R. (1974). Review: *The Technique of Psychoanalytic Psychotherapy*, Vols. 1 and 2. *American Journal of Psychiatry* 131:1054.

SPITZER, R. L., Chairperson (1980). *Diagnostic and Statistical Manual of Mental Disorders*. 3rd ed. Washington, D.C.: American Psychiatric Association.

STONE, L. (1975). Some problems and potentialities of present-day psychoanalysis. *Psychoanalytic Quarterly* 44:331–370.

——— (1981). Notes on the noninterpretive elements in the psychoanalytic situation and process. *Journal of the American Psychoanalytic Association* 29:89–118.

SZASZ, T. S. (1960). Three problems in contemporary psychoanalytic training. *Archives of General Psychiatry* 3:82–94.

THOMPSON, C. (1958). A study of the emotional climate of psychoanalytic institutes. *Psychiatry* 21:45–51.

UCHILL, A. B. (1979). Deviation from confidentiality and the therapeutic holding environment. *International Journal of Psychoanalytic Psychotherapy* 7:208–219.

CHRONOLOGICAL BIBLIOGRAPHY OF THE WRITINGS OF ROBERT LANGS

1959

A Pilot Study of Aspects of the Earliest Memory. Paper presented at the joint meeting of the Section of Neurology and Psychiatry of the New York Academy of Medicine and the New York Neurological Society, May 22, 1958. Abstract: *Archives of Neurology and Psychiatry* 81:709.

1960

A method for the clinical and theoretical study of the earliest memory. *Archives of General Psychiatry* 3:523–534 (with M. Rothenberg, J. Fishman, and M. Reiser).

1962

Placebo reactions in a study of lysergic acid diethylamide (LSD-25). *Archives of General Psychiatry* 6:369–383. (with H. Linton).

Subjective reactions to lysergic acid diethylamide (LSD-25). *Archives of General Psychiatry* 6:352–368 (with H. Linton).

1964

Empirical dimensions of the LSD-25 reaction. *Archives of General Psychiatry* 10:469–485 (with H. Linton).

Retrospective alterations of the LSD-25 experience. *Journal of Nervous and Mental Diseases* 138:409–423 (with H. Linton and I. H. Paul).

1965

Earliest memories and personality: a predictive study. *Archives of General Psychiatry* 12:379–390.

First memories and characterologic diagnosis. *Journal of Nervous and Mental Diseases* 141:318–320.

Individual differences in the recall of a drug experience. *Journal of Nervous and Mental Diseases* 140:132–145 (with H. Linton Barr and I. H. Paul).

1966

Manifest dreams from three clinical groups. *Archives of General Psychiatry* 14:634–643.

1967

Manifest dreams in adolescents: a controlled pilot study. *Journal of Nervous and Mental Diseases* 145:43–52.

Stability of earliest memories under LSD-25 and placebo. *Journal of Nervous and Mental Diseases* 144:171–184.

1968

Lysergic acid diethylamide (LSD-25) and schizophrenic reactions. *Journal of Nervous and Mental Diseases* 147:163–172 (with H. Linton Barr).

1969

Discussion of "Dream Content in Psychopathological States" by Milton Kramer. In *Dream Psychology and the New Biology of Dreaming*, ed. M. Kramer. Springfield, Ill.: Charles C Thomas.

1971

Altered states of consciousness: an experimental case study. *Psychoanalytic Quarterly* 40:40–58.

Day residues, recall residues, and dreams: reality and the psyche. *Journal of the American Psychoanalytic Association* 19:499–523. (Reprinted in R. Langs, *Technique in Transition*, pp. 43–69. New York: Jason Aronson, 1978.)

1972

LSD: Personality and Experience (with H. Linton Barr et al.). New York: Wiley.

A psychoanalytic study of material from patients in psychotherapy. *International Journal of Psychoanalytic Psychotherapy* 1(1):4–45. (Reprinted in R. Langs, *Technique in Transition*, pp. 71–111. New York: Jason Aronson, 1978.)

1973

The patient's view of the therapist: reality or fantasy? *International Journal of Psychoanalytic Psychotherapy* 2:411–431. (Reprinted in R. Langs, *Technique in Transition*, pp. 113–138. New York: Jason Aronson, 1978.)

The Technique of Psychoanalytic Psychotherapy. Vol. 1: New York: Jason Aronson.

1974

The Technique of Psychoanalytic Psychotherapy. Vol. 2: New York: Jason Aronson.

1975

The patient's unconscious perception of the therapist's errors. In *Tactics and Techniques in Psychoanalytic Therapy,* vol. 2: *Countertransference,* ed. P. L. Giovacchini, pp. 239–250. New York: Jason Aronson. (Reprinted in R. Langs, *Technique in Transition,* pp. 139–154. New York: Jason Aronson, 1978.)

Therapeutic misalliances. *International Journal of Psychoanalytic Psychotherapy* 4:77–105. (Reprinted in R. Langs, *Technique in Transition,* pp. 155–188. New York: Jason Aronson, 1978.)

The therapeutic relationship and deviations in technique. *International Journal of Psychoanalytic Psychotherapy* 4:106–141. (Reprinted in R. Langs, *Technique in Transition,* pp. 189–230. New York: Jason Aronson, 1978.)

1976

On becoming a psychiatrist: discussion of "Empathy and Intuition in Becoming a Psychiatrist," by Ronald J. Blank. *International Journal of Psychoanalytic Psychotherapy* 5:255–280. (Reprinted in R. Langs, *Technique in Transition,* pp. 325–355. New York: Jason Aronson, 1978.)

The Bipersonal Field. New York: Jason Aronson.

The misalliance dimension in Freud's case histories: I. The case of Dora. *International Journal of Psychoanalytic Psychotherapy* 5:301–318. (Reprinted under the title "Misalliance and Framework in the Case of Dora" in R. Langs, *Technique in Transition,* pp. 231–252. New York: Jason Aronson, 1978. Also reprinted in *Freud and His Patients,* ed. M. Kanzer and J. Glenn, pp. 58–71. New York: Jason Aronson, 1979.)

The Therapeutic Interaction, Vol. 1: *Abstracts of the Psychoanalytic Literature.* New York: Jason Aronson.

The Therapeutic Interaction, Vol. 2: *A Critical Overview and Synthesis.* New York: Jason Aronson.

1977

The Therapeutic Interaction: A Synthesis. New York: Jason Aronson.

Psychoanalytic interaction. In *International Encyclopedia of Psychiatry, Psychology, Psychoanalysis, and Neurology,* vol. 9, ed. B. B. Wolman, pp. 189–195.

New York: Aesculapius. (Reprinted under the title "Framework, Misalliance, and Interaction in the Analytic Situation: Three Encyclopedia Articles" in R. Langs, *Technique in Transition*, pp. 295–325. New York: Jason Aronson, 1978.)

Psychoanalytic situation: the framework. In *International Encyclopedia of Psychiatry, Psychology, Psychoanalysis, and Neurology*, vol. 9, ed. B. B. Wolman, pp. 220–225. New York: Aesculapius. (Reprinted under the title "Framework, Misalliance, and Interaction in the Analytic Situation: Three Encyclopedia Articles" in R. Langs, *Technique in Transition*, pp. 295–325. New York: Jason Aronson, 1978.)

Therapeutic misalliance. In *International Encyclopedia of Psychiatry, Psychology, Psychoanalysis, and Neurology*, vol. 11, ed. B. B. Wolman, pp. 146–150. New York: Aesculapius. (Reprinted under the title "Framework, Misalliance, and Interaction in the Analytic Situation: Three Encyclopedia Articles" in R. Langs, *Technique in Transition*, pp. 295–325. New York: Jason Aronson, 1978.)[1]

1978

The adaptational-interactional dimension of countertransference. *Contemporary Psychoanalysis* 14:502–533. (Reprinted in R. Langs, *Technique in Transition*, pp. 501–535. New York: Jason Aronson, 1978. Also reprinted under the title "The Interactional Dimension of Countertransference" in *Recent Studies in Countertransference*, ed. L. E. Epstein and A. H. Feiner, pp. 71–103. New York: Jason Aronson, 1979.)

Discussion paper: responses to creativity in psychoanalysts (reply to Harold J. Searles, M.D., "Concerning Transference and Countertransference"). *International Journal of Psychoanalytic Psychotherapy* 7:189–207. (Reprinted under the title "Reactions to Creativity in Psychoanalysts" in R. Langs, *Technique in Transition*, pp. 473–499. New York: Jason Aronson, 1978.)

Dreams in the bipersonal field. In R. Langs, *Technique in Transition*, pp. 537–586. New York: Jason Aronson, 1978. (Reprinted under the title "The Dream in Psychotherapy" in *The Dream in Clinical Practice*, ed. J. M. Natterson, pp. 333–368. New York: Jason Aronson, 1980.)

Framework, misalliance, and interaction in the analytic situation: three encyclopedia articles. In R. Langs, *Technique in Transition*, pp. 295–325. New York: Jason Aronson, 1978. (Adapted from three contributions to *International Encyclopedia of Psychiatry, Psychology, Psychoanalysis, and Neurology*,

---

[1]The three preceding articles were originally published separately and later reprinted as one chapter in *Technique in Transition*.

ed. B. B. Wolman: "Psychoanalytic Interaction," vol. 9, pp. 189–195; "Psychoanalytic Situation: The Framework," vol. 9, pp. 220–225; and "Therapeutic Misalliance," vol. 11, pp. 146–150. New York: Aesculapius, 1977.)

Interventions in the bipersonal field. In R. Langs, *Technique in Transition*, pp. 627–678. New York: Jason Aronson, 1978. (Reprinted in *Contemporary Psychoanalysis* 15:1–54, 1979.)

The Listening Process. New York: Jason Aronson.

Misalliance and framework in the case of the Rat Man. In R. Langs, *Technique in Transition*, pp. 253–293. New York: Jason Aronson, 1978. (Reprinted under the title "The Misalliance Dimension in the Case of the Rat Man" in *Freud and His Patients*, ed. M. Kanzer and J. Glenn, pp. 215–231. New York: Jason Aronson, 1979.)

Misalliance and framework in the case of the Wolf Man. In R. Langs, *Technique in Transition*, pp. 275–293. New York: Jason Aronson, 1978. (Reprinted under the title "The Misalliance Dimension in the Case of the Wolf Man," in *Freud and His Patients*, ed. M. Kanzer and J. Glenn, pp. 373–385. New York: Jason Aronson, 1979.)

A model of supervision: the patient as unconscious supervisor. In R. Langs, *Technique in Transition*, pp. 587–625. New York: Jason Aronson, 1978.

Some communicative properties of the bipersonal field. *International Journal of Psychoanalytic Psychotherapy* 7:87–135. (Reprinted in R. Langs, *Technique in Transition*, pp. 413–472. New York: Jason Aronson, 1978. Also reprinted in R. Langs, *The Listening Process*, pp. 549–615. New York: Jason Aronson, 1978. Also reprinted in *Do I Dare Disturb the Universe? A Memorial to Wilfred R. Bion*, ed. J. S. Grotstein, pp. 441–487. Beverly Hills, Calif.: Caesura Press, 1981.)

Technique in transition. In R. Langs, *Technique in Transition*, pp. 1–41. New York: Jason Aronson, 1978.

Technique in Transition. New York: Jason Aronson.

Transference beyond Freud. In R. Langs, *Technique in Transition*, pp. 357–379. New York: Jason Aronson, 1978. (Also published under the title "Transference Beyond Freud: Reality and Unconscious Processes" in *The Unconscious*, vol. 2, ed. L. Chertok. Tbilissi Symposium, 1978.)

Validation and the framework of the therapeutic situation: thoughts prompted by Hans H. Strupp's "Suffering and Psychotherapy." *Contemporary Psychoanalysis* 14:98–104. (Reprinted under the title "Validation and the Framework of the Therapeutic Situation" in R. Langs, *Technique in Transition*, pp. 381–411. New York: Jason Aronson, 1978.)

1979

On the formulation and timing of interventions. *Journal of the American Academy of Psychoanalysis* 4:477–498.

The misalliance dimension in the case of Dora. In *Freud and His Patients*, ed. M. Kanzer and J. Glenn, pp. 58–71. New York: Jason Aronson. (Reprinted from "The Misalliance Dimension in Freud's Case Histories. I. The Case of Dora." *International Journal of Psychoanalytic Psychotherapy* 5:301–318, 1976.)

The misalliance dimension in the case of the Rat Man. In *Freud and His Patients*, ed. M. Kanzer and J. Glenn, pp. 215–231. New York: Jason Aronson. (Reprinted from "Misalliance and Framework in the Case of the Rat Man." In R. Langs, *Technique in Transition*, pp. 253–273. New York: Jason Aronson, 1978.)

The misalliance dimension in the case of the Wolf Man. In *Freud and His Patients*, ed. M. Kanzer and J. Glenn, pp. 373–385. New York: Jason Aronson. (Reprinted from "Misalliance and Framework in the Case of the Wolf Man." In R. Langs, *Technique in Transition*, pp. 275–293. New York: Jason Aronson, 1978.)

The Supervisory Experience. New York: Jason Aronson.

The Therapeutic Environment. New York: Jason Aronson.

1980

Interactions: The Realm of Transference and Countertransference. New York: Jason Aronson.

Intrapsychic and Interpersonal Dimensions of Treatment: A Clinical Dialogue (With Harold F. Searles, M.D.). New York: Jason Aronson.

On the properties of an interpretion. *Contemporary Psychoanalysis* 16:460–478.

Some interactional and communicative aspects of resistance. *Contemporary Psychoanalysis* 16:16–52.

Supervision and the bipersonal field. In *Psychotherapy Supervision: Theory, Research and Practice*, ed. A. K. Hess, PP. 103–125. New York: Wiley.

The Therapeutic Experience and Its Setting: A Clinical Dialogue (with Leo Stone, M.D.). New York: Jason Aronson.

Truth therapy/lie therapy. *International Journal of Psychoanalytic Psychotherapy* 8:3–35.

1981

Modes of "cure" in psychoanalysis and psychoanalytic psychotherapy. *International Journal of Psycho-Analysis* 62:199–214.

Resistances and Interventions: The Nature of Therapeutic Work. New York: Jason Aronson.

1982

Countertransference and the process of cure. In *Curative Factors in Dynamic Psychotherapy*, ed. S. Slipp, pp. 127–152. New York: McGraw-Hill.

A new dawn for psychoanalysis. *Voices: The Art and Science of Psychotherapy* 18:57–60.

The Psychotherapeutic Conspiracy. New York: Jason Aronson.

Psychotherapy: A Basic Text. New York: Jason Aronson.

Supervisory crises and dreams from supervisees. *Contemporary Psychoanalysis* 18:575–612.

1983

Unconscious Communication in Everyday Life. New York: Jason Aronson.

AUTHOR INDEX

SUBJECT INDEX

Abreaction, 426

Abstinence, rule of, 195, 201, 458; *see also* Therapist self-disclosure

Acting out, 76–97
 and adaptive context, 76–77
 and communication in Type B field, 348
 to destroy secure frame, 93, 95
 and management of frame, 89, 94, 95, 359–360, 433
 role evocation in, 87; *see also* Role responsiveness
 in therapist, 68–69, 80, 83, 219
 transference and nontransference, 77, 88

Action discharge, 33, 81

Action language, 457–464
 theory-making, advantage of, 463–464

Action, structuralization of, 458

Adaptation-evoking contexts, x; *see also* Adaptive context

Adaptive context, 5, 18, 38, 76, 87–88, 99–100, 112, 125, 324–325, 466, 469
 analogies of, 336, 340–341, 369–371, 454
 direct representation of, 117, 144, 405, 466
 examples of, 38, 43–44, 47, 83, 112, 119–120, 173, 258, 279–284, 424, 467, 469–470, 477–478
 extratherapeutic contacts as, 279–280
 fading of, 280

frame (ground rules) management as, 102

frame modifications as, 52, 220, 228; *see also* Frame; Frame deviation

identification of, 106, 118–119, 166, 178, 405

in interpretations, 84, 93, 103, 364, 459

missing, 61–63, 82, 89, 103, 104–105, 167, 261, 365, 380, 406, 417

missing in absurdist drama, 371, 374, 376–377

in mother-child interaction, 336, 340–341

in nonclinical situations, 370–371

omitted, 46, 50, 78, 114, 116, 134, 142, 232, 238, 242, 280

as organizer of patient's material, 75, 120, 125, 268, 466

primary, 127, 129, 138, 143

in secure frame, 434

secured frame as, 88, 93, 102, 231, 290–291

silence as, 50, 102, 403, 405–406, 424, 469

and Type A communicative field, 324

in Type C communication, 316, 365–366, 376–377

and Type Two derivative listening, 179

unconscious perception of, 481

see also Derivative playback; Psychotherapeutic frame; Therapist behavior

505

healthy, in symbiotic phase, 332
meaning in, 205
in mothers, 330, 332, 342
as reaction to disturbance,
    illustration of, 383
in therapist, 327, 332
therapy of, 320, 326, 427–428
communicator, fictional character
    as, 372–373
patients, 16
therapist response to, 327
and Type B-A therapist, 326
Type B-A communicative mode,
    297, 311, 314, 326
dynamics of, 356–357
as effort to cure mother, 341
as response to Type A listening,
    326–327
in therapist, 326
therapy of, 311–312, 357
Type B-C
communicative field, 311–312, 314,
    387, 460
countertransference in, 359
communicative mode, 297
linguistic characteristics,
    example of, 387
in patient as most difficult to
    work with, 327
communicator, as character
    disorder, 334
Type C
communicative field, 4–5, 15, 85, 87,
    304, 316–318, 320, 327–328,
    345, 460
cliche in, 318
in clinics, 231, 247
in drama, 371–391
influence of therapist in, 65, 349,
    354–355
language in, 317–319
as normal among in-laws, 377
participants preserving sanity in,
    389
and research findings, 319

and separation–individuation, 331,
    341–342
communicative mode, 58, 60, 81,
    296–297, 316, 354
as absence of verbalization capacity,
    technique in, 406
as acute disorder, 334
as adaptive context in *The
    Homecoming* (Pinter), 374
and alexithymia, 350
analogy of, in Pinter's, plays, 372
constitutional factors in, 352–353
and derivative blindness in
    Pinter's work, 376
derivative commentary of, 81, 86,
    92, 210, 328, 365
developmental aspects of, 65, 317,
    328, 330–331, 335–336,
    341–342, 348–349, 352–353
difficulties in treatment of, 354,
    363, 374
dynamics of, 348, 351–354,
    357, 363
example of, 92
interpretation with, 360–361
and lack of neurotic symptoms, 350
language in, 390
medication in treatment of, 354
in mother and infant, 329–332,
    335–337, 340, 342, 351
in psychosomatic patient, 349–350
review of literature on, 349–354
therapy of, 65, 71–72, 317, 328,
    348–349, 354–358, 364–366
as "trauma screen," 353
in Type B character, 391
see also Alexithymia
communicator, 16, 350, 353
diagnosis in, 349–350
example of, 382
response to Type B attack, 386, 389
therapist, 354
Type One derivative, 4–6, 9, 16, 58, 79,
    89, 134, 167, 437–439
dynamics in, 439